# THE PREMODERN CHINESE ECONOMY

Until five hundred years ago China's technology was the most advanced in Eurasia and as recently as two hundred years ago its standards of living surpassed those of most other civilisations. However, the economies of the West and smaller developing countries then overtook the Chinese economy. China had reached its developmental limits and deadlock set in.

Covering the time span from the Shang to the Qing Periods (1520 BC–1911 AD), Gang Deng examines important factors in the decline of the Chinese economy from medieval sophistication to modern underdevelopment. These factors include:

- resource endowments
- socio-economic structure
- property rights
- state and bureaucracy
- ideology and values
- geo-political environment
- internal rebellions
- external invasions and conquests

*The Premodern Chinese Economy* is a comprehensive analysis of China's economic history and provides essential background to the study of this country's modern struggle for growth and development. Deng's emphasis on comparative analysis offers new insights into the concept of underdevelopment and theories of transitional economics. This will become a major reference work in the fields of Chinese studies, economic history and development studies.

**Gang Deng** was born in Peking and educated in Melbourne. He currently lectures in Economic History at the London School of Economics and has published widely on aspects of premodern Chinese economy.

# ROUTLEDGE EXPLORATIONS IN ECONOMIC HISTORY

# THE PREMODERN CHINESE ECONOMY

## Structural equilibrium and capitalist sterility

*Gang Deng*

London and New York

First published 1999
by Routledge
2 Park Square, Milton Park, Abingdon, Oxon, OX14 4RN

Simultaneously published in the USA and Canada
by Routledge
270 Madison Ave, New York NY 10016

Transferred to Digital Printing 2007

Typeset in Garamond by
Puretech India Ltd, Pondicherry. http.//www.puretech.com.

*British Library Cataloguing in Publication Data*
A catalogue record for this book is available from the British Library

*Library of Congress Cataloguing in Publication Data*
Deng, Gang, 1953–
The premodern Chinese economy: structural equilibrium and
capitalist sterility / Gang Deng.
p.   cm.
Includes bibliographical references and index.
ISBN 0–415–16239–4
1. China – Economic conditions – To 1644.   2. China –
Economic conditions – 1644–1912.   3. China – History – Shang
dynasty – 1766–1122 B.C.   4. China – History – Ch' ing dynasty –
1644–1912.   I. Title.
HC427.6.D46   1999
330.951–dc21      98–25901 CIP

ISBN10: 0–415–16239–4 (hbk)
ISBN10: 0–415–45864–1 (pbk)

ISBN13: 978–0–415–16239–5 (hbk)
ISBN13: 978–0–415–45864–1 (pbk)

**Publisher's Note**
The publisher has gone to great lengths to ensure the quality of this
reprint but points out that some imperfections in the original
may be apparent

FOR JANE AND TORREY ORTON

# CONTENTS

# FIGURES AND TABLES

## Figures

## Tables

# PREFACE

This book is the final part of my trilogy dealing with the long-term economic history of premodern China. Together with my earlier works on the literati (*Development versus Stagnation*, 1993) and the maritime sector (*Chinese Maritime Activities and Socio-economic Consequences*, 1997), this book can, I hope, add in a small way to the debate on China's economic history for the understanding of this long-lasting civilisation, its success and failure.

Ironically, my comparative advantage in undertaking research such as this has owed much to the notorious 'Cultural Revolution' during which I was sent, aged only 15 at that time, to a labour camp in Heilongjiang near the Sino-Soviet border. Towards the end of the 'revolution', after spending six long years in the camp, I consequently underwent a Stalin-type brain-washing programme and was officially recognised as being cleansed of my non-proletarian family background and its related 'original sin'. Ridiculous as it may sound, I was even granted a quasi-peasant status by the authorities, as high a non-monetary reward as one could ever dream of during the Dark Age of the 'revolution'. Although for me the brainwashing never worked, only stimulating my brain-shielding, the six-year-long hard labour did bring me down to earth and helped me develop a sense of reality, including an understanding of how institutions worked and what ordinary day-to-day peasant life was like in China. Later on, a heavy dosage of Western training, which was first arranged by my best friends, Dr Jane Orton and Mr Torrey Orton, only reinforced this sense.

I would like to take this opportunity to thank the London School of Economics for funding this project. My gratitude goes in particular to Mrs Pip Austin, whose help made the project go much more smoothly and faster than planned, which has been unprecedented in my career.

I am deeply indebted to Professor Eric L. Jones of the University of Reading and the University of Melbourne for his continued support, guidance and advice in relation to this project since 1990. I am very grateful to Professor Patrick K. O'Brien of the Institute of Historical Research, London, Professor Ramon H. Myers of Stanford University, and my LSE colleague Dr Gareth Austin, who kindly read the manuscript and made invaluable comments.

Dr John Singleton, my former colleague in Wellington, New Zealand, offered his comments on the early draft. Two other LSE colleagues, Dr Larry Epstein and Dr Max-Stephan Schulze, provided me with important references concerning West European agriculture and peasantries.

Retrospectively, I would also like to thank those former colleagues who commented on my paper 'Structural Equilibrium and Capitalist Sterility in China: A New Insight', one of the humble beginnings of this project, at the Bi-annual Conference of the Economic History Society of Australia and New Zealand, July 1992 in Perth, Australia.

Last but not least, I wish to thank my wife Lucy and my children Alexander and Belinda, who have put up with my stinginess in giving them time in the evening, at weekends and during the holidays on the one hand and my constant demand for their support on the other. Their understanding and support has been critical for my academic life in general and for this book in particular, given that the whole family moved during this period from Wellington to London. With all the normal stresses associated with such a move, remarkably, interruption to this project, a project which owed so much to them, was kept minimal.

# ABBREVIATIONS

| | |
|---|---|
| AEHR | *Australian Economic History Review* |
| CBW | Cihai Bianji Weiyuanhui (Compilatory Board of the *Encyclopaedia*) |
| CA | *Current Anthropology* |
| CR | *China Reconstructs* |
| EEH | *Exploration in Economic History* |
| EHR | *The Economic History Review* |
| HJY | *Haijiaoshi Yanjiu (Research in the History of Sea Communication)* |
| IA | Institute of Archaeology, the Chinese Academy of Social Sciences |
| IHNS | Institute of the History of Natural Science of the Chinese Academy of Social Sciences |
| JAS | *Journal of Asian Studies* |
| JCE | *Journal of Comparative Economics* |
| JEH | *Journal of Economic History* |
| JPS | *Journal of Peasant Studies* |
| KG | *Kaogu (Archaeology)* |
| KR | *Keji Ribao (Science and Technology News)* |
| LY | *Lishi Yanju (Research in History)* |
| MAS | *Modern Asian Studies* |
| MPL | Marginal (physical) product of labour |
| MRP | Marginal revenue product |
| NGM | *National Geographic Magazine* |
| NK | *Nongye Kaogu (Agricultural Archaeology)* |
| PEAO | Population elasticity to agricultural output |
| PP | *Past and Present* |
| RR | *Renmin Ribao (People's Daily)* |
| SA | *Scientific American* |
| WW | *Wenwu (Cultural Relics)* |
| XW | *Xinhua Wenzhai (Xinhua Compilation)* |
| ZDB | Zhongguo Dabaikequanshu Bianji Weiyuanhui (Compilatory Board of the *New Encyclopaedia Sinica*) |
| ZDC | Zhongguo Ditu Chubanshe (Compilatory Board of the *Maps of China*) |

ZJY      *Zhongguo Jingjishi Yanjiu* (*Study of Chinese Economic History*)

ZKY      Zhongguo Kexueyuan (Chinese Academy of Sciences, *Academia Sinica*)

ZNK      Zhongguo Nongyie Kexueyuan (Chinese Academy of Agricultural Sciences)

ZNS      *Zhongguo Nongshi* (*Agricultural History of China*)

ZNZ      Editorial Board of Zhongguo Nongmin Zhanzhengshi (*A History of Peasant Rebellions in China*)

ZSY      *Zhongguoshi Yanjiu* (*Study of Chinese History*)

ZW      Zhongguo Wenhua Yanjiusuo (Institute for Advanced Chinese Studies)

# 1

# INTRODUCTION:

## Problems and a new insight

## 1.1 Paradoxes in Chinese economic history

### 1.1.1 First paradox: shocks, disasters and perpetuation of the Chinese system

China puzzles us by her resilience in spite of a long history that has been full of shocks and disasters, both natural and man-made: periodic droughts and floods, internal riots, potential and actual foreign invasions and occasional alien conquests. Despite so much misfortune, China revived time and again from the ashes like a phoenix.

Most remarkably, after conflicts with and defeats by the modern economic and military might of the West were added to the disaster list, China stood up in one piece in spite of the heavy bombardment by major colonial powers in the second half of the nineteenth century (which numbered as many as eight in one joint campaign) and the ferocious, all-round attacks by the Japanese in the first half of the twentieth century. This is indeed a rare case, if not a miracle, in which a country targeted for colonisation remained independent despite such devastating blows.

Why did Chinese or 'Sinic' civilisation not vanish as many of its ancient counterparts have done throughout history? More fundamentally, considering the Chinese track record of survival, which civilisation has greater vigour, Western or traditional Chinese? If the Chinese civilisation does, what is the point of promoting the Western civilisation? This is the first paradox.

### 1.1.2 Second paradox: from development to underdevelopment

China has a rich history of inventive genius and sophistication across a wide spectrum. She also enjoyed cultural and economic supremacy, at least in Asia, until the seventeenth century. To elaborate these points, technology and commercialisation, the two accepted factors of importance in economic development, can be taken as evidence.

1

Chinese achievements in science and technology have been presented in Joseph Needham's gigantic work *Science and Civilisation in China* (1954–94) and numerous other works in the English language, especially since the 1970s. There is very little doubt that China, the homeland of a list of inventions including silk, gunpowder, the compass, paper-making and block printing, was one of the most creative societies and consequently led the world in technology for a long time. Not surprisingly, these technological achievements had a profound impact on the economy (Hartwell 1963, 1967; Elvin 1973: chs 9–10, 13). As for commerce, it has been estimated that markets were established in China not later than the Warring State Period (475–221 BC) (Chao 1986: 2). As economic growth continued, the sheer volume of trade certainly impressed outsiders like Ibn Batuta, a Moroccan traveller who was sent on an embassy to Yuan China, and Marco Polo,[1] who had a merchant background himself, in the fourteenth century in spite of the fact that some figures might not be accurate (Wright 1854). Apart from professional merchants, who always existed in premodern China, ordinary peasants participated regularly and actively in market activities: an ordinary farmer traded a considerable percentage of his crop for cash (Latourette 1964: 575), although it is argued that 'the bulk of commerce of premodern China was confined to a very few geographical favoured regions' (Rawski 1972: 6).[2] Some changes favourable to commerce, including the use of paper currency and the establishment of credit institutions, also took place in China much earlier than in Europe (Elvin 1973: chs 11–12). It has been said explicitly that capitalist elements, not just the market, were evident in China long before Christ (Jones 1988: 74).

China therefore seems to have had nearly all the important ingredients for further development and even possessed at times major characteristics of an incipient industrial revolution in the Han and Song periods respectively (Elvin 1973). Moreover, as China seemingly came within a hair's breadth of industrialising later in the fourteenth century (Jones 1981: 160), there was almost every likelihood that she would become the first industrialised society. Not so long ago, up to *c.* AD 1800, China claimed roughly a third of the total world manufacturing output, ahead of the West by a tenth of the world total. The tide changed around 1830 when the West managed to surpass China by a small margin of 1.3 per cent in the world total. In 1900, China's share of manufacturing output slid to 6.2 per cent while the West's rose to 77.4 per cent (Huntington 1996: 86; see also Kennedy 1987: 149). Needless to say, the country did not capitalise on her achievements and so did not pass the threshold for industrialisation before Western Europe. As a result, not only has China been ruthlessly surpassed by Europe, but also she has fallen to the very bottom of the developmental pyramid with one of the lowest per capita incomes in the contemporary world.

Why did China not develop further? How could this fairy tale of the hare–tortoise race become real in history? It helps little to dismiss these issues by casting doubts upon whether China ever reached those heights at all since few will disagree that the Occident caught up with and surpassed the Orient step by step following the Crusades (Landes 1994). For many researchers, China presents a haunting paradox between development and stagnation, between advancement and backwardness, which is recognised as one of the greatest enigmas in world history. At least four aspects can be identified to explain this situation.

First, if one supposes that the European pattern of economic development, a pattern which is full of revolutionary changes, is the universal path for other civilisations, it would be unacceptable to jump to the conclusion that the general principles which worked in Europe did not operate in a large country like China. Then one has to face the following questions: (1) Why did the Chinese not take off after the glorious proto-capitalist Han or Song, but instead had to wait after the Han for a millennium till the Song, and again wait after the Song for another millennium till modern times with the total delay of, shockingly, two thousand years? (2) What went 'wrong' in China so that a quantum leap towards industrialisation did not take place?

Second, if one believes that economic development towards capitalist industrialisation is an inevitable process and that the European way of implementing such change was only one of many ways to do so, the question then becomes whether it would have been possible for China to have evolved to the stage of industrialisation if sufficient time had been given. This approach is largely counter-factual.[3] The reality is that since capitalist industrialisation was invented and ripened in England, for the rest of the world it has been a matter of diffusing the new system, often in the 'reverse engineering' fashion, through substituting artificially created factors for the 'natural prerequisites', as convincingly argued by scholars like Alexander Gerschenkron (1962) (see also Harley 1991). Therefore, during the post-industrial revolution era, the key issue is about the ability of a civilisation to carry out such a diffusional process, not about the possibility of reinventing the wheel. It is also a fact that in the past hundred years or so China did poorly in adopting industrialisation: she started late and moved slowly with extraordinary difficulty in implementing the known task vis-à-vis the success story of neighbouring Japan. The point is that if China had difficulties not only in inventing but also in copying capitalist industrialisation, can one still assume that she would have entered industrialisation in a 'natural course' of her developmental history? In addition, even if the 'sufficient time' scenario is acceptable, on what account should one consider a period of two thousand years from the Han onwards, as demonstrated earlier, not long enough for the slowest motion of growth to accumulate and reach a 'take-off' point?

Third, if one is sceptical about the validity of a universally applicable development pattern, since so many societies have been left out, another question emerges: why did China approach capitalism at least twice in history? Moreover, was China during the Han and Song periods on her 'normal'

3

track? If the answer is 'yes', why did China have to break with her promising proto-capitalism?

Finally, quantitatively, China's performance in the past was impressive by any standards. Regarding population size, according to Simon Kuznets's estimate world population reached 275 million around 1000 BC (1966: 34), while the Chinese were estimated to number 90–100 million for around the same period (Ho 1970; Ge J. 1993). For the earlier period around 1 BC, the estimated figures for the world and China are 250 million and 70 million, respectively (Llewellyn-Jones 1975: 24–5). More accurately, a recent linguistic grouping of the world's population indicates that in 1992 Mandarin speakers made up 15.2 per cent of the world total while Chinese speakers all told made up 18.8 per cent (Huntington 1996: 60–1). As its population share in the world total has halved since AD 1000, China's population claimed a greater share and importance in the world prior to AD 1000. But over the very long term until the Second World War, China never faced a real challenge from other population heavyweights. In terms of territorial space, China occupies roughly the same size as Europe. It has been calculated that in 1900, China's land territory occupied 11.1 million square kilometres (4.3 million square miles), or 8.2 per cent of the world total (Fullard 1968: 5). Her share declined in 1920 to 10.1 million square kilometres (3.9 million square miles), or 7.5 per cent of the world total, owing to the loss of Mongolia (1.57 million square kilometres; see Huntington 1996: 84; Anon. 1995: 27). It is worth noting that earlier, in 1858–60, under the Sino-Russian Aihui and Beijing treaties, tsarist Russia obtained over 1 million square kilometres from Chinese Siberia and 440,000 square kilometres from Chinese Turkestan. In 1881, Russia gained a further 70,000 square kilometres from Chinese Turkestan. By the turn of the twentieth century, the lost land areas, totalling over 3.08 million square kilometres, accounted for 24.4 per cent of the Qing territory (CBW 1989: 1596). So, until the end of the nineteenth century, the maximum percentage share of China's territory in the world total was 9.3 (7.5 × 1.244). Given that all political units of large size established in ancient and medieval world history disappeared, China being the sole exception, and that in modern world history up to the Second World War, among the four territorial superpowers – Canada, the United States, the Russian Empire and China – the first three were established after the sixteenth century, China is the undisputed champion in territorial possession.

Here, fundamentally, if one agrees that China has the longest continuous history and that China has qualified as the most populated country in the world with the Chinese as the largest single ethnic group on this planet since the beginning of the Christian era with at least 20 per cent of the world total, which civilisation has represented the developmental mainstream in the long term, the West or China? If China did, because of her overwhelming size and population, all the developmental criteria will have to be radically altered with the entire developmental issue turned upside down. If the

4

West did, then how should one regard China's 'quantitative victory' in terms of human biomass, survival time and territorial space, which have had few parallels in world history?

In this context, China's past presents a challenge to the scholarly world, a challenge that is second only if not equal, to the issue of the Industrial Revolution.

## 1.2 Critique of theoretical frameworks

Many theoretical frameworks have been used to tackle China's paradoxes. They have obvious merits, and have contributed to the understanding of premodern Chinese economic performance. But, without exception, they are also caught by the paradoxes in one way or another. Eleven main frameworks have been singled out to demonstrate our plight in dealing with the paradoxes.

### 1.2.1 Main frameworks and their individual problems

#### 1.2.1.1 Ideological determinism

The establishment of ideological determinism owed much to G. W. F. Hegel (1770–1831), the German philosopher whose theoretical model demonstrates what may be called a cult of the power of logic. Hegel believed that socio-economic development is determined by spirit, a way of thinking that has greatly influenced later thinkers, as clearly shown in Max Weber's *The Protestant Ethic and the Spirit of Capitalism*, claiming a close link between the Protestant ethic and Western capitalism (Weber 1930; cf. Tawney 1926).

The advantage of this model is that one can show an ultimate reason for differences in developmental performance because religions, ideologies and ideas are not difficult to identify and trace. And those religions, ideologies and ideas are often unique to different civilisations or 'cultures'. Thus, conclusive answers can easily be drawn from a spiritual origin. Many scholars have followed this Hegelian–Weberian line to reinterpret socio-economic development in different parts of the world. In the Chinese studies, scholars pointed out that 'deficiencies', in relation to economic development, in ideology and cultural values under the Confucian–Taoist alliance, froze Chinese creativity and misled and wasted Chinese energy and talent, locking the country in stagnation and backwardness (e.g. Fairbank 1957; Qian W. 1985).

Although it promotes cultural studies, this model has some obvious weaknesses: ideological determinism has a strong flavour of fatalism, as if development is pre-programmed at the beginning of time. In other words, choices have been made for later generations long before they are born. This is irrational in itself. More seriously, it is counter-factual. It is known that in history some peoples who shared the same or a similar culture or belief pattern had very different economic development paths. In European history, for example,

Protestantism originated in Germany and later spread out to the northern part of Western Europe and offshore England. But why did the Industrial Revolution not break out in Germany, the Protestant homeland, or take place simultaneously throughout the Protestant world? Moreover, why did Germany as well as the other European countries have to take considerable trouble to create artificial conditions to replace some key prerequisites in order to transplant industrialisation, as recognised by the Gerschenkronian School (see Sylla and Toniolo 1991)? Similarly, one can ask why the Confucianism-converted Japanese succeeded in industrial diffusion while the Chinese, who had patented Confucianism, did not; nor did, until very recently, the other peoples living under Confucian states such as the Koreans and Vietnamese.

### 1.2.1.2 Developmental stage models

Developmental-stage models try to divide socio-economic development into different stages. A systematic attempt was made by Karl Marx, who labelled those stages as (1) primitive communism, (2) slavery, (3) feudalism, (4) capitalism and (5) 'scientific' communism, a stage of Marx's own creation. Later, Walt W. Rostow, defying the Marxian politicisation of human history, reinterpreted history as having four developmental stages: (1) a traditional society, the starting point, which is a predominantly agricultural economy with limited trade and industries; (2) economic take-off when a traditional society manages to shake off the timeless harness of extensive growth (characterised by a small increase in per capita income); (3) industrial maturity, when an industrial structure becomes entrenched in society; and (4) the age of high mass consumption, when human welfare is guaranteed with an affluent nirvana (1960: ch. 6). According to Rostow, it took a dedicated society between 54 and 80 years to go through all the stages (*ibid*.: 38, 59). The stage models arguably owed much to Darwinism, which hypothesises a common developmental pattern in the natural world among species from their primitive forms to more advanced ones (for Marx, see 1976a).

What Marx and Rostow have in common is the viewpoint that there is a unilinear pattern dictating economic development everywhere in the world. Unfortunately, such a unilinear pattern cannot explain why certain societies did not go through some of the stages that are so central to the models: China has not had a stage of slavery or feudalism as a dominant system in the past three thousand years, not to mention the fact that China has had enormous difficulties in adopting and adapting capitalist industrialisation. In effect, Marx himself realised this problem and admitted that there existed a so-called 'Asiatic Mode of Production', neither slavery nor feudal, but of despotic state ownership, which is a major compromise to his theory (Pryor 1980). What Marx totally neglected was the fact that China did have sophisticated private land ownership instead of state-communal dualistic land ownership of the traditional Indian–Russian type, a key factor which made China more like early modern Western Europe (Moulder 1977: 15). He then treated the Orient without discrimination as an exception in the hope that his theory could be kept intact. But if one accepts that China was one of the greatest civilisations with one of the largest populations in world history, Marx's expelling of China can hardly be justified. Similarly, Rostow's hypothesis is unable to accommodate a traditional economy like China, with extensive trade activities and industrial undertakings. China's past exemplified a non-linear growth over a period of time much longer than a linearist is accustomed to comprehend.

Second, both Marx and Rostow imply that once development begins, there is no way back and a society is destined to go up along all the steps. This is a major misunderstanding and/or abuse of the essence of Darwinism, which expounds the view that development is highly conditional/selective and setback is common through stagnation and extinction. In reality, socio-economic development has never been 'one-way traffic': in Eurasia alone, the glory of ancient Babylonia and Egypt evaporated long before the birth of the next lasting civilisation to emerge on their sites; and China appears to have repeatedly made sharp U-turns in her development (for the plight faced by Chinese scholarship, predominantly Marxist, see Huang 1990: 3–5).

Third, the Marxian–Rostowian view cannot explain why development in the world can never be synchronised as suggested by their unilinear models. Instead, in the past, non-synchronisation was the norm, as some societies developed faster than the others in a race: (1) China was surpassed by the West; (2) continental Western Europe was surpassed by industrialised Britain; (3) Britain was then surpassed by the United States. While treating Britain as a special case with some peculiar exogenous factors, both Marx and Rostow committed major violations of their own linear law (for Marx, see 1976b, Volume 3 of *Das Kapital*; Rostow 1960: 33–5).

### 1.2.1.3 Market model

Aristotle and Thomas Aquinas were among the pioneers in studying the market. Later on, William Petty and Adam Smith linked the market to wealth. Karl Marx followed suit and went further by recognising the market as one of the revolutionary forces in the downfall of feudalism and the rise of capitalism. Although he also viewed the market as the source of social alienation, and therefore wished its elimination (1976a), Marx left a legacy. After him, a great many scholars have seen the market as a locomotive, or even the sole propulsion, of economic growth, the best example being Sir John Hicks's ideas as expressed in his *Theory of Economic History* (1969: 7).

According to Hicks, Europe had very favourable conditions for the market economy to grow, including the rise of an agricultural surplus, specialisation, professional traders, the establishment and maintenance of law and order, money and credit, as well as mercantile policies (1969: 23–6, 42, 68–71). Hicks ignores the fact that these conditions also existed at the other end of the Eurasian continent in China. As early as the sixth century BC individual private land ownership was established and became the dominant form of ownership before Christ. China had not only the most productive agriculture in the world, but a sophisticated monetary system and credit institution as well. In addition, extensive domestic and international market networks, backed by producers' private ownership and basic property rights, existed in China for millennia (see Elvin 1973; Liang F. 1980: 398–411; Sun G. 1989: 548, 559; Chen X.W. 1991: 49–50; Quan H. 1993: 8; Yan H. 1994: 107; Deng 1993a, b 1997; cf. Hicks 1969: ch. 5). Professor Albert Feuerwerker explicitly said that (1984: 304) 'from the Song onward, China's economy was essentially a market economy in which most of the economic results were determined by decisions made and actions taken in the private sector.' China was also considered by the premodern Europeans as one of the most orderly and lawful societies on earth (Waverick 1946; cf. Hicks 1969: 69–71). A recent work by Morgan Kelly shows that Song China had a market expansion to reach the point of 'economywide market', or simply a market economy, with no parallel in the world until the eighteenth century (Kelly 1997: 952–62). The question is why these conditions, imperative for Hicks's market-driven growth, did not lead China anywhere near the achievements of her West European counterparts. Hicks praised the geographic advantage of Europe, claiming that the city-state of Europe was a unique gift of the Mediterranean (see Hicks 1969: 38–9).

However, Hicks fails to explain why his most celebrated European city-states, so unique to Europe and so favourable for capitalist growth, should also be so short-lived, and why Europe, the most promising land for capitalism, had to wait for many centuries for offshore England to start over again. His model also cannot explain the fact that when the market economy ushered in an era of industrial growth in Western Europe, trade strengthened serfdom in Central Europe and Russia, which contradicts his market–modern growth formula (see Hicks 1969: 112–13). Therefore, Hicks's model is unsatisfactory even in explaining what occurred within Europe. The statement that the Asians had defective geographic surroundings eventually leads his model to geographic/environmental determinism (*ibid.*: 38–9; cf. Deng 1997: chs 1–2).[4]

Another commonly recognised key factor in the market model, as well as the spirit model, is entrepreneurship or entrepreneurial spirit (mainly risk-taking with readiness to try out a new market and new technology), or the degree of it, an idea which was spearheaded by Joseph A. Schumpeter (see Scherer and Perlman 1992). China's problem is often attributed to the lack of entrepreneurship or entrepreneurial spirit. But this claim is incompatible with both the rates and range of Chinese inventions and innovations in premodern times and the returns from commercial activities. The following table shows trade duty in China imposed on private merchants, with standard rates from 10 to 30 per cent of goods' value (based on Zhu Y. AD 1119 vol. 2; Ma D. AD 1307 vol. 20: ch. 'Shidi Yi'):

| Period | Trade duty revenue collected | Minimum total value traded |
|--------|------------------------------|----------------------------|
| *Song* | *(in mint bronze coins $\times 10^6$)* | *(at a 10% tax rate, coins $\times 10^6$)* |
| AD 1049–53 | 530 | 5,300 |
| 1064–7 | 630 | 6,300 |
| 1127–61 | 2,000 | 20,000 |
| *Ming–Qing* | *(silver, in kg)* | *(silver, in kg)* |
| 1615 | 1,010 | 10,100 |
| 1571–1644 | 142,190 | 1,421,900 |
| 1815 | 22,400 | 224,000 |

Although the information is fragmentary, the sheer amount of revenue underlines the very considerable scale of Chinese entrepreneurial activities. Evidence also shows that apart from a common practice of government profiteering in China (see Appendix A), merchant groups were active almost throughout in premodern Chinese history. Prominent groups included the Anhui Group, the Shanxi Group, the Shaanxi Group, the Shandong Group, the Ningbo Group, the Guangdong Group, and the Fujian Group, which in the Ming–Qing Period practically controlled the trade of salt, tea, cotton, transport and money-lending (Zhang H. and Zhang H. 1993). Another main group, called the Maritime Group, dominated China's exporting business even under the alleged bans of Ming–Qing times (see Deng 1997: ch. 4). Therefore, the allegation of lack of entrepreneurship or entrepreneurial spirit seems groundless in the light of Chinese business history. On the whole, the market model has a long way to go to produce any sound explanation for China's puzzle.

Most fundamentally, according to both classical and neo-classical economics, the market can optimise resource allocation and thus enhances economic growth. But, in theory, the market does not automatically lead to economic development as we know it. So, ultimately, the market leads to the Ricardian 'stationary state', rather than sustained technological change and industrial revolution. By definition, therefore, to rely on the market to achieve economic development is not compatible with the classical and neo-classical economics.

### 1.2.1.4 Class model

Karl Marx was also responsible for the establishment of the class model. There are two interrelated aspects in this model. First, a society constitutes rival classes with contrasting economic interests: slaves and their masters under slavery, serfs and feudal lords under feudalism, wage workers and capitalists under capitalism. Second, these rival classes are not only factors of the given economic systems, but also the driving forces of socio-economic change. For instance, the class struggle between slaves and masters led to the decline of the Roman Empire and created an opportunity for the Frankish tribes to take over with their military duty-based feudalism. Later on, the class struggle between the European serfs and lords led to the decline of feudalism and cleared the ground for capitalism. Such a long chain of class struggle can be ended only under communism, an ultimate stage of human perfection. Marx's historical vision is of all the ruling classes being first progressive and later conservative, while the ruled classes were inferior, exploited and revolutionary.

The problems with this approach are evident. The model is strongly moral judgement-based and thus biased and subjective. It is extremely doubtful whether one should divide population into different interest groups in the way Marx portrays: throughout a history of thousands of years, the Aborigines of Australia have never seen something called class and class struggle. Even in a most discriminatory society, one can always find supra-class behaviour. On the other hand, clashes often occur within the same class. Thus, class and class struggle are in no way the key to understanding human society and its function. This has been proved by the practice of communism. Under the communist system, classes are artificially determined by the authorities just for the sake of the class struggle, the best examples including Stalin's mass political purges, Mao's Anti-Rightist Movement and Cultural Revolution, and the Khmer Rouge's genocide. Such class struggle either held back economic development (as in Maoist China) or led to self-destruction (as in the case of the Soviet and Khmer Rouge régimes). Most importantly, as mentioned earlier in relation to the developmental stage model, slavery, feudalism and capitalism are not universally applicable: they were largely absent in Chinese history. Marx's model thus completely misses out the East Asian mainland where the majority were landholding peasants, much more equal than those highly polarised societies with 'haves' vis-à-vis 'have-nots' in Europe (for China, see Fei 1939: 191–4; Tawney 1964: 34–5, 38, 71; Buck 1968: 194–7; Mousnier 1971: 237–41; Hsu 1980: 10–11, 13–14, 66–7; Chao 1986: chs 7–8).

### 1.2.1.5 Population models

The population model was first put forward by Malthus, an English clergyman who lived in the eighteenth century and worried about the ongoing population crisis in rural Britain. He stressed the correlation between economic resources and the size of population in order to raise the alarm about the constant danger of overpopulation. The model begins with two premises: (1) human sexuality is natural and largely uncontrollable; and (2) the law of diminishing returns from production inputs cannot be avoided. Consequently, the rate of population growth is much greater than that of food production. Thus, sooner or later the unchecked population growth will reach a crisis point and lead to war, starvation and disease. He thus argued that human society is far from perfection, because it cannot even cope with the growth of its own biomass (Malthus 1914).

In the Malthusian model population has only a negative impact on socio-economic development. This model is one of the most frequently used tools in explaining China's past. Kang Chao's monograph (1986) typifies such application: over population is portrayed as the matrix of all the difficulties in Chinese economic growth. The main problem for such a hypothesis comes from three assumptions: (1) that there were few technological and/or structural changes, especially in the later period of the Empire; (2) that the supply of land in China was near-perfectly inelastic; and (3) that there was no preventive check on China's population growth. Recent research suggests the opposite.

First, China's rural economy was much more dynamic than one might think during the Ming–Qing Period, when a vigorous population increase occurred. In places like the Yangzi Delta, similar to Tokugawa Japan, rural surplus labour was absorbed almost completely by handicraft industries so that the previous balance between labour and land inputs in farming remained more or less intact (Li B. 1996a, b)

Second, during the Ming–Qing Period, vast interior regions of the Yangzi –Han Plain (*jianghan pingyuan*), mainly comprising Hubei and Hunan provinces with a total land area of some 400,000 square kilometres, which had been rather marginal paddy-farming areas compared with Jiangsu and Guangdong till the end of the Yuan Dynasty, were transformed in to a highly productive, remarkably commercialised and urbanised region, known as a regular net exporter of large quantities of rice, raw cotton and cloth. This new development was supported by a new method of land utilisation and reclamation (known as *weihuan* or 'diked paddies'), new crops and new market opportunities. Total annual grain output of the region rose from 1,700 million *jin* during the Chenghua's reign (AD 1465–87), to 3,700 million *jin* (2.21 million metric tons; 1 Qing *jin* = 596.82 grams) during the Yongzhengs reign (AD 1723–35). Of this output, 2,300 million *jin* were marketed, an astonishing 62 per cent (Zhang J. 1995: 42). Yet during this period of some five hundred years, the population in the plain multiplied over tenfold (including immigrants) (Zhang J. 1995: 41). Similarly, Shandong, a province with one of the poorest man-to-land ratios in Ming–Qing times (Liang F. 1980: 207, 263, 272, 274), managed (1) to double its acreage cultivation, (2) to adopt a multi-cropping system, and (3) to adopt a range of new plant species. Consequently, in spite of its doubled population, Shandong in the Ming–Qing Period maintained its position as a net exporter of salt, wheat, dry fruits, soya bean products (loose beans, bean cakes and oil), peanuts and peanut oil, raw cotton and cotton cloth, raw silk and silk cloth, raw and processed tobacco, pottery and mats with an estimated total value of 55–60 million *liang* of silver a year (2,051.6–2,238.1 metric tonnes) (Xu T. 1995). If the population peak of Shandong (33,266,055 persons in 1851) is taken as a basis, the export share per head is 1.65–1.80 *liang* of silver (61.5–67.1 grams), which is a considerable economic surplus by premodern standards. A recent study shows that in the seventeenth and eighteenth centuries, the average price of rice varied between 0.94 and 2.18 *liang* per *shi* in the Yangzi Delta (see Wang Y. 1992: 40–7). Another study indicates that a similar price range, 1.03–1.93 *liang* per *shi*, existed in Guangdong and Guangxi during the eighteenth century (see Marks 1991: 102). The yearly average rice consumption of a Chinese adult was 2.17 *shi* (*ibid.*: 77). On the basis of this information, a subsistence wage can be reconstructed by multiplying the price range by the yearly amount of rice consumed per person. The result is 2–4.7 *liang* of silver (74.4–175.3 grams) a year. Thus, the amount of 1.65–1.80 *liang* export share represents 35–90 per cent of minimum wage.

Third, evidence shows that in some of the richest farming areas of Jiangsu, population control was practised, resulting in a growth rate of 0.3 per cent a year (Li B. 1996a: 3; 1996c).

In addition, research has also indicated that the increase in food prices, the often-quoted evidence for the alleged deterioration of the man-to-land ratio in Qing times, was the symptom of a 'price revolution' caused by the oversupply of cheap monetary silver over time, together with the impact of China's first synchronisation with the business cycle of the capitalist world (see Appendix B; Eng 1993; Guo C. 1996; Wang Y. 1996; also Geiss 1979: 159–64; Cartier 1981: 464). The price change had little to do with the actual condition in food supply, which seemed to be sufficient from China's domestic production without foreign imports. It is thus highly likely that during the Ming–Qing Period there was no crisis concerning the man-to-land ratio in the advanced farming regions where rural 'overemployment' rather than 'underemployment' was the norm (Li B.Z. 1985, 1996a,b), while the other regions may have not reached the threshold of such a crisis. If so, a Malthusian explanation becomes very shaky: an increased population alone cannot justify the assertion of overpopulation simply because the other two factors – technology and land input – were both elastic and dynamic.

In contrast with the Malthusian model, Boserup's, argument is that the heavier the population pressure the more creative people become. Thus, the solution to the population problem is provided by human creativity. In other words, population pressure is viewed as not only a positive force but also an endogenous factor for economic development. In tracing the long-term trend of technological changes in agriculture throughout the world, Boserup concluded that major steps have been taken by humankind to combat population pressure: food supply has been increased by progressive intensification of farming, moving from forest–fallow cultivation to, eventually, multi-cropping (1965: chs 1–2, 4–5). Recently, Richard Sullivan has developed a similar model to show that the greater the population size, the larger the pool of intelligence, the easier the process of invention and innovation (Sullivan 1984: 270–89). In both the Boserupian and Sullivanian models, technological improvement is the key to solving population crisis: as long as a society can manage to maintain a rate of technological changes above that of population growth, there will be no subsistence crisis with the impact of the law of diminishing returns avoided (see also Grigg 1980: 46).

It seems obvious that if one allows technology to improve, the Malthusian model will not work. However, if the Boserupian–Sullivanian model is right about the correlation between population growth and technological change, why did densely populated India and China not have sustained technological and economic development in history? Also, if the size of population is the stimulus of economic growth, why did mainland Asia not become industrialised before Europe? Unable to sort out this dilemma, Boserup treats China as an exception in that the Chinese went too far in population growth, thus moving away from the so-called 'Boserup space', an optimal and harmonious range for population growth and technological advancement, which caused her to retreat practically to the Malthusian camp (Boserup 1981: 87–90; Coleman and Schofield 1986: 123; for the Malthusian–Boserupian link see Lee 1986). In contrast, Mark Elvin insists that continuous technological change in late traditional China was a stabilising factor allowing the Chinese to cope with population pressure without being caught in a Malthusian crisis (Elvin 1975: 112–13).

In addition, there is in the long run a time bomb in the Boserupian process: increasingly intensive land utilisation leads to polarisation between land productivity and labour productivity, as revealed by Boserup's own observation that the farmers worked longer hours after each increase in intensity caused by the population shock (Boserup 1965: 53). This is also recognised as the general trend with the modern Green Revolution (Hazell *et al.* 1991: 19–20; Watanabe 1992: 39–40). This productivity trade-off is illustrated by Figure 1.1 where point a represents a land/capital-intensive choice and point b, a labour-intensive choice. At point b the labour-intensive choice lands the land/capital productivity at the higher end but the labour productivity at the lower end. In the long run, because of the labour-intensive nature of the Boserupian process, even if one allows the technological level to rise continuously over time, the population-responsive society may win some battles on the Boserupian front but eventually lose the war against the Malthusian crisis when the farmer approaches the physical as well as the human biological limit for tillage in terms of the hours available a day.

### 1.2.1.6 *Technological determinism*

In the early 1970s Professor Mark Elvin, identifying China's 'Medieval Economic Revolution', was among the few economic historians who recognised the significance of the Chinese experience in long-term world economic history. To explain why the Chinese failed to go further to launch their own industrial revolution, Mark Elvin pointed out that it was because of the

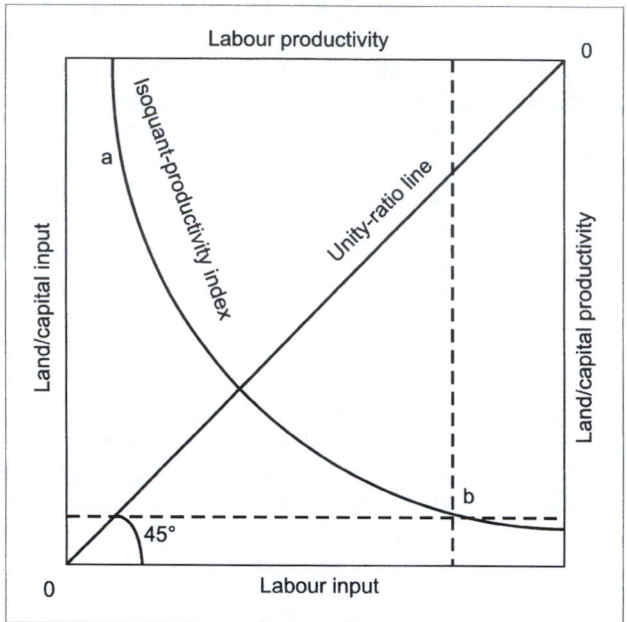

*Figure 1.1* Trade-off between land/capital and land productivities

lack of growth in Chinese traditional technology, as presented in his 'high-level equilibrium trap' (Elvin 1973: 313; see also Fei and Liu 1977). The key condition for Elvin's model is diminishing returns in the very long term, which means that given sufficient time a traditional society, as inventive and innovative though it might be, would eventually be trapped and that only modern science-based technology can offer a relief by dramatically stretching the productivity frontier. But that relief, as suggested by Elvin's trap, is likely to disappear in the long run, for diminishing returns will set in one day in the distant future. Thus this is basically a Malthusian model. On the other hand, the notion of 'quantitative growth, qualitative standstill' implies that (1) the Chinese economy reached optimal resource allocation, and (2) technology was an exogenous factor in the Chinese system (Elvin 1973: chs 17 and 18). A similar attempt has been made to portray Song China as a case of one-off growth of the Smithian type that is characterised by better resource allocation without technological breakthrough (Kelly 1997). This echoes the Ricardian 'stationary state'.

From the viewpoint that China did not go any further to achieve an indigenous industrialisation, Elvin's model seems very convincing. However, also taking the Boserupian model into account, one faces a difficult choice: the Chinese were evidently very creative, as demonstrated by Joseph Needham.

So, they should not have been trapped. The acid test of Elvin's trap hypothesis will have to come from a comprehensive analysis of the living standard during Ming – Qing times, especially after 1600. So far, there is little evidence to show (1) that at the macro level China imported large quantities of food from other countries or (2) that China suffered a long-lasting and large-scale famine during that period in spite of the fact that she did have frequent disasters of all sorts: mass armed rebellions, alien invasions and conquest, floods, droughts and locust plagues. Instead, new plant species, ranging from cash crops (such as American cotton, tobacco, peanuts and chili) to staple-food types (like potato, sweet potato and maize), were actively diffused across China and fed the rising population (Wang Y. 1964: 232; Shi S. 1979: 694; Lin G. 1982; Yang B. 1982; Zhang K. and Li G. 1983: 94–5; ZNK 1984: 91–3; Tang Q. 1986: 213–24, 278; Guo W. 1988: 383–5, 421–2). In addition, it has been commonly agreed that during Ming–Qing times, China's commercialisation and urbanisation maintained a reasonable level which in turn depended on agricultural surplus (see Fu Y. 1966; Wu C. 1985; Zhang J. 1995). As mentioned earlier, the increase in population and food price did not qualify the Ming–Qing Period for a Malthusian crisis. Most obvious of all, both the phenomenon of the continuation of Chinese population growth to this day (today's population is easily triple the number at the Qing peak) and the limited modern scientific and technical inputs in China's agricultural production indicate a great leeway permitted by premodern farming: as late as the mid-1930s, as much as 25 per cent of agricultural growth was owed to streamlined traditional technology (Buck 1968: 203). Thus by late Qing times the economy may not have been trapped by the combination of traditional farming methods and an increased number of people.

After all, it is doubtful whether modern technology alone was responsible for the rise of the West and the fall of China. In Europe, the trial-and-error-based traditional technology accommodated some revolutionary changes: the geographic discoveries of the Columbus–da Gama type in the fifteenth century and the long line of improvements of the prime mover prior to 1765 in the hand of artisans like James Watt, to name just a few. The point is that China reached more or less the same level of technology (with a list of 'relevant' inventions ranging from the mechanical clock and the printing machine to the water-powered spinner) and thus had a similar capacity or potential. What was missing in China was that the economy failed to take full advantage of the indigenous technology. So, the reason for China's failure is likely to have been much more than just technical.

Francesca Bray put forward another hypothesis, which may be called the 'rice black hole' theory (1986). She claims that rice cultivation, characterised by its unique scale of diseconomies, is like a black hole to suck in any amount of capital and labour inputs without reaching the point where the marginal labour product equals zero. In other words, in rice farming there are no diminishing returns and the productivity potential can never be fully realised. Because of this black hole, she argues, rice-farming Asia has little surplus labour and capital available for non-agricultural and non-rural development. The credibility of such a model is indeed questionable if one considers that (1) a long-time rice producer, Japan, has not been sucked in by this black hole; and (2) China, an economy which has not yet achieved industrialisation, has never had a mono-crop agriculture with rice. It is clear that wet rice cultivation was not a necessary factor for the developmental status in Asia. Bray realises such potential self-contradiction, especially taking rice-growing Japan into account (1986: 217). Thus she treats Tokugawa Japan as a petty commodity producer that could overrule the black hole. However, she ignores the fact that China, a country which was responsible for the invention of the first paper currency in world history, was far more ancient and active a petty commodity producer than Tokugawa Japan. Also, her theory fails to indicate how an Asian rice economy can break away from its black hole without external shocks.

### 1.2.1.7 Dualism/transition model

The dualistic model was established by Arthur Lewis to explain the mechanisms by which a non-industrial or non-capitalist society can be transformed into an industrial one. His premise is that labour productivity (measured by the marginal product of labour) is substantially higher in the capitalist sector (mainly the industrial sector) than in the non-capitalist sector (mainly the 'traditional' agrarian sector). As a result, capitalist industries can afford to offer much higher wage rates than agriculture. Such a wage difference attracts labour from farms to factories. Thus, siphoning labour from rural areas is all the transition is about. His model suggests that an economy with dual sectors self-generates growth and structural change (in terms of 'unlimited supply of labour' to the high return-yielding sectors).

China had a long history of traditional industries and commerce which yielded returns much higher than those from farming (Deng 1997: chs 4–6). But there is no evidence for any transition of the Lewisian type, including during the periods when the Han and Song economic revolutions took place. This suggests that a sizeable capitalist sector in the economy, not just high returns, is a necessary condition to the model. Moreover, from the neoclassical viewpoint, Lewis's model will work only under two conditions: (1) the absence of any institutional barrier against labour mobility from agriculture to industry, and (2) perfect competition between the two labour markets with perfect information flow. To meet these conditions, the society ought to have at least one sector that has well-established capitalism. In Tsarist Russia, for example, economic dualism under the government-led industrialisation scheme proved to be a threat to social stability and was partly responsible for the rise of communism because of the enormous cost that fell upon the peasantry, the very class that should have been content, according to Lewis (Gerschenkron 1963: 130). If so, the actual transition period should be over before the Lewisian process can even begin. This is logically problematic since the very prerequisites of such cross-sectional transition mean a universally accepted capitalist entrepreneurial profit-maximising behaviour, as portrayed by Lewis's thesis: (1) population constantly pursues a high wage rate and has no hesitation in crossing the border to enter the non-agricultural sectors; (2) because of such inter-market mobility, no market will have to face the problem of being stuck in a situation of marginal product of labour (MPL) approaching zero; (3) no room is left for surplus population in agriculture; and (4) the society will become, almost painlessly, industrialised. Such a happy ending is the central point of Lewis's model for the process of industrialisation, which was counter-factual in both the first industrialised economy, England, and in a late industrialiser, Russia, as shown by Karl Marx in Volume 3 of his *Das Kapital* and Alexander Gerschenkron in his *Economic Backwardness in Historical Perspective* (1962: 69).

At the pure theoretical level, the model is also problematic. According to Lewis, if a society has a dual economy (i.e. traditional agriculture coexisting with industry), the surplus rural population will leave agriculture for industry to establish a new livelihood. This is what the process of specialisation, urbanisation and, above all, industrialisation is about (Lewis 1954). But, conceptually, this transition will sooner or later come to a halt owing to the innate market mechanisms. This situation can be portrayed by the marginal analysis. To begin with, a marginal revenue product (MRP) curve can be derived from the curve of the marginal physical product of labour (MPL) through multiplying the latter by a price level. Thus, MPL can be regarded as a proxy for the marginal revenue product curve. Moreover, the marginal revenue product curve is often taken as a demand curve of the labour market. Therefore, MPL can also be regarded as a proxy for the labour demand curve. With free competition, in the sectoral labour markets, the equilibrium wage rates ($W_1$, $W_2$) and equilibrium employment levels ($Q_1$, $Q_2$) are determined at the point where a downward-sloping demand curve and an upward-sloping supply curve intersect. This intersection occurs before the marginal physical product curve approaches the zero point. In Figure 1.2, such an intersection is at points $a_1$ in market A and points $a_2$ in market B. According to Lewis's theory, rural labour will leave agriculture after point $a_1$ which is distant from the earlier-mentioned labour input floor MPL = 0 at point $b_1$. In other words, in a dual economy, a surplus agrarian population will leave the agricultural sector much earlier than the point where labour input no longer makes any neo-classical economic sense.

At points $a_1$ and $a_2$, the market reaches an equilibrium wage rate and Keynesian full employment in that all the workers who accept the wage deal are employed, and that the idle labour ($Qm_1 - Q_1$, $Qm_2 - Q_2$) is the result of voluntary unemployment. However, the voluntary unemployment

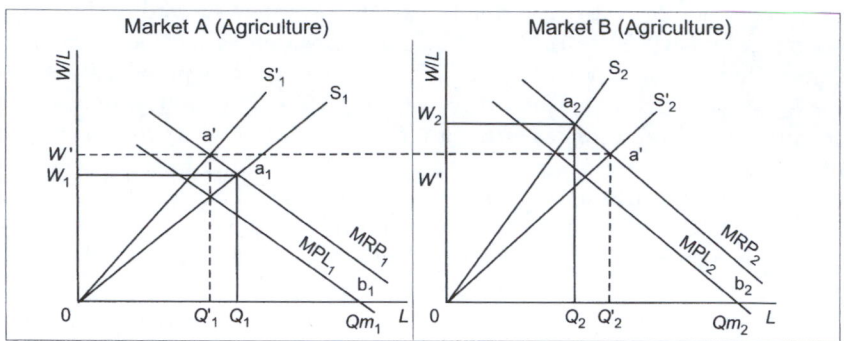

*Figure 1.2* Labour markets under economic dualism

labour is mobile. If a higher wage rate is offered either inside or outside a particular sector, this amount of labour will be attracted. As illustrated in Figure 1.2, when market B offers a wage rate at $W_2$ which is higher than $W_1$ at market A, a proportion of unemployed labour (between $Qm_1$ and $Q_1$) of market A will join the labour supply at market B. This will cause a supply shock to Market B, and the labour supply curve $S_2$ will shift down to $S'_2$, which in turn shifts the original equilibrium wage rate $W_2$ down to $W'$. Eventually, the loss in labour supply at market A will push its own labour supply curve from $S_1$ up to $S'_1$, and consequently causes the wage rate to increase from $W_1$ to $W'$. In the end, (1) market B receives more labour than before while the labour force at market A gets a higher wage than the starting point; (2) a universal wage rate is established between these two markets, and an inter-market equilibrium is reached; and (3) labour stops moving to market B. Unless the flow of labour between these two markets is blocked, the market mechanism will produce this result. The same principle works for capital input markets as well: if the industrial sector offers higher returns, the amount of agricultural capital in excess of the equilibrium input level will be transferred to industry, instead of staying in agriculture, and vice versa. Not realising this function of the market economy, Arthur Lewis claims that (1) a permanent gap (called the wage 'cliff') in wage rate can be maintained between the capitalist and the non-capitalist sectors, and (2) the only way to lower the wage rate in the capitalist sector is to undertake mass immigration from the labour-abundant subsistence economies of India and China (1954). In contrast, the marginal analysis indicates that if a surplus population is locked in the agricultural sector, it is not because of relative poverty as claimed by Arthur Lewis, but because of a market equilibrium.

Moreover, the dualistic model does not take the seasonality of agricultural production into account. Seasonality becomes crucial in peasant economic behaviour because it determines the fluctuation of the peasant marginal physical product of labour (MPL). In normal circumstances, during the busy seasons (for land preparation, sowing and harvesting) the peasant MPL increases dramatically instead of remaining at zero. So, by definition, an abundant labour supply is available, mainly during the slack seasons. However, this seasonal surplus in labour supply does not automatically make the rural population idle. Empirical evidence shows that in a traditional economy it is very common for the rural population to take up by-employments during the slack seasons to offset the lowered MPL in farming (for France see Hohenberg 1972: 234; for Russia see Mathias and Postan 1978: 330–41; for Japan see Francks 1992: 118–19, 139–40, 154–5; for India see Rothermund 1993: 75, 112–13, 131, 147). Once by-employments are considered, the peasant MPL is likely to be maintained above zero all year round. This is particularly relevant if the economy is open to international trade and the peasant by-employments are linked to the world market, which functions as the 'vent for surplus' and thus sustains the by-employments in the traditional sector. If this is the case, according to Lewis's own logic the temptation for people to leave the traditional sector diminishes even during the slack seasons because of the opportunity cost incurred by their by-employments.

Furthermore, Lewis's model only tells us the labour-supply side of the story, implying (1) an 'unlimited demand for labour' and (2) perfect interchangeability between farmers and factory workers as employees. This is certainly not true in reality throughout the history of industrialisation (see Sylla and Toniolo 1991). Evidence shows that the modern sector requires a labour force with some minimal skills. So, the demand for labour from the modern sector includes not only the quantity but also the quality of the factor. Poor quality of labour can backfire and reduce the quantity of labour demanded. For example, to overcome the problem of unskilled labour, in later industrialisers such as the United States, special-purpose machine tools had to be developed to replace labour of poor quality (see Harley 1991: 37–8), which in turn set up a ceiling for the quantity of labour demanded by industry. Therefore, even if one still considers the supply side only, as long as the rural labour and factory labour are not interchangeable parts without some hard training, the labour supply to industry will never be unlimited, owing to an inevitable skill barrier. Since labour demand from and supply to the industrial sector are both limited, the coexistence of the two economies can be perpetuated and this makes the transition of the traditional sector difficult.

Last, fundamentally, to undertake a Lewisian transition, a society has to solve the problem of food demand and supply. If one assumes the absence of food imports from the world market, the speed of such a transition depends entirely on how much surplus the agricultural sector can produce to feed the growing urban population, not on the free will of the farming quitters. From the neo-classical viewpoint, if food shortage occurs because of, for example, rapid industrialisation, the food price will be pushed up, and so will the real wage of food producers, with or without change in the marginal product of agricultural labour. The farmers, now receiving an increased income, will have little incentive to quit farming. So, to make Lewis's model work, a society will have to maintain an adequate food supply at any given time, which contradicts Lewis's implication that the agricultural sector suffers chronic low productivity as seen from the low marginal product of labour. If what Lewis means is to include foreign trade for food, his model becomes immediately inconclusive because the transition partly depends upon the performance of other food-exporting economies. To rescue the model, one must assume that revolutionary changes in farming technology should be taken into account whereby the food supply is secured. But any such change will certainly increase the marginal product of labour in agriculture, improve the real wage rate and thus keep the farmers within the sector. To summarise, either food shortage or improvement of farming technology will stop labour from joining industry.

### 1.2.1.8 Institutional model

The institutional model was first established by the German Historical School in the nineteenth century whose founder, List, rejects a universal developmental path and believes that each country has to find its own way to prosper. He argues that institutions such as law and order, banking and the postal service are imperative to foster socio-economic development in some countries. Following this line of thought, in the 1970s North and Thomas established a 'new economic history' which was marked by their joint book *The Rise of the Western World*. They claim that developmental success in the West owed much to an economic organisation/institution which efficiently balanced across sectors: (1) the social cost and private cost; (2) social returns and private returns; (3) the social cost and private returns; and (4) the private cost and social returns. The private rate of return is the sum of the net receipts which the economic unit receives from undertaking an activity. The social rate of return is the total net benefit (positive or negative) that society gains from the same activity; – it is the private rate of return plus the net effect of the activity upon everyone else in the society. This total balance sheet of all costs and returns, very similar to Pareto's optimal point for the market, generated and sustained individual incentives to produce more and better until a society reached industrial revolution. North and Thomas thus argued that the Industrial Revolution was not the source of modern economic growth but rather the outcome of it (1973: 1–3). According to North and Thomas, the core of this institution was producers' property rights, which raised the previously stifled private rate of return on developing new techniques for production (*ibid*.: 8, 157). They went further by saying that the failures – the Iberian Peninsula in the past, and much of Latin America, Asia and Africa in our times – have been a consequence of inefficient economic institutions, mainly the lack of property rights (*ibid*.: 157).[5]

This model, however, cannot explain why premodern China did not develop in spite of the fact that individual private ownership not only was common but also was established very early. To take land as an example, private ownership was legalised as early as in 594 BC and became the norm after the Warring States Period (476–221 BC) (see, for example, Liu Z. *et al.* 1979: 113, 132–59). As a result, land-holding peasants formed the majority of the Chinese Empire. This is demonstrated by the residual of this old institution: in the 1930s, at least 70 per cent of the rural households still belonged to the category of free landholders (see Tawney 1964: 34; Chao 1986: ch. 8). R. H. Tawney thus pointed out that the typical figure in Chinese country life is not the hired labourer but the land-holding peasant (1964: 34). From the Han to the Qing periods (Qin: 221–207 BC; Qing: 1644–1911 AD), agrarian reforms in China were aimed mainly at reinforcing private land ownership through either the redistribution of already privately owned land or the privatisation of state-owned land (especially on frontiers and in other marginal areas). Not surprisingly, China did not have a real need for radical reform to change the type of land ownership as Japan and Russia did in the mid-eighteenth century to dissolve their feudal systems. China's private land ownership laid the foundation for what can be called 'pan-commercialisation' at the grass-roots level, which can be described as 'small farms and great market circulation' (Zhang Zhongmin 1996). The establishment and maintenance of private rights did not, however, lead China to industrial capitalism. Instead, the economy was characterised by overwhelming agricultural dominance. By the end of the nineteenth century, there had been no apparent trend for the economy as a whole to shift to any other pattern: what modern researchers have found is some 'sprout of capitalism', weak, primitive and sporadic, which was more like a form of proto-industrialisation than capitalism (Li J. 1957: chs 5–6; 1962: ch. 15; Elvin 1973: 164–78; Liu C. 1982; Bray 1984: 565–6). In other words, producers' property rights were not a sufficient condition for economic growth and they alone did not help China develop towards industrialisation.

In addition, Douglass North believes that the impetus for changes in property rights comes from population growth, and that the higher the population density the more advanced the economic institution (North 1981: chs 7, 9). Because of this, the criticism of the Boserupian model in relation to Chinese economic history is also relevant to the institutional model: if population is the dynamo of institutional progress, why did China not lead the world? In particular, why did China reject private ownership and practise communism in the 1950s–1980s?

### 1.2.1.9 *Bureaucratic determinism*

Related to the institutional model is what can be called 'bureaucratic determinism' or 'buro-determinism'. Professor John K. Fairbank reached the conclusion from his research that what stifled China's developmental potential was the Chinese imperial bureaucracy. On the one hand, as a neatly organised institution with enormous coercive power, the Chinese bureaucracy was able to put the merchant class under constant check and to crack down upon any undesirable or 'non-orthodox' growth in the economy. On the other hand, as an attractive profession for career advancement, it was able to siphon a continuous supply of the best-educated and most talented citizens to serve the Establishment so that the highest-qualified human capital went to waste (Fairbank 1957, 1965, 1980; Perkins 1967; Balazs 1972; Qian W. 1985; see also Wittfogel 1957). One may question the validity of viewing China as a unified political entity in the long run. However, the fact that over the past two thousand years the mainland Chinese lived under one government for 70–75 per cent of the time justifies such generalisation.

Although plausible, bureaucratic determinism cannot explain why in traditional China urban centres and trade (regional, inter-regional and overseas) were common and science and technology flourished (see Needham 1954–94; Skinner 1964–5, 1977; Elvin 1973). Most important of all, as Professor Eric L. Jones repeatedly stresses, the first recorded intensive growth (or growth in per capita terms) occurred in Song China, centuries ahead of Europe and Japan (Jones 1988; Goudsblom *et al.* 1996: ch. 5). These achievements at least indicated that the institutional barrier was not any more prohibitive in bureaucratic China than in places where an authoritarian bureaucracy was absent. Compared with early modern states in Western Europe and Japan, the Chinese state was rather weak and inefficient which makes it dubious to blame the Confucian government for what it virtually had no control over (Jones 1988: ch. 8).

Bureaucratic determinism receives ammunition from the comparative front. A key point made in Professor Joel Mokyr's *Lever of the Riches* is that China's failure was rooted in its centralised state structure, which overruled internal competition, while inter-state competition, which worked with the same rule and result as market competition, led Europe to an optimal locus in developmental probabilities up to the point of the Industrial Revolution (Mokyr 1990: ch. 9). Plausible too, this hypothesis does not explain why and how this centralised state also managed to foster or at least to tolerate growth in China ahead of that in Europe until the sixteenth century, and possibly longer. In other words, why and how could optimal or near-optimal points also be reached under the Chinese system? So, competition among political units seems not to have been a necessary condition for growth to take place in mainland Asia prior to the sixteenth century.

### 1.2.1.10 Petty farming, landlordism and government rent-seeking determinism

The term in the above heading is an awkward one but popular in contemporary studies of Chinese economic history. It is a mixture of (1) the Marxian conception of property ownership-based class differentiation, the need for so-called 'primitive capital accumulation' and the formation of a proletariat; and (2) the Smithian–Ricardian doctrine of the power of economies of scale, which is based on the social division of labour, the consequent surplus from enhanced productivity for capital formation and accumulation. It is a revisionist view in that China is treated as a unique case in which petty owner-farmers and small landlords prevailed *vis-à-vis* the large feudal holdings in much of medieval Europe and pre-Meiji Japan.

Scholars of this school commonly hold that (1) there was little surplus on the peasant part because petty land holding farms could barely maintain subsistence living because of their low productivity and heavy tax burden while tenants on larger estates were ruthlessly exploited to the very limit by rent-seeking landlords; and (2) there was no capital formation for modern growth by landlords or government because the former were interested only in reinvesting in land and maintaining an extravagant lifestyle while the latter had only non-productive fiscal policies. They thus claim that China's growth potential was retarded by small-scale agriculture, weakness in the social division of labour, shortage in capital formation/accumulation and a deficiency in the formation of both capitalists and proletariat. In their eyes, Chinese petty farming with the parasitical landlords and state was the worst enemy of indigenous capitalist growth. Often, Western imperialism is also added as another key retardant of a native modern growth (Han D. 1957, 1986; Sanlian Books 1957; Xie G. 1980; Yin J. 1980; Li W. 1981; Fang X. 1981–1984, 1986; Liu C. 1982; FDL *et al.* 1983; Li S. 1984: 319–25; Wang J. 1984; Wu C. 1985; Xu D. and Wu C. 1985; Han D. 1986; Zhou Y. and Xie Z. 1986; Cao G. 1989). A typical study in English was done by Philip C. C. Huang, who suggests that the 'familisation' of rural production in the Yangzi Delta, China's most advanced farming zone since around AD 1000, led to economic 'involution' – China did not just stagnate but hopelessly withered (1990).

The landlord rent-seeking hypothesis needs to be tested against history. For us to suppose that landlord exploitation was able to take place, China's total agricultural output must have been capable of providing a surplus, as demonstrated by the distance between the production frontier and the subsistence living line in Figure 1.3. The total amount of surplus is represented by the shaded area $QQ'ab$. According to the landlordism hypothesis, this shaded area was taken by landlords as rent and little surplus was left for the tenants, whose total subsistence wage bill is marked by the area of $0QbL$. Here, the demographic indication is that the tenant population will more or less stay at $L$, and that the main driving force of population growth will have to come from the landlord class, which possesses and translates its rent into an extra human biomass within the range of $L–L'$ Under these circumstances, population growth will be modest simply because the landlords have a strong incentive to maintain their standard of living above that of their tenants. Indeed, the Tokugawa feudal land system put the Japanese

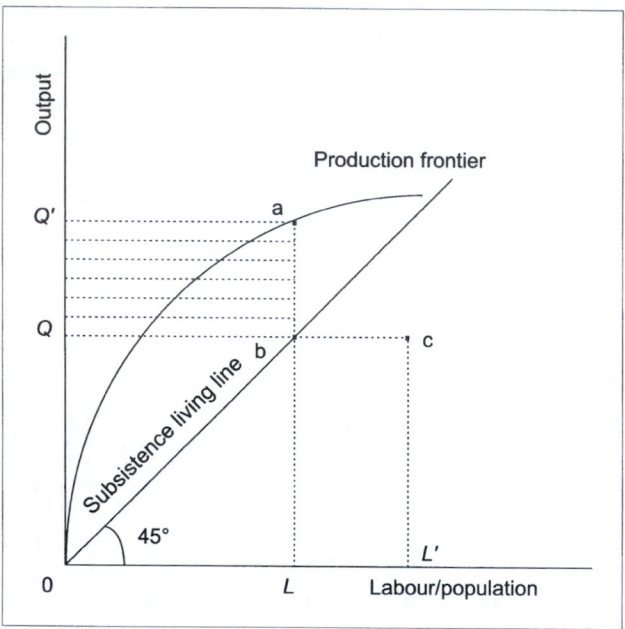

*Figure 1.3* Rent-seeking and population check

population under such a check, as is convincingly shown by Feeney and Hamano (1990). Heavy government rent-seeking has a similar effect on land-holding farmers.

The alleged rampant growth of landlordism is often related to the Ming–Qing Period. However, China's population also exploded during this period, which probably began in the first half of the eighteenth century and ended China's long-term demographic stability at 30–50 million people. The starting point of this growth is inferred from the average growth rate of 1.45 a year based on the data for 1741–1851 and 1863–87. With this rate, it would take about 45 years to double the population. The population reached 143.4 million by 1741, doubled by 1790 to 301.5 million, and peaked by 1851 at 432.2 million, before dropping back by 1863 to 240 million and bouncing back by 1887 to 377.6 million (Liang F. 1980: 4–11; 251–4, 256–7). From the data for 1741–1851, the population growth rate was 1 per cent a year; from those for 1863–87, 1.9 per cent a year (*ibid.*; cf. McEvedy and Jones 1978: 167). So, there was little sign that a rent-seeking-cum-population check, valid in feudal Japan, existed in Ming–Qing China.

One possible explanation is that the Chinese landlords generated the population growth. If so, the annual growth by this class would have to be ridiculously high: 2.5–4.8 per cent if landlords and their families made up 40 per cent of the total population (which is doubtful); 3.3–6.3 per cent if they represented 30 per cent; or 5–19 per cent if they constituted 10 to 20 per cent (which are the more likely proportions: see Chang 1955; Rawski 1979: 23; Wang D. 1982: 69–70; Wang X. 1987: 171). These rates are beyond not only human social capacity but also the biological capacity for reproduction. In other words, the fact that China's population went from $L$ to $L'$ contradicts the landlordism hypothesis.

To elaborate this point further, it is commonly agreed that during the Ming–Qing Period the tenancy rate was higher in south than in north China. Landlordism determinism would be expected to generate less vigorous population growth in the south than in the north. But evidence shows just the opposite in the following set of data covering a century (based on Liang F. 1980: 258, 262). They come from the Qing poll tax records and are thus reasonably accurate.

| Province | Year | | | | | |
|---|---|---|---|---|---|---|
| | 1749 | 1757 | 1767 | 1791 | 1839 | 1851 |
| *North China* | | | | | | |
| Fengtian | 100 | 105 | 174 | 202 | 532 | 636 |
| Zhili | 100 | 103 | 120 | 167 | 160 | 168 |
| Shanxi | 100 | 101 | 110 | 140 | 155 | 165 |
| Shaanxi | 100 | 105 | 109 | 125 | 178 | 178 |
| Gansu | 100 | 104 | 202 | 267 | 270 | 271 |
| Shandong | 100 | 103 | 107 | 96 | 130 | 139 |
| Henan | 100 | 125 | 129 | 165 | 184 | 186 |
| Anhui | 100 | 104 | 108 | 135 | 172 | 174 |
| Mean | — | 106 | 132 | 162 | 223 | 240 |
| *South China* | | | | | | |
| Jiangsu | 100 | 108 | 113 | 152 | 200 | 211 |
| Zhejiang | 100 | 123 | 139 | 187 | 240 | 254 |
| Hubei | 100 | 106 | 111 | 262 | 428 | 449 |
| Hunan | 100 | 101 | 103 | 188 | 227 | 238 |
| Sichuan | 100 | 107 | 118 | 354 | 1,394 | 1,785 |
| Jiangxi | 100 | 108 | 139 | 231 | 290 | 291 |
| Guizhou | 100 | 108 | 112 | 168 | 175 | 177 |
| Guangxi | 100 | 125 | 153 | 210 | 245 | 254 |
| Fujian | 100 | 105 | 106 | 166 | 236 | 264 |
| Guangdong | 100 | 104 | 107 | 251 | 382 | 440 |
| Yunnan | 100 | 104 | 110 | 182 | 346 | 380 |
| Mean | — | 109 | 119 | 214 | 378 | 431 |

Here, two points can be made. First, south China, where the tenancy rate is believed to have been high, also had a high population growth rate, which means that the agricultural surplus accessible to the landlord class was not as great as one might think, not enough to prove a considerable check on population increase. Second, the north, where the tenancy rate was low, at the same time experienced impressive population growth, which suggests that the Chinese government was not efficient in tapping off agricultural surplus so that enough was left in private hands to support more and larger families. This situation is portrayed in Figure 1.3, where the area $QQ'ab$ is 'translated' into $LbcL'$ as a result of the extra population. After all, rent-seeking alone did not stop the Japanese of the late Tokugawa Period from moving towards industrialisation.

It has remained controversial whether a dramatic increase in the tenancy rate did occur and whether the petty peasant economy really sank in Ming –Qing China (Chao 1981; Li B.Z. 1984, 1985, 1996a, b; Xu T. 1995; Guo C. 1996; Wang Y. 1996; Zhang J. 1995: 42). Evidence from a field study of land ownership in Jiangsu in the 1920s shows that the tenancy rate was kept very low (based on Li B.Z. 1996a: 6; cf. Buck 1937: 445–7). The percentages are the proportions of total cultivated land.

| County | Number of villages under investigation | Small holding | Medium holding | | Proportion of total land under cultivation |
|---|---|---|---|---|---|
| | | 1–5 *mu* (%) | 5–15 *mu* (%) | 15–20 *mu* (%) | (%) |
| Shanghai | 7 | 29 | 61 | 9 | 100 |
| Fengxian | 6 | 2 | 44 | 51 | 97 |
| Nanhui | 7 | 6 | 40 | 48 | 94 |
| Chuansha | 4 | 14 | 58 | 26 | 98 |
| Taicang | 6 | 16 | 47 | 35 | 98 |
| Baoshan | 5 | 41 | 42 | 15 | 98 |
| Songjiang | 7 | 7 | 37 | 54 | 98 |
| Qingpu | 5 | 30 | 50 | 15 | 95 |
| Jinshan | 5 | 5 | 34 | 55 | 94 |
| Jiading | 8 | 14 | 50 | 33 | 97 |
| Chongming | 9 | 48 | 35 | 13 | 96 |
| Mean | – | 19 | 45 | 32 | 97 |

Highly compatible with the 'petty farms–extra population' paradigm, the high proportion of freeholders in Jiangsu, a phenomenon which has been defined as 'pan-medium-size landholding', refutes both the landlordism and government rent-seeking hypotheses.

It is worth noting that such a land distribution pattern was very similar to that of Japan after the 1873 Land-Tax Reform. The percentages are of the shares of privately owned land in the total cultivated land (based on Francks 1992: 133). For comparison, hectares used in the original data are converted to *mu*.

| Year | Small and medium holding | | | Share in total land under cultivation | Large holding | |
|---|---|---|---|---|---|---|
| | <7.5 mu (%) | 7.5–15 mu (%) | 15–30 mu (%) | | 30–75 mu (%) | >75 mu (%) |
| 1908 | 37.3 | 32.6 | 19.5 | 89.4 | 9.4 | 1.2 |
| 1935 | 33.7 | 34.3 | 22.5 | 90.5 | 8.1 | 1.4 |

China's land distribution pattern was also similar to the landholding pattern of South Korea after the 1947–8 Land Reform periods. The South Korean landholding pattern has been recognised as a celebrated case of a successful modern land reform and a solid footing for equity. For comparison, hectares used in the original data are also converted to *mu*. The percentages are the proportions of privately owned land out of the total cultivated land as in 1974 (based on Hasan and Rao 1979: 206):

| Small holding | Medium holding | | Share in total land under cultivation | Large holding |
|---|---|---|---|---|
| <7.5 mu (%) | 7.5–15 mu (%) | 15–45 mu (%) | | >45 mu (%) |
| 10.6 | 29.7 | 52.9 | 93.2 | 6.8 |

If one transcends the *parti pris* of the Marxian–Rostowian linearism with the West European–Japanese model as the yardstick, China's petty peasant agriculture was at least not less successful than that of any other pre-industrial economies in world history. Again, stagnation and regression were common in the pre-industrial world. So, what appeared to be a problem here was not uniquely Chinese but rather universal. Interestingly, few scholars see a problem in such a petty peasant economy by the Song Period (AD *960–1279*) and many even applaud the same peasant economy as a functional, humane and incentive-generating model whose performance supported the lasting Chinese civilisation. Moreover, the dividing of large land estates into smaller landholding farms has been commonly practised by agricultural reformers of modern times: from the Meiji Land-tax Reform (1873–6), through Stolypin's land reform in Russia (1906–11) to more recent postwar land shake-ups in Taiwan and South Korea. It is also no secret that the success of current rural economic reform under Deng Xiaoping lies chiefly in the re-establishment of petty farms to replace China's failed three decades' long experiment with agricultural collectivisation (see for example Chinn 1979; Kueh 1984; Lardy 1983, 1986; Lin, J. 1987; McMillan *et al.* 1989; Putterman 1988; Nee *et al.*, 1989; Nee and Su 1990). The small farm is thus seen in contemporary China as the saviour of the rural economy. The question is: why should the creation of petty farms become a prerequisite for modern growth in those cases, while the Chinese system operating with the same principle is blamed for underdevelopment? Or, why has the petty farm, coming full circle after the failure of Stalinism–Maoism, become such an economic dynamo in contemporary China? Such an apparent double standard reveals the fact that the petty farm was not a sufficient condition for China's underdevelopment.

Thus, China's problem seems not to have been rent-seeking by landlords or government nor the inability of the petty peasant to produce a surplus but a high propensity and high efficiency in channelling agricultural surplus to population growth. At this point, it is inevitable that we should go back to Malthusianism.

### 1.2.1.11 *World-system determinism*

Attempts have been also made to explain China's underdevelopment in the macro-context of the world. Orthodox Leninists and Wallerstein both indicate the existence of a developmental hierarchy in a super-macro system concerning the entire world (Lenin 1960; Mao 1965; see also Wallerstein 1974–86). Within the system, economic development of an individual society is dictated by other players. Imperialist and colonialist powers, as the extension of their domestic bourgeoisie, exploit the underdeveloped countries, as the extension of their domestic poor. It is in the interest of such powers not to see modern development in the Third World. It is an appealing thought. But given that China and Western Europe reached more or less the same technical and economic levels around the seventeenth century (Hartwell 1963; 1967; Elvin 1973, 1988; Bray 1984), world-system determinism does not tell us how and why some underdogs eventually became top dogs and vice versa, as if the world order is given both *ab extra* and *a priori*.

Similarly, we are told by J. A. Goldstone that there existed a macro system across Eurasia. The key societies (namely England, France, Germany, the Ottoman Empire, China and Japan) synchronised in at least two areas of development during the early modern period: population growth and resource constraints (as seen in food prices, elite employment opportunities and government budgets), and that crises and 'revolutions' were the universal result (1991: ch. 1; 352–3, 355, 359–60). If this is true, why did revolutions in seventeenth-century England, eighteenth-century France and, to a certain extent, nineteenth-century Japan usher in a new era of industrial growth, but did not prove so helpful to their Ottoman and Chinese counterparts during the seventeenth and nineteenth centuries? Or, why did a further develop-mental synchronisation have to fail, which left mainland Asia to old poverty but led Western Europe to new abundance?

### 1.2.2. Common problems with the models

The sheer number of the models, 11 in all (for a shorter line-up of theories/model regarding China's economic development see Lippit 1987: ch. 3), shows just how many variables need to be taken into account in dealing with the Chinese experience of the past millenna. It also indicates just how far apart scholars are in solving China's paradoxes: some are diametrically opposed as in the cases of Malthus versus Boserup, developmental stages versus the Asiatic Mode of Production, Marxism (historic materialism) versus ideological deter-minism, institutionalism and bureaucratic determinism, and so forth.

The first common problem is that although these models have offered sens-ible explanations of why China declined, they cannot explain equally satisfac-torily why China rose in the first place, or vice versa. The cause of this problem is the seeming inconsistency or incompatibility between China's 'victory' and 'failure', which forms the very core of China's paradoxes.

The second common problem lies in the use of Europe as a universal bench-mark. The contributory factors to European growth are often taken as the basics (such as the type of mindset, the kind of government policy and its impact, the status of the merchant class, the degree of domestic and foreign trade, the extent of urbanisation, the timing for changes and so forth). If a society had those conditions/factors, growth is expected to have taken place. If not, something must have been wrong. In searching for an answer, anything which made China distinct from the West is inevitably considered to have been responsible for China's downfall. The use of this reference system can be misleading because the underlying concern is eventually why, with so many factors in common, China was not another Europe. This is where the paradoxes begin. At this point, it is easy to see where ideological determinism and bureaucratic determinism came from: Confucianism and a centralised bureaucracy are singled out mainly because of their absence in Europe.

Nevertheless, this is not to say that all these models and hypotheses are worthless. They are valid in explaining the developmental phenomenon in many parts of the world or some parts of the Chinese past. But when dealing with the long-term premodern Chinese history as a whole, they become in one way or another inadequate. Even if all the aforementioned theories and hypotheses are to be combined to form a synthesis, the common problems are still there.

The long-lasting history and rich experience of the Chinese have made China an unignorable 'factual' and thus 'counter-theoretical' (as opposite to the vision that 'China as a counter-factual'). It thus necessitates new ways to look at and decode China's paradoxes.

## 1.3 Areas to examine and theoretical tools

### 1.3.1 Areas and elements

Obviously, China's developmental path in the past millennia was unique: it was not like Europe which experienced development to reach industrialisation; nor was it like the ancient civilizations of Egypt, Babylonia and the Maya, whose progress came to a full stop. The recognition of this uniqueness should not be interpreted as exceptionalism to treat China as another planet which operated with a set of rules totally different from those for the rest of the world.

On the other hand, understanding premodern China necessitates a detachment from the stereotype of the 'developmental norm'. The seeming inconsistency or incompatibility between China's victory and failure may just be notional, if one transcends the 'unilinear trap'. For this reason, areas to examine will have to be different from the conventional choice – such as resource endowments and allocation, input and output, technology and productivity, income and living standard, commercialisation and urbanisation, population and human capital, classes and government, policies and mindset or 'culture' – with analytical approaches equally different from the conventional. The reason is simply that (1) they represent 'trees' but not the 'wood'; and (2) they are either the conditions for or the outcomes of the Chinese socio-economic developmental path rather than the cause of it.

The main areas to examine are: (1) the dominant socio-economic structure; (2) the main interrelations between the economy and the social and economic institutions; (3) the behavioural patterns of economic agents; and (4) the self-regulating mechanisms for perpetuating non-industrial and non-capitalist growth. They transcend the scopes of resource endowments and allocation, input and output, technology and productivity, income and living standard, commercialisation and urbanisation, population and human capital, and so forth, and thus allow us to see the wood. After all, it is the 'wood' that made China different from, for example, the capitalist, industrial forerunners of the West in spite of the fact that China's 'trees' sometimes appeared strikingly similar to those of their Western counterparts.

Within these four agenda areas, elements subject to close attention include: (1) institutions, especially land ownership types and their impact on the economy; (2) behavioural patterns of the peasantry and other classes; (3) government economic policies, their making, function and impact; and (4) peasant armed rebellions and alien conquests, two main shocks to the system, their functions in and impacts on the socio-economic structure. The reason why these elements are chosen is that, generally speaking: (1) institutions accommodate the socio-economic structure of a society; (2) influenced by institutions, economic behaviour affects later development; and (3) government economic policies reflect institutions and the socio-economic structure of a

30

society. In these aspects, premodern China was no exception. Periodic peasant armed rebellions and alien invasion/conquests played an important part in regulating the economy; unique to premodern China, they are thus included.

### 1.3.2 Theoretical approaches and tools

#### 1.3.2.1 Conventional factorial approach versus equilibrium analysis

Many scholars believe that China's problem was due to deficiencies in certain factors, which can be defined as the 'factorial approach'. First, the Chinese social structure and institutions (class structure, ownership type, family system, authoritarian régime, educational system and so on) had a negative impact on economic development (Sanlian Books 1957; Fairbank 1965: pt. 1; Perkins 1967; Yin J. 1980; Fang X. 1981; Liu C. 1982; Wang J. 1984). Second, Chinese traditional technology had its limit and eventually became exhausted before scientific experiment-based modern technology came about (Elvin 1973; Du S. *et al.* 1982; Bray 1984 and 1986; Qian 1985). Third, Chinese ideology and cultural values froze Chinese creativity and squandered their energy and talent (Fairbank 1965: pt. 1; Qian 1985). Fourth, China's physical environment and natural resources locked the Chinese in a non-capitalist trend (Lee 1969: 13–17; Hicks 1969; Bray 1986; Chao 1986). Fifth, China's population was a burden on development (Elvin 1973; Chao 1986).

The factorial approach has contributed a great deal to the understanding of premodern China. However, apart from disagreement among scholars as to which factors should be regarded as more important than the others, this approach often implies that other conditions being equal, improvement or removal of the factors would have led to progress. This is counter-factual not only because a society cannot go back to its past, but also because 'other conditions' are very rarely equal among different civilisations. Moreover, the impact of those alleged deficiencies was not always obvious: one can always find opposite cases in which those deficiencies were either largely absent or even favourable to development. For instance, even with so many 'negative factors' China was evidently quite capable, at the highest level, of adopting new technology from the outside world, including post-Renaissance Europe. During the seventeenth and eighteenth centuries, it was rather fashionable among the Chinese upper classes to learn the 'Western knowledge' (*xixue*). Top court officials like Xu Guangqi (1561–1633) and Emperors Kangxi (r. 1661–1722) and Qianlong (r. 1736–96) were particularly involved. Western books were translated and Western equipment duplicated (see, for example, Deng 1993a: chs 3–5; Liu L. 1996). Second, Confucianism which 'confined' the Asian mind for so long, has helped several places with their industrialisation in the past hundered years. The countries that have been positively affected by Confucianism are Taiwan, Hong Kong, Singapore,

South Korea and Japan, with a combined population of 197.2 million, large enough to be noticeable (Anon. 1995: 19–36). Third, population pressure did not always present a problem in pre-Qing China, and even to the recent past China was still self-sufficient in grain.

China's problem was not just factorial. It was a problem of a series of interlocking factors in some kind of counterpoise or equipoise. Therefore, equilibrium analysis, commonly used in economics since the Marshallian model in the late nineteenth century, is preferable because it emphasises the mutuality and sees things through a network of elements rather than as factors in isolation; and such an analysis does not have to be static (Schumpeter 1954: 963–71). In effect, some scholars have already begun to adopt this approach to study China. Feuerwerker used the concept of 'equilibrium' to show conditions and factors which maintained socio-political stability in Chinese society (1976: 21–2). Fairbank's theory of 'dynastic cycle' implies also an equilibrium in explaining how the Chinese Empire revived so many times and survived for so long (Fairbank 1965: ch. 4; Fairbank and Reischarer 1979: 70–5). Finally, Mark Elvin's 'high level equilibrium trap' says it all (Elvin 1973: ch. 17).

However, what has been lacking is a study of China from the angle of an all-round equilibrium. To contribute to the decoding of the Chinese past, the present study will examine counterpoises or equipoises and their mechanisms from this new angle to see how an all-round equilibrium confined China and whether it was responsible for both China's success in surviving so long and her failure to pursue industrial capitalism.

Although equilibrium is the focal point in this monograph, factors as 'bricks' for construction will receive attention as they deserve. Thus the equilibrium approach leads to a synthesis.

### 1.3.2.2. Framework: a panorama analysis

Professor Eric L. Jones has established a comparative framework with the thrust of a macro- and multidimensional structural analysis which can be defined as a 'panorama analysis' or a 'panorama model'. It has an obvious advantage compared with its mono- or bi-dimensional counterparts.

The long name of the Jonesian model itself shows just what is involved in it and how demanding it is in use. First, there is the knowledge requirement: one needs to be very fluent with economic histories of the main civilisations in both the short run and the long run before any decent questions can be raised and comparisons made. Second, there is the mind-quality requirement: one will have to face a constant struggle for an acultural, apolitical, non-fatalistic, non-static and non-normative assessment of economic performances of different societies under a comparative scrutiny. Moreover, the model can be divergent, which equally causes difficulties for the researcher: unless a convergent point is defined and firmly grasped at all times, one easily gets lost in a maze. Here, an obvious trade-off for sophistication is the loss, to a degree, of user-friendliness.

Under the comparative microscope, Jones detected important structural differences among various societies at the family, communal and state levels. He argues that these differences in the social fabric produced very different results in socio-economic development as seen from what he calls the 'European miracle' versus the stagnation in the rest of the Eurasian world (Jones 1981). To decode how histories evolved, he also took pains to trace the determinants of these structures and exogenous factors affecting them, ranging from natural endowments to alien invasions.

The advantage of the structuralist model lies in that it does not tie the development issue to any particular area. Rather, it deals with a range of conditions for economic development: some conditions work as building bases and bricks, some as catalysts and buffers, some as blockers or inhibitors. These conditions are not necessarily designed for economic purposes in the beginning but have great impacts on economic life. This also means that the structuralist model is flexible enough to accommodate or complement most other models, a marked comparative advantage for studying China.

Extremely powerful, such an encompassing framework offers a useful framework with which to contemplate and probe into the core of China's paradoxes: it is clear that what made China different from other main civilisations in world history was its unique structure, which was characterised by a centralised government structure (regardless of the actual number of political entities coexisting), a successful agricultural sector and a sizeable traditional industrial sector with a marked degree of urbanisation and commercialisation, and a stable landholding peasantry with individual or quasi-individual property rights. Or, to put it another way, China had a unique structure which contained many factors commonly in existence in many societies, but the peculiar proportions of the factors, in both the spatial and temporal terms, were unique to China. By analogy, it is like the difference in the isomers in the natural world: the same molecules but with a different structure and thus different properties (as in diamond and graphite). The multidimensional, macro, panorama approach enables the present study to transcend the constraints and 'representative problem' incurred by micro and short-term case studies, and allows, at the same time, the present analysis to take advantage of the existing models, theories and hypotheses to understand China's socio-economic past.

## 1.4 Chinese names and historical periods

In this book, Chinese names are spelt according to the *pinyin* system, a standard practice since the 1970s. For the convenience of the reader, Chinese historical periods are listed in Table 1.1.

*Table 1.1.* Chinese historical periods

| Name | Time |
|---|---|
| 1 Neolithic Period | *c* 7500–3500 BC |
| 2 Xia (Hsia) | *c* 2000–1520 BC |
| 3 Shang | *c* 1520–1030 BC |
| 4 Zhou (Ch'ou) | *c* 1030–221 BC |
| (a) Western Zhou | *c* 1030–771 BC |
| (b) Spring and Autumn | 770–476 BC |
| (c) Warring States | 475–221 BC |
| 5 Qin (Ch'in) | 221–207 BC |
| 6 Han | 206 B.C.– AD 220 |
| (a) Western Han | 206 B.C.– AD 24 |
| (b) Eastern Han | 25– AD 220 |
| 7 Three Kingdoms | 221–265 |
| 8 Jin (Chin) | 266–420 |
| 9 Northern and Southern | 479–580 |
| (a) Qi | 479–502 |
| (b) Liang | 502–557 |
| (c) Chen | 557–589 |
| (d) Northern Wei | 386–534 |
| (e) Eastern Wei | 534–550 |
| (f) Northern Qi | 550–577 |
| (g) Northern Zhou | 557–581 |
| 10 Sui | 581–618 |
| 11 Tang (T'ang) | 618–907 |
| 12 Five Dynasties | 907–960 |
| 13 Song (Sung) | 960–1279 |
| (a) Northern Song | 960–1127 |
| (b Southern Song | 1127–1279 |
| 14 Jin (Tartar Ch'in) | 1115–1234 |
| 15 Yuan ( Yuen, Mongol) | 1271–1368 |
| 16 Ming | 1368–1644 |
| 17 Qing (Ch'ing, Manchu) | 1644–1911 |
| 18 Republic (Nationalist) | 1911–1949 |
| 19 People's Republic (Communist) | 1949– |

*Sources*: Based on CBW 1979: vol. 3 and Chao 1986.

# Notes

1 It has been speculated whether Marco Polo ever reached China (see Wood 1995). Even if Marco Polo's journey is treated as fictitious, China's prosperity and wealth in the past is undeniable, in view of the medieval records of neighbouring Korea, Japan, Ryukyu, Vietnam and Tibet, not to mention the rich archaeological evidence within and outside China.

2 Scholars have suggested that the absence of market activities was one of the key features of the European peasantry (see Macfarlane 1978: 21–3).

3 Robert W. Fogel was responsible for the invention of indirect measurement of growth through a counter-factual method as he tried to work out the impact of railways on the economic growth of the USA (1964). Fogel's way of thinking is typical of modern economics and modern sciences: factors can be isolated and measured with the assumption that other conditions are held constant or equal. Unfortunately, in the field of historical studies one cannot take 'other things' as being 'equal' which is in principle an ahistorical approach. Instead, the historian's task is to see which conditions differed from place to place, and when, how, why and to what extent these conditions changed over time. By analogy, 'other things being equal', would have implied that natural evolution would have resulted in only one common type since all the early species would have developed the same way. The very purpose of studying natural evolution would be in jeopardy.

4 Such a view is still around and influential (for a comparison of Europe and China see Diamond 1998).

5 To be fair, in developing his theory, Professor Douglass North later downplayed the importance of property rights and put more emphasis on 'transaction costs' (North 1981). However, the 'property rights–capitalist industrialisation' paradigm formed a milestone in economic history theories and thus should be treated seriously.

# 2

# MAIN FACTORS IN THE CHINESE SOCIO-ECONOMIC SYSTEM

The focus of this chapter is the main factors in China's socio-economic domain: namely the predominance of agriculture in the economy, prevailing private individual land ownership, the landholding peasantry as the majority, the physiocratic state, the centralised government and Confucian ideology. Although they had innate links with each other which are sometimes crucial for understanding of premodern China at this stage, these factors are mainly dealt with in isolation. This method of analysis occasionally leads to some inevitable repetition. But the advantage is that it is possible to see the individual pattern and impact of the evolution of each factor over time.

The term 'peasantry' has been long debated, and so have been its main features (e.g. Chayanov 1925; Redfield 1965; Moore 1966; Wolf 1966; Lipton 1968; Dalton 1972; Galeski 1972; Shanin 1973–4; Scott 1976; Ennew *et al.* 1977; Harrison 1977; Patnaik 1979; Popkin 1979; Feeny 1983; Ellis 1988). The present research has adopted the term for a grouping purpose since it serves the macro-approach well.

## 2.1 Predominant agriculture in the economy

### 2.1.1 Background: settled agriculture in prehistoric times

How and why the archaic proto-Chinese began farming has remained largely a mystery. Nevertheless, archaeological studies have succeeded in pinpointing when and where prehistoric farming began on the East Asian mainland. Sufficient evidence, including that of carbon dating, indicates that sedentary agriculture was established widely in China during the Palaeolithic Period (? – 7500 BC): more than 300 cultural sites, many with primitive farming tools, have been discovered in over 80 per cent of the provinces of modern China (Institute of Archaeology 1984: 1; Pannell and Ma 1983: 47–9; Tong Z. 1986: 16). This means that the Chinese were among the earliest users of agriculture in the Eurasian continent (Cipolla 1978: ch.1).

Agriculture occurred more widely on the East Asian mainland in the following Neolithic Period (7500–3500 BC), which is marked by the geographic distribution of 18 major sites of Neolithic cultures between latitudes 18 and 36° N, covering all the main economic regions of modern China and offshore Taiwan (Blunden and Elvin 1983: 53; Pannell and Ma 1983: 50–1; Yan W. 1987: 38–49). Among the total items unearthed at those sites, high proportions of farming tools (30–94 per cent of the total) have been discovered (Pannell and Ma 1983: 50–1; Wang Z. 1986; Institute of Archaeology 1987; Yan W. 1987: 38–49; Cui X. 1987; Anxi Culture Bureau 1987; Balinyouqi Museum 1987).

Studies have also shown that at the early stage of Chinese civilisation, various tribes were to a great extent isolated from one another (Anon. 1986). For instance, in the Yellow and Yangzi river valleys alone, there existed at least seven identifiable independent Neolithic cultural systems (Institute of Archaeology 1965; Cultural Bureau of Shandong Province and Jinan Museum 1974; Guo W. 1988: ch. 1; Zeng 1988). The following information reflects agriculture-related excavations in the Yangzi Delta only. The continuity of the trend is obvious (Fan Y. 1995).

| Name | Location | Carbon dating | Products | Tools |
|------|----------|---------------|----------|-------|
| Luojiajiao | Zhejiang | >7,000 years | Cultivated rice | Bone spades |
| Hemudu | Zhejiang | 7,000 years | Cultivated rice | Bone spades |
| Majiabang | Jiangsu | 6,300 years | Cultivated rice | Stone spade |
| Liangzhu | Jiangsu | 5,200 years | Cultivated rice and silk | Stone plough |

Consequently, up until 4000 BC the technical level of these sites, in terms of artefacts, varied from pure pottery to a mixture of pottery and bronze (Tong Z. 1986). Such a difference in development is more distinguishable between regions at a distance. For example, in Henan, North China, dry-farming products supplied the main diet (An 1984: 65; Institute of Archaeology 1984: 9–11; Anon. 1985). In parts of South China, such as Zhejiang, people relied heavily on cultivated rice as a staple food (Pannell and Ma 1983: 53; Bray 1986: 9; Li S. 1987; Yan W. 1987). Cultural and economic integration across regions occurred much later (Li S. 1987: 94; Gong W. 1987; Zeng 1988).

In this context, although some of the original Neolithic cultures vanished, agriculture survived. For instance, the Longshan Culture in the Yellow River Region, which is well known for its high-quality thin black pottery (the 'eggshell pottery'), completely disappeared, and later cultures in what had previously been the Longshan domain represented a much lower level of pottery technology. However, tillage did not stop with the disappearance of the early farming tribes. Agriculture proved to be immortal in the hands of successive farming tribes. All this suggests that agriculture developed simultaneously and widely across the land from Palaeolithic to Neolithic periods. These developments predated any of the Chinese written records, including the Inscriptions on Bones and Tortoise Shells (*jiaguwen*) of 3000 BC.

Such findings strongly refute the accepted hypothesis that agriculture in protohistorical China originated from a single centre in the Yellow River region and later diffused to other regions (see Ho 1956). This view is not only misleading but also biased towards what can be called 'Han ethnocentralism' or 'Han chauvinism', systematically playing down the importance of indigenous peoples in China's history. The evidence demonstrates the opposite. Wheat and rice were introduced between 5000 BC and 4000 BC to the heartland of the Yellow River Valley from other regions. Wheat came from the east coast; rice from the Yangzi River Region (ZNK 1984: ch. 1; Tang Q. 1986: chs 1–2). Both regions were at this stage homes of non-Chinese (see Appendix C). The introduced crop species eventually replaced millet in importance and became the pillar of the Chinese farming output, a position they have maintained for the past five thousand years (Tang Q. 1986: 57–60). The plough and irrigation techniques were also introduced from non-Chinese tribes and revolutionised farming in China (see appendix C). Recent ethnographic research into Chinese blood and gene types provides further support for the existence of multiple centres of the Chinese agricultural settlement (Zhao T. 1986; Mao H. 1987).

After the Neolithic Period, the Chinese became progressively more specialised in agriculture: they expertly developed multi-cropping, fertilisation, drought-resistant strains of seed, inventions and innovations in a wide range of farming tools, sophisticated water control and irrigation techniques, and so forth (Deng 1993a). As Mark Elvin states (1973: 129), 'by the thirteenth century China thus had what was probably the most sophisticated agriculture in the world, India being the only conceivable rival'.

### 2.1.2 Agriculture's long-term dominance: a choice from archaic to late traditional times

Concerning China, it has been appropriately stated that 'from time immemorial agriculture had been the major occupation of the Chinese' (Latourette 1964: 485), and it continued to be the basis of the economy for millennia throughout China's premodern history (Blunden and Elvin 1983: 50).

Up to late 'traditional times' – that is, the Ming–Qing Period – there are two aspects in the form of quality and quantity in relation to agricultural dominance in the Chinese economy. Quantitatively, according to a conservative estimate based on Professor Albert Feuerwerker's comprehensive survey of the literature, (1) the agricultural sector provided the population with 80 per cent of the total employment; (2) about 80 per cent of the total cultivated land was engaged in grain production; (3) around 70 per cent of the total

GDP was produced by the agricultural sector while the grain production alone had a share of some 60 per cent of the GDP; (4) the agricultural sur-plus–output ratio was at least 0.25, which supported 20 per cent of the non-agricultural population of the Empire; and (5) this situation lasted for about a millennium from the ninth century onwards (Feuerwerker 1984: 299, 302, 312–13). Qualitatively, up to the closing years of the Qing Dynasty (1644–1911), there was no apparent trend in China for the economy as a whole to shift to nomadism or industrialisation, even though the degrees of commercialisation and urbanisation in Han, Song and Ming times are often regarded as the dawn or 'sprouting' of indigenous capitalism (Li J. 1957: chs 5–6; 1962: ch.15; Elvin 1973: 164–78; Bray 1984: 565–6). China may have failed in commerce and industries but, like ancient Egypt, Babylonia and Rome, it never failed in agriculture (Lee 1969: 13–17).

This success story of agricultural development over a very long period has been attributed partly to favourable natural endowments and good returns from farming, and partly to deliberate reinforcement by the Chinese of agri-cultural dominance: continuous reinvestment in land preservation, water con-trol, new farming methods and new crop species time and again resharpened the comparative edge of agriculture over other sectors.

### 2.1.2.1 Environmental conditions

Although settled agriculture did not necessarily mean simultaneous agricul-tural dominance in the economy, there has been no evidence so far that the Chinese were, in the long term, heavily engaged in non-agricultural activities at the expense of agriculture. Now, the question is: why did the Chinese establish an economy in which agriculture dominated, given that other poss-ible choices existed in the form of nomadism, craft industry and commerce? Assuming that the Chinese choice was rational, then the reason they devoted themselves to agriculture to such a degree was likely to be due to the higher and/or more stable returns from agriculture as compared with any other sec-tors of the economy in premodern times. Such returns were due partly to a reasonably favourable physical and biological environment (see Cressey 1934: chs 1–4).

Professor Ping-ti Ho's early work 'The Loess and the Origin of Chinese Agriculture' implies that favourable natural conditions in the Loess Plateau worked as an inductive factor for the early start of dry farming in East Asia (Ho 1969). China, not just the Loess Plateau, is situated in a vast oasis where good physical and biological environments exist, surrounded by drought and typhoon-flood belts. First, modern statistics show that 40 per cent of the country belongs to the temperate or subtropical zones with 8–12 frost-free months per annum. Second, extensive river systems in particular cover south China, the dry area in north China being well compensated by the monsoons (see Spencer and Thomas 1971: 183; Barker et al. 1985: 23). Third, about 30 per cent of the land has an average annual rainfall of more than 400 mm; the average annual irradiance is 50–70 kcal/cm$^2$ (Needham 1961; 1986: 23–181; Hsieh 1973: 23–51; ZKY 1978; Bray 1984: 3–46). Fourth, there are ten main soil types all over the East Asian mainland, most of them being suitable for cultivation (either in their virgin or improved forms), in the vast 'farming block' consisting of the Loess Plateau, North Plain (*huabei pingyuan*), Sichuan Basin, Yangzi Valley Plain and Pearl River Delta (ZKY 1978 ch. 3; Deng 1993a: 50–2). By the Tang Period (A.D. 618–907), this block covered some 2.4 million square kilometres in a total territory of 4 million square kilometres (102–125° E, 22–40° N) (ZDC 1990: 134). Finally, and more specifically, the four adjacent regions in the block – the North Plain, Sichuan Basin, Yangzi Valley Plain and Pearl River Delta – have the topographic advantage of being flat, which aids tillage, transport and communication.

Given that farming is a year-long process because of the natural growth cycle of the plants in most parts of China (25° N and above), returns are not immediate but delayed. Under this circumstance, immediate inputs, rather than delayed returns, were likely to be the main concern of the proto-Chinese. This was particularly significant compared to other activities with more immediate returns such as hunting, gathering and looting. From the input point of view, a favourable environment (soft soil, suitable temperature, irradiance, rainfall and so forth) helps to lower the starting cost of production: fertile and light soil requires cheap and easy-to-make tools, but offers a high rate of seed germination, which means low capital inputs and fewer tilling hours. This low cost offered an easy head start which made farming at least as attractive as other alternatives (see Jones 1991: 8–9). Moreover, the favourable environment lowers the cost of crop maintenance during the growth season: if nature looks after the crop with suitable temperature, irradiance and rainfall, farmers have an easy life between planting and harvesting. Finally, at the end of the year, because of the favourable environment, the yield proves the early inputs worthwhile. Logically, the Palaeolithic and Neolithic farming individuals would have to be offered this resulting output in each production cycle, generation by generation, before they became professional farmers. In this sense, the proto-Chinese farmers were 'lured' by the combination of the low tillage cost advantage and the more or less guaranteed yearly returns. This helps to explain why so large a proportion of the proto-Chinese became so involved in farming so early in history (Anon. 1986; Zhang Z. 1987; Gong W. 1987; Li S. 1987; Yan W. 1987).

In contrast, Europe's relatively harsh climates and poor soil made farming less attractive and the opportunity cost for undertaking non-agricultural activities low. This point is supported by the development of non-agricultural sectors in medieval times, as shown in domestic and international trading zones, regular fairs, seaports. Among them, there were the shining stars of city-states, and later, the wide spread of industrial by-employment in the seventeenth and eighteenth centuries in the Swiss and French Alps, the Netherlands' Twente, and Germany's Elbe, Silensic and Black Forest areas (Jones 1968).

This, however, should not be interpreted as a view of environmental determinism, as it might seem in the eyes of some readers. That the proto-Chinese became specialised in agriculture manifests only a normal relationship between the given resource endowments, economic constraints and returns from some human activities on the one hand, and the opportunity cost for undertaking other activities on the other. The ranking of returns from a range of activities, which might later develop to different economic sectors, showed, to a certain degree, 'environmental favouritism'. The existence of this environmental favouritism reflects the fact that at any given time and in any given place humans have only limited freedom and limited ability to alter nature for their own benefit. This favouritism sometimes and/or in some places worked as a promoter of economic divergence; in other times and/or in other places it functioned as a prohibitor against such divergence – all because of the uneven geographic distribution of resources (not only in terms of minerals and soil types but also in the forms of annual rainfall, frost-free period, irradiance and so forth). Rational choices thus had to be made according to specific environmental favouritism. Those tribes that made rational choices had a better chance to survive, grow and develop. Irrational choices certainly existed. But they led to economic disasters and even instability and extinction of civilisations. A better way to describe this is 'environmental advantage compatible choice', a concept that shows the interaction between object and subject in philosophical terms. This choice is a result of the interaction between conditions of the environmental world and human efforts (Ho 1969: 3–4). Environmental favouritism can change and the old environmental advantage compatible choice may backfire. If this change happens, the society has to go back to square one to decide on another environmental advantage compatible choice. Even so, the rule still applies. It is thus unrealistic to believe that human communities would automatically go for a package of divergency. In this context, the Chinese relatively convergent, pro-agrarian choice was rational, not blindfold.

Once a significant proportion of the Chinese population became professional farmers, farming gained its momentum, and inertia regarding economic decisions set in even though the low-cost advantage declined when the Chinese moved from zones best suited to farming to marginal regions. They were now equipped with skills and knowledge to alter some of the conditions in their favour to obtain similar returns. By the time recorded history finally began in China, farming and its success had been widely 'franchised' to those marginal regions in parts of west China, south China and Manchuria (Anon. 1986; Zhang Z. 1987; Gong W. 1987; Li S. 1987; Yan W. 1987), with the application of better tools, the practice of irrigation and the improvement of crop species, and so forth. Gradually, over a period of millennia, the landscape of the rest of the East Asian mainland was altered. This alteration probably speeded up when the returns from farming in those old, most environmentally ideal regions declined owing to overcultivation. The final result was the stunningly high-yield level across China. This legacy can be seen up to the present. Recent studies indicate that out of the total 100 million cultivated hectares in China, 80 per cent fall within high-yield (above 4,125 kg/ha) and medium-yield (2,625–4,215 kg/ha) categories, and 50 per cent are categorised as flood- and drought-proof (Zhang B. and Mu Z. 1987; ZDC 1990: 7; see also Tregear 1970: 49).

Retroactively, farming in China went a very long way generation by generation from its humble Palaeolithic–Neolithic origin held in the hands of millions of worker bee-like landholding and landowning farmers. Probably as early as 2000 BC, the Chinese professional farmer was no longer an interchangeable part in a mixed economy of farming, hunting and handicraft industry. Leaving agriculture now bore a considerable opportunity cost and was thus harder to do. The combination of agricultural dominance and the prevailing 'high-yield agriculture' then reflects entrenched economic 'path dependency'.

### 2.1.2.2 Evidence of environment compatible choice and soil alteration

Among all the natural conditions, soil types were to the proto-Chinese the most important single factor affecting output level. The proto-Chinese gradually became aware of the geographic distribution and productivity capacities of many soil types in relation to farming output and responded accordingly to get the best results out of tillage (Wang Y. 1980; Deng 1993a: 50–2). So, the strong agricultural propensity among the proto-Chinese was not solely a gift of God but a result of a long line of nature–human interplays as well. Such a mechanism of environment-compatible rational choice of farming by the proto-Chinese is strongly supported by archaeological findings during the recent decades of the Neolithic crop diffusion. The two most significant cases were wheat in 5000–4000 B.C. and rice in 4000–2000 BC.

From recorded ancient times to this day, north China has been known as a wheat-growing zone. However, the origin of the wheat species (*Triticum aestivum*) was not the interior of China. The region in which wheat cultivation was invented has been identified as the Laimu Region (in what is now Laiwu City, 117°22′ E, 36°11′ N) of Shandong Province near the east coast, which was the centre of the nomadic *yi* people ('Eastern Barbarians') during the Xia (*c*.2000–1520 BC) and Shang periods (*c*.1520–1030 BC) (Wang X. 1985: 357–8, 435–6). Palaeographers have indicated that the Chinese words *lai* and *mu*, both for wheat, came from the place-name of Laimu (Hu X. 1958: 244; Wang X. 1985: ch. 5; Tang Q. 1986: ch. 2). The archaeological evidence for the earliest diffusion of wheat to the interior of China dates back to 5000–4000 BC in Shanxian County (111°6′ E, 34°30′ N), the western end of Henan

Province, the first footing for wheat to enter the domain of the proto-Chinese (Guo W. 1988: 30), which is some 1,200 km west of Laiwu. Later, in the second wave of diffusion, wheat cultivation extended from Laimu southwards: a large quantity of carbonated wheat dated to 3000 BC has been found in Boxian County (now Bozhou; 115°20′ E, 33°33′ N), Anhui Province (*ibid.*), which is only some 640 km south of Laimu. The astonishing difference in diffusion times (1,000–2,000 years) and distance (Boxian being half the distance between Laimu and Shanxian) suggests deliberate human choices. Even if this choice was finalised through trial and error over time, it will not change the nature of the conscious diffusion of the crop. So, instead of a gradual 'crawling' inch by inch, the westwards diffusion was through 'skipping' the distance to the Loess Plateau, where farming was most advanced at that time in north China.

Even if one accepts the traditional theory that wheat was introduced to the Yellow River Valley from Central Asia, it will not change the nature of the statement: Central Asia was the region occupied by the 'Western Barbarians' (both *di* and *rong*). The only difference is that credit should then go to the indigenous peoples in the West. There is still a possibility that wheat was introduced from two independent sources, from both East and West (see Appendix C).

Such a process recurred later in the spread of rice (*Oryza sativa*). Archaeological findings have identified Hemudu (121°6′ E, 30°2′ N) in Yuyao County, Zhejiang Province, as the starting point of rice cultivation in East Asia. The rice samples have been carbon-dated to 5000–4600 BC, considerably later than wheat (Yan W. 1982; *cf.* Swaminathan 1984: 63–8). During the period 4000–3000 BC, rice spread in Jiangsu, Anhui and west Hubei, leaving a vacuum in east Hubei and north Jianxi. In the following period of 3000–2000 BC, rice cultivation rapidly expanded along the southern banks of the Wei and Yellow rivers and the northern banks of the Han and Yangzi rivers, covering much of the plains in north China and the Yangzi Valley, and 'sneaking' to the Pearl River region along a narrow corridor. Most dramatic of all, between 2000 and 1000 BC rice cultivation 'flew' 1,000 km from the tip of the front of its last expansion to the Jinsha River Valley in Yunnan (Yan W. 1982; An Z. 1988).

Given that the macro-climatic pattern in China is generally in favour of farming, the skipping phenomenon and its patterns were heavily dictated by soil types, with deliberate human choices involved. In terms of wheat, the crop's original place, Shandong, is a region of Brown Earth (*zongrang*), semi-acidic, full of humus, fertile in its virgin form and good for wheat, soya beans and fruit trees. The first wheat recipient region is a region of Mellow Drab Soil (*loutu*), full of humus, fertile but heavier than its Shandong counterpart. The skipped belt (112–116° E) is covered by the inferior Damp Soil (*chaotu*) and Drab Soil (*hetu*). The former is not only infertile but also vulnerable to drought, flood and salinisation; the latter, poor in its virgin form, requires improvement by human manipulation, deep ploughing, irrigation and fertilisation being important methods. It is not so surprising that it took 1,000–2,000 years for some part of this Drab Soil region to become suitable for wheat growing. Similarly, the homeland of rice, Hemudu, is located at the southern tip of a belt of Wet-Rice Soil (*shuidaotu*), fine, iron rich and impermeable. The skipped region has Yellowish Brown Soil (*huangzongrang*) and Red Earth (*hongrang*). The former is aluminium-rich, semi-acidic fertile soil but does not hold water easily; the latter is iron and aluminium rich, acidic, not only infertile in its virgin form but also having difficulty in retaining fertiliser. In both cases, great investment is needed to improve the soil for rice cultivation. Like the diffusion of wheat, during the first phase (4000–3000 BC) rice was first grown in the region with the most suitable soil types, Wet-Rice Soil and types of similar composition. During the second phase of rice dissemination (3000–2000 BC) the crop 'invaded' regions of less favourable soils: part of the Damp Soil Region (Henan and Anhui), part of the Yellowish Brown Soil Region (Henan, Hubei), and the entire Brown Earth Region (Shandong). During the third phase (2000–1000 BC), it moved on to more marginal soils: the rest of the Damp Soil Region (Hebei and Henan) and the Drab Soil Region (Shanxi) in the north, the Red Earth Region (*hongrang*, rich in aluminium and iron, acidic, poor in humus and poor in its virgin form, in Jiangxi and Hunan) in the south, and the Yellow Soil (*huangrang*, acidic, with humus but little phosphate, in Hunan and Hubei) in the west. During this phase, rice also established an enclave in Yunnan, in a pocket of Wet-Rice Soil within a region which predominantly has Red Earth and Purple Soil (*zisetu*).

The pattern of wheat and rice diffusion also shows that the first round of diffusion was almost entirely determined by soil type, and thus very little innovation took place. During the later rounds, the proto-Chinese were gradually able to transcend the difference in soil types, which required technological innovations. In both case, it took a millennium to improve inferior soil for the alien crops to settle firmly in marginal lands. This process is highlighted in Figure 2.1. For wheat, during the first diffusion phase the crop moved westwards from belt 1 to belt 4. During the second phase of the diffusion, it moved southwards from Belt 1 to Belt 2. In the case of rice, during the first phase the crop 'travelled' westwards from the eastern belt 10 to the pocket 10 in the middle. During the second phase, it went northwards to belt 2, westwards to belt 6 and southwards to belt 9. During the third phase, it spread southwestwards to belt 8, further northwards in belt 2 and to belt 3. Meanwhile, it 'jumped' further southwest to enclave 10. This phenomenon is also reflected in Figure 3.6 in Chapter 3. Arguably, this pattern of moving in accordance with soil quality reveals what can be called a 'Ricardian sequence'. This sequence also shows the pattern of risk management in Chinese agriculture since the difference in soil quality incurred risks in farming the new crops.

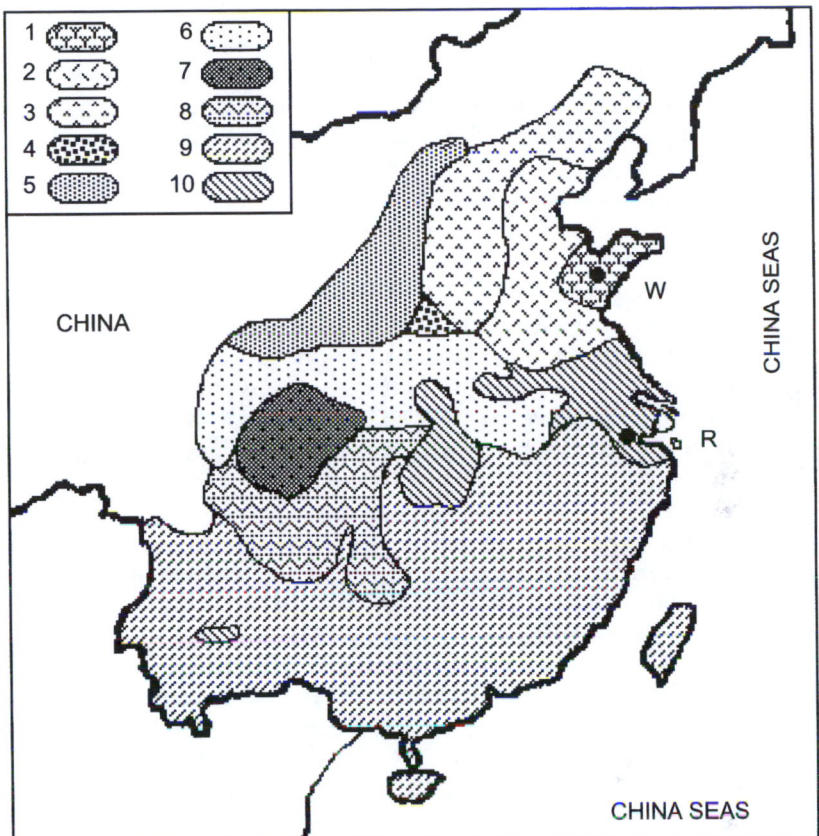

*Figure 2.1* Main soil types and wheat and rice dissemination in China

*Notes*

Border lines indicate the contemporary land boundary of China. W, the original location of wheat; R, the original location of rice; 1, Brown Earth (*zongyang*); 2, Damp Soil (*chaotu*); 3, Drab Soil (*hetu*); 4, Mellow Drab Soil (*loutu*); 5, Loess (*haungmiantu*); 6, Yellowish Brown Soil (*huangzongrang*); 7, Purple Soil (*zisetu*); 8, Yellow Soil (*huangrang*); 9, Red Earth (*hongrang*); 10, Wet-Rice Soil (*shuidaotu*).

So far, it has been assumed that no evolution took place in crop species *per se*. In reality, early farmers were likely to engage in seed selection, crop domestication and cross-breeding either by sheer accident or by deliberate act. Thus, the human physical and intellectual inputs in understanding agriculture were likely to have been much greater than one might think. This was also the result of human choice.

45

### 2.1.3. *Impact of agricultural dominance: the agricultural cult*

Under such long-term agricultural dominance, non-agricultural activities had to compete against the agricultural sector. Nomadism, craft industry, commerce and other services were considered only sidelines (Chao 1986: 17). In this section, the impact of long-term agricultural dominance is examined only from an ideological angle.

At the grass-roots level in Chinese society, the common belief in the importance of agricultural prosperity was a powerful and popular quasi-religion, one which can be defined as an 'agriculture cult'. This cult was embodied in the worship of Shennong (Divine Master of Agriculture, *c.* 2800 BC), who was a part-real, part-legendary king, and of Huangdi, Yao, Shun (before the twenty-first century BC) and Yu (*c.* twenty-first century BC), who were the early agricultural administrators in Chinese history (Werner 1961: 186, 419, 446–7, 585, 597; Lee 1969: 35–43, 46; Li M. 1986; Lin X. 1987).

This cult is also revealed by the idea of *xiangtu* (home orientation, literally meaning 'home with land'). According to *xiangtu*, the last thing one should do is to leave home and land. Such a mentality is often regarded as the core of the conservative personality of the Chinese race (Shang X. 1989: 26–33 and chs 2–3). However, it does not mean that the Chinese stuck to their birthplaces (and marital places for women). To the Chinese, home could be built and removed. Families could split up and migrate in a practice called *fenjia* (dividing family property and living apart), and acquire new territories. But the precondition for establishing a home was the possession of arable land. Thus, the core of the *xiangtu* concept is *tu*, or arable land and farming.

Another example is the concept of society, *sheji* in the Chinese language, an ancient but still standard word. Here, *she*, alone, means 'land' or the 'Earth God', an equivalent to Gaia or the Virgin Mary in the European tradition (Cotterell 1986: 166, 190); *ji*, 'millet' or the 'Grain God', is an equivalent to Demeter in ancient Greece, or Saturn of ancient Italy (*ibid.*: 153, 183). When *she* and *ji* are combined, the result is a new word which means 'society' or 'state'. This reflects the Chinese view of the world: (1) it is agriculture that provides the basis for a society; (2) land and grain are of primary importance and human relationships (including society and state) are considered secondary. Such a direct link between agriculture and society differentiates China from, for example, Europe. In Latin, the word *societas* indicates human relationship, and *status*, a political organisation. Both *societas* and *status* have little to do with farming, although the ancient Romans were agricultural.

The Chinese agricultural cult was institutionalised and became a ritual in ordinary people's life. To take the Ming Dynasty as an example, a report was filed that across China, every *li* [1 *li* = 0.5 km] and among every 100 households, one altar to the Earth God and Grain God was built for people to pray. In a rotary system one household works for a year to act as the head of the communal ceremony, in charge of the maintenance of the altar and the organising of the spring and autumn ceremonies, including preparing materials and arranging the date. A sheep and a pig are used as sacrifices with plenty of wine, fruit, candles and incense (see Wu Y. 1988: 54). In Ningbo Prefecture (*ningbo fu*) of south China of that time, on the fifteenth day of the first month, people of all the villages gathered in the local temples to pay their worship to the gods, chanting the Buddhist scriptures and praying for a good harvest and good fortune. In the eighth month, every village offered sacrifices to the gods in local ceremonies. Dragon-boat racing was conducted under the name of 'Celebration of the Year [of Harvest]' (*ibid*.: 55).

Such an agricultural cult was not practised just at the grass-roots level. The upper classes were heavily involved. For instance, according to many clan regulations, all the members, rich and poor alike, were asked to have first-hand experience in tillage to understand fully the meaning of the saying 'Food is People's God' (*min yishi weitian* ) (Wu Y. 1988: 37). It is recorded that in AD 628 there was a drought in the capital and with it a locust plague. Emperor Taizong of the Tang (r. 627–49) went to the Royal Estate to inspect the grain and saw the locusts. He gently held several insects with his hands and prayed: 'Food is people's lifeline. Eating the grain, you harm the people. If your visit is due to some wrongdoings of the ordinary people, I would like to take the responsibility. So, if you are really intelligent, you should eat my heart, but not the grain to harm the people.' The emperor then swallowed the insects (Xu T. and Li Y. 1995: 356).

The agriculture cult, together with the physiocratic ideology, set the tune for the Chinese behavioural pattern in other areas. For instance, according to orthodox Buddhism, monks should not work but should rely on begging and keep away from material production. When this agricultural religion was introduced to China, the Chinese monks abandoned this doctrine and involved themselves greatly in agricultural production. They went one step further and established a new doctrine (see Ch'en 1973: 145–51; Yu Y.S. 1987: 457–9): 'one day no work, one day no food' (*yiribuzuo, yiribushi*). Later, Chanzong, the radically modified form of Chinese Buddhism, further took everyday labour as the way of self-cultivation (see Le S. 1986: 95–6).

### 2.1.4. Impact on the economy: inadequacy and bias in capital accumulation and investment

It has been noted that in the Chinese agricultural sector in late premodern periods, the capital formation rate was low in per capita terms and investment in labour-saving techniques was limited, although land reclamation and investment in labour-intensive farming techniques were evident (see Elvin 1973; Chao 1986). This was closely linked to the non-development of a primogeniture system and of a prevailing land tenure system of the European type (for Europe, see Macfarlane 1978: 87–8): in China, for each younger generation, the family estate was subdivided (Needham 1969: 196; Elvin 1973:

250). The outcome was that individual families could not accumulate sizeable resources in the same way as Europeans did. In other words, with the growth of population, capital de-formation took place: land and farming equipment were divided among sons into smaller and smaller units. Moreover, the pressure on resources pushed up the prices of materials for building equipment, which hindered investment and reduced the opportunities for technological changes in agriculture, as suggested by Elvin (1973: chs 17–18). According to a neo-classical view, society normally readjusted scarcity in supply by generating new technology, including new methods and new materials, to meet the increased demand (Mokyr 1990: ch. 9). Thus, the shortage of capital accumulation and investment was likely to have been double-edged. But one thing is certain: a low level of capital accumulation and investment had a negative impact on specialisation and economies of scale (Jones 1981: 131).

Since resources availability and accessibility are always limited at any given time and in any given place, the leaning towards agricultural dominance in the Chinese economy itself implies a shortage of resource available to non-agricultural sectors. Under the constant pressure of competition from the agricultural sector, resources for development in non-agricultural sectors were constrained by at least 'relative scarcity' of things like the shortage in aggregate physical materials, capital investment, time (as an economic resource), land and inputs of human intelligence (see Elvin 1993; Deng 1993a; for its striking effects, see, for example, He B. 1992; Brook 1989). To take the seafaring sector as an example, in spite of its long history of technological development, good market opportunities, high trade returns and the noticeable political influence of sea merchants, the participation rate in maritime activities among the Chinese population was only some 2 per cent of China's total. In addition, there were few cases in which rich maritime merchants did not invest in land (see Deng 1997: chs 5–7).

## 2.2 Private individual land ownership

What most obviously made China differ from other ancient civilisations was probably the extent and duration of the private individual land ownership.

### 2.2.1 The establishment of private land ownership

A prominent feature of land-ownership types in China was the existence of a strong, long-term bias against feudal land-ownership types, although it has been recognised that during the Zhou Dynasty (c. 1030–221 BC) the Chinese political and economic systems were organised according to a feudal principle: the king (tianzi, literally 'Son of Heaven') divided the country and distributed land among his lords, a process which was called 'Grand Distribution of Land' (dafengjian). On the basis of this, a great many mainland Chinese scholars in history and archaeology thus have asserted with sketchy evidence that China was first a slave society and then a feudal society, in order to prove how universally correct Marxist dogma is (see, for example, Fan W. 1964–5; Bai 1982).

Nevertheless, evidence suggests that the Chinese had only a weak feudal system during Zhou times if it had one at all. This can be seen in three dimensions (see Fan W. 1964–5: vol. 1; Bai 1982: chs 4–5). First, the power of the Zhou kings is reported to have been very weak, so weak that the kings virtually did not even have the power to enforce the law for basic things such as collecting regular taxes from dukedoms (for the Tax Law, see Dai S. Western Han Period: ch. 'King's Regulations'). Tax default and evasion were universal. For example, Lu Dukedom, the closest ally of the Zhou court, paid its annual taxes only seven times in a period of 242 years, the tax being evaded 97 per cent of the time (Fan W. 1964–5 vol. 1: 164). Second, fighting between political units of different levels was common, indicating that both law and order and the feudal hierarchy were poorly established and ineffectively maintained. Third, ignorance on the past of the Zhou authorities eventually caused the feudal social order and feudal landholding to collapse and led to political anarchy which marked an epoch of non-feudal private individual land ownership (Yang S. 1984; Hao T. 1987). With it, the formation of a landholding and landowning peasant economy took shape rather than there being a move to market-based industrial capitalism as asserted by the linearist hypothesis of Marxism (see Marx 1976a, b; Rostow 1960, 1975).

Moreover, evidence suggests that Zhou's feudalism was only partial or incomplete. First, feudal landholding never took over the entire society: until the Spring and Autumn Period (770–476 BC) there was communal–tribal landholding and private land ownership in non-feudal areas, which eventually spread out without too much trouble from the Zhou authorities (Han L.Q. 1986: 78–108; Wu Y. 1988: 46–7; Chao F. 1996). Second, even in the areas under Zhou feudal rule, land was often directly distributed and redistributed among the farmers by court official People's Affairs Ministers (*da situ* and *xiao situ*) without the involvement of the lords (Zhou B. 1981: 59). Third, apart from prisoners of war, who were treated like slaves or serfs, there is no evidence to show that the majority of the farming population in Zhou consisted of landless slaves and/or serfs (Jian B. and Zheng T. 1962: ch. 2; Li W. 1994). Thus, even if the Zhou system is taken as having been a full-blooded feudal one, it is a big question as to just to what extent China was 'feudalised' and for how long.

As for the ultimate reason why the Chinese moved to a private individual land-ownership system, it is an open-ended question. From fragmentary information, the new ownership type owed much to a favourable incentive–output correlation associated with the legalised freeman status of a farmer. This correlation became the drive to strengthen the economic and military power of a political unit as well as to enrich the affected population from the Spring and Autumn to the Warring States periods. During this turbulent episode of Chinese history, those political units that established this incentive–output correlation and protected private land ownership proved to be superior to those units that still stuck to the old Zhou system. This superiority led to official abandonment of the feudal land ownership after the sixth century BC in the key kingdoms, with military/administrative duties and landholding distinctively separated.

Apart from the obvious production incentive under private land ownership, given that the feudal system was weak in China, it is plausible to assume that the Chinese system of individual land ownership and a free peasantry were derived directly from a tribal/communal origin, after the family became the basic unit of tribal life (see ZNK 1984: chs 1–2; Ye W. 1991). The main evidence comes from the Chinese inheritance system, which was the key indicator of property rights (see Macfarlane 1978: chs 1, 3–4). After all, the human life cycle provides the ultimate acid test of the nature of rights to possess and dispose of property within the basic economic unit.

The Chinese practice was characterised by equal inheritance under which parents bequeathed their real estate property – farming land and permanent houses, normally excluding chattels and women's dowry – equally among their sons (and sometimes daughters), known as 'dividing family real estate property and living apart' (Latourette 1964; Fairbank 1965: 25; Feuerwerker 1976: 82; Chao 1986: 109). The earliest law for equal inheritance of real estate was established by Shang Yang (c. 390–338 BC) when he launched a reform in Qin Kingdom (Sima Q. 91 BC: 'Biography of Master Yang'). Shang Yang's idea was to institutionalise this practice so that the state was able to have an expanding tax base for revenue and an increasing number of households for army recruits (Xing T. 1995). By the Tang Period, such an inheritance system had been well defined. Regarding all assets – family land, houses and other properties – subject to inheritance, according to the 'clause for inheritance' (*yingfen tiao*) of Tang law, they were to be equally divided among all the sons. Assets belonging to the mother were not subject to inheritance. If a son had passed away, the son of the dead (the grandson) was to inherit the share. If all the sons had passed away, the assets were to be divided equally among all the grandsons (see Shi F. 1987: 267–8).

More interestingly, according to the laws of the Tang, Song and Ming, there was no discrimination against the rights of descendants from concubines (Shi F. 1987: ch. 10). Arguably, from written records, individual inheritance rights were established in China much earlier than any known cases in Eurasia. In England, such rights developed in AD 1540 at the earliest (see Macfarlane 1978: 86). Equal inheritance was practised much later in France – after the 1789 Revolution.

For a long time, the Chinese real estate (farming land and permanent houses) inheritance system thus differed not only from the West European practice (which was characterised by primogeniture) but also from that of many other civilisations in Eurasia (which was marked by indivisible family

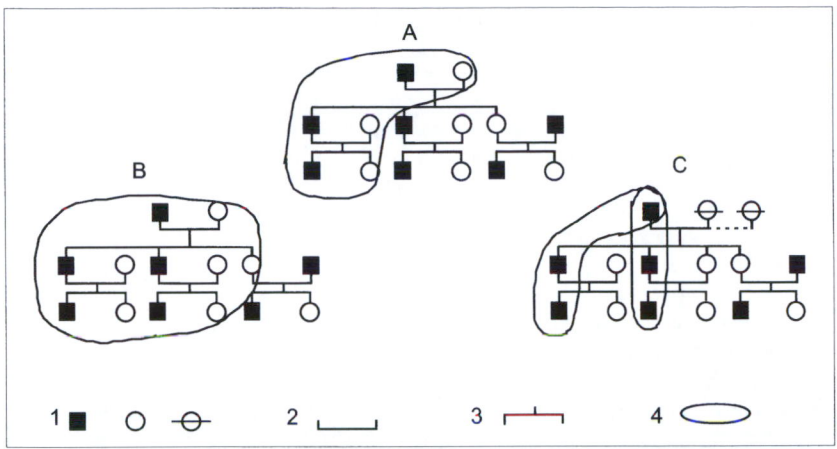

*Figure 2.2* Patterns of peasant real estate inheritance systems in Eurasia
*Source*: Macfarlane 1978: 33.
*Notes*
A, Real estate inheritance system of the West European peasantry; B, real estate inheritance system of the 'classic peasantry'; C, real estate inheritance system of the Chinese peasantry. 1: Square, male; circle, female; barred circle, concubine; 2: marriage line (solid line, basic relationship; broken line, optional relationship); 3: descent line; 4: inheritance sphere.

property), as shown in Figure 2.2. This explains why Chinese women were not obliged to change their maiden names after marriage: unlike their European counterparts, Chinese wives were not a part of the inheritance deal although they were sometimes able to claim their shares from their own fathers' properties. In effect, keeping their maiden names was an insurance policy for such an inheritance right.

The central issue of these real estate inheritance systems is what comes first: the integrity of the estate or the basic production needs of individual family members. The European systems (patterns A and B) ranked the integrity of the estate higher than individual needs while the Chinese system (pattern C) was diametrically opposite. In this sense, the European systems can be defined as an 'estate integrity-oriented' system and the Chinese an 'individual needs-oriented' system. Therefore, these inheritance patterns imply not only different methods of handling properties but also different property rights and their related institutions. From economics' point of view, the estate integrity-oriented system suggests that land was more scarce than labour while the individual needs-oriented system the opposite. At least, this was the case when these systems were first established. Thus, these systems also reveal difference in economic conditions in resource accessibility and allocation. These differences, which can be highlighted in a simplified checklist below (for

England and Eastern Europe see Macfarlane 1978: chs 1, 3–4), were not trivial, and to a great extent influenced later developments.

| Features | China (from 221 BC) | East Europe (16th century) | England (16th century) |
|---|---|---|---|
| *General* | | | |
| 1 Kinship tie | √ | √ | — |
| 2 Early and universal marriage | √ | √ | × |
| 3 Geographic mobility | √ | × | √ |
| 4 Social mobility | √ | × | √ |
| 5 Household as the unit of production, reproduction and consumption | √ | √ | × |
| 6 Relative income equality | √ | √ | — |
| 7 Prevailing small landholding | √ | √ | — |
| *In common with China* (China as 100) — | | 70 | 30 |
| *Property rights-specific* | | | |
| 8 Individualised land ownership and landholding | √ | × | √ |
| 9 Land transaction through the market | √ | × | √ |
| 10 Regular market activities | √ | × | √ |
| *In common with China* (China as 100) — | | 0 | 100 |

Here, in terms of general features, there were more features shared by the East Europeans and the Chinese (70 per cent). But property rights were common (100 per cent) to the English and Chinese. Those points for China will be elaborated from this chapter onwards.

The comparison between the European and Chinese real estate inheritance systems also raises related issues of (1) just how monogamous the peasantries were in the past, and (2) which pattern was the mainstream as judged by the temporal duration, spatial scope and affected population size of a system.

To allow the Chinese practice to work, the prerequisite has to be the recognition of the internal equal and/or joint property rights among family members (mainly male members), which can be viewed as the natural extension of the internal equal and/or joint rights enjoyed by all male members within a tribe. Under this internal ownership system, the economic resources are collectively owned within the basic unit. The existence of such equal tribal rights has been verified by ample modern anthropological findings. Indeed, the Chinese *fenjia* process repeated, in a highly condensed way, the long evolution of the fission of the early Chinese tribes. By analogy, it is similar to the development of the embryo, which repeats the main evolution stages in natural history. The significance of these internal property rights and the consequent equal division of family property was that economic interest totally overruled the Confucian family order, which was characterised by a chain of obedience in accordance with seniority in the family hierarchy. Typically, the younger brothers were obliged to follow the elder brothers' instructions, and the elder brothers those of the father. When it came to family property, such a pecking order was no longer valid (Li X. 1986: ch. 6). Under Qing law, it was normally regarded as a criminal act to sue the family superior: even if the defendant were guilty, the plaintiff faced a two-year gaol sentence (Shi F. 1987: 262–3). But this did not apply to property division. If the family property was not evenly divided and the rights of the inferior members of the family were violated, the inferior were entitled to sue the superior; and the law protected the plaintiff (*ibid.*). This is the only exception in which the law fully protected the inferior (*ibid.*).

These internal equal and/or joint property rights and, with them, household collective ownership are extremely important in decoding the 'Chayanovian behaviour' among the peasants (Appendix D). In particular, they explain well (1) why a peasant family-cum-firm aims at total employment instead of full employment simply because all the production factors are shared; (2) why such a firm calculates only the average product of labour instead of the marginal product of labour because the average measure is the only suitable yardstick for sharing; and (3) why the firm self-exploits its labour to the point where the total output is maximised and thus the marginal product of labour equals zero because to maximise each share the firm has to maximise the total output. These two facts in a peasant economy – total employment and zero marginal product of labour – are recognised by economists like Arthur Lewis (1954: fig. 1). The only way to 'reset' the clock was to remove labour from the family firm, which would in turn increase the distance to the zero point for the marginal product of labour. In premodern China, corvée service for public works and military service to guard the borders served such a purpose. This was one of the reasons why labour-saving technology never died out in Chinese agriculture.

In contrast, a free wage-worker owns his or her own labour, which is not shared. What a wage-worker can share with the others is the wage. So, it is rational for the wage-worker to watch the marginal product of labour during production. In a crude way, this is to see how busy the worker is. The busier, the greater the marginal product of labour. The worker can then be assured of the security of his or her job. Likewise, to the owner of the enterprise, his or her profit is private property. The profit margin, as well as the total wage bill, is determined by the marginal product of labour. Therefore, in the best interests of both parties, the wage-worker and the enterprise owner, (1) the average product of labour has little meaning; (2) the marginal product of labour should not approach zero; and (3) the total output should not reach the maximum level. So, the marked difference in calculation of the average product of labour and the marginal product of labour between a

Chayanovian firm and a capitalist firm is deeply based on two distinctively different types of ownership. However, this does not mean that a family-cum-firm has only the Chayanovian behavioural pattern. It can easily have a dualistic pattern: within the family, Chayanovian behaviour; outside the family, as an economic unit, market behaviour. The marginal product of labour is then calculated for the whole firm, not at the individual level. Such complexity and sophistication puzzles economists, who tend to seek clear-cut and black-and-white models for the peasant household economy (see Appendix D).

The overwhelming success of such a historical transition from Zhou's feudal land ownership to private individual land ownership can be largely attributed to the lack of resistance from the feudal classes during the critical period of the Warring States when China was at a crossroads. Post-Qin China had only occasional brief flirtations with feudalism: the revival of feudalism occurred when the Chinese Empire became deranged and fragmented in crises. Thus, feudalism in post-Qin China was, at best, a local and occasional phenomenon while non-feudalism was the long-term mainstream (see Appendix E).

### 2.2.2 Expansion of the ownership system

Given that private land ownership, which made the formation and perpetuation of a landholding peasantry possible, prevailed in premodern China prior to 200 BC, the most important feature of economic system in the following Qin Period was undoubtedly the institutionalisation of this ownership as the fundamental institution of the Chinese agrarian economy (Su J. 1985: 481–92; Chao 1986: 2). By Qin law, private land and other assets were strictly protected. For instance, (1) lost domestic animals were to be returned to the owner so long as the owner was able to prove the marks and ages of the animals; (2) the county magistrate was responsible for arbitration if a civil dispute occurred; and (3) severe penalties were applied to theft (Su J. 1985: 481–92). This system continued virtually unchanged for more than two millennia although the Qin itself was a very short régime.

In post-Qin China, owning land was at the very centre of economic life for the ordinary Chinese, which can be defined as the Chinese 'land ownership fetishism'. This makes a lot of sense because to an ordinary Chinese to lose land often meant bankruptcy. As a result of a lasting development, in the eighteenth century as much as 92 per cent of registered land was privately owned, which left a narrow margin of only 8 per cent for state ownership (Feuerwerker 1984: 313). Among these property owners, smallholders were the majority. In the Qing dynasty, for example, the average farm size was 20–30 *mu* (1 Qing *mu* = 0.67 ha) in the north and 12–15 *mu* in the south, and 'there were few large agricultural holdings comparable to the great estates of Europe and other parts of Asia, to the latifundia of South America, or the commercial farms of the United States' (Feuerwerker 1976: 81). The hangover of this system can be strongly felt in modern times: up to the 1910s and 1930s, at least 70 per cent of rural households still belonged in the category of freeholders (Tawney 1964: 34; Chao 1986: ch. 8), although the acreage of landholding varied (Fei 1939: 191–4; Tawney 1964: 34–5, 38, 71; Buck 1968: 194–7; Myers 1970; Chao 1986: 107).

Here, it is crucial to clarify the point that although in absolute terms a Chinese landholding was, on average, only a fifth the size of its English counterpart under the manorial system, a direct comparison between China and England is not sound because of the complexity of environmental conditions and quality of human capital (farmers' knowledge and skills), which in the end makes the average size of farms almost meaningless (cf. Chao 1986: 222). For example, studies of landholding sizes in India's cotton-growing region (1872–1910) and Japan (1908–15) show that 70 per cent of Indian farmers, categorised as 'smallholders', had 4–20 hectares and that the same percentage of Japanese smallholders had only 0.5–1 hectares (see McAlpin 1975: 295; Francks 1992: 133). A direct comparison leads to a conclusion that since they had some 20 times as much land as the Japanese the Indians were thus better off than the Japanese. However, during the period 1888–1917, peasant savings in Japan increased 5.6 times and peasant investment 2.3 times (Minami 1986: 96). This means a significant growth in Japanese real income. In contrast, Indian agriculture experienced stagnation (Mishra 1985). In addition, parts of India had severe famine, which sometimes cost the lives of at least 20 per cent of the population (Ambirajan 1989: 367), a sign of a fall in and even a collapse of rural income. Here, different landholding sizes mean very little in agricultural performance. By analogy, different landholding sizes in different economies are like inconvertible national currencies which mean nothing across the national boundaries regardless of their face values. To enable a meaningful comparison, the establishment of an exchange rate is imperative. The very function of this exchange rate is to transcend the face value of theses national currencies. So, a straight comparison of the absolute farm sizes across different parts of the world is as absurd as exchanging inconvertible currencies. A better index is the population-supporting capacity of a unit of land; even more relevant, the population-supporting capacity of each farmer.

The Chinese land-ownership system required certain conditions for its expansion in space and its perpetuation over time. There were at least three: (1) the replication mechanism of the ownership system within the Chinese basic economic unit – the family; (2) the accessibility of arable land through the territorial expansion of the Chinese empire; and (3) the intensive methods of land utilisation with the advancement of Chinese agronomy to produce more food from the same acreage.

In terms of the replication mechanism, the Chinese family structure, also the basic landholding and landowning unit, carried the 'genes'. The process took place through the Chinese equal inheritance system, the dominant inheritance system until the 1949 Communist takeover of the mainland (Latourette 1964; Fairbank 1965: 25; Feuerwerker 1976: 82; Chao 1986: 109). Such a practice was feasible because of (1) the natural function of human reproduction; (2) the recognition of equal property rights among male family members; and (3) the diseconomies of scale in farming. This equal inheritance practice strongly suggests a strong tribal/communal origin, another face of the same coin of non-feudal tradition in China's ancient past. In comparison, feudal primogeniture was a process of replicating the manors and tenants.

To turn the human reproduction instinct into a socio-economic mechanism to preserve and perpetuate private individual land ownership was the greatest invention next to that of the ownership itself. The key factor was not the blood line, but rather the recognition of the internal equal property rights among male members of the family. The diseconomies of scale in farming, a marked characteristic of agricultural production even in modern times, helped too. This means not only that land can be divided but also that a smaller plot does not necessarily lead to a decrease in land productivity. Then, nothing would stop the Chinese from replicating.

Not surprisingly, China's expansion always had a land link between its home bases of interior China and the newly captured areas, such as in the colonisation of Korea in the Western Han Period (206 BC – AD 24) and that of Vietnam in the Tang (AD 618–907). This was probably the reason why before the nineteenth century the Chinese population spilt out mainly to land-rich Southeast Asia and refrained from going any further, offshore Taiwan having been the main exception. Only after the nineteenth century did the Chinese finally begin to migrate overseas in large numbers. By that time, the world had changed: it was already three centuries since the Europeans' period of great geographic discovery, and China had already been drawn into the world market.

### 2.2.3 Evolution in ownership types

There were two main types of such ownership over time: (1) freehold with a sole owner and complete rights to the land; and (2) leasehold with multiple owners and divided rights over the land. Transactions of the first ownership type had been very common since the Warring States Period. According to a well-known poem written in 1194 by Xin Qiji (1140–1207) of the South Song Period, 'the ownership of land changes eight hundred times within one thousand years' (*qianniantian huan babaizhu*) (Tang G. 1988: 1541). Although it may exaggerate the frequency of land transactions, the poem certainly reflects this common practice of the property market. In England such a market developed only during the sixteenth to seventeenth centuries, but is considered nevertheless to have been ahead of the rest of Europe and India

(Macfarlane 1978: ch. 4, esp. pp. 93–4, 130). The existence, function and duration of the property market in premodern China have been sometimes overlooked and denied by Western scholars, who obviously have no access to primary sources of Chinese economic history (see, for example, Macfarlane 1978: 130).

The traditional freehold ownership type later mutated to a dual ownership which was characterised by the coexistence of freeholding and permanent leaseholding in the same property. This type of ownership was increasingly popular in the Ming–Qing Period, when the empire faced shortages of new land. Dual ownership was characterised by the division between the freeholding rights and leaseholding rights (or the rights to till the soil) between the owner and the tenant and, further, the subdivision of the leaseholding rights among tenants. It is worth noting that the same trend occurred in India even after independence. As Byres points out, the landlord class were not necessarily freehold owners; rather, they owned the property rights in the soil, which were superior over property rights in land *per se*. These soil property rights allowed this class to extract agricultural surplus from farmers (Byres 1974: 230).

The key was establishment of the 'permanent tenancy rights' or 'permanent leaseholding rights' (*yongdianquan*) by Song law in AD 994 (Tuo T. 1345 : ch. 'Economy'; for the Ming–Qing Period, see Zhou Y. and Xie Z. 1986: ch. 7; for land deeds, see Yang G. 1988: ch. 2). By this law, the freehold rights and the leasehold rights over the same land became permanently separate. From this separation, the door for the further splitting of property rights was wide open, especially with the development of fixed rent (called *tiebanzhu*, literally 'hard iron rent') gradually replacing share-cropping. By the early Qing Period, as shown in the Qing lawsuit cases, the fixed rent had become the dominant type in the south and affected about one-third of tenancy deals in the north (Zhou Y. and Xie Z. 1986: 141). In addition, to cope with the increase in land-hungry peasants under a combination of population growth and shrinkage of the amount of land under cultivation during Ming–Qing times, the Chinese invented a multi-party ownership system with well-defined 'surface or topsoil cultivation rights' (*tianmian quan*), 'subsoil or base land rights' (*tiandi quan*) and numerous other subrights (Marsh 1961: 62). All the partial ownership rights were subject to trade and mortgage. As a result, a piece of land may have belonged to several private owners at the same time. It was an ingenious solution to the Chinese land-ownership crises. This multi-party ownership system spread widely during Ming–Qing times. Thanks to an increasing yield level in Chinese agriculture, such fragmentised land ownership worked well. Table 2.1 shows the division of land-ownership types from Song to Qing times. Here, the primary rent is called 'land rent' (*tianzu*), and the secondary and tertiary rents, 'soil rents' (*pizu*). In practice, the rents in the aggregate in ownership types 2 and 3 in Table 2.1 could be in excess of the primary rent. In effect, the subleasing party had an incentive not only

*Table 2.1* Land-ownership types from Song to Qing times

| Type | Landholder | Leaseholder(s) | Rent(s) | Defined property rights | Tiller |
|---|---|---|---|---|---|
| 1 *Yitianliangzhu* | 1 | 1 leaseholder | Share-cropping: 30–50% output | √ | √ |
| 2 *Yitiansanzhu* | 1 | 1 main leaseholder | Fixed rent: 1–2 *shi* per *mu* | √ | ≈ |
| | | 1 sub- leaseholder | Responsible for the secondary rent | √ | √ |
| 3 *Yitiansizhu* | 1 | 1 main leaseholder | Fixed rent: 1–2 *shi* per *mu* | √ | ≈ |
| | | 1 sub- leaseholder | Responsible for the secondary rent | √ | ≈ |
| | | 1 second sub- leaseholder | Responsible for the tertiary rent | √ | √ |

*Sources*: Based on Fei 1939; Rawski 1972: 190; Yang G. 1988: ch. 2; Li S. 1995.
Note
Measures: (1) 1 Song *shi* = 92.97 g; 1 Ming *shi* = 150.32 g; 1 Qing *shi* = 144.97 g. (2) 1 Song *mu* = 0.058 ha; 1 Ming *mu* = 0.070 ha; 1 Qing *mu* = 0.067 ha. Symbol ≈ indicates that it may or may not apply.

to pass his own rental burden on to the subleaseholder but also to make some profit out of his property rights, in this case the 'soil tillage rights'. The sub-leasing party may not be the actual tiller but a middleman, a broker of the tillage rights.

No doubt, to support this dual ownership with multiple agents, the agricultural sector needed to be extremely productive. Evidence shows that there was a positive relationship between the number of multiple agents and the degree of multiple cropping: in the Pearl River Delta, where 3–4 crops a year could be expected, ownership type 3 was common; while in the Yangzi River Valley, where double cropping per annum, was the norm, ownership type 2 was practised. In the Yellow River Region, where the multiple cropping index was at best 1.5 per year, ownership type 1 prevailed. Within a region, the ownership types varied from plot to plot. Normally, the more productive land tended to have the more complex ownership type. From this pattern, it is clear that the numbers of leaseholders on the same land depended on the point where the marginal revenue of the land was equal to the marginal input of labour/capital on the one hand and the income of the tiller equal to the subsistence living on the other. As long as the marginal revenue was in excess of the subsistence living, there would be some room for another layer of subleasing. After all, it was the population-supporting capacity of the land yield that determined the number of the agents. Data show that during the mid-Qing Period in Jiangsu, Jiangxi and Fujian, the ratio between the rents and tillers' income varied between 1:1 and 1.5:1, which was only a slight deterioratin from the 50–50 share-cropping tradition (Li S. 1995: 46–7; cf. Zhou Y. and Xie Z. 1986: ch. 3). However, with the increase in the total output, the same or similar rent:income ratio was able to support more investors.

Taking full advantage of the highly productive agriculture in China, one of the best in the premodern world, this multiple ownership was an ingenious invention to cope with the shortage of land supply and create an investment vehicle without much input of new physical resources (such as new land area). Moreover, it was a sophisticated and flexible system to accommodate the different needs of the investors. Evidence shows that in Ming–Qing times, free-holding was increasingly less profitable owing to the 'sandwich effect' from government land taxation, which was exclusively applied to landholders, and the fixed rent arrangement, whose rate seemed to perpetuate for several centuries. In comparison, leaseholding was much more attractive because the subleasing party enjoyed all the benefit from being neither eligible for land tax nor obliged to undertake tillage. The leaseholding land was thus called the 'no tax land' (*wushuitian*) and was in high demand in market specu-lation (Li S. 1995: 46). This situation is shown from the profit yield ratio between the freehold property rights (for the primary rent) and the leasehold property rights (for the secondary rent), which, for example, was about 0.75:1 in Fujian at the end of the sixteenth century (*ibid.*). Accordingly, the market price for freehold property rights was much lower than that of leasehold prop-erty rights for the same land – so much so, that there was a strong trend for large landholders from a commoners' background to divide their properties into smaller plots and sell the freehold rights but retain the leasehold rights in order to capture the economic benefit as tenants. Smaller landholders fol-lowed suit, purely for the purpose of tax evasion. Landowners often sold their land to the so-called 'gentry' class because the latter had both political influ-ence to protect their tenants and economic incentives to buy land under the tax exemption law (and thus were not disadvantaged by landholding).

Indeed, with this intriguing mutation, the investors' (or rent-seekers') ben-efit was maximised: (1) the subleasing party had the secondary rent and paid no tax; (2) the 'gentry class' accumulated land and enjoyed the primary rent and the tax exemption. There was probably little change in the group who tilled the soil, who were subject to exploitation regardless of just how many layers of subleasing agents were above them. The only party which was worse off in the whole change was the Chinese state, which now received much less tax revenue from the land, given the increasing number of tax-free households. The loss of the land tax revenue contributed greatly to the crises of the Ming–Qing state.

This leads a to reinterpretation of Chinese economic history, especially of the Ming–Qing Period. For example, according to orthodox Marxists, the large freeholding 'gentry class' in China were the worst exploiters in society and thus should be among the first groups to be eliminated. In Ming–Qing time, since the rent yield from freeholding was very limited, owing to the fixed rent, the landholders needed to own much more land than otherwise to gain any economies of scale in rent-seeking. In contrast, evidence indicates that the leaseholders, being tenants themselves in legal terms, were much more exploitative towards the tillers and gained proportionally more out of their property rights than the landholders (Li S. 1995).

At this point, it is important to see the advantage of the long-term, macro-scale and wide-scope approach in history studies, using not a decade or a century but a millennium, not a village or a county but a country as a unit. Short-term 'snapshot' or even medium-term approaches often fail to identify a tendency or trend. The 'telescope' local or regional approaches are often hardly representative for a country like China, which is the size of Europe, and easily lead to overgeneralisation. This is a matter of seeing the trees or the wood. It is naive to believe that once one sees and understands all the trees, one automatically sees and understands the wood. In the real world, even the simplest arithmetic addition in temperature and/or number of molecules can lead to a break point at which physical, chemical and biological properties change. Similarly, an increase in population density of individual animals changes their behavioural pattern. To take individual private land ownership as an example, modern observers often pay too much attention to the Ming–Qing landless peasants and the problem of landlord exploitation, on the basis of which a conclusion is often reached that class struggle of the European style was evident in traditional China (Buck 1968; Bray 1986: Appendix C). This is easily misleading, although some scholars such as Marsh are well aware of this conceptual problem and deliberately use 'stratum' to define China's social stratification in premodern times (Marsh 1961: 24). A long-term and macro-scale approach thus provides a better insight: the weight of land-ownership and landholding crises in China should not be overplayed. Such crises were often only regional, and a general crisis in landholding and landowning was relatively rare in premodern China. This is the advantage of the long-term, macro-scale and wide-scope study.

The point here is that by definition the wood is not just a simple aggregate of the trees. The trees and the wood are related but not identical, and the difference between the two is not trivial. This necessitates specialisation in the study of the trees and that of the wood. The former cannot replace the latter, and vice versa, although they can supplement each other.

### 2.2.4 Impacts of the ownership system

#### 2.2.4.1 'Pan-private land ownership'

Chinese non-feudal individual/family land ownership led to a peculiar result: what can be called 'pan-private land ownership', with most people in Chinese society possessing land properties. There is good reason to believe that this majority consisted of around 70 per cent of the Chinese population. On Professor Fei Hsiao-t'ung's account, in the densely populated Jiangsu Province during the first half of the twentieth century few did not own land at some stage of their life (1939: 177).

### 2.2.4.2 Extensive and intensive expansions of farming under land ownership

As for the accessibility of arable land, a condition necessary for the sustainable expansion of the Chinese landholding and landowning peasant economy, this ongoing replicating of the peasantry, with its population growth, was to reach a point where the average size of a farm became too small to support a family without a technological breakthrough (in terms of new tillage methods, new crop species and so forth). To avoid this land shortage crisis, the society had to find new land to cater for and cope with the constant replication of small landholding and landowning farms. This task was successfully fulfilled by the Chinese state through a steady, systematic and ruthless internal colonisation on the East Asian mainland. Without exception, most new territories soon became 'agrarianised', until the empire reached its geo-ecological limits for premodern farming. In contrast, during the nineteenth century, Indian peasants practised subdivision of family land among sons while India had little room to expand its territory. The result was a decline in labour productivity which was partly responsible for the widespread poverty of that time (Rothermund 1993: 48–9). The pattern of agriculture-related territorial expansion raises an intriguing issue: just how alienated was the Chinese state from the interests of the general public? Even if the state was not for the people, it certainly had mutual interests with the people and thus cooperated and compromised with them. In other words, it was a 'giver-and-taker' state. It fed the peasantry with new land and in return demanded revenue. The Chinese peasantry, on the other hand, were a class of 'takers-and-givers'. They received land with the territorial expansion and paid tax for the benefit.

In this long process of territorial expansion, a centralised state proved to be efficient at attaining economies of scale by minimising military and administrative costs and maximising the prey. From the Han Dynasty onwards, after major campaigns, military and paramilitary colonies (*tuntian*) were established as the first echelon to transplant small landholding and landowning farms in newly established frontiers (Lee 1969: 33–133). So, after the entire south was firmly colonised during the Song Period, civilian farmers of the Song moved in and the south was filled with small farms. During the Qing Period, under the constant pressure for new land, the Qing conquerors finally gave in and opened up the far northern territory beyond the Great Wall, the Manchu 'holy land' known as Manchuria and Siberia, for the growing number of farms to cultivate. The new land was soon filled up again just as South

China had been in previous times. Indeed, in this process, the Chinese completely counter-conquered the Manchus in terms of land ownership. So, it is no exaggeration to state that the Chinese benefited greatly from their strong centralised state as organised violence pushed indigenous peoples off their land to make way for Chinese farms. The Chinese government also sponsored internal migration under the nationwide scheme of 'moving farmers from overcrowded regions to thinly populated regions' (*yi zhai bu kuan*) (see Zheng X. *et al.* 1984).

Apart from this extensive growth pattern, which was generated by small farms, private land ownership was able to accommodate intensive farming as well. This was particularly true when the territorial expansion came to a halt. Technologically, the Chinese, including the bureaucratic elite, made continuous efforts to increase single-factor and total-factor productivities (land, as well as capital and labour). The developmental pattern was dictated by the changes in the man-to-land ratio: when China had plenty of fresh land, labour-saving was the main innovative effort, as was the case during the Tang and Yuan periods when a new plough type and a new set of farming tools were invented and diffused (see Deng 1993a: chs 3–4). When China's expansion paused, land-saving became the focus of technological attention, as seen during the East Han, Southern Song, Ming and late Qing in the increase in the use of ultra-marginal land, the adoption of multi-cropping and the introduction of new crop species (*ibid.*). By the end of the Qing, the process of 'horticulturalisation' of farming, called 'intensive and meticulous cultivation' (*jinggeng xizuo*), had moved a long way from its humble beginnings during the Song (see Deng 1993a).

The Chinese efforts paid off. The mechanism of replication not only maintained over time a stable owner-farmer stratum in a vast agrarian empire, but also created the largest single peasantry in the world, capable of feeding a fifth to a quarter of the total world population with some 7 per cent of the world's cultivated land, undisputed evidence of China's agricultural success in both extensive and intensive dimensions.

### 2.2.4.3 *Impact on the political structure*

With rapid growth in individual private landholding, a centralised bureaucracy and a standing army began to take shape. By the Warring States Period (475–221 BC), all the competing political units had a centralised structure which indicated the accomplishment of this transition. In the following Qin Period, behind the spectacular façade of his empire-building, Emperor Qin Shihuang (r. 221–210 BC) invented very little, if anything at all. His main contribution was to streamline and institutionalise the existing non-feudal system. Under a single centralised government China was divided into coherent administrative units of prefectures (*jun*) and counties (*xian*) to make vertical control easier. All the officials were salaried government employees, selected from the population, and the careers of the bureaucrats (meritocrats, to be more precise) depended on their merits, not their social position at birth, in order to prevent special-interest groups from monopolising state power. Accordingly, administrative positions were not inheritable by the descendants of bureaucrats. State budgets were financed by regular taxes (either in kind or in labour) collected at fixed rates from free citizens. A standing army was organised on the basis of conscription from all registered households, and the defence walls of separate kingdoms along the northern frontier were linked up to make a complete line, known as the Great Wall, against barbarian invasions (Zhou B. 1981: 67–8; Yu 1986; Guisso *et al.* 1989: 88–9).

The fact that private individual land ownership and a landholding peasantry pre-dated the Chinese Empire by centuries gives a hint that dominant individual private land ownership and the free peasantry were among the determinants for the establishment of the Chinese empire. With little doubt, the Chinese Empire from the Qin onwards was built on the basis of this ownership and peasantry. This in turn explains, first, why the imperial government took pains to measure and periodically register farming acreages and incomes across the country. For example, in the Tang Dynasty, by law, officials surveyed household income levels once every three years (Zhou B. 1981: 212). Second, it explains why landowners resisted government regulations, sometimes violently, by concealing acreage to avoid land tax, so much so the Chinese government sometimes had to switch to a household tax or poll tax to replace land tax. Third, it explains why the taxation department of the central government had a long payroll for tax watchdogs and why tax collection was given priority in local administration (*ibid.*: 50). It is also the case that not all these measures would have been necessary in the running of a feudal system.

The Chinese centralised state and standing army were ready to capture new land in East Asia for the landholding and land-owning peasantry. It was no accident that the Chinese Empire expanded only overland: throughout history, the Chinese systematically carried out land colonisation until in all directions they reached the point where the land was no longer suitable for agricultural settlement: in the north there is the Gobi Desert; in the south, tropical jungles; to the east, the sea; and to the west, the Himalayas.

Also, in China, because of the prevailing pattern of private individual landholding and landowning, the authorities and landowners were two separate entities, and rent and tax were also separate, unlike in feudalism, under which defence, administration and land ownership overlapped, and rent and tax were combined. The Chinese land-ownership system and the free peasantry thus laid the foundation of a non-class-based official–civilian relationship, the officials being selected from the vast base of the general public. This is evidently shown from the family backgrounds of all the 'Imperial Examination

Table 2.2 Backgrounds of 'Imperial Examination Champions', 618–1904

| Period | A. Geographic distribution | | | | | | | | | | | | | | | | | | | Unknown | Total |
|---|---|---|---|---|---|---|---|---|---|---|---|---|---|---|---|---|---|---|---|---|---|
| | HeB | HeN | SD | SX | SS | GS | AH | JS | HuB | HuN | SC | ZJ | FJ | GD | GX | JX | GZ | LN | HL | | |
| Tang | 10 | 14 | 3 | 4 | 5 | 3 | 1 | 8 | — | 1 | 4 | — | — | — | 2 | 2 | — | 1 | — | 88 | 146 |
| 5 Ds | 1 | — | 3 | 1 | 1 | — | 2 | 1 | — | — | 1 | — | 2 | 1 | 1 | 1 | — | — | — | 11 | 26 |
| N. Song | — | 17 | 9 | 2 | 1 | — | 2 | 4 | 4 | 1 | 5 | 2 | 7 | — | — | 3 | — | — | — | 9 | 66 |
| S. Song | — | — | — | — | — | — | 2 | 4 | — | 1 | 1 | 11 | 10 | 1 | — | 3 | — | — | — | 16 | 49 |
| Liao | 5 | — | — | — | — | — | — | — | — | — | — | — | — | — | — | — | — | 1 | — | 47 | 53 |
| Jin | 5 | 1 | 4 | 4 | — | — | 1 | — | — | — | — | — | — | — | — | — | — | — | 2 | 4 | 20 |
| Yuan | 2 | 1 | 1 | — | — | — | 1 | 17 | 2 | 1 | 1 | 1 | — | — | — | — | — | — | — | 26 | 32 |
| Ming | 4 | 2 | 4 | 0 | 2 | 0 | 6 | 17 | 2 | 2 | 1 | 19 | 10 | 3 | 0 | 19 | 0 | 0 | 0 | 0 | 90 |
| Qing | 3 | 1 | 5 | — | 1 | — | 8 | 47 | 3 | — | 1 | 21 | 3 | 1 | 2 | 2 | 2 | — | — | 15 | 115 |
| Total | 30 | 36 | 29 | 11 | 10 | 3 | 22 | 81 | 9 | 4 | 13 | 54 | 32 | 6 | 5 | 30 | 2 | 2 | 2 | 217 | 597 |
| Percent | 5.0 | 6.0 | 4.9 | 1.8 | 1.7 | 0.5 | 3.7 | 13.6 | 1.5 | 0.7 | 2.2 | 9.0 | 5.3 | 1.0 | 0.8 | 5.0 | 0.3 | 0.3 | 0.3 | 36.4 | 100 |
| Regional share | | | | | | | 23.6 | | | | | | | | | | 39.4 | | 0.6 | | |

64

| Period | B. Social and economic background | | | | | | | | Total |
|---|---|---|---|---|---|---|---|---|---|
| | Royal family | Bureaucrat | Scholar | Farmer | Poor | 'Cotton clothes' | Non-Han | Unknown | |
| Tang | 3 | 28 | 1 | — | 2 | 1 | — | 111 | 146 |
| 5 Ds | 0 | 1 | — | 1 | — | — | — | 24 | 26 |
| N. Song | 0 | 16 | — | — | — | 2 | — | 48 | 66 |
| S. Song | 0 | 4 | 2 | — | 1 | 2 | — | 41 | 49 |
| Liao | 0 | 1 | — | — | 1 | 1 | 3 | 50 | 53 |
| Jin | 0 | 3 | — | — | 2 | — | — | 14 | 20 |
| Yuan | 0 | 4 | — | — | 2 | 2 | 14 | 10 | 32 |
| Ming | 0 | 14 | 1 | 1 | 4 | — | — | 71 | 90 |
| Qing | 0 | 17 | 5 | 1 | 7 | 1 | 3 | 81 | 115 |
| Total | 3 | 88 | 10 | 2 | 16 | 8 | 20 | 450 | 597 |
| Percent | 0.5 | 14.7 | 1.7 | 0.3 | 2.7 | 1.3 | 3.4 | 75.4 | 100 |
| Class share | | | 16.9 | | | | | 83.1 | |

*Sources:* Based on Zhou Y. 1995.

*Notes*

5 Ds, Five Dynasties; N. Song; Northern Song; S. Song; Southern Song. Abbreviations of regions (in the form of provinces of modern China) are: HeB, Hebei; HeN, Henan; SD, Shandong; SX, Shanxi; SS, Shaanxi; GS, Gansu; AH, Anhui; JS, Jiangsu; HuB, Hubei; HuN, Hunan; SC, Sichuan; ZJ, Zhejiang; FJ, Fujian; GD, Guangdong; GX, Guangxi; JX, Jiangxi; GZ, Guizhou; LN, Liaoning; HL, Heilongjiang. The term 'cotton clothes' (buyi) was often used for commoners with no official position.

Champions' (*zhuangyuan*) in the Palace Examinations for bureaucrat recruits from 618 to 1904, including a total of 597 events in 1,286 years.

These champions were those who scored the highest in each examination. It was the greatest achievement for a Confucian scholar. The 'champion' title was conferred by the emperor himself in a grand imperial ceremony and a good official post was secured. So, the champion was an national hero and immediate celebrity. Customarily, a permanent memorial archway was built in the champion's home village or home town to mark such an occasion. His name was recorded in local gazetteer as well as Imperial archive. In most cases, the family backgrounds of these champions were well exposed in the best interests of the family/clan in order to capitalise on such an event. Therefore, the family backgrounds of these champions had the best possible chance to become well known. From the data of Table 2.2, surprisingly, as many as 75.4 per cent of these champions' family backgrounds were 'unknown', which traditionally was a euphemism for 'poor' and 'obscure'. This contrasts with the identified home places of those champions: only 36.4 per cent are unknown. Since most champions with non-identified home places also belonged to the category of 'unknown' families, a proportion of 39 per cent (75.4 per cent minus 36.4 per cent) of these champions in the 'unknown' category almost certainly had very low-class backgrounds, so low that apart from their names and champion titles nothing about them was worth mentioning. This, for the first time in Chinese studies, quantitatively unveils the composition of the bureaucrat recruits.

It is worth noting that to ensure fair competition, the imperial state from the Northern Song Period onwards went to the length of (1) establishing a strict quota for candidates with a bureaucratic background; (2) making examination papers the top national secret; (3) carrying out full body-searching of all the examinees; (4) locking up the examination site as well as examinees' cabins; (5) having all the essays hand-copied by professional transcribers with a uniform calligraphy before marking; (6) instituting severe punishments, including the death sentence by hanging and decapitation, for fraud and dereliction; and (7) arranging double-marking by separate inspectors and triple-marking of the best essays by the emperor himself (Shen Z. 1995: 6–14; for Qing times see Song Y. 1992: 174–9). In 1684, sons of two court officials passed the examination, which caused wide suspicion. Emperor Shunzhi (r. 1644–61) had no choice but to cancel the imperial degrees and deprive five officials of their posts. Earlier, in a sensational incident in 1657, seven imperial examiners found guilty of irregularities were beheaded immediately, their private property being confiscated and a total of 109 close relatives exiled (*ibid.*). Such a punishment was otherwise imposed on felons only for treason.

From the data of Table 2.2 in the context of examination rules, several extremely important observations can be made. (1) The aggregate share of the lower-class families was 83.1 per cent, while that of the upper classes was a meagre 16.9. Such a ratio (83.1:16.9) was roughly the ratio in society between the lower classes and upper classes in traditional China (see Deng 1993a: Appendix 1; Chang 1955: ch. 1; Marsh 1961: 13–15; Ho 1962; Mousnier 1971: 256; Feuerwerker 1976: 48; Hsiao 1979: 7; Jing J. 1981: 53; Wu H. 1984: 64–6; Hucker 1985: 1–96). This means, first, that Confucian high education was not designed only for the rich. Members of poor and obscure families/clans were able to produce brilliant results. Second, the costs of education were thus much lower than one might think. This is supported by an analysis of the age groups of the Qing champions: about 58 per cent of them were under 35 when they succeeded in the examination (Song Y. 1992: 188). This shows just how ridiculously untrue it is that there was lifetime study and struggle for the Imperial Examination among the Confucians, as portrayed in the eighteenth-century novel by Wu Jingzi in his *Rulin Waishi* (*An Unofficial History of Confucian Scholars*). Third, the common belief that the privileged families (bureaucrats and established scholars) monopolised official positions immediately collapses before the evidence: a humble share of 16.4 per cent among the top winners in the competition. Fourth, the competition was almost certainly fair and open, not only because of the above ratios and shares, which show a high degree of political equality, but also because of the fact that members of the royal family had to go through this purgatory to gain recognition. Fifth, the geographic distribution of the champions matched the economic gravity of premodern China: more southerners topped the examinations than northerners (39.4:23.6), which was consistent with the capacity for surplus and the development of specialisation in the south from the Tang Period onwards (see Deng 1993a: 29–30; 156–8). This disparity developed further in the Ming–Qing Period. During the Qing, among all the 144 Imperial Examination Champions, the southerner-to-northerner ratio was 87:13 (Song Y. 1992: 109). Undoubtedly, the traditional view that the bureaucrat recruits were overwhelmingly rich kids is not merely biased and exaggerated, but actually groundless.

This has a very serious implication for the composition of the bureaucrats. It is known that the north dominated state politics of the Chinese Empire, as seen in the capital cities, public expenditure, the transport networks, the army barracks and the Great Wall, and so forth. If, as alleged, the bureaucracy was monopolised by a group of privileged gentry, the northerners should also have dominated the Imperial Examinations and thus the positions of champion. The fact that the southerners outwitted the northerners shows that Chinese politics were subject to economic power.

Finally, these data provide positive evidence that lower classes' interests were able to be represented at all levels of the bureaucracy. This was not only supported by the orthodox Confucian ideology of 'people as the foundation' (*minben*), but also manifest in the bureaucratic recruitment process and social mobility. The Chinese peasantry were able to find allies in officialdom at a personal level, as the best-educated peasant sons were recruited by the bureaucracy. At best, the so-called Chinese 'gentry class' can be termed a 'spiritual/intellectual aristocracy' (*jingshen guizu*) – a group of citizens who held public offices not because of their superiority in blood but because of their superiority in education. The peasant interests were thus internalised in the Chinese politics through this bureaucratic recruitment process. Such an earthy link between bureaucrats and the agricultural economy is reflected by a recent study of Liukeng Village, Le-an County (27°21′ N, 115°40′ E), in a remote part of Jiangxi, a province which was long considered, in premodern times, a less developed region and thus poor. Liukeng Village is a tiny village by Chinese standards with currently 800 households living in an area of 3.6 square kilometres. However, between 1015 and 1874 this village had 34 students who obtained the degree of 'Presentee' (*jinshi*), the highest academic qualification of the Imperial Examination. Of them, one became, in 1148, the Champion of the Examination (*zhuangyuan*). Between 1009 and 1891, the village supplied to the Chinese bureaucracy 278 officials, with a frequency of one new official in every 3.2 years. Some reached the ranks of minister and prime minister (Zhou L. 1997: 16–8, 232–48). This internalisation of rural interest in bureaucracy had the important side-effect of minimising opportunities for the government to become too alienated from public interests, mainly peasant interests.

There is a certain degree of ambiguity regarding the dignity of a Chinese official. A Chinese official was not fully qualified as a civil servant by the modern standard. He was certainly not a feudal master by any medieval European or Japanese standard, either. Fundamentally, the fact that his position was not inherited but earned by his merit made him in nature a proto-civil servant. The main difference between a proto-civil servant and a real one lies in that the former was more prone to venality and power abuse. After all, the modern civil service system originated from the traditional Chinese bureaucracy, which itself explains a lot. The main misconception among the Marxists about the Chinese bureaucracy is blindly to label a Chinese mandarin a feudal master like those in Marxist textbooks.

In comparison, the European and Japanese serfs or their equivalents had less power under their lords and state politics because, under a feudal system, the rigidity of the class system provided little leeway for such non-class relationships to exist, although internal rigidity of feudalism was sometimes offset by external competition among feudal units.

Finally, it becomes clear that to originate an industrial revolution it takes not just a particular level of technology, status of agricultural productivity or degree of commercialisation/urbanisation. From an institutional point of view, feudalism was a precondition, or at least a blessing. Thus, it was not sheer coincidence that before industrialisation, Europe and Japan both had feudal land ownership (Jones 1981: 226). It is reasonable to state that the reasons for the failure to shake off the agrarian deadlock in China resulted from a failure to separate the peasantry from the land for an alternative path of economic development (Fairbank 1965: 237). The difficulty in driving the peasantry off the land was attributed to the political and economic power this class possessed. It was also a result of the prevailing private landholding and landowning and the sheer number of peasants in society as producers, tax-payers, soldiers and bureaucrats. In terms of political influence, it was the Chinese peasantry who maintained the agricultural dominance. The key to their power was private land ownership. In a narrow sense, Volume 3 of Marx's *Das Kapital* was right about the 'primitive accumulation of capital' in Europe as the first step to industrialisation.

### 2.2.4.4 Impact on law

Chinese law in premodern times was designed to protect landowners. The best example is shown by the provisions of 'inheritance by daughters', 'inheritance by the near relation' and 'inheritance through the adoption of a son as an inheritor'. Generally, if a family did not have a male descendant, female descendants were entitled to inherit the family property. If a family did not have any descendant, male or female, the near relation was entitled to inherit.

In principle, if a family had none of the above, the government was entitled to confiscate the family property. However, from Song to Qing times, the law allowed either the widow (if she survived her husband) or the chief of the clan (if no one in the family survived) to re-establish the inheritance through the adoption of a son for the family, a practice called *liji*, meaning 'adopting a son by the widow', and *mingji*, 'adopting a son by the clan' (Wang Z. and Xu Y. 1986: 112–13; Xing T. 1995). Other concessions included inheritance by an outsider according to the will of the owner, which was applied if there was no descendant of the family, and inheritance by the caretaker, which was applied if there was no descendant of the family and the caretaker had shared the house with the owner for at least three years (Shi F. 1987: 268–9).

Here, the point is that if the Chinese state had been rent-seeking, it would have taken this golden opportunity to confiscate the family property instead of giving the family a second and third chance. It seems that the Chinese lawmakers understood that if they were too mean the law would backfire and burn themselves and their own folk, especially their own descendants as property inheritors.

### 2.2.4.5 Impact on Chinese economic life

The impact of this private individual land ownership on Chinese economic life was multifold. First, the Chinese land-ownership system provided ordinary people with an essential factor of production and the security of employment. In contrast, under feudalism peasants did not have such security, because their ability to continue tilling land was ultimately subject to decisions of the military defence duty-based landowning feudal class. This is not to say that a feudal tenant did not have any right. He did. But tillage rights by definition differ from landholding and landowning property rights. It was the latter that gave the landowners the power to evict tenants. Moreover, the Chinese inheritance system served the peasantry as a means to reach total employment whereby the marginal product of labour stays at zero (see Appendix D). Such an employment pattern was bound to hide any form of underemployment or unemployment. Ultimately, it is the producers' privately owned land that provided the Chinese with the means, and a sense, of self-employment. As this self-employment always blurs the definition of underemployment or unemployment even in a highly developed modern economy, the only reliable indication of underemployment or unemployment is the bankruptcy of a production unit. The feudal system seldom created such an illusion to the same degree, simply because a feudal tenant (a serf, for example) did not have the same control over non-labour factors of production, particularly land, as the Chinese small landholders. In other words, a serf was not self-employed. Rather, his employment depended on the demand for his labour and capital (seed, fertiliser, plough and so forth) from the feudal landowner. The prevailing agrarianisation of China's territory and continuity in agricultural specialisation among the general population also resulted in a general tolerance among peasants towards the government's anti-merchant policies and trade monopoly, while the feudal system seldom produced such a consensus.

Second, it strengthened the agricultural dominance in the economy. Given that the majority of the Chinese were engaged in tillage, an immediate consequence was a less divergent economy. In contrast, the feudal system helped to consolidate the social division of labour among all the classes because of the exclusive land-ownership system *per se*. To take the landowning upper classes as an example, under feudal primogeniture the younger sons of aristocrats had to seek alternative professions or careers, typically in the army, the church and commerce. In China, the equal inheritance practice, which was protected by law, guaranteed the sons of landholders entry to the farming profession, although whether these sons could also make a good career out of it was another matter.

Third, the Chinese land-ownership system provided the society with grounds for relative equality, which was also the result of human relationships that were not based on slavery or feudalism. As employment was stable and income differentials were limited among the self-reliant owner peasants, the principle of equality prevailed. This principle is crystallised in a Confucian maxim: 'Our anxiety is not for poverty but for inequality in society' (*buhuanpin erhuanbujun*) (Kong Q. c. 479 BC: ch. 'Jishi'). This was the case even during the later dynasties when China experienced increasing land fragmentation owing to the replication of the small landholders (Chao 1986: 107). To take the end of the Qing Dynasty as an example, although China was in a series of severe crises, the income level differentiation between the upper and lower strata has been estimated at only 14:1 (Chang 1955: 447–50, 475–

7), while under the 'most equal society' of Stalin's or Mao's communism such a gap is easily over 10:1 (Lardy 1983: 163–72). Needless to say, the Chinese equal inheritance system reflects nothing but equality in spite of the fact that it was meant for internal property division. Comparatively, Leveson and Schurmann point out (1969: 92), 'Feudal primogeniture perpetuates inequality, since land is left concentrated in individual hands. For this reason . . . dynasts on the Han model favoured constant pressure for the fragmentation of landhold-ings to counteract any proto-feudal, anti-central private aggrandizements.'

Fourth, Chinese land ownership bonded the peasantry 'voluntarily' to land, although most farmers were legally free from personal bondage. In compar-ison, under the feudal tenancy arrangement, peasants appeared bonded to land but were in effect bound to their feudal master. The outcomes were very different. Historically, once feudal classes – aristocrats and peasants alike – were free from dependence on their old professional paths, they took the opportunity to enter non-agricultural sectors, although they probably immediately depended on the market. It was a trade-off. So, in feudal Eur-ope/Japan, once the personal bondage was removed (either by force or peaceful means), peasants left the land. In China, unless force (either political or eco-nomic) was used, the peasantry adhered to land. In other words, the Chinese landholding and landowning peasant was willing to be bound to the land through his private land ownership. In this context, the opportunity cost for a feudal peasant to leave agriculture was lower than that for a landholding and landowning free farmer. Fairbank thus points out that private individual land ownership in premodern China gave the peasantry the incentive to per-petuate the keeping of agriculture in their own hands, separation of land from the peasantry being extremely difficult (Fairbank 1965: 237). Similarly, Brenner argues that the reason for rural poverty and a self-perpetuating cycle of backwardness was the freedom and property rights enjoyed by the peasantry. He concludes that it is the absence of such rights that manoeuvred English society towards development (Brenner 1982).

So, ironically, although their status as free citizens allowed the Chinese to choose their occupations, either in or out of agriculture, individual private land ownership largely limited their choices and resulted in what can be called a 'self-confinement effect'. This self-confinement at the micro level was the basis of China's 'path dependency' at the macro level. Thus, the Chi-nese experience shows that private ownership did not necessarily lead to a high degree of commercialisation and economic divergency. To achieve the latter, other conditions were required.

It is not at all surprising that the Lewisian model (Lewis 1954) of indus-trial transition cannot explain why in China peasants were not free to be released from agriculture for capitalist development in the Song Dynasty (a period when China spearheaded a medieval economic revolution) and the Ming–Qing Period (a period when China had frequent exchange of ideas and goods with the West). Thus, unlike feudal Europe and Japan, which left leeway for the rural population to work in the industrial sector, a compound of private land ownership and free citizen status formed a colossal barrier in China to the transformation of an agrarian economy to an industrialised one.

### 2.2.4.6 Hangover in contemporary China

Immediately after the Communist takeover in mainland China in 1949, the Chinese peasantry was manipulated into farming under Stalinist collective land ownership (Shue 1980: chs 2, 7). Remoulding the largest peasantry in the world was taken by the Chinese Communist leadership as a great triumph of the Communist movement. However, only a generation later, in the 1970s, the Chinese Communist leadership was forced to abandon the notorious commune system for ever and to move back to the time-honoured state of land-holding and landowning peasantry. The fact that the Chinese peasantry has successfully broken the Communist system in rural China and sparked the sweeping economic reforms in other sectors of the Chinese economy shows again the strength of the unarmed peasantry in the face of the armed-to-the-teeth 'proletarian dictatorship'.

## 2.3 Free peasantry: backbone of the agrarian economy

### 2.3.1 Concepts of peasants and the peasantry

There has long been debate about how the premodern professional farmers should be viewed. There have been two main schools of thought. Leninism–Maoism insists that no such a thing as the peasantry existed and that the rural population was always divided according to property possession and income levels. The 'haves' belong to either the feudal, or the bourgeois or the petty-bourgeois classes; the 'have-nots', to the proletariat or semi-proletariat (see Aston and Philpin 1985; also Ennew *et al*. 1977). In contrast, the populists and neo-populists regard the farming and rural groups as more or less a homogeneous stratum because of the similarities in their lifestyle, production and consumption pattern and mindset (see Harrison 1977; Davies 1990: 47–8; *cf*. Patnaik 1979).

The present study favours the populist approach for two reasons. First, not only were there obvious similarities among peasants, but also there was inter-group mobility among them. So, it is naive to view the class division among peasants – if it did exist – as static and perpetual. Even if one follows the authentic Marxist hypothesis of class division, most premodern peasants resembled the modern 'middle class' more than the city pauper owning little more than their bare hands.

Second, and more importantly, the human and socio-economic disasters that were incurred by the Leninist–Maoist policies for dealing with farming communities and rural population in the processes of the Soviet brand and the Chinese brand of communist socialisation indicate that any such class division is totally arbitrary and demoralising. In both the Soviet Union and mainland China, much of the alleged rural class struggle was created by propaganda to whip up hatred among rural communities so that the closed communities were prised open and opportunities created to lay the power basis for the Communists. Later on, when agrarian reforms finally took place in both the Soviet Union and mainland China from the late 1970s onwards, differences in property possession and income levels occurred naturally among once equally positioned communist peasants; very few officials made a fuss about this return to inequality. Times had changed and the officials may well have become more pragmatic. But one thing is certain: the differences in property possession and income levels among the peasants did not matter and should not have mattered so much. This provides us with strong counter-evidence that the populist approach is much closer to the truth than Marxism–Leninism.

### 2.3.2 Origin and the duration of the free peasantry

The establishment of private individual land ownership was heavily entwined with the rise and perpetuation of the free peasantry in China. The Chinese peasantry in premodern times was based on extensive land properties owned by ordinary people. In Tawney's phrase (1964: 34), 'the typical figure in Chinese country life is not the hired labour, but the landholding peasant'. Similarly, Rawski maintains in a sweeping way (1972: 3) that 'for at least the last millennium, Chinese agriculture has been dominated by a large number of free, small-scale farmers, working under a system of private land-ownership'. Such a peasantry occurred as early as the Spring and Autumn Period (770–476 BC), the period of the dissolution of tribal/communal land ownership, the chessboard-field system (*jingtianzhi*, commonly translated as the 'well–field system'[1]) as described by Mencius (Warring States Period: ch. 'Duke Tengwen Shang'), and the feudal Zhou landholding, and *pari passu* the establishment of private land ownership and private property rights (Elvin 1973: 23–4). In comparison, the landowning free peasantry in Europe and Japan either occurred rather late or existed as a sideline under the dominance of feudalism (see Landsberger 1974: pt. 1; Critchley 1978).

The reason why the early Chinese were so pro-free peasantism is not yet clear. It may again have had something to do the strong clan or tribal tradition and the absence of a persistent threat from outsiders during prehistoric periods. The main evidence is that the proto-Chinese tribes formed inclusive alliances under their early kings during the Xia Period rather than undertaking military action against each other as was the case later, in the Warring States Period (Fan W. 1964–5 vol. 1; Bai 1982: chs 2–3). Confucian ideology of *datong*, or Great Harmony, reflects this earthly paradise. In contrast, in Europe, class distinction and personal bondage under the feudal system were primarily designed for tribal defence under the pressure of outside com-petition for resources, the social structure of the Frankish Barbarians being a good example (see Critchley 1978). Compatible with China's near-defence-free situation during the early stage of the civilisation, although a division of labour took place later on for defence purposes (as seen in the standing army, arsenal and the Great Wall), Chinese society lacked a high degree of specialisation in the defence forces. In medieval Europe and Japan, such specialisation was displayed not only by the designated military class of fight-ers (knights and *samurai*) and officers (lords and *daimyo*) but also by the specially designed weapon system consisting of carefully bred warhorses, heavy-duty armour and high-quality cold steel. These horse, armour and cold steel were constantly on the shopping list of the Chinese army from the Western Han Period onwards (206 BC – AD 24) (see Deng 1997: table 5.2). Later, from the Tang to the Ming, a pattern of foreign trade was established and maintained, known as the 'tea for warhorses' exchange (*chama hushi*). As a good example, in 1485 Japan shipped 38,610 swords to China (see Li J.M. 1990: 57). Given that during the early fifteenth century the Ming had 2.8 million troops with a total of 28,000 commanding officers down to the company level (see Zhao X. *et al.* 1987: 404, 410–11), these swords were sufficient to equip all the Ming officers.

It should be stressed that the existence of a free peasantry itself was not exclusively Chinese. What was uniquely Chinese, though, was its long-term stability, which no other peasantry has matched. Some studies indicate that, in spite of the twin facts that from the end of the Ming Dynasty onwards the proportion of landless tenants increased and that during the Qing China was conquered by the nomadic Manchus, the basic social structure in China did not change until the turn of the twentieth century (Skinner 1971; Rawski 1972: 3; Jing J. 1981). No other premodern civilisation matched the Chinese persistency in such complex agrarian growth.

### 2.3.3 Status of the peasantry

There were two legal categories of peasant in ancient China: free and semi-free. When combined with the two main ownership types (freehold and lease-hold), the permutation is free landholders, free leaseholders (non-feudal tenants) and semi-free leaseholders (quasi-feudal tenants). By definition, land-holders were free. Regardless of their landholding and landowning status, free peasants constituted the majority of the peasantry through most of premodern Chinese history. Semi-free leaseholders had a sporadic existence throughout post-Qin history and mainly existed in state-owned estates such as the milit-ary farming colonies along the frontiers (*yimin shibian*) (for the Qing Period, see Weng D. 1990: 829–33).

The free peasantry-based social structure was reflected in some distinctive phenomena in Chinese history. For instance, (1) farmers in Chinese society were accorded a fairly high status in legal terms: they were ranked above all the working classes and merchants and entitled to special help from the government such as land, loans and exemption from taxation; (2) the Chinese peasantry had access to political power through the Imperial Examination system: by law their sons had equal access to officialdom with the candidates of the upper strata.

This high status give us a clue as to why (1) the government of each dynasty, whether run by Chinese or non-Chinese, always took as a matter of paramount importance the establishment and maintenance of the census register system of counting the number of peasants; (2) in Chinese history massive peasant insurrections often broke out, and the peasants were from time to time responsible for changes of régime, as well as changes in government policies. First, since the majority in China were free peasants, the census register system was the only effective means of controlling the subjects of the Empire in order to raise revenue via taxation and obtain young soldiers from the population. The best example is that after having captured the capital city, Xianyang, and toppled the Qin Dynasty, the first thing Liu Bang (256–195 BC; 202–195 BC), the founder of the Han Dynasty, wanted was the Qin imperial census record to impose tax (Ban G. AD 82: ch. 'Xiaohe Zhuan'). Any modern government does the same in a free citizens-based society. To facilitate government registration, some institutions were established at the grass-roots level. For instance, during the Northern Wei (AD 386–534) and Sui (AD 581–618) dynasties the 'Three Heads System' (sanzhangzhi) ensured tax revenue and prevented tax evasion (Zhou B. 1981: 181, 192). Second, in the absence of a rigid system of aristocracy, the masses were to a certain degree free from personal bondage to a particular group in society, and political centralisation became imperative to keep a smallholders' society secure and orderly. This in turn provided the basis for China's empire-building. Third, although a centralised political power transcended conflicts between individuals, the state still often found itself in the position of public enemy number one – a policy that could affect the lives of the masses and trigger discontent in the populace, or even result in mass armed rebellions (Moore 1966; Landsberger 1974: 43–5).

In contrast, after the collapse of the Western Roman Empire, a feudal system first developed in Europe as a response to the need for protection from outside attacks. Peasants placed themselves under the protection of the local lord, who acquired land in return for military service in support of his overlords or king. These estates were autonomous; the peasants were bound to the owner of land – the lord – and could be transferred to the new landowner. Therefore, although a serf stayed in the same estate without a physical move, he may have been transferred many times with changes of landowner. The fact that the serf did not move was solely because the land asset was not portable. In Chinese, land estate is called an 'immovable asset' (budongchan), which is extremely accurate. So, conceptually, the serf was bound to the owner, not to the land. At best, the feudal lord was directly bound to the land and the serf was bound to the land indirectly via his lord. To equate a serf and a landholding and landowning free peasant – who was truly bound to the land through his possession of an estate – is entirely misleading.

Thus under the European/Japanese feudal system the upper classes were dominant and the peasantry were the lowest stratum of society (Morse 1969: 3467–8). In post-Qin China, although the upper classes or strata appeared to play a role similar to that of their European/Japanese counterparts, the landholding free peasantry was the true dominant stratum in society (Marsh 1961: 13–15; Ho 1962: 17–41; Mousnier 1971: 237–41; Hsiao 1979: 7; Jing J. 1981: 53; Chao 1986: chs 7–8). It was a hidden fact because of the striking contrast in education, lifestyles and authority/responsibilities between an ordinary peasant and a high-ranking mandarin. In modern Chinese history Maoists knew it only too well and thus won the civil war against the West-supported KMT in 1940s by flattering the peasantry and promising the peasants an ideal world.

Of course, from Qin to Qing the tide changed occasionally and feudalism or quasi-feudalism played a part, examples being in Han and Jin times. But feudalism was never the mainstream and the status of the peasantry was never completely uprooted: even under the Communist régime the peasantry was recognised as one of the ruling classes and was ranked above military personnel, party cadres and scientists–technicians.

### 2.3.4. Types of landholding and landowning

In premodern China, land ownership and landholding were not necessarily identical, especially in later periods of the empire's history. Here, landholding included freehold and leasehold. In any case, freehold was the mainstream and leasehold was often transitional and had a strong tendency to move to freehold or quasi-freehold. In other words, the Chinese peasantry was always a landholding stratum. Here, the focus is on state-owned land because it embodies the principle of individual landholding without private land ownership.

Such a situation is reflected in the state-owned farming estates where the individual peasants did not necessarily possess the land but had tillage rights (which were often permanent) and had first choice when the land was privatised (which was the fate of most state-owned land; see Li Y. 1996). One of the forms of state land was that of *tuntian*, or 'agricultural colonies', which continued to be established from the Han Dynasty onwards until the last dynasty, the Qing. In 122 BC, the Western Han state established agricultural colonies along the northwestern frontier of China, to which 600,000 people were sent (Ban G. AD 82 vol. 24: 'Economy'; see also Fu Z. and Wang Y. 1982: 319–36). In these colonies, land and capital (including seed, animals and other equipment) were provided by the government. The farmers were also entitled to be provided with one year's means of livelihood if the place had not previously been cultivated (Ban G. AD 82 vol. 69: 'Biography of Zhao Chongguo'). Agricultural colonies were also established in the central areas of China. In the Eastern Han Dynasty, for instance, there were colonies in six inland areas including the capital region (Xu T. Southern Song Period: 'Economy'). During the Three Kingdoms Period (AD 2221–265), agricultural colonies were spread over all the kingdoms. In Wei Kingdom, 80 per cent of soldiers were once involved in tillage along the Huai River (Chen S. *c*. AD 280 vol. 28: 'Biography of Deng Ai'). Following the model of the Three Kingdoms, the authorities of the Northern and Southern Dynasties established colonies widely. Later, in the Tang Dynasty, there were 1,147 agricultural colonies occupying a total area of 57,000 *qing*, or 307,800 hectares (Zheng X. *et al*. 1984: 172), and sometimes two-thirds of the Tang soldiers were employed in these colonies (Lee 1969: 68). These colonies continued to be established in the Song, Yuan, Ming and Qing Dynasties (*ibid*.: 73, 85–6, 104, 113, 117; Liang F. 1980: 322–8, 360–4, 420–2, 464). In all the colonies, as a consequence of state ownership, a network of agricultural supervision was established, attached to the Agricultural Board of the central government (Zheng X. *et al*. 1984: 114, 119; Zuo S. 1986). In most cases, as a standard practice, when soldiers retired from service, ownership of the land in the farming colonies was then granted to the individuals who had tilled the land. So, in the state-owned land, individual landholding normally led to individual land ownership.

Share-cropping was the standard condition of tenancy, which proved to be very effective in enabling cooperative interests of the state and individual farmers. According to records, rent in these colonies varied between 60 per cent and 80 per cent of total production, which indicates fairly high agricultural productivity and surplus (Fang X. AD 646: 'Biography of Fu Xuan'). There was little doubt that the farmers on state-owned land had the incentives to produce. In Qing times, one of the highest-quality rice species was developed in such a colony near Tianjin (Jiang C. 1987). Moreover, in most cases, the proportion of the state-owned land was very limited. By 1887, Qing agricultural colonies had occupied 3,412,310 hectares (509,300 *qing*), about 6 per cent of the total cultivated land of China (Liang F. 1980: 384–5). Clearly, the Chinese state had the intention both of keeping a conscription system rather than a professional army, and of rebuilding small freeholders' farms when conditions allowed, given that the farmers in these colonies were soldiers or paramilitary civilians who were in effect state-sponsored migrants in most cases.

Apart from military farming colonies, state land estates were also distributed among civilian farmers in well-established agricultural regions. Individual farmers were granted permanent leaseholding rights until they retired. Governments obtained rent and tax in kind under this system. Such schemes took different names, the best known being 'Land Allowed to Citizens' (*zhantian*), 'Land Allocated to Citizens' (*shoutian*), and 'Land Equalisation System' (*juntianzhi*). Although the first system was set up in AD 280 under the Jin Dynasty (Fang X. AD 646 vol. 26: 'Economy' no. 16), the idea can be traced back to the chessboard-field system of the Zhou Dynasty under which farmers were also granted landholding rights to farm (Li J. 1962: ch. 9). The most cited system was the Land Equalisation System of the fifth century AD (Wei S. AD 554 vol. 7: 'Biography of Emperor Gao Zu'). Interestingly, the system was first designed not for the farming Chinese but for the Xianbei, a nomadic people who entered the interior of China in order to conquer it and had to solve the problem of high unemployment among the conquerors. With two-thirds of the Xianbei population becoming idlers, Emperor Xiaowen (r. AD 471–499) in desperation launched a reform of the economy in AD 485, following the advice of a Chinese scholar, Li Anshi. The reform delivered a desirable result: the Land Equalisation System enabled all able men and women to obtain state land so that agricultural production was resumed and recovered (Tang Z. 1956; Elvin 1973: 47–51). Records show that in AD 485 the system allowed each married couple to till 80 *mu* of land, 60 *mu* for grain and 20 *mu* for 50 mulberry trees, five jujube trees and three elm trees (Wei S. AD 554: ch. 'Economy'). As a result, the Xianbei themselves were converted to settled farmers. This system was then inherited by the following Sui and Tang Dynasties, functioning for three hundred years before privatisation took place (Emperor Xuanzong AD 738: vol. 3; Liang F. 1980: 476–85; for archaeological evidence see Du S. 1996). It has been recognised that the Land Equalisation System was a transitional landholding type from state ownership to private ownership for the purpose of rebuilding the agricultural economy after some major disturbance such as wars. Under Tang and Five Dynasties laws, idle land was automatically subject to a government land redistribution scheme and was granted to land-hungry farmers according to their family size. Once it was redistributed, the land was recognised as 'Ever-holding Land' (*yongyetian*). The government had no right to take it away as long as it was under cultivation. So, practically, these granted land plots were privatised at the moment of redistribution. It is recorded that the authorities of the ten kingdoms during the Five Dynasties collectively possessed more idle land than in any other historical period in premodern China. But before long, the state-owned share dropped back to the previous level of less than 10 per cent of the total (Wu J. 1996; for the early Ming Period, see Cao S. 1995). Such a phenomenon of short-term fluctuation in the proportion of private landholding and landowning recurred at the beginning of most new dynasties. Since the old equilibrium was maintained over time, such fluctuation can be largely, if not completely, ignored.

On a much smaller scale, there was state-owned *zhitian* ('Salary Land'), allocated to officials of different ranks (Liang F. 1980: 292, 472–5, 488–92). As a normal practice, the land was tilled by tenants under a share-cropping scheme. The acreage varied from time to time and from rank to rank. For the highest rank, it was 75 hectares (1,500 *mu*) during the North Wei Period,

64.8 hectares (1,200 *mu*) during the Tang, 116 hectares (2,000 *mu*) during the Song and 112 hectares (1,600 *mu*) during both Yuan and Ming (CBW 1978: 151). Salary land sometimes occupied a considerable proportion of state-owned land. For example, during the period between 1068 and 1076, the total acreage of salary land was 136,242 hectares (2,349,000 *mu*), representing 37 per cent of the total state-owned land (Liang F. 1980: 290, 292). Even so, this 37 per cent was only 0.5 per cent of the total land under cultivation in China at that time (*ibid.*).

In addition, there existed the 'Imperial Land Estates (Torbert 1977: ch. 3). The Imperial Land Estates were first established in the Han Dynasty and lasted until the end of the Qing Dynasty (Fu Z. and Wang Y. 1982: 203–11; CBW 1978: 151–3). Evidence shows that in Ming times the imperial estates run by the princes occupied half the cultivated land in Henan in central China and 70 per cent of that in the Chengdu Plain in western China (Guo W. 1988: 347). In Qing times, between 1644 and 1820, the Imperial Land Estates increased from 132 to 1,078 locations (CBW 1978: 151; Guo W. 1988: 348), while between 1764 and 1818 the total land area increased by 170 per cent to 239,677 hectares (3,577,275 *mu*) (Torbert 1977: 85). But, as with the Salary Land, even in 1818 the Imperial Land Estates occupied only 0.54 per cent of the total cultivated land in China (*ibid.*). The land of the imperial estates was cultivated by ordinary tenants under the supervision of stewards or managers appointed by the Imperial Household Department (*nei-wufu*). The rent was a source of income for the royal family. In 1764, for instance, the revenue from the imperial estates was 11,950 tonnes of grain (164,818 *shi*) and about 892 kg of silver (28,555 taels); in 1818, it was about 3,093 tonnes of grain (42,671 *shi*) and 4,396 kg of silver (140,674 taels) (*ibid.*: 89). As a result of this system some members of the imperial family became directly involved in agricultural production, such as Duke Wei of the Jin Dynasty, who became the vegetable and fruit supplier to the capital city (Wang Y. 1964: 25). The Ming princes Zhu Quang and Zhu Xiao both practised farming (*ibid.*: 126–7, 128–9), and the Qing prince Hong Jiao introduced many southern varieties to the North through his estate (*ibid.*: 225–6). Their farming practice was very likely to have been carried out on imperial estates. However, evidence shows that during the Ming, the Imperial Land Estates were on the decline over time. Only one-third of the estates were passed on to the younger generation of the princes in Imperial Land Estates in Kaifeng. The most important single factor was heirlessness, the cause of 50 per cent of cases where land was lost (Ma X. 1996: 69–70).

The long-term trend of state land of different kinds was to increase. In the eleventh century, it constituted 1.37 per cent of the total cultivated land in China, while in the Qing Dynasty it increased to 3.3 per cent (Liang F. 1980: 290; Guo W. 1988: 349). Still, it was an insignificant part of the Chinese agricultural economy. The point is that the state's having such a small share of the land meant a small proportion of tenants on these estates, too small to have any noticeable impact on the Chinese landholding system.

### 2.3.5 Peasant dual household-cum-economy

From the 1920s onwards, a long-lasting debate on the definition and behavioural pattern of peasant household-cum-economy has yielded some fruitful results, in spite of the fact that it has been entangled heavily with differences in criteria ranging from 'efficiency in resource allocation', 'profit/returns maximisation', 'utility maximisation' to 'economic optimisation'. A distinct type of economic organisation, the peasant economy has even been labelled as a separate mode of production (Harrison 1977; Siskind 1978).

So far, three main opinions have been formed concerning the behavioural pattern of a peasant household: (1) the 'resource rational but non-capitalist' opinion, which views a peasant household as a self-sufficient unit but not a return-maximising enterprise (Chayanov 1925; Dalton 1969; Scott 1972, 1976; see also Feeny 1983); (2) the 'market rational and capitalist' opinion, which views a peasant household as an enterprise little different from a capitalist firm, functioning on the principle of marginal product of revenue to maximise returns (Schultz 1964: 37, 72; Popkin 1979; cf. Lipton 1968); and (3) the 'resource-market rational and dualistic' opinion, which views a peasant household as having one foot in the 'subsistence economy' and the other in the market economy (Ellis 1988: 13; Huang 1990: pt 1). Although these opinions are backed by some empirical evidence, the 'dualistic opinion' has been the only one which has been tested, in a completely unintended way, on a large scale in the largely peasant society of Russia in the early twentieth century, under an unusual circumstance known as the 'food dictatorship' during the Soviet 'War Communism'. In response to the Bolshevik policy, the Russian peasantry, which had been reasonably commercialised under the tsar, first practised grain hoarding to boycott the ruthless robbery and then undertook black-market trade for profit. During this period, Russian peasants took feeding themselves as the priority and making profit as secondary. They did both extremely successfully. Their collective efforts effectively made the Soviet food control collapse and ushered in an era of the so-called 'New Economic Policy' designed to restore the old, time-honoured market system (Nove 1992: chs 3–4; Gregory and Stuart 1994: ch. 3; see also Gatrell 1986: ch. 4). Even so, this was what can be called a 'snap shot' observation in terms of geographic location and duration of time. Among other things, archaeological evidence shows that humans began settled farming at least 10,000 years ago. Since then, farmers have gone a long way in their economic behavioural evolution. Reflecting only the latest hundred years in that evolutionary process, the above opinions needed to be treated with caution for a study of long-term history. Such doubts will evaporate when the Chinese peasantry comes into the picture.

There is strong evidence from each dynasty that (1) agriculture and commerce, in which the rural population actively participated, coexisted most of the time; and (2) peasants were shrewd opportunists towards market opportunities but seldom had a total commitment to the market economy. As G. W. Skinner points out (1971: 272–3), the Chinese peasant was a permanent member of two communities, his village and his market town, which embraced 15–20 villages, some 1,800 households within an area of 45 square kilometres (for case studies, see Zeng X. 1996 and Wang X. 1996). Even under the communist command economy, the Chinese peasantry often managed to outwit the procurement system to get maximum income from their output (Kelliher 1992: 125–35, 240). Therefore, a dualistic behavioural pattern is most suited to such a study although further qualification is needed of how the peasantry oscillated between the two poles (see Appendix F). Fundamentally, the market was not necessarily a 'natural direction' for people who were self-reliant, a point that has been proved in many civilisations. It is often neglected that self-reliance is linked but not identical with self-sufficiency. The former often needs others' products/services to supplement one's own while the latter does not. The differentiation between the two types is critical to the understanding of the need, or the degree of the need, for the market.

The coexistence of self-reliance and the market is related to risks and risk management, as well as productivity, divergence and specialisation. In other words, it is a matter of variety and security of economic returns and livelihood. Unless a society was able to develop a range of varieties in production and consumption and was able to guarantee business security in market-oriented development, which often means an increasing dependency between individuals, people preferred to keep their economic independence from other economic agents. Such economic independence was offered by cultivation of self-owned land. This behavioural pattern does not exclude some pockets of highly commercialised rural communities which produced mainly for the market. These pockets belonged to, in the orthodox sense, the market economy. But their share in the entire economy was often insignificant.

A consequence of agricultural dominance and private individual landholding and landowning in premodern China was that self- or semi-self-reliance was at the household level: ordinary peasants produced most of what they needed and were involved in market activities for supplements, largely to trade surplus products up to the Ming Period. This formed the foundation of an economy of dualism: self-reliance as the dominant type on the one hand, and trade as the auxiliary on the other. The limited use of money was a clear indication of such a situation. Fairbank thus maintains that (1965: 49) 'the creation of credit among the villages was retarded by the relative self-sufficiency of the peasant household and its dependence upon short-term purchases from sources close at hand'.

However, apart from the Stone Age (Palaeolithic and Neolithic periods) such micro-level self-sufficiency was only relative, there being a wide spectrum between total self-sufficiency and specialisation and economic dependency. Self-sufficiency and self-reliance can function to different degrees at micro and macro levels, respectively. These two levels sometimes synchronised, sometimes did not. Such a distinction of levels is extremely important because although China was self-sufficient at the macro or aggregated level in its long-term premodern history, it does not necessarily mean that self-sufficiency was also the case at the micro (village and household) levels. This difference is common in most continental economies, even during the modern era, as seen in the difference between domestic and foreign trade. Whether economic divergence could continue to progress and replace self-sufficiency at both macro and micro levels is indeed another matter. The long-lasting dualism shows clearly that in China's case it was neither 'natural' nor inevitable for the market to override self-sufficiency and self-reliance (see Appendix D).

### 2.3.6 Impact on society

#### 2.3.6.1 Impact on state politics

The existence of this landholding free peasantry had a profound impact on Chinese state politics. First, the function of the peasantry was all-round and critical to the status and the survival of the empire: this stratum provided the state with its main sources of tax revenue, manpower for civil projects and soldiers for the standing army guarding the Great Wall and other frontiers against attempted barbarian invasions from the north. Across over 4,000 miles from the sea to the heart of the desert, the Great Wall was built along the natural dividing line between arable land and non-arable land, between the Han Chinese (Sinitic) and the non-Chinese (Altaic–Turkic, Mongol and Tungus–Manchu). It was thus not only a defence line, but also a permanent demarcation line to separate two different types of economies (see Anon. 1980b, 1991, 1995: 31). Although scholars like Arthur Waldron have questioned the purpose and function of the wall (1990), no one denies its utility as a defence line and a demarcation line between two different types of economies until the 1920s (Waldron 1995: 92, 101, 105, 108, 154, 170–1, 202, 205). This means at least two things: (1) the wall was a material manifesto of Chinese agricultural interest; and (2) it was a result of China's agricultural prosperity considering the enormous capital, labour and material inputs to build and maintain this greatest man-made defence line in the whole of premodern human history.

To take the military services as an example, in the Northern Dynasty (AD 386–581) able-bodied male adults had to serve in the army for 30 to 45 days a year (*ibid*.: 180–1). In the Tang Dynasty, every two to three households supported a soldier on duty (*ibid*.: 195). The Ming troops along the wall amounted to nearly a million men out of the total population of 60 million (Zhang T. 1735: ch. 'Military'; Liang F. 1980: 4–10). Inevitably, how to treat the peasantry remained a repertoire agenda in state politics throughout the entire post-Qin history. In return, the state provided the society, mainly the peasantry, with public goods: law and order. Public projects such as farming technology, water control and famine relief were mainly geared towards peasant needs as well. This was an enlarged and institutionalised reciprocal 'patron–client' relationship with clearly defined rights for the two parties, as defined and described by James Scott (1972), a fundamental relationship which is often overlooked *vis-à-vis* the disproportionately appealing appearance of the spectacular state machinery.

Second, the recognition of the peasant status led to the door of officialdom being opened to peasant sons through the imperial examination system (Marsh 1961: 12). Naturally, those officials who had a rural background would act favourably towards agriculture or even represent their farming families. Either attitude reinforced the existing pattern of agricultural dominance.

Third, after all, China was seldom ruled by a military dictatorship. The Chinese state power had to be mandated to the ruling clique by the landholding peasantry. It was based on a principle of legitimacy, not built upon exclusively by the physical intimidation of the large population (an impossible task even during modern times for tyrants like Hitler and Stalin; see, for example, Fukuyama 1992: ch. 2). For one thing, ruling a vast empire like China by physical force would incur prohibitive costs and thus become unfeasible in the long run. If the government failed to deliver the expected public goods, it lost its legitimacy to rule China (e.g. Wong 1997: pts 2–3). Given that there were constantly millions of able-bodied farmers who had basic military training, armed insurrections were a natural outcome if the government lost public support from the allegedly passive, authority-craven and exploited peasantry.

This agricultural favouritism in Chinese state politics was so obvious that it is no exaggeration to say that to a great extent the Chinese peasantry collectively manipulated state politics.

### 2.3.6.2 *Impact on the merchant class*

The existence of such an ever-growing peasantry served to inhibit the rise of the merchant class, which was viewed as a rival to the power of both the peasantry and the state. The rise of a powerful merchant class was thus incompatible with the Chinese system, although this did not at the same time mean that trade activities were also incompatible. This is the reason why in Chinese history merchants were ranked so low in the social hierarchy for so long. The consequence was profound, as pointed out by scholars like Joseph Needham, the Chinese failure being deeply rooted in the anti-merchant social atmosphere. In contrast, in Europe the rise of the bourgeoisie was very much a welcoming event to the nation-state where merchants felt very much at home in state politics, liaising directly with monarchies. He explicitly argues that unlike in

Europe the social structure in China prevented development of the bourgeoisie class (Needham 1969: 32). In terms of the balance of power, the merchant class was viewed as a threat which demeaned the emperor (Jones 1969: 205).

However, it is incorrect to suggest that such anti-merchant social atmosphere would have resulted in the non-development of trade and the market in China. In a private ownership-based economy, trade will take place as long as there exist (1) surpluses in products and labour, and/or (2) a certain degree of specialisation or division of labour. In this sense, a merchant class, especially a strong merchant class, was neither a necessary nor a sufficient condition for trade and the market to emerge. This was precisely the pattern in premodern China, a society which contained a considerable degree of market activities which coexisted with (1) a weak professional merchant class, (2) a high participation rate among ordinary peasants in market activities, and (3) the persistent involvement of the state in trade, with a strong commitment by the government to anti-merchant policies. In Skinner's account, the Chinese peasantry were largely responsible for the establishment and maintenance of local markets across the country, as many as 45,000 local markets in Qing China (Skinner 1964–5; and especially Skinner 1971: 272–3). Some Chinese scholars have defined this phenomenon as 'petty production at the household level and great circulation of commodities in the economy' (xiaoshengchan daliutong) (Zhang Z. 1996).

Given that the market capacity was limited at any given time and in any given place, when a large proportion of the peasantry were market active, less room was left for professional traders to operate. As the Chinese government provided a political or ultra-economic check on the growth of the merchant class through trade legislation and state monopoly on key markets, the Chinese peasantry delivered an operational check at the grass-roots level on the growth of the merchant class with its own active involvement in market activities at all levels as producers and consumers. As a main social and economic force against the merchant class, the peasant check was as effective as, if not more so than, the government check. So, the weakness of the Chinese merchant class could hardly have ultimately resulted from its defects by birth but rather resulted from the overall socio-political and socio-economic environment, which was dictated by the overall social structure and balance of power among competing classes. So far, very few scholars have recognised this 'double-check' phenomenon in Chinese economic history.

In light of this analysis, many opinions about the role and influence of the Chinese government need to be re-examined. For instance, Murphey (1954: 357) and Fairbank (1965: 38, 51) argue that the merchants' inability to rise as an independent force in China was the result solely of the Chinese government's constant control, oppression and hindrance by means of, for example, taxation and state monopoly. This view is the result of superficial observation. In world history, the rise of the merchant class was not a gift but a trophy. It is extremely doubtful whether state power would have been able to manipulate a class for so long. Given that the occasional triumph of the merchant class was often accompanied by temporary weakening of the landholding and land-owning peasantry in traditional China – Song times being a very good example – the worst enemy to the merchant class was probably the free peasantry, not the state. This also indicates that for the merchant class in China to have risen would have required a revolutionary change in China's social structure, not merely in the state's policies.

It is plausible to state that, for the survival of the Chinese Empire, the society did not need a strong and independent merchant class. It is probably true also that the Chinese government attitude was never truly unconducive to commercialisation, but only inadequate, simply because it tended to leave much of the market to an ocean of unprofessional rural residents and to 'unplug' the power for the merchant class.

### 2.3.6.3 *Impact on demographic pattern*

China has been taken as a classical case of overpopulation. For example, Eric L. Jones argues (1969: 1) that China fell victim to vicious cyclical elements of overpopulation which in the end retarded China by perpetual involvement in subsistence, labour-intensive agriculture. Similarly, Mark Elvin states (1973: 314) that in the late dynasties a high-level population–technology equilibrium trap held China back from further development because the increased population ate up the technology-permitted surpluses.

It is generally agreed that the Chinese extensive family system is responsible for the population crisis. However, in tracing the ultimate cause of the family system, answers are often given referring to the Chinese culture, values and mindset. But where did these values and mindset come from? Confucianism does not instruct the Chinese to have larger families. It is now clear that the landholding and landowning free peasantry itself was the ultimate reason for the Chinese demographic pattern. Undoubtedly, the central link between the ownership type and population growth was the Chinese system of equal land inheritance. Once such an inheritance system was well entrenched, the biological link of family lines began to function as the carrier of the 'genes' to replicate the small landholding and landowning system. So, only under a private individual land ownership system did lineage matter so much to the majority of the Chinese. In turn, the majority in society had a strong incentive to keep the ownership going by keeping the land within an extensive family. So, to a great extent, the Chinese traditional lineage, private individual land ownership and the equal inheritance system worked hand in hand as a package of a self-fulfilling institutions with a clear, rational economic purpose. In contrast, under a feudal system lineage was relevant mainly to the land-controlling upper classes.

Chinese matrimonial behaviour was affected and conditioned accordingly. For the Chinese, the precondition for a marriage was landholding or land ownership. As a result, the 'threshold' for a Chinese male to marry was much lower than for his counterpart in feudal or quasi-feudal Europe and Japan where the lower classes had to consider their occupations and income, rather than landholding, before they could think of marriage. As the saying goes, 'once you own a piece of land and a cattle, you will marry a woman to bear your children and have a sweet home' (*liang mu di, yi tou niu, laopo haizi, re kongtou*), which can well be taken as 'land-centrocism' in Chinese matrimonial behaviour. A recent study, based on Chinese legislation and the Chinese marital code, shows that during premodern times the 'ceiling ages for the first marriage' were 30 and 20 for men and women, respectively, and that the 'floor ages for the first marriages' were 20 and 16 for men and women, respectively ( Jiang X. 1995: 42–3). The study also indicates that although polygamy existed, it was mainly practised among the well-off classes (*ibid.*: ch. 2). Given the biological balance among the Chinese between the male and female, polygamy was almost certainly a minority practice because of the need to sustain a civilisation based on landholders. In other words, given the constraint of the sex balance among the Chinese population, a sustainable landholding and landowning peasantry with the prevailing equal inheritance had to rely on monogamy. Otherwise, unmarried single males, or a large proportion of them, would certainly have lost their land due to heirlessness. Moreover, during the post-Song period in particular, there was a great emphasis on widows' integrity, which rejected remarriage or any form of sex life for widows (called *zhenjie* 'chastity'), and this served as an effective check on the birth rate (*ibid.*: 132–41). Furthermore, the secret and focus of the Taoist sexual techniques is to have intercourse without ejaculation, arguably designed for the polygamous male to serve his multiple sex partners each day (*ibid.*: 47–58, 308–9), which effectively worked as a means of male contraception although only in a very limited way. Therefore, the main contributors to China's population growth were (1) the young marriage ages, and (2) the prevailing anti-celibacy; both were 'programmed' by the Chinese system of property ownership.

As the landholding-based commitment to family perpetuance prevailed among landholders, the majority of the population, China had a constant demographic push which was much greater and longer lasting than that in premodern Europe and Japan (Chao 1986: 8–9, 11). It is thus unconvincing to suggest that the marital behaviour of the Chinese was derived from their cultural values and social obligations (ibid.: 9, 30). This is particularly true considering that the Europeans and the Japanese had distinctively different cultural backgrounds but had a similar matrimonial pattern.

The impact was multifold. First, as the overwhelming majority in society, if the peasantry preferred to have big families, society would sooner or later suffer from a population explosion. Second, owing to the land-ownership system, not only was there a natural desire among, and incentive for, the Chinese peasantry to have more children, but also it was imperative for the ordinary farming household to have more children in order to satisfy the requirement of labour supply to family farms and property inheritance. Indeed, having children was a type of investment in terms of both labour input and property-holding within the family. Third, for landholding and landowning individuals, having children was commonly taken as a combined insurance policy and old-age pension scheme, which was (and still is) called *yang-er fanglao*, literally 'having children to provide pension'. All these concerns and factors reinforced each other.

A common belief is that the old-age pension was automatically provided by the younger generation within the traditional Chinese family structure. It is a romantic view on two accounts. First, the fact that laws were made to implement this pension arrangement means that in traditional times there was a tendency for the younger generation to avoid this family obligation. Second, what was commonly practised was, in effect, for the youngest son to live with the aged parents after the division of the family assets. The youngest son now had practically a double share from the family asset pool. It was the extra share that made him obliged to provide the parents with their pension. It can also be viewed as the case that the parents took the youngest son as a 'pension hostage'. Everything was based on cool-minded, careful calculation and there was nothing rosy about this pension arrangement. After all, China was not a communal society of collective ownership but a society of private landowners. This was reflected by complex pension deals and pension hostage.

## 2.4 Physiocratic state

A physiocratic state can be defined as an 'agrarian bureaucratic state' (Goldstone 1991: 41). According to M. C. Wright, the security of the agricultural producer was the essential aim of political economy in traditional China because the land tax provided the great majority of the state's funds. The principle 'exalt agriculture', and its corollary 'disparage commerce', had been emphatically reiterated in the Classics and Histories, where agriculture continued to be regarded as the only desirable basis for the economy (1957: 148). John K. Fairbank highlights that this elite class found their security in land and office, not in trade and industry. This bureaucratic stratum upheld the agrarian sector at the expense of the development of a merchant class (Fairbank 1965: 51). These accounts are simplified but quite accurate.

### 2.4.1 Origin of physiocracy

The idea of protecting agriculture was crystallised in *nongben*, meaning physiocracy or agricultural fundamentalism (see Broadbent 1978: 104; Zhao K. 1984; Guo W. 1988: 6; Yan S. 1988). This physiocratic ideology originated no later than the Spring and Autumn Period (770–476 BC), and was shared by nine major schools of thought of that time: Taoism, the Yinyang school, the

Legalists, the School of Logicians, Mohism, the Political Strategists, the Eclectics, the Agriculturists and Confucianism. All of them claimed either directly or indirectly that agricultural prosperity was the prerequisite to making a political unit powerful (see Chen 1911: ch. 11).

Undoubtedly, Confucianism played an important role in philosophising physiocratic ideas and indoctrinating the view of agriculture as the most respectable economic activity in China (Chao 1986: 106). For example, in *Guoyu*, one of the Confucian classics, the idea of physiocracy is expressed as follows:

> The greatest business of the people is agriculture. From agriculture, the millet which is used for the sacrifice to God is produced; the density of population grows; the expense of the business is supplied; social harmony and peace arise; the multiplication of wealth begins; and the characters of honesty, great-mindedness, integrity and solidity become a general habit of the people.
>
> (quoted in Chen 1911: 381)

Confucianism also indoctrinated the Chinese social hierarchy in which the peasantry was recognised as higher than other working classes and the merchant class was placed at the bottom of the class ranking. Arguably, Confucianism was at best a theoretical source of physiocracy to reflect the Chinese socio-economic reality, since it did not create farming or the landholding and landowning peasantry.

The ideology had several aspects. First, agriculture was regarded as *benye*, or the 'Principal Occupation'. Priority was given to the protection of the agricultural sector of the economy, while other sectors which competed with agriculture for labour, capital and other resources were confined so that agricultural dominance was not undermined (Twitchett 1968; Lau 1984: 21). Second, farming as an occupation received great respect and farmers were accorded considerable dignity: they ranked in society above other commoners such as artisans (*gong*) and merchants (*shang*), as observed as early as the seventh century BC by Guan Zhong (? – 645 BC) (see also Fairbank 1965: 17–27; Mokyr 1990: 230–1). Third, to encourage and protect agriculture as well as to assist the peasantry were considered the dominant economic policy by the governing institutions (Lee 1969: pts 1–2).

Surrounding this 'policy core', there was often a physiocratic package. Policy measures employed included (1) control of grain prices by establishing the floor price level and buying in surplus grain in good years, exemplified in the policy of Li Kui (*c.* 455–395 BC); (2) the protection of private land ownership, as in the deeds of Shang Yang (*c.* 390–338 BC); (3) assistance with irrigation projects, under such policies as those of Sang Hongyang (152–80 BC); (4) demonstration of new and better techniques, as in the policy of Emperor

Wudi (140–88 BC); (5) famine relief, as in the undertakings of Emperor Zhaodi (86–74 BC); and (6) periodic land allotment, as proposed in the agrarianism theory and corresponding policy of Li Anshi (AD 43–493). Moreover, tillage (*litian*) was one of the criteria for awarding titles to citizens and for exempting farmers from taxation (for the Warring States Period see Shang Y. 338 BC: ch. 'Jinling' and Guan Z. Warring States Period: ch. 'Shanquan-shu'; for the Qing Dynasty see Cheng Q. 1865 vol. 9: 635). Furthermore, members of 'marginal classes' of non-landholding individuals and non-scholars such as artisans and merchants were persuaded to buy land to join the mainstream, as practised in post-Song times. Often, sons of these marginal classes became landholders and/or scholars rather than following in their fathers' footsteps, thanks to the class mobility mechanism in society. Last but not least, it was not unheard of for emperors, 'the Sons of Heaven', to 'practise farming' on the imperial farms in order to identify themselves with the peasantry and to set an ultimate example for the younger generation to follow ( Ji X. 1955: 54; Lee 1969: 67, 159; Merson 1989: 12–13). In the context of its origin, it is not surprising that this physiocratic ideology dominated government economic policy-making until Qing times (AD 1644–1911) (Broadbent 1978: 104; Zhao K. 1984; Yan S. 1988). After being long absent in medieval Europe, a physiocratic state occurred only briefly in the eighteenth century when this oriental ideology was introduced to French politics through Quesnay (Waverick 1946; Schumpeter 1954). Therefore, it is largely irrelevant to talk about a physiocratic Europe.

Among all these measures, in terms of supporting the small landholding and landowning farms, the most important were the following three: (1) a low tax rate; (2) grain price control; and (3) low-interest loans, which were designed to help small farmers to sustain their production cycle. The tax rate, for example, is estimated as 10 per cent of the household's total output from Han to Tang times (see Appendix G). From the Song to Qing on average the government tax revenue counted for merely 7.1–9.3 per cent of the total agricultural GDP or 5–7 per cent of China's total GDP (Feuerwerker 1984: 299–300, 302). Given that the Chinese agricultural sector was able to produce about a quarter of its products as surplus (*ibid.*), the amount which the Chinese state tapped was only one-third of that surplus.

One may argue that this figure was a formal tax rate and that informal taxes and duties should also be included. There is little doubt not only that informal taxes and duties existed – and they sometimes got out of control and destroyed the economy – but things went wrong with formal taxes as well. Policy fluctuations were common. Excessive rent-seeking haunted the Chinese Empire. However, heavy tax on agriculture was recognised by both the Confucian elite and ordinary peasants as non-physiocratic, unorthodox and abnormal. Although the picture was not so black-and-white, in most cases physiocracy prevailed in the end, as evidently shown from the aftermath of each major peasant rebellion throughout Chinese history.

However, physiocratic dominance in the Chinese state politics did not mean that there was no room for non-agricultural activities. Quite the contrary, physiocracy in China allowed the market to exist and sometimes to prosper. For instance, Sima Qian (145–86 BC), the best-known historian in the whole of premodern Chinese history, believed that trade was indispensable in society. So much so, in his *Book of History* (91 BC) he included a section on market activities ('Shihuo Zhi') and merchant biographies, which became a standard for writing dynastic histories. Of course, the market was not 'free'; it was regulated and controlled to protect the agricultural sector. But no matter how tight the state monopoly on some domestic and most international trade appeared to be, there was always a place for trade and trade expansion as long as farming was not sacrificed. It is indeed quite another matter as to whether the professional merchants felt comfortable with such control. In this context, the stated status of the merchant class reflected the real place of that class in society. Scholars often blame the Chinese state for 'putting the merchant class down'. Oddly enough, few scholars have blamed the Chinese state for honouring and collaborating with the peasantry too much, as if the peasantry naturally deserved it. The same attitude should have been consistently applied to all classes.

### 2.4.2 *Physiocracy and people as the foundation*

Physiocracy in premodern China was supported by and entwined with the ideology of *minben*, *min* meaning 'the amorphous, indeterminate mass of peasants' (Hall and Ames 1987: 139), and *ben* 'basis' or 'foundation'. Therefore, *minben* can be translated as 'People as the Foundation' or 'the Peasantry as the Foundation'.

Interestingly, in spite of the philosophical and political differences between Confucianism and Taoism, scholars from both sides tried to find a way to reach social harmony and took a strong stand against the tyrannical policies of Legalism. The idea which both Confucianism and Taoism came up with was this *minben*. After the political and socio-economic disaster caused by the Qin Legalists (Jia Y. *c.* 200–168 BC), *minben* became well entrenched in China's political thinking (see Chen 1911: 77–9), which can be taken as a sign of the social and political consciousness of the Chinese literati (Liu Z. 1987). As a result, in modern China, even the ruthless ruler Mao Zedong had to disguise himself as a benevolent sage by labelling his régime as one of 'serving the people' (*weirenmin fuwu*).

In Lao–Zhuang philosophy, or early Taoism, *minben* was embraced in its *laissez-faire* framework known as *wuwei erzhi* (literally 'order and equilibrium will be achieved without ruler's intervention'). Taoism had its turn to serve the state to guide policy-making in the early period of the Han Dynasty, because of the total bankruptcy of the heavy-handed Legalist approach under the previous Qin régime. The Legalists' rejection of the *minben* principle made the Qin pay a heavy price in that it was the shortest-lived dynasty in Chinese history (see Fan W. 1964–5 vol. 2: 50; Shao Q. 1985: 6; Sun C. 1986: 618). Confucianism was later favoured because the Taoist potential for passivity and the *laissez-faire* attitude became exhausted (see Ban G. AD 82 vol. 56; Jian B. 1983: 485–93). Confucianism, by comparison, was more active, disciplined and utilitarian. The idea of *minben* was also more explicitly manifested by the Confucian School (see Shao Q. 1985). According to orthodox Confucians, humans are the most precious beings between Heaven and Earth (Zhang Z. 1987). Mencius explicitly states that (1) the people are of supreme importance; (2) rulers have to win the people's support and (3) an effective way to win people's support is to ensure that they do not starve in bad years (for an English translation, see Lau 1984: 291, 145, 21). Mencius further held (Mengzi Warring States Period: ch. 'Lianghui Wang') that 'only he who is able to protect people is entitled to become the ruler' (*baomin erwang*).

The legitimacy of government, according to *minben*, was indeed conditional: government had to ensure that the masses were employed, fed and thus relatively content (e.g. Wong 1997: pt 2). Otherwise, the emperor would lose Heaven's favour and a rebellion could be justified as an antidote to disequilibrium. In world history, there were probably more mass armed rebellions of peasants against the corrupt central authorities in China than anywhere else: for instance, from 1644 to 1721, across China there were 176 armed rebellions, an average of more than two each year (Xie G. 1956). Sometimes these rebellions succeeded in overthrowing the target dynasties, including the Qin, Han (both Western and Eastern), Sui, Yuan and Ming (Jin G. and Liu Q. 1984: 115–19).

The unique phenomenon of rebelling to change dynasty was another face of the same coin of the Chinese landholding free peasantry-based society. In comparison, frequent massive armed rebellions did not occur under a system such as the medieval feudalism of Europe or Japan, in which the majority of the people were restrained by a decentralised social structure, often characterised by personal legal and economic bondage. In such societies, a census register system was neither necessary nor possible, because of the principle, 'my subject's subjects are not mine'. Nor was it necessary in medieval Europe for mass armed rebellions to be organised to change unbearable social conditions: there were many other bloodless means of breaking out of personal bondage, for instance by escaping from individual masters or overlords. It can thus be safely assumed that in Europe more peasants or serfs preferred becoming free bourgeois to joining in violent rebellions, simply because the potential cost of the latter was much higher than that of the former. Furthermore, in both Europe and Japan the decentralised political system, the personal bondage which existed within the small, separate political units, as well as the economic differences between these, handicapped any attempt at organised manoeuvres by the ruled in rural areas. Further, since the free citizens of the political alliance of independent city-states in medieval Europe were not the social majority, they could not play the same role as their Chinese counterparts. In the case of the free Germanic and Slavic communes, there was no need for the members to rebel, since the underdevelopment of private ownership hindered the alienation of the political power from the public interest (Engels 1942). Therefore, ideas like 'People as the Foundation' was not very relevant in feudal Europe and Japan.

Naturally, in order to gain and maintain this legitimacy, the ruler had to protect and encourage agriculture as the means to satisfy the peasantry. This was the link between *minben* and physiocracy. On the whole, physiocracy and the principle of People as the Foundation were simple justifications and confirmations of the importance of agriculture and the peasantry in pre-modern Chinese society. Of course, they also reinforced the agricultural dominance and the rights of the peasantry.

The best example of the *nongben–minben* paradigm in action can be seen in the policy of Emperor Taizong (AD 627–49) of the Tang Dynasty. Drawing a lesson from the previous tyrant, Sui (AD 581–618), who was destroyed by rebels, Emperor Taizong resumed the old dogma of *minben* and openly recognised that (1) it is the people that maintain the monarch (*min yang jun*); (2) it is the people that select and allow the monarch to rule (*min ze jun*); and (3) it is conditional for people to follow and obey the monarch (*min guiyu jun*). His policy was designed to establish harmony between the people and the ruler by practising abstinence among the ruling class and *laissez-faire* towards the ordinary people: tax and corvée were reduced or exempted, and agriculture was protected and promoted (Liu Z. and Zhang F. 1991: 70–3). As a result, the Tang Dynasty was prosperous and long lasting.

From the above analysis it is easy to understand just how misleading the so-called 'oriental despotism' is when applied to the Chinese case. The Chinese state, including the monarch, Imperial Court and the bureaucracy, was not God and could not have a free hand to do whatever it wished to, because the power of the Chinese state needed to be mandated in the name of *tian* (or *t'ien*, meaning Heaven or the deity which has the transcendent power over society) by millions of ordinary free peasants. As Hall and Ames point out (1987: 145), 'in the Confucian tradition, there is a frequent association between *t'ien*, conventionally rendered "Heaven", and the masses (*min*)'; *'T'ien* has compassion on the masses (*min*): whatever they desire, *t'ien* is sure to effect'; and *'T'ien* sees as the masses (*min*) see; *t'ien* hears as they hear'.

Therefore, the Chinese political system should not be interpreted as total-itarianism or absolutism because the ruling clique never obtained such power even when it tried – the illusion of the state's total control in premodern China being rooted in the sophisticated bureaucratic machine of the Chinese Empire (Wittfogel 1957); nor should it be interpreted as a form of upper-class democracy because the Chinese system lacked political equality. At best, the Chinese established and maintained a system equivalent to what is often called 'soft authoritarianism'.

### 2.4.3 Determinatives for physiocracy

Why did the Chinese state have to be physiocratic? Why not mercantile like some European states in the sixteenth and seventeenth centuries? These two questions strike modern observers. It is often believed that physiocracy was a creation of the government or the upper class. In a sense it was, given that policies had to be made and implemented by some organisation in society. However, since such policies were so consistent in spite of the periodic changes of government, some having not even been Chinese in origin (such as those of the Tartar Jin and Manchu Qing), it seems that there were some 'invisible hands' in control of the process. In other words, a physiocratic state in China did not occur by accident. Rather, it was a result of a carefully calculated purpose and accomplishment of that purpose. The purpose was to protect economic interests and promote a type of economic life. Analysis of agricultural dominance and the power of the Chinese peasantry shows that agricultural fundamentalism in China was not a free choice by governments, but a 'must' if they wanted to rule the country, as seen from physiocracy and the principle of the People as the Foundation.

The invisible hands were primarily the social structure, and secondarily Confucian belief and empire-building. In contrast, by the seventeenth and eighteenth centuries, Europe had already developed an advanced financial system including the creation of government bonds and annuity investments that were guaranteed to be as safe as land. Governments in Europe greatly extended their role in capital markets and were also responsible for the appearance of mortgage markets (Jones 1988: 137). No parallel existed in China. It can thus be suggested that a non-agricultural alternative, which was discovered by European societies, diminished the need to protect agriculture.

Then, the question becomes: why did the Chinese fail to find a similar alternative? The answer is that Chinese society did not provide a strong incentive to seek any alternatives, as demonstrated (1) in the unique replication of small landholding and landowning households, and (2) in the fact that the landholding and landowning peasantry was a main determinant of physiocracy.

From the peasant point of view, physiocracy and *minben* ideology provided the public with a yardstick to judge government socio-economic policies and to ensure that those policies did not become empty talk. If the majority of the population became worse off, it was the government that was to blame. Bad administration would give enough reason for the peasants to rebel to change the government. The Chinese state could not afford to ignore the interests of the majority that were constituted by the peasants.

From the Chinese elite's point of view, there was a correlation between agriculture and peace. They were fully aware of the danger of massive peasant armed rebellions and of the fact that a crisis was often preceded by misconduct on the part of the ruling group. They believed that the central power must be careful in handling the peasants and agriculture because only wise rulers could occupy the throne for long, a lesson drawn by imperial historians from the downfall of the glorious Qin Dynasty (Lee 1969: 148). A golden rule was to ensure that the masses were properly fed, as described in *Huainanzi* (*Duke of Huinan*) as follows (Liu A. 179–122 BC): 'Food is the foundation of people's life; people are the foundation of the country; the country is the foundation of the monarch.'

From the Chinese state point of view, physiocracy was in fact the ramification of the agricultural and free peasantry's dominance in Chinese lives. First, the peasantry was the stratum of agricultural performers and thus embodied the interest in agriculture. Second, peasants were the overwhelming majority in China's population. Third, the Confucian education–civil service system provided a path for peasant sons to become bureaucrats, which was also encouraged by law. This further safeguarded and reinforced the peasant interest: peasant sons in power were more likely to protect agriculture simply for the sake of their own farming families. Fourth, Agriculture was, as mentioned earlier, the main source of government revenue and for manpower for public works and defence forces. Agriculture was thus central to social stability in China: ultimately, it determined the ebb and flow of the latter. Throughout Chinese history, whenever and for whatever reasons agriculture was disturbed and weakened, social disequilibrium would occur and the country would either be defeated by barbarians through the weakening of the Chinese standing army, which relied on the agricultural sector for soldiers and the food to feed them, or collapse internally following peasant armed rebellions due to peasant discontent (for disturbances of agriculture and fall of dynasties see Wang 1936). On the other hand, the more prosperous the agriculture, the stronger the country, with greater tax revenue and a more generous supply of food and fighting men; and the stronger the country, the less trouble the barbarians and the peasants would cause. It is easy to understand why agriculture became an issue on the ancient Chinese political agenda and was so closely watched over by the central authorities (Chen 1911: 50, 55; chs 21, 26, 30–1). That it became a matter of life and death for any dynasty in dealing with agriculture and the peasantry means the Chinese state had virtually no choice but to be physiocratic. Obviously, peasantry and agriculture were the cause and the physiocratic state was the effect.

At this point, many hypotheses about China need to be re-evaluated. For example, according to mainstream opinion, the Chinese state was perceived to be hostile towards commercial activities and as favouring agriculture, which consequently caused China's inability to become industrialised (Perkins 1967: 478). This view seems plausible at first glance. However, when we trace further to ask why the Chinese state had to be so anti-merchant (which is by definition different from anti-market), the ultimate reason can only be established in the Chinese 'mindset'. Such argument ignores the basis of public choice: a society does not live on mindset but on economic activities, inputs and outputs, investment and returns. Mindset does not belong to any of these economic categories.

### 2.4.4. *Impacts of physiocracy*

#### 2.4.4.1 *Reinforcement of agricultural dominance*

No doubt physiocracy reinforced agricultural dominance in the economy. 'Coaxing and enticing people into agriculture' (*quannong*) was a standard economic policy guide right from the beginning of the empire's history. Accordingly, tillage (*litian*) became one of the criteria for awarding titles to citizens and for exempting farmers from taxation in the Qin Kingdom of the Warring States Period (see Shang Y. 338 BC: ch. 'Jinling'; Guan Z. Warring States Period: ch. 'Shanquanshu'). Later, the virtues of 'Piety and Tillage' (*xiaodi litian*) were established by Emperor Huidi (r. 194–188 BC) of the Han Dynasty as the criteria for selecting model citizens to enjoy corvée exemption (Ban G. AD 82: ch. 'Biography of Emperor Huidi'), and from then on it also remained among the criteria for the selection of bureaucrats until the Tang (Xu S. 1838: 17, 27). In the Yuan Dynasty, an elderly and skilful farmer was appointed Head of Farming Group (*shezhang*) to take charge of tillage and the local security of 50 households (Zheng Z. 1938: 202). Under Qing law, successful farmers were to be appointed to the official position of Eighth Grade (*bapin*) to assist agricultural affairs (Cheng Q. 1865 vol. 9: 635; Lee 1969: 117). Li Yinggui, an expert in growing double-cropping rice, even became closely allied to Emperor Kangxi (Kong X. 1983). Monetary reward was available, too. In 1828, a magistrate of Suzhou Prefecture honoured four farmers who successfully put the method of pit cultivation into practice with an official banquet and a prize in silver bullion (Chen Z. 1958: 369).

#### 2.4.4.2 *Check on the growth of professional merchants*

An immediate consequence of the physiocratic policies was discrimination against the activities of the merchant class. Although it is speculative to pinpoint the Chinese physiocratic state and its policies as the prohibitive factor responsible for the lack of capitalist development in traditional China, the policies certainly made such a development more difficult than otherwise. This is particularly true in terms of the lack of government support for pro-merchant institutions – commercial laws and pro-market property rights – as Eric L. Jones points out that in China the 'political structure did not establish a legal basis for sufficient new economic activity outside agriculture' (1990: 20).

The rationale for the anti-merchant attitude and policies was multifold. First, technically, it was easier for government to collect tax and recruit young soldiers from settled farming households than from mobile merchants, a fact that was repeatedly pointed out by officials throughout Chinese history.

In other words, without modern technology, the monitoring costs were much higher in dealing with merchants than in dealing with land-bound farmers. Such a lower cost in financial administration itself provided the government with enough of an incentive to protect the agricultural sector. In the end, it became a self-realising cycle: because it was cheaper to tax the agricultural sector, the sector was protected and nurtured for taxation purposes. So, when observations are made, as in Murphey's remark (1954: 358) that 'the imperial revenue was at most periods largely from the land tax and from the government trade monopolies', modern scholars tend to neglect the historical dynamics of this self-realisation. Moreover, technically, it was more feasible to impose state control on a weaker group such as the merchants than a strong group like the peasantry. Once again, it was a matter of the social cost and social benefit.

Second, in a typically Chinese view of 'zero-sum gain' towards resource allocation, merchants were regarded as the main competitor for resources against the peasants and the state. This 'zero-sum' view was natural in that a premodern society did not have a device with which to measure economic gains or a clear vision of the process of value-adding outside agriculture (as theorised by classical economics in the analyses of Smithian 'trade-accounting cost' and Ricardian 'trade-opportunity cost'), both crucial in the development of capitalism. Accordingly, enrichment of merchants was viewed as having been achieved at the expense of peasant welfare and government revenue (Fu Z. and Wang Y. 1982: 358; Han L.Q. 1986: 421). This was true not only in China but also in France, as seen from the influential School of Physiocracy headed by François Quesnay (1694–1774), who excluded commerce completely in his input–output model. Since the Chinese had freedom to choose their own occupations between the agricultural and non-agricultural sectors (Chao 1986: 2, 3, 5), a potential danger existed that more profitable sectors of the economy would attract too much labour and capital from agriculture. Typically, as an ancient (Han Dynasty) saying goes, 'to become rich from poverty, working in agriculture is not as effective as crafts industry while crafts industry is not as effective as commerce' ('*yongpin qiufu, nong buru gong, gong buru shang*') (Fu Z. and Wang Y. 1982: 358; Han L.Q. 1986: 421). Hence, the agricultural sector was protected by the authorities by means of the blocking of any flow from agriculture and the guiding of other sectors such as industry and trade in directions which were of benefit, or at least not harmful, to agriculture. That a constant effort was required to check the over-growth of the merchant class was only part of the 'social engineering'.

Finally, empirically, the masses in premodern China, who consisted of millions of small landholding and landowning farmers, had a strong sense of equality, an ideal of Great Harmony (*datong*). They could tolerate to a great extent a rich state but not rich individuals. This was the reason the government trade monopoly seldom upset the peasantry.

### 2.4.4.3 Bias in technological development

The physiocratic state, together with the agricultural cult, helps to explain why technological development became so highly selective and so clearly agriculture biased. Although the Chinese proved to be highly creative in a wide range of fields, a great many Chinese inventions and innovations withered before reaching their full potential, as revealed by Needham's work (1954–90). In contrast, agriculture was one of the few areas which received constant scholarly attention throughout long-term Chinese history (Deng 1993a). This was largely due to the systematic promotion and support of agriculture with the physiocratic state functioning as a filter and amplifier in the manipulation of the developmental path for science and technology. This manipulation was possible because there existed a degree of bureaucratic conformity; and different ideas were often seen as unsafe and therefore there were incentives to discourage innovations (Fairbank 1965: 114). Within the 'safe' areas of study, useful results were counted as merits. To take technical books as an example, agricultural books (*nongshu*) were written and published consistently, even during the chaotic periods, by different levels of government, with a wide range of intellectuals being involved. As a result, agriculture and its related fields (such as water control and irrigation for production, transportation and communication for internal migration and food distribution) became exceptions when Chinese science and technology on the whole slowed down and stagnated in the later dynasties (Elvin 1973: 298).

Of course, the Chinese monarch often appeared apathetic towards technological progress. This is not surprising. The monarch was largely a symbol of the empire, and the 'dirty work', including administrative routine and contingent treatment and the encouragement of technological process, was done by the bureaucrats at the front and thus often became hidden. A great deal of work was done at local and individual levels without any involvement of the central authorities (Deng 1993a). So, the reason why the monarch could be lazy was precisely the existence of the hard-working Confucian bureaucracy. In the realm of agriculture, China's technological development was achieved in private hands or from the joint efforts of the bureaucracy and individual farmers. In that sense, Mokyr's viewpoint that in premodern China technological development was a dependent variable to state is questionable (Mokyr 1990: ch. 9). The difference between China and Europe was not whether and how the state was involved. Rather, the difference was that in China the development was a dependent variable to a peculiar pro-agricultural socio-economic structure and thus biased towards farming interests. The Chinese state was heavily involved as one of the parties in this biased technological development. There is no evidence that the Chinese state monopolised the entire process of technological development over any length of time in premodern China (see Deng 1993a, 1997). So, the importance of the government's role should not be overplayed. Typically, Mokyr maintains that by the fifteenth century, the role of the imperial government in both invention and innovation was far less remarkable than it had been in medieval times, and no other entity in China was in a position to replace the state in promoting technological progress (Mokyr 1990:238). There were no substitutes for the state in China. In Europe, precisely because technological change was private in nature and took place in a decentralized, politically competitive setting, it could be sustained in the long run.

## 2.5 Centralised government

### 2.5.1 Structure

The Chinese government is well known for its centralisation, as shown in Figure 2.3. Quantitatively, the proportion of bureaucrats in the total population was very small even by modern standards. However, this small army of bureaucrats successfully ran a huge empire containing easily, from AD 1000

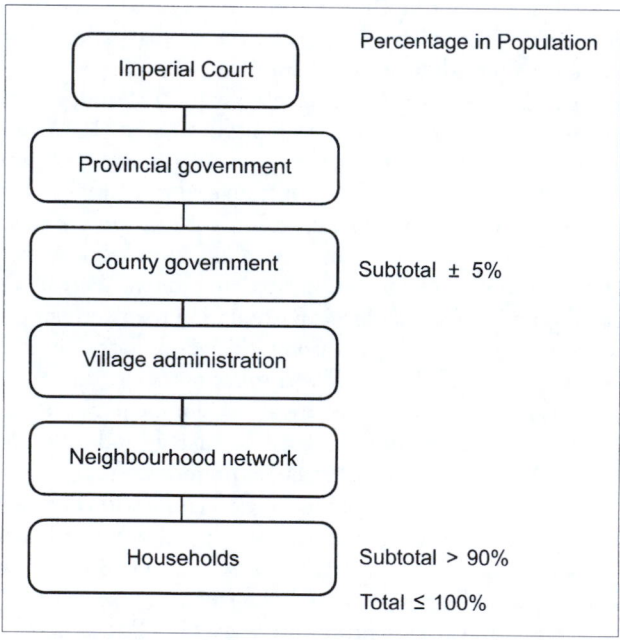

*Figure 2.3* China's administrative structure

*Source*: Based on Chang 1955: ch. 1; Marsh 1961: 13–15; Ho 1962; Mousnier 1971: 256; Stover 1974: 272; Feuerwerker 1976: 48; Hsiao 1979: 7; Jing J. 1981: 53; Wu H. 1984: 64–6; Hucker 1985: 1–96.

at the latest, one-fifth to a quarter of the human race. Given that such a vertical structure was the administrative framework of the Chinese Empire for some two millennia, its record of efficiency is impressive.

### 2.5.2 *Reasons and origin*

The reason the Chinese established and maintained a highly centralised political system since the Qin Dynasty was not the Chinese ideologies (Confucianism, Legalism, Taoism, Buddhism and so forth). For instance, Confucianism does not contain a constitution but a code of behaviour. Nor does it indicate that society should be run by a single political centre. Instead, during the period when Confucius and Mencius lived, China was not united and multiple power centres were the norm. Confucianism stratifies society in different layers and tells people their responsibilities. Through Chinese history, Confucians served with ease coexisting political centres, the best example being the Three Kingdoms Period (AD 221–65). In addition, Confucianism served well in politically decentralised Tokugawa Japan. Legalism emphasises coercion to establish authority, which may be interpreted as a guide for political centralisation. However, in Chinese history, coercionists were never popular and the most coercive régime, the Qin (221–207 BC), lasted less than a generation. As for Taoism and Buddhism, they are far more distant from political centralisation and often lead to self-government or even anarchy. Thus, there must have been other reasons for the establishment and perpetuation of political centralisation in premodern China.

The main reasons for the establishment and maintenance of a highly centralised political system in China were the need for arbitration in internal disputes and the need for national defence against external invasions. Both functions were crucial to the survival of the empire. First, as already mentioned, in a society where the majority of people are free citizens, an authority is needed to settle disputes, an authority which can transcend individual interests. So, a centralised state suited a society of legally free citizens who were loosely related to each other at an impersonal level with little personal bondage. Not surprisingly, all free citizen-based societies in the modern world have a centralised political system. For the same reason, free citizens of modern nations need a centralised authority as an arbitrator which can transcend individual interests, and which at the same time can act as a protector to safeguard individual welfare against violation from inside society and plunder from outside invasions. In comparison, in a society where the majority is not free, such a task can be undertaken by slave masters or feudal lords within their domains. Second, and more importantly, China was vulnerable to nomad invasions. This was not only because of the topographic features of the East Asian mainland, but also because of the evident military superiority enjoyed by those nomadic tribes over the scattered Chinese individual farmers who were easy prey for the nomads (see Weng D. 1990). Recent studies also suggest that the livelihood of nomads beyond the Great Wall was far more vulnerable to climatic changes than that of the settled Chinese farmers. Plunder by those nomads was thus a way to survive in the harsh environment (Lan Y. 1996a; Gao W. 1996).

To build a permanent defence system along the northern border with the Great Wall, a strategy to substitute 'capital-intensive' military hardware for low-quality soldiers, proved to be very effective in the long run. Indeed, the Great Wall reveals just how unique China was as a civilisation throughout world history. China's uniqueness was not so much due to the conflicts between a settled agrarian society and a nomadic society; such conflicts were common in Eurasia. Rather, it was the capacity to build and maintain such an expensive system to protect an agrarian oasis. No other agrarian society was able to show that it could afford a parallel system. Also, the very fact that the Chinese built and maintained the wall and the army shows just how determined they were to take their comparative advantage in manpower and economic surplus, both being the products of successful agriculture, to counterbalance the ferocious nomadic warriors. No doubt, to command this basically peasant army, a centre was needed. So, the ultimate reason for China to perpetuate a centralised government still lies in the existence of the individual landholding and landowning free peasantry. Against this background, and considering the longer history of farming in China, the prototype of this administrative structure may have originated from some kind of military organisation invented by proto-Chinese tribes. The evidence that the early chiefs or kings of the proto-Chinese tribes (like the *yan* and *huang*) were capable military commanders supports this hypothesis (Wang X. 1985).

To show just how critical this command centre, the Great Wall and border-guards were to the survival and expansion of the Chinese civilisation, the Manchu invasion and conquest can be seen as counter-evidence. When the Chinese command centre collapsed and the gate of the Great Wall was open, it was easy for a nomadic tribe to take over the Chinese territory, considering the fact that the elite Manchu Eight Banners (*baqi*) had only 20,000 members *vis-à-vis* approximately 51.7 million Chinese (Hong Z. *et al.* 1735; Liang F. 1980: 10). The Manchu Banners to Chinese ratio was 0.0004:1, some 130 times lower than the Chinese bureaucrats:non-bureaucrats ratio of 0.0526:1 (Chang 1955: ch. 1; Marsh 1961: 13–15; Ho 1962; Mousnier 1971: 256; Feuerwerker 1976: 48; Hsiao 1979: 7; Jing J. 1981: 53; Wu H. 1984: 64–6; Hucker 1985: 1–96).

The function of wars in the making of socio-economic systems is overlooked by most economic models. At best, wars are taken as an exogenous factor and unwanted shocks to an economic system. However, whether one likes it or not, (1) wars formed a normal part of premodern life in China; and (2) wars played a crucial role at every single step of making of the socio-economic systems throughout Chinese history. To a great extent, the success of the

Chinese civilisation was the success of its adaptability to wars. Therefore, war should be considered as an endogenous factor in the Chinese economic system and its function as the most decisive input in the making of the system simply because of the high returns, known as 'the winner takes all'.

Finally, that civil disputes could lead to a centralised political structure has been suggested in the Japanese studies of the Tokugawa Period (1603–1867), during which a new order was established to minimise clashes among different interest groups (the 'inner' *daimyos* versus the 'outer' *daimyos* and the *daimyos* versus the Tokugawa Shogun), as highlighted by the *sankin kotai* system (see for example Francks 1992: 20–4). This has given Tokugawa Japan the designation of 'centralised feudalism', a self-contradictory but factual term. That foreign invasion resulted in incentives to build a strong army and strong commanding centre has been positively identified in tsarist Russia after the Tartar invasion from the Crimea in 1571 (Nove 1992: 11). Therefore, the Chinese experience was not unique.

### 2.5.3 Flexibility in decision-making

However, such political centralisation should be understood in relative terms. It is an exaggeration to say that in premodern China all the decisions were made by the Imperial Court as, for example, Fairbank holds (Fairbank 1965: 114). Evidence shows that each government level of the Chinese Empire had considerable autonomy in decision-making. Such autonomy, depicted by the traditional Chinese phrase 'Heaven is high and the emperor is far away' (*tiangao huangdiyuan*), was based on (1) a universally applicable rule and code, and (2) a homogeneous agency to implement the rule and code.

Therefore, under the Chinese political system, the decision-making process was only conditionally centralised. Under normal circumstances, imperial law and Confucian doctrine were followed as the guideline at each level by a homogeneous bureaucratic class for routine tasks, and the decisions were thus highly localised with minimum intervention from the top (Jin G. and Liu Q. 1984: 28–9; see also Zheng Z. 1938). Indeed, Confucian education and imperial bureaucrat recruitment ensured this mechanism of a local-ised and simplified decision-making process in order to respond to social issues straightforwardly without necessarily involving the Imperial Court at all. In effect, local initiatives were encouraged, as shown in the Chinese his-tories and official local gazettes: initiatives and merits of local officials were reported and praised. This explains why, to run their domains, Chinese offi-cials not only took orders vertically from the top but also cooperated horizon-tally with their counterparts from other districts. Some top Qing officials like Zuo Zongtang (1812–85) and Li Hongzhang (1823–1901) even regularly reported to and consulted their family members, particularly their mothers and brothers, for administrative advice (Zuo Z. *c.* 1885; Li H. *c.* 1901). Zuo Zongtang was an influential court official who in 1862 was appointed

Governor of the Minzhe Region and concurrently Minister of War (*minzhe zongdu* in charge of the coastal Fujian and Zhejiang provinces) with a ducal title of Guardian of the Heir Apparent (*taizi shaobao*, Second Grade) (Lü Z. 1994: 104, 636; *cf.* Hummel 1967). Li Hongzhang (nicknamed the 'Oriental Bismarck') was the leader of the Westernisation Movement, and reached his career pinnacle around 1868 when he occupied the position of Governor of the Huguang Region and concurrently was Minister of War (*huguang zongdu* in charge of Hubei and Hunan provinces), Assistant Premier (*xieban daxueshi*, literally, Assistant Grand Secretary of First Grade) and Grand Guardian of the Heir Apparent (*taizi taibao*, First Grade), a ducal title, an honour granted to only a few outstanding top officials (Lü Z. 1994: 40, 104, 334; *cf.* Hummel 1967).

Strict central control was applicable only to the military. After all, Chinese officials were meritocrats whose careers depended greatly on political and administrative improvisation to earn their scores, not on blindly copying others, including the court ( Yang Z. 1992; Tang J. and Zheng C. 1993; Tian Z. 1994; Zhang Y. *et al.* 1995).

The central authorities by and large played a surveillance role. The 'big brother' syndrome of Stalin's style did occur, but very briefly, during the Legalist régime (221–210 BC) of the Emperor Qin Shihuang, who is believed to have diad of exhaustion because he went too far in involving himself in all matters concerning his empire by distrusting his bureaucracy . No doubt, Confucianism had the advantage, for running a huge empire like China, of low cost.

Such flexibility was in effect a matter of life or death for the empire. In the absence of a rigid system of nobility, the masses in China were to a certain degree free from personal bondage to a particular group in society. They enjoyed some basic rights. Many were militarily trained. If those rights were violated for long enough and on a large enough scale, rebellion would break out. The centralised governing structure in China had its advantage in lowering the social cost of organising the society. It also had a main drawback: any policy of the state could affect the lives of the masses on a large scale. If discontent spread widely peasants often protested collectively. If the governing institutions did not respond and stop their misrule of society, local armed rebellions often followed. If the governing institutions still did not show any significant improvement in policies, rebellions often spread and toppled the non-physiocratic régime. The Chinese peasantry was 'incorruptible', though it was far from being a revolutionary force in any sense: insurrections were always based on selfish peasant interests and aimed at stopping non-physiocratic initiatives. So, a certain degree of flexibility at the local level was crucial to avoid the synchronisation of discontent in different parts of the empire and thus to minimise the possibility of rebellion.

Evidence shows that in the long term the real danger was not that the Chinese state apparatus had a change of heart and wooed the merchant class, but that it over-reacted towards, for example, commercialisation. It was partially because of the difficulty in keeping a good balance between overdoing it and not doing enough. In premodern China it was politically safer to overdo it in order to please the mighty peasantry.

### 2.5.4 Nature of the Chinese state

The Chinese bureaucracy is often labelled a 'totalitarian régime'. Typically, this is reflected in the work by K. A. Wittfogel, who refined the Marxian 'Asiatic Mode of Production', a theory which is based on a hypothetical causality called 'hydraulic agriculture leading to a centralised state' (Wittfogel 1957; see also Krader 1975; Brook 1989). The fundamental problem with the application of such a model to China is twofold.

#### 2.5.4.1 Lack of irrigation, or lack of control over it

Irrigation in China's agriculture was lacking, at least by the standard of the paradigm of 'hydraulic agriculture leading to a centralised state'. This is evident quantitatively in both spatial and temporal senses.

In the spatial sense, such a lack can be highlighted by the following facts: (1) in China, until the 1930s about half of the cultivated land was not irrigated at all; (2) of the other half, only about two-thirds was reasonably watered at a rate of 40 per cent or more. Farming in north China, the heartland of the empire, long relied on rainwater from the monsoons, not water from rivers (Ho 1969). According to Buck's investigation, by the 1930s most farming regions north of the Yangzi River had an irrigation rate of 9 per cent or less of the total acreage (Buck 1937: 187). In South China, where watering networks did exist, irrigation was highly localised and small scale. Consequently, praying for good rainfall to bring a good harvest (*qiyu*) was conducted religiously by the crown as a regular ritual. But no such ceremony was carried out for irrigation. This situation is shown in the following data (based on Buck 1937: 187):

| | Land total | Irrigated land in all | Irrigated at 40–100% | Irrigated at 80–100% |
|---|---|---|---|---|
| | I | II | III | IV |
| Ratio | | | III:III | IV:III |
| Sub-percentage | | | 100.0% | 21.5% |
| Ratio | | II:II | III:II | IV:II |
| Sub-percentage | | 100.0% | 68.4% | 14.7% |
| Ratio | I:I | II:I | III:I | IV:I |
| Percentage | 100.0% | 50.7% | 34.7% | 7.5% |

Thus, irrigated farming was not, as alleged, the main trademark of Chinese agriculture. Rather, Chinese agriculture was at best a 50–50 mixture of dry and irrigated farming. This was the case in the post-Tang period for over a millennium after the south was firmly colonised, as numerous historical records show.

Also in the spatial sense, China's irrigation was predominantly small scale. This has been proved by archaeological evidence of small-scale irrigation by well water in North China ( Yang S. 1992: 177–8). By the 1930s, the 'heavily irrigated' pockets, where over 80 per cent of the cultivated land was watered, accounted for only 14.7 per cent of all the acreage under irrigation or 7.5 per cent of land in China proper, scattered along the Jiangling, Yangzi, Lancang, Wu, Xiang, Min, Pearl and Han rivers and around Lake Poyang (Buck 1937: 187). After all, there has been no nationwide integrated irrigation system or project in China during recent times; the much talked about, and ambitious plan called 'manoeuvring river water from the south to the north' (*nanshui beidiao*) is yet to be carried out (Guo Q. 1979). Overall speaking, during the entire premodern era, water control rather than irrigation was the main concern among the Chinese elite (Song X. 1954). In the long run, the only projects on a nationwide scale in terms of resource allocation under the central administration were the Great Wall, a permanent defence line against the northern nomads, and the Grand Canals, an artery to link the north and south for transport, which had little to do with irrigation or water control.

In the temporal sense, South China, where an irrigation network did exist, was recognised as a marginal land for at least 1,000 years after the establishment of China's political unification in 221 BC (Bray 1983: 9–15; 1984). Clearly, the 'totalitarian state', if it did exist in China, had become well entrenched long before any cross-regional irrigation was in place.

Most significant, majority irrigation networks were constructed and maintained by the private sector (for Sichuan, see Lan Y. 1996b). So, it is not surprising that in Chinese history there was no single ruler whose name was associated with great irrigation projects. If irrigation, or the control over it, was as essential to establish and maintain legitimacy as the Asiatic Mode hypothesis asserts, China's crowned rulers, 386 in all (according to official records 146 kings and 240 emperors from the twenty-first century BC to 1911; see CBW 1989: 2345–406), would have had sufficient incentive to capitalise on any possible opportunity to link themselves to it. Had such an opportunity been lacking, they would certainly have created it, or simply have 'cooked' the history, for that matter. The absence of any such attempts shows just how irrelevant irrigation was to state power. The closest one can come to something of this kind was the deed of the legendary King Yu (*c.* the twenty-first century BC) of the Xia Dynasty, a capable agricultural administrator who supposedly led his people in fighting a lasting flood in the upper and middle reaches of the Yellow River in China's dry-farming region, a campaign known as 'Yu's harnessing rivers' (*dayu zhishui*) (Fan W. 1964–5: 93–4; Lee 1969: 35–43, 46). Modern scientific research has indicated that the probability of any lasting flood in that region was very low during Yu's time and that the alleged flood control projects were in effect the work of nature instead of human efforts (Ma Z. 1982). Even if we count King Yu as an 'irrigation king', the percentage is a negligible 0.26 per cent among all the rulers, not enough to qualify as a phenomenon. From Yu on, two directions were taken by the Chinese state as nationwide programmes. But neither was irrigation-driven: (1) investigation of rivers as demonstrated by *King Yu's Hydrography*, or *Yuji Tu* (Needham 1959: fig. 226; Cao W. 1987); and (2) disaster control rather than irrigation, known as disaster management (*huangzheng*) (See for example Will 1990; Will and Wong 1991; Wong 1997: pt 2).

In terms of science and technology, apart from paddy field management, very few works by premodern Chinese scholars were on the subjects of river irrigation and large-scale irrigation engineering. In comparison, hundreds of treatises were written on farming, giving clear evidence that the authorities and the literati paid much attention to crop species, farming methods and their diffusion. The point is that farming was an area over which the state had little control as a sector, much less than irrigation, over which the state might have taken some control. Logically, according to 'hydraulic determinism', the control of water should not have been given up by an authoritarian ruler (Deng 1993a). Yet premodern China was not a desert island and water control by a single centre was neither necessary nor feasible. Evidence also shows that when the Chinese government invested in water conservancy projects, instead of running those projects as state-owned enterprises it often passed on the tasks of maintenance and administration to local communities, which were customarily headed by landholding 'gentries' (Feuerwerker 1984: 131–4). If the control of water had been the imperative factor for the making of the 'hydraulic farming and centralised state' paradigm, the Chinese state certainly did not have the will to take the advantage over its population. Most damaging of all to the Asiatic Mode is the fact that China's irrigation systems have been highly localised, not centrally controlled. According to Marx's own logic China should have had a decentralised political system, at least at the macro level.

China as a whole does not qualify as a 'hydraulic empire', much less so than pre-WWII Japan (Francks 1992: ch.7). The last resort by hydraulic determinists is to take the Grand Canals as hard evidence of the hydraulic state. The very fact that the construction of the Grand Canals did not match the timing of the formation of the empire refutes such an attempt. The construction of the canals lagged behind the establishment of the empire for, shockingly, eight hundred years. This shows just how irrelevant were the canals to the making of China's political structure. Also, considering the fact that, from the Sui Period (AD 581–618) onwards, North China was heavily reliant on imported grain that was taxed in the south, the function of the canals only shows the economic dependence of state power on small farms, not the other way around. The alleged 'hydraulic farming– totalitarian state' causality is therefore utterly counter-factual in China, not to mention its unconcealed bias towards geographic determinism.

### 2.5.4.2 *Lack of total control*

Total or near-total government control was never sustained at any point in Chinese history in areas including capital, land, labour and resources such as water. On the contrary, opposite, numerous works have suggested that China often suffered from a relatively weak, incompetent administration and inadequate policies, especially during later dynasties in areas other than civil dispute arbitration and national defence (see, for example, Wright 1957; Feuerwerker 1984). This is precisely why Mr Lee Kuan Yew defines Chinese values and structure as 'communitarian' (Huntington 1996: 108), something close to Tonnis's *gemeinschaft*.

More importantly, it has been estimated that from the Han to the Qing on average the government tax revenue accounted for merely 7.1–10 per cent of total agricultural GDP (Appendix G; and see also Feuerwerker 1984: 299–300, 302); the lion's share of it was left in private hands. As a result, the bureaucracy and military were often underfunded (Wong 1997: chs 6 and 10). This tax rate in turn limited the power and ability of the Chinese state to extract more revenue from the economy, something which cannot be explained by the totalitarian hypothesis.

The more accurate term for the nature of the Chinese state is 'soft authoritarian': not democratic but not totalitarian, either. Totalitarian control in premodern China was no more than a façade. First of all, the imperial bureaucracy was a form not of military dictatorship but of civilian administration which was manned by 'culturally homogeneous' bureaucrats with Confucian training. The nature of the civilian government can also be seen in the fact that the Chinese took every opportunity to disparage the warrior stratum (*wufu*) which obtained state power by force, and often made the warrior stratum hand over state power to the educated professional administrators, although the Chinese army had impressive records in the periodic campaigns of the empire's territorial expansion during early dynasties (Fairbank 1983: 68–9). Fairbank calls such a paradox the unique 'Chinese militarism' and differentiates such a non-feudal military tradition from those of Europe and Japan (*ibid.*). Such distaste for military régimes was rooted in the nature of the Chinese socio-economic structure and the need for economic administration. Obviously, without such distaste for military government, the centralised civilian government structure would long ago in Chinese history have been replaced by feudalism.

What confuses scholars educated in the Western democratic tradition is the seeming uniformity and the high degree of homogeneity of the Chinese system. Although both can lead to efficiency, uniformity and homogeneity differ by definition. The former is of the Nazi–Soviet type, and the latter the Chinese–Tokugawa Japanese type. There is, though, a noticeable difference between the Chinese and Tokugawa Japanese homogeneities: the former was chiefly a culture-based or learned quality, the latter largely race-based (see Minami 1986: 3–9). This is the reason why a Western observer claims that

China is a civilisation pretending to be a state and Japan is a civilisation that is a state (Huntington 1996: 44).

It is homogeneity that the Chinese Empire was built upon, a quality which was largely a result of Confucianism-regulated conduct. China's administrative efficiency was achieved through the combination of macro 'fuzzy' control from the top and micro-autonomous improvisation at the lower levels. This explains why the Chinese bureaucracy was normally able to respond quickly to problems and needs at all levels of society without involving the imperial court at the same time. So, the secret of the efficiency lies in the flexibility of the system, not in its coerciveness. It is not surprising that this imperial bureaucracy, invented by the Chinese before Christ, was transplanted first to premodern East Asia (Korea, Vietnam and Japan) and then to modern western Europe (the British Empire), gradually spreading to the rest of the world.

### 2.5.4.3 Lack of initiative

Much research has been done to reveal the tasks of the centralised governing structure in China. A clear outline is presented by Feuerwerker that by its legislative and judicial actions the Chinese government was expected to defend state and society against external enemies, to suppress internal rebellion, to maintain the social order, and to affect the economy (Feuerwerker 1976: 69).

Apart from these tasks, the Chinese state did not take many initiatives. There is reason for believing that the premodern Chinese economy came close to being 'under-governed': infrastructure improvements were only marginally enough to support a long-term, balanced, essentially non-intensive growth (Jones 1988: 141–2). In other words, China never managed to generate the 'original push' from the government to kick-start a sustained market-oriented growth. Behind this ossification were the dictating conditions from agriculture and the peasantry, and the state had little freedom to move away from the assigned track.

### 2.5.5 Impact of the centralised political system

The centralised political structure had an obvious advantage in empire-building. The extraordinarily long life span of the Chinese Empire is self-evident in this aspect.

Under the Chinese form of centralised administration, significant progress was made; Mokyr argues that under the Chinese system interested and enlightened emperors actually encouraged technological progress (Mokyr 1990: 231). To take transport techniques as an example, the Chinese achievements permitted cheaper long-distance carriage of goods in larger quantities between the main economic areas in the country, particularly between north and south. Passes were made through previously unpassable places in mountain ranges. Separate waterway systems were linked. Sea travel also developed and new frontiers were opened up for China's increasing trade operations. With them, the foundations of a nationwide market were laid. By the mid-Ming Period, China had 28 national highways, 53 provincial main roads and, 120 main land and water transportation hubs (Yang Z. 1994). Other examples include agronomy, astronomy and weaponry (see Needham 1954–94; Deng 1993a). However, it may be argued that the favourable conditions for technological development provided by the centralised government seemed to be cancelled out to a certain degree by the anti-merchant policies. Therefore, governmental impact on such advancement was probably neutral overall.

The main negative effect of Chinese political centralisation was the eliminating to a great extent of political competition on the Asian mainland. So, in China 'there was little opportunity for the promotion of new social institutions to take advantage of Chinese inventive genius' (Merson 1989: 78). The key was the unique socio-economic environment in China. In comparison, in the European continent such political competition was always present after the fall of the Roman Empire. To take the city-state phenomenon as an example, these entities grew largely outside the rural feudal system and became political centres in their own right. The decentralised nature of the European feudal system also meant that the city-based merchant class could formalise their own laws and financial practices without being drawn into a subjugating political system that possessed integrative and unifying powers, as did the Chinese political system (Murphey 1954: 351; see also Elvin 1973: 177).

Chinese cities in premodern times were a different breed. They arose first and foremost as administrative centres, and the group which dominated many of the cities was the 'gentry class', a Europeanised terminology which really means the 'bureaucratic and quasi-bureaucratic stratum'. China's politicised cities, coupled with the country's relative geographic isolation, hindered extensive foreign trade and ran counter to the conditions needed for city-states of the European style.

Moreover, the existence of reactionary rulers was not uniquely Chinese; 'such rulers existed in Europe as well, but because no one controlled the entire continent, they did no more than switch the centre of economic gravity from one area to another' (Mokyr 1990: 231). Thus, the Chinese structure rather than their rulers should bear the responsibility for the consequence of central control.

## 2.6 Confucian ideology

Confucianism is commonly viewed as both the core of the code of conduct for Chinese people of all walks of life and the guideline to the imperial government for ruling the country. These two roles are intermeshed. Therefore, the philosophy should be examined accordingly. From this angle, the Confucian doctrine is a package consisting of the 'way' (*dao*), 'will of Heaven' (*tian*), 'authoritative humanity' (*ren*), 'harmonious social order' (*li*), 'moral integrity and virtue' (*de*).

### 2.6.1 Confucian doctrine and its application

#### 2.6.1.1 Way (dao) and Heaven (tian)

In the field of Chinese studies, *dao*, or the 'way', has been customarily associated with Taoism (*daojia*, literally meaning the 'School of the Way'). However, the concept of *dao* played a central role in the making of Confucianism. To begin with, Confucius and his disciples treated *The Book of Changes* (*Yijing*, or *I Ching*), a work written no later than the eleventh century BC, some five centuries before Confucius, as the number one text among their classics. Second, Confucius himself wrote *Commentaries on 'The Book of Changes'* (*Yizhuan*) to promote *The Book of Changes*. As demonstrated in either the original eight divinatory diagrams (*bagua*) or the derived sixty-four divinatory diagrams (*liushisi gua*), the essence of *The Book of Changes* is the recognition of the existence of a cosmic order with its innate 'natural law' to govern the relationship between nature and society and that among groups within a society (see Liu D. 1992; Liu D. and Lin Z. 1993; Luo Z. 1995: preface).

Later, in Han times, Dong Zhongshu (179–104 BC), a leading Confucian at that time, invented an ingenious framework to depreciate the status of the monarch by putting *tian* (Heaven) above all rulers (Dong Z. *c.* 104 BC: ch. 'Zhi Zhi'; see also Ban G. AD 82: 'Biography of Dong Zhongshu'). Dong wrote in his *Many Dewdrops of Spring and Autumn* (*Chunqiu Fanlu*): 'The cardinal principle of Confucius' *Spring and Autumn Annals* is that the subjects yield to the monarch while the monarch yields to Heaven' (Dong Z. *c.* 104 BC: ch. 'Yubei'); and also: 'If the committing of evil and crimes by monarchs brings calamities to the people, Heaven will deprive the monarchs of the power to rule' (*ibid.*: ch. 'Yao Shun Bu Shanyi, Tang Wu Bu Zhuansha'). In addition, Dong claimed that 'Heaven changeth not, likewise the way changeth not' (CBW 1980 vol. 'Zhexue': 173), which further indicates the eternal nature of Confucian doctrine and the irreplaceability of the Confucian literati in social life. After Dong, *tian* and *dao* became principles to dictate Chinese political behaviour.

Here, there are two essential points made by Confucian literati. First, the will of Heaven was independent of the monarch. In Xun Kuang's phrase (Xun K. 313–238 BC: ch. 'Tianlun'), 'Heaven has its own way to rule which does not exist for the sage king Yao nor does it disappear because of the tyrant king Jie' (*tianxing youchang buweiyaocun buwei jiewang*). Second, the right to interpret the 'will of Heaven' was monopolised by the Confucian literati. Thus, the behaviour of the Chinese, including the monarch, was checked by the literati. From the Han Dynasty onwards, Chinese monarchs had to accept the social role designed for them by the *dao*, if they did not want to lose power. They did not have free will to rule the country (Chen 1911: 62; Yang 1961; Huang 1981).

This heaven-mandated power through *dao* possessed by the Confucian literati was effective. Not only was the education of princes and princesses taken as a bounden duty by the Confucian literati in order to make the younger generation of the royal family truly Confucian, but also the Confucianism-trained monarchs had to adhere to their given position. Emperor Taizong (r. AD 627–49), one of the founders of the Tang Dynasty, was reported as saying (Xu S. 1838/1984: 22) that 'If Confucian literati work for the ruler, China will become prosperous; if they do not, China will suffer chaos' (*deshi zechang, shiren zeluan*). He even wrote a book entitled *The Norm for Monarchs* (*Difan*), systematically instructing his descendants how to behave and run the country properly by Confucian standards. It contains 12 chapters which cover all the important areas of state management: (1) 'Rule for the Monarch' (*Juntipian*), (2) 'Enfeoffment' (*Jianqinpian*), (3) 'Searching for Able and Virtuous Administrators' (*Qiuxianpian*), (4) 'Managing the Bureaucracy' (*Shenguanpian*) (5) 'Remonstration and Admonition' (*Najianpian*), (6) 'Eliminating Slanderers' (*Quchanpian*), (7) 'Avoiding Extravagance' (*Jieyingpian*), (8) 'Promoting Frugality' (*Chongjianpian*), (9) 'Rewards and Punishments' (*Shangfapian*), (10) 'Physiocracy' (*Wunongpian*), (11) 'Military Forces' (*Yuewupian*) and (12) 'Confucians' (*Chongwenpian*) (Li S. *c.* AD 649a). Following this model, Emperor Taizu of the Ming wrote *Instructions on State Management* (*Zishi Tongxun*) (Liang J. and Wang Y. 1995: 50).

As a result of the *tian* and *dao* principles, the relationship between the Confucian literati and the monarch was dual: politically, the Confucians were inferior as a group of subjects of the monarch; while morally and intellectually, they were superior as the teachers and advisers of the monarch, who consequently had little free will to rule the country (Chen 1911: 62; Yang 1961; Huang 1981).

### 2.6.1.2 Sage-like humanity (ren)

*Ren* was the legacy of an earlier idea of 'Serving Heaven and Protecting People' (*jingtian baomin*) (Fan W. 1964–5 vol. 1: 150–2; Hsiao 1979: 101–8). *Ren* embodied people's dignity and value as human beings, and the harmony of society. Confucius mentioned *ren* more than a hundred times in his *Analects* (for an English translation see Legge 1892: vol. 1), explaining that it meant cherishing or loving one another, as in *renzhe airen* (ch. 'Yan Yuan' of *The Analects*), and also that it was the essence of civilisation: *renzhe ren ye* (Zi S. n.d.).

Later, Han Yu (AD 768–824) in his book *Yuandao* (*Original Way*; Han Y. *c.* AD 824) wrote that '*Ren* means universal fraternity' (*bo-ai wei zhi ren*). In the Southern Song Dynasty (1127–1279), Zhu Xi (1130–1200), the founder of

Neo-Confucianism (Needham 1962: 496–505, 557–80; Tu 1974), claimed that the fundamental difference between animals and human beings is that the latter have the nature of benevolence, righteousness, etiquette and intelligence (*ren yi li zhi*, see Zhu X. *c.* 1200: vol. 4). Of these qualities, Zhu took benevolence to be the most important.

So, what is *ren*? *Ren* can be translated a dozen ways of which the most popular are 'benevolence' and 'love' (see Hall and Ames 1987: 112). According to these translations, *ren* was a passion and the authorities were passion-givers. But, when applied to the ruler, such translations do not reflect well the essence of *ren*. In an extreme case, *ren* is translated as true 'personhood' (see C. J. Smith 1991: 35), which completely ignores the purpose of *ren* as a code of conduct for the ruling clique, not for the ruled. In particular, such translations fail to reflect the Confucian concern of the danger of alienation from the administration caused by the power–corruption effect. Confucius believed that the ruler should set the highest example of *ren* (*qishen zheng*) by taking good care of the ruled and should never rule arbitrarily nor oppress the people. Concerned that government should not hinder the economy but assist it in all possible ways, he wrote in *The Analects* that the ruler should 'not employ people in busy seasons' (*shimin yi shi*) (ch. 'Xue Er'); and that he should 'enrich them': (*fuzhi*) (ch. 'Zi Lu'). He also told a ruler that 'Light taxation results in people's affluence' (*bo fulian ze minfu*) (*ibid.*: ch. 'Xianjin'). Xun Kuang articulated the *ren* concept with perfection of human society and the ultimate equity (see Ho 1962: 8). Later, in Han times, Dong Zhongshu (179–104 BC), another leading Confucian, condemned the tyranny of the previous Qin monarchs and called for the restoration of a benevolent government (Dong Z. *c.* 104 BC: ch. 'Zhi Zhi'; see also Ban G. AD 82: 'Biography of Dong Zhongshu'). Moreover, he advised the government to restrict the amalgamation of landholdings and to reduce taxes and the corvée (Ban G. AD 82: 'Economy'). As Professor Ho Ping-ti points out (1962: 5), 'In fact, when Confucius' whole system of thought is analysed, it is obvious that he regards rule by the wise and virtuous as the very foundation of good government.'

According to Confucius, 'benevolent government' (*renzheng*), a concept which was directly derived from *ren*, was the political programme of his school of thought (Hsiao 1979: chs 2–3). He believed that a benevolent government should ensure that its people had enough to eat (Chen 1911: 50, 307, 382–3; Xin L. 1987: 90–1). This was so important to the Confucians that *zushi*, or 'plenty of food', was considered the basis of civilising people. The principle was to enrich people before civilising them (Hsiao 1979: 110), as the way to realise the Confucian ideal. In *Master Guan's Book* (*Guanzi*), the same idea is described: 'When granaries are full, the ordinary people will know propriety and moderation; when clothing and food are sufficient, the ordinary people will know honour and shame' (*cf.* Rickett 1985: 52). The same ideal was later maintained by Mencius (see Lau 1984: 7).

From the above, although the generality of *ren* is something about 'bene-volence' and 'love', it is mainly designed to regulate the behaviour of the rulers by enlightening them on their true position in society and on ingratiat-ing themselves with the masses. In this context, what *ren* asks for is a govern-ment which can represent and protect ordinary people's interests, as Mencius said (Mengzi Warring State Period: ch. 'Gaozi'), '*Ren* is to win people's sup-port' (*ren renxinye*). The authorities should thus be a 'feeling-minder', a helper and a caretaker, rather than a passion-giver. According to the *ren* criterion, the ruler should show sage-like behaviour, while the centrality of sagehood in Chinese culture is understanding and helping people. So far, the best transla-tion of *ren* is 'authoritative humanity' (Hall and Ames 1987: 114, 187). Yet the term 'authoritative' does not indicate the quality desirable in rulers. Therefore, in order to indicate all the qualities of the ruler required by Chi-nese society, better translations of *ren* are (1) 'Understanding the Feelings and Hardships of People, and Doing Something to Help Them' (He *et al*. 1991: 26–9), or (2) 'Oriental sageness' or 'sage-like humanity' (Ma Z. 1993: ch. 5).

But who were these people *vis-à-vis* the ruler? As I have demonstrated, over-whelmingly they were free peasants or, to use the legal term, free citizens. Undoubtedly, the basis and premise of Confucianist *ren* was a society of free cit-izens. A useful test is provided by feudal Japan during the Tokugawa–Meiji Era. The Japanese stripped Confucianism of its humane essence by isolating loyalty (*zhong*) from other qualities such as 'understanding others' hardships' (*ren*), and 'wisdom' (*zhi*). In a feudal society, to understand common people's hardships and practise sage-like humanity was much less relevant. The obviously cor-rupt form of Confucianism in Japanese hands betrays the fundamental differ-ence in social structures between premodern China and Japan. Confucianism in its Japanese form was deliberately used to benefit the feudal relationship.

The great political taboo in the eyes of Confucianism is to rule the people despotically, as reflected by Mencius' dogma that 'tyranny is fiercer than a man-eating tiger' (*kezheng mengyuhu ye*). There exists ample evidence that Con-fucius and Mencius were both critical of despotism, and believed in the application of *ren* as an ethical means of checking despotism and mismanage-ment. According to Confucius (Ronan 1978: 79),

> [T]he true aim of government . . . was the welfare and happiness of all the people, brought about by no rigid adherence to arbitrary laws but by a subtle administration of customs that were generally accepted as good and had the sanction of natural law.

Xun Kuang (313–238 BC) put it more frankly thus: even if a man were a des-cendant of a ruler, if he failed to observe proper conduct and justice, he ought to be relegated to the common ranks (see Ho 1962: 7).

Aware of the real danger of alienation of the state power, Confucianism warns the rulers of the inevitable consequences should they act as tyrants.

This is the whole purpose of *ren*. Therefore, far from being rhetorical, the Confucian *ren* functioned as an ideological regulator in a non-democratic society, making it clear to the rulers as to who was the true social determinative: the common people, not the dynasts. Therefore, to practise *ren* was not something the rulers offered as a gift or goodwill gesture to the populace, it was imperative for the survival of any régime. Confucianism only recognised this relationship, it certainly did not create such a relationship.

*Ren* was a powerful tool for both the ruling and the ruled: it was the crucial link between the interests of the common people and the goal of the centralised authorities. It was also a criterion by which to judge government performance, a criterion which was universally accepted among all strata. So, fundamentally, the *ren* doctrine reflects the ever-existing dilemma in Chinese society: landholding individuals had to mandate power to the state for law and order and other public goods, while such power easily leaned towards alienation from the general public. A moral code for the monarch provided a positive check, given that the head of state was conscious of his role as 'people's protector'. Insurrection was a negative check if the monarch was no sage, as Confucius's political maxim goes (Xun K. *c.* 238 BC: ch. 'Duke Ai'): 'The ruled are to the ruling as water is to a boat: not only does water support the boat, it can also capsize the boat' (*Junzhe, zhouye; shurenzhe, shuiye. Shui ze zaizhuo, shui ze fuzhuo*). An old Chinese saying is even more direct: 'Armed rebellions only result from oppression by officialdom' (*guanbi minfan*). If the committing of evil and crimes by monarchs brings calamities to the people, Heaven will deprive the monarchs of the power to rule. As a means of bringing society back into order by force, armed rebellion was regarded by Confucians as just (Mousnier 1971: 240).

Confucian *ren* shows such a sound grip of the very nature of Chinese society that there was no other concept in the Chinese language able to match it. In premodern China, the relationship between the state and the ordinary citizen was a complex one: at the micro level and in the short term, to individuals and inferior groups the transcending power of the state had a despotic appearance; while at the macro level and in the long term, state power was a dependent variable and thus was humanity-based. Also, at the micro level and in the short term, individuals and small groups were powerless and had little influence on state politics; but at the macro level and in the long term, the common people as a whole were the determinative in state politics. Therefore, to understand the relationship between the Chinese state and ordinary citizens, it is crucial to draw a clear-cut demarcation line between micro and macro levels, and between short and long terms. To a great extent, such a paradox exists in modern democratic societies as well, although there is much less illusion about the powerlessness of the individual electors. The Chinese rulers had to practise *ren* because they had few other options under this symbiosis between the free landholding peasantry and the centralised bureaucracy.

### 2.6.1.3 Etiquette (li)

On the basis of *ren*, Confucius and his school paid close attention to *li*, which is often translated as rites or etiquette. The rite itself is a means to an end: a stable social order. As Xun Kuang points out, 'without etiquette population will not grow [because of wars]; without etiquette noble causes will not be realised [because of disputes]; without etiquette a country will not have peace' (313–238 BC: ch. 'Self-cultivation'). Thus, the Confucian rites or etiquette should be defined as 'rule by rites or etiquette' (*lizhi*). During the warring Spring and Autumn Period (770–476 BC), Confucius set himself the task of restoring the Social Order of the Zhou Period (*zhouli*). Confucius put it, in *The Analects* (ch. 'Yunyuan') as a simple rule of thumb: 'Not to look at, listen to, say and do what is incompatible with the etiquette' (*feili wushi, feili wuting, feili wuyan, feili wudong*); 'once self-abnegation is practised and rites are resumed, society will enter the *ren* status' (*yiri keji fuli tianxia guirenyan*) (Kong Q. *c.* 479 BC: ch. 'Yan Yuan').

*Li* matches perfectly with *ren*: *ren* is the ideal quality of and the criterion for the social relationships between the monarch and the officials, between the ruling and the ruled, between the aged and young; while *li* is the status of such relationships (Wu Y. 1988: ch. 4). This is the reason why the Confucians took the *Book of Rites* (*Liji*) as one of the obligatory classics for over two thousand years. So, a better interpretation of *li* is 'harmonious social order'. No doubt *li* has an appearance of social hierarchy, which often causes all sorts of misunderstandings about Chinese civilisation.

### 2.6.1.4 Moral integrity and virtue (de)

In addition, Confucius believed that the best way to establish and maintain *li*, or social order, was to use 'moral integrity and virtue' (*de*) to civilise people instead of using force to keep society harmonious and quiet by reducing civil disputes at all levels. Confucianism believes that moral integrity and virtue (*de*) is a vehicle with which to reach 'harmonious social order' (*li*) and 'sage-like humanity' (*ren*) through four interlocking stages: (1) self-cultivation (*xiushen*) which should be done at the individual level; (2) family management (*qijia*), which is at the level of the family; (3) establishment and maintenance of order in society (*zhiguo*); and (4) realisation of nationwide lasting peace, or equilibrium (*pingtianxia*). Obviously, Confucianism in its Chinese origin was designed and implemented in order to condition and regulate the behaviour of people in all walks of life: emperors, bureaucrats and commoners alike.

The true colour of Confucianism becomes more obvious when compared to other schools of thought. The Legalists (*fajia*) held that there is no need for the monarch to care for or compromise with the masses, and that the interest of the monarch is the only purpose of society; the power of the monarch should be absolute. Thus, law and severe punishment should be applied to keep society in good order, while law (*fa*) and 'rule by law' (*fazhi*) was nothing but the embodiment of the monarch's will. *Fa* (law) in the hands of the Legalists was truly despotic and inhumane, representing a political philosophy absolutely opposite to that of Confucian *ren* (sage-like humanity). It is the Legalist attitude that fits the category of 'oriental despotism'. Emperor Qin Shihuang's failure as that of a great Legalist monarch shows that the Legalist approach and methods were not workable in China in the long run: the Legalist régime was extremely short-lived and insignificant, occupying only 1–2 per cent of the life span of the Chinese Empire. Indeed, China never had 'rule of law' because the crucial conditions of independent law-making and execution of law were missing. Even so, China did not fit the 'oriental despotism' stereotype, simply because of the prevailing Confucian humanity. China was not black-and-white but grey.

Modern observers often ask why premodern China was so lacking in law. If we understand the fate of the Qin Dynasty and the historical reason why Confucianism replaced Legalism, the lack of written law was quite natural. First, the disastrous outcome of the Legalist régime gave the rule of law and rule by law a bad name. Second, the Confucian 'way' (*dao*), 'will of Heaven' (*tian*), 'sage-like humanity' (*ren*), 'harmonious social order' (*li*) and 'moral integrity and virtue' (*de*) were adequate to maintain social order. Third, it is obvious that Chinese society did not have the mechanism, as a modern Western society does, to practise rule by law, because there was no independent peasant institution to judge government's doings. On the other hand, Taoism believes that individuals should make all the decisions and that the best the authorities can do is to do as little as possible (*wuwei erzhi*). So, law to Taoism is a nuisance. Certainly Taoism recognises the nature of the free citizen-based society in China and the existence of individual rights. However, it has gone to the other extreme by denying the need for an administrative centre in China, crucial for the maintenance of social order and national defence (as well as offence). Still, Taoism proved far more popular than Legalism in premodern China.

Obviously, among Legalism, Taoism and Confucianism, the latter was the best-balanced ideology, defining the places, rights and responsibilities for all the social forces and strata and providing ways to accommodate and bring about cooperation between different interests in society. Thus, the long-lasting dominance of Confucianism in the Chinese political arena was the result of its serving Chinese needs rather than the result of its promotion by the ruling groups. Otherwise it is hard to explain why Legalism, a philosophy which was highly favoured by some of the most powerful rulers in premodern Chinese history, failed so early and so badly. In other words, Confucianism was highly internalised in Chinese society because of its flexibility, virtue and low cost of operation. Next was Taoism, more flexible but more difficult to practise. Legalism was most rigid and 'expensive' to have.

## 2.6.2 Confucian attitude towards agriculture and trade

In terms of economic thought, Confucianism has been viewed as in favour of agriculture (see Chen 1911: chs 21, 26, 30–1). This is generally true. In particular, Confucianism sees multiple functions in farming in terms of self-respect, self-reliance and self-cultivation, not just for food supply and livelihood (for Mencius's opinion, see Lau 1984: 107).

However, this does not necessarily mean that Confucianism is against all trade. According to Confucian doctrine, only when trade (or any other activity) creates a threat to social tranquillity should it be suppressed. Even then, it should not be eliminated (see Yan S. 1988). At this point, it is helpful to review the Confucian attitude towards commerce. For instance, it is recorded in *Master Zuo's Chronicle* (*Zuozhuan*) that Confucius commented that 'Zang Wenzong is neither benevolent [*ren*] nor knowledgeable on three accounts respectively. He invaded Zhanqin, abandoned six border markets and married Zhi Pu as his concubine' (Zuoqiu *c.* 454b BC: ch. 'Wengong Ernian'). Here, in Confucius's own eyes, closing markets and invading others' territory were equally evil. Mencius, the most prominent disciple of Confucius, reportedly gave his advice to rulers that:

> The members of the literati will serve the régime if the ruler respects and employs the able and virtuous; merchants will stay and work at the market if heavy tax is exempted; travellers will make trips if tolls are lifted; farmers will till if agriculture is not taxed, only corvée being imposed.
>
> (Mengzi Warring States Period: ch. 'Gongsun Chou Shang')

He did not discriminate against merchants at all. Moreover, according to Menciu , the ideal social order should accommodate commerce as an organic part:

> Merchants are lawful and there is no counterfeit at the market. Children, although young, are not cheated in trade. Cloth is traded for what it is worth by length; hemp and silk by weight; cereals by volume; shoes by size.
>
> (*ibid.*: ch. 'Teng Wengong Xia')

In addition, Confucianism does not condemn personal wealth, merely the 'wrong' ways to get rich and to use the wealth. In *The Great Learning* (*Daxue*), it is stated that:

> There are golden rules for getting rich. First, to make more money than is spent; second, to create wealth fast but use it slowly. [If these rules are followed] one will always be wealthy. The righteous

people use their wealth as a means to become successful. The sinful use their influence as a means to become rich.

(Zeng S. *c.* 436 BC/1993: 3)

Unmistakably, the merchant class and trade activities are sometimes ranked rather favourably by Confucius and Mencius. This attitude was naturally welcomed by the populist Confucians. It is worth mentioning that Zi Gan, one of Confucius's own students, resigned from his official post in Wei Kingdom, became a full-time trader and eventually accumulated great wealth (Sima 91 BC: ch. 'Biographies of the Economic Sectors'). Zi Gong, another student of Confucius, was known for his money-making tactics and serious wealth of the top rank (*ibid.*). Obviously, Confucius's training did not prevent these two from doing earthly business; rather, the training probably helped their money-making careers.

It is fair to say that Confucianism was never blindly anti-trade or blindly pro-agriculture at the expense of commerce. At worst it was ambivalent towards trade. This assessment is justified by the track record of Confucianism serving the empire as the state philosophy. Throughout its 2,050-year long service life (*c.* 140 BC–1911), which officially began from Dong Zhongshu's success in convincing Emperor Wudi (r. 140–87 BC) with his 'Three Counter-arguments' (*tianren sance*) (see Dong Z. *c.* 104 BC), for the best part of 1,500 years (over 73 per cent of its total service time) there was no ban on international trade. The attribution of the Ming–Qing maritime trade bans to Confucianism as state philosophy can account for only 60 years, less than 3 per cent of the total time of its service, a negligible amount. Moreover, in Tang–Song times for over six hundred years (30 per cent of the total service time) there was little negative attitude towards trade activities, both domestic and overseas (see Wang 1958: 46–89). From this track record, two interpretations are possible: either Confucianism had limited influence on government trade policies, or Confucianism was neutral, with regard to trade policy.

As the Confucian ideology *per se* left very limited room for state Confucians or the bureaucrats to use it for anti-trade purposes, ideas had to be found from other schools of thought. Among these schools, Legalism was notorious for its anti-trade and anti-merchant bias. The highlight of Legalist policy-making activities was Sang Hongyang's historic victory in 81 BC at the Imperial Conference known as the 'Debate on Trade of Iron and Salt' (*yantie zhiyi*). This victory paved the way for state monopoly over 'key' markets (wine, iron and salt). However, at the conference Sang represented a minority and his victory was due solely to the support of Emperor Wudi (see Huan K. Han Dynasty). The rival majority were mainly Confucians. To judge by this episode, the state trade monopoly was evidently anti-Confucian. In addition, after the conference, the Confucian lobbyists did not disappear from the scene: throughout Chinese history they reappeared whenever government monopoly caused too much hardship for the ordinary people. Most unfortunately, the intrusive

Legalist trade policies were often mistaken for the practice of orthodox Confucianism.

In principle, orthodox Confucianism does not easily take sides to avoid radical and extreme shifts which may tip an existing social order. If one term is used to define Confucianism, it should be 'orderism' because Confucianism is more concerned than anything else with the balance of political and/or economic power among individuals and strata and between state and society. This includes the economic sector. The track record of trade policies of the Chinese Empire at least shows what a significant role Confucianism played in balancing the Legalist prejudice in the long run. In other words' the fact that Chinese economic history was not shaped according to the Legalist anti-trade and anti-merchant blueprint owed much to the overwhelming influence of Confucianism.

### 2.6.3 Pragmatism of Confucianism seen from the role of the literati

There are always some serious doubts about the pragmatism of Confucianism – more so when one treats it as a religion. The best way to judge this Chinese philosophy is to transcend the Confucian classics and see what the Confucians did in history. Since the majority of the Chinese literati were Confucians or semi-Confucians, this stratum can be taken as a proxy for the Confucians.

A great many works have studied the Chinese literati. Although few ignore the existence of this stratum, a wide range of viewpoints exist as to its functions. The dominant view is that the Chinese literati were a socio-political force but not an economic force in Chinese history. This illusion comes mainly from the political and ideological role played by this stratum of Chinese society. Modern scholars are so deeply influenced by this cliché that even those, like Joseph Needham, who are experts on the development of civilisation, science and technology in China have ignored the role of the literati in Chinese economic history. A more extreme view portrays the literati as useless parasites on society, living in an ivory tower with little knowledge of practical life. Often, in support of this view, Confucius is quoted as having criticised some scholars, as he did, for 'not working with their able bodies and being unable to distinguish crops by their appearance' (*sitibuqin, wugubufen*). These two views can be said to compose the mainstream.

Evidence shows that the mainstream opinions are faulty: the literati were largely responsible for the development of Chinese agronomy and thus played an important role in the a progress of Chinese agricultural technology in the long run (Deng 1993a).

If this is not enough, evidence from essays by the best-qualified Confucian scholars indicates that Confucians were concerned with very earthly things, such as people's living standards, government economic policies, management of the bureaucrats, law and national defence, as well as 'higher' things such as philosophy, rites and so forth.

Table 2.3 contains data for essays by 12 outstanding scholars during the Tang Period. These essays were taken later as samples for those who applied to sit the examinations. To show what was in these scholars' agenda, the method used here is (1) to use the sentence in an essay as the basic unit, and (2) to classify the content of the sentence under eight categories ranging from social order to philosophy.

It is obvious that 'hard topics' such as social order and its maintenance, government and the economy received great attention (averaging 63.8 per cent in aggregate). 'Soft topics' such as education, regulations and philosophy attracted much less attention than one might think (averaging 10.6 per cent in aggregate). More interestingly, most essays pointed out problems in the Chinese system and criticised the Establishment, including the Imperial Court, for either not handling problems properly or simply ignoring them (see Shen Z. 1995). Some of these scholars were later appointed to high and influential positions in the Tang government. Among them, six became Prime Minister or *de facto* Prime Ministers of the Third Grade (*zheng sanpin*): Zhang Jianzhi (AD 625–706) – Prime Minister (*zaixiang*); Zhang Shui (667–730)

*Table 2.3* Quantitative information of outstanding essays for the Tang Imperial Examinations

| Year (AD) | Name | A | B (%) | C (%) | D (%) | E (%) | F (%) | G (%) | H (%) | J (%) | Total (%) |
|---|---|---|---|---|---|---|---|---|---|---|---|
| 688 | Zhang Shui | 33 | 63.6 | 12.1 | 0 | 0 | 0 | 9.1 | 0 | 15.2 | 100 |
| 689 | Zhang Jianzhi | 38 | 39.5 | 50.0 | 0 | 0 | 0 | 2.6 | 0 | 7.9 | 100 |
| 694 | Xue Ji | 24 | 12.5 | 0 | 25.0 | 33.3 | 0 | 0 | 0 | 29.2 | 100 |
| 712 | Zhang Jiuling | 35 | 22.8 | 31.4 | 2.9 | 11.4 | 8.6 | 0 | 0 | 22.9 | 100 |
| 714 | Sun Ti | 71 | 8.4 | 12.7 | 8.0 | 0 | 19.7 | 14.1 | 5.6 | 32.4 | 100 |
| 721 | Yang Ruoxu | 77 | 24.7 | 15.6 | 5.2 | 31.2 | 1.3 | 0 | 0 | 22.0 | 100 |
| 800–3 | Bai Juyi | 129 | 0 | 0 | 40.2 | 0 | 27.2 | 7.0 | 5.4 | 20.2 | 100 |
| 806 | Gu Duyu | 26 | 73.1 | 19.3 | 0 | 3.8 | 0 | 0 | 0 | 3.8 | 100 |
| 806 | Yuan Zhen | 60 | 31.7 | 11.6 | 31.7 | 1.7 | 3.3 | 1.7 | 0 | 18.3 | 100 |
| 821 | Shen Yazhi | 89 | 20.2 | 50.5 | 6.8 | 0 | 1.1 | 2.3 | 0 | 19.1 | 100 |
| 825 | Shu Yuanbao | 75 | 24.0 | 32.0 | 28.0 | 0 | 0 | 0 | 1.3 | 14.7 | 100 |
| 828 | Liu Fen | 117 | 34.2 | 22.2 | 5.1 | 0 | 0.9 | 15.4 | 0 | 22.2 | 100 |
| Average | | — | 29.6 | 21.5 | 12.7 | 6.8 | 5.2 | 4.4 | 1.0 | 19.0 | – |

*Source*: Based on Shen Z. 1995.

*Note*

A, total number of sentences in essay. Issues dealt with: *B*, social order and its maintenance; *C*, government, including management of the bureaucracy, selection of qualified personnel and governmental structure; *D*, economy including economic policies, people's livelihood, production and market activities; *E*, national defence; *F*, education, including moral and knowledge; *G*, regulations including law and rites; *H*, philosophy; *J*, others.

and Zhang Jiuling (673–740) – *de facto* Prime Ministers called *zhongshu ling*; Xue Ji (?) – *de facto* Prime Minister called *canzhi jiwu*; Yuan Zhen (779–831) and Shu Yuanbao (?–839) – *de facto* Prime Ministers called *zhongshu menxia pingzhangshi*. Bai Juyi (772–846) held the position of Guardian of the Heir Apparent (*taizi shaofu*) of the Third Grade. Sun Ti (?) was appointed Tutor of the Heir Apparent (*taizi shaozhanshi*) of the Fourth Grade (see Shen Z. 1995). Shen Yazhi (?) worked as Emperor's Secretary (*neigongfeng*). Thus, they not only thought about those issues but also had the opportunity to put their ideas into practice.

### 2.6.4 *Tension within and true colour of Confucianism*

There were two types of Confucianism, as identified by Albert Feuerwerker: state Confucianism (so-called Confucianism for *raison d'état*) and populist Confucianism (Confucianism for general will), and obvious tension existed between the two (Feuerwerker 1984: 308–9). However, scholars like Feuerwerker only recognise populist Confucianism as a tool for 'local gentry'. In effect, populist Confucianism serves lower classes as well. Confucianism was not exclusively designed for the ruling class, as Marxists assert. Thus, Leon E. Stover is right about recognising Confucianism as 'jack-o'-both-sides' (Stover 1974: ch. 15).

There is little doubt that such division did exist and that tension between the two poles was always there. On the whole, state Confucianism emphasised the importance of the national interest while populist Confucianism emphasises communal and individual rights and interests. Both sides claimed the genuineness and orthodoxy of their brands of Confucianism. In most cases, both sides had to compromise, and the ultimate determinant for the pendulum to swing was inevitably the political and economic strength of the two sides. In addition, Confucianism of the state brand frequently received shocks, mainly from the Legalist School (*fajia*) and Taoism (*daojia*) in terms of policy-making; while Confucianism of the populist brand received such shocks from Taoism and Buddhism (*fojia*). So, the tension was not just internal but external as well.

However, even if one takes Confucianism solely as a state philosophy, it is undeniable that from the Western Han Period onwards, the state philosophy helped at least with: (1) promoting social order and stability through defining justifiable methods (which was reflected by the Confucian doctrine of *xiu qi zhi ping*, meaning self-cultivation, family management, national administration and the maintenance of the whole social order); (2) legitimating justice in human relationships by defining duties/responsibilities and rights among individuals as well as groups (as in the 'monarch–minister/father–son' paradigm [*junchen–fuzi*], a social order in accordance with political and biological/kinship rankings exemplified by the monarch versus the minister and the father versus the son); and (3) accommodating and compromising conflicting interest groups (which was reflected by the Confucian doctrine of the 'Golden Mean' (*zhongyong*)).

So, generally speaking, Confucianism was a tool to help keep China in one piece but was not responsible for the creation of the empire. Neither was it a device designed exclusively for the ruling class, as claimed by Marxists with the bias of the class-struggle hypothesis. Rather, it was a code of conduct for all the members of Chinese society regardless of their social and economic backgrounds. Thus, it served both the ruling (as seen from day-to-day state administration) and the ruled (as seen from daily household management, frequent and peaceful social mobility and occasional violent rebellions), although here the class category is admittedly oversimplified. Arguably, in China the universally applied Confucian principle dramatically lowered the costs of running a huge empire and helped China avoid the fate of the Western Roman Empire (for Europe, see McNeill 1963, 1979).

## 2.7 Remarks

The main factors in the Chinese socio-economic system, namely the predominance of agriculture in the economy, the prevailing private individual land ownership, the landholding peasantry as the majority, the physiocratic state, the centralised government and Confucian ideology, developed in the unique environment and socio-political conditions of the East Asian mainland. They in turn had their impact on shaping the Chinese economy and its growth path. Although at this point these factors are mainly dealt with in isolation, one does not have to search hard to see some obvious links among them. These links are the focal point of the next chapter.

## Note

1 The chessboard-field system had nine plots in each unit of *jin* (chessboard). Eight of the nine plots were household holdings of eight families. The remaining was the plot to pay tax in output.

# 3

# TRINARY STRUCTURE

## Origin, tension and equilibrium

In Chapter 2, the main factors in the Chinese socio-economic system were revealed in the light of their origins, extents, and importance in the long-term economic history of China. Also, interrelationships between these factors were referred to, though in a very limited way. Such interrelationships suggest a greater system embracing all these main factors. More significantly, the duration of these factors in Chinese history suggests some kind of individual equilibria in the relevant areas.

In turn, the track record of the premodern Chinese economy in terms of duration suggests an overall equilibrium which was built upon those interlocking individual equilibria. It is the task of this chapter to examine this greater system and the overall equilibrium.

## 3.1 Trinary structure: a macro institution

### 3.1.1 *The structure*

The interrelationships can be described as a 'trinary' or 'tripartite' structure with three interlinked counterpoises within one system: (1) agriculture and its dominance; (2) the landholding and landowning free peasantry; and (3) centralised physiocratic or 'agro-centric' government. The interrelationships are represented by a triangular interlocking pattern as shown in Figure 3.1.

Within this triangular interlocking framework, each counterpoise played its part. First, as the dominant sector in the economy, agriculture provided the majority in society with the basis for a livelihood (employment and income); the peasantry in turn provided agriculture with manpower, social interest and attention. Second, agriculture provided government with resources whereby revenue was tapped on a regular basis; in turn the government provided agriculture with political protection. It has been suggested that it was the fiscal need of the Chinese government which caused the protecting and promoting of agriculture in the economy (Fairbank 1965: 52). One might argue that a premodern government did not have to be pro-agriculture just for the sake of fiscal revenue: it could support the non-agricultural

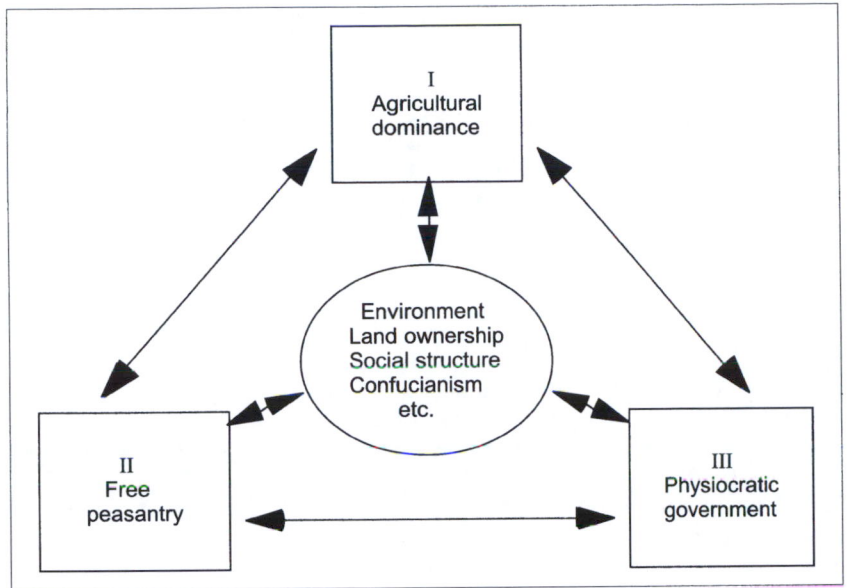

*Figure 3.1* Trinary structure

*Note*
Arrows indicate mutual relationships.

classes and milk industries and commerce, as happened in medieval Europe. Some studies support this view, showing that during the Ming–Qing Period, as much as 80–90 per cent of the total employment was provided by the agricultural sector with a share of 70 per cent of China's total GNP (Feuerwerker 1984: 299, 302, 312–13; Chao 1986: ch. 3). In other words, taxing agriculture was not as beneficial as taxing some other sectors since the per capita GNP in agriculture was 12.5–22.2 per cent lower than the unity ratio. However, if one also accepts the role played by the resource endowments in shaping an economy, the source for government revenue was to a certain degree endowment-specific. Moreover, from the viewpoint of the total sum, the agricultural sector was undisputedly the main, indispensable taxpayer. Such a tax structure remained unchanged until the very end of the Qing in spite of the fact that the revenue capacity of the land tax halved from over 70 per cent of the total tax revenue in 1753 to about 35 per cent in 1908 (Wang 1973: 80). The following data for toll tax (*lijin*) and salt tax (*yanshui*) are adjusted according to the share of the rural population (80 per cent) in China's total by applying a weight of 80 per cent to indirect tax figures with the assumptions that (1) salt consumption was price and income inelastic, and (2) toll taxes on roads and bridges were evenly spread among the population. The resulting data show that the agricultural sector was responsible for 57 to 75 per cent of the total tax revenue (raw data based on Wang 1973: 74):

| | Direct tax (*in* liang) | Indirect tax (*in* liang) | | Total tax revenue | Percentage of total |
|---|---|---|---|---|---|
| | Land | Toll | Salt | (*in* liang) | |
| 1903 | 35,360,000 | 18,200,000 | 13,000,000 | 105,460,000 | 63 |
| *Adjusted* | — | 14,560,000 | 10,400,000 | — | 57 |
| 1904—5 | 127,763,000 | 42,537,000 | 81,000,000 | 300,949,000 | 83 |
| *Adjusted* | — | 34,029,600 | 64,800,000 | — | 75 |
| 1908 | 102,400,000 | 40,000,000 | 45,000,000 | 292,000,000 | 64 |
| *Adjusted* | — | 32,000,000 | 36,000,000 | — | 58 |
| 1910–11 | 69,000,000 | 43,000,000 | 57,000,000 | 249,100,000 | 68 |
| *Adjusted* | — | 34,400,000 | 45,600,000 | — | 60 |

Third, the peasantry provided the government with the basis of mandate to rule, sources of personnel for the bureaucracy and soldiers for the army; the government in turn provided the peasantry with political protection and public goods such as law and order, transportation, communication, land acquisition and distribution, and disaster management like famine relief and water control.

The three counterpoises in effect became three equipoises. As agricultural dominance, centralised physiocratic government and free and often landholding and landowning peasantry are intimately interlocked and form a super-framework of mutuality, an incentive system took shape which reinforced the structure. Comparatively, it was this free landholding peasantry that made China different from other great agrarian societies. Scholars like Barrington Moore sensed some unique characteristics of the Chinese peasantry but failed to spot the nature of the class (see Moore 1966: 202–3, 205, 207–8, 213–14).

The factors within the ellipse are some key conditions/factors compatible with the three counterpoises. With this trinary structure, they become convergent within a framework of mutuality: the influences of religious and political beliefs (Confucianism, Taoism and Buddhism), environmental factors (endowments of natural resources, climatic and geographic conditions), land (ownership type and distribution), technology (such as tools and species) and social institutions (such as families and centralised bureaucracy) were all accommodated and interacted. In addition, the general socio-economic equilibrium gained a certain momentum and was able to influence movements of other aspects of Chinese life, especially non-agricultural activities. Resistance against the system would then largely be neutralised. Thus, this convergence was not just cultural, political or technological, respectively: it embraced subequilibria in many areas.

### 3.1.2 *The purpose*

Ultimately, the system was designed to feed the population (*yangmin*). It was based on the recognition of subsistence as a fundamental right, a right with which a traditional agrarian civilisation could be successfully formed and smoothly operated (see, for example, Scott 1976: 35–55, 176–92). Thus, the centrality of this framework is (1) employment opportunity, mainly in farming; and (2) food availability (in terms of either agricultural output, peasant income or government revenue). As Moulder points out, to supply enough food to the population in order to prevent armed rebellions was one of the major tasks of the Chinese imperial government (1977: 62). This approach was very similar to that of 'entitlement' in modern scholarship (Sen 1981).

To take the interrelationship between government and the peasantry as an example: if the majority of people (mainly peasants) were employed and had enough to eat, government would have a peaceful rule. Here, both parties have active roles to play: if through employment the peasantry had the resources (capital, land and labour) for agricultural production, sufficient food was likely to be produced. If government managed to maintain the momentum of food production by protecting and promoting agriculture, and by assisting the peasantry (either actively with the guidance of better farming practices and hand-outs of capital and land, or passively with reduction of tax and famine relief), the peasantry was likely to concentrate upon food production. On the other hand, in a premodern society which lacked a continually updated information flow among the masses, employment opportunities and the availability of food ultimately formed the most reliable and accurate gauge for the ordinary people to measure and judge the patron's performance in the fulfilment of its obligation set up in accordance with the patron–client reciprocity norm (Scott 1976: chs 2, 6). If any of these conditions was not met – unemployment was high and food supply was short and the subsistence of the peasantry was threatened – the legitimacy of the government was doomed.

Such a correlation was theorised by the ancient Chinese literati, as clearly reflected in Mencius's well-known maxim 'food is people's god' (*min yishi weitian*). It was with the emphasis of food availability as the vital strategic point in state politics that the ideology of 'people as the foundation' (*minben*) was developed by the Confucian School as the obligatory guide for the rulers to reign over China in an acceptable way. If a ruler understood the 'masses–employment/food–government' paradigm and practised physiocracy, he achieved 'sage-like humanity' (*ren*), and his reign was secure (Mengzi Warring States Period: chs 'Gongsu Chou Shang' and 'Lilou Shang'). As Emperor Kangxi of the Qing (r. 1662–1722) once said, 'Since ancient times, the model for long-lasting peace has been essentially to ensure people's livelihood. To achieve that is to have land reclaimed for farming so that surpluses are produced and income become inexhaustible' (Wei Z. *et al.* 1995: 49). This correlation, as demonstrated in Figure 3.2, formed the basis for the Chinese

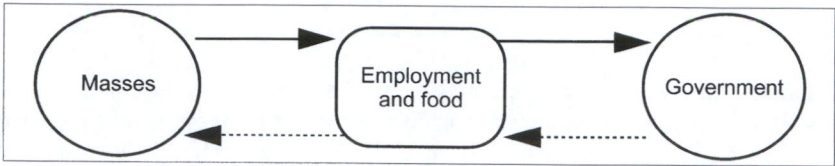

*Figure 3.2* The Confucian *minben* paradigm

Note

Arrows indicate reciprocity between the masses and the state. Solid lines, how legitimacy and mandate of political power takes shape; broken lines, how sage-like humanity and physiocracy feeds back.

granary systems for food-price regulation and famine relief (*canglin*) consisting of the Ever-Stable Granaries (*changpingcang*, first established in 54 BC), the Local Community Granaries (*shecang*) and the Charity Granaries (*yicang*) (see, for example Will 1990; Will and Wong 1991).

In the context of these mutual needs, the practice of physiocracy by the Chinese state was not at all a result of the noble-mindedness, thoughtfulness or sagacity of the authorities as romanticised by the Chinese upper classes. Rather, it was the imperative condition to remain in power. In other words, the ruling elite had few alternatives: throughout Chinese history, he who was capable of satisfying people's need for employment and food ruled China. Such a trinary equilibrium was uniquely Chinese.

In contrast, medieval Europe was marked by (1) decentralised administration; (2) exclusive property, mainly land, ownership; and (3) competing economic institutions as embodied in markets, city-states and nation-states. These three factors were largely absent individually let alone in their combination in China. As a result, capitalist elements found themselves able to develop in Europe and ushered in, during the late medieval period, a mercantile era and then an industrial era, two important steps in capitalist development. During these eras, governments in Europe not only were in favour of trade but also cooperated with the merchant–entrepreneur stratum. In Britain, for example, state interference was present in the process of 'labour force changing hands' from the feudal class to the entrepreneurial class through manoeuvring labour from rural areas to the cities (as in the case of the Poor Law from the sixteenth to the nineteeth centuries; see Gardiner and Wenborn 1995: 607–08), crucial to capitalist development. Not surprisingly, these mercantile and industrial steps were completely missed out in China, an economy that was under the trinary structure.

### 3.1.3 Critiques

At this point, some further critiques can be made on the validity of some existing models and theories in explaining the Chinese experience in the past. First, the establishment and maintenance of China's trinary structure and its equilibrium created a distinctive 'mode' or pattern of economic development, a mode which cannot be explained by a Hegelian–Marxian 'natural process' of development because in a normal situation there is no serious conflict but harmony or quasi-harmony between those equipoises, whereas in the Hegelian–Maxian Scheme conflict between dialectic forces is the key to further development. Second, this trinary structure cannot be explained by Marx's Asiatic Mode of Production either, because of the prevalence of land-holding and landowning small farmers in the economy, whereas to make the Asiatic Mode of Production work requires the absence of this large number of small landowners. Third, it cannot be explained by the Malthusian model or the Boserupian model: it indicates that the Chinese failure in industrialisation may have had very little to do with the demographic pattern because the trinary structure was by and large intact, with the Chinese population fluctuating over time and thus population-neutral. Fourth, it cannot be explained by the Lewisian model or the Rostowian model (Lewis 1954; Rostow 1960): these models cannot explain why the pattern of sector-led, unbalanced economic development was not workable in China over a period of millennia because of the overwhelming check from a 'traditional sector'. Fifth, the Marxian model cannot accommodate this trinary structure, which explains why there was not much chance for a 'progressive' class such as the progressive bourgeoisie to grow in China or for the old, conservative classes to perish. Last but not least, the Chinese experience challenges the vision that development with a capitalist bias is a universal path simply because China's trinary path was factually a sustained pattern in its own right.

Against this background, it is easier to understand that the problem with premodern China was not just the deficiency of some isolated factors alone such as government performance and policies, land shortage and Confucian ideology; it was the result of a joint force from a well-structured framework, including both 'hardwares' (such as the conditions for the economy, the structure of society and the function of bureaucracy) and 'softwares' (such as economic policies, values and ideology).

## 3.2 Origin and development of the structure

The main factors revealed in Chapter 2 are related to but not identical to the trinary structure. The key to understanding the trinary structure is to know how such a package of agricultural dominance, centralised physiocratic government, and landholding and landowning peasantry took shape.

It is far too simple to explain this phenomenon by pointing out that the Chinese were naturally born farmers as numerous works have claimed. They were not. The Chinese were very good at many other things: commerce, academic studies, handicrafts, city-building and so forth (see Needham 1954–94; Skinner 1964–5, 1977; Deng 1997). Or that the natural environment in China was best suited for agriculture (see typically Ho 1962). It was not.

Any lasting land fertility relies on human inputs. Also, China was so large and regional differences were only too obvious; for example, soil types and vegetation differend widely (for the soil types, see Figure 2.1; for vegetation see JKY 1987: Appendix 15; for contemporary cropping systems see C. J. Smith 1991: figure 5.2). The present analysis rejects any idyll-like romantic narration of Chinese economic history.

The specialisation in farming and the favourable natural enviroment offer, at best, half the explanation. The other half comes from political and military competition among different units during the long period from the Shang (*c.* 1520–1030 BC) to the Qin (221–207 BC). There were two decisive incidents in which the agriculture-based units defeated trade-active units. The first was the victory of the Zhou Kingdom (*c.* 1030–841 BC) over the suzerain Shang, and the second, that of the Qin Kingdom (841–221 BC) over its six counterparts. Although one of the most intriguing periods of Chinese economic history, it has so far been conspicuously understudied.

This was a period of evolutionary change, which took about a millennium to complete, in a dynamic, sometimes painful, process of trial and error entwining with shocks and mutations, tinkering and restoration. The impact of this change was so profound that the period can thus be defined as the 'Zhou–Qin Evolution'.

### 3.2.1 The Zhou–Qin Evolution: an institutional invention

#### 3.2.1.1 Starting point: pastoralism and migrating handicrafts under the Shang

With a territory of some 1.6 million square kilometres covering the North Plain and Loess Plateau (roughly 105–125° E, 30–40° N) (Song X. 1991: 201), the Shang Dynasty was established by a tribe which probably originated in the region of what are now Shanxi and Henan provinces. From the fragmentary information, the Shang ruling tribe were nomads turned military conquerors, who imposed taxes on the captured regions (Yang S. 1992: ch. 4). On the whole, the Shang had a mixed economy of pastoralism and migrating handicrafts with ten identifiable subsectors: (1) quarrying, (2) building construction, (3) pottery, (4) the making of bone tools, (5) bronze-making, (6) wine-making, (7) textiles, (8) transport, (9) animal husbandry and (10) farming (Li J.: 1990; Luo C. 1996). Among these subsectors, the Shang were particularly good at civil engineering, bronze-making, pottery, textiles, transport and trade. Their achievements are very impressive by premodern standards. Apart from the Shang domain, a wide economic divergence existed on East Asian mainland from the Palaeolithic till the Bronze ages (see Deng 1993a: ch. 2, A. 2).

Looking at civil engineering, we find that the Shang were active city-builders. In an area of 42,000 square metres at the site of the Yin Ruins, as

128

many as 57 large buildings in a complex have been discovered. The main building in this complex alone has a floor area of 1,230 square metres with 25 pillars erected on bronze bases. The discovery of the Zhengzhou Ruins, another site of a Shang city, shows that it was once a walled city of approximately 3.1 square kilometres. At both the Yin and Zhengzhou sites, the detectable walled area is 24 square kilometres with a total urban settlement of some 190 square kilometres, larger than any known city in the following Zhou Period (Chen 1994: 736). The total urban area to walled city ratio is thus 8:1. Given that the Shang tribe moved their capital 10 times (Fu Z. 1980 vol. 1: 23–4; Song X. 1991: 206–18), 10 such large cities would have to be built successively, with an estimated aggregate walled floor area of 240 square kilometres and a total urban area of 1,900 square kilometres if the same ratio for urban area to walled city ratio is applied.

It is known that the total length of the wall at the Zhengzhou Ruins is 6,960 m and that of Yanshi 5,330 m (Yang S. 1992: 447). To judge from some Shang remains, the walls are often 3 m high with a base 20 m wide (*ibid*). It may be supposed that the minimum cubic earthwork (as with a triangular cross-Section) for a metre-long wall is thus 30 cubic metres ($3 \times 20 \times 1 \div 2$). The total earthwork for these two walls is at least 370,000 cubic metres in volume. This amount was only a part of the construction operation. If all the permanent buildings are included, the total workload would be much greater. In addition, walled castle towns of various sizes were also built. The data for the three known sites are as follows (based on Song X. 1991: 43–4, 47–8, 50–1, 66; Yang S. 1992: 447–8):

| Location | Castle floor area | Walled-town floor area |
|----------|-------------------|------------------------|
| Yanshi Ruins | 40,000 m$^2$ | 2,100,000 m$^2$ |
| Yuanqu | — | 140,000 m$^2$ |
| Panlong Ruins | — | 75,400 m$^2$ |

According to the unearthed Shang oracle inscriptions, there were 48 castled kingdoms in the Shang territory (Chen M. 1956: 269–301; Liu X. 1995: 19). If the Panlong castle town was a prototype of these castle towns, the total walled area could reach some 3,620,000 square metres. Undoubtedly, systematic construction and maintenance of walled cities, a phenomenon of the Chinese civilisation, originated in the Shang Period.

If we suppose that the Shang had at any given time one capital of 24 square kilometres and 48 castled towns of 30 square kilometres, the total walled area was likely to be around 50 square kilometres. To apply the above urban settlement to walled city ratio of 8:1, the aggregate castle town-cum-urban area would be some 400 square kilometres at any given time. The aggregate urban area could occupy some 0.3 per cent of the total Shang territory. It has been estimated that around 5 per cent of the total population under the Shang reign was urban (Chen M. 1956: 269–301; Liu X. 1995: 19). Given that King Zhou, the last ruler of the Shang, had an army of 170,000 (Fan W. 1964–5 vol. 1: 131; *cf*. Sima Q. *c*. 91 BC: ch. 'Yin Benji'), and if we suppose that the Shang army recruited one soldier from each household of five people, it would have taken at least 850,000 residents to sustain the army. If this figure is right, the Shang urban population is likely to have been around 50,000 people (*cf*. Yang S. 1992: 44–50).

To move on to look at bronze-making, in terms of metallurgy the Shang artisans were able to produced copper (with a melting point of 1,084.5°C) and three types of copper-based alloys (copper–tin bronze, copper–lead bronze and copper–tin–lead bronze) with various metal proportions in order to obtain different chemical and physical features to suit different purposes. To refine the ingredient metals and make the bronze, the Shang artisans used furnaces and crucibles with charcoal as the main fuel (Zhang Z. 1977: 31–7; Yang S. 1992: ch. 7). At the Yin Ruins, over 600 carved jade ornaments have been unearthed from a workshop, suggesting that tools such as drills and chisels made of hard metals other than bronze were in use (Song X. 1991: 45; Yang S. 1992: 397). In casting, the Shang used stone, clay (pottery) and wax to make moulds (Yang S. 1992: 401–10) and were able to perform permanent casting and investment casting (also known as 'lost wax casting') to make high-quality pieces (Zhang Z. 1977: 37). The products were sometimes cast at one go, sometimes in several stages.

The operation was on a large scale by premodern standards. The Shang bronze workers were capable of performing mass production and did so, as seen from standardised arrowheads unearthed. Techniques of tin-plating on a copper base also developed (Zhang Z. 1977: 30). The site of a main bronze-making centre discovered at the Yin Ruins, once the Shang capital, covers 10,000 square metres with a total of 19,000 casting moulds and some 2,000 finished bronzes excavated (Song X. 1991: 45; Yang S. 1992: 397). At another site, a patterned bronze quadripod weighing 875 kg (and measuring 123 cm × 77 cm × 110 cm) has been discovered together with over a hundred casting moulds (Guo B. 1978: 14).

In this context, it is no longer a puzzle why the Shang tribe as a whole migrated as many as 16 times (Fu Z. 1980 vol. 1: 26–9) and consequently moved their capital city 10 times of which 8 have been confirmed by modern research (*ibid*.: 23–4; Song X. 1991: 206–18; for archaeological evidence, see Guo 1986). Modern research shows that the Shang migratory activities were voluntary and had little to do with natural or man-made disasters such as floods, droughts or wars. In fact, the locations of the Shang capital cities coincided with copper mines, essential for bronze-making (Fu Z. 1980 vol. 1: 23–51; Yang S. 1992). In comparison, the following Zhou Dynasty moved the capital only once in 770 BC, and that move was forced by a political, military and economic crisis. Thus, the Shang migratory behaviour was induced by economic needs from a high level of commercial and industrial activities and a low level of farming engagement.

The Shang was probably the starting point of China's speciality in ceramics. So far, over 250,000 pottery pieces have been unearthed. Produced for everyday uses, they range from containers and cooking pots to building components (Zhang Z. 1977: 29; Yang S. 1992: 471–92). The estimated firing temperature for some of the pieces was 900–1,000°C, a height which the Shang artisan had already achieved with their metallurgy (Zhang Z. 1977: 27). The Shang artisans also knew how to glaze their pieces (*ibid.*: 24–9).

Archaeological discoveries indicate that the Shang artisans knew how to plain-weave wool, hemp and cotton and how to jacquard-weave silk. They almost certainly invented the loom (Yang S. 1992: 493–513). In 1976, the tomb of Fuhao, the wife of a Shang ruler, was discovered in Henan. With it, six types of woven silk cloth, some dyed, were unearthed (Anon. 1980a: 18).

The Shang people were known for their obsession with vehicles for transport. Legend has it that Wang Hai, the seventh king of the Shang, invented the cattle cart and Xiang Tu, the eleventh king, invented the horse cart (Fan W. 1964–5 vol. 1: 108). It is believed that this Wang Hai drove his newly invented cattle cart trading among different tribes until he was murdered by the Barbarians of the North (*di*) while on tour (*ibid.*). He was the first recorded king-martyr of commerce in Chinese history.

The use of horse carts for transport by the Shang is reflected by the practice of using 'funerary horses with carts' which have been discovered in Shang tombs (*chemazang*) (Zheng R. 1987; Yang S. 1992: 205). So far, at least 40 such archaeological excavations have been made. In one grave, 37 horses were carefully buried (Zheng R. 1987; Yang S. 1992: 205). Archaeological evidence shows that the Shang carts that have been unearthed in different regions have the same tread (distance between the wheels of both sides). This implies that the Shang had a standardised highway network (Yang S. 1992: 518). This fact, together with evidence of the use of money, means the Shang are likely to have had a cross-regional market. Legend has it that the Shang were even capable of sailing, not only around China's coast but across the Pacific. This legend has some support from discoveries in Mexico, Ecuador and Peru. So far, apart from Sinicised tools of the Neolithic Age, some 140 ancient Chinese characters have been identified on relics on the other side of the Pacific (Fang Z. 1983; cf. Lin W. 1986; see also Jennings 1978: 350–65), suggesting a maritime link between the archaic Shang Chinese and Central and Southern Americans. Although a demanding task for the Shang with primitive maritime technology, such a trip was not entirely impossible (Deng 1997: ch. 1).

It has been generally agreed among Chinese historians that the Shang Period marked the first upsurge, in terms of both scale and scope, of commercial activities in Chinese long-term history. Chinese classic books indicate that the trade volume in the capital city Yin was the greatest of all (Anon. Zhou

Dynasty: ch. 'Shangshu Pangeng'; Anon. Spring and Autumn: ch: 'Shangsong Yinwu'). It had nine market-places which were packed with cattle carts loaded with wine jars and horse carts full of roast meat (Li F. AD 983 vol. 83: ch. 'Diwang Shiji'). The excavated items from the site of the Shang capital city in Henan include precious stones, sea turtle shells, rhinoceros horns, elephant tusks, whale bones and cowries whose origins were far away from both north China and its immediate periphery. They were probably the result of Shang trading. A recent study has identified the Shang horses as being a breed from Asia Minor. Although it remains unknown how these animals were introduced to China, there is a good likelihood that they too were obtained through trade (Yang S. 1992: 212).

Evidence also shows that Shang commerce developed to the level of the formation of professional merchants and the use of currency (called *bei* and *peng*, probably cowrie), as demonstrated by the large quantity of currency cowries, over 6,000 pieces discovered in one tomb (Guo B. 1978). The scope of the Shang merchant activities was great. It covered an area including most of the land to the northern bank of the Yangzi River and what is now Korea (Lü Z. 1983: 60–1). After the historic defeat of the Shang by the Zhou in *c*. 1030 BC, trading activities of the Shang tribe did not stop. Members of the overthrown Shang upper classes continued their old profession of making a living by 'travelling on cattle carts as long-distance traders and making money to maintain parents at home' (*zhao qianniu yuanfugu yong xiaoyang fumu*) (Anon. Zhou Dynasty: ch. 'Jiugao'). The Shang tribe was so heavily involved in trade that the meaning of the Chinese word *shang* ('trade' and 'traders') was derived from them.

So far as agriculture is concerned, the cultivated land area under the Shang is estimated to have been 460,300 hectares (6.87 million modern *mu*) (Liu X. 1995: 24). Conservatively, to suppose that (1) the Shang practised long fallow in a three-year cycle, and (2) the maximum land yield level was 150 *jin* per *mu* (about 1.2 metric tons per hectare), this aggregate land area was able to feed a total of 941,000 adults at the subsistence level of living (at 500 g of unhusked grain per day). This estimate is compatible with the Shang army-based estimate of a minimum population of 850,000 (170,000 soldiers each from a household of five). In terms of farming technology, archaeological studies of the Shang oracle inscriptions (*buci*) show that cattle were used to pull ploughs in tillage, the range of crops being millet, barley, wheat, rice and legumes (Deng 1993a: 46–7).

Shang oracle inscriptions also indicate large numbers of domestic animals. Sheep/goats, horses and cattle in their thousands were regularly used by the crown for sacrifices to gods and ancestors, a sign of prosperous animal husbandry in the economy (Guo M. 1977: 179; Guo B. 1978: 41; Wen S. and Yuan T. 1983: 234–7). In addition, official posts were established for horse-related matters and raising horses was an established profession (Yang S. 1992: 50–1, 255).

However, although within the Shang territory agriculture was widely spread and the Shang ruling tribe paid close attention to things such as rainfall and harvests, there is little evidence that the Shang ruling tribe itself, especially among the male population, actually practised substantial farming of any kind. There has been a long-standing debate among Chinese scholars on the identity of the stratum of *zhong* or *zhongren* (literally meaning 'the masses') during the Shang Period. Some have suggested that this group were free citizens who farmed during peaceful times and fought wars when confrontations broke out (Hou W. 1992: 1598–9). However, it remains unclear whether this stratum consisted of members of the Shang tribe. Therefore, the existence of such a free-citizen class that performed tillage itself does not qualify the Shang tribe as a farming clan. The fact that a large number of the Shang soldiers mutinied against their commanders implies that the main body of the army was recruited from non-Shang tribes.

It is worth noting that archaeological findings show that socio-economic life under Shang rule was organised similarly to the Indian caste system with five main race-based strata. Evidently, the *qiang*, a western nomadic tribe, were made a caste of the Shang king's herdsmen, and the Zhou, a cast of farmers. The Shang tribe was at the top of the society as the military conquerors who were particularly keen on 'hunting', an ancient form of war exercise (Yang S. 1992: ch. 5).

Alternatively, the farming pattern during the Shang Period has been identified by some scholars as 'shifting agriculture', which is characterised by women having chief responsibility for tillage tasks (Fu Z. 1980 vol. 1: 23–51; Yang S. 1992). Even if the ruling Shang tribe was to a certain degree agrarian, the male members of the tribe specialised in non-agricultural activities. Boserup suggests that there was a withdrawal of women as the main labour force from tillage (Boserup 1970: 26). Logically, if the Shang tribe did not dirty their hands in ploughing, as is suggested by archaeological and textual evidence, the Shang males may have never become involved in replacing their women in farming and thus never farmed at all.

The Shang had an ambivalent attitude towards agriculture as seen in (1) the existence of 'king's inspecting farmers' (*xingtian*), presumably serfs of some kind within direct Shang control, and (2) the practice of 'forecasting and foraging wheat harvest' (*gaomai*) by king's agents in each autumn before the king sent the army to plunder the grain, probably outside the Shang domain (Yang S. 1992: 121, 189, 250). Obviously, the Shang ruler needed farming products but did not himself farm even as a gesture. In contrast, under the succeeding Zhou, the farming ceremonies by the king called 'opening of tillage' (*gengji*) and 'planting of five crops' (*gongqin*) were carried out as required by law (Dai S. Western Han: ch. 'Monthly Ordinance'), a tradition which not only was passed on generation by generation till the end of the Zhou (Lü B. Warring States Period: ch. 'Mengchun Ji'), but also became mandatory from the Han Dynasty onwards (Ji X. 1955: 54; Lee 1969; Merson 1989: 12–13).

This non-agrarian bias was compatible with the pattern of metal tool production and distribution which were monopolised by the Shang tribe. As archaeological discoveries show, during the Shang, most strata enjoyed the fruits of the Bronze Age. The army was equipped with bronze helmets, suits of armour, spears, dagger-axes, swords and arrowheads; the merchants rode on carts with bronze joints and nails, pulled by horses with bronze ornaments and bridles; the priests used bronze utensils to service their ceremonies; chefs had bronze utensils of various sizes, bronze table sets of plates, mugs, jars, bottles; musicians had bronze bells, drums, gongs; craftsmen had a range of bronze tools such as needles, chisels, adzes and axes to work on different materials. In contrast, the Shang farmers still lived in the Neolithic Age, using predominantly stone, wood and bone tools (Song X. 1991; Hou W. 1992: 891–2). Among the 2,000 items excavated from a bronze workshop at the Yin Ruins, including ceremonial utensils, weapons, music instruments, industrial tools and gear for horses and carts, not a single piece of farming equipment was found (Song X. 1991: 56, 88; Hou W. 1992: 892). So far, among all the Shang bronze tools unearthed all over China, only 32 have been positively identified as exclusively tools for farming, while the total number of unearthed Shang farming tools made of wood, bone and shells is 4,864 pieces. The non-metal tools to bronze tools ratio, shockingly, is 152:1 (Yang S. 1992: 132–7, 151–2). This shows that although the Shang artisans had no technical difficulty in making farming tools, they could not be bothered. Such 'metal discrimination' was not only sectoral but also regional: archaeological evidence has shown that the amount of bronze items diminished at a steady rate from the capital city and core area (in what is now Henan) to Shang's colonised and well-controlled subcultural regions and to Shang's semi-colonised periphery (Song X. 1991: chs 2–4; Yang S. 1992: ch. 7). This shows that the supply of bronze was carefully ranked by the Shang ruling tribe. Why? One may argue that this was a case of resource scarcity and that the metal was thus used for more value-added products. That may well have been the case. However, this assumption becomes shaky before the facts (1) that according to *Master Guan's Book*, there were 467 copper-mining sites within China's territory (Guan Z. Warring States Period: ch: 'Dishu'), and modern research has identified 36 copper-mining sites for the Shang (Yang S. 1992: 380); and (2) that this 'bronze discrimination' ended almost overnight when the physiocratic Zhou tribe drove the Shang out of office: immediately, bronze started to be used for farming tools (Bai Y. 1985). The most feasible reason seems that the Shang government did not, as a matter of policy, give agriculture priority, an attitude that was reflected in tool-making.

Four points can be made from the above observation. First, the Shang Period presents a rare case in the entire history of China in which a ruling tribe was so versatile, so mobile and so active in craft industry and commerce. The Shang elite were almost certainly literate, as shown by the large number of oracle bone pieces (so far 154,600 in all) and the vocabulary of some 4,700 characters, the same number as the basic modern Chinese language requires (Song X. 1991: 89–90). Second, it may be no exaggeration to state that the Shang economy, or a large part of it, was market-oriented. Third, the Shang ruling tribe had very limited interest in farming. Lastly, what can be called 'agricultural fetishism' was not so obvious in society. Given their advances in handicrafts and trade and their ruling position, the Shang are likely to have had most of their food supplied from other professional farming groups through a combination of market exchange, taxation and naked plunder. From the scope of the excavation of Shang bronze wares in the non-bronze-making regions, the exchange seems to have been both regular and extensive.

### 3.2.1.2 Stage 1: changes during the Western Zhou, c. 1030–771 BC

The growth of the Shang mixed economy was interrupted by the rise of the agrarian Zhou. The Zhou had their permanent base in Shaanxi, the western part of the Loess Plateau, an area which was favourable for farming. According to modern data, this plateau is covered with deep and easy-to-till soil (50–150 m deep) and the region has a frost-free period of eight months per annum. In addition, the region benefits from an extensive network involving two of China's main rivers (Lee 1969: 28; Hsieh 1973: 23–51; Geelan and Twitchett 1974: 13; Needham 1961: ch. 4; 1984: 3–46; 1986: 23–181). Prior to AD 1000, the local climate was almost certainly warmer and wetter than today, which was an extra bonus for agricultural development (Zhu K. 1979; Wang C. 1987).

It was not a sheer accident that the Loess Plateau became the very heartland of agriculture in north China, where farming settlement can be traced back for 7,000–8,000 years by carbon dating, starting from the Palaeolithic Period (? – c. 7500 BC) (Wang Z. and Wei L. 1995: 69; see also Ho 1969). Topographically, the plateau is a natural fortress with an elevation of 800–1,200 m, surrounded by the Ordos Desert to the north, the Qinling Range to the south, Mount Liupan and Mount Helan to the west and the Taihang Range to the east (Needham 1961 vol. 1: 69). These economic and military advantages have made Shaanxi a region of strategic importance in Chinese political history: from the Zhou to Mao's Communist era, those who controlled that region are likely to control North China and thus the entire Chinese Empire.

Unlike the Shang, the Zhou tribe were known as both excellent dry farmers and fearless soldiers. For generations their chiefs served the Xia authorities (c. 2000–1520 BC) as the Agricultural Minister although this tradition seems to have been interrupted under the succeeding Shang (Hou W. 1992: 1285). An ancestor of the Zhou tribe, Qi, is believed to have instructed his people how to grow a range of crops. He was posthumously honoured by the name of *ji*, after the most popular millet species of that time, or vice versa (Anon. Zhou

Dynasty: ch. 'Yiji'). The Zhou tribe built a strong army in response to the military pressure from the neighbouring Barbarians of the North (*di*) and the Barbarians of the West (*rong*). The marriage between a prosperous agricultural sector and a strong army laid the foundation for the Zhou to become a 'supertribe' whose power was demonstrated by Zhou's consecutive victories over numerous barbarian tribes (*di* and *rong*). Finally, in 1066 BC Zhou's 48,000 elite troops, led by 300 chariots, defeated a much larger Shang army of 170,000 fighting men (Fan W. 1964–5 vol. 1: 131).

With the historic victory of the Zhou, several changes took place which significantly altered the developmental path of the Chinese economy from its track under the Shang. First, a system was established to distribute land, with the chessboard field (*jingtian*) as the standard unit. Conventionally, this system is translated in a word-for-word fashion as the 'well–field' system, which is totally misleading because there was no actual well in the field. What the 'well' means here is the way in which the chessboard is divided like the Chinese ideographic character *jing* for 'well'. Each chessboard had nine evenly divided plots, eight of which were granted to eight households for private, autonomic farming. The remaining plot, known as 'communal plot for taxation' (*gongtian*), was tilled collectively by the eight households and the output was exclusively used to pay government rent-tax (Li J. 1962: ch. 9; Sun Z. 1966; Fu Z. 1981: vol. 1; Ma Z. 1985; Li W. 1994). This is illustrated in Figure 3.3.

As indicated by both the textual and the archaeological evidence, the farmers were free citizens with their own household economies and certain kinds of

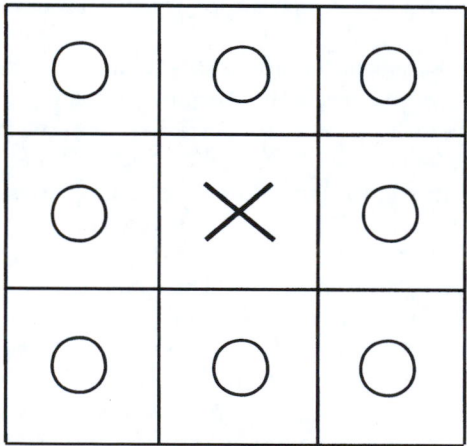

*Figure 3.3* Chessboard field of the Zhou Period

Note

The circles indicate plots for households, the cross represents a plot under collective farming for taxation purposes.

property rights (Xie W. 1990: 268–76). Accordingly, the official positions of Chief Minister of Labour (*da situ*) and Local Minister of Labour (*xiao situ*) were established. Holders of these offices were in charge of both land distribution and labour employment management (Anon. *c*. third century BC: ch. 'Land Officials – Ministers of Labour'). A recent study suggests that one chessboard was an equivalent of 18.7 modern hectares (see Zhu S. 1985: 92). So, each household's plot occupied 2.08 hectares. These figures were for good farming land. The land area was doubled for 'medium fertile land' and tripled for 'inferior land' (Ban G. AD 82: ch. 'Economy I'). From the way the chessboard was organised, the Zhou property rights were likely to have been communal, which was compatible with the individual household's economies within a community. In comparison, the Shang practice of Forecasting Wheat Harvest (*gaomai*) clearly indicates the absence of such property rights among the farmers (for *gaomai* see Yang S. 1992: 121, 189, 250).

Second, Zhou agriculture was land-intensive under fallow: every three years, farmers moved to a rotary chessboard (Gongyang G. Warring States Period: entry 'Fifteenth Year under Duke Xuan'). Thus, the ranking of land fertility and the distribution of land became imperative for the chessboard-field system (*jingtianzhi*) to function. Consequently, official positions were established and the study of soil types occurred. The former marked the chessboard-field system, the first known land distribution framework in Chinese history; the latter, the first systematic attempt in the history of Chinese agronomy (Deng 1993a: 47–8, ch. 4.B). Moreover, from available records, a certain degree of uniformity in farming technology occurred, probably under Zhou government initiative, known as *leisi* and *ougeng*. The spade-plough (*leisi*), a digging tool with a metal edge and a pulling rope adherent to the shaft, was commonly applied. It was operated by two farmers called 'ploughing in pair' (*ougeng*) – one digging in soil and another pulling the spade with a rope to turn the soil. An intermediate stage to the development of the animal draught plough, the spade-plough was almost certainly designed for household farming with either a husband-and-wife team or father-and-son team (Hou W. 1992: 1290; Wang Y. 1980: 132–3; Li B. 1981: 21–6), which also supports the notion that there was an autonomous peasant economy at the micro level. This is consistent with the Zhou family structure. Recent work based on textual and archaeological evidence has identified that during the Zhou (1) families were predominantly paternalistic; (2) the nuclear and extended families were the main types; (3) the household was the basic economic unit, with 2–7 members; (4) the lower classes tended to have small families; and (5) the household as the basic registration unit for the government census had developed widely across China by the fourth century BC (Xie W. 1990: ch. 7). In comparison, according to a recent study, the Shang social structure was based on primitive communes with internal marriages among blood relations (Zhang S. and Li X. 1990: 7–8).

The Zhou chessboard system certainly represented a more sophisticated family structure as the basis of a socio-economic unit.

Third, on the basis of the chessboard-field system, a sophisticated social structure was built in a military fashion: each 10 chessboards (80 families) formed one regiment called *cheng* (literally 'ten per cent'), each 10 regiments one division called *tong* (literally 'unit'), each 10 divisions one army called *feng* (literally 'grand unit'), and each 10 armies one group army of 80,000 soldiers called *ji* (literally 'territorial unit'). In addition, by law, every 64 chessboards were to provide 4 warhorses, 12 head of cattle and 3 suits of armour (Jian B. and Zheng T. 1962 vol. 1: 57). When a new land was conquered in a process of military migration, the chessboard-field system was replicated to guard the prey (Si W. 1957: 167; Wang B. 1979: ch. 2). The prolonged Shang practice of plundering harvest was stopped and farmers' property rights (communal, private or both) were protected.

Zhou's victory was thus a turning point in Chinese history on three counts: (1) it showed the economic and military power of an agriculture-based over that of a mixed economy; (2) agriculture was promoted with an unprecedented effort; (3) land property rights were protected; and (4) a more sophisticated social structure emerged.

### 3.2.1.3 Stage 2: changes during the Spring and Autumn to the Qin, 770–207 BC

From the very beginning under its first king, Wu (r. 1066–1062 BC), the Zhou Dynasty established a decentralised political system containing numerous units (*guo*), as many as 71 at one time, responsible for paying taxes to the crown (Hou W. 1992: 1286). This planted the seed of internal competition among these units with a clear tendency for their numbers to be reduced. By 841 BC, China had reached an equilibrium with 12 main units including one kingdom (Eastern Zhou) and 11 dukedoms (Lu, Qi, Jin, Qin, Chu, Song, Wei, Chen, Cai, Cao and Yan). Also, the superiority of the agriculture-based power was not always secure. The Zhou army under King You (r. 781–771 BC) was defeated by the nomadic Barbarians of the West (*quanrong*), who conquered the Western Zhou territory by force. With the loss of the western territory, You's successor, King Ping, moved the capital eastward in 770 BC, which marked the era of the Spring and Autumn Period (770–476 BC).

With the weakening control of the Zhou crown, Xiong Tong, the ruler of Chu, proclaimed himself king in 704 BC. In the following Warring States Period (457–221 BC.), the tension among the competitors intensified when the number of main units decreased to 10, with two kingdoms (Zhuo and Chu) and eight dukedoms (Qin, Wei, Han, Zhao, Yan, Tianqi, Qi and Jin), by 458 BC. The number was further reduced to eight, with four kingdoms (Zhou, Chu, Wei and Tianqi) and four dukedoms (Qin, Han, Zhao and Yan), by 344 BC. Finally, by 325 BC all the remaining dukedoms had upgraded.

A turning point occurred in 256 BC when the Zhou Kingdom, first the only kingdom and later the kingdom of the kingdoms, was wiped out by Qin. With it, Qin rose as a super-kingdom and united China 35 years later. The establishment of the Qin Empire dragged the economy from a crossroads back to the course set by the Zhou.

What the Qin had in common with the Zhou was its base in the dry-farming region Shaanxi, its farming expertise, its physiocratic bias and its agriculture-based economic and military power. These features become more obvious when the Qin is compared to the other political units. Like the previous Shang, the other kingdoms which coexisted with the Qin were unmistakably biased towards handicrafts and commerce. For example, the Qi Kingdom was known for its silk production and dominated the silk market in China (Chen C. 1995). Yue indulged in trade under the best-qualified business tycoons of the time, such as Ji Ran and Fan Li (Sima Q. 91 BC: 'Biography of the Economic Sectors'; see also Fang J. 1995). Commercial interests were carefully protected in the Chu, Wei, Jin and Qi kingdoms, which granted merchants special rights and discounts (Zuoqiu M. *c.* 454a BC: 'Jin History No. 4', 'Qi History'; *c.* 454b BC: Entry 'The Second Year under Duke Min'). In 651 BC, with the initiative of Duke Huan of the Qi, a treaty was signed (Kuiqiu Treaty) at an all-states summit to ban government interference in inter-state trade activities (Mengzi Warring States Period: ch. 'Gaozi Xia'). Guan Zhong (?–645 BC) of the Qi Kingdom, a prominent scholar and politician of the time, even claimed (Guan Z. Warring States Period: ch. 'Guoxu') that 'A kingdom with 10,000 chariots must have merchants worth 10,000 units of currency to match it; and a kingdom with 1,000 chariots, merchants worth 1,000 units.' It is not surprising that modern scholars have been arguing that in China the sprouting of capitalism began during the Spring and Autumn–Warring States Period (Fu Z. 1981).

The Qin Kingdom was largely left out of this commercial race and was regarded as a marginal state in terms of commercial development. Qin benefited, mainly passively, from incoming traders of the other states. Seeing a gap arising from the lack of influence of money in Qin politics, Lü Buwei, a successful merchant of Wei (now Henan) origin, took advantage to invest in the Qin crown prince, which yielded him handsome returns: Lü was later appointed Prime Minister (*xiangguo*) and practically controlled the politics of the kingdom during his heyday (Sima Q. 91 BC: 'Biography of Lü Buwei'). But commercial backwardness did not handicap Qin's rise as a champion among the competing powers. This was especially true after Shang Yang (*c.* 390–338 BC), a Legalist by training, was employed in 356 BC as a policy adviser by Duke Xiao of the Qin. According to Shang Yang, 'Once attracted by farming, men become simple-minded and thus reliable to fight the war' (Shang Y. 338 BC: ch. 'Agriculture and War'). He specified that for a strong political unit to be built, peasants should ideally make up 90 per cent of the total population (*ibid.*), and made this his target in his reform. The first reform, masterminded by Shang Yang, took place in 359 BC with radical measures aiming at building a landholding, tax-paying and soldier-conscripting peasantry with two key features: (1) 'promoting farming and confining trade' (*zhongnong yishang*) through discriminative taxes; and (2) dissolving the extended family types and promoting the nuclear family as the taxable unit. In fact, extended families embracing several generations occurred in Han times but in the long run were not a norm. This family type occurred exclusively among the super-rich. So, Shang Yang's reform did not create any new family pattern. Rather, it streamlined the existing pattern under the Zhou (Xie W. 1990: 270–1, 276–8). Moreover, the fact that to increase employment in agriculture became Shang Yang's target means that the farmers had come to constitute a much smaller proportion in the general population by the time of the reform.

A year later, Shang Yang launched his second reform (1) to replace the age-old chessboard-field system with tax-liable household farms so that the farmers had more incentive to produce more and better; (2) to privatise state land and to permit trade in land properties; (3) to attract farmers from other kingdoms to settle in Qin by offering tax advantages and private ownership (called *laimin*, literally 'attracting immigrants') in order to maximise the recruitment of native Qin males for the army; (4) to establish the system of prefectures and counties (*junxianzhi*) under a single commanding centre to allow the Qin state apparatus to govern territories of a great many times its core area; (5) to establish a universal census register system for taxation and army recruitment purposes; and (6) to standardise weights and measures to lower the transaction costs in tax collection (Shang Y. 338 BC; Zheng L. 1989).

The main consequences of the Qin reform in the agricultural sector were at least three: (1) the reinforced property rights; (2) the abandonment of fallow; and (3) the spread of the plough. These were closely entwined. By definition, the abandonment of fallow went hand in hand with private land ownership. In other words, land held in common encouraged fallow whereas private land ownership led to crop rotation. The ultimate reason for that lies in the degree of land scarcity. Once fallow ceased to exist, the maintenance and improvement of land fertility depended greatly on human inputs whereby the plough, which had been the tool for reclamation and sowing, became an indispensable tool for the maintenance and improvement of land fertility. Not surprisingly, by the early Han Period fallow had come to be regarded as backward, inefficient and even barbaric. Its domain retreated to lands in China's periphery. The plough was promoted by imperial order and crop rotation-based intensive farming encouraged (see Deng 1993a: chs 3–4).

After the reforms, obtaining superiority in food supply and military power, the Qin Dynasty was ready to build an empire on the East Asian mainland. That Qin knocked its rivals over one after another like dominoes showed just how powerful Shang Yang's new institution was. Its military superiority was clearly shown in the life-sized terracotta infantry and cavalry unearthed from Emperor Qin Shihuang's tomb. The 'army' was equipped with advanced weaponry of that time (bronze-cast and chrome-treated dagger axes, spears, swords and a crossbow mechanism, as well as a horse bridle, and possibly armour for the infantrymen, have been discovered). It includes nearly 6,000 foot soldiers and 2,000 cavalrymen with chariots and horses. This indeed reflects the emperor's military accomplishments (Guisso *et al.* 1989: 56–69). If the Zhou's victory over the pro-commercial Shang was more or less accidental, Qin's over its six rivals was certainly not. Instead, the whole process was carefully planned and executed. From the available data, the impact of this early reform was profound: during the Ming–Qing Period, as much as 80–90 per cent of total employment in China was still provided by the agricultural sector (Feuerwerker 1984: 299, 302, 312–13; Chao 1986: ch. 3).

In spite of some coherence, there were marked differences between the Zhou and the Qin in their socio-economic institutions: land-ownership types and structure and sophistication of the state were the main discrepancies. First, the Zhou agricultural economy was based on communal or collective application of land, a resource that in theory belonged to the crown, while that of the Qin was based on privately owned individual land. According to the unearthed 'Qin Code Written on Bamboo Slips' (the *Yunmeng Qinlü*), household properties were carefully defined and protected. For example, in the clause for 'household internal crime' (*jiazui*), the law exempts the son from being charged with criminal offences such as injuring the father's employees or stealing the father's livestock only if the son lives with his father. In the clause for 'stealing from the employer's parents', the law exempts from charge the servant who steals from the employer's parents only if the parents do not live with the employer (see Xie W. 1990: 269). Second, the Zhou was characterised by a decentralised administrative structure in which the ruler had very limited power and did not rule the territory efficiently even for tax revenue: Zhou rulers were on occasion (like King Li) even expelled by the Zhou citizens, who enjoyed full rights (Sima Q. 91 BC: ch. 'Biographies of the Zhou'). Qin represented the opposite, an 'over-engineered' state machine, which was a much more effective administrative network than that of the Zhou (Yang S. 1984; Hao T. 1987) and which was characterised by a centralised bureaucracy with the ruler at the top of his impersonal tiered administrative network. It took a nationwide rebellion to overthrow the ruler. Given that in the premodern world it required a certain degree of social homogeneity to run such a centralised bureaucracy, the establishment of the Chinese bureaucracy means that the Qin land-ownership reform was successful in consolidating a more or less homogeneous peasant landholding and landowning peasantry across China. The establishment of the Qin state apparatus in turn reflects (1) the completion of a structural change, and (2) the beginning of the dominance of the agricultural sector in the economy. Also, the combination of landholding peasantry and physiocratic bureaucracy offered society little chance to turn back to a less regulated economy as in the Shang and late Zhou periods unless some sort of revolution occurred. Later on, we will see that even alien conquerors were unable to change the inertia of the interlocking trinary system.

The superiority of the Qin system becomes more obvious when the Qin is compared with its rival units. The Qin was not the only unit which underwent socio-economic reforms. During the Spring and Autumn–Warring States Period, as a matter of life and death, reforms were carried out in all main political units. These reforms were all under the influence of the Legalist School and were often carried out earlier in the other kingdoms than in Qin, as highlighted below:

| Year | Kingdom | Reformer | Policy |
|------|---------|----------|--------|
| 685 BC | Qi | Guan Zhong | 'Differential rents/taxes on land output capacities' (*xiangdi shuaizheng*) |
| 594 BC | Lu | — | 'Taxing on land under cultivation' (*chu shuimu*) |
| 548 BC | Chu | — | Tax on land according to its output level |
| 540 BC | Zheng | Zi Chan | Tax on land area under cultivation (*qiufu*) |
| c. 435–401 BC | Wei | Li Kui | 'Maximising agricultural production' (*jin dili*) and 'controlling fluctuations in food prices' (*shan pingdi*) |

No doubt the reforms in those kingdoms almost certainly resulted in a better incentive system. However, the reforms outside the Qin were mainly meant for distribution and redistribution of surplus instead of distribution and ownership of land, which proved to be crucial to Qin's success. The closest thing to the Qin reforms was the reform under Li Kui (455–395 BC) in Wei Kingdom aiming at 'maximising agricultural production' and 'controlling fluctuations in food prices' (Ban G. AD 82 pt 1: ch. 'Economy'; Li R. 1986). Still, the key element of private ownership was missing in Wei's reform. As a result, these kingdoms experienced only short-term prosperity after the reforms. As a good example, in spite of a policy of negative tax to attract immigrants, the economies of Lu and Qi kingdoms soon went bankrupt (Zuoqiu c. 454b BC: Entry 'Twenty-fifth Year under Duke Zhao of Lu').

Apart from property rights, those kingdoms which did not practise physiocracy also paid a heavy price. Later, the Qin rulers found themselves caught in a similar situation when Emperor Qin Shihuang, the big-headed victor, drove 60 per cent of the eligible male adults (mainly landholding peasants) to the very limit (1) by treating large numbers of farmers, 1.2 million of them, as forced labourers in building the Great Wall (*changcheng*), national highways (*chidao*), imperial palaces (*efanggong*) and the Underground Mauso-leum, and (2) by sending 800,000 troops consisting of peasant soldiers to fight the Huns (*xiongnu*) in the north and Viets (*baiyue*) in the south. In 209 BC his non-physiocratic policy triggered a nationwide armed rebellion of the seemingly docile and meek peasants (Shi W. 1986: 18–19). This rebel-lion consequently ended the glorious 635–year-long history of Qin (841–206 BC). Only then did Chinese history realise what a monster it had created – the mechanism to bring the system back on track.

Both the Qin monarch and the peasantry benefited from the agriculture-based power and triumph. First, Qin's victory confirmed the winning physiocracy–agriculture formula which provided the Qin with an abundant supply of revenue and well-fed and well-disciplined peasant soldiers, crucial to the Qin cause of unification. Second, as the Qin ruling class gained huge territorial possessions, the peasantry were rewarded immediately after Qin's historic victory under a nationwide scheme of 216 BC called *shi qianshou zishitian*, literally 'allowing the commoner-farmers to claim and own land' (Sima Q. 91 BC: ch. 'Biography of Emperor Qin Shihuang'). Private individual land ownership expanded and prevailed as the Qin system was replicated in all the newly captured areas that once belonged to the defeated kingdoms.

To sum up, by the establishment of the Qin Empire, China had moved a long way from the Shang in terms of socio-economic structure and institu-tions. In particular, with the rise of the Qin, Shang Yang's reform package had a profound impact on the making of the Chinese socio-economic structure: it provided the first workable model for the trinary equilibrium to function (see Sadao 1978: 547). Therefore, the establishment of the trinary structure was the result of a long period of military struggle between the agricultural tribes/states and non- or semi-agricultural tribes/state during the turbulent late Shang (eleventh and tenth centuries BC) and the Warring States (475–221 BC). The Zhou and Qin states were both establishments of agro-centric militarism. During the Shang Period when a mixed economy prevailed, physiocracy was at best an exception, not the rule. During the Zhou the tables were turned. After a relatively short period of the dominance of a mixed economy during the Warring States, the establishment of the Qin Empire marked a long era in which the dominance of a mixed economy became an exception, not the norm.

Here four points can be made. First, no matter how productive farming appeared, this was not a sufficient condition for the ancient Chinese to adhere rigidly to it. Second, agricultural favouritism was not a sheer technology-based choice for production but rather an institution which combined eco-nomic and political interests and incentives, and natural endowments. Third, the entrenchment of agricultural dominance was not a God-given practice but the result of an institutional choice through long-lasting violent conflicts among different competing groups. Finally, military power played a crucial role in the shaping of the macro, cross-regional economy on the East Asian mainland.

This is not to say, however, that military power and conquest were solely responsible for the making of the Chinese 'pan-agrarian' economy. Nor does it mean that a military group was able, of its own free will, to change the economy. Military power was a necessary but not a sufficient condition to convert much of the empire to a farming zone. Other conditions included endowments such as geographic locations, climatic patterns and soil types at the very least. Military power becomes critical in the choice of an economic system (production, distribution and consumption) when the same geographic locations, climatic patterns and soil types allow various types of economy to flourish, be it farming, pastoralism or trade. What the military power did in the Zhou and Qin periods was, through coercion, to lower the opportunity costs incurred from other choices. Such military power-based choice did not always work, the best examples in Chinese history being the Northern and Southern Dynasties (AD 420–581) and the Mongol Yuan (AD 1271–1368). The former period was marked by a time of warfare and schism during which China was broken into pieces by nomadic invaders from the north and west (Elvin 1973: 44). The Xianbei, one of the 'Five Barbarian Tribes' (*wuhu*), conquered north China and established the Northern Wei in AD 386. In the process, agriculture in the North fell into ruin: production was disrupted, farmers killed, and cultivated land abandoned. As the expansion of the Northern Wei ceased, and with it the spoils of war, which had been an important income source for the ruling class, two-thirds of the Xianbei population became idlers. The combination of the decline of farming and exhaustion of the spoils of war resulted in a severe economic crisis. Emperor Xiaowen (r. AD 471–99) was compelled to launch a reform in AD 485 by rebuilding agriculture through re-establishing the landholding and land-owning peasantry (Tang Z. 1956; Elvin 1973: 47–51). During the Mongol invasion of China, a suggestion was made to the Mongolian emperor, Taizong, (Song L. 1371 vol. 153: no. 146) that 'Since the Chinese are useless to our cause, they should be killed off so that their land can be converted to grazing land.' Such a plan was carried out in the occupied regions. After their 40-year-long campaign against China, the Mongols finally conquered the whole of China in AD 1279. During and after the campaign, millions of Chinese were killed or captured to be slaves or serfs (*quding*); vast agrarian areas were enclosed as grazing land; horses belonging to the Chinese were confiscated, and horse-raising was forbidden in Chinese communities; autumn tillage for the second crop was forbidden in the North so that the land could be used for grazing after the summer harvest (Wang Q. 1586; Perkins 1969: 23–4, 197–9; ZNK 1984 vol. 2: 51–3; Zheng X. *et al.* 1984: 242–4, 254–5). This policy of transforming the Chinese agrarian economy was stopped only because of the loss of revenue, at the suggestion of Yelü Chucai, a high-ranking courtier of Persian origin (Wright and Twitchett 1962: 19–20, 189–216). So, military power-based choice was highly conditional: the military ruler had only a limited number of choices. This is particularly so when the economy was not at a crossroads but on a well-set-up developmental path simply because a crossroads economy had less resistance than one following a path, owing to the differences in opportunity costs, a phenomenon known as 'path dependency' (see Mokyr 1990: ch. 7; Rosenberg 1994: pt 1). This was because of the opportunity costs induced by the existing patterns of economic activities including resource allocation, skills and technology. In a crossroads economy, choices bore more or less equal weight because of the similar opportunity costs for those choices. In a well-established economy, the opportunity cost for resuming the same pattern was often the lowest. So, it was rational to go for the old path unless the old pattern faced a major crisis and thus lowered the opportunity costs for a change to take place.

In this context, early China was far less static and far less homogeneous than one might think; and consequently, adopting this choice was far less straightforward and far less smooth than one might imagine. From the invention of settled farming to the invention of the trinary structure, the Chinese saga began as a random process and became convergent much later. To a great extent, the success story of the agriculture-based civilisation in China really began in the Zhou Period.

From the above analysis, even if the early choice of settled agriculture among the proto-Chinese was spontaneous owing to the returns yielded from tillage, the rise of the communal land property rights (under the Zhou chessboard-field system) and household and individual land property rights (under the Qin privatisation scheme) and the establishment of an agro-centric government on the East Asian mainland were certainly not a 'natural' process. They were the result of bloody wars among rival units and violence-backed policing. Considering that the agrarian states were able to manoeuvre resources effectively in their military build-ups, their victory seemed inevitable. After all, it is a game of the quality of the military machine. Throughout history, this Chinese peasant army usually proved to be as effective as the nomads, the main exception being the Tartar–Mongol joint invasion in the eleventh and twelfth centuries.

### 3.2.2 Nature of the change

Regarding the origin of the trinary structure, much of the credit should go to the Legalist School which helped, by deliberate policy, to create a competitive environment for the Chinese to try out different structures and institutions. It is not completely surprising that the structure/institution that emerged victorious from the most severe competition, lasting five centuries, was able to overshadow China for the entire life span of the Empire – two millennia – in spite of the fact that the Legalists' short-term goal was merely the survival of those political units.

Confucianism had very little input in forming this structure. Having great difficulty in obtaining high office in the entire Spring and Autumn–Warring States Period, Confucius and his disciples were at best lobbyists and were never associated with any reform. Indeed, Confucians were blacklisted by reformers. Shang Yang treated Confucianism as heterodoxy and had Confucian books banned to reduce resistance from the public. Even worse, on his way to the unification of China, Qin Shihuang not only had Confucian books destroyed but had Confucians buried alive as well, an incident called *fenshu kengru*. This was mainly because the conciliatory voice of Confucianism was out of tune with wartime politics. Not until the Han Period (206 BC–AD 220), when the era of aggressive and extensive Legalist reforms was over, was Confucianism adapted to serve the winning structure, for its conciliatory nature was able to reduce the tension within the framework. Confucianism and Legalism played distinctly different roles at different times and they exchanged their positions accordingly between heterodoxy and orthodoxy.

### 3.2.3 *Immediate impact of the change on society*

In this context, it is easy to understand why the merchant class had a raw deal later on: they and their protectors were defeated and subjugated first by the Zhou and then by the Qin, in spite of the fact that the pro-commercial states seemed to be stronger than the pro-agricultural states either in terms of suzerainty (Shang) or sheer number (six states in the Warring States Period). The distaste for merchants and their activities was thus rooted in discontent with Shang's mercantile rule, which was characterised by the ruling class's extravagant lifestyle, and exploitation, robbery and suppression of the farming regions in north China. As losers, the merchants were abased sharply, as proved to be the case in the later history of China too. This is simply because although the wars were over, the disgrace of the merchant class was deliberately maintained in the best interest of the winning party. When one considers the fact that the Chinese word for 'trade' and 'traders' is identical with that for 'the defeated Shang tribe', it must indeed have been a dirty word in post-Shang times. Indeed, the policy of promoting farming and confining trade served as a reminder to these defeated merchants. At this point, it is worth noting also that the Zhou used 'funerary horses with carts' not only on a much larger scale than did the Shang but also with a strong implication of horse massacres instead of animal sacrifice for purely ceremonial purposes. For example, the burial pit (5 m × 215 m) unearthed in Zibo (118°2 E, 36° 41′ N), Shandong Province, contains as many as 600 horses, enough for 150 chariots of that time. Given that there were 1,000 such chariots with 4,000 horses in the Zhou army, the horses sacrificed were equivalent to 15 per cent of the army's total (Chen 1984). A more recent discovery at Fufeng County (107°17′ E, 34°10′ E) of Shaanxi Province unveiled the chilling fact that some 100 adult male horses were pushed into a burial pit 12 m deep and were badly injured before being buried alive (Wang Z. and Bian J. 1996). It is almost certain that the Zhou punished horses because the Shang loved them. Although the practice of horse massacres during the Zhou sounds irrational, it makes sense in the context of the Zhou's repression of Shang mercantilism since the horse was a symbol of the Shang merchant power and activities. This is further supported by the Zhou chessboard-field system (*jingtianzhi*), a system which was designed to plug loopholes by which the merchants could rise by locking the population into farming. The raw deal for the merchant class in post-Zhou China was to some extent like anti-Semitism towards Jews in medieval and early modern Western Europe (for the French peasant attitude towards the Jews, see Burns 1984: 131, 136–7, 140–1, 151, 160–4). The main difference was that the Chinese merchants had only a class identity while the Jews had both a class and an ethnic identity.

The psychological burden together with the political pressure seems to have been too great for the merchant class to shake off, which explains at least three phenomena in Chinese history: (1) why Chinese merchants, sometimes ridiculously wealthy, seldom challenged the state's power by, for example, building castles and establishing private armies on China's soil to protect their interests, although there were no financial nor technological difficulties for them in undertaking such tasks; (2) why Chinese merchant diasporas have done better outside Chinese territory ever since archaic times (Deng 1997: chs 3–4); and (3) why individual merchants felt safe only after joining other social groups. Typically, the younger generation of the merchant households tried to enter officialdom through Confucian education and the Imperial Examinations while the merchants themselves were always ready to invest in land to join the rankes of the landholders.

The weakness of the merchant class can be seen more clearly from the striking difference in how the peasantry reacted to the coercionary state. When Emperor Qin Shihuang uprooted large numbers of merchants with their parents and offspring from their urban bases to the frontiers (*zheshu*, literally 'exile on military services'), he did so without too many difficulties (Sima Q. 91 BC: ch. 'Biography of Emperor Qin Shihuang'). It was a completely different matter when he began to treat 'settled commoners' (*lüzuo*, literally 'residents under the neighbourhood registration') the same way: unlike the defeated merchants, these commoners, mainly peasants, revolted and overthrew his dynasty (*ibid.*; see also Ban G. AD 82: ch. 'Biography of Cao Cuo'). Although the ruled class itself, the peasantry was far more confident in resisting pressure from above. This is repeatedly shown by the history of peasant armed rebellions in China. So, we need to trace the innate weakness of the merchants as a class back to these historic defeats rather than just looking at the timeless policy of 'promoting farming and confining trade' at its face value.

## 3.3 Equilibrium as a pursued status

### 3.3.1 *Variables and terms for the equilibrium*

From a conventional approach, an economic system can be expressed as a production function with many variables. For example, a production function for a premodern economy, or any economy, can be written as: $Q = f(L, K, R, T, I, G, \cdots)$ where $Q$ is the total output; $L$, labour inputs; $K$, capital inputs; $R$, resource endowments (including land and climatic patterns); $T$, technology; $I$, social institutions; $G$, government policies; and so forth. The objective was to generate maximal total output. Such an approach is very useful but will not suit the purpose of the present study, which emphasises the interrelationships among the variables rather than the relationship between the total output and the variables. Also, the interrelationships are viewed as conditions for an equilibrium, not as inputs. Thus, a different approach is needed. So, instead of dealing with variables, the present study pays more attention to terms for a general equilibrium, written as:

$$F = f(x, y, z) \tag{3.1}$$

where $F$ can be defined as the objective function for social harmony under the trinary structure. Under such a harmony, utility maximisation or near-maximisation can be realised individually or collectively in society. To reach utility maximisation is thus to reach the maximum of $F$. The trinary variables in the function are: (1) $x$ – the proportion of agricultural output in GDP as the index of agricultural dominance in the economy; (2) $y$ – the proportion of rural population in the total population as an index of the size of the peasantry; and (3) $z$ – the proportion of funds to assist agriculture out of total government economic expenditure as an index of physiocratic policies.

It needs little explanation that the rural population was the overwhelming majority in premodern China, amounting to between 79 per cent and 93.1 per cent of the total in different periods, the long-term average estimated as being 86.6 per cent of the total (Chao 1986: ch. 3; see also Feuerwerker 1984: 299, 302, 312–13). So, the value of $y$ is known. In Chinese history over the long term (till the first half of the nineteenth century) there were few cases in which commercial projects were financed by government. Although the state did provide services (such as the distribution and redistribution of state land, construction and maintenance of irrigation and water control systems, famine relief schemes and the establishment of agricultural colonies), data concerning government expenditures on agriculture are not available. Thus, it is difficult to know the size of agriculture-related funds/investment in the total government economic expenditure (the value of $z$). Likewise, apart from population size and government taxation, the agricultural output as a proportion of GDP (the value of $x$) is unknown.

Alternatively, the proportion of agricultural tax revenue in the total government revenue can be taken as an index of agricultural dominance in the economy, and the reciprocal of the rate of agricultural tax can serve as an index of physiocratic policies. The function becomes:

$$F = f(u, y, w) \tag{3.2}$$

where $u$ is the proportion of the tax revenue from agriculture, and $w$ stands for $1/R$ ($R > 0$), $R$ being the tax rate. Among these three variables, $u$ and $w$ need some explanation. If the main source of the tax revenue is agriculture, the economy is very likely to be dominated by agriculture. As the majority of the Chinese population consisted of peasants, household tax (*hufu* or *hudiao*) and poll tax (*kofu* or *dingyin*) were mainly from rural communities. Moreover, sometimes the Chinese government deliberately combined household or poll tax with land tax, good examples being the 'two seasonal taxes' (*liangshui fa*) in the Tang Dynasty, the 'combined tax and corvée in one' (*yitiaobian fa*, literally 'one-whip method for tax and corvée') in 1581 under the Ming Dynasty and the 'poll tax from land' (*tanding rudi*) in the Qing. Such treatment shows how closely household/poll tax and land tax were related, which suggests that the majority of households owned land. Moreover, agricultural tax was often dealt with by the Bureau of Agriculture (*sinong*), the very organisation which was also in charge of the promotion of agricultural production (Zhou B. 1981: 183). In addition, household tax and poll tax were often collected in kind: silk or hemp products, which were the typical household products in rural China. This shows how the agricultural sector dictated the types of tax revenue received by the state. All these reveal the actual weight of the agricultural sector in the economy. Again, although data are lacking, there is little doubt that the tax revenue from the agricultural sector was the main source of government revenue in premodern China (see Murphey 1954: 358).

### 3.3.2 Terms for the equilibrium

Hypothetically, in a state of 'general equilibrium', the critical values $x$, $y$, and $z$ (or $u$, $y$, $w$) at which the function is optimised are found by setting the first-order partial derivatives equal to zero and solving simultaneously:

$$F_x = F_y = F_z = 0 \tag{3.3}$$

Or,

$$F_u = F_y = F_w = 0 \tag{3.4}$$

And hence:

$$dF = \frac{\partial F}{\partial x}dx + \frac{\partial F}{\partial y}dy + \frac{\partial F}{\partial z}dz = 0 \tag{3.5}$$

Or,

$$dF = \frac{\partial F}{\partial u}du + \frac{\partial F}{\partial y}dy + \frac{\partial F}{\partial w}dw = 0 \tag{3.6}$$

Such a trinary equilibrium can be partially illustrated in a three-dimensional diagram in which a vertex is reached at point e (see Figure 3.4).

If time is taken into account to make the equilibrium more dynamic, a constraining function $g(x, y, z)$ or $g(u, y, w)$ can be added. A new function can then be formed by setting the constraint equal to zero, multiplying it by the Lagrangian multiplier $\pi$, and adding the product to the original function. Thus

$$F(x, y, z) = f(x, y, z) + \pi g(x, y, z) \tag{3.7}$$

Or,

$$F(u, y, w) = f(u, y, w) + \pi g(u, y, w) \tag{3.8}$$

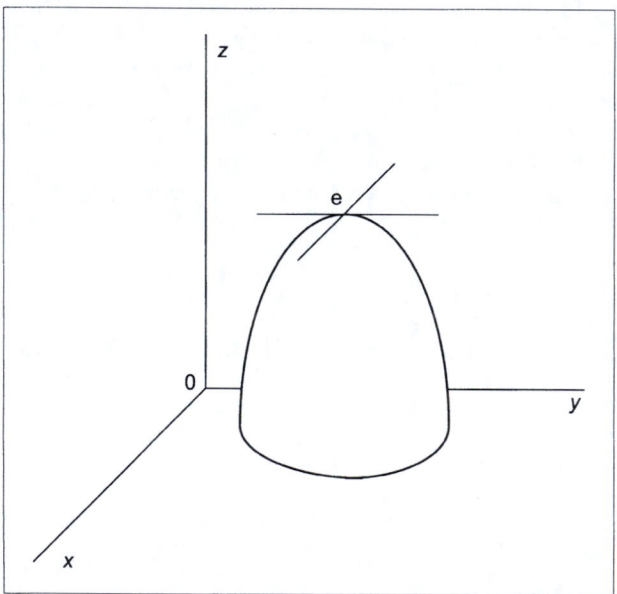

*Figure 3.4* The trinary equilibrium

The critical values $x$, $y$, $z$, (or $u$, $y$, $w$) and $\pi$, at which the function is optimised, are found by setting the first-order partial derivatives equal to zero and solving simultaneously:

$$F_x = F_y = F_z = F_\pi = 0 \tag{3.9}$$

Or,

$$F_u = F_y = F_w = F_\pi = 0 \tag{3.10}$$

### 3.3.3 Tension within the structure

In reality, the trinary equilibrium was by no means a nirvana. Its establishment and maintenance were highly conditional. Internal tension came from two interlocking factors; (1) land accessibility to private individual land ownership versus limited supply of land; and (2) peasant interest versus government and landlord rent-seeking.

The tension derived from several constraints. The first such constraint was land availability: only when land was readily available could land ownership be materialised to satisfy a growing population. Land constraint in land supply included both absolute shortage of land and relative shortage of land. The former was the physical limit of land supply on earth; the latter, the distribution of the land among the farmers. The second constraint was the maintenance of the minimal real income, or ultimately, the minimal food availability to individuals in society. Unlike the ancient Roman Empire, which provided free food to her citizens with full rights, the majority of the citizens of the Chinese Empire had to feed themselves from the establishment of private individual land ownership during the Spring and Autumn Period onwards, except during famines. On the other hand, the invention of the centralised bureaucracy resulted in government taxation, which had to be extracted from households' income in the zero-sum game fashion. Thus, the food issue in traditional China often took the form of tax régime and tax burden. In particular, the Chinese peasantry was extremely sensitive and responsive to state taxation because it was the single most important external determinant in relation to individual real income measured by food at the end of each production cycle (mainly the yearly agricultural harvest). In other words, through the link of real income in food, taxation and tax burden these became internalised in the household economy of ordinary Chinese. This taxation–real income correlation in turn made the tax burden a tangible and accurate gauge with which to measure government performance: a good government would benefit the Chinese population with light tax and/or exemption of tax to secure food availability to ordinary citizens (for tax exemption rates during the Ming–Qing Period, see Will 1990: 245). Moreover, the uniformity of state taxation in the Chinese Empire made a simultaneous, nationwide judgement of government performance an easy task for ordinary citizens at the grass-roots level. Later on, we will see that such a mechanism is the key to understanding simultaneous mass rebellions in China's long history.

The third constraint was competition for resources from other sectors of the economy. This was closely associated with social mobility (see Eberhard 1962; Ho 1962; Hsu 1965). Apart from an excessively rent-seeking state, which often harmed agriculture as well as the peasantry, the dominant position of the agricultural sector in the economy could be undermined, as sometimes happened, by competition from growing industrial and service sectors, a situation which was also incompatible with the physiocratic policies of the government. Moreover, as sometimes happened, alienation of the peasantry could take place when a large number of free landholding peasants either lost their land under the pressure of taxation and personal debts or voluntarily gave up their farming profession for better returns from flourishing commerce, a situation which weakened agricultural dominance and challenged physiocratic administration.

### 3.3.4 Evidence of the equilibrium reached

The maintenance of an equilibrium was a harder question. Constraints, tensions and crises from either area could cause the system to collapse. Remarkably, the structure survived for two thousand years. So, an equilibrium did exist. This equilibrium was not just a product of the imagination: it existed in the long-term history of premodern China. The most telling evidence for the equilibrium reached is the existence of the dynastic cycle and the periodic 'piping times of great peace and prosperity', or Golden Ages (*taiping shengshi*) (see Shen Y. 1994).

In his cycle model, Fairbank rightly pointed out that the Chinese Empire was stable in terms of the duration of the major dynasties (Fairbank 1965: ch. 4; Fairbank and Reischaver 1979: 71). More precisely, the Zhou ruled China for some 774 years (including both the Western and Eastern, *c.* 1030–256 BC); the Western Han, 230 years (206 BC–AD 24); the Eastern Han, 195 years (AD 25–220); the Tang, 289 years (AD 618–907); the Northern and Southern Songs, 167 and 152 respectively (960–1279); the Ming emperors reigned for 276 years (1368–1644) and the Manchus, 267 years (1644–1911). These major dynasties reigned in China for more than twenty-three centuries, about 80 per cent of post-Shang history (1030 BC–1911). The essence of this cycle model is the lasting stability of the Chinese Empire.

In each dynasty, there was a period that constituted a Golden Age. The first recorded such period occurred in the Western Zhou Dynasty (*c.* 1030–771 BC), as 'Under the reign of King Cheng and King Kang, great peace prevailed and order was maintained without corporal punishment for forty years' (Li M. *et al.* 1990: 64). During the Han, from Emperor Huidi (r. 194–188 BC) to Emperors Wendi (r. 179–157 BC) and Jingdi (r. 156–141 BC) people were free from tax burden for over sixty years. As a result, population increased dramatically; the government granaries were so little used that the stored grain became rotten; and money in the Treasury was not spent for so long that the threads of coins decayed. After Emperor Aidi (r. 6–1 BC) was crowned the Palace and Treasury were full, ordinary people became wealthy. Although the economy was not as good as under the Emperors Wendi and Jingdi, population reached a record level (Zhou B. 1981: 71, 73).

Such stability also existed in short-lived régimes. For instance, the Sui Dynasty (AD 581–618) has been regarded as a very unpopular régime, known for heavy taxation and hopeless corruption and power abuse. However, in the first 25 years of the dynasty, between AD 581 and 606, the society enjoyed prolonged peace, and population increased in spite of the country being hit many times by floods and droughts. The annual event of transferring the collected goods from taxation through Tongguan in Henan Province and Puban in Hebei Province to the capital occupied the main roads day and night for several months. The official report in AD 592 said that the Treasury and granaries were all full and a new storage depot was built to take in the goods (Zhou B. 1981: 190–1).

This great peace and prosperity were based on the trinary equilibrium, a status which not only impressed European visitors (such as Marco Polo in the thirteenth century and the Jesuit commissionaires after the seventeenth century) but also qualified China as a model for Europe to follow in as late as the eighteenth century (Maverick 1946).

The Golden Ages had several aspects in common: prosperous agriculture, a contented peasantry, good government and peace. For general historians the signs of a Golden Age also include a stable territory, flourishing scholarship and arts, improved social welfare with an increase in public works, and the limitation of taxes (see Wright 1957: 43–4; see also Feuerwerker 1976). For economic historians, the signs are slightly different, including: (1) stable food prices, (2) abundance in government granaries, (3) a light tax burden, and (4) an increased population.

Here, a question emerges: if the equilibrium was periodical, what was the mechanism by which the society returned to the equilibrium after major dislocation of the trinary structure cause by shocks and disturbances such as demographic pressure, unchecked commercialisation and alien invasions/conquests? In other words, why and how did China return to its 'norm' after the system cracked and had a chance to change itself? Crucial to an understanding of the Chinese past, this issue will be dealt with step by step in Chapters 4, 5 and 6.

## 3.4 Intra-equilibria

The critical question about the trinary equilibrium is not only how to keep the balance among those counterpoises, but also how to keep the balance within each counterpoise. Such balances, which can be defined as intra-equilibria, are equally important to the trinary equilibrium.

### 3.4.1 Fragmentation and concentration in landholding and landowning

#### 3.4.1.1 The Chinese dilemma

Keeping a balance between private individual land ownership and land concentration was not an issue under feudalism since individual land ownership and the market transaction of land were largely absent. Primogeniture perpetuated inequality in landholding and landowning and thus in the feudal system. As long as the feudal class was in control of socio-economic life, stability was to be expected.

In contrast, such a balance was needed in China to make the trinary equilibrium work. But a balance like that was not to be obtained with ease: the absence of primogeniture made it much harder to achieve the development of private land ownership and a real market in real estate, stability or equilibrium. On the one hand, wealth did not beget more wealth because of the land-splitting process caused by the practice of equal inheritance of land among sons (Cipolla 1970: 275), a tradition which dates back as far as the Xia Dynasty (c. 2000–1520 BC), initially within the upper class (see Li M. et al. 1990: 37). The danger with equal inheritance was that with population growth landholding would become smaller and smaller with a bias towards labour-intensive farming (for the French case see Hohenberg 1972: 233). Once the landholding shrank below the minimal size, the livelihood of an owner–farmer was jeopardised. On the other hand, owing to the market mechanism, land was transferred from one group to another and land concentration was often the result: from as early as the Warring States Period (475–221 BC), landowners had freedom to transfer properties (Zhou B. 1989: 49). Because of that, in traditional China, it has been said, land could hardly remain in the same family for more than two or three generations (Cipolla 1970: 275). Although exaggerated, this statement does show the common practice in the Chinese economy. Most land transactions were implemented through the market in peaceful times, and outside the market in troubled times. No matter by what means, once such transactions took place on a large scale, the stability of a landholding and landowning peasantry was undermined: a land tycoon class emerged, as well as a landless tenant class. With a functional property market, such a process was indeed inevitable. Obviously, if a great many farmers lost their land, free peasantry-based agriculture would not last. However, such alienation did not occur in the long term: throughout Chinese history, a balance between private individual land ownership and land concentration was maintained (for a comparison see Appendix H).

### 3.4.1.2 Stability in landholding and landowning

Therefore, the answer to whether the Chinese smallholding system itself was able to survive and be maintained in the long run is affirmative. This is shown in Table 3.1. The probability for stability is 25 per cent (6.25% × 4, at the northwestern quadrant), and so is instability (6.25% × 4, at the southeastern quadrant). Semi-stability accounts for 50 per cent (6.25% × 8, at both the northeastern and southwestern quadrants). In all, there is a 75 per cent chance for China's land-ownership situation to be manageable. Most interestingly, this 75 per cent was roughly the proportion of landowners in society over the long term, which can hardly be accidental. The probability for China to have prevailing state land ownership against ownership by small farmers (category III) or prevailing large landholdings (category IV) is at maximum 25 per cent. Therefore, it is groundless to assume that the Chinese system was unstable in nature. Quite the opposite.

This stability is confirmed by empirical evidence. First, in Ming–Qing China land accumulation and concentration was a very slow process (Chao 1981: 727). Second, during the period 1481–1640 under the Ming, the price of paddy land in south China remained fairly stable within the range of 8.4–10 *liang* of silver (313.3–373.0 grams) per *mu* (or 4,475.7–5,328.6 grams per hectare (*ibid.*: 728) in spite of the onslaught of the price revolution which caused food price to double (see Appendix B). This

*Table 3.1* Stability in China's land-ownership types

| A \ C  \ B |  I | II | III | IV |
|------|------|------|------|------|
| I | stable 6.25% | stable 6.25% | semi-stable 6.25% | semi-stable 6.25% |
| II | stable 6.25% | stable 6.25% | semi-stable 6.25% | semi-stable 6.25% |
| III | semi-stable 6.25% | semi-stable 6.25% | unstable 6.25% | unstable 6.25% |
| IV | semi-stable 6.25% | semi-stable 6.25% | unstable 6.25% | unstable 6.25% |

*Note*

A, Status of land-ownership types; B, Trend of change in land-ownership types; C, Result. I, Prevailing small and middle landholdings; II, prevailing state land ownership in favour of small farmers; III, prevailing state land-ownership against small farmers; IV, prevailing large landholdings. The percentages are the chances for events to take place.

implies that an increase in paddy yield level offset the inflationary effect of the price revolution. Third, during 1641–81, when Manchuria was not yet open to peasant immigration and new arable land was largely unavailable, the price of paddy land in south China dropped steadily by 44 per cent. It took about ninety years for the nominal land price to recover its 1641 level (*ibid.*: 728–9), which was much slower than the recovery speed of China's population after the wars at the end of the Ming and the beginning of the Qing. If the inflationary effect of the price revolution is taken into account, it was not until 1821 that the real price of paddy land recovered (*ibid.*).

### 3.4.1.3 Measures, macro socio-economic instruments and China's track record

In theory, stability in landholding and landowning can be achieved through the manipulation or neutralisation of market forces. The Chinese did just that. Interference from the Chinese values and government policies retarded the 'natural' process of alienation.

First, individual peasants were always reluctant to sell their land. The worst thing that could happen to a Chinese rural household was to become landless, a situation which was described in Chinese literature as 'no room for a tile above head, and no room for a needle under feet' (*shangwu pianwa, xiawu lizhuizhidi*). Losing land was considered an economic disaster. Such reluctance served as a conscious check on land sale.

Second, government rescue projects often provided the poor and land-hungry with low-interest loans and land allotments. With the cheap loans, the poor did not have to sell their land. Also, land allotment helped the landless regain their position straight away. The conditions for such policies were: (1) that the government had enough resources for the loans either in cash or in kind; (2) that land was available at the government's disposal; and (3) that the government was efficient in detecting peasant financial difficulties and in implementing the above tasks. Fortunately, the Chinese state often had resources against famine and other shortages (see, for example, Will 1990: pts 2–3 and Appendix A). Fresh or unclaimed land was created by wars and internal colonisation; and the Chinese bureaucracy was powerful enough to carry out those salvation tasks. The best example of government loans were those under the 'green sprout loan scheme' (*qingmiaofa*) under the administration of Wang Anshi (AD 1021–86): cheap loans were made available to the needy peasants to cover difficult periods of temporary shortage when the new crop was still in the blade and the old one was all consumed (Wu H. 1984). Allotment of state-controlled land to able-bodied citizens with no discrimination across the country was originated in the Western Han Period (206 BC – 24 BC), standardised in the Northern Wei Period (AD 386–534), and inherited by the Sui and Tang dynasties (AD 581–618 and 618–907, respectively) (Zhou B. 1981: 151–69, 193, 195, 198–201). Government land redistribution took two dimensions: (1) during peaceful times, it was through organised internal emigration of peasants from land-hungry regions (*xiaxiang*) to land-abundant regions (*kuanxiang*); (2) immediately after wars, it was through the establishment of agricultural colonies in prewar agricultural regions or newlyconquered lands where unclaimed land (*wuzhudi*) became available.

Third, in terms of market manipulation, the trade of land properties was targeted and restricted by government: land trade was, from time to time, either forbidden or controlled by the authorities. For instance, according to laws under both the New Régime *xinzheng*, during the Eastern Han Period (AD 9–23) and the Jin Dynasty (AD 265–420), sale of land allotments under the 'king's land scheme' (*wangtianzhi*) and 'land equalisation scheme' (*juntianzhi*) were not allowed (Zhou B. 1981: 116, 145–6). Moreover, marginal land was brought into cultivation to increase the supply of land. By Song times, the cultivation of marginal land had gone so far that not only were hillsides and river banks regularly tilled but also plots were created on wooden rafts floating on lakes (see Chen F. 1149). Furthermore, there was a ramification of property rights on land estates as discussed in Section 2.2.3.

These measures effectively offset both land concentration (which was caused by the market mechanism) and land fragmentation (which resulted from the Chinese equal inheritance system). Up to the end of the Qing Dynasty, the free landholding and landowning peasantry remained largely intact in spite of the fact that the Chinese population multiplied while the cultivated land area shrank (Deng 1993a: ch. 6). To a great extent, the credit should go to the political power in China, which from time to time overrode the market on behalf of the public interest.

However, this does not mean that land-shortage crises did not occur in premodern China. They did. But in most cases such a crisis was local and of short duration. If the crisis became universal, the economy moving away from an equilibrium, society sometimes approached the critical point for the peasantry to respond with mass insurrections. To re-obtain their land and social status, the Chinese peasantry did not hesitate to resort to radical means of 'expropriating local tyrants and distributing their land among the poor' (*datuhao fentiandi*), as echoed in Mao's writings (Mao 1967 vol. 1: 23–59, 87–90). The paramount goal of the peasantry was to restore the timeless trinary equilibrium in the empire.

In this context, all sorts of symbols were used by the peasantry for armed insurrections, including the Taoist 'five decilitre grain charity' (*wudoumi jiao*) in Han (206 BC–AD 220) and Jin (AD 265–420) times, the Buddhist 'white lotus' (*bailianjiao*) in Yuan (1271–1368) and Ming times (1368–1644), and the Christian 'Heavenly Kingdom of Great Peace' (*taiping tianguo*) in Qing times (1644–1911) (see Appendix J). Therefore, Marxism–Stalinism–Maoism was just another sign-board for the rebellious peasantry, who could not care less about the 'isms'. What they cared about was 'every farmer having his own land to till' (*gengzhe youqitian*).[1]

Nevertheless, in spite of the fact that the proportion of landlords in China's total population is unknown, it is known that in premodern China landless farmers occupied only a small proportion of the rural population throughout Chinese history. So, in a long battle between land amalgamation caused by market forces and equal land allocation resulting from government intervention to protect small landholding farmers, a long-term equilibrium of landholding existed (Li J. 1957: ch. 7; 1962: chs 8–10, 16; Fan W. 1964–5: *passim*; Fu Z. and Wang Y. 1982: chs 4, 11; Zheng X. *et al.* 1984; Gao M. 1987).

### 3.4.2 State power and official corruption

#### 3.4.2.1 Uprightness versus kakistocracy

After Emperor Qin Shihuang (r. 221–210 BC) had unified China and established a centralised governing structure consisting of the monarch and the bureaucracy, the 'power–corruption' correlation began to haunt Chinese politics. Corruption and power abuse occurred at all levels of the bureaucratic institutions: from head of state at the top to district officials at the bottom. This gives the impression that China was a haven for corruption, which raises the crucial question of how to keep a balance between state power and official corruption. This was critical to maintain the trinary equilibrium.

No doubt the state in China was corruptible. However, every régime also had to face the choice between a combination of a high degree of corruption/power abuse and a short-lived reign, and a combination of a low degree of corruption/power abuse and a long-lasting reign, as shown in the following formula:

$$t = a + \frac{b}{K} \quad (a \geq 0;\ b > 0;\ K > 0) \tag{3.11}$$

where $t$ is the length of time for a régime to rule the country, $a$ and $b$ are constants and $K$ is the degree of corruption and power abuse. Other conditions having been equal, if a régime wanted to last, it had to control corruption and power abuse. In other words, if a good government represented the long-term interests of the ruling clique, while corruption and power abuse stood only for the short-term interests, it was rational to control $K$ if the survival of the régime was the aim.

This reveals the truth behind the seeming paradox in Chinese history: the centralised political structure generated enormous power and thus had an irresistible tendency towards corruption/power abuse, but the empire was one of the longest-lasting institutions in world history. The question is:

although corruption/power abuse repeatedly brought the end of régimes, why did the Chinese Empire *per se* not die of corruption/power abuse? Obviously, the Chinese system allowed corruption and power abuse ($K$) to exist. Or, more correctly, it had room for such abuse ($K > 0$). On the other hand, to survive, China also had some kind of built-in mechanism to check corruption/power abuse. Thus, the problem was not whether corruption/power abuse was allowed, but how to keep a balance between uprightness and kakistocracy. Within the ruling clique of premodern China, there existed two parties vulnerable to corruption/power abuse: the monarch on the one hand, and the bureaucracy on the other. Under an interlocking surveillance structure (*jian-cha*), the Chinese system allowed one party to become corrupt at any given time. If the other party was still 'clean', corruption/power abuse was controlled at a manageable level. Certainly, the two parties might become corrupt at the same time, but statistically the chances of this happening were not great. Therefore, although China was far from having been a corruption-free zone and was known for numerous notoriously unscrupulous dynasts and officials, nevertheless the empire survived for millennia. Much of the credit should go to the effectiveness of China's self-regulating system: in the long term, a balance was kept between good administration and corruption/power abuse. Excessively rent-seeking kakistocracy, also known as the 'predatory state', was not the mainstream. This was the main reason why the country remained a unified entity for most of the time in the long run. To suppose that the probability of having an uncorrupt monarch is 50 per cent and so is that of having an uncorrupt bureaucracy, the chance of having a full stability is 25 per cent ($50\% \times 50\%$, quadrant I). The chance of having semi-stability is 50 per cent ($25\% \times 2$, quadrants II and IV). This gives the system a 75 per cent chance of staying stable. This is illustrated in Figure 3.5.

This insight challenges Leon Stover's 'alternative view' that China was such a custom-dominated society that the monarch was no more than a prisoner of the society (see Stover 1974). The Chinese monarch did have a range of choices and played a significant role in the socio-political and economic equilibrium.

### 3.4.2.2 China's track record

The best examples of unchecked corruption/power abuse and excessive rent-seeking in China's history are the Qin Period under Emperor Shihuang and the late Sui Period under Emperor Yang (r. AD 605–617). It was recorded in the *History of the Han Dynasty*:

> In ancient times the corvée burden had been no more than three days per annum and the government still had sufficient labour supply.... The Qin Dynasty broke the norm by imposing multiple corvée services on the people: the alternate monthly corvée for the local

prefecture (*gengzu*), the bi-annual military service at the frontier (*shubian*) and the bi-annual corvée for national projects (*liyi*). The total corvée burden was 30 times heavier than before.

(Ban G. AD 82 vol. 24: ch. 'Shihuo Zhi')

From the above information, the Qin corvée burden for each able-bodied male can be estimated as 90 days per year (multiplying three days by 30) for an able-bodied male citizen. Later, under the reign of Emperor Yang (r. AD 605–617), the corvée burden was increased dramatically. In AD 604, several hundred thousand corvée labourers were sent to dig a long defence trench across three provinces. In AD 605, 2 million corvée labourers were employed to build the new capital city of Luoyang; 1 million were employed to build the Grand Canal, and another 10,000 were employed for the emperor's inspection tour along the canal (Fan W. 1964–5 vol. 3: 30–47). In AD 607, 500,000 corvée labourers were employed to extend the national highway. The sheer workload in the construction of the Grand Canal (2,500 km in length) and that of the new highway system (1,500 km long) alone was back-breaking

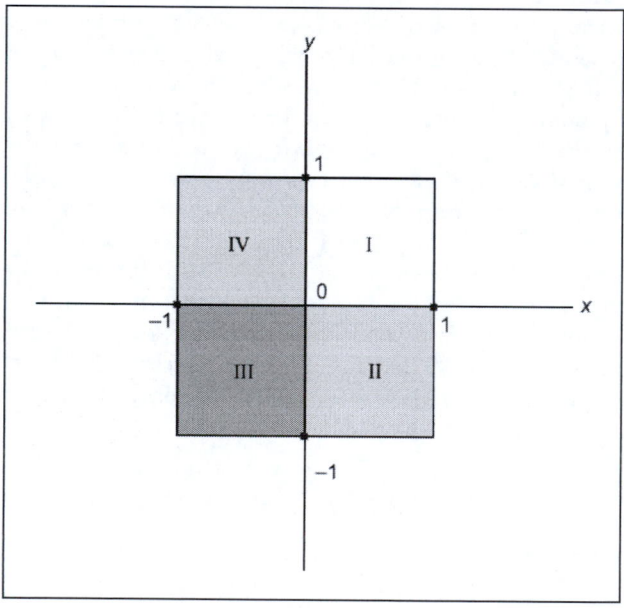

*Figure 3.5* Stability probabilities of the Chinese Empire

Notes

Axes $x$ and $y$ are bureaucracy and the monarch respectively, two key stability determinants in the Chinese system. Situation (1), proper function of $x$ and $y$; situation $(-1)$, malfunction of $x$ and $y$; quadrant I, fully stable zone $(x > 0, y > 0)$; quadrant III, unstable zone $(x < 0, y < 0)$; quadrants II and IV, semi-stable zones $(x > 0 > y, x < 0 < y)$.

for a total of 8.9 million households (for the construction see Han L.F. 1986: 14–15 and Cressey 1934: 24–6; for the population size see Liang F. 1980: 6). If we suppose that the households were all eligible for the tasks, each would be responsible for 0.28 m of the canal and 0.17 m of the highway plus distance travelled and provisions, which would have to be provided by the same population either directly (as in the case of self-provision, commonly practised under the Chinese corvée law) or indirectly (as in the case of government provision which came from a tax on the population).

In the same year, another million corvée labourers were sent to build and maintain the Great Wall; in 608, the number was lower but still significant at the level of 200,000 people (*ibid.*). In addition, from 611 to 614, the emperor launched three wars against Korea. During the wars, large numbers of corvée labourers were employed. In 612, the invading army had 1,133,800 men. Its supporting team consisting of corvée labourers was reported to have twice as many people as the army (*ibid.*). Under Emperor Yang, the average number of corvée labourers for national projects was about 2 million, or 730 million corvée man-days a year. According to the census of AD 609, Sui China had a population of 46,019,956 people in 8,907,546 households (see Liang F. 1980: 6). If all the households were eligible for corvée services, the burden for each household would have been 82 days per annum, which is already very close to the burden under Emperor Qin Shihuang. That was not all. The Sui army had 1–2 million troops and the soldiers were mainly young peasants on corvée under the 'regional recruitment scheme' (*fubing*) (Zhou B. 1981: 184). The military service was thus another 365–730 million man-days. If military service is also taken into account, the total corvée burden in the Sui Dynasty was 1,095–1,460 million man-days per annum. The burden for each household would then have been between 123 and 164 days a year, occupying 34–45 per cent of a man-year. In contrast, during the Northern and Southern Dynasties (AD 420–581), the corvée service was between 20 and 45 days per annum for each able-bodied adult male (Zhou B. 1981: 180–1), the rate being 5.5–12 per cent of the time in a year (365 days) with anaverage of 8.8 per cent of the time in a year. According to an official record, by the time the Sui collapsed, the total grain stock in government possession from taxation was sufficient to feed the country for 50–60 years (Xu T. and Li Y. 1995: 308). This killing burden of corvée and taxation during Qin and Sui times represented an appalling degree of corruption/power abuse. The consequences were the same: these two dynasties were notoriously short-lived.

However, in the long term, China had an impressive track record for maintaining overall socio-political stability. After the Qin, there were only four main periods when the Empire split up and the Chinese lived under more than one government: the Three Kingdoms (AD 220–265), the Northern and Southern Dynasties (AD 420–581), the Five Dynasties (AD 907–60) and the Tartar Jin–Southern Song (1115–1279). These periods totalled 423 years, 20 per cent of the 2,132-year-long life span of the empire (221 BC–AD 1911), slightly lower than the theoretical ratio of 25 per cent. The stability had much to do with government self-regulation to check excessive rent-seeking behaviour. This is evident in the long-term rates of land and household/poll taxes.

The estimation of land tax rate from the Han to the Tang periods is shown in Table 3.2. From the data, the estimated long-term land tax rate is within the range of 0.7–5.2 per cent of a household's grain total output, averaging of 1.6–2.5 per cent. One may argue that the estimated grain output levels were likely to have been those at the top of the rank and thus would make the land tax burden appear lighter than it otherwise would have been. Such a problem can easily be solved by weighing the calculation. For instance, the estimated yield levels can be reduced to half. This makes the tax burden rise to 1.4–10.4 per cent, averaging 5.9 per cent. Even so, the tax burden was still light (see Appendix G).

In Han times, poll tax was imposed at 20 coins (*qian*) for a child and 120 coins for an adult (Zhou B. 1981: 92). During the Jian-an Period (AD 196–219) of the Eastern Han Dynasty the household tax was two bolts (*pi*) of silk cloth and 446 g of silk floss (2 *jin*; 1 Eastern Han *jin* = 223 g) (*ibid.*: 153). During the Western Jin Period (AD 265–316), household tax was 3 bolts of silk cloth and 669 g of silk floss (3 *jin*; 1 Jin *jin* = 223 g) (*ibid.*). During the Northern Dynasties (AD 420–589), under the Song régime (AD 420–79), the household tax was 4 bolts of cloth; under the Liang–Chen régime (AD 520–589), the household tax was about 12.3 m of cloth (5 *zhang*; 1 Liang =

*Table 3.2* Land tax rates from the Han to the Tang periods

| Period | Tax[a] | Converted figure[b] | Land productivity[c] | Rate (%) |
|---|---|---|---|---|
| Eastern Han | 4 | 1.15 | 53.6–80.4 | 1.4–2.1 |
| Eastern Jin | 3 | 0.78 | 79.1–111.1 | 0.7–1.0 |
| Northern Dynasty[d] | 3 | 1.05 | 79.1–111.1 | 0.9–1.3 |
| Sui[d]  (1) | 3 | 1.57 | 75.7–113.6 | 1.4–2.1 |
| (2) | 7.5 | 3.93 | 75.7–113.6 | 3.5–5.2 |
| Tang | 3.3 | 2.42 | 75.7–113.6 | 2.1–3.1 |
| Average | | | | 1.6–2.5 |

*Source*: Based on Liang F. 1980: 7; Zhou B. 1981: 153, 158, 160, 195–6, 198–9; Deng 1993a: 160.

*Notes*

a In *sheng* per *mu*.

b Based on Liang F. 1980: 545, Chao 1986: 66, Deng 1993a: xxv.

c Estimates of land productivity (see Deng 1993a: 160).

d From the Eastern Jin (317–420 AD) to the Northern Dynasties (420–589 AD), the land tax and poll tax were combined at five *shi* (piculs or hectolitre) per male adult a year (Zhou B. 1981: 158, 160); based on this, the tax amount in kind can be estimated as not greater than three *sheng* per *mu*, based on the information that under the long-lasting Land Equalisation System an average of 160.45 *mu* of land area was possessed by each household (Liang F. 1980: 7).

2.45 m) and 42 g of silk floss (3 *liang*; 1 Liang–Chen *liang* = 14 g) (*ibid.*: 159–61). Later, in the Sui Dynasty (AD 581–618), each household in silk- producing regions was taxed 1 bolt of silk cloth plus 125 g of silk floss (3 *liang*; 1 Sui *liang* = 42 g), while in the non-silk-producing regions each household was taxed 1 *pi* of flax cloth plus 2,005 g of flax fibre (3 *jin* 1 Sui *jin* = 668 g) (*ibid.*: 196). In Tang times, the arrangement became 6.2 m of silk cloth (2 *zhang*; 1 Tang *zhang* = 3.11 m) plus 75 g of silk floss (2 *liang*; 1 Tang *liang* = 37 g) or 7.5 m of flax cloth (2.4 *zhang*; 1 Tang *zhang* = 3.11 m) plus 1,791 g of flax fibre (3 *jin*; 1 Tang *jin* = 597 g) (*ibid.*: 198). In AD 769, the Tang government decided to tax households in cash according to nine grades between 500 and 4,000 coins (*wen*) (*ibid.*: 206–7). Owing to the lack of data concerning fibre processing productivity, the household/poll tax rate has remained largely unknown. However, from modern observation, it takes about an hour to weave 2–3 yards (*chi*) of plain cloth 1 yard wide on a traditional loom. The traditional measure of bolts (*pi*) meant either 50 or 100 yards (*chi*), which took between 17–25 and 34–50 hours to weave. The amount of work involved can be estimated, as shown in Table 3.3.

If all the work for hemp growing and processing, mulberry-tree growing, mulberry-leaf picking, silkworm raising and silk processing is taken into account, the figure for work hours is certainly much higher than that for the weaving process only. If we suppose that the work hours of the pre-weaving processes were 5–10 times that of the weaving, the time worked by each family to pay for household tax can be estimated as 12–24 person-days or 24–48 person-days. Moreover, supposing that the average household had two adults and three children, and that each child took a minimum of 0.1 adult workload, the total household adult person-work hours per year can be estimated as 839.5 days (365 days × 2.3). Furthermore, if we suppose that only half of those

*Table 3.3* Estimated weaving hours for household tax from the Han to the Tang periods

| Period | | Cloth (chi) | Modern chi[a] | Work hours[b] | Work days (12 h) |
|---|---|---|---|---|---|
| Eastern Han | | 100–200 | 69.7–139.4 | 27.9–55.8 | 2.3–4.7 |
| Western Jin | | 150–300 | 121.3–242.6 | 48.5–97.0 | 4.0–8.0 |
| Northern | (1) | 200–400 | 158.4–316.8 | 63.4–126.8 | 5.3–10.6 |
| | (2) | 50 | 40 | 16 | 1.3 |
| Sui | | 50–100 | 44.6–89.2 | 17.8–35.6 | 1.5–3.0 |
| Tang | | 20–24 | 19.8–39.6 | 7.9–15.8 | 0.7–1.4 |
| Average | | | 75.6–144.6 | 28.8–57.8 | 2.4–4.8 |

*Source*: Based on Liang F. 1980: 7; Zhou B. 1981: 153, 158, 160, 195–96, 198–99; Deng 1993a: 160.
*Notes*
a Conversion is based on Liang F. 1980: 540–4.
b Based on an average weaving productivity of 2.5 yards per hour.

household total work days (419.8 days) were used for non-grain-growing activities, the rate of household tax can be estimated as between 2.9–5.7 and 5.7–11.4 per cent of a household's total non-grain-growing work days, averaging between 4.3 and 8.6 per cent of those days. This rate is halved if the total number of household work days (839.5) in a year is used as the denominator.

Sometimes land tax and household/poll tax were combined; examples include the 'two seasonal taxes' (*liangshui fa*) of the Tang Dynasty, the 'combined tax and corvée in one' of the Ming Dynasty and the 'poll tax from land' (*tanding rudi*) in the Qing. According to Tang law in AD 769, under the 'two seasonal taxes' the tax collected was 7–11 litres (*sheng*) of grain per *mu* (Zhou B. 1981: 206), which can be converted to a modern measure of 5.14–8.07 litres per *mu*. Considering that the estimated grain yield levels were between 75.7 litres per *mu* of wheat and 113.6 litres per *mu* of rice (Deng 1993a: 160), the tax rate was between 6.8 and 7.1 per cent. This is slightly lower than Professor Feuerwerker's estimate that the long-term average government revenue from the agricultural sector was 7.1–9.3 per cent of the total GDP of the sector with the dynastic rates ranging from 4 to 13 per cent (Feuerwerker 1984: 300). Although fluctuating from time to time, the tax rate was normally around 10 per cent of the household's total output. Such a rate was institutionalised and observed by all Confucian governments in a self-regulating manner.

To increase the tax burden was one of the taboos in state management, and any such increase was religiously avoided by responsible monarchs and/or bureaucrats (for the monarchs see Lai Q. and Chen S. 1995: 273–95; Wei Z. 1995: 279–85). To take the Qing Period as an example, in 1687 Emperor Kangxi (r. 1662–1722) is reported to have been very pleased to know that the tax exemption in Shaanxi and Jiangning had reached a record level of 6 million tael (*liang*) of silver, saying, 'To show my love for the people, this 6 million taels is barely enough.' On another occasion, in 1702, after he realised over 5 million taels of silver fiscal surplus, instead of keeping the surplus, Emperor Kangxi instructed the Imperial Treasury to exempt four provinces – Yunnan, Guizhou, Guangxi and Sichuan – from taxation for one year (Wei Z. *et al.* 1995: 279, 283). Given that in 1685 the total Qing land tax revenue was 24,449,724 taels (Liang F. 1980: 392), the 5 million taels was equivalent to 20.5 per cent, and the 6 million, 24.5 per cent of the revenue. The exemptions were not trivial.

In Qing times, there were four main sources of government revenue: the land tax, the grain tribute, the taxes on domestic commerce and the salt monopoly. Among them, the land tax made up two-thirds of the total tax revenue. The rates of land tax and the grain tribute were fixed, and the rate for taxes on commerce and salt monopoly were also inelastic. The Qing government had to rely on the sale of official ranks to raise funds for its financial needs (see Wright 1957: 149). Such sale is often viewed as an act of corruption/power abuse. It certainly was. However, if such sales were designed to target the rich and avoided impoverishing the ordinary peasants, even if only for the sake of maintaining the political power of the rulers, such corruption/power abuse was morally acceptable among the peasants. At the end of the Qing, after the Taiping Rebellion swept the richest regions in the 1850s, the Qing government lost as much as 90 per cent of its regular revenues, which was fatal to Manchu rule and a blessing to the rebels. But the correlation between a heavy tax burden and armed rebellions was so obvious that in Chinese history, increasing taxes became taboo. In 1868, when two court officials could not resist the temptation to raise funds by increasing of taxes in order to finance Emperor Tongzhi's 'self-strengthening' reform (1862–74), they were condemned and severely punished: one was stripped of office and the other banished to a remote province some 3,000 km away (*ibid.*: 155). The emperor's edict on this incident declared that the Qing government would not, under any circumstances, increase taxes and would abide by the principle of perpetuation of fixed taxes (*ibid.*: 155–6). In both cases, Qing self-regulation was obvious. Such a self-regulating mechanism to check excessive rent-seeking explains the paradox raised by Feuerwerker (1976: 75): on the one hand the Chinese political system was indeed corruptible, and the Qing government was notorious for corruption/power abuse; on the other hand the Qing did not collapse or die of corruption/power abuse. The régime's demise was caused by something else.

Therefore, in China's history as a whole, the importance of corruption and power abuse should not be overplayed. Otherwise, it is puzzling why on the on hand the Chinese system seemed to permit open corruption and on the other hand it had the self-discipline not to squeeze the peasantry too hard (see, for example, Moore 1966: 171–2). No doubt, the tax burden upon the peasantry could be increased either through changes in tax law which affected the whole country or through power abuse by local officials who acted in an illegal manner. If these happened, the government moved away from physiocracy and the political consequence was often catastrophic.

### 3.4.2.3 The mechanisms

The secret of China's stability was 'tolerable corruption/power abuse': one party at a time, as demonstrated in Figure 3.5. The weapon to fight against corruption/power abuse was fourfold: (1) a universally accepted Confucian code of conduct; (2) consistent categorisation of monarchs and bureaucrats; (3) unobstructed information channels, and (4) functional surveillance systems between the literati and the monarch.

#### CONFUCIAN CODE OF CONDUCT

To Confucianism, corruption or power abuse is controllable; as the maxim goes, 'once self-abnegation is practised and rites are resumed, society will enter the *ren* status' (*yiri keji fuli tianxia guirenyan*) (Kong Q. *c.* 479 BC: ch. 'Yan Yuan').

Here, self-abnegation (*keji*) and resumption of rites (*fuli*) mean, respectively, individual control at the micro level and social control at the macro level over corruption and power abuse. When these two types of control are combined, society reaches the status of long-lasting peace and prosperity. Therefore, *keji fuli* is in effect an anti-corruption manifesto. Confucianism made the bureaucracy conscious of the needs of society (mainly of the peasantry) and the responsibility of the state. Once such needs and responsibility were clear, it was easy to follow the Confucian norm as a code of conduct. The essence of the code was to run China like a big family, which was reflected in the formula of 'self-cultivation, family management, establishment and maintenance of order in society, realisation of nationwide lasting peace' (*xiuqizhiping*). Each of these steps was the preparation for the next (Wu Y. 1988: 213–15). This family-based social order often gave the outsiders the impression that the Chinese Empire was a 'familistic state' (Fairbank 1965: ch. 2). Considering that the Confucian code was openly taught in society and the Confucian ethics were known at the grass-roots level, a set of criteria was given to ordinary citizens with which to judge the performance of the state and individual officials. The code then became a weapon against corruption and power abuse at all levels. Certainly, the Confucian moral check was not as efficient as the rule by law in modern democratic societies, but it was a reasonable arrangement for a centralised political structure in premodern times; at least it was humane and open.

Under a centralised reign, corruption/power abuse usually takes the form of excessive taxation. If this rent-seeking avaricious activity is not checked, the value of $F_W$ in equation (3.4) becomes greater than zero, which means that the economy moves away from the status of trinary equilibrium. Also, $K$ in equation (3.11) will increase and cause $t$ – the duration of the régime – to fall. This explains why the Confucian ideal of 'self-cultivation, family management, establishment and maintenance of order in society, realisation of nationwide lasting peace' also crystallises in the principle of 'light tax and corvée' (*qingyao bofu*). Dong Zhongshu (179–104 BC), a leading Confucian in the Western Han Dynasty, condemning the tyranny of the previous Qin monarchs, called for the restoration of benevolent government to conform to 'the will of Heaven' (Dong Z. *c.* 104 BC: ch. 'Zhi Zhi'; see also Ban G. AD 82: 'Biography of Dong Zhongshu' and 'Economy') and maintained 'Only lightening tax and exempting corvée to relieve people's hardships can lead to great order and peace across the land' (Ban G. AD 82 vol. 24: ch. 'Shihuo Zhi'). The logic behind this principle is simple: if corruption and power abuse were checked, the process of deterioration was reversible; and if tax and corvée burdens were controlled, corruption and power abuse would be checked.

## CATEGORISATION OF MONARCHS AND BUREAUCRATS

Applying the Confucian code of conduct, monarchs and bureaucrats were customarily categorised by imperial dynastic historians and Confucian writers into two opposing types: (1) 'judicious monarchs' (*mingjun*) versus 'fatuous monarchs' (*hunjun*), and (2) upright officials (*qingguan*) versus venal officials (*tanguan*). Two points can be made regarding this practice. First, all the deeds of the judicious monarchs and upright officials fit in well with the trinary equilibrium; while those of the fatuous monarchs and venal officials violate the equilibrium. Second, all the judicious monarchs and upright bureaucrats were highly praised, and all the fatuous monarchs and venal officials condemned (Li G. 1987; Xiao L. 1987; Li Z. 1990; SGC 1991; Niu C. and Qin G. 1992; Shi Y. 1992; Wei Z. and Yan J. 1992; Li Z. 1993; Yang C. and Shen G. 1993; Zhang J. *et al.* 1993; Li S. 1994; Sun Y. 1994; Dong S. 1995). Accordingly, apart from the official dynastic histories, numerous books were produced by and for the monarchs and bureaucrats to tell the ruling class what mistakes should be avoided; for example, Wu Jing's *Essence of State Administration under the Zhenguan Reign* [AD 627–49] (*Zhenguan Zhengyao*), Sima Guang's *Comprehensive References for State Management* (*Zizhi Tongjian*), Bi Yuan's *Enlarged Comprehensive References for State Management* (*Xu Zizhi Tongjian*); and *Emperor Tangtaizong's Instructions on State Management* (*Tangtaizong Zhiguo Shengxun*), *Emperor Songtaizu's Instructions on State Management* (*Songtaizu Zhiguo Shengxun*), *Emperor Mingtaizu's Instructions on State Management* (*Mingtaizu Zhiguo Shengxun*), *Emperor Kangxi's Instructions on State Management* (*Kangxi Zhiguo Shengxun*) and *Emperor Qianlong's Instructions on State Management* (*Qianlong Zhiguo Shengxun*) (Lai Q. and Chen S. 1995; Liang J. and Wang Y. 1995; Xu C. and Li Y. 1995; Xu T. and Li Y. 1995; Wei Z. *et al.* 1995). There is no secret that the Chinese ruler had an incentive to have his personal history rewritten in accordance with the Confucian line of sagehood. Often, the more corrupt he was, the stronger the incentive. This practice was, and still is, commonly called, rather accurately, 'a whore disguising herself as a lady of chastity' (*biaozi li paifang*). From the positivist viewpoint, the ruler is a compulsive liar, and lying should be condemned. However, from the normativist viewpoint, although the ruler is a liar, his lying nevertheless reinforces a social norm: at least the value of chastity is appreciated by the whore. So, in a normative social setting the normative liar and his normative lie are not only acceptable but also have their irreplaceable utility in the public life.

INFORMATION CHANNELS

In premodern China, an information-collecting system kept the bureaucratic machinery informed both externally of developments in society and internally of developments within the state apparatus itself. It is another important weapon for checking corruption.

In the Qin Dynasty, the Prime Minister (*chengxiang*) took charge of the collecting of information through all the government channels, to report to the emperor (Wu Y. 1988: 95). In Han times, information collecting and processing were the responsibility of a group of middle-ranking officials (*lang*) of the Imperial Secretariat (*shangshutai*), to minimise the influence upon the system from senior ministers (*ibid.*: 96–9). In the early Sui Dynasty, a system under the Bureau of Imperial Representatives (*yezhetai*) was established which paralleled the normal administrative network as an alternative channel of communication with the central government (*ibid.*: 96–7). In Tang times, the Imperial Academician (*hanlin xueshi*) and eunuchs formed another channel for information and communication purposes. Empress Wu Zetian even established an accusation system: letterboxes (*gui*) were set up at each gate of the Imperial Palace for people to communicate with the government (*ibid.*: 98–9). Also in the Tang Dynasty, Imperial Inspectors (with four ranks: *guanchashi, xunchashi, anchashi, caifangshi*) were sent to the provinces and counties to obtain first-hand information (*ibid.*: 99). The later dynasties (such as the Song and Ming) simply duplicated the early systems until an important innovation was made by the Qing called 'confidential memorial to the throne' (*mizhe, mizou* or *zoushu*) to link officials, especially those of lower ranks, to the emperor (*ibid.*: 99–102). Confidential memorials dealing with local and national policy issues were used to inform the monarch of what was going on in different parts of the empire and what should have been done, and thus formed the most important monarch–official communication channel (*ibid.*: 109–11). The idea behind these channels was to reduce the chance for information manipulation by bureaucrats at different levels in order to run the empire smoothly with minimal mistakes and less corruption. The stability of the main dynasties in Chinese history suggests that these networks worked efficiently.

SURVEILLANCE SYSTEMS

Carefully designed surveillance systems played an extremely important role in keeping a good balance between power-generated corruption/power abuse and good government for the empire. Such systems targeted two categories in the state: the monarch and the officials. The basic issues were (1) how to confine the selfish interests of the monarch and the officials and (2) how to ensure that power was not easily abused (Peng B. and Gong F. 1989; Pu J. 1990: chs 6–13; Zhu Y. and Lin Y. 1992; Tang J. and Zheng C. 1993: chs 4–10; Tian Z. 1994: 249–310). The Confucian literati and the monarch each played a role in solving these problems, which can be defined as the 'Confucian literati versus monarch' formula and the 'monarch versus bureaucrats' formula.

*'Confucian literati versus monarch'*    In the long run, Confucian literati and the Chinese monarch were bonded together through weal and woe. The mission-minded Confucian literati believed that people could and should be civilised through education and that a better world would be built through civilising human beings, including the monarch. Naturally, throughout Chinese

history education and supervision of the monarch were considered the vocation of Confucian literati: to admonish and restrain the monarch so that he became responsible for the well-being of society and, equally importantly, set a good example for his subjects so that social harmony was to be reached and maintained. The Confucian principle includes rules (1) that 'True Confucians in officialdom must put the Way [*dao*] of Confucianism into practice' (*shi yi xingdao*) (Yan B. 1986: 146); and (2) that 'True Confucians should follow the Way [*dao*] of Confucianism but not the will of the monarch' (*congdao bu congjun*) (Xun K. *c*. 238 BC: ch. 'Chen Dao'). Mencius claimed more frankly that 'The purpose for a Confucian to work for the king is solely to guide him to reach benevolence' (*junzi zi shijun ye wuyin qijun yi dangdao zhiyu ren eryi*) (Mengzi Warring States Period: ch. 'Guozi Xia'; *cf*. Lau 1984: 257). The ultimate goal of Confucian education and supervision was to produce 'sage kings' or 'paragon kings' for society (see Dobson 1983: 155–7). To achieve that, the monarch must be educated/trained to accept the ideal and values of sage-like humanity (*ren*). The Confucian literati also took the education of princes and princesses as a bounden duty in order to make the younger generation of the royal family truly Confucian (for the Qing Dynasty see Feuerwerker 1976: 35–8).

It is easy to imagine that conflicts between Confucian values and the will of the monarch often occurred. In such a situation, a true Confucian should stick to his principles and if necessary he should resort to resignation (Lau 1984: 221; see also Yan B. 1986; Zhang D. 1987), or even to so radical a step as deposing the ruler (Lau 1984: 219). Confucius himself maintained very straightforwardly (Kong Q. *c*. 479 BC: ch. 'Wei Linggong') that 'Those who have a lofty ideal will not harm *ren* in order to survive, but will sacrifice [their lives] and kill [evil rulers] to reach *ren*' (*zhishi renren wuqiusheng yihairen youshashen yichengren*). Obviously, Confucius foresaw the constant tension between the Confucian literati and the Chinese monarch. The former represented the intellectual and civil power, while the latter embodied the political and, more often than not, the military power. As analysed in Chapter 2, in the philosophical framework of Heaven (*tian*) and the Way (*dao*), the monarch was checked by the Confucian literati, and the 'muscles' had no free hand before the brains. In reality, from the Han Dynasty onwards, most Chinese monarchs accepted and adhered to their position below Heaven as designed by the literati and willingly cooperated with the literati for the sake of peace. This explains why Chinese monarchs sometimes issued edicts publicly confessing their errors (*xiazhao zuiji*) in order to ask forgiveness of the people, a practice which is unthinkable in the eyes of Oriental despots.

The check upon the monarch also took the form of Confucians' participation in top-level decision-making. In the running of the empire, the decisions were often made jointly between the monarch and his administrators. In the Ming Dynasty, for example, Imperial Academicians (*neige daxueshi*) from five imperial colleges were actively involved in the top-level decision-making process (Wu Y. 1988: 100). The check against corruption/power abuse by the monarch was thus on the spot. On some complex issues, an 'emperor-chaired conference' (*yuqian huiyi*) was held as a forum for open debates on policies. Often, hundreds of officials attended. In Han times, 127 such conferences were held at an average internal of one conference each 3.4 years (*ibid.*: 119). The best-known conference was the one on the state monopoly of the salt and iron trade (*yantie huiyi*) in 81 BC, which laid the foundation of government commercial policy for the later dynasties.

The check from the literati can be seen from remonstration and admonition (*jianzheng*). The first recorded case of remonstration occurred during the Xia Period (*c*. 2000–1520 BC) when King Jie, one of the early tyrants, exhausted the national wealth by building his palaces (*yaotai*). A minister (*dafu*) named Guan Long remonstrated upon this matter (Li M. *et al*. 1990: 32). Guan consequently lost his life and became the first recorded martyr of remonstration and admonition. Remonstration and admonition thus had a sensitive nature: if the monarch was narrow-minded, such action could cost one's career and even one's life. The literati established two ways of dealing with the monarchs: the direct way (*zhijian*) and the indirect way (*qujian*), depending on the personality of the monarch. According to their qualities, monarchs were classified by the Confucian literati into three categories: the first class (sages or paragons), the second class (upright) and the third class (tyrants). Xun Kong pointed out in his *The Way to Work as Officials* (*Chendao*) that to work with a sage monarch, no remonstration and admonition were needed; to work with an upright monarch, remonstration and admonition should be direct; to work with a tyrant, remonstration and admonition were crucial and should be done indirectly (see Wu Y. 1988: 122). This showed that the 'Confucian literati versus monarch' formula was jealously guarded by the literati, to whom the problem was not whether but how moral checks should be employed.

Even so, upright officials repeatedly performed their mission of remonstration and admonition. Among them are Zhang Chang (? – 47 BC), Gong Sui (?), Yang Zhen (? – AD 124), Yu Yuan (AD 426–79), Le Yun (?), Wei Zheng (AD 580–643), Ko Zhun (AD 961–1203), Yelü Chucai (1190–1244) and Hai Rui (1514–87) (Wei Z. and Yan J. 1992: 38–50, 75–82, 102–4, 119–24; Chen G. and Yuan H. 1995: chs 4–5; see also Luan B. and Qin J. 1994). To show their determination, Le Yun of the Northern and Southern Dynasties and Hai Rui of the Ming Dynasty even brought their own coffins with them to the court when remonstrating with the emperors (Wei Z. and Yan J. 1992: 121, 247). With the persistence of the literati, remonstration and admonition had gradually become institutionalised by the early Tang under the reign of Emperor Taizong (r. AD 627–49), a great supporter of remonstration and admonition who was quoted as saying, 'Taking remonstration and admonition makes a monarch a sage king' (*shoujian zesheng*) (Xu C. and Li Y. 1995: 210). The Confucian literati versus monarch mechanism confirms to a degree

Leon Stover's view (see Stover 1974) that the Chinese monarch was a prisoner of the society in that he had little freedom to break away from what may be called the 'custody of the literati', although Stover's view is rather one-sided, failing to consider the balance of power between the monarch on the one hand and the bureaucracy on the other.[2] The literati, often labelled the 'Chinese gentry', benefited by its role: among other things, members of the class often enjoyed a reduction in tax. At the end of the Qing Period, such reduction varied from 15 to 46 per cent, the mean reduction rate being 30.5 per cent (see Wang 1973: 40).

The Confucian literati versus monarch mechanism was not foolproof. Occasionally, the monarch violated this rule and lost the support of the literati. The outcome was often disastrous. The first emperor, Qin Shihuang, responsible for the notorious 'burning books and executing Confucians by burying them alive', trusted very few literati members (Guisso *et al.* 1989: 164–7). His atrocity contributed to the quick demise of his régime. No doubt the external shock from outside the Establishment in the form of mass rebellions provided the ultimate check, an issue which will be dealt with in Chapter 4.

*'Monarch versus bureaucrats'* According to the Confucian norm, the Chinese monarch has an active role to play, either for the sake of the Confucian ideal or for the sake of the survival of a dynasty. Emperor Qianlong of the Qing (r. 1736–95) points out:

> If the order or turmoil of the country should depend only on the Prime Minister, the emperor then becomes no better than a puppet. After all, employing the Prime Minister is the job of the emperor. It is a taboo that the monarch stays away from the reality and passes his own responsibility to manage the state affairs on to the Prime Minister.
>
> (Xu C. and Li Y. 1995: 32–3)

A Chinese emperor acted, more often than not, as the ultimate arbitrator in state affairs rather than the highest administrator. This determined the role of the monarch as a surveillant to the system rather than a policy-maker for everyday dealings. The common impression that the Chinese monarch was heavily involved in all sorts of decision-making chores is false. In effect, this method of running the empire was found only under Emperor Qin Shihuang (221–209 BC), an aggressive monarch who was known for his preference for making all the decisions by himself. He personally went through some 120 *jin* (about 31 kg; 1 Qin *jin* = 258.24 g) of documents written on bamboo slips every day before going to bed (Guisso *et al.* 1989: 166). In addition, Qin Shihuang made nationwide inspection tours as part of his campaign to strengthen his control over the newly conquered regions. During the period between 219 BC and 210 BC, he travelled four times along the coastal provinces (Sima Q. 91 BC: ch. 'Qinshihuang Benji'). It was recorded that during his last tour in 210 BC, the emperor travelled by boat from Mount Jiuyi (in Hunan Province) along the rivers for some 1,600 km to the sea, and then travelled along the coast to Zhejiang, Jiangsu and Shandong Peninsula for another 1,400 km. Overworked, he died on the trip.

After the Qin, very few emperors worked as hard as Emperor Qin Shihuang, but they worked more efficiently, with the full assistance of the bureaucracy. As long as their activities conformed to Confucian values, local governments were encouraged to act autonomously (Fairbank 1957: 169–72). The best evidence is that local governments often initiated their own projects and even imposed their own taxes (Feuerwerker 1976: 90–2; Deng 1993a: chs 2, 5). For the monarch, the principle used to control the huge bureaucratic machine was the so-called 'centralising the process to deal with major issues and decentralising the process for minor issues' (*daquan dulan xiaoquan fensan*), a golden principle of devolution which survived premodern China and became one of the paramount tenets of Mao Zedong, a self-praising 'new democrat' who ruled modern China just like any of the old dynasts in the past. The mechanism of 'monarch versus bureaucrats' was just the other face of the 'Confucian literati versus monarch' of the same coin. This may appear to be paradoxical to a 'black-or-white' mould of thinking: under a centralised framework there should be no local autonomy of any sort; whereas under a decentralised system there should be no central control. However, reality often falls in the 'grey' zone. For instance, Tokugawa Japan has been characterised as having 'centralised feudalism' (Mathias and Postan 1978: 140; see also Hall 1991: chs 1, 5, 10, 11, 13). There is no reason why post-Qin China should not be labelled as having 'autonomous centralism'.

However, once the principle of 'centralising the process to deal with major issues and decentralising the process for minor issues' was practised, there was a real danger that the red tape and corruption/power abuse among officials, especially among senior administrators, would jeopardise the stability of the empire. The best examples are: (1) the takeover of the Wei Kingdom by Sima Yi (AD 179–251), an influential official, ruled by the *de facto* king, Cao Cao, during the Three Kingdoms Period (AD 220–80); and (2) the takeover of the Tang Dynasty by Wu Zetian (r. AD 684–704), who began as a concubine of two successive emperors. A modern version of this kind of takeover can be seen in the activities of Mao's diehard loyalists called the 'Gang of Four', headed by Mao's unauthorised spouse Lan Ping (commonly known as Jiang Qing) under the banner of the notorious Cultural Revolution during the 1970s.

The dilemma between the decentralisation of decision-making (or devolution) and the danger of losing power made the politicking of the monarch an art: the Chinese emperor had to rely on the bureaucracy and, at the same time, had to watch very carefully every move of this self-moving machinery to make sure that the bureaucracy did not go too far.[3] It was thus crucial for the monarch to have a wide range of information flow from below. The emperor had his surveillance network for fighting official corruption and power abuse (Wu Y. 1988: 102–18).

The first strategy was to split up the power of government departments. For example, in the early Sui Dynasty (AD 581–618), a 'three-department system' (*sanshengzhi*) was established. The three departments, Prime Ministry (*shangshusheng*), Imperial Secretariat (*zhongshusheng*) and Imperial Liaison Office (*menxiasheng*), were in charge of administration, legislation and evaluation of policies respectively. A policy edict was first drafted by the Imperial Secretariat, then discussed and evaluated in the Imperial Liaison Office before being issued and executed by the Prime Ministry. The heads of the three departments (*shangshuling*, *zhongshuling* and *shizhong*) were all equally ranked as Prime Ministers (*zaixiang*), all personally responsible to the emperor. The aim of this arrangement was to minimise the chance of bureaucrats possessing too much power and maximise the chance of having different opinions and feedbacks. This Sui structure was inherited by the later dynasties with limited modifications (Wu Y. 1988: 96–8, 104).

The second strategy was to impose extensive surveillance (*micha*) on both officialdom and society. There were two purposes for such surveillance: (1) to collect information and policy feedback from society, and (2) to watch officials and ordinary people to prevent corruption/power abuse and armed rebellions. Four systems were established (Wu Y. 1988: 105–11; Wang X. 1991): 'imperial commissioners' (*xunxingfa*); the imperial detective network (*zhenjifa*), confidential memorials to the throne (*mizoufa*); and the 'neighbourhood responsibility network' (*baojiafa*). The post of imperial commissioner began in the Western Zhou Dynasty (*c.* 1030–771 BC) in the form of 'travelling commissioners' (*xingren* and *qiuren*). They were sent to the provinces and were responsible for reporting to the monarch new developments in different areas. The commissioners, called prefectural surveillants (*jianjun yushi*) in Qin times, were posted in each of the 36 prefectures (*jun*). In the early Han Dynasty, Emperor Wudi (r. 141–87 BC) sent his Prime Minister across the country as an inspecting commissioner. The system continued until 106 BC, when the country was divided into thirteen administrative/surveillance regions and the 'inspecting commissionership' (*cishi*) was designed (Wu Y. 1988: 106–7; Wang X. 1991). The imperial detective network was an ancient Chinese counterpart of the FBI. In the Ming Dynasty, the network, combining the 'imperial task force' attached to the court (*dongchang* and *xichang*) and surveillance agents in all provinces and government departments, was responsible for watching, reporting and prosecuting unlawful officials on a regular basis (Wu Y. 1988: 107–9). The practice of 'confidential memorials to the throne', a supplementary to the imperial detective network, encouraged officials to watch each other (*ibid.*: 109–12). Unlike the first three

systems, which were exclusively designed for internal surveillance of officialdom, the 'neighbourhood responsibility network' was designed to control
civilians and prevent attempts at rebellion. If a crime was committed by an
individual, his or her family and neighbours were to be punished. However,
from the making of the surveillance network, it is obvious that the empire
laid more emphasis on the control of the bureaucracy than of the ordinary
people.

The third strategy was to separate honour, salary and rank from executive
power. Junior officials were deliberately employed as watchdogs of the monarch against well-entrenched senior officials who were more likely to become
corrupted by power. Later on, when these young watchdogs were promoted
and became senior, they were in turn watched by some fresh blood. Junior
bureaucrats were thus constantly brought into the system just for the purpose
of surveillance. Impeachment of high-ranking officials were practised, too, as
a part of the surveillance mechanism (Wei Z. and Yan J. 1992; Li S. 1994). To
make sure that surveillance agents did their job, recruits were sometimes
brought from outside the normal bureaucratic channels. For example,
Emperor Tang Zhuangzong (r. AD 924–6) of the Five Dynasties (AD 907–
60) employed entertainers, and Emperor Taizu (r. 1368–98) of the Ming
Dynasty hired Buddhist monks as agents (Wu Y. 1988: 107). In addition,
eunuchs were readily used for surveillance purposes (Yu H. 1993). It was an
ongoing process to keep corruption and power abuse by privileged groups in
the bureaucracy within an acceptable level.

Under the surveillance network, officials were watched and their performance assessed. In the Tang Dynasty (AD 618–907), the officials were
graded according to a nine-scale system varying from excellent (*shangshang*)
to poor (*xiaxia*) to determine promotion, demotion in rank and salary, and
termination of careers (Lu X. 1991: 76–7). This system was inherited by
the later dynasties including the Song, Ming, Qing and even the Republic
(*ibid.*).

Interestingly, during the Sui–Tang Period (AD 581–907), the surveillance
system also bore the responsibility of 'remonstration and admonition' and
thus became a watchdog of both the bureaucracy and the monarch
(Wang X. 1991: 76). In Tang times, the sphere of influence of the surveillance system also expanded to (1) assessing officials' performance, (2) conduct-
ing censuses and evaluating the tax burden, (3) inspecting conditions of
agricultural production and government granaries, (4) routine policing, (5)
recruiting the talent to work for the state, and (6) investigating unlawful
activities of officials and local thugs and bringing them to justice (*ibid.*:
76–7).

Such extensive surveillance heavily overlapped the policing function of the
state and thus often gives modern observers an impression that premodern
China was a police state or under military dictatorship, especially when taking the 'neighbourhood responsibility network' into account. However, if we

understand the enormous task the Chinese monarch faced in running a gigantic bureaucracy with the power–corruption temptation, such institutional checks were indeed crucial. Given that the bureaucrats were extremely underpaid for the responsibilities they bore (for one case see Zhang D. 1970), temptation was sometimes irresistible; and, as a result, the network of extensive surveillance became indispensable.

On the whole, the Confucian literati tended to overplay the importance of the formula of 'Confucian literati versus monarch' and overemphasize the responsibility of the monarch; while the Chinese monarch tended to overplay the importance of the formula 'monarch versus bureaucrats' and overemphasize the responsibility of the bureaucrats. This is shown from a debate in AD 642 between Emperor Taizong (r. 627–49) of the Tang and his top advisers (Xu T. and Li Y. 1995: 60). The emperor asked, 'Which situation is worse, a monarch making a mess with his bureaucrats tidying up or the bureaucrats making a mess with their monarch tidying up?' The emperor used the Northern Qi, a régime which had a bad emperor but an excellent minister, as a case to justify the shunning of his share of responsibility. The response from Wei Zheng (AD 580–643) was:

> If the monarch understands the principles, he watches all the wrong-doings in society. . . . If the monarch is fatuous and does not follow remonstration and admonition, even if he has capable administrators like Bai Lixi in the case of the Yu Kingdom and Wu Zixu in the case of the Wu Kingdom, he will not be able to avoid disasters and the fate of defeat and demise.

But both sides accepted the two formulae, 'Confucian literati versus monarch' and the 'monarch versus bureaucrats'; and both parties recognised that a delicate balance was required to keep the Chinese state within the trinary structure. This interrelationship between the Confucian literati and monarch rejects either the Oriental despot determinism (which overplays the importance of the monarch) and the Confucian bureaucracy determinism (which overemphasizes the role of the Confucian officials; see, for example, Stover 1974).

## 3.5 Life under the trinary equilibrium

Regarding life under the trinary equilibrium, five areas are to be examined: (1) territorial expansion; (2) prosperity of the agricultural sector; (3) room for the market; (4) demographic pattern; and (5) general living standards.

The purpose here is not to search for the ultimate causality but to see different aspects or correlations of economic life under the trinary equilibrium on two counts: (1) the causality is rather blurred in a multidimensional system such as the trinary structure and equilibrium; and (2) in the historical dynamics these aspects of economic life were by and large the developments themselves.

### 3.5.1 *Territorial expansion of the Chinese Empire*

As mentioned earlier, the trinary equilibrium required new land to feed the system. This is demonstrated by Figures 3.6 and 3.7 (see also Fitzgerald 1972). In terms of the speed of agricultural expansion, the data are as shown in the tables on pp. 177–8, taking the measurements of the longest distance between the last and the new farming frontiers.

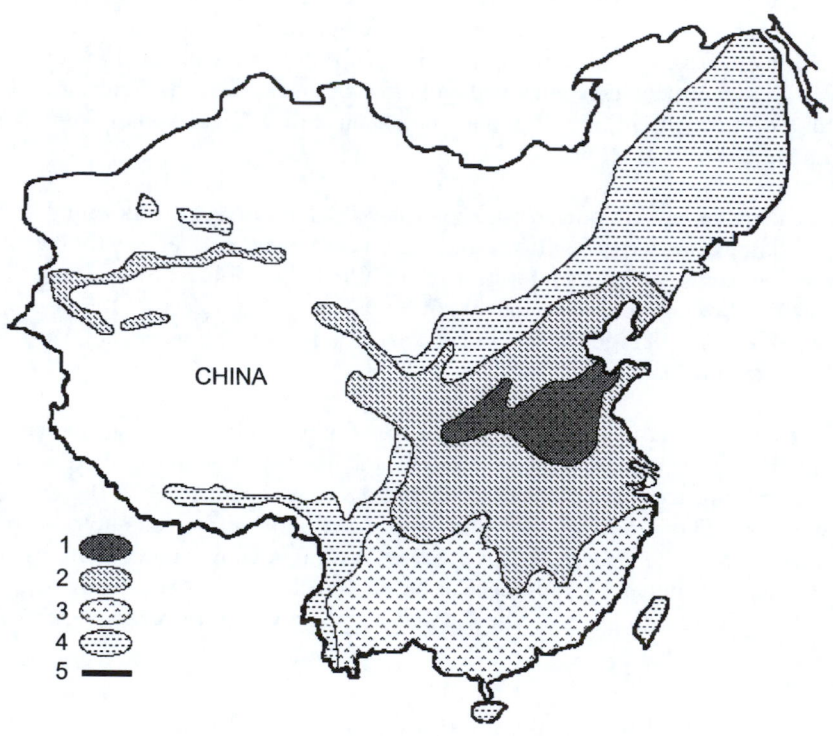

*Figure 3.6* Geographic expansion of farming zones up to the Qing Dynasty

*Source*: Based on information from Chen D. and Hu J. 1983: ch. 2; Hou W. 1992: 5, 811, 1538.
*Notes*
1, Western Zhou at *c.* 1030 BC; 2, Western Han at *c.* 100 BC; 3, Sui–Tang: the sixth to eighth centuries AD; 4, Ming–Qing: the fourteenth to nineteenth centuries; 5, land boundary of Qing China. The expansion of the farming zone was not necessarily consistent with registered land under cultivation for taxation purposes (*cf.* Liang F. 1980: 4–13, 122–5).

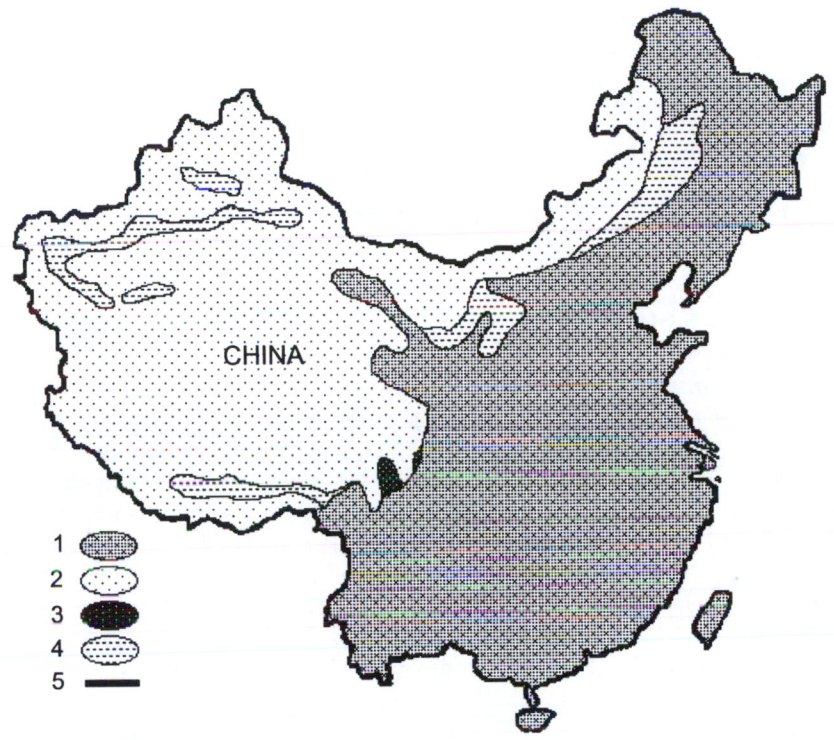

*Figure* 3.7 Modern division between farming and pastoral zones

*Source*: Based on information from Chen D. and Hu J. 1983: 148.

*Notes*

1, Current farming zone; 2, current pastoral zone; 3, expansion of the farming zone since the Ming–Qing situation; 4, penetration of the pastoral zone into the traditional farming zone; 5, land boundary of modern China.

| Period | Duration (years) | Distance spread (km) | Speed (km/year) |
|---|---|---|---|
| Zhou–Western Han | 930 | 2,810 | 3.02 |
| Western Han–Tang | 900 | 940 | 1.04 |
| Tang–Qing | 1,000 | 1,260 | 1.26 |

In terms of scale, by the Qing Period the empire had been enlarged by 27.3 times from its Zhou domain (*c*. 1030 BC) and the farming zones 12.7 times during the same period:[4]

| Period | Duration (years) | Arable land $(10^3 km^2)$ | Index | Increase from the last period (%) | Decadal rate (%) |
|--------|------------------|---------------------------|-------|-----------------------------------|------------------|
| Zhou | — | 405.0 | 100 | — | — |
| Western Han | 930 | 2,794.5 | 690 | 690 | 2.10 |
| Tang | 900 | 3,807.0 | 940 | 136 | 0.34 |
| Qing | 1,000 | 5,548.5 | 1,370 | 146 | 0.38 |
| 1980 | 70 | 5,346.0 | 1,320 | −3.6 | −0.53 |

Arguably, the speed of expansion was higher than its European counterpart, which was about 1 km a year (Cavalli-Sforza 1974; Lewin 1997: 33).

Three points can be made here. First, the extensibility of the Chinese agricultural zone in terms of geographic out-stretching ended in the Qing Period, probably around the end of the eighteenth century. Second, the demarcation line between the farming and non-farming zones has been very stable since the Qing, the line being dictated mainly by topographic and climatic factors (see Chen D. and Hu J. 1983: 51; JKY 1987: appendices 4, 7, 11–15). Third, the farming zone contains a high population density: over 125 persons per square mile at a recent reading (see JKY 1987: appendix 17; C. J. Smith 1991: figure 7.2). It can be suggested that the premodern Chinese were fortunate in that land supply was at times quite abundant: it was only by the late Qing Period that arable land really became exhausted and reached its natural limit in all directions.

This expansion over time indicates that China managed well in terms of increasing the supply of land to ease the land shortage in absolute terms: with territorial expansion, the land supply increased absolutely. Most interestingly, the contemporary farming zone in China has contracted from its traditional past, a clear indication of the geographic limit the farming zone reached in the past (see Figure 3.7).

In this context, the 'relative shortage of land' was particularly relevant to the day-to-day life of the premodern Chinese. The term 'relative shortage of land' means the constraint associated with the allocation of the existing arable land, which was determined partly by demographic status and partly by market mechanisms. However, sudden population growth is rare because it is dictated by both the natural, biological process of fertility and collective efforts in society. The impact of the market mechanisms is more immediate. The maintenance of land ownership by individuals was subject to their financial situation, often determined by their farming performance and sometimes marketing skills to make both ends meet. Less skilled and less fortunate farmers tended to have difficulty in maintaining their income at the subsistence level which one day could lead to loss of their land plots to well-to-do buyers, a process which can be described as landholding and land-ownership concentration. Such concentration upset the initial near-egalitarian land allocation among the rural population and consequently caused a relative shortage of land. Therefore, even if the orthodox physiocratic state favoured the pattern of egalitarian family farming units for obvious economic and political reasons such as taxation and social stability, there was a strong tendency to move away from that equilibrium owing to demographic and market dynamics.

On the demand side, as mentioned earlier, the fight against the relative shortage of land was conducted via ultra-economic interference in the property market to control land trading in order to minimise the inevitable polarisation among the small landholders. On the supply side, the relative shortage was largely offset by (1) the relative increase in land supply through continuous progress in land-saving technology in farming to increase the yield from a given plot size and employ, as well as feed, more people (see Bray 1984; Deng 1993a), and through subdividing land property rights to create the secondary and tertiary property rights of the same plot for trade (see Chapter 2); and (2) redistributing land under government-sponsored internal migration schemes to move population from land-hungry regions (*zhaixiang*) to land-abundant regions (*kuanxiang*).

But, on the whole, to obtain new land was far more straightforward, as seen in the process of internal colonisation of south China and China's frontiers in the north and west. This internal colonisation on the East Asian mainland has been confirmed by textual, archaeological and anthropological studies. Recent mapping of the blood and gene types among the ethnic Han provides fresh evidence for the hypothesis that the 'Chinese race' is far from being geographically homogeneous. Instead, the Han are descendants of multiple, region-specific origins, which match closely the internal colonisation (Zhao T. 1986; Mao H. 1987; Liu B. 1987). So, the Han group is more of a cultural and economic concept than a genetic concept. It is very demanding to maintain a stable farming system of owner-holders by checking the market-led polarisation among the landowners by means such as bans on property sales during certain periods and provision of credit for farmers in financial trouble. Thus, the increase in the absolute supply of land through territorial expansion was in the long term very effective in maintaining and replicating the Chinese landholding and land-owning peasant economy.

Given Figure 3.6, China faced the possibility of a land shortage crisis during the Qing Period when the economy was finally hit by both the 'absolute shortage of land' due to the exhaustion of new land and the relative shortage of land due to the lack of any new land-saving technology. However, the fact is that with a very limited input of modern technology in agriculture and little new land, China's population still kept growing during much of the twentieth century and consequently China has become the first demographic billionaire in human history. Clearly, China has yet to reach the very limit.

### 3.5.2 *Performance of the agricultural sector*

The prosperity of the agricultural sector in premodern China can be revealed by the position of both the total agricultural output and agricultural productivities.

#### 3.5.2.1 *Total output of agriculture*

Owing to lack of data, the total output of agriculture is completely unknown. The way to get around this difficulty is to take population and its growth as a proxy for the total output from the agricultural sector.

Chinese population growth was impressive. But external invasions and conquests, internal chaos and epidemics did result at times in Malthusian 'positive checks', which often claimed millions of lives at one time. To reflect the Chinese demographic achievement, it is reasonable to take the high points of Chinese population as the basis. These points were (see Appendix I) 56 million in the Western Han Dynasty (206 BC–AD 24), 46 million in the Sui (AD 581–618), 53 million in the Tang (AD 618–907), 74 million in the Southern Song (1127–1279) and Tartar Jin (1115–1234) combined, 60 million in the Yuan (1271–1368), 63 million in the Ming (1368–1644) and 399 million in the Qing (1644–1911).

If it is supposed that (1) it takes 0.5 kg of husked cereal each day to maintain an adult and half that amount to maintain a child under the age of 15 at the subsistence level of living, and (2) children consist of one-third of the total population, it requires about 425 tonnes to maintain a million people per day (350 tonnes for the adults and 75 tonnes for the children), or 155,125 tonnes per year. If we use this as the standard, the total food required for the various periods is as follows:

| Period | Population | Aggregate food required (tonnes) |
| --- | --- | --- |
| 206 BC–AD 24 | 56 million | 8,687,000 |
| 581–618 | 46 million | 7,135,750 |
| 618–907 | 53 million | 8,221,625 |
| 1127–1234 | 74 million | 11,479,250 |
| 1271–1368 | 60 million | 9,307,500 |
| 1368–1644 | 63 million | 9,772,875 |
| 1644–1911 | 399 million | 61,894,875 |

If the Qing is taken as an exception, the average aggregate food required to maintain the Chinese population at the subsistence level of living is about 9.1 million tonnes. These estimates are almost certainly the tip of the iceberg regarding what was produced, consumed and taxed.

Between the Tang (AD 618–907) and the Ming (1368–1644) dynasties large quantities of grain were collected as annual land tax until tax in cash was introduced during the Qing (1644–1911) (Liang F. 1980: 284–5, 288–9, 304, 332–3, 344, 353–4, 356, 358), the conversation into the metric system being done in accordance with the dynastic variations of the Chinese measure of *shi* (see Deng 1997: table 3):

| Period | Grain collected as land tax for a year | |
|---|---|---|
| | *in* shi | *in tonnes* |
| 742 BC–AD56 | 25,000,000 | 1,040,250 |
| 997 | 31,707,000 | 1,474,058 |
| 1021 | 32,782,000 | 1,525,035 |
| 1077 | 17,887,257 | 831,579 |
| 1085 | 24,450,000 | 1,136,680 |
| 1329 | 10,960,053 | 509,533 |
| 1393 | 29,420,970 | 2,211,280 |
| 1457 | 26,560,220 | 1,996,266 |
| 1502 | 29,775,519 | 2,237,928 |
| 1542 | 29,206,733 | 2,195,178 |
| 1578 | 26,638,405 | 2,002,143 |
| 1551 | 26,085,916 | 1,960,617 |
| 1628–44 | 26,396,260 | 1,983,943 |
| 1633 | 28,270,343 | 2,124,799 |
| Average | | 1,659,164 |

If we suppose a tax rate of 10 per cent of the total agricultural output, the long-term average tax revenue (1,659,164 tonnes) leads to an average total output of 16.6 million tonnes, which comfortably surpasses the 9.1 million tonnes minimum for the aggregate human consumption. In addition to tax, the Chinese granary system often stores large quantities of grain. As reported in AD 749, the grain reserve in all granaries amounted to over 4.5 million tonnes (108,718,840 *shi*) (Liang F. 1980: 287; for the Qing period see Will 1990; Will and Wong 1991). Since the stored grain had to be renewed regularly, it is reasonable to assume that the total grain output was in the neighbourhood of 20 million tonnes per year. In other words, the maximum surplus in grain was likely to be some 50 per cent (9.1 million tonnes ÷ 20 million tonnes) from the Tang to the Ming periods.

### 3.5.2.2 Labour productivity

There is little doubt that after AD 1000, especially during the Song and the second half of the Qing periods, progress in total agricultural output was mainly achieved by improvements in productivity with new and better technology (Deng 1993a: chs 4–5). The trend was for intensive farming to become the mainstream of Chinese farming practice, and agricultural productivity per unit of land area soared continuously (*ibid.*: ch. 6, pt B. 4). This legacy strongly influences Chinese agriculture to the present day. Some of the ancient Chinese farming techniques have even been introduced to Third World countries to help solve their food problems today (Bainbridge 1988). Thus, the development pattern of Chinese agriculture has provided a positive case for the Boserupian hypothesis (Boserup 1965).

Owing to the lack of data, labour productivity in premodern China has remained unknown. But, if data for the total population and for the labour force in agricultural production are available, labour productivity can be calculated by the following formula:

$$Y_L = \frac{P_T}{P_W} \tag{3.12}$$

where $Y_L$ is the value of labour productivity, $P_T$ is the total population standing for the total food output of the agricultural sector and $P_W$ is the total number of agricultural workers standing for the total wage bill paid in kind (grain). With the constraint of data shortage, to realistically estimate the labour force in farming necessitates the calculation of (1) total non-agricultural population and (2) intra-agricultural surplus-dependent population. Here it is assumed that the same living standard is applied across economic sectors.

TOTAL NON-AGRICULTURAL POPULATION

According to Kang Chao, the non-agricultural population occupied between 6.9 and 21 per cent of the total Chinese population in premodern times, with an average of 13.4 per cent (Chao 1986: ch. 3). If these figures are applied to data from government censuses, the size of the non-agricultural population can be estimated (for the fluctuations in China's total population, see Appendix I). Again, to take the peak points as the basis to measure, the figures are 3.86–11.76 million in the Western Han Dynasty (206 BC–AD 24), 3.17–9.66 million in the Sui (AD 581–618), 3.66–11.13 million in the Tang (AD 618–907), 5.11–15.54 million in the Southern Song (1127–1279) and Tartar Jin (1115–1234) combined, 4.14–12.60 million in the Yuan (1271–1368), 4.35–13.23 million in the Ming (1368–1644) and 27.53–83.79 million in the Qing (1644–1911). The proportion of officials in the Chinese population was very small, varying between only 0.03 per cent and 0.7 per cent and averaging 0.26 per cent (Jin and Liu 1984: 26). If we suppose that each bureaucrat had a family of five persons, the size of the 'bureaucrat-related population' can be estimated as between 80,000 (Yuan) and 5.19 million (Qing), with an average of 620,000 if excluding the Qing Dynasty, or 1.06 million if including the Qing.

These people, including merchants, artisans, servants and bureaucrats and their families, were dependent on agricultural surplus at any given time. On the basis of the above information, the size of the total non-agricultural population can be estimated as 7.02–21.37 million on the long-term average (as shown in Table 3.4). It is important to point out that China's long-term urban population has often been underestimated by some scholars whose data show little change over time and cannot explain the Song phenomenon (see, for example, Rozman 1973: 102, 279–82).

Here, one may argue that size of the total non-agricultural population raises a chicken-and-egg problem because it is hard to tell whether the limited size of the non-agricultural population was the cause or the result of the trinary equilibrium, which may have been the case in pre-Qin times. But, in the post-Qin era, it was almost certain that the limited size of the non-agricultural population was a result of the trinary equilibrium, which conditioned or overshadowed the growth of the private commercial sector.

POPULATION DEPENDENT ON INTRA-AGRICULTURAL SURPLUS

Conventionally, the concept of 'agricultural surplus' is understood as the amount of agricultural output in excess of the need for maintaining the farmers and their families. Table 3.4 is based on that way of thinking.

*Table 3.4* Non-agricultural population in the major dynasties

| Dynasty | Year | $A^a$ | B | C |
|---|---|---|---|---|
| Western Han | 2 BC | 3.86–11.76 | 5.37–18.63 | 12.00 |
| Eastern Han | 157 AD | — | — | — |
| Sui | 609 | 3.17–9.66 | 4.76–18.86 | 11.81 |
| Tang | 755 | 3.66–11.13 | 3.44–17.56 | 10.50 |
| Song | — | 5.11–15.54 | 10.68–32.99[b] | 21.84 |
| Yuan | 1291 | 4.14–12.60 | 6.78–20.92 | 13.85 |
| Ming | 1381 | 4.35–13.23 | 7.06–21.90 | 14.48 |
|  | 1474 | 4.35–13.23 | 6.39–20.74 | 13.57 |
| Qing[c] | 1833 | 27.53–83.79 | 5.60–19.70 | 12.65 |
| Average |  | 7.02–21.37 | 6.26–21.41 | 13.84 |

*Sources*: Based on Liang F. 1980: 4-13; Jin G. and Liu Q. 1984: 26. See also Chang 1955: ch. 1; Marsh 1961: 13–15; Ho 1962; Mousnier 1971: 256; Feuerwerker 1976: 48; Hsiao 1979: 7; Jing J. 1981: 53; Wu H. 1984: 64–6; Hucker 1985: 1–96.
*Notes*
A, Total non-agricultural population; B, Percentage of non-agricultural business population in China's total; C, Mean value.
a In million.
b Calculation based on the census datum for 1110 AD.
c An estimate based on the population peak in Qing times and the 0.26 per cent of average proportion of officials in the total population.

For the purpose of the present study, that concept cannot satisfy a more explicit calculation of labour productivity simply because it neglects the dependent population within the agricultural sector. If the dependent population within the agricultural sector – the young, old and disabled (the sick and pregnant, for example) – are also counted, the size of the agricultural surplus-dependent population was much larger. Thus, the concept of 'intra-agricultural surplus' is created to identify the boundary of surplus within the agricultural sector. This new concept can be defined as 'the amount of agricultural output in excess of the need to maintain the farming labourers themselves'. Intra-agricultural surplus is counted as a component of the total agricultural surplus. If the minimal dependent number was one person at any time within a family of an average size of five people (or 20 per cent), the proportion of agricultural surplus-dependent population within the agricultural sector in the total Chinese population could be estimated as between 15.8 and 18.6 per cent with an average of 17.3 per cent, as based on Chao's figures (1986: ch. 3). If the agricultural sector employed 80 per cent of the total population, the number of dependents during the demographic peak periods within the agricultural sector can be estimated as 8.85–10.42 million in the Western Han Dynasty (206 BC–AD 24), 7.27–8.56 million in the Sui (AD 581–618), 8.37–9.86 million in the Tang (AD 618–907), 11.69–13.76 million in the Southern Song (1127–1279) and Tartar Jin (1115–1234) combined, 9.48–11.16 million in the Yuan (1271–1368), 9.95–11.72 million in the Ming (1368–1644) and 63.04–74.21 million in the Qing (1644–1911). These figures represent the 'deadweight' within the agricultural sector at any given time.

To estimate the proportion and size of the total agricultural surplus-dependent population, we can simply combine the estimates of the total non-agricultural population figures with the figures for dependants within the agricultural sector. Thus, estimates of the proportion of agricultural surplus-dependants in the total population are between 22.7 and 39.6 per cent, averaging 31.2 per cent, resulting from the addition of Chao's two sets of estimates: (1) the non-agricultural population – between 6.9 and 21 per cent of the total Chinese population with an average of 13.4 per cent; and (2) agricultural surplus-dependent population – 15.8 and 18.6 per cent with an average of 17.3 per cent (based on Chao 1986: ch. 3).

The size of the agricultural-dependent population during the high points of population growth is thus estimated to have been 12.71–22.18 million in the Western Han Dynasty (206 BC–AD 24), 10.44–18.22 million in the Sui (AD 581–618), 12.03–20.99 million in the Tang (AD 618–907), 16.80–29.30 million in the Southern Song (1127–1279) and Tartar Jin (1115–1234) combined, 13.62–23.76 million in the Yuan (1271–1368), 14.30–24.95 million in the Ming (1368–1644) and 90.57–158 million in the Qing (1644–1911). These figure are very useful in terms of establishing the performance of Chinese agriculture.

Given that the estimates of the proportion of agricultural surplus-dependants in the total population are between 22.7 and 39.6 per cent, averaging 31.2 per cent, the total number of agricultural workers ($P_W$) can be estimated as between 77.3 and 60.4 per cent, averaging 68.8. The value of $Y_L$, or the estimated labour productivity in terms of the food-providing capacity of each farmer, is thus between 1.29 and 1.66, averaging 1.48. This means that a Chinese farmer was able to feed about 1.5 people.

The above estimation is made upon the conservative assumption that 80 per cent of the rural population was exclusively engaged in tillage. If we allow a non-grain-growing subsector (weaving, for example) or a higher percentage of dependent population (more than one dependant per household) to be included, the estimate of labour productivity will be much higher. For instance, if a quarter of the rural labour is reasonably assumed to have been engaged in producing fibre and cloth, the number of total agricultural workers should be reduced by 25 per cent, and the proportion of agricultural workers ($P_W$) in the total population becomes 58 and 45.3 per cent, averaging 51.7. Consequently, the value of $Y_L$ becomes 1.72–2.21, with an average of 1.97. That means a farmer was able to feed about two people, an increase of 33.3 per cent from the earlier figure. In Riskin's and Lippit's accounts, in the early twentieth century, what China was able to produce above its population's subsistence level of living amounted to about one-third of its GDP. This sheds some lights on the surplus capacity of the economy (Riskin 1975: 74; Lippit 1987: ch. 4).

In reality, the combination of a constant dependent population (as part of the human life cycle) and the development of by-employment is likely to have lowered the value of $P_W$. In addition, this estimated capacity is conservative since a growing population must begin with an increasing surplus capacity whereby a growing size in surplus-dependants in society was fed. Thus, the above estimates of labour productivity should be taken as the minimum. Mencius (372–289 BC) of the Warring States documented in his *Master Meng's Book* that with a farm of 100 *mu* (1 Warring States *mu* = 0.142 ha) the best farmer was able to produce enough to feed nine people, a second-grade farmer eight people, a medium-grade farmer seven people, a low-grade farmer 5–6 people (Mengzi Warring States Period: ch. 'Wanzhang Xia'). According to *History of the Ming Dynasty*, it took 40,000 farmers in state-owned agricultural colonies to feed an army of 190,000 men. To include those farmers themselves, the food consumer: farmer ratio was 5.75:1 (Zhang T. 1735: ch. 'Economy'). If the family dependants of these farmers are taken into account, the supporting capacity of the farmers is almost certainly greater than 6:1.

Considering the estimated average land productivity during that time to be 0.732 *shi* (1 *shi* = 75 kg) of wheat per modern *mu* (0.67 ha), an average total grain output from 100 Warring States *mu* can be estimated as 15.67 *shi*, or 1,175.4 kg (see Deng 1993a: 160). Further, if we assume that an average adult consumes, among other things, 175 kg of grain a year, this 1,175.4 kg is enough to feed 6.72 persons, which is very close to the medium level (7 persons) in Mencius's record for his time. Joel Mokyr indicates that premodern China's labour productivity did not decline until 1800 (Mokyr 1990: 224), which is a fair comment. It is plausible to suggest that the supporting capacity of a Chinese farmer did not decline dramatically. A recent study indicates that the labour productivity was doubled from the Qin to the Qing periods and that during the Ming–Qing Period one rice farmer in the south was able to support 9–10 adults at the subsistence level of living (Hu J. 1983: 14–22).

Judging from the performance of Chinese labour productivity, one may regard China as a case of low marginal product of labour and go further by suggesting that following the neo-classical line: (1) a very low-level marginal product of labour in agriculture means that the allocation of labour resource in the economy was not optimised; (2) a low marginal product of labour and thus a low agricultural wage rate means the existence of surplus labour in the agricultural sector; and (3) the fact that cheap labour existed in the agricultural sector is a signal of a need for transition to industrialisation. These points are relevant only to a capitalist system. So, a low marginal product of labour alone does not justify the need for capitalist industrialisation, a normative and ahistorical view that should be avoided (see Appendix D).

### 3.5.2.3 Land productivity

Land productivity can be derived from the size of total population and total acreage of cultivated land at any given time in the following formula:

$$Y_K = \frac{K_T}{P_T} \tag{3.13}$$

where $Y_K$ is the value of land productivity in terms of the providing capacity of each unit of land (in *mu*; 1 modern *mu* = 0.067 ha), $K_T$ is the aggregate acreage of land under cultivation and $P_T$ is the total population, standing for the total food output of the agricultural sector. Here it is assumed that the same level of technology is applied across economic sectors. Obviously, the higher the value of $Y_K$, the higher the land productivity.

It is known from Appendix I that the value of $Y_K$ was between 0.104 and 0.094, averaging 0.099, in Han times; between 0.035 and 0.046, averaging 0.041, in Tang times; 0.114 in Northern Song times; between 0.067 and 0.156, averaging 0.115, in Ming times; and between 0.029 and 0.435, with an average of 0.233, in Qing times (see Appendix I, Column F of Table I.1). If we take the average $Y_K$ value of Han times as 100, an increasing trend of $Y_K$; is revealed: 100 (Han), 41 (Tang), 115 (Song), 116 (Ming) and 235 (Qing), which points to technological improvement and changes in production function. This trend is compatible with the change in China's grain yield level, which was improved from then by 110 per cent in the Han, 151.8 per cent in the East Jin, 155.2 per cent in the Sui and Tang, 189.5 per cent in the Song, 263.3 per cent in the Yuan and by 355.7 per cent in the Ming–Qing (see Deng 1993a: 160).

The result was that the Chinese traditional technological development reached a near-optimum level of yield per unit of land area (Elvin 1973: 306; Deng 1993a: chs 4, 6), and built the largest national agricultural economy in the premodern world.

The advancement in land productivity continuously reduced the minimum size of the farm needed to maintain subsistence living, whereby (1) the time bomb of land shortage (either in the absolute or relative senses) was defused time and again, and (2) what is known as the 'trend of universal middle-peasants' (*zhongnonghua*, meaning that the majority of the rural population joined the 'peasant middle class' in both landholding and standard of living) was fostered in post-Song China (see Li B.Z. 1985, 1996a, b).

### 3.5.2.4 Critique of the man-to-land ratio approach

The man-to-land ratio approach is often used to explain the reason why in certain societies, capital-intensive production, or manufacturing and capitalist industrialisation, failed to take place (Bray 1984, 1986; Chao 1986). The reasons why the man-to-land ratio approach has become popular lie in the facts: (1) Europe enjoyed a favourable man-to-land ratio prior to and throughout the process of industrialisation (Perkins 1969: 13–17; Chao 1986: 223); (2) Europe enjoyed a relatively large agricultural surplus which financed industrialisation (Kuznets 1966: 103); and (3) Europe for a long time had a lower agricultural output potential than China, which became an advantage for its later development (Gerschenkron 1962: 72). Obviously, (2) and (3) have little to do with man-to-land ratio *per se*; and (1) alone does not explain the European production function and living standards.

In the light of the above analysis, the 'man-to-land ratio approach' (see Chao 1986) needs to be re-evaluated, especially considering the long term. By definition, a man-to-land ratio shows only a degree of land scarcity under population pressure, which is caused by the supply of land being less elastic to the growth of human biomass. A man-to-land ratio does not however, show, any technological change, or any change in the production function, although it may be loosely related to technological status of the economy. Not surprisingly, with the same man-to-land ratio there may exist a wide range of possibilities for production functions. On the other hand, when a man-to-land ratio changes, the production function can remain the same. More particularly, the marginal product of labour can differ under the same man-to-land ratio, and different man-to-land ratios may coexist with the same level of marginal product of labour. The same can also be said of the marginal product of capital and land. In all, the same man-to-land ratio can result in very different total outputs.

It is obvious that a declining man-to-land ratio does not necessarily mean a deteriorating agricultural economy or living standards. In theory, once the curve of marginal product of labour/capital is shifted upwards with the upgrading of technology, agricultural productivity and the total output level increase and the decline in labour/capital marginal product (which is caused by the law of diminishing returns) is simultaneously offset (see the TP, APL and MPL curves in Appendix D). Thus, an economy with land scarcity does not necessarily fall into a vicious circle of labour intensiveness and low labour productivity. Throughout Chinese history, the development of science and technology had a strong bias towards agricultural improvements (Deng 1993a), which indicates that the production function in agriculture experienced continued changes and the alleged impact of the deteriorating man-to-land ratio may well have been offset and neutralised. Therefore, it is risky to rely on the man-to-land ratio to analyse the long-term economic history of China.

If population is growing, an increasing man-to-land ratio often indicates technological progress, while a constant man-to-land ratio indicates territorial expansion. This is illustrated in Figure 3.8, in which the curve OB stands

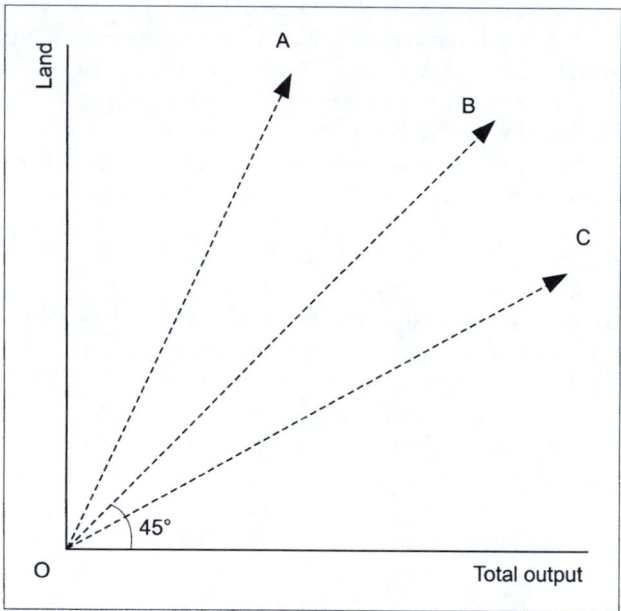

*Figure 3.8* Land input and total output

*Note*

OB, no technological change; OA, technological degeneration; OC, with both technological change and population increase.

for a territorial expansion path with no technological improvement since the land under cultivation and the total output increase at the same speed simultaneously and the man-to-land ratio remains constant. OA represents a technological degeneration path since the total output level falls behind expansion over land. OC on the other hand demonstrates a rapid technological advancement path since the total output increases at a much higher speed than that of the land expansion. In this sense, the man-to-land ratio is irrelevant to population status.

To take change in man-to-land ratio in isolation as the sole indicator for overpopulation is misleading, and can be called 'demographic determinism'. Unfortunately, the demographic determinist argument is often overwhelming in dealing with Chinese economic history: overpopulation led to labour-intensive production which in turn caused the population to expand further. For example, Bray believes that population growth and agricultural intensification worked hand in hand: surplus population and multicropping rice production were a perfect match (Bray 1986).

Moreover, by definition, the general living standards in a society are measured not by man-to-land ratio but by per capita GNP, which is a quotient of total output divided by total population. Therefore, an increasing man-to-land ratio does not mean much before we know anything about the corresponding GNP. In this context, the man-to-land ratio is again irrelevant to determine living standards.

In addition, although land-saving inventions and innovations change the man-to-land ratio, with a farmer tilling less land, the absolute amounts of land and labour may reduce in producing each unit of agricultural products. From this point of view, most technological progress saved both land and labour. The so-called land-saving innovation is only a relative concept.

It is worth noting, first, that periodically the deteriorating man-to-land ratio was reversed by heavy losses of population in civil wars and external invasions throughout premodern Chinese history (see Appendix I). So, the clock was from time to time reset. For instance, when China, particularly the north, was depopulated during alien conquest first by the Jin Tartars and then by the Mongols, the resulting man-to-land ratio appears to have been favourable to a capital-intensive pattern of agriculture. This, however, did not develop. No revolutionary change took place to lead China to a stage of proto-capitalist agriculture as over-optimistically suggested by Bray (1984: 587–616). The point is that when the country was depopulated by war, capital in the form of draught animals, farming implements and houses was destroyed as well. So, a single element such as the man-to-land ratio alone cannot be used to account for agricultural growth. Second, and more importantly, there is no persuasive evidence that European technological progress was predominantly labour-saving in early modern times: only 3.7 per cent of the total English patents of the eighteenth century belong to the 'labour-saving' category (Mokyr 1990: 165), which means that labour was plentiful in industrialising England so that capital and land-saving became the mainstream in inventions and innovations. This seriously challenges Chao's assertion that the Anglo-European Industrial Revolution was a labour-saving phenomenon (1986: 227). It also raises doubts about the claim that once an abundant labour supply reached a certain point, the entire technical structure was geared to a labour-intensive pattern (Elvin 1973: 306, 308, 314; Chao 1986: 227; Merson 1989: 79).

The real problem about premodern China is not why the man-to-land ratio became poorer and poorer, but why, given the land and labour productivities achieved by the Chinese, a part of the agrarian population was not released from agriculture to facilitate industrial growth. The Chinese seem to have deliberately stayed in agriculture despite Chinese agriculture reaching the point where a farmer was able to feed at least two persons, as shown in the above analysis. In other words, the Chinese problem was more institutional than technical.

### 3.5.2.5 Technological progress in agriculture

It is commonly believed that China had an increasing population, expanding cultivated land areas and eventually stagnant technology (see Needham 1954–90; Chao 1986). This view is now highly questionable, because what we can see in reality was a completely different picture: with a steady population growth and without the import of foodstuffs, the Chinese cultivated acreage shrank in both the relative sense (seen from the man-to-land ratio change) and the absolute sense (seen from the reduction of the total acreage under cultivation) (see Figure 3.9). This was the case not simply during the periods when the Chinese Empire fragmented – for example, towards the end of the Tang (AD 618–907) and Northern Song (AD 960–1127) dynasties – but also when the empire's territory was stable or even expanding such as during the Mongol Yuan (1271–1368) and Manchu Qing (1644–1911) dynasties. By 1662 the cultivated area in China had shrunk to 72 per cent of what it had been eighty years earlier (Jones 1990: 13). There was no sign that this abandonment was involuntary.

This is a serious paradox: with a high rate of population growth and limited arable land, why did the Chinese abandon their valuable cultivated land? The only possible answer to this mysterious behaviour lies in Chinese technology and its progress. The practice of land abandonment indicates that revolutionary changes had taken place in technology. Empirical evidence shows that advancement of agricultural technology in China never stopped, whether in Ming–Qing times or over the country's long-term history (Deng 1993a). These changes, such as the introduction of high-yield species and multi-cropping, meant that peasants were no longer able to or needed to till the same acreage to produce the some quantity of food (Li B. 1996a, b).

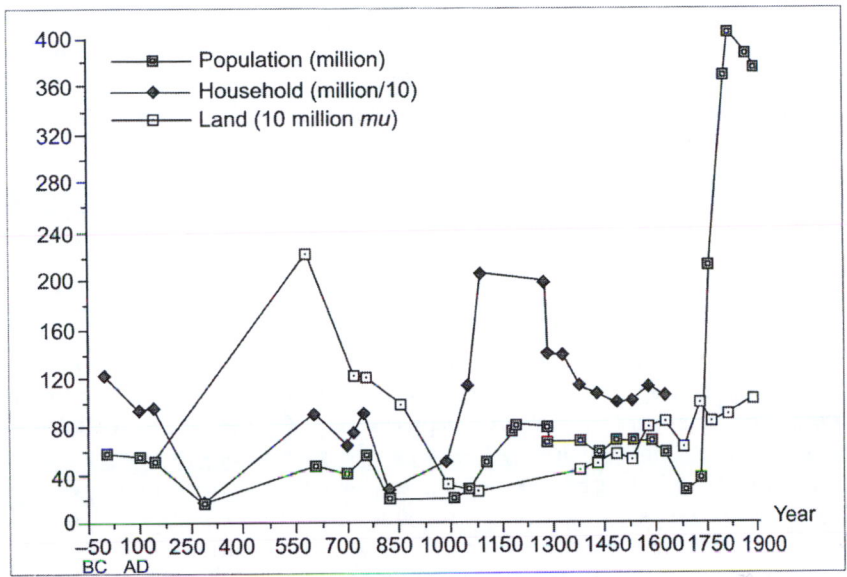

*Figure 3.9* Long-term trend of population and registered land under cultivation
*Source*: Based on information in Appendix I.

Moreover, given that the population did not stop growing in later dynasties, and therefore that China needed to produce a much larger total output from a smaller acreage, the rate of technological progress must have been higher than that of population growth and land area shrinkage combined. Furthermore, considering that Chinese society consisted of a majority of landholding and land-owning peasants, those technological changes must have spread out quickly and widely before abandonment of farming allotments made the aggregate figure of land shrinkage noticeable. This phenomenon thus challenges an often-heard assertion that, as Eric L. Jones puts it, 'an immediate and lasting night [of technological stagnation] fell on China after the twelfth century' (Jones 1990: 13). This phenomenon also throws some doubt on Mark Elvin's model for the Chinese past: owing to the fast rate of population growth the benefit of technological development was eventually eaten up by the increased population after the Song Dynasty (Elvin 1973: pt 3).

### 3.5.2.6 Expenditure pattern

Although in premodern China the government did not have a free hand to squeeze the peasantry, it did have a rent-seeking tendency, which is reflected

191

by periodic increases in taxation. When this was taking place, it reduced the peasant capacity to invest and reinvest in the economy. If a proportion of the after-tax savings of peasants was devoted primarily to investment in farming, and only the remaining funds were used in non-agricultural investment, an increase in taxation would always hit non-agricultural investment first. This is demonstrated by the following formulae:

$$I_{n+1} = I_{a(n+1)} + I_{b(n+1)} \tag{3.14}$$

$$I_{n+1} = Y_n - (i_n + \beta/K_n + W_n + R_n + T_n) \tag{3.15}$$

where $I$ stands for the total fund for investment; $I_a$ and $I_b$, investment in agriculture and non-agriculture respectively; $Y$, total income of the year; $i$, interest as capital returns; $\beta/K$, capital depreciation; $W$, wage bill; $R$, rent; and $T$, government tax on agriculture. The starting period is marked by $n$, while the next period is marked by $n + 1$. Suppose the tax rate is increased by 30 per cent; other things being equal, the value of the investment fund for the next period is reduced. If peasants give agriculture priority by not reducing the investment in farming ($I_a$), the only way they can pay the extra tax is to reduce the investment fund for non-agricultural projects ($I_b$). Also, to a certain extent, an increase in the tax burden is tolerable to the peasantry as long as the fund $I_a$ is still there. In other words, to them the maximum sacrifice is $I_b = 0$. Thus, $I_b$ is the cushion against a tax increase. Of course, the same thing can be said of increases in wage and rent.

More importantly, since the Chinese merchants were attracted to the peasantry and the 'bureaucratic gentry' and spent their fortune in purchasing land and official titles, the capital formation rate in non-agricultural sectors was reduced. Sometimes, those merchants simply withdrew completely from trade to return to the land. Eric L. Jones argues that there was a lack of sufficient incentives to draw out the fullest investment responses in commerce (Jones 1990: 18). Such trade-quitting behaviour indicates that the Chinese did not just overlook investment in non-agricultural sectors, but the Chinese system channelled the funds from trade, for instance, back into agriculture.

Mark Elvin relates population burden to the lack of demand for non-agricultural goods and services (1973: 312): 'A falling surplus per head of population meant, of course, a reduction in effective demand per person for goods other than those needed for bare survival.' By definition, this can take place through an inward shift of the utility function of the population, as commonly practised in the name of frugality in spending during the recessions of modern business cycles. If the demand for non-agricultural goods and services was weak, there was little point in investing. This is another reason for the shortage in investment in the non-agricultural sector.

192

All the above points suggest that the shortage of non-agricultural investment in premodern China was not technological nor demographic, but structural.

### 3.5.3 Room for the market and its characteristics

In the trinary structure, the Chinese imperial apparatus was the guardian of both agriculture and the free peasantry; physiocracy was expected to be the dominant state policy and functioned as a regulator to stop alienation caused by market mechanisms and excessive rent-seeking. A rise of the merchant class and accordingly the emergence of a high degree of market undertakings would present a threat to the system and thus needed to be eliminated. So, there is little doubt that the trinary structure stifled a high degree of development in commercialisation.

#### 3.5.3.1 Supply of and demand for agricultural surplus

Nevertheless, commercialisation and urbanisation always existed in China. The trinary structure did accommodate trade activities. The periods which were marked by promising urbanisation and commercialisation often occurred during the periods of the trinary equilibrium. In this context, it becomes easier to understand why the Chinese merchant class was, in the long term, an active minority.

To begin with, agricultural dominance does not necessarily mean that the Chinese products were short in variety and surplus. Owing to the high level of agricultural productivity and the range of regional differences, agricultural surplus did exist and took a wide variety of forms. As mentioned earlier, between the Northern Song (AD 960–1127) and the Qing (1644–1911) dynasties, an average of 401,000 tonnes of rice was transported each year by the Chinese government under the scheme of the 'annual shipping of rice to the north' (*caoyun*) (Liang F. 1980: 293–4, 303, 375, 394, 396). In terms of variety, the Qing Imperial agronomic treatise entitled *Compendium of Works and Days* (*Shoushi Tongkao*) listed 3,525 rice varieties, making an average of 16 rice varieties for each of 217 administrative divisions (E E. 1742: chs 21–2). Given that Chinese rice is of two major types (glutinous and non-glutinous), and each type has three subtypes (early-ripening, middle-ripening and late-ripening), six varieties would be the minimum number required to cover all the possible combinations. The existence of surplus and variety within the peasant economy was the foundation of market activities, and premodern China was no exception (see Skinner 1964–5, 1977).

The variety was not just a phenomenon exemplified by the grain types, and surplus did not only take the form of grain. Owing to the seasonality in the production cycle in farming, by-employment and sideline production in craft industries was very common in rural China, one example being silk production, which made China known to the premodern world. The typical production pattern in a rural household was called 'tilling by the husband and weaving by the wife' (*nangeng nüzhi*). What is so significant is that under this pattern at least one adult in a household was engaged in non-tillage activities on a regular basis, not just during the off-season periods. Such division of labour and by-employment at the grass-roots level certainly fuelled the market activities of the peasantry. This pattern also determined the way in which tax was paid by each household: grain and cloth. The Chinese farmers did not stop at by-employment; they went further to produce cash crops. To take tea production as an example, the undertakings were on such a large scale in south China that between 1750 and 1875, China was the main supplier of tea, as well as silk, to the rest of the world (see Lin M. 1991: 12–15; Deng 1997: ch. 5). Indeed, these farming household-made cash crops became the backbone of China's foreign trade during the Qing Period: between 1760 and 1833, tea and silk formed at least 90 per cent of the total value of Chinese exports to Britain (see Deng 1997: ch. 5).

On the demand side, it is known that the non-agricultural population varied between 3.17 million and 83.79 million, with an average of 7.02–21.37 million (see Table 3.4). This group formed the cornerstone of urbanisation in premodern China. To take artisans as an example, through generations of practice some Chinese crafts were able to mature and reach perfection. As a result, China gave the impression, to the medieval world, of being a country with style, class and abundance, which was clearly reflected in Marco Polo's *Travels* (see Wright 1854). Slightly exaggerating, Mokyr maintains that 'Europeans had always wanted things that only the Orient could produce; the Oriental empires had little interest in Europeans and their products' (1990: 231). The point is that Chinese artisans had to be fed by agricultural surplus, and had to be maintained for generations before their skills were able to become crystallised in products of high quality. In that sense, Chinese artisans, and indeed the entire non-agricultural population, were the products of Chinese agricultural surplus over time. This does not take into account the intra-agricultural exchange, which was not trivial (see Skinner 1964–5, 1971, 1977). In Skinner's account, China's multiregional, multilayered trading network consisted of as many as 45,000 market towns, each of which affected 15–20 villages (Skinner 1971: 272–3). It is fair, then, to state that the agricultural surplus was stable in the economy.

### 3.5.3.2 *Demand for and supply of non-agricultural products*

The technological status of Chinese agriculture in post-Han times, marked by metal tools (such as hoes, ploughs and sickles) and mechanical devices (including water pumps, milling machines and looms), made agricultural production a difficult task without the inputs of non-agricultural capital goods (see Elvin 1973; Bray 1984; Deng 1993a). These capital goods needed special resources and skills to produce and were certainly made by the artisan class for the market. On the other hand, although agricultural surplus existed in the economy, these artisans did not get 'free lunches' from tax revenue and thus had to get food, at least partly, from market trade with farmers.

Thus, there is little doubt that a degree of commercialisation existed in and served the trinary framework either from the viewpoint of a necessary vent for agricultural surplus or from the viewpoint of a result of exchange between agricultural and non-agricultural sectors. It is a case of interdependence between urban China and rural China.

However, China had, at the most, a proto-market economy. First, the areas where trade was allowed were limited. Market control by the state in China had been common since the time prior to Christ, such as the monopoly of some 'key' domestic staple markets such as salt, wine, metal and weapons (Zhou B. 1981: 51–7, 110–13, 173–7, 214–16, 268–76). Control was also imposed upon foreign trade (Deng 1997: ch. 4). Second, the key to a full development of the market economy from a non-market base lies in market penetration and marketisation of the agricultural sector (Jones 1981: ch. 5). The development of the market sector in traditional China never reached this level.

### 3.5.3.3 Pan-merchanting of the peasantry

According to modern anthropological studies, peasants in a traditional society were natural, active market participants (see, for example, Kroeber 1948: 284). The most striking characteristic of the market under the trinary structure, though, was what can be called 'pan-merchanting of the peasantry', an ocean of trade-active peasants scattered in tens of thousands of market towns (Skinner 1971: 272–3; Gates 1996), equipped with household produce in the form of either agricultural surplus or seasonal by-employment and full-time sideline production. On Perkins's and Feuerwerker's accounts, during the Ming–Qing Period and throughout the early twentieth century as much as 20–40 per cent of China's agricultural output was traded (Perkins 1969: 115; Feuerwerker 1976: 86).

But, as far as the specialisation and development of labour division are concerned, this pan-merchanting of the peasantry functioned more as an obstacle than a booster. To take cotton as an example, the crop was widely produced as a cash crop in the Yangzi River Valley during Ming–Qing times. Peasants in the valley also possessed the expertise to spin and weave cotton. But, despite the advantage of processing cotton, peasants spun only enough for their own consumption and sold the rest as raw material. Cotton-rich China ended up importing foreign cotton instead of exporting finished cotton products (Fairbank 1980 vol. 11: 17–18, 21). Under the trinary equilibrium landholding and land-owning farmers did not have a strong enough incentive to move away from agriculture full time, although they may well have become qualified part-time traders, craftsmen or entertainers. The only exception was the affiliation to the bureaucracy: to have a son well educated, pass the Imperial Examination and become an official was every farmer's dream, rich and poor alike. This shows just how close a link there was between the peasantry and the bureaucracy: the peasantry saw officialdom as enjoying the highest status individuals could attain in society, while the government saw the peasantry as a pool of talent to supply the bureaucracy. This is clearly a case of symbiosis. Both parties were agriculture-based, hence although joining the bureaucracy was the end, it was only a natural extension of one's career in the agricultural sector. In other words, the opportunity cost for members of the Chinese peasantry to quit farming and join officialdom diminished, because, apart from the prestige of being an official, agriculture was certainly the recognisable ground for such a type of pseudo-specialisation. The Chinese bureaucracy was, to a great extent, a group of learned peasant sons, and the peasantry to the same extent formed the supporting majority for the physiocratic party in power.

The combination of the 'pan-merchanting' and government monopoly formed an anti-merchant market alliance in the economy. Very limited room was then left for professional merchants. The effect was to elbow the merchants out of certain markets and to confine them in others. This worked as an inhibitor to the full growth of the professional merchant class. The best retaliation from the merchant class was to join the land-holding and land-owning class in the fashion that 'if you can't beat them, join them'.

Therefore, the impression is wrong that the Chinese authorities physically monitored and controlled the merchants day and night, 365 days a year. The surveillance cost would have been too high. Certainly, premodern China lacked a sound financial and legal system conducive to commerce. China had no history of mercantilism as Europe did. But this had more to do with the lack of need to protect commerce than the incompetence of the state. The opportunity cost of not protecting commerce may have been high, but the cost of not protecting agriculture was almost certainly higher, at least in the short run. As Professor Mark Elvin points out, the way in which the government acted greatly impaired the economy of China's coastal provinces, especially Fujian (Fukien), and hence might have 'deprived China of stimuli which could have triggered new scientific and technological departures' (Elvin 1973: 215). The check provided by ordinary peasants who participated in market activities in the capacity of part-time or casual petty merchants proved to be more effective. Purely from a surveillance point of view, watching by the jealous eyes of millions of ordinary peasants made it an impossible task for merchants living in a rural area to conceal their wealth for long from the taxman. If they decided to move to the cities, they immediately put themselves under the thumb of the mandarins. The merchants could, as they often did, bribe the villagers and urban mandarins to secure their wealth. But, as a deduction of private wealth, handing out bribes was not different from paying taxes.

The impression is also wrong that the Chinese government was capable of curbing the merchants single-handedly with state coercion. In Chinese history, merchant activities were tolerated by the state when they were under control. For instance, by the nineteenth century titles and ranks were bestowed on some merchants (Perkins 1967: 479), and government tax did not place a tremendous burden on internal trade (*ibid.*: 480). However, this does not mean that the general attitude towards merchants changed in a revolutionary way, as is suggested by some researchers (*ibid.*: 479–80). The secret of Chinese success in controlling merchants was through the peaceful process of integrative social mobility. Officialdom and farming functioned like two opposite magnetic poles to attract elements from the merchant class: individual merchants either purchased land to join the peasantry, or purchased education, and even official titles, to join the elite club. As Needham puts it (1969: 202), 'Wealth as such was not wisdom, and in China affluence carried comparatively little prestige. The ideal of every merchant's son was to become a scholar, to enter the imperial examination and to rise high in the bureaucracy.' As a result, the Chinese merchant class always had one foot outside commerce, and the professional merchant class was to a great extent 'de-merchanted', the members being part-time farmers or part-time 'gents'. As entrepreneurial spirit and its influence diminished, China had no leader for capitalist development.

Such a socio-economic environment has created some paradoxes. For example, merchants in China developed a wide range of standardised marketing practices, such as using uniforms, trademarks, shop names, labels, packaging, quality control stamps, trading language and a credit system (Elvin 1973: 162, 281, 294; Wu Y. 1988: 64–6). But they did not have an autonomous organisation in the European style: even the merchant organisations were organised in China by the government and functioned like a branch of the administration network. No merchant solidarity of the European style existed. Nor did autonomous control by merchants of price, quality and output exist, as they did in Europe (Jones 1988: 102–3). Regarding commercial activities, Chinese merchants not only relied on the government for money supply, permits and quotas for lucrative 'key markets', but also depended on the government for the invention and operation of bills of exchange (Zheng X. *et al.* 1984: 371), unthinkable in the Western European context. Not until 1797, over one and a half centuries after their invention, were bills of exchange operated by private merchants in Shanxi (*ibid.*: 371–2; Zhang Z. 1995: 167–82). The Chinese merchants were neutralised and dissolved in the trinary structure and never became mature and independent enough to challenge the structure or change the path of economic development.

In contrast, under a rigid feudal system, merchants were largely excluded from landholding and they had few other choices but to pursue a career as full-time merchants. Moreover, they had to protect themselves by forming guilds and even establishing city-states. This is a clear-cut picture of the class distinction and class struggle of Marxism. In China, the social mobility mechanism blended 'classes' within the trinary equilibrium. That is one of the reasons why the Marxist approach of class theory always causes confusion in dealing with socio-economic development in both premodern and modern China. Marxists have made endless attempts to cast the Chinese population in the class mould of the European style. Not surprisingly, their results are shaky.

### 3.5.3.4 *Pseudo-capitalism*

The trinary system was even flexible enough to allow pseudo-capitalism to develop, a status of specialisation, commercialisation and urbanisation that China achieved from time to time throughout history. In Han times, for instance, merchants earned 20 per cent profit and the capital city, Chang-an, had nine market-places and goods were traded according to their nature and sorts. These places were so crowded that people and vehicles could hardly move on the streets. Apart from the capital, there were 100,000 households in Lizi City, where the local merchants were wealthier than their counterparts in Chang-an (Zhou B. 1981: 108–9). Sometimes, the well-to-do maritime merchants became richer than the monarch (see Deng 1997: ch. 5).

In terms of commercialisation, China was once ahead of Europe in some areas. While Europe was still bartering and using precious metals as a form of liquidity, China was already in a basically cash economy where barter was no longer the norm. To respond to a shortage of money supply in copper coins, the Chinese began to develop a credit system (Elvin 1973: ch. 11). Moreover, trade along rivers and by sea was more advanced in Song China than in Europe and Japan at that time (around AD 1000). China remained in this position until the Ming Dynasty. Also during this period, public goods such as canals and roads were vigorously created, which benefited the traders (Jones 1988: 78).

Although commercialisation in premodern China was largely based on surplus products, as the first stage of commercial development such surplus-based commercialisation is not uniquely Chinese. The real problem is why the Chinese did not go further to enter the next stage of capitalism, given that China had some important instruments such as market, currency and credit. Obviously, the reason was not due to a lack of trade or commercial activities in China, either in terms of multitude or techniques, but because of something else. A parallel also existed in Europe: early commercial regions such as southern Italy and parts of the Netherlands were not the first places to have capitalist industrialisation. After all, trade is only one of the conditions for capitalist development.

### 3.5.3.5 *Incompetent cities and retarded merchants*

In the eyes of Marco Polo, premodern China had impressive cities which belittled any of their European counterparts in size, population and organisation (Wright 1854). But there were some fundamental differences between the Chinese and European cities.

First, the merchant class was actively involved in the establishment of European cities, while in China, cities were mainly built by the authorities. Second, although both European and Chinese cities were once administrative centres (Murphey 1954: 350), the former were quickly changed into trading centres, while Chinese cities remained administrative centres (*ibid.*: 351, 353). Third, consequently, China did not have a history of city-states, an institution which played an important role in the formation of capitalism (Hicks 1969: 38), one of the main reasons being that China did not produce an independent bourgeoisie class.

The status and role of the Chinese merchants has induced some very intriguing discussions about Chinese society and government. The most common view blames the Chinese authorities for their iron-fisted handling of merchants and in the stifling of capitalist tendencies. In other words, the Chinese government was too coercive, which made the merchant class weak and incompetent. This may sound plausible if the factors are examined in isolation. Whether the Chinese government viewed the merchant class as a threat or not does not change the fact that in Chinese society the only powerful rival to the government was the peasantry, not the merchants. Just for the sake of the balance of power, the Chinese government should have left the merchants alone or formed an alliance with them to form an anti-peasant united front. Unlike in Europe, such an alliance never occurred successfully in post-Qin China in the long term. Instead, the Chinese government often entered into an alliance with the peasantry against the merchants. The only explanation is that the merchant class was alien to the trinary equilibrium, and thus needed to be controlled.

Premodern China had at most some room for sporadic and tenuous rudiments (commonly known as 'buds') of capitalism or pseudo-capitalism to appear, but never created any leeway for them to grow.

### 3.5.4 **Demographic pattern**

The analysis of the non-agricultural population shows the overall population structure in the long term. In the light of the analysis, it is easy to understand that 'overpopulation' is indeed a relative term. By definition, if a society can still feed its population, it is not overpopulated, no matter what sort of man-to-land ratio it faces. Therefore, the head count per unit of land area, known as 'population density', can be a very misleading measure of whether a society is overpopulated. An industrialised society is far too crowded by the standards of an agrarian society; an agrarian society is too crowded in the eyes of tribes-men practising hunting and gathering. Moreover, population is not just a biological concept, but also a socio-economic concept which embodied occu-pational skills. A large population with more sophisticated skills often enjoys a higher standard of living than people in a thinly populated, primitive society. So, population quality is as important as population quantity.

The sign of overpopulation is a rapid decline of population in a short per-iod (shorter than a generation's time) through starvation, for example. So, the very fact that the Chinese population steadily increased in Qing times, for instance, suggests the opposite. Of course, such a process is conditional: society needs peace and tranquillity. If a war breaks out and consequently the normal production cycle is interrupted, the existing equilibrium will end and the society will then become overpopulated overnight. A natural dis-aster has a similar effect. Such a disaster-induced overpopulation can take place even in the most thinly populated areas on this planet and thus should be taken as an abnormal case. Thus the criterion by which to judge whether a society is overpopulated is to see whether the population is fed. Population growth is reliable evidence with which to refute the notion of overpopulation. It is quite a different matter to ask how well the population is fed. The former is about the population size that a society can afford to have; the latter, the quality of life, which depends not only on population size but also the distri-bution of income. Confusion often occurs as a result of the overwhelming appeal of assessment of society's welfare in terms of per capita income.

In terms of the demographic pattern, what matters is how the population responds to the fluctuations of the total output of agriculture, which can be defined as 'population elasticity to agricultural output' (PEAO). The formula is:

$$e = \frac{\partial P}{\partial Q} \cdot \frac{Q}{P} \qquad (\partial P \geq 0; \ \partial Q > 0; \ 0 \leq e \leq 1) \qquad (3.16)$$

Or,

$$PEAO = \frac{\text{percentage change in population}}{\text{percentage change in agricultural output}}$$

We assume that under normal circumstances the change in agricultural out-put ($\partial Q$) is positive and the change in population ($\partial P$) is not negative; and that the value of PEAO ($e$) is between unity and zero. If $e$ is greater than unity, the society is overpopulated: population growth surpasses that of the total output in agriculture. If $e$ is below zero, the society has either net popu-lation loss (negative reproduction rate of human biomass) or net output loss (underproduction in the agricultural economy). If $e$ is unity, increases in population and agricultural output synchronise perfectly, and the society reaches zero economic growth, or a stationary state, which is similar to what is described in the Quesnay–Ricardo model except for an expanding population (Schumpeter 1954: 243, 563–4). Thus, if the agricultural output and population increase or decrease in the same direction and to the same degree, a society has a sensitive or high PEAO. If agricultural output increases while the population increases at a slower rate, or remains stationary, or even moves in the opposite direction, a society has a low PEAO. Obviously, PEAO has a direct influence on both population growth and living standards which is measured in per capita output/income.

China had, and still has, a high PEAO: the population closely follows the increase in the total output of agriculture. As mentioned earlier, in premodern China such behaviour was not primarily derived from ideology or culture. It was dictated by: (1) private individual land ownership; (2) the equal inheritance system; (3) freedom of decision-making at the grass-roots level; and (4) reasonable fertility of the adult population due to reasonable nutrition and reasonable surplus to support a dependent population including pregnant mothers and children under labouring age.

In general, with an increase in agricultural output, there was a strong incentive for ordinary households to have children and to have more of them, chiefly for economic reasons. Without modern technology it was difficult to store food for long. Sun-dried cereals kept in cool, dry storage conditions can probably last for ten years at the maximum. Processed meat lasts a much shorter time. An alternative way to store agricultural surplus is to use the 'food chain' to convert the surplus into more durable and/or more valuable goods through food consumption by livestock and/or by extra family members. There is a limit for this conversion through livestock, determined by the physical size of the farm and the animal's optimal age for working or for slaughter. Also, it is rather difficult to convert meat through livestock. But the conversion of the surplus grain and meat can always take the form of maintaining more children, who are both valuable and durable. Therefore, when modern technology for grain/meat storage and the market for surplus grain/meat are absent or limited, feeding extra family members is a rational way to dispose of agricultural surplus.

This is particularly true as empirical evidence shows that the returns from the investment in children are both long delayed and very limited. A recent study of India indicates that until the 1980s children in non-modernised rural India were still regarded as an 'investment good'. They began to work at the age of 5 and to yield net economic returns at the age of 15 (Balasubramanyam 1984: 19). Given that the Indian life expectancy at birth was 52 (in 1981), which can be taken as a proxy for an average life cycle, the investment was likely to be nearly one-third (15:52, or 29 per cent) of a human life. Since this investment period was much longer than that for a draught animal in both absolute and relative terms, it was probably not a very profitable way to make returns, not to mention the fact that the net yield from a

15-year-old child was hardly sufficient to support the parents. At best, the Indian youngsters served as an 'age pension scheme' for the end of their parents' lives when the latter could no longer support themselves. So, not only was the investment in children very long term but also it yielded very limited returns. It thus is a paradox that the rural Indians were still so keen on such investment. Here, what has been commonly overlooked is the function of children in relation to surplus product management or, simply, 'waste management' in the production cycle.

To have more children was determined not only by the 'age pension scheme' and surplus product management, but also by institutions, mainly property rights. Private property rights gave ordinary households the incentive to have children just for the sake of keeping the ownership within the family. With the combination of high productivity in agriculture and private property rights, the Chinese economy produced two kinds of 'crops': grain and children. Therefore, a high PEAO was a built-in product of the Chinese system.

By comparison, under a feudal system there was an institutional barrier to family expansion. As a result, both celibacy (in England) and infanticide (in Japan) were practised on a noticeable scale. Then, technological progress in agriculture along with a low population growth rate led to surplus, mainly in the form of agricultural products. With the constraint in storage, trade, or the incentive to undertake trade, arose. Moreover, improvement in technology and labour productivity sometimes made a part of the existing labour force redundant, which created surplus labour in the agricultural sector. These two types of surpluses provided the foundation for industrialisation. Industrialisation in turn brought about more technological change in agriculture, and the process started all over again until a large proportion of the rural population was sucked into industries and the gravity of the economy shifted to the industrial sector, this being known as a 'structural change of the economy'. This applies to Meiji Japan, where the creation of a landholding peasantry was a component of the package for industrialisation, known as the 'Japanese Mode of Production' (Tomlinson 1985: 677–8; see also Hayami and Ruttan 1971: 1), instead of a component of a package of 'agrarianisation' as in Zhou–Qin China.

Therefore, an unemployed and dispensable labour force, not a man-to-land ratio, is a much more relevant criterion by which to judge whether the agricultural sector is overpopulated. Throughout history, such an unemployed and dispensable labour force in the agricultural sector has been a prerequisite for industrialisation and capital-intensive farming to take place. If the farming population was not bound to land property ownership, as was the case under feudalism, the rural surplus population could be dismissed from land within a short period of time. Therefore the worst enemy of the rise of industries and capital-intensive farming is not the population size and density, but the 'man-to-land bondage'. Population density is thus not necessarily a barrier to more capital-intensive production. By definition, in an agrarian society, only when a minimal size of surplus population becomes available from agriculture can industries obtain a steady labour supply and grow. In contrast, in premodern China, such a man to land bondage was particularly strong because of the private individual land ownership and equal inheritance system, which gave the peasantry a strong incentive to maintain a tie to the land, rather than seeking alternative careers to make a living. To ask why the Chinese peasants did not want to leave land is to ask why landholders did not want to give up their property and, ultimately, why there was value for land as an economic resource. In the light of this analysis, it is easy to see how superficial and misleading it is to blame the population density in China for a non-capitalist development trend.

With a high degree of PEAO, technological inventions and innovations in premodern China led to agricultural surplus, but not at the same time to a dispensable rural population. The surplus became a source for population increase. So, the greater the technological change, the greater the total output and the greater the population size.

It is worth noting that most Third World countries today have a high degree of 'population elasticity to income', which is just another form of high PEAO. The effect is well known: population growth closely chases income growth. Although it is often taken as the first and inevitable stage of modern economic growth, according to the 'demographic transition model' (see Osborn 1960: 90–1), such a phenomenon reveals that a high PEAO is not uniquely Chinese. It did not result from Confucianism or other traditional values. In mainland China, after the devastating Cultural Revolution the government had to impose the most extreme means in human history to keep the birth rate under control among the 'de-Confucianised' young generation born in the 1960s and 1970s. It is now clear that the Chinese government's ambition has failed: a high PEAO tendency has recurred in rural China, having been fuelled and refuelled by the *de facto* private landholding under the economic reform under Deng Xiaoping. So, those Chinese values at best strengthened and rationalised the existing high PEAO pattern.

To sum up, demographic determinism is based on false causality. The Chinese population size was indeed innocent in relation to the economic development status of premodern China, and so was the Chinese demographic behavioural pattern, simply because neither of them was the cause of the problem. The cause was closely related to the trinary equilibrium. With hindsight, feudalism was a blessing to capitalist industrialisation. England, despite noticeable technological advancement, experienced only a slight population growth between 1650 and 1750. It is obvious that the English inheritance system contributed at least partly to the moderate population growth. As a result, PEAO was low and the society was able to spend the surplus income on non-agricultural activities which stimulated markets (see Jones 1968: 59).

### 3.5.5  General living standards

With continuous progress in agricultural technology (see Deng 1993a), a population with a high PEAO did not necessarily lead to a decline in living standards (Mokyr 1990: 219). There is no evidence that, at least before the eighteenth century, China suffered chronic food shortage. So, although they reflect the output levels of Chinese agriculture, the sheer size and the increasing tendency of the Chinese population certainly do not indicate a low standard of living in comparison to, say, China's neighbouring countries, including Tokugawa Japan. Some comparative studies have suggested that around the mid-eighteenth century the average living standards in China (lumped with the Third World) were as high as in China's European counterparts (Bairoch 1993: 95), and during the same period the living standards in China's advanced regions were decades ahead of those in advanced European regions (Pomeranz 1997), which seems to be well supported by solid evidence from European visitors' own accounts of that time (see, for example, Barrow 1804: 527; Ellis 1818 vol. 2: 128–9; Bairoch 1993: 106–8).

#### 3.5.5.1  Hidden abundance

Standard of living is a function of at least four variables, namely (1) output level, (2) technology, (3) population size, and (4) income distribution. Household consumption pattern can be added, although data are often not readily available. To see the trend, scholars commonly compare population growth, cultivated land area and technological progress embodied in output level. If cultivated land area grows at the same speed as population, technology being held constant, people are at least not worse off. If cultivated land area grows faster than population, it is assumed that people become better off. If cultivated land area is held constant, technological progress and population growth work on the same principle. When technology and population are both held constant, income distribution plays the role of determining how people live with the given aggregate yield. The benefits of better technology and less population pressure may be cancelled by a less favourable income distribution system offering fewer incentives. At the same time, a favourable income distribution system that does offer incentives may offset technological difficulty and population pressure and thus allows the society to enjoy a living standard similar to that achieved by a technologically more advanced and less populated society. In reality, these three variables have different trends and different degrees of development, resulting in far more complex combinations.

A stereotype argument is that (1) after Song times the momentum of technological development in Chinese agriculture not only slowed down but stopped; (2) the expansion of cultivated land in China did not keep up with the speed of population growth, especially in the Ming–Qing period; and (3) living standards must have been on the decline. Premodern China is often taken as a classic case of the Malthusian crisis (see Chao 1986). As mentioned earlier, however, evidence shows that technological development did not stop in premodern China, which undermines the very basis of the Malthusian hypothesis.

More encouragingly, according to Perkins (1967) and Mokyr (1990), significant decline in total agricultural output did not occur in China, nor did the income level and living standards decline. One study explicitly suggests that medieval China had minimal income differentials by modern standards and that the ordinary Chinese enjoyed a higher standard of living than their European counterparts probably until the eighteenth century (Bairoch 1986). Although there is a lack of data concerning living standards in premodern China, some testing of the Perkins–Mokyr hypothesis can still be conducted. Logically, when foreign trade is absent, a society must have enough surplus before it can contain extra population simply because children are dependent on adult providers. Women, during a certain period of their pregnancy and immediately after giving birth, join the dependent population, too. Therefore, even just to replace the existing population (i.e. zero population growth) requires a certain degree of surplus from agriculture. Otherwise, the normal life cycle of society cannot be maintained. Considering the production cycle of agriculture, which is characterised by seasonal processes and, in particular, an annual harvest, deferred consumption of agricultural output is the way of life, as is basic management of the household economy. The time lag between two harvests makes savings crucial. Such deferred consumption and inter-seasonal saving also make hidden abundance possible at the household level.

PATTERN 1: ONE STEP FORWARD AND ONE STEP BACKWARD

Assume a young peasant couple establishes a family in year 1 with a new baby. The very facts (1) that this family has financially survived during the wife's pregnancy and the break after the birth, and (2) that this family is supporting a new dependant mean sufficient surplus existed before year 1. The surplus is hidden because it is now embodied in the nine-months'-long pregnancy and in the life of the new baby. But, in theory, this family must begin with abundance before it grows. It is indeed another matter that such surplus is later substituted by or materialised in the increased dependent population (the pregnant wife plus the baby), because the disposable surplus may well be saved, invested or consumed by the working couple, instead of their using it for the new baby-related expenses. This correlation can be expressed in the following formulae:

$$I_{(i)} = Q_{(t1+t2)} + S_{(t1+t2)} = A_{(i-1)} - \{K_{(i-1)} + E_{(i-1)}\}$$
$$(i = t_1 + t_2)$$

(3.17)

$$I_{(i)} = P_{(i)} = P_{W(t1+t2)} + P_{D(t2)}$$
$$\{P_{(t1+t2)} = Q_{(t1+t2)}; \; P_{D(t2)} = S_{(t1+t2)}\} \tag{3.18}$$

where $I_{(i)}$ stands for the total income of period $i$, which can be divided into two sums ($Q$ and $S$) in two subperiods ($t_1$ and $t_2$): $Q_{(t1+t2)}$ is the amount (wage bill) required to maintain the working population during period $i$, while $S_{(t1+t2)}$ is the amount of intra-agricultural surplus. $A_{(i-1)}$ represents the total output of the previous period $i - 1$. $K_{(i-1)}$ is the capital expenditure in period $i - 1$, $E_{(i-1)}$ is the material expenditure in period $i - 1$. $P_{(i)}$ stands for the population size during period $i$, $P_W$ is the working population and $P_D$ the dependent. Logically, the dependent population only can occur in subperiod $t_2$. The hidden abundance can be measured by the intra-agricultural surplus $S_{(t1+t2)}$, or the dependent population $P_{D(t2)}$.

The standards of living during the entire period $i$ is measured by $M$ in the per capita term, which is a quotient of total output or income ($I$) divided by total population ($P$), as follows:

$$M_{(i)} = \frac{I_{(i)}}{P_{(i)}} = \frac{Q_{(t1+t2)} + S_{(t1+t2)}}{P_{(i)}} \tag{3.19}$$

However, income is not evenly distributed through the entire period $i$, there is considerable difference between subperiods $t_1$ and $t_2$. During subperiod $t_1$ the hidden abundance takes the form of disposable income $h$, and the living standard of the household is improved in the per capita term, and thus:

$$h = M_{(t1)} - M_{(t2)} \tag{3.20}$$

$$M_{(t1)} = \frac{I_{(t1+t2)}}{P_{W(t1)}} > M_{(t2)} = \frac{I_{(t1+t2)}}{P_{W(t1+t2)} + P_{D(t2)}} \tag{3.21}$$

As long as a society has a minimal rate of population growth, the living standard in subperiod $t_1$ is higher than that in subperiod $t_2$, represented by the value of $h$. Since the time lag is constant, owing to the agricultural production cycle and human reproduction cycle, the hidden abundance ($h$) is bound to exist in one of the subperiods and thus should not be ignored.

According to this time-lag approach, at the macro level, before each wave of new babies there is a wave of uplift in income in per capita terms: abundances make it possible to have more children. Certainly a baby boom may offset the increase in living standards later on, but that is a consequence, not a cause. In other words, improvement in per capita income must occur first, and growth in population follows. Otherwise, it is impossible to have any population increase. Therefore, the cycle must begin with abundances even in the strictest Malthusian terms.

Considering that Chinese society consisted of a majority of landholding peasants, and that they were the main contributors to population growth at any given time, it is almost certain that the living standards of ordinary farming households improved from time to time across the country. This is particularly true if we take the Chinese hyper-growth of population in Qing times into account: in a space of some 150 years between 1680 and 1833, the population enlarged 22.33 times, with a rate of 2.05 per cent per year (see Appendix I). Such an increase in population can be converted to agricultural surplus. From the time-lag point of view, the population enjoyed from time to time a rise in per capita income. In our case, it was annually 1.5 per cent from where the income level had been (either at the subsistence level of living or above). One may see the second half of the seventeenth century as a special case because of the heavy losses in human life after the nationwide armed rebellions at the end of the Ming Dynasty and the alien conquest at the beginning of the Qing. Therefore, the hyper-growth in population was largely the result of a low demographic base. The problem can be avoided by skipping the second half of the seventeenth century. Even so, the Chinese population grew very fast: between 1626 and 1833, it increased 6.72 times, which makes the annual growth rate 0.99 per cent.

Obviously, the conventional Malthusian approach is static, which often indicates that the Chinese fell into a trap of population deadlock. The present approach is more dynamic and shows that the Chinese problem was what may be called 'population fetishism': given the disposable agricultural surplus and the possibilities of sustained improvement in living standards, there was a lack of stimuli in Chinese society for ordinary people to seek a better life to substitute more children. In other words, the improvement in the Chinese living standards fell behind the potential promised by the level of agricultural surplus.

In the light of the time-lag approach, the population problem may have very little to do with intensive farming practice *per se*, as often suggested (see, for example, Bray 1986; Chao 1986). Peasants may deliberately stay in the agricultural sector when their marginal physical product of labour approaches or even reaches zero (see Appendix D), whereas the basic drive for more and more intensive farming is to prevent the marginal physical product of labour from reaching that point.

With this pattern, the per capita income of the population takes one step forward in subperiod $t_1$ and one step backward in subperiod $t_2$, the assumption being that the surplus is just enough to provide for the wife during her pregnancy, her after-birth break and a new baby. Hence, the surplus eventually disappears during the period of family establishment ($t_2$). The income level oscillates over time and in the long term stagnates. The conditions for such oscillation are (1) that new land is always available and tilled at the same speed as population growth or that technological change takes place at the same speed as population growth, and (2) that disasters, either natural or man-made, are at an acceptable level so that the cycle can start again.

PATTERN 2: TWO STEPS FORWARD AND ONE STEP BACK

If a society manages to produce food at a faster rate than the rate of human reproduction with an interval between births and infant deaths at a minimum, it enjoys a gradual improvement in per capita income as 'two steps forward and one step back'. If we agree with the Boserupian model, and thus agree that $M = f(L)$, income ($M$, per capita GNP) being the function of population size or labour input (L), such an outcome can be expected. This is illustrated as follows:

$$M_{(i+1)} = f(L_{(i+1)}) = n \cdot M_{(i)} f(L_{(i)}) \qquad (n > 0) \qquad (3.22)$$

And, hence:

$$M_{(t2')} = \frac{I_{(t1'+t2')}}{P_{W(t1'+t2')} + P_{D(t2')}} > M_{(t2)} = \frac{I_{(t1+t2)}}{P_{W(t1+t2)} + P_{D(t2)}} \qquad (3.23)$$

$$\{P_{W(t1'+t2')} \geq P_{W(t1+t2)}; \; P_{D(t2')} > P_{D(t2)}\}$$

where $t_{1'}$ and $t_{2'}$ represent the subperiods of the next round in the cycle. The per capita income level is higher even when more children are born because a higher income is generated in period $i + 1$. There was a real possibility for this to take place in the context of hyper-growth of population in late dynasties of the empire.

### 3.5.5.2 Living standards vis-à-vis hyper-growth of population

The ratio between the income increment in the current period and the income level in the previous period (equation (3.20)) can be taken as the 'rate of change of per capita income level' ($\mu$).

$$\mu = \frac{M_{(i-1)} - M_{(i)}}{M_{(i)}} \qquad (3.24)$$

If technology is held constant, owing to the law of diminishing returns the value of $\mu$ will be negative. And, with population increase, sooner or later per capita income will drop below the subsistence level and the population will stop growing, as indicated in the Malthusian paradigm. However, the value of $\mu$ can be 0, if a society manages to generate new technology, should the rate of technological progress equal the rate of population growth. The value of $\mu$ will be positive if the speed of technological progress exceeds that of population increase.

Owing to the lack of data concerning the quality of life in premodern China, it is hard to evaluate the benefit of technological progress, although evidence indicates that such progress never stopped (Deng 1993a). Here population size and its increase rate will not help, because we have to know the total agricultural output before we can know anything about the actual living standards. Thus, the value of $\mu$ is unknown. However, although the value of $\mu$ cannot be found in the size of population, some indication can be found in the speed of population growth.

It is commonly agreed that the capacity for child-bearing is a function of women's nutritional condition, while women's nutritional condition is a function of living standards. Logically, a hyper-growth of population in Qing China means that the Qing women became more fertile than before. This becomes much clearer if we compare all the peak points of population growth in premodern China, as follows:

| Period | Increase by (%) | Annual growth rate (%) | Growth over 30 years (%) |
|---|---|---|---|
| AD 705–55 | 42.50 | 0.71 | 23.62 |
| 1053–1100 | 101.48 | 1.50 | 56.00 |
| 1426–84 | 21.04 | 0.33 | 10.38 |
| 1680–1833 | 2,232.00 | 2.05 | 83.86 |

The rates in Qing times are undoubtedly the highest in premodern China: 37 per cent higher in annual terms and 50 per cent higher in generational terms than the second highest period (in the Northern Song), and 4.2 and 7.1 times higher than the lowest annual and generational growth rates respectively in Ming times. Considering that during the Northern Song Period, the neo-Confucian philosophy of Zhu Xi (1130–1200) was on the rise and remained dominant in the Ming–Qing Period, suggestions of behavioural disruption caused by cultural factors can be largely eliminated. According to this analysis, the value of $f$ during the hyper-growth periods can be estimated as greater than zero.

To achieve such high population growth rates, the Qing women had to be fit enough to bear children either more intensively/frequently during a short period within their child-bearing age, or more extensively by extending their child-bearing period. The improved fertility status should be taken as evidence of improved nutrition and medical care conditions, which reflected a reasonable standard of living at the time.

## 3.6 Remarks

The most important factors and features in relation to the Chinese enigma are not mindset, or technology, population size, physical environment, per capita income level, market, and so forth. They are the Chinese land ownership system, a free peasantry, physiocratic government and the consequent trinary equilibrium. The origin of the trinary structure was derived from a combination of economic endowments and military – or, more correctly, military– economic – power in north China. The main characteristic of the structure was its equilibrium and self-regulating mechanisms.

The impact of the trinary equilibrium was multifold and double-edged. On the one hand, in terms of benefit, it fostered Chinese agriculture, the most successful in the premodern world. It also contained a remarkable degree of market activities and urbanisation. The equilibrium thus laid the foundation for a lasting civilisation to prosper for at least one and a half millennia up until the end of the seventeenth century. So, until the eighteenth century, Europeans regarded China as the most orderly, creative, industrious and productive society in the world and as a model for Europe to follow (Waverick 1946).

On the other hand, in terms of costs, this equilibrium reinforced problems, including the overprotection of agriculture, biased development in technology and the economy, and shortage of investment in non-agricultural sectors. The phenomenon of the trinary equilibrium was closely related to what may be called 'the perpetuation of the peasant economy', 'capitalist sterility' or 'industrialisational sterility' in China. Occasional growth such as in Han and Song times soon languished in the inertia of the trinary system.

Now, judging Fairbankian–Needhamian 'bureaucratic determinism' from these factors and their functions, it is easy to see why blaming the Chinese bureaucracy can be misleading and why traditional bureaucracy-oriented reforms in China have been and will be limited in their impact. China's three-pronged problem needs a package of reforms.

## Notes

1 It is indeed less significant to examine the reasons why the peasant rebels in the twentieth century followed communism.
2 Strictly speaking, Maoist China departed a long way from the trinary tradition by abolishing Confucianism as the state philosophy and by abandoning the Imperial Examination-based bureaucrat recruitment system. Known as the 'cadre system', the transplanted Leninist bureaucrat recruitment system is characterised by the monopoly of the so-called 'professional revolutionaries' in the bureaucracy and state politics. Structurally, what Leninism has created is a monopolistic party machine in society, something traditional China did not have (see Stover 1974: 272–4). It is in nature a closed system and thus a much narrower channel for social mobility. Worst of all, the Leninist system itself provides no check on the head of

the party, who acts like a high priest with the exclusive right to communicate with God. To criticise or admonish a Communist leader is a crime even within the Communist Party hierarchy and even if the criticism is strictly based on Leninist–Maoist doctrine. To bring down a Communist guru thus necessitates a conspiracy and a *coup d'état* of the Byzantine style. It is not surprising that the communist system will collapse. What is so amazing is that such a system lasted for seventy years in Russia.

3 Ironically, having become aware that his bureaucracy was out of his personal control, Mao Zedong, the *de facto* monarch, equipped with Marxism–Leninism, launched his 'Cultural Revolution' to destroy the bureaucracy. This clearly reveals how little has changed in modern China: the pattern of monarch versus bureaucracy is still working in China's non-democratic structure in the late twentieth century.

4 Modern China's territory shrank by 15.5 per cent from 11.4 to 9.6 million square kilometres after the independence of Mongolia.

# 4

# DISEQUILIBRIUM, CATACLYSM AND RECOVERY

Normally, the agricultural foundation – the landholding and land-owning free peasantry and the physiocratic government – worked together well and harmony was achieved. To the satisfaction of all, the agricultural sector was prosperous, peasant interests and rights were protected, and the rulers enjoyed sufficient revenue and political tranquillity. In Chinese history this equilibrium nourished many culminations of technological and cultural developments: the highlights of Chinese civilisation in the past.

However, this equilibrium was a dynamic one: it was highly conditional with internal tensions. There was a 25 per cent chance for the trinary equilibrium to fall apart. China was thus not a country of static tranquillity, but a land which suffered periodic crises. Political and economic alienation sometimes caused Chinese society to move away from its 'normal' track:

> The governing class loses first the will and then the ability to meet the high standards of Confucian government. Its increasing luxury places a strain on the exchequer. Funds intended for irrigation, flood control, maintenance of public grain reserves, communications, and payment of the army are diverted by graft to private pockets. As morale is undermined, corruption becomes flagrant.
>
> (Wright 1957: 44).

Often, a socio-political and economic cataclysm followed. In effect, Fairbank's dynastic cycle reflects such periodic crises (Fairbank 1965: ch. 4; Fairbank and Reischaver 1979: 70–5).

But, on the other hand, the empire survived over time. So, the purpose of this chapter is to find out why and how a disequilibrium occurred and why and how the equilibrium was restored.

## 4.1 Disequilibrium: the trinary crisis

### 4.1.1 Characteristics and nature of the crises

On the whole, the trinary crisis was characterised by (1) widespread corruption of the state apparatus (including both the monarch and the bureaucracy at various levels), which became excessively rent-seeking and exceedingly collaborative with large landowners; (2) failure of the self-regulating surveillance mechanism, which led to incompetence of the governing institutions so that corruption became unchecked and rampant on a large scale; (3) widespread discontent among the masses due to an increasing tax burden, landholding and land-ownership concentration and a consequently lowered living standard; (4) rebellions breaking out, first on a local, small scale and then on a large, even national, scales; and (5) the devastation of huge areas, with heavy losses in human lives and capital and a sharp decline in economic activity.

It is important to know that economic difficulties were there throughout Chinese history, even during the Golden Ages. However, whether China had a trinary crisis largely depended on the performance of the state. The centralised imperial apparatus was designed to control such alienation. Only when the regulating mechanism failed to function did a real crisis begin. The malfunction of the Chinese governing institutions was itself largely due to simultaneous corruption of both the monarch and bureaucracy, who pampered each other. Here, the concept of corruption is used in a broad sense which covers delinquency, power abuse, graft, embezzlement and so forth.

Regarding the performance of the Chinese state, one area where things did often go wrong was fiscal policy. From time to time, power abuse of the bureaucracy resulted in an excessive tax burden on the population. As the first documented case in Chinese history, the financial expansion in Qin times imposed a unprecedented tax burden 30 times heavier than before (Ban G. AD 82 vol. 24: ch. 'Shihuo Zhi'; see also Zhou B. 1981: 564–5). This type of fiscal crisis was widely recognised by the dynastic historians and modern scholars of China (Wang 1936).

Another area was landholding and land-ownership concentration, which led to landholding and land-ownership crises. The weakened physiocratic authorities made it possible for the power of the 'landlord' class to increase, which presented a threat to the small landholders and landowners: with an increase in landholding and land-ownership concentration and consequently an increase in the number of landless rural poor, the peasantry found themselves under the thumb of local strongmen, losing their properties, freedom and their usual way of life. Commercialisation and urbanisation could also encroach on the power and status of the peasantry to a certain extent (Landsberger 1974: 31): the peasantry sometimes felt the grip of competition from merchants, who were often viewed as dispossessors, especially when wealthy merchants invested in land property and clashed head on with the interests of the less fortunate peasants in a zero-sum game fashion. All these would cause social tranquillity to collapse. To take the end of the Qing Dynasty as an example, it has been estimated that in the 1880s a share of 25 per cent of the cultivated land was owned by absentee landlords, an evil sign of landholding and land-ownership concentration (Chang 1955: 477). The problem of landholding and land-ownership concentration went beyond the life of the Empire until the recent past. During the first half of the twentieth century, in Manchuria, where land was rather abundant, 10 per cent of the rich farmers/landlords owned 60 per cent of the total cultivated land, while the poor peasants, who made up 70 per cent of the total population, had only 20 per cent of the land (Marsh 1961: 68). Between the nineteenth and twentieth centuries, landholding and land-ownership concentration and ownership crisis led China twice to a communist utopia which promised to solve the land distribution and a land-ownership problem once and for all, the first being the Christian Heavenly Kingdom of Great Peace (*taiping tianguo*, 1850–64) and the second Stalinist–Maoist 'New China' (1949–76).

Often, fiscal and landholding problems became entwined. Typically, (1) with government's favouring large landholders, tax exemption was granted to the privileged; (2) revenue to maintain the standing army and welfare of the bureaucrats was then obtained by squeezing the small landholders; (3) the bankruptcy rate among the small landholders soared, which in turn reduced the taxation basis; (4) a vicious spiral occurred with a further squeezing of the small landholders; (5) poverty-stricken peasants were forced to rise up to stop such a spiral.

Natural disasters such as unfavourable weather conditions and pandemics might play a role in the process. But evidence shows that they could trigger a trinary crisis but they were not the cause, which will be elaborated later.

### 4.1.2 Types and causes of corruption

Two types of corruption existed: power-pulled and low income-pushed. Arguably, the salary of the Chinese bureaucrats was pegged to the income of the middle peasantry, a standard practice known as the 'system of low-level salary' (*dixinzhi*). Ideologically, it had a strong egalitarian and physiocratic thrust. Financially, it kept the government nominal budget low, which in turn kept taxation low. A low tax rate was dictated by physiocracy, which was in turn dictated by the trinary structure. Thus, the paradoxicality that China's powerful bureaucrats were constantly underpaid is illusory.

Until the Ming Period, the main source of officials' salaries was the state-owned and state-allocated 'land for official post' (*zhitian*) in accordance with official ranks. The land was leased out to farming tenants. The rent from the land was earmarked for the salary of the official himself and all the administrative expenses including office hands, travel and entertainment. The following data show the acreages for the highest and lowest ranks, *mu* being converted to its modern measure and figures in parentheses being the area in hectares (based on CBW 1978: 151; see also Liang F. 1980: 292, 472–5, 488–92):

| Period | Highest rank (mu) | Lowest rank (mu) | Mean (mu) |
|---|---|---|---|
| Northern Wei | 1,500 (75.0 ha) | 600 (30.0 ha) | 1,050 (52.5 ha) |
| Sui | 500 (38.0 ha) | 100 (7.6 ha) | 300 (22.8 ha) |
| Tang | 1,200 (64.8 ha) | 200 (10.8 ha) | 700 (37.8 ha) |
| Song | 2,000 (116.0 ha) | 200 (11.6 ha) | 1,100 (63.8 ha) |
| Jin | 3,000 (174.0 ha) | 200 (11.6 ha) | 1,600 (92.8 ha) |
| Yuan | 1,600 (112.0 ha) | 100 (7.0 ha) | 850 (59.5 ha) |
| Ming | 1,600 (112.0 ha) | 100 (7.0 ha) | 850 (59.5 ha) |

If the data for China's mean grain yield levels on good farming land in good years are applied as proxies (Wu H. 1985: 194; see also Deng 1993a: 161), the resulting officials' gross incomes are as follows, taking 50–50 share-cropping as the norm across all periods (figures in parentheses are the yield in tonnes):

| Period | Yield level (jin/mu) | Highest rank (jin) | Lowest rank (jin) | Mean (jin) |
|---|---|---|---|---|
| Northern Wei | — | — | — | — |
| Sui | 257 | 128,800 (64.4 t) | 25,760 (12.9 t) | 77,280 (38.6 t) |
| Tang | 334 | 400,800 (200.4 t) | 66,800 (33.4 t) | 233,800 (116.9 t) |
| Song | 309 | 618,000 (309.0 t) | 61,800 (30.9 t) | 339,900 (170.0 t) |
| Jin | — | — | — | — |
| Yuan | 338 | 540,800 (270.4 t) | 33,800 (16.9 t) | 287,300 (143.7 t) |
| Ming | 346 | 540,800 (276.8 t) | 33,800 (17.3 t) | 287,300 (147.1 t) |

Of course, in reality the actual sums depended on local weather conditions, soil types, tillage patterns and the skills of tenants. Although it is still not clear just how much an official was able to receive as a salary from this lump sum, the amount was limited.

A better indication of the salary comes from the Qing record. The annual monetary income for the Qing officials was between 33.1 taels (*liang*) of silver (1,234.6 g for the ninth rank (*jiupin*) and 180 (6,714 g) taels for the first rank (Sun X. 1988: 192–3; see also Feuerwerker 1976: 65).[1] In contrast, the living allowance of a Qing duke was 10,000 taels of silver a year, 55–301 times higher than the officials received (see Sun X. 1988: 192–3). Merchant tycoons during the Ming–Qing Period enjoyed even more. So far, it is known that (1) in the Ming–Qing Period, the average trade value of each registered large cargo ship in a return trip was normally some 55,000 taels of silver (trading with Japan) and 200,000 taels (trading with South and West Asia); (2) the gross profit rate usually varied from 100 to 500 per cent; (3) in Qing times the crew/passenger-ship ratio was often between 21 and 90 (Sun G. 1989:

601). The income range of sea merchants ($I_m$) can be calculated by the annual value of goods for trade on each merchant ship ($V_t$), the profit rate ($r$) and number of merchants involved ($n$), according to the following equation:

$$I_m = \frac{rV_t}{n} \tag{4.1}$$

The resulting income level for each merchant is, in round numbers, 600–13,700 taels (22.4–511 kg per year. The greater figure is of course only an indication because there was no ceiling for a sea merchant's annual income. This is not too far from the range of the government tax-based estimates (500–10,000 taels), and within the recorded range of sea merchants' returns from several hundred up to several tens of thousands of taels of silver a year depending on the capital inputs (see Zhu D. 1986: 157–8).

Yet the officials bore great responsibilities in society. A governor-general administered an area as big as a country in Europe (Wei Q. 1989: pt 1; Pu J. 1990: chs 6–13; Yang Z. 1992: chs 5–18; Tang J. and Zheng C. 1993: chs 4–10; Tian Z. 1994: 91–112; see also Chu and Saywell 1984); while a county magistrate at the bottom of the official ladder was responsible for a wide range of duties: (1) moralising the locals; (2) practising law as a judge of the local court; (3) promoting agriculture and sericulture; and (4) tax-collecting (Zheng Z. 1938; Lu X. 1991: 75).

So, the responsibility of officials was not reflected by their income; nor was their salary sufficient to maintain a high society lifestyle. In Qing times, middle-ranking bureaucrats living in the capital, Beijing, constantly needed financial support from their relatives and sometimes had to quit their positions and return to their home region to make a living (Zhang D. 1970: 46–54). The relative poverty of the bureaucrats was not uniquely a Qing phenomenon. As early as the Western Jin Dynasty (AD 267–316) the real income of the officials was too low to support their families, which led to a petition to the throne to increase salaries (Zhou B. 1981: 145), probably the first recorded industrial action from civil servants in world history. In AD 971, Emperor Taizu of the Song (r. 960–76) issued an edict addressing this problem:

> Corrupt officials cause political unrest. This begins with the inadequate salary which causes hunger and cold among officials. This leads to their scrambling for income at the expense of the ordinary people.... From now on, new bureaucrat recruits in provinces and counties are allocated tenants for their salaries in accordance with the ranks of the provincial and county official positions.
>
> (Zhao K. *c.* AD 976/1995: 57)

Earlier, in 970, the emperor commented on the same problem by saying, 'It does not make much sense to discipline the officials to be free from corruption while they are paid so poorly' (Lai Q. and Chen S. 1995: 122). But few were able to challenge this 'system of low-level salary'. A typical cliché was to promote a simple, ascetic life, as reported in Emperor Kangxi's *Maxims from Family Instructions* (*Tingxun Geyan*):

> Frugality keeps officials uncorrupt. Without embezzlement, are officials, in power or retired, able to afford beautiful houses, desirable wives and concubines, numerous valets and large circles of friends? Should asceticism be better than corruption? As the saying goes: 'Frugality nurtures uprightness while extravagance leads to embezzlement.' This tells us the inexorable law.
>
> (Xuan Y. *c*. 1772/1994: 263)

It was no secret that extra income could be tapped by power in Chinese history. In general, power is the hot-bed of corruption. Centralised power is a stronger inducer of corruption than decentralised power. Income-hungry bureaucrats under a centralised political structure lean even more towards corruption. Moreover, a high society lifestyle has a 'demonstration effect' on officials as to what material comfort can be obtained. In addition, there is often no limit in the short run to the extent to which corruption can run rampant. Overall, the opportunity cost for corruption is lowest among the powerful, poorly paid and high society-coexisting officials under a centralised political structure. This cocktail, the worst of all, was what China had, which made the Chinese bureaucrats highly corruptible.

An estimate suggests that the aggregate actual income of Qing officials was 12 times higher than their 'legal income' (including salaries, rewards and allowances), the major proportion being extra-legal income from power abuse and rent-seeking (Marsh 1961: 64). For higher ranks, with their greater power, there was a tendency to obtain yet more extra-legal income. The actual income a Qing governor-general received, according to Fairbank, could have been some 140 times higher than his nominal salary (Fairbank 1983: 115). In an extreme case, He Shen (1750–99), Grand Secretary of the Qing Court, managed to accumulate a corrupt fortune of 80 million taels of silver, a sum over 400,000 times his annual salary (Marsh 1961: 65; Feuerwerker 1976: 74). With such alienation, the Chinese bureaucracy was turned into 'organised corruption' (Fairbank 1965: ch. 5).[2]

In light of this analysis, given that corruption was inevitable and to a great extent tolerated (as described in Chapter 3), the victory in the war against corruption was always a temporary one. Ultimately, severe corruption brought an end to the old régime, but it soon started all over again under a new régime. This formed a corruption cycle that largely overlapped the Fairbankian dynastic cycle.

The Chinese ruler hence had two faces: benevolence and ruthlessness. When the ruler was fully aware of the socio-political mechanism, he was likely to follow the orthodox Confucian rule of practising honesty and uprightness. If, however, he could not resist the temptation of power which was mandated by his people, he could become ruthlessly rent-seeking. But sooner or later, the social mechanism would violently remind him of his place.

### 4.1.3 From corruption to crises

However, raking in extra-legal income did not always harm the peasantry and the trinary equilibrium. To exploit the merchant class was an option for that purpose in terms of lower costs and better returns. To begin with, more wealth could be milked from a smaller number of merchants. For example, during the period of the Southern Dynasties, the Governor of Guangzhou reportedly received from maritime merchants a bribe up to 30 million bronze coins (*qian*) each time he passed the gate of the walled city to inspect the port (Xiao Z. AD 514–26: ch. 'Wangzengru Zhuan'). This type of exploitation of merchants could easily gain the consent of the peasantry and thus had little impact on the trinary equilibrium. Merchants, low in the Chinese class pyramid and highly mobile as they were, did not have the will or need to engage in armed rebellions against the fiscal pressure. They simply turned away from the worst rent-seekers. In the case of Port Guangzhou, the number of merchant ships dropped sharply to as low as three per year from their previous hundreds (Li Y. AD 659: ch. 'Xiaoli Zhuan'). Throughout Chinese history, no trinary crisis ever resulted from exploiting the merchants.

But when the corrupt state turned to the peasantry, especially the small landholders, the consequence could be explosive. Once distortion was out of control and the doom of the trinary equilibrium became obvious, society could face a chaotic consequence. The population responded with two types of popular rebellions: (1) tax rebellions against fiscal pressure, and (2) landholding rebellions against the unchecked power of the 'landlords'. Tenant rebellions against excessive rent ('rent rebellion') were a ramification of the landholding rebellion.

If the imperial apparatus managed to fix the distortions in time – which was claimed by Confucianism to be the lawful duty of both bureaucrats and monarch, and which was expected by the general population to be the governing institutions' responsibility – the equilibrium could be saved. In this context, the surveillance system of the empire played a vital role in maintaining social tranquillity. In Chinese history, numerous corrupt cases were brought to light and the guilty were punished by confiscation of property and often they faced capital punishment (see Cheng X. *et al.* 1994; Liang J. and Wang Y. 1995: 214–17, 264–5; Wei Z. *et al.* 1995: 151–7, 161–71; Xu C. and Li Y. 1995: 241–65; Xu T. and Li Y. 1995: 317–28). A good example of confiscation is provided by a description of a family ordeal in the partly autobiographical novel *Dream of the Red Chamber* (*Hongloumeng*) (Cao X. *c.* 1763). Cases of capital punishment were not uncommon. In 1693, Emperor Kangxi instructed his provincial governors of Guanxi, Guizhou, Sichuan and Yunnan that in 1694 these four provinces were to be totally exempted from the land-poll tax, that illegal tax collection was a criminal offence and that the guilty officials should be exposed and severely punished (Wei Z. *et al.* 1995: 433–4). In 1781, Emperor Qianlong issued an edict on a case of unlawful taxation and embezzlement in Gansu Province that those officials who embezzled over 10,000 taels were to be beheaded (Xu C. and Li Y. 1995: 254–5). In 1786, for the crime of unlawful taxation and embezzlement, Emperor Qianlong ordered Wang Danqi, a provincial governor, to be executed and the other guilty ministers to die through 'committing suicide' (*ibid.*: 261).

Together with the punishment for embezzlement, sweeping reforms were often launched to clean up the governing institutions. The best examples are the deeds of a long list of reformers: Shang Hongyang (152–80 BC), Liu Xiu (6–57 BC) and Wang Mang (45–23 BC) of the Han Dynasty; Li Chong (AD 450–98) and Tuoba Hong (467–99) of the Northern Wei; Liu Yan (715–80), Yang Yan (727–81) and Wang Shuwen (753–806) of the Tang; Chai Rong (921–59) of the Five Dynasties; Fan Zhongyan (989–1052) and Wang Anshi (1021–86) of the Song; Wanyan Yong (1124–89) of the Tartar Jin; Yelü Chucai (1190–1244) and Hubilie (Kublai, 1215–94) of the Yuan; Xia Yuanji (1366–1430), Zhou Chen (1381–1453), Ouyang Duo (1487–1544) and Zhang Juzheng (1525–82) of the Ming; Tian Wenjing (1662–1732), Yinzhen (1678–1735) and Zaichun (r. 1862–1874) of the Qing (Wright 1957; Wu H. 1984; Xu M. and Jing C. 1992). Among them, Liu Xiu, Wang Mang, Tuoba Hong, Cai Rong, Wanyan Yong, Hubilie, Yinzhen and Zaichun were emperors.

Sometimes an unpopular monarch had to step down. As Fairbank described, when surplus revenues were used for the purposes of corruption and many members of the ruling class found new ways to cheat the taxation system, placing extra strain on taxpayers, the emperor was then seen as having failed to follow the Confucian doctrine as the majority of the population were angry and objected to the changes made. A new emperor was chosen who might solve the problem (Fairbank 1965: 93). According to Mencius, the mechanism for changing the monarch was in the hand of the Confucian bureaucrats. In his phrase (Mengzi Warring States Period: ch. 'Wanzhang Xia'), 'Confucian officials must remonstrate when the monarch makes mistakes. If the monarch repeats his mistakes, the officials should dethrone him.' Mencius's rationale is that an unbenevolent and unjust monarch morally dethrones himself first; thus 'the killing of the tyrant King Zhou was like the execution of an evil man of the ordinary rank, not the head of the state' (*canzei zhiren weizhi yifu, wen zhu yifu zhou yi weimen shijun ye*) (*ibid.*: ch. 'King Lianghui Xia').

Without exception, these reformers tackled the tax burden and landholding and land-ownership concentration in order to defuse the trinary crisis. The last such effort was probably made in the Tongzhi (T'ung-chih)

Restoration and Reforms (1862–74), initiated by Zaichun (better known as Emperor Tongzhi, r. 1862–74). The reform package was multifold. First, the land tax was radically reduced by 30 per cent and was more equally distributed as the key to reasserting political control of the country against the aggressive Taiping rebels. Second, great efforts were made by the Restoration officials to improve the troubled agriculture sector by increasing the area under cultivation, increasing land productivity, improving water control, as well as reforming the land tax. Third, efforts were made to rebuild dikes along the Yellow River, the 'Sorrow of China', to reduce the threat of flood to the adjacent farming regions. In addition, proposals were made to reclaim some 30,000 hectares of wasteland in the north (Tianjin and Zhili) through improving water control works (see Wright 1957: 163–4). It is worth noting that, in contrast to the pro-agricultural efforts, the Tongzhi government had no policy of reviving commerce.

However, if the corrupt force was too powerful to be eliminated by the state itself, a more powerful remedy was needed. As Wright described (1957: 44), corruption could be retarded by the vigorous training of officials; if, however, the corruption went unchecked, the people expressed their disaffection in a great rebellion. The armed mass rebellion which turned the society upside down in a cataclysm served as the remedy.

## 4.2 Cataclysm: popular armed rebellions

Popular armed rebellions were probably the most striking characteristic of premodern China in comparison with its counterparts. As a phenomenon in premodern China, they have received some scholarly attention. But few know exactly what occurred, owing to the lack of data. To begin with, no one knows just how many rebellions have taken place in Chinese history. From the official record there were several thousand incidents within just three years from AD 613 to 615, probably one thousand events a year (Wei Z. AD 656: ch. 'Report of the Imperial Historians'). According to Parsons, during the period 1629–44, there were as many as 234,185 insurrections in China, averaging 43 events per day, or 1.8 outbreaks per hour (Parsons 1970: 187). These figures are too great to be realistic unless the Chinese had nothing else to do but rebel.

One way to get around this problem is to count only the major recorded incidents. The criteria are (1) scale in terms of rebels' numbers, (2) scope in terms of affected areas, and (3) duration of time. However, these criteria should not be applied too rigidly. For instance, some small rebel groups managed to attack the Imperial Palace, or occupied huge areas, or lasted for a reasonable length of time. In those cases, it is likely that the original official records understated the rebel numbers to mask the seriousness of the crises. The result is a collection of 269 main events in 2,106 years as shown in Appendix J, which makes the present analysis manageable.

### 4.2.1 A comparative survey

Compared to those faced by other civilisations, the Chinese rebellions were massive, extensive, frequent and long-lasting.

First, popular rebellions often had large numbers of participants, more massive than their counterparts in other societies: in a major incident the Chinese rebels easily numbered several hundred thousand, sometimes several million. Massive rebellions were rather rare in countries such as England, Ireland, India and Japan (Moore 1966: 254–75, 330–41, 353–70; Clark and Donnelly 1983; Dobson 1983; Bix 1986: xxi–xxii; Bagchi 1992: 34–7). In Meiji Japan, for instance, the rural protesters in a major event amounted only to 3,000 to 10,000 (Bowen 1980: 16, 30, 50). During the 1773–4 Cossack rebellion in Russia, the rebels numbered between 15,000 and 42,000 (Landsberger 1974: 231, 245). Although they attracted in all 55,000 people, the French rural revolts in 1637–41 had a peasant army of a mere 8,000 men (Bercé 1990: 114, 322). In England, the number involved in the 1381 peasant rebellion is more impressive: between 20,000 and 100,000 (Dobson 1983: 160, 244, 263, 381). They were dwarfed by the Chinese. In terms of the violent conflict between the rebels and the government forces, the closest case in Europe was probably the Russian 'Great Cossack Peasant Uprising' in 1773–4 in which the rebels' combat resembled a real army against the troops of the tsar (Landsberger 1974: ch. 6). As a result, the Chinese probably produced more rebellion martyrs (and casualties) with heroic stories than any other main civilisation of the ancient world. According to various records, the martyrs often reached tens of thousand after a successful crackdown by the government forces (see Zhang S. and Zheng X. 1983).

Second, the rebellions in China covered a wide area: the only places where major rebellions were not reported were Heilongjiang in the northeastern tip (the homeland of the ethnic Manchus), Outer Mongolia in the north (the homeland of the Mongols) and Qinghai and Tibet in the far west (the homeland mainly of the Tibetans). A major event easily affected an area equivalent to the whole of Japan or one modern nation in Europe. This had few parallels in premodern world history.

Third, no other country's rebellions had the same degree of regularity as in China. In medieval continental Europe and England, peasant revolts did break out and shake the state as in the cases of Wat Tyler and the Lollards in England, the 'Jacques' of the Beauvaisis and the 'Croquants' of Normandy, Thomas Münzer in Germany, and Stenka Razin and Pugachev in Russia (Chesneaux 1973: 7; Landsberger 1974: pt. 2; Clark and Donnelly 1983; Dobson 1983). However, these events were only occasional. Regarding the popular, peaceful resistance movement of M. K. Gandhi (1869–1948), it was a one-off event and a product of ethnic and nationalist consciousness during the colonial era, which is by definition a different type of rebellion.

Fourth, peasant armed rebellions in China were more long-lasting than their counterparts in some other societies such as Europe and Japan. For instance, the 1773 'Great Cossack Peasant Uprising' in Russia and the 1882 Fukushima Incident in Japan both lasted a year (Bowen 1980: 8); while the 1381 uprising in England lasted somewhere between only a few days and a fortnight (Dobson 1983: pts III–V). In nineteenth-century Ireland, two of the powerful rural revolts endured for several years (Clark and Donnelly 1983: 25), which is probably the record for Europe. In China, the longest-lasting rebel movements endured for more than 40 years under Liu Bei (AD 221–63), Li Te (AD 301–47) and Wang Gang (1630–71).

Finally, in terms of the consequence, the Chinese mass rebellions destroyed and/or replaced régimes. They overthrew at least six main dynasties: the Qin, the Han (both Western and Eastern), Sui, Yuan, Ming and Qing (Li G. et al. 1958; Zhang S. and Zheng X. 1983; Jin G. and Liu Q. 1984: 115–19; see also Li Z. 1993; Sun Y. 1994), and numerous régimes within a dynasty. Between 209 BC and 1864 they established at least 48 régimes of their own, among which four became the main dynasties: the Western Han, Eastern Han, Tang and Ming (see Table 4.1).

In comparison, in no single case in Europe, India or Japan did peasant rebels succeed in replacing a régime but not the timeless socio-economic structure. The nature and consequences of insurrections were different between China and Europe/Japan, too. In Europe and Japan, most 'rebellions' were at best a form of petition, rather than a process of changing the régime (Landsberger 1974: ch. 3; Dobson 1983: 371; Bowen 1980; Bix 1986). The best examples were the London uprising in 1381 and the rising in Périgord in 1637–41. The London rebels greatly outnumbered King Richard's guards and Wat Tyler obviously had some leadership qualities while the king was a youngster of only 14 years of age. However, the king and his advisers turned the tables and put down the revolt without too much difficulty (Landsberger 1974: ch. 3; Dobson 1983: pt 3). It would have been a completely different story if a young monarch with a few guards had encountered rebels in China. In the French case, under the attack of the king's troops, the rebels' communes barely lasted for a month (Bercé 1990: 124–9, 145–8). The European peasants played a decisive role probably only in the 1789 French Revolution and 1917 Russian Revolution (Landsberger 1974: 35–6). But in both cases, the French and Russian socio-economic structures were subject to a major change. The same thing can also be said concerning M. K. Gandhi's resistance movement in modern India during the first half of the twentieth century.

Rebellions also broke out specifically against a well-off stratum instead of the state. In 1875, the Indian rebels in the Deccan Riots targeted the much-hated money-lenders rather than the Establishment under the British rule and thus had no intention to change the colonial régime (Rothermund 1993: 46; see also Bagchi 1992: 34–7). In 1918 Japan, the widespread Rice Riots were to stop the profiteering rice traders and left the Japanese state intact (Francks

*Table 4.1* Rebel-installed régimes in premodern China, 220 BC–1911

| Name | Founder | Period | Affected area |
|------|---------|--------|---------------|
| 1 Zhangchu | Chensheng | 209 BC | AH, JS |
| 2 Western Han* | Liu Bang | 206 BC–AD 8 | Whole of China |
| 3 Shigeng | Liu Xuan | AD 23–5 | HuB, HeN |
| 4 Fuhan | Wei Xiao | 23–35 | — |
| 5 Longxing | Gongsun Shu | 25–7 | — |
| 6 Jianshi | Liu Penzi | 25–7 | — |
| 7 Eastern Han* | Liu Xiu | 25–220 | Whole of China |
| 8 Shu | iu Bei | 221–63 | SC |
| 9 Chenghan | Li Te | 303–47 | SC |
| 10 Xingping | Tang Yuzhi | 485 | ZJ |
| 11 Jianyi | Yong Daoyi | 500 | SC |
| 12 Zhin | Poliu Hanbaling | 523–6 | GS |
| 13 Tianjian | Mozhe Niansheng | 524–5 | GS, NX, S′X |
| 14 Zhin | Du Louzhou | 525–8 | HeB |
| 15 Guang-an | Ge Rong | 526–8 | HeB |
| 16 Luxing | Xianyu Xiuli | 526 | HeB |
| 17 Yonghan | Liu Jinggong | 542–3 | SC |
| 18 Dashi | Liu Jialun | 614 | S′X |
| 19 Changda | Zhu Can | 615 | AH |
| 20 Qinxing | Xue Ju | 617 | GS |
| 21 Wei | Li Mi | 617–8 | HeN, HeB |
| 22 Xia | Dou Jiande | 617–23 | HeB |
| 23 Liang | Xiao Xian | 617–8 | HuN, GD |
| 24 Tang* | Li Yuan | 618–907 | Whole China |
| 25 Mingzheng | Li Zitong | 620 | SD |
| 26 Song | Fu Gongshi | 623–4 | JS |
| 27 Baosheng | Yuan Chao | 762–3 | ZJ, JX |
| 28 Luoping | Qiu Pu | 860 | ZJ |
| 29 Qi | Huang Chao | 878–84 | SD, HeN, AH, HuB, HuN, ZJ, FJ, GD, JS, S′X, JX, GX |
| 30 Yingyun | Li Shun | 994–5 | SC |
| 31 Desheng | Wang Ze | 1047–8 | HeB |
| 32 Yongle | Fang La | 1120–1 | ZJ, AH, HeN |
| 33 Tianzai | Zhong Xiang | 1130 | HuN, HuB |
| 34 Dasheng | Yang Yao | 1133–5 | HuN, HuB |
| 35 Tianshun | Yang An-er | 1214 | SD |
| 36 Tianwan | Xu Shouhui | 1351–60 | SD, SX, HeB, S′X, GS, SC, LN, FJ, ZJ, JX, HuB, HuN, GD, GX |
| 37 Zhou | Zhang Shicheng | 1354–57 | Lower Yangzi (6 provinces) |
| 38 Song | Han Lin-er | 1355–66 | AH |
| 39 Ming* | Zhu Yuanzhang | 1368–1644 | Whole of China |
| 40 Longfeng | Tian Jiucheng | 1397 | S′X, GS |

| 41 Dongyang | Huang Xiaoyang | 1449–50 | GD |
| 42 Desheng | Li Tong | 1465–6 | HuB, SC, HeN, S'X |
| 43 Dacheng Xingsheng | Xu Hongru | 1622 | SD |
| 44 Dashun | Li Zicheng | 1644–5 | S'X, HeB, HeN, SX, SD, HuB, JS, GD |
| 45 Daxi | Zhang Xianzhong | 1644 | SC |
| 46 Yonghe | Zhu Yigui | 1721 | TW |
| 47 Shuntian | Lin Shuangwen | 1786–8 | TW |
| 48 Taiping Tianguo | Hong Xiuquan | 1851–64 | JS, JX, HuB, HuN, GD, GX, SC, FJ |

*Source*: Based on Appendix J.

*Note*

An asterisk indicates dynasties which were directly established by rebels. Abbreviations of regions (in the form of provinces of modern China): AH, Anhui; FJ, Fujian; GD, Guangdong; GS, Gansu; GX, Guangxi; GZ, Guizhou; HeB, Hebei; HeN, Henan; HuB, Hubei; HuN, Hunan,; JS, Jiangsu; JX, Jiangxi; LN, Liaoning; NX, Ningxia; SC, Sichuan; SD, Shandong; SX, Shanxi; S'X, Shaanxi; TW, Taiwan; ZJ, Zhejiang.

1992: 56, 105, 144). Such rebellions belong to a category irrelevant to the present study.

### 4.2.2 Long-term patterns

At least three patterns can be identified in the dynastic breakdown from the data of Table J.1 in Appendix J. First, the number of participants had a tendency to decrease and stayed relatively stable after the Han Dynasty (206 BC– AD 220). This means that smaller numbers of rebels were able to achieve a similar goal after the Han (see Figure 4.1). In other words, the efficiency of

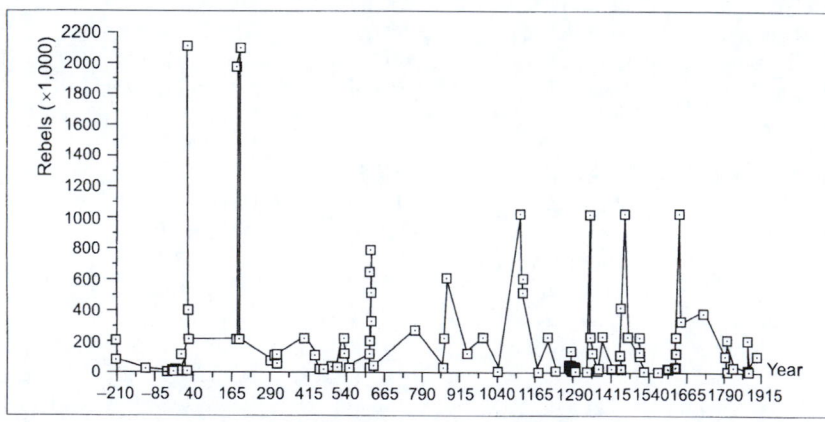

*Figure 4.1.* Fluctuations in the dynastically aggregated number of rebels

*Source*: Based on Appendix J.

the rebels increased in both the absolute sense (in the sheer head count) and the relative sense (*vis-à-vis* the growth in the total population).

Second, when the stance of the fluctuations in scale (in the number of rebels) is compared to the change in the scope of the rebellions (as counted in provinces affected), it is evident that the rebels became more mobile after the Northern and Southern Dynasties till the Ming Period (see Figure 4.2). This improved mobility reflects an improved efficiency of the rebellions.

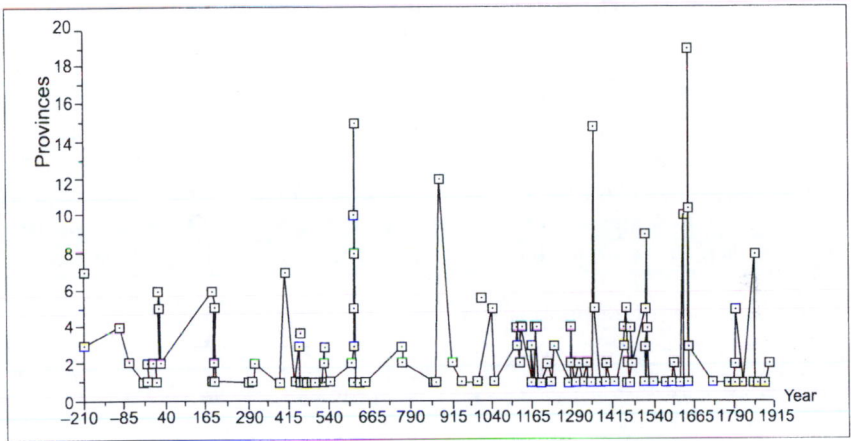

*Figure 4.2.* Changes in the scale of the rebellions

*Source*: Based on Appendix J.

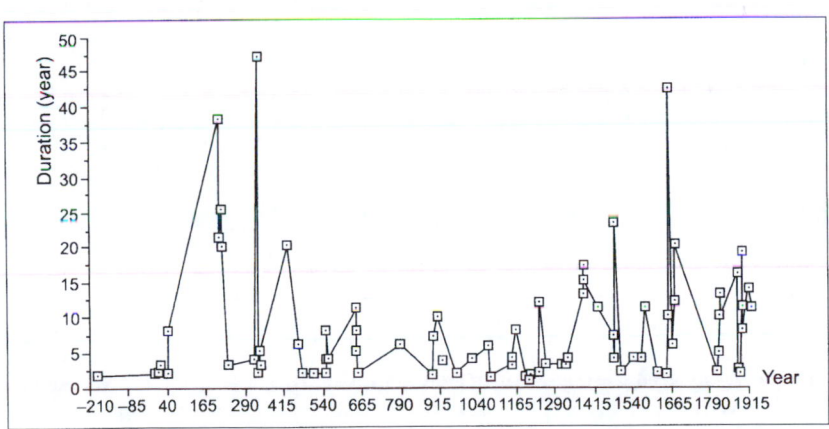

*Figure 4.3.* Dynastically aggregated durations of the rebellions

*Source*: Based on Appendix J.

Third, there were two peaks in rebellions (see Figure 4.3). The first one was between the Eastern Han and Western Jin; the second, in the early Qing. In between, there was a long period of relative stability, which implies a balance between the Chinese state and the rebel forces.

### 4.2.3 Identity of participants

Owing to the lack of official records it is difficult to trace precisely who the participants were, although numerous studies have indicated (1) that nearly all the rebellious events began in rural China, and (2) that the majority of participants were peasants (e.g. Xie G. 1956; Li G. *et al.* 1958; Xie T. and Jian X. 1980; ZNZ 1982, 1985; Zhang S. and Zheng X. 1983; Li B.C. 1985; Zhu D. 1985). This claim is now strongly supported by quantitative data.

For the present purpose, China can be divided by five demarcation lines into four macro-regions according to topographic features (Table 4.2 and Figure 4.4): NE (the *amb* quadrant, an area north of the Huai River, east of the

*Table 4.2* Regional breakdown of armed mass rebellions, 210 BC–1900

| Period | Time | Incidents | NE[a] | NW[a] | SE[a] | SW[a] | Other | Scope[b] | Scale[c] | Duration[d] |
|--------|------|-----------|------|------|------|------|-------|---------|---------|------------|
| I | 208 BC | 2 | 2 | — | — | — | — | 7 | 270 | 3 |
| II | 99 BC–AD 191 | 42 | 19 | 11 | 5 | 3 | 3 | 13 | 7,332 | 113 |
| III | 294–399 | 11 | 2 | 1 | 3 | 1 | 4 | 11 | 750 | 75 |
| IV | 432–544 | 27 | 5 | 7 | 4 | 11 | — | 11 | 1,109 | 21 |
| V | 611–20 | 43 | 27 | 9 | 6 | — | 1 | 12 | 2,548 | 24 |
| VI | 621–875 | 12 | 5 | 1 | 4 | 2 | — | 13 | 1,100 | 26 |
| VII | 920–42 | 2 | 1 | — | 1 | — | — | 3 | 100 | 1 |
| *Subtotal (1)* | *800* | *139* | *61* | *29* | *23* | *17* | *8* | *70* | *13,209* | *263* |
| | | | | | | | | | | |
| VIII | 993–1278 | 45 | 30 | 2 | 12 | 1 | — | 17 | 2,490 | 33 |
| IX | 1280–1353 | 22 | 8 | — | 12 | 1 | 1 | 16 | 1,509 | 49 |
| X | 1375–1646 | 46 | 8 | 5 | 27 | 5 | 1 | 19 | 5,070 | 146 |
| XI | 1721–1898 | 17 | 4 | 2 | 6 | — | 5 | 15 | 988 | 99 |
| *Subtotal (2)* | *810* | *130* | *50* | *9* | *57* | *7* | *7* | *67* | *10,057* | *327* |
| | | | | | | | | | | |
| Total | 2,106 | 269 | 111 | 38 | 80 | 24 | 15 | 137 | 23,266 | 590 |
| Mean | — | — | — | — | — | — | — | — | 2,115 | 54 |
| Percentage | | 100.0 | 41.4 | 14.2 | 29.8 | 9.0 | 5.6 | — | — | — |

*Source*: Based on Appendix J.

Notes

Numbers are rounded where necessary. Dynasties: I, Qin; II, Han; III, Jin; IV, Northern and Southern; V, Sui; VI, Tang; VII, Five Dynasties; VIII, Song; IX, Yuan; X, Ming; XI, Qing.
a NE, NW, SE and SW are consistent with Figure 4.4.
b Counted in provinces of modern China.
c Number $\times 10^3$.
d Aggregate number, in years.

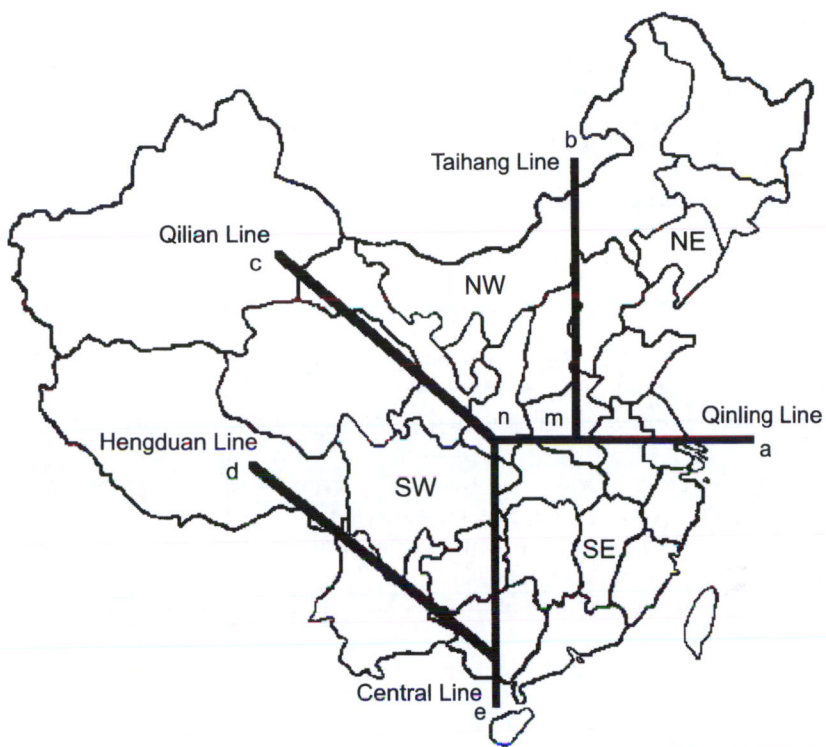

*Figure 4.4.* Rebellion zones, 210 BC–1900

Source: Based on (1) Table 4.2; (2) Fullard 1968: 2–5; and (3) Anon. 1991.
Note
The contemporary China territory is used for the demonstrative purposes only. For the maximum size of the Chinese Empire, see Figure 3.6.

Taihang Range and west of the Bo Hai and Huang Hai coasts), NW (the *bmnc* quadrant, an area north of the Qinling Range, east of the Qilian Range and Chaidamu [Qaidam] Basin, west of the Taihang Range), SE (the *ane* quadrant, an area north of the Nanhai coast, south to the Huai River, east of the Qinling Range and Upper Yangzi River, west of the Donghai coast) and SW (the *cned* quadrant, an area north of the Yun-Gui Plateau, south of the Qinling Range, east of the Hengduan Range, west of the Qinling Range and Upper Yangzi River).

Over 70 per cent of all the outbreaks took place in the northeast and southeast regions, two macro-regions which have been known as the heartlands of dry farming (since 1000 BC) and paddy farming (since around AD 700), respectively (Buck 1968: 187). This is highly consistent with the notion that the participants of the armed rebellions in premodern Chinese were predominantly peasants.

## 4.3 Causes of the rebellions

In light of the above analysis of data, it is clear that (1) the Chinese rebellion phenomenon was unique in terms of scale, scope and frequency; and (2) the majority of participants were peasants. The next issue to be raised is why the Chinese rebelled.

### 4.3.1 *Natural disasters and population explosion?*

The Chinese dynastic historians often attributed the outbreak of peasant rebellions to natural disasters (floods, droughts, locusts, crop plagues, epidemics and so forth) and population pressure. The present study challenges this view.

Quantitative data shows that natural disasters were rebellion neutral: not only did the trend of rebellions move generally in the opposite direction to that of the natural disasters, but also rebellions remained rather lethargic when the disasters intensified after the Tang Period (see Figure 4.5). So, natural disasters did not cause rebellions. At best, they might lower the threshold for the outbreaks.

The same can be said of population pressure. Figure 4.6 reveals that there is no correlation between population growth and either the number of peasant

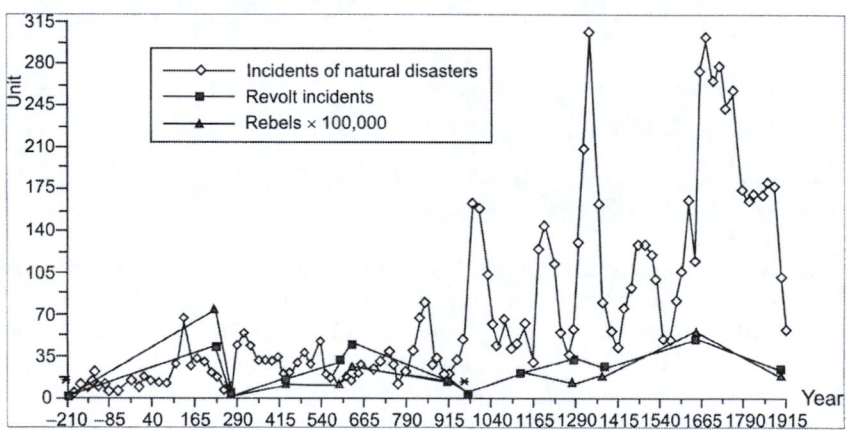

*Figure 4.5.* Natural disasters and rebellions, 210 BC–1900

*Source*: Based on Table 2.1 and Chen G. 1939.
*Note*
Natural disasters are aggregated numbers, including main incidents of floods, droughts, plagues and others.

228

rebellions or the number of rebels. The figure also indicates that there was no correlation between changes in the man-to-land ratio and the number of rebellion events as well as rebels.

Arguably, the disaster-pull and population-push models were attempts to cover up the real cause of the rebellions: it was natural for the dynasts and dynastic historians to blame bad weather conditions and human biomass.[3]

### 4.3.2 Abject poverty

Among the Marxists, peasant rebellions in China are commonly explained as the result of 'abject poverty': peasants were exploited to the point of starvation from time to time so they rebelled to fight for a chance to live (see Xie G. 1956; Li G. *et al.* 1958; Xie T. and Jian X. 1980; ZNZ 1982, 1985; Zhang S. and Zheng X. 1983; Zhu D. 1985). This view is paradoxical. Most obviously, rebellious individuals had to be fit enough to fight. If the society suffered starvation on a large scale, instead of rising up, a large number of people would simply die straight away. Even if the starving did manage to rise up, they would almost certainly not last long enough to make an impact.

From the data in Table 4.2, a great many Chinese rebellions did last for some time, which meant constant material support from someone and somewhere. The existence of these surplus resources thus contradicts the notion of abject poverty. So, logically, from the pure biological coefficient, it was the prospect of starvation, rather than the actual starvation itself, that caused rebellions. It is thus safe to suggest that it is relative poverty, not absolute poverty, that caused the Chinese to rebel.

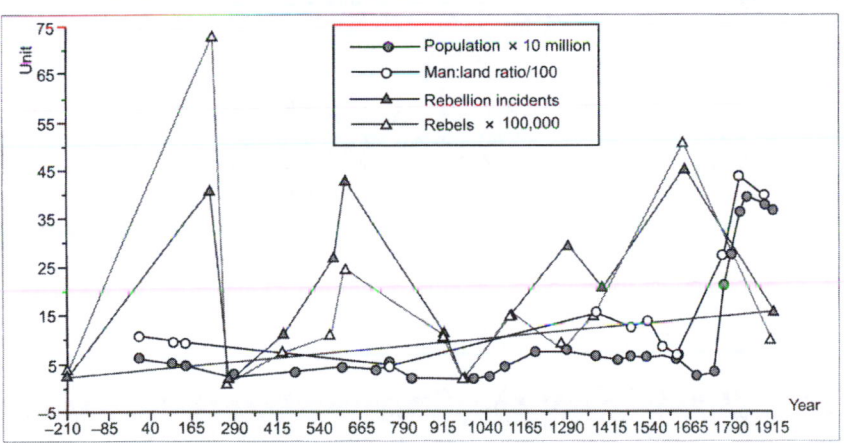

*Figure 4.6.* Population pressure versus rebellions, 210 BC–1900

*Source*: Based on Appendix J; Liang F. 1980: 4–11.

In contrast to the view of abject poverty, there is strong evidence that it was the relatively well-off peasants who rebelled most frequently, as shown from the uneven geographic distribution of insurrections (see Figure 4.7). The Chinese rebellions were highly concentrated in most developed economic regions rather than remote and less developed areas. There were three of them: (1) four northern provinces (which are marked 'A') in the middle and lower reaches of the Yellow River Valley: Hebei, Shandong, Henan and Shanxi; (2) two provinces in central and western China (marked 'B') in the middle reaches of the Yangzi River: Hubei and Sichuan; and (3) three south-

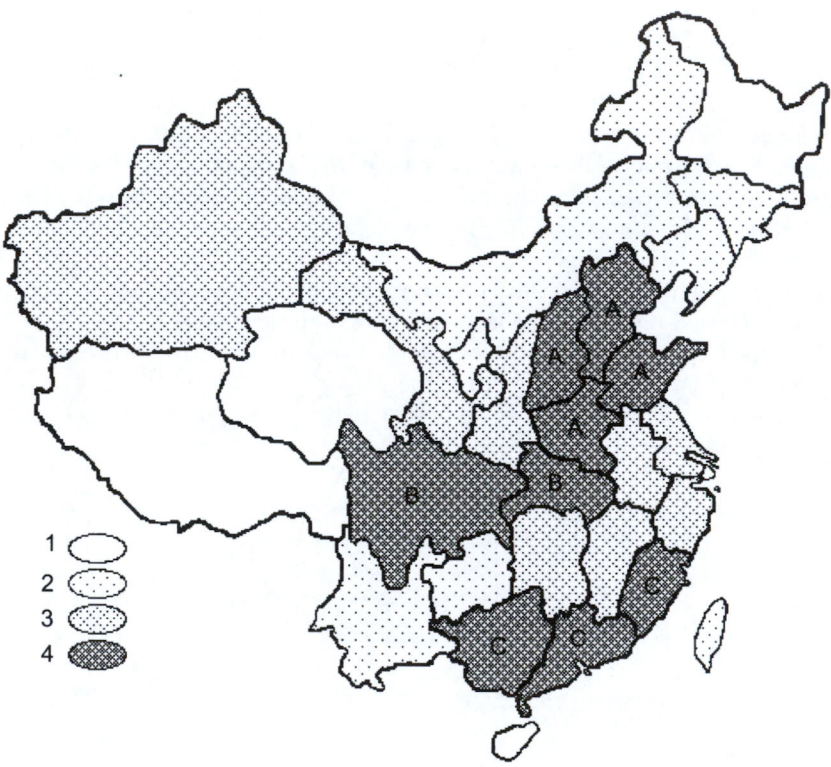

*Figure 4.7.* Geographic distribution of main armed rebellions, 210 BC–1900

*Source*: Based on Appendix J.
*Note*
The contemporary China territory is used for demonstrative purposes only. For the maximum size of the Chinese Empire, see Figure 3.6. 1–Rebellion-free areas; 2–revolt incidents numbered 1–5; 3–revolt incidents numbered 6–10; 4–revolt incidents numbered over 10. A–The middle and lower reaches of the Yellow River; B–and upper and middle reaches of the Yangzi River; C–the Xun–Pearl river drainage and coastal Fujian.

eastern provinces (marked 'C') along the southern coast: Guangxi, Guang-dong and Fujian.

The four northern provinces cover the Loess Plateau and most of the North Plain, the main theatre for dry farming throughout Chinese history, and commonly recognised as the cradle of Chinese civilisation. The two provinces in central and western China formed a vast wet-farming area with high yields. Sichuan was regarded as the 'Region of Affluence in China' (*tianfu zhiguo*). The three southeast provinces were a rich multi-cropping rice-growing region. These areas are roughly the same size and had all been well populated by Han times (see Fairbank 1965: 6).

So, the most rebellious peasants were not those 'marginal peasants' who lived in the marginal farming zones and who were usually very poor. The reason is multifold: (1) densely populated, advanced regions were strongholds of the peasantry and thus the insurrection centres where the imperial army was hopelessly outnumbered by the peasants; (2) better educated and thus better informed, peasants in these advanced regions were more conscious of economic and political crises; (3) with more surplus the advanced regions had a great capacity for supporting rebellions. The rebellions were thus based on and relied heavily on the conditions of the peasant economy.

### 4.3.3 *Trinary disequilibrium*

Now, on the one hand, it is clear that rebellions had little to do with China's population growth and man-to-land ratio. So, a Malthusian or natural disaster explanation, although popular, helps little. On the other hand, it has been recognised that (1) in most cases rebellions in China were initiated by protests of the rural poor, who acted as the instigators (Wang 1936); (2) if the conditions were not largely improved, rebellions became inevitable; (3) if the rebellion was successful, the rebellious 'bandits' were recognised by society as the righteous forces (see Wright 1957: 44). Here, although the view of 'the rural poor' should be discounted as the 'relatively impoverished peasants', a causality can be sensed.

As demonstrated in Chapters 2 and 3, the institutions that distinguished Chinese from feudal Europe and Japan were (1) small landholding and land-owning peasantry, and (2) centralised bureaucracy, both being components of the Chinese trinary structure. Earlier in this chapter, it was shown that in feudal Europe and Japan, armed mass rebellions were not only rare but also less effective in terms of overthrowing and replacing the government and monarch. Indeed, in the premodern world, no other peasantry had the same strength as the Chinese, which overpowered the state so many times. All these provide a clue that the cause of peasant rebellions in premodern China was institutional and directly related to the collapse of the trinary equilibrium.

The correlation between the peasant armed rebellions and the trinary crises is demonstrated in Figure 4.8 containing data for fluctuations in political units *vis-à-vis* populous armed rebellions over two millennia. By definition, in the absence of foreign invasions, the fragmentation of the empire reflects either the weakening of the trinary equilibrium (weakened agriculture, crippled government and an impoverished peasantry) or the collapse of the structure. Within four periods of five centuries each (210 BC–AD 290, 290–790, 790–1290 and 1290–1790), the rebellious incidents had the same trend as that of the political units, a main exception appearing between AD 665 and 790. The aggregate durations of the rebellions followed more or less the same pattern as the incidents. Figure 4.9 reveals the correlation further. Given that the replacement of an emperor normally meant a change of government, the frequency of emperor replacements meant socio-political instability. Such instability was consistent with fluctuations in the incidence of the rebellions.

One step further from the general, visual trends shown in Figures 4.8 and 4.9 is to measure quantitatively correlation coefficients (1) between rebellions and the number of political units coexisting in China, and (2) between rebellions and replacement of emperors, using the following formulae:

$$r = \frac{S_{xy}}{\sqrt{S_{xx}} \cdot \sqrt{S_{yy}}} \tag{4.2}$$

$$S_{xy} = \sum_{i=1}^{n}(x_i - x)(y_i - y) \tag{4.3}$$

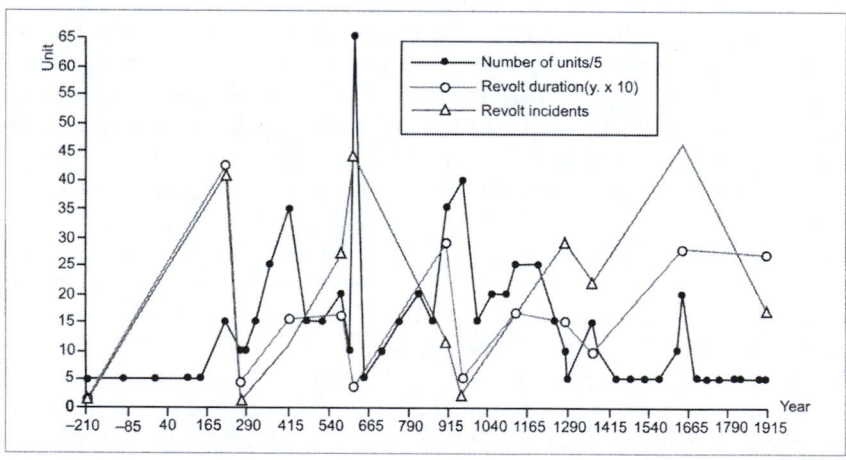

*Figure 4.8.* Political units versus rebellions, 210 BC–1900

*Source*: Based on Appendix J; CBW 1989: 2345–2405.

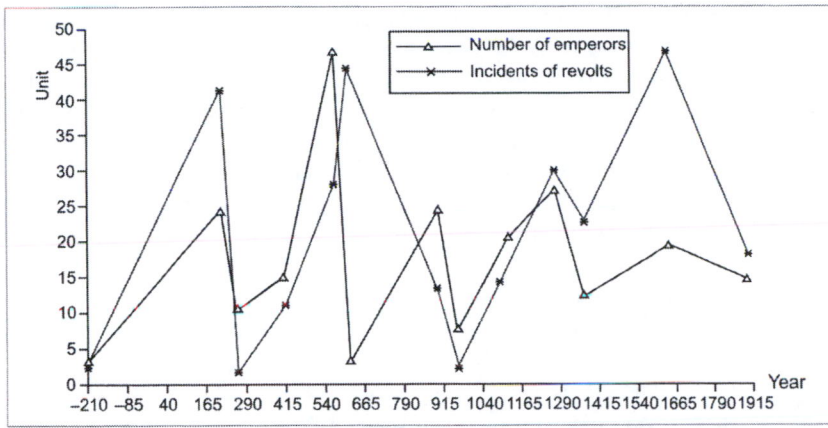

*Figure 4.9.* Replacement of emperors versus rebellions, 210 BC–1900

*Source*: Based on Appendix J; CBW 1989: 2345–2405.

$$S_{xx} = \sum_{i=1}^{n} (x_i - x)^2 \tag{4.4}$$

$$S_{yy} = \sum_{i=1}^{n} (y_i - y)^2 \tag{4.5}$$

where $S$ is the sum total; $x$ and $y$ are two variables; $x_i$, $y_i$ the values of these variables in period $i(1 - n)$; $x$ and $y$, the average values of the variables in period $1 - n$. The item $r$ is the correlation coefficient, whose value ($0 \leq r \leq 1$) indicates how closely two variables ($x$ and $y$) are related, zero in value meaning no correlation and unity, the closest correlation. The results are shown below:

| Category | $S_{xy}$ | $S_{xx}$ | $S_{yy}$ | $r$ |
|---|---|---|---|---|
| Number of political units ($x$) versus rebellion duration ($y$) | 27.04 | 11.79 | 42.21 | 0.05 |
| Number of political units ($x$) versus rebellion incidents ($y$) | 142.88 | 11.79 | 54.76 | 0.22 |
| Replacement of emperors ($x$) versus rebellion incidents ($y$) | 673.94 | 41.10 | 54.76 | 0.30 |
|     Subperiod I (210 BC–AD 600) | 810.40 | 34.04 | 34.51 | 0.69 |
|     Subperiod II (AD 700–1400) | 261.40 | 16.67 | 20.41 | 0.77 |

Three points can be made. First, the correlation between rebellion duration and the number of political units coexisting in China, a sign of the collapse of the empire, is insignificant. Second, the correlation between rebellion incidents and political units was only loosely related. Here, the implication is clearly that the peasant rebellions did not result in, or simply did not aim at, the breaking up of the empire. Indeed, peasants needed the empire, which embodied the kind of institutions required by the survival and growth of the peasant household economy. Third, the correlation between rebellion incidents and replacement of emperors was much closer than that between rebellion incidents and the number of political units, especially during the two subperiods. The increase in the value of $r$ in AD 700–1400 shows that the correlation was closer. This tells us that the rebellions resulted in both personnel and policy changes of the empire without jeopardising its fundamental socio-economic structure. In other words, the peasantry wanted the empire and the trinary structure but not corruption in governing institutions. Thus, these coefficients are highly consistent with the analysis so far regarding the trinary structure, its equilibrium and self-regulating function.

## 4.4 Main characterisitcs of the rebellions

### 4.4.1 Peasant behavioural dualism

In peaceful times, the Chinese peasants maintained, in Fairbank's phrase, a highly civilised life in very poor conditions by modern Western standards (1983: 21) and were extremely obedient before the authorities. But during the troubled times they became extremely militant. This behavioural dualism has often puzzled observers because they cannot see the link between the two extremes. Evidence shows that the Chinese enjoyed a living standard no lower than that of the West Europeans up to the seventeenth century and probably after that (see, for example, Mokyr 1990: ch. 9; Pomeranz 1997). So, it is groundless from the criteria of the modern Western lifestyle to assume that the Chinese were, or should have been, miserable and discontented.

The illusion comes first from the Confucian norm of filial piety and fraternal duty (*xiaodi*), which is often understood as rules of obedience both within the family and without (Fairbank 1965: ch. 2). However, if we know that Confucian filial piety and fraternal duty is not one-way traffic going from the powerless inferior to the powerful superior but a two-way exchange between inferior and superior, the puzzle evaporates.

In the Chinese family life cycle, in the initial stage the parents were providers and guardians of the younger generation; in return obedience of the younger generation as beneficiaries to the elder was expected. Later on, when the parent generation retired and became dependent on the younger generation, the tide changed: although respect to the elder was still maintained, most decisions were made by the younger. In terms of decision-making, both the obedience of the younger and the interference of the older diminished. Of course, the cycle resumed for the next round of the guardian–

234

beneficiary relationship. In essence, the filial–fraternal obedience was not a relationship between the ruling and the ruled. Rather, it was a relationship of interdependence with mutual understanding and mutual support.

Similarly, the Confucian sage-like humanity (*ren*) versus etiquette (*li*), a recognised extension of filial–fraternal obedience, operated in the same way, but transcending the family–kinship limit. Thus, sage-like humanity was not charitable behaviour on the part of the giver or benevolence from the superior, but an exchange behaviour based on mutual understanding and mutual support from the top to the bottom in the social pyramid. The coercive appearance is one-sided only if one views the relationship from the angle of the inferior, where responsibilities and rights seem to separate each other permanently (see Fairbank 1965: ch. 2). Indeed, it is hard to imagine that a long-lasting civilisation could be built on the basis that the young and the inferior had only duties but no rights.

There existed some minimal conditions for such an interdependent relationship to function which in practice set up a threshold for rebellion to take place in society as well as in the family (for a family case see Jia Baoyu in *Dream of the Red Chamber* [*Hongloumeng*] (Cao X. *c.* 1763)). Before the deteriorating socio-political and economic situations and the unilateral violation of the duty from the top pushed the inferior to this threshold, the inferior would act obediently. This was rational because an individual peasant, for example, could hardly fight against the state apparatus that was designed to control a large population with its organised violence. But once millions of peasants were pushed towards the critical point, the issue of government wrongdoings became explosive and the peasantry then organised themselves to fight against the corrupt state apparatus in order to protect their immediate and future interests. This was rational, too, because once the discontented peasants outnumbered the government forces, the cost of victory over the state was sharply reduced and the chances of winning increased. Under this circumstance, rebellions did not just offer hope, half the battle was won. To sum up, collectively the Chinese peasants behaved obediently to the state not because they were helpless and powerless but because they were reasonably content. They became aggressive and militant when they were no longer contented. Parsons thus points out that the main reason for the revolts to break out was not religious but was the fact that peasants were fed up with the corrupt governing institutions (Parsons 1970: 199).

That the scattered Chinese peasants pulled their heads together to fight for a common goal in rebellions creates another paradox: the self-centred and selfish peasants who under normal circumstances could not care less about the others' welfare (Shang X. 1989: 26–8) periodically in their rebellions became solidified, strong and motivated by public interest (Li G. *et al*. 1958; Liu Z. *et al*. 1979; Zhang S. and Zheng X. 1983). One thing is sure: this cohesion was not always present. Rather, it was highly temporal. It was 'coerced solidarity' rather than a voluntary one. It occurred only when the peasants faced unusual coercion, which may be defined as the 'diamond effect': the peasants were like graphite, which is normally soft and shapeless. However, under high pressure graphite becomes diamond, which is the hardest substance in the natural world. The Chinese trinary crises provided such pressure. If the Chinese state ignored the 'natural law', it would have to face the diamond, which could easily cut the state apparatus into pieces.

The diamond effect reveals the fact that in traditional China the major conflict was between the ruling elite and the majority peasantry. This should not be taken as a view of Marxian class struggle, which simplifies all the social relations into two bare categories, the exploiting and the exploited, with little room to negotiate, compromise and cooperate. The Marxian class struggle hypothesis thus distorts rather than explains and decodes the actual social relations, as shown by the practice of communism in the past eighty years worldwide. Together with private land ownership and social mobility, this diamond effect betrays the overwhelming individualistic personality of the Chinese peasants *vis-à-vis* the common recognition of the collective nature of the same peasantry. This is another dualism which is demonstrated in Confucian and Taoist values (Munro 1985).

This leads to an answer to a puzzling question: why did the Chinese peasantry have such power, a power which surpassed the power of autocratic dynasts and determined the fate of numerous régimes? A satisfactory answer cannot be found by using the European/Japanese model, where individual private land ownership did not develop to the same extent as in post-Qin China. Nor can it be found in the degree of so-called economic exploitation of the masses, simply because such exploitation was always part of the life of ordinary people under slavery, feudalism, capitalism and indeed Stalinism even according to the strictest Marxist measurement. The secret lies in (1) the well-entrenched private individual land ownership and its derived landholding types, (2) the peasantry as the dominant stratum in long-term Chinese history, and (3) the public sense of fair and just government. So, the power of the peasantry was determined by the Chinese institutions: mainly land ownership and the trinary structure.

This behavioural dualism makes a lot of sense when China is compared to feudal Europe and Japan. In pre-industrial England, for example, manor owners had the lawful power to evict their tenants, a power which was made possible by the Enclosure Movement (Moore 1966: 467; Critchley 1978). Although doomed, the peasantry could not stop the Enclosure Movement, a form of concentration of land which drove tenants off the land (Moore 1966: 20–39). Instead of rural rebellion, such alienation triggered profound socio-economic changes and eventually ushered in the British 'Industrial Revolution' (Chambers 1972; Jones 1974; Yamamura 1979). Also, in a decentralised feudal system, the personal bondage which existed within the small, separate political units, as well as the economic differences between these, handicapped any attempt at organised manoeuvres of large numbers of people in rural areas. Nor was it necessary in medieval Europe for there to be organised mass rebellions to change unbearable social conditions: there were many other, bloodless means of breaking out of personal bondage under feudalism, for instance by protesting against individual masters or overlords to obtain a better deal, or simply by escaping from individual masters or overlords to become, for example, free bourgeois, known as 'voting with feet' (Moore 1966: 256). Moreover, since the free citizens in medieval Europe were not the social majority, they could not have the same influence as the Chinese peasants. In the case of the free Germanic and Slavic communes, there was little need for the members to rebel, since the underdevelopment of private ownership hindered the alienation of the political power from the public interest (cf. Engels 1942). The overall impression one gains from this comparison is that institutional barriers to peasant rebellions existed in Europe, India and Japan. Such barriers were largely absent in premodern China.

### 4.4.2 Shifting of centres of rebellion

Another interesting characteristic is that the rebellious centre of gravity, in terms of rebellion frequency, changed through time. There are two distinctive stages and the watershed was the Song Dynasty (AD 907–1271).

Before the Song Dynasty, rebellions were concentrated along the 'A' and 'B' belts (Figure 4.7), including eight provinces: Hebei, Shandong, Jiangsu, Anhui, Henan, Shanxi, Shaanxi and Sichuan. During the second stage, rebellions were concentrated along the 'B' and 'C' belts (Figure 4.7), including ten provinces: Shandong, Shanxi, Hebei, Henan, Jiangsu, Hubei, Hunan, Guangxi, Guangdong and Fujian. This phenomenon is illustrated in Figures 4.10 and 4.11. Such a shift in the rebellious centre of gravity suggests that rebellions followed economic centres.

The timing of the shift deserves some special attention. Evidence shows that by the Tang Dynasty (AD 618–907), North China (zhongyuan) had become more advanced than the south in most areas such as science and technology, the economy, arts and scholarship, and the North dominated the Chinese economy. After the Song Dynasty (AD 907–1271), the south surpassed the north on all the above counts and replaced it as the dominant force in the economy (Zhang J. 1957; ZNK 1984 vol. 2: 4–5; Zheng X. et al. 1984: 161–3). The dramatic change in southern agriculture was driven by what can be called the 'rice–cotton revolution' in Song times: (1) early-ripening rice varieties revolutionised the old tillage pattern and opened up a new era of multiple cropping in South China; (2) cotton as a cheaper alternative replaced the traditional silk and flex/hemp (ma), and became the main source of fibre in everyday life, which revolutionised the timeless pattern of grain–mulberry–hemp cultivation (Li J. 1957: 36–43; Zhang J. 1957: 156–60). The resultant labour saving from silkworm-raising and silk–hemp processing provided the required input for multiple cropping.

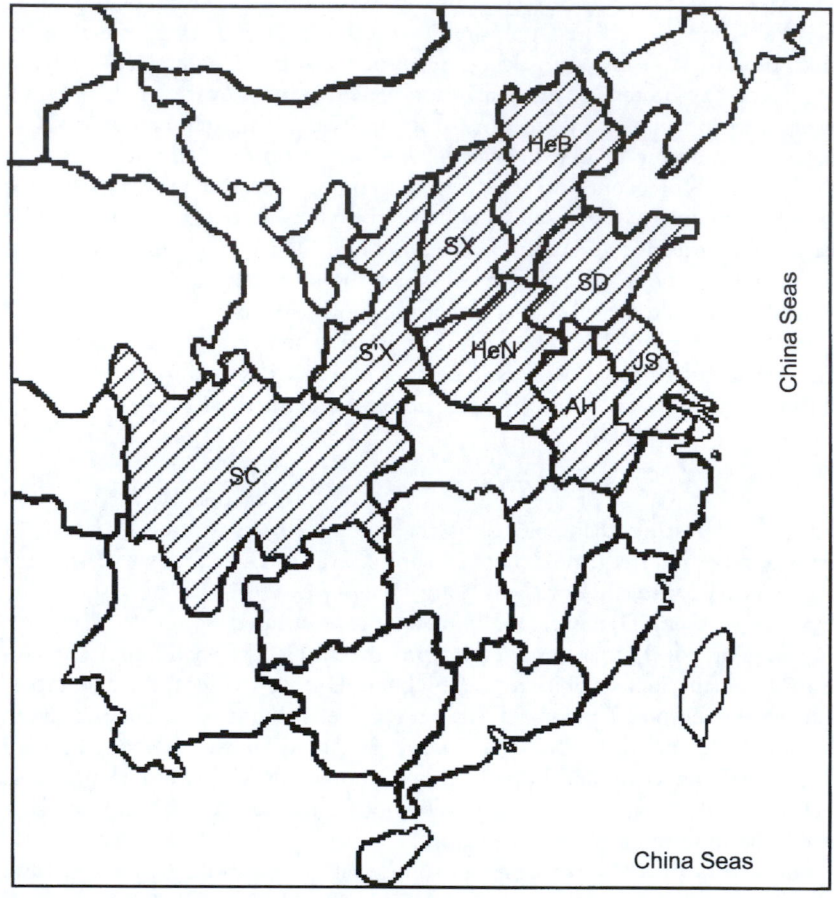

*Figure 4.10.* Geographic distribution of rebellions, 210 BC–960 AD

*Source*: Based on Appendix J.
*Note*
Only part of China's territory is illustrated. The provinces shown are provinces of modern China: AH, Anhui; HeB, Hebei; HeN, Henan; JS, Jiangsu; SC, Sichuan; SD, Shandong; SX, Shanxi; S'X, Shaanxi.

The superiority of the south can be seen from its agricultural performance. Grain shipment from the south through the Grand Canal (*caoyun*) in post-Sui history was the most obvious case (see Table 4.3; see also Needham 1971: 317–18; Elvin 1973: 54–5, 58–9, 102–3; Zhou B. 1981: 189). It is evident from both the magnitude and the south-to-north ratios that the south was

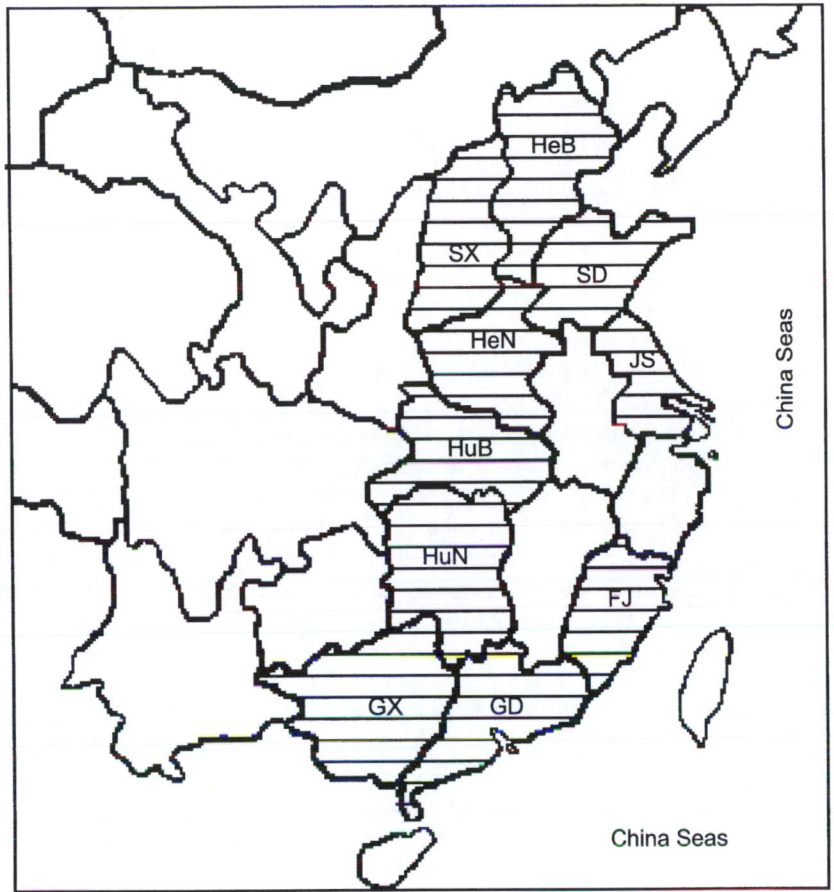

*Figure 4.11.* Geographic distribution of rebellions, 960–1911

*Source*: Based on Appendix J.
*Note*
Only part of China's territory is illustrated. The provinces shown are provinces of modern
China: FJ, Fujian; GD, Guangdong; GX, Guangxi; HeB, Hebei; HeN, Henan; HuB.
Hubei; HuN, Hunan; JS, Jiangsu; SD, Shandong; SX, Shanxi.

more advanced than the north in agricultural output. During the same period, the population density in one province along the Yangzi River was 2.5
to 3 times higher than in a province in the Yellow River region, which can
also be seen as a sign of higher land productivity in the south whereby the
greater population was supported (Zhang J. 1957: 159).

239

*Table 4.3* Quantity (*shi*) of grain contributed to the state

| Period | Year | North | | South | | S:N ratio |
|--------|------|-------|------|-------|------|-----------|
| Song | 1065 | 1,007,000[a] | (668,749) | 5,755,000[a] | (3,821,896) | 5.71 |
| Yuan | 1299 | 2,932,945[b] | — | 6,890,311[b] | — | 2.35 |
| Ming | 1578 | 4,412,105[a] | (4,737,277) | 10,674,633[a] | (11,461,353) | 2.42 |
| Qing | 1753 | 668,652[a] | (692,389) | 4,076,182[a] | (4,220,886) | 6.10 |
| | 1766 | 521,084[a] | (539,582) | 4,266,679[a] | (4,418,146) | 8.19 |

*Source*: Based on Liang F. 1980: 293–4, 303, 375, 394, 396.

*Notes*
S:N–South:North.
a Grain transported to capital.
b Tax collected in kind. Numbers in parentheses are converted to the modern measure.

By the Ming Dynasty, southern farmers produced approximately 70 per cent of the total grain output in China (Song Y. 1637: 1). This is supported by land-tax revenue obtained from the south in Ming times. Suzhou Prefecture (*fu*) had 1.1 per cent of the total cultivated land of China while it produced about 10 per cent of the country's total land-tax revenue, which suggests that agricultural productivity in Suzhou Prefecture was 10 times higher than the average level (Zhang J. 1957: 159).

After this shift of the economic centre, the centres of peasant insurrections shifted, for at least two reasons: (1) south China became a new stronghold of the peasantry, and (2) the south began to bear most of the tax burden of the country. Therefore, the Song Period was not only a watershed for the south's importance in the premodern Chinese economy but also a watershed for a regional distribution of rebellions: before the Song rebellions were concentrated in the northeast; after the Song, in the Yuan (1271–1368), Ming (1368–1644) and Qing (1644–1911) dynasties southern rebellions dominated the Chinese political arena.

Five provinces in the northeast overlapped in these two periods: Shandong, Shanxi, Hebei, Henan and Jiangsu as the axis of the rebellious movements. This raises a problem of why the peasant rebels always had one foot in the northeastern region. This has something to do with the location of the nerve centre of the Chinese bureaucratic machine: the northeast had been the political core of the empire since Qin times, no matter how the territories fluctuated. Because of that, this area was always targeted when the rebels attempted to overthrow the ruler and seize state power.

### 4.4.3 Peasant organisers

Peasant organisations always existed in Chinese society, either legally or illegally. During peaceful times, those secret societies – under all sorts of religious or political banners such as clans and tongs, Taoism, Buddhism, Christianity – were underground and often harmless to state power. Peasant organisations were compatible with the free-citizen status of the peasants. However, they often had paramilitary capacity, like the long-lasting Five Decilitre Grain Charity Movement (*wudoumijiao*) early in Chinese dynastic history and the White Lotus Buddhist Movement (*bailianjiao*) in later times (see Appendix J).

Observers are often confused by the non-orthodoxy, or non-Confucian colours, of these peasant societies as if these organisations fundamentally differed from the upper-class systems in terms of ideology and programmes. Superficially they did. However, in the context of the function of the Chinese peasant rebellions, these differences only show different tastes between upper and lower strata. It did not really matter much how these peasants combined in order to rebel as long as they were able to rise up in large numbers. The test again is pragmatic: after the major rebellions, the Chinese peasantry supported without exception a Confucian régime, including the Han, Tang, Song and Ming. Fairbank thus overplayed the importance of the link between the names of the peasant organisations in rebellions and the political ideals of the peasants, seeing the Buddhist White Lotus Movement (*bailianjiao*) and the Christian Heavenly Kingdom of Great Peace (*Taiping Tianguo*) as a new pattern (Fairbank 1965: ch. 7; Shih 1967; Feuerwerker 1975: 20–3, 28).

With an acute crisis, all the hidden social networks which had been on stand-by began to produce a cohesive force to organise the scattered peasants. These organisations had no difficulty in converting themselves to a well-organised army in a short space of time, given that many peasants had served in the Chinese army and/or were involved in martial arts training. Witchcraft was popular, too. The leaders of the first mass rebellion in the Qin Dynasty, Chen Sheng and Wu Guang, relied greatly on witchcraft to mobilise their fellow peasants (Zhang S. and Zheng X. 1983: 7).

But the external pressure was imperative. Only under persistent, universal and simultaneous pressure from above did the Chinese peasants become increasingly united. With an increasing degree of unity, the peasants became more and more militant, a situation which can be called the militarisation of the peasantry (Kuhn 1970: ch. 3). When a government crackdown became impossible because of its military weakness due to the paralysis of the bureaucratic network and/or the heavy loss of tax income, the rebels were able to defeat and replace the government by their collective efforts.

At the individual level, rebels hibernated during the time of the trinary equilibrium, as did peasant organisations. Once conditions were right and insurrections broke out, many ordinary peasants acted heroically and showed their leadership qualities. They became candidates for the roles of high-ranking commanders or officials, and even grabbed the crown for themselves, the best example being Zhu Yuanzhang, the founder of the Ming Dynasty.

## 4.5 Nature of the rebellions

The nature of the Chinese peasant armed rebellions was reflected by the right, aims, motives and incentives to rebel, which will be dealt with one by one in this section.

### 4.5.1 The right to rebel and the aim of rebelling

In China, law did exist but morality had the ultimate say. Thus, it is correct to believe that in China ultimately the successful execution of laws and policies depended on moral authority (Fairbank 1957: 172, 1965: ch. 5). The reason was multifold. First of all, it was part of the clan tradition. Within the clan, the chiefdom and custom were combined in one. The Confucian idea of 'internal sage and external wise ruler' (*neisheng waiwang*) manifests such a milieu. Second, it was based on a society of relative homogeneity so that a common custom or code of behaviour was widely accepted and applied. Third, the centralised Chinese political structure did not have much room for an independent judicature. As a result, practising law could be disastrous, as shown by the tyrannic Qin model. As an alternative, in China a combination of strong moral standards and weak law persisted. The advantage of this combination was that the state power was under the surveillance of millions of eyes of the commoners, who did raise their voice to stop a bad government. So, in long-term Chinese history, morality often triumphed over law.

Precisely because of the lack of law to control state corruption, when the ruling class failed to represent desirable moral and policy standards, the ruled were entitled to rebel and replace unpopular régimes at the people's will. This explains why peasant insurrections were often morally sound although unlawful. In this context, when mass rebellions broke out it was the ruler or the governing institutions that should be morally blamed, which is crystallised in an old Chinese idiom: 'official oppression leads to rebellions' (*guanbi minfan*). As Marsh correctly points out, old dynasts lost the mandate to rule China when the ordinary Chinese felt extreme 'duress', and such dynasts could be legitimately overthrown (Marsh 1961: 43). And overthrown they were (Li Z. 1993; Sun Y. 1994). As a result, the Chinese trinary equilibrium is more of a morality-guarded equilibrium than a law-guarded equilibrium. To restore such an equilibrium often needed unlawful activities such as rebellions. In this sense, the reason why rebellions took place was frequently structural rather than emotional. Moreover, in law-lacking China, the rebellion was a built-in factor in the socio-political and economic systems.[4] This led to the right to rebel among the ordinary citizens (Fairbank 1965: 54).

The recognition, definition and endorsement of the right to rebel existed in China in the time before Christ. It had multiple aspects. First, the right to rebel was reflected in Chinese popular thought. The heroes in the three classics *The Romance of the Three Kingdoms* (*Sanguo Yanyi*), *Water Marsh* (*Shuihuzhuan*) and *Journey to the West* (*Xiyouji*) are all rebels. In *Water Marsh*, all the rebels, 108 of them, are in one way or another forced to fight against the state. In *Journey to the West*, the Monkey King, Wukong, has a humble past in his life: he has no birthright and works as the bodyguard of a Buddhist pilgrim to India as punishment for his previous wrongdoings, namely causing havoc in Heaven, where the most powerful monarch, the Great Jade Emperor (*yuhuang dadi*), operates his mighty state apparatus (Tang C. 1979). The monkey normally obeys his master. But, coming across evil, he rebels against his master and fights vigorously against the bad, as shown by the main plot of the *Journey to the West*: first, the monkey destroys the Heaven Palace (*tiangong*); second, he fights for and earns his title of 'Heavenly Great Sage' (*qitian dasheng*). What is interesting is that the evil themselves are often mutants of good characters, equivalents of corrupt monarchs and officials who were once 'good guys' in their lives. From the literature, rebellion is a sacred right, if not a mission, of the ordinary people.

Second, Chinese society did not rule out the possibility of peasants themselves becoming leaders or rulers. In this context, it is no exaggeration to say that the Chinese peasantry did have the 'genes' of rebellion. Arguably, the genes were the result of the social mobility in traditional China, to replace a monarch having been regarded a possibility because of the mobility (Li Z. 1990; Yang C. and Shen G. 1993; Zhu D. 1994). As the Chinese sayings go, 'everybody could become an emperor, one day it may well be my turn' (*huangdi renren zuo, jintian dao wojia*); and 'one may take over China by force [regardless of one's background]' (*datianxia*). Even if the odds were against most individual attempts, the chance did exist (see Appendix J).

Third, the right to rebel was theorised by Confucianism in two interrelated aspects: (1) to get rid of corrupt government and (2) to restore the old order. Both required violence. This also explains why the seemingly peace-loving Confucians paid considerable attention to military arts. The theory of warfare is a part of Confucian classics, which can be seen especially in *Master Xun's Book*, written during the Warring States Period (Xun K. *c.* 238 BC). Military training such as horsemanship and archery (*qishe*) is included in the Confucian curriculum (ZDB 1985: 229–30). If the Confucians had been trained solely as civil officials, they would have had no need for military training. In a sense, the Confucians were ready to rebel, too. Mass rebellions against the corrupt authorities were regarded as necessary and just, or even 'natural' (Mousnier 1971: 240): as the Confucian political maxim goes, 'The ruled are to the ruling as water is to a boat: not only does water support the boat, it can also upset the boat' (*junzhe zhouye, shurenzhe shuiye; shui ze zaizhuo, shui ze fuzhuo* (Xun K. *c.* 238 BC: ch. 'Duke Ai'). Dong Zhongshu (179–104 BC), a prominent Confucian since the Han Period, pointed out more specifically in his *Many Dewdrops of Spring and Autumn* (*Chunqiu Fanlu*) that if the committing of evil and crimes by monarchs brings calamities to the people, Heaven will deprive the monarchs of the power to rule (Dong Z. *c.* 104 BC: ch. 'Yao Shun Bu Shanyi, Tang Wu Bu Zhuansha'). Confucians also saw insurrections and wars as the means of establishing order and peace. Confucius explicitly maintained in his *Analects*, 'He who wants to be a ruler must first establish order and peace in war and then practise *ren* (Kong Qiu *c* 479 BC: ch. 'Zi Lu'). Confucianism thus offered the peasantry a licence to rebel. It is worth noting that the Confucian concept of the justifiable rebellion included tyrannicidal practices. A tyrannicide was regarded by Confucians as a national hero, as in the ancient case of 'Jing Ke's assassinating the King of the Qin' (*jingke ci qinwang*) in 227 BC and modern cases like 'Wang Jingwei's assassinating the Regent Zaifeng of the Qing' in 1910.[5] In contrast, strongmen's or warlords' rebellions to divide China were condemned by Confucianism as betrayals or treasons. The standard expressions by Confucians are 'usurpation' (*jianyue*) and 'collapse of the etiquette and ruin of the music' (*libeng yuehuai*).

Confucianism thus sent two opposite messages to the peasantry: obedience to authority and insurrection against authority, which forms another paradox. Most scholars tend to overlook the rebellious side of Confucianism because it does not seem to fit in with the general picture of the Chinese civilisation. In effect, both obedient Confucianism and rebellious Confucianism were highly conditional: if the government is good, citizens should obey; if the government is corrupt, citizens should rebel. Such dualism in Confucianism reflects the complexity of Chinese society and conditionality of the trinary equilibrium. In this context, the key concept of the Confucian legitimacy to rule China, Heaven's will, was in effect the peasantry's own will. Such a will was expressed in two ways: during the periods of equilibrium, it is reflected by people's support of and obedience to the governing institutions; during the crises, it is reflected in protests and rebellions. The best examples are the slogans created by rebels: (1) 'The old heaven is dead and is replaced by the new heaven above yellow scarfs' (*cangtian yisi, huangtian dangli*), in AD 184 under the leadership of Zhang Jiao, Zhang Bao and Zhang Liang, known as the 'Yellow-Scarf Uprising' (Zhang S. and Zheng X. 1983: 435); (2) 'Imposing the Way on behalf of Heaven' (*titian xingdao*), during 1120–2 under the leadership of Song Jiang (Shi N. Early Ming Period). The hangover of this legitimacy issue remained valid in China during the first half of the twentieth century (Thaxton 1983).

This Confucian endorsement of rebellions was particularly significant. First, it confirms the peasants' political and economic rights. Second, it justifies the participation of members of the Confucian literati in peasant rebellions. It was recorded that even Confucius's own descendant, Kong Fu (*c.* 264–208 BC), joined the rebels as Chen Sheng's adviser to topple the Qin Dynasty (CBW 1989: 1262). Many elite members not only joined the rebels but also provided leadership for the rebellions. Thus, they were an organic part of the rebellions in premodern China. Without the help of Confucianism, the Chinese peasantry would have had less chance of success. Because of this,

Confucianism should be taken as an important component in the Chinese rebellions. It is misleading to take Confucianism as an exclusive tool in the hands of the ruling clique to protect their selfish interests.

Third, as a result of the above reasons, instead of denying the existence and deeds of the rebels, Chinese imperial historians customarily included the biographies of rebel gurus in Chinese dynastic histories (Chen T. 1994), as well as of all the rebels-turned-dynasts (Zhu D. 1994). This was the ultimate recognition of the right to rebel.

Finally, unlike the French dream of a mythical utopia (Bercé 1990: 274–6), the Golden Ages of the Chinese Empire and Confucian teaching provided the peasantry with a tangible yardstick with which to decide who was responsible for the crises and was thus the target for rebellion. From their track record, the Chinese rebels seldom missed this target; the main exception was the Boxers, who were completely confused at a time when China was under unprecedented pressure from the West.

The justification for peasant rebellions in Chinese culture was compatible with the social status of the landholding and landowning free peasantry, and became a common belief at the grass-roots level of society. Rebellions were thus to a great extent institutionalised: society expected violent uprisings to take place in a deteriorating socio-economic situation. This attitude towards mass armed rebellions would have been almost unimaginable in Europe and Japan. For instance, after the 1381 rebellions in England, peasant actions were considered unfortunate or bad luck rather than necessary (Dobson 1983: 333–4). The Chinese ruling class understood the rebellious mechanism perfectly well and sometimes deliberately used or manipulated the peasant force in its own interests, an example being the Boxer Rebellion in 1889–1900, which at first adapted the banner of 'supporting the Qing and eliminating the Westerners' (*fuqing mieyang*).

### 4.5.2 Aims, motives and incentives to rebel

The analysis of Confucian teaching and the Chinese trinary structure/equilibrium in Chapters 2 and 3 reveals the mass consciousness of the economy and socio-political and socio-economic structures. The Chinese peasantry never blindly followed government orders. Instead, the performance of the Chinese state was constantly watched and evaluated by the peasantry with the trinary equilibrium as the norm and the Confucian sage-like humanity as the criterion by which to judge. So, the Chinese rebels seem to have had clearer political and economic aims and programmes than their European or Japanese counterparts: they knew what they wanted and how they could achieve it.

Not surprisingly, the immediate aim of rebellions was to stop state corruption, which was reflected in the rebels' repertoire of attacking key government institutions and military installations in order to bring down the government

(Li Z. 1990; Yang C. and Shen G. 1993; Zhu D. 1994). This was helped by the fact that the centralised Chinese political structure gave peasants a single and easily recognisable target. In feudal Europe, because the majority of the population was administered by a decentralised system, massive discontentment resulting from a single source was rare. In addition, the Chinese bureaucrats were selected mainly according to their qualifications, not their wealth or blood. This meant that the ordinary Chinese tended to despise the bureaucrats instead of viewing them as god-like figures. So, there was little psychological barrier to prevent rebels from acting against officials. The rebels' final aim was to restore physiocratic policies by replacing the government (Li Z. 1990; Yang C. and Shen G. 1993; Zhu D. 1994). In effect, the Chinese rebels had a model to follow since the Han Period, which included basic processes of (1) organising the general peasant population, (2) attacking political and military targets, (3) replacing the old régime with a new one, and (4) restoring the old socio-economic order.

The motives of the Chinese rebels were reflected in the manifestos of the rebels themselves. 'Equality' was repeatedly used, as shown in Table 4.4. Here the term should be understood in the context of the Chinese trinary equilibrium; it had very little to do with a communist utopia. As mentioned before, private land ownership was both the dominant form of land-holding and the foundation of the free peasantry in premodern China, which differed from feudal Europe and Japan where private, individual land ownership was out of reach of the peasant majority (Landsberger 1974: pt 1; Critchley 1978). Thus, economic equality in the eyes of the Chinese rebels meant land distribution on an equal basis so that every able-bodied citizen was able to undertake tillage. The repetition of the demand for equality meant that the aim was highly standardised and hardened. This becomes more obvious when peasant rebels established their own régimes: the new government's priority was often to establish or replicate landholding and land-owning family farms.

No doubt Confucius's claim that 'our anxiety is not for poverty but for inequality in society' (*buhuanpin erhuanbujun*) (Kong Q. *c.* 479 BC: ch. 'Jishi') further facilitated peasant demand for equal land distribution and possession.

During the trinary crises, the incentives to rebel were often great, partly because of corruption (the disappearance of light taxation, erosion and dispossession of landholding and land ownership, the loss of hope for social mobility, the decline in living standards, the threat of unemployment, and the possibility of starvation) lowered opportunity costs for the rebellion, and partly because the returns from rebellion were immediate. Mass rebellions meant citizens' collective denial of the existing social order either at the local or the national level, which led to (1) the rejection of state authority and the power of the larger landholders, (2) organised default on tax and rental payments, and (3) the immediate redistribution of the wealth belonging to

*Table 4.4* Rebels' aims, 859 BC–1864

| Leader | Period (AD) | Claimed aim | Action taken |
|---|---|---|---|
| Qiu Pu | 859 | Heavenly equality (*tianping*) | — |
| Huang Chao | 874–84 | Heaven-assisted equality (*tianbu pingjun*) | Wealth redistribution |
| Wang Xiaobo | 993–5 | Levelling the poor with the rich (*junpinfu*) | Wealth redistribution |
| Zhong Xiang | 1130–5 | Equalising the respected with the humble and levelling the poor and the rich (*dengguijian junpinfu*) | Land redistribution |
| Zhu Yuanzhang (Buddhist) | 1351–68 | Stripping the rich to benefit the poor (*cuifu yipin*) | Wealth and land redistribution |
| Ye Zongliu | 1445–8 | Equality | — |
| Liu Tong | 1465–6 | Equality | — |
| Li Zicheng | 1627–46 | Equalising landholding and exempting tax (*juntian mianliang*) | Land redistribution and Tax exemption |
| Hong Xiuquan (Christian) | 1851–64 | All farmers sharing all the land (*tianxiatian tianxiaren tonggeng*) | Land redistribution |

*Sources*: Based on Li G. *et al.* 1958; Fan W. 1964–5; Feuerwerker 1975: 29; CBW 1979: 4766–816; Liu Z. *et al.* 1979; Zhang S. and Zheng X. 1983: 167, 174, 199, 230, 266, 313.

the government and the upper classes (in the form of incomes and properties). Therefore, rebellions paid, at least in the short run.

The aims, motives and incentives to rebel reveal the nature of the mass armed rebellions in premodern China as a response to trinary disequilibrium. From the viewpoint of outbreaks, these motives and incentives were the internal factors while the government pressure was the external factor. It took both internal and external factors to realise a rebellion.

# 4.6 Effectiveness, success, function and consequence of the rebellions

## 4.6.1 *Effectiveness of the rebellions*

As a violence-based instrument, rebellion was extremely efficient in determining the fate of a régime in premodern China. So, although rebellions were by nature a reactive response to corruption of the Chinese state, the free landholding and landowning peasantry was by far the most powerful counterpoise to corrupt state power. As mentioned earlier, the armed rebels overthrew at least six dynasties and numerous régimes within a dynasty.

The bloody rebellion was an effective way to 'vote' out the unwanted, corrupt state apparatus. In essence, it was the military power of the peasant rebellions that provided the ultimate solution of the trinary crises. Mao Zedong was thus correct by claiming that power comes from the barrel of a gun in the hands of millions of peasant followers as the antithesis of the Soviet city-based, worker-centred model (*qiangganzi limian chu zhengquan*) when instigating his brand of revolution among the Chinese peasantry in the 1930s and 1940s. But either he did not understand the true function of the peasant rebellions in premodern China or he deliberately manipulated the peasantry for his own purposes. Mao and his revolution benefited the peasantry little: consider merely the compulsory collectivisation in the early 1950s, almost immediately after the land-redistribution reform, and the nationwide man-made famine in the later 1950s (Kelliher 1992: 23–5). In that sense, he did far less than most founders of the dynasties in rewarding the peasantry who established the new régime. It is not surprising that even under the iron-handed rule of communism, which systematically dismantled the traditional fabric of Chinese society, peasant power eventually prevailed soon after Mao's death as both the initiator and locomotive of China's economic reform, which was by nature pro-private land ownership and anti-communism (ibid.: 25–30, 35–6, 100–1, 146n, 178–89, 233–53).

### 4.6.2 Success rate

Although nothing in Chinese history could have been so dramatic and so decisive as popular revolts in changing the tide of government policies, this is not to say that the rebels were always able to replace a rotten régime. From the data shown in Appendix J, the ratio between the establishment of a régime by the rebels and building a lasting dynasty was 12:1 (or 8.3 per cent) while the ratio between rebellions and successes in establishing new régimes was 5.6:1 (18 per cent). So, overall, the rebels' success rate in establishing a lasting dynasty was 1.5 per cent.

So, in terms of overthrowing and replacing an undesirable régime, the conditions (both internal and external) were demanding. Overall, there were four major internal conditions for a great rebellion to succeed in taking over the state power: (1) competent leadership, (2) military superiority, (3) support from the general public and (4) support from the literati. Such support was critical in obtaining legitimacy, manpower and revenue for the rebels' cause. To achieve that, the rebel leadership customarily offered peace, land, light taxation and a revival of the physiocratic state. Regarding how a policy package worked best, there were plenty of examples available in the Chinese histories for a would-be new ruler to copy. These examples were all along the lines of the trinary equilibrium. On the other hand, logically, if the rebels did succeed in replacing the corrupt régime, the momentum from a functional pattern to win people's support during this rebellion would lead to the restoration of the trinary structure. The whole process was highly convergent and standardised. The rebellion itself was therefore a carrier of the trinary genes.

The external conditions for a rebellion's success were largely determined by government actions against corruption and rebellions. The defusing of a rebellion by minimising the diamond effect through tackling state corruption has been mentioned earlier. In terms of dealing with rebellions, both a stick and a carrot were used. Rebels were from time to time cracked down upon by government forces. Sparing no effort, the Chinese state even invited foreign forces, the best-known cases being (1) the Hun cavalry (Shatuo), which in AD 883 crushed the rebellion under Huang Chao, and (2) the Western troops which during 1862–4 defeated the Taiping rebels (Zhang S. and Zheng X. 1983: 185, 385). The carrot was a practice called 'offering amnesty and official position' (*zhao-an*). In AD 623, Du Fuwei, the commander of the main force of peasant rebels, was offered and accepted an amnesty and official position, which practically ended a six-year-long armed struggle which had defeated the Sui's elite troops. In 1121, rebel leader Song Jiang accepted an amnesty and official position from the Song court (ibid.: 445, 451; see also Li G. *et al.* 1958: 167–85). Later, in 1861, Song Jingshi accepted the Qing amnesty and an official position (Li G. *et al.* 1958: 378). However, the carrot was far less effective, which shows the peasant political disillusionment with the corrupt régimes. In contrast, the resistance to amnesty from the Ming–Qing smugglers was considerably less: during the period 1796–1820, a total of 7,043 illegal maritime activists received an amnesty from the Qing state, an average of 293 cases a year (Zhang Z. 1986: 187). This marked difference was closely related to the different social statuses of the merchants and peasants.

What one should bear in mind, however, is that no matter how successful the government counter-attack to the rebellion was, changes normally took place in state affairs, tending towards the restoration of the trinary equilibrium, unless the state apparatus completely collapsed. The state had little choice. Without dramatic changes, the rebellion would become more widespread or break out anew.

Therefore, no matter how demanding replacing an unpopular régime looks, to judge from the success rate, one should not conclude that régime replacement was the only indicator of rebels' success. Given that peasant uprisings themselves were often sufficient to transform the government personnel and policies whereby corruption would be stopped, the replacement of a rotten régime was indeed optional. In effect, as long as the trinary structure and equilibrium was restored after a rebellion, the peasantry would calm down and return to their household farming regardless of the name of the régime and regardless of whether the peasants themselves had won a military victory or suffered a total defeat. In this context, the success rate of the Chinese peasant armed rebellions was much higher than the rate of régime replacement.

### 4.6.3 The function of the rebellions

Rebellion in China had several political and socio-economic functions: as a deterrent to corruption, a catalyst for change, a terminator of the alienated structure, a redistributor of wealth and a restorer of the old system. Since all these points have been referred to in one way or another, they will be dealt with briefly here just to complete the argument.

First, considering the existence of the right, incentive and organisation for rebellions to take place, the potential of a rebellion, rather than its actual outbreak, served as the sword of Damocles to the Chinese ruler. Evidence shows that the Chinese monarch and bureaucrats were fully conscious of and sensitive to this factor. Although the Chinese state was not mistake-proof and alienation-proof, the lesson from the Qin was well learned. For example, Emperor Taizong of the Tang (r. AD 627–49) wrote in his *Self-Warning* (*Zijian Lu*):

> When I saw the crowned prince on a boat, I asked him, 'Do you understand the boat?' 'No,' he answered. I then lectured him: 'The boat is like the monarch; and water, the citizens. Water is capable of supporting the boat as well as capsizing it. When taking the throne, shouldn't you be scared!'
>
> (Li S. *c.* AD 649b/1994: 78)

This was no doubt copied from the chapter 'Duke Ai' of *Master Xun's Book* (*Xunzi*) (Xun K. *c.* 238 BC). The emperor is also reported to have commented on the demise of the Sui Dynasty and said, 'I always take the Sui lesson to warn myself not to burden the people. Only when the ordinary people are content is there no rebellion' (Xu T. and Li Y. 1995: 427); and 'A larger territory does not guarantee lasting peace if the people are worn down, which is the matrix of rebellions' (*ibid.*: 410). Therefore, although they had little hope of overthrowing a régime, rebellions of the smallest calibre survived as early warning shots to alarm the state.[6]

Second, rebellions functioned as a catalyst for change even if the state targeted by a rebellion eventually got the upper hand in the civil war. After all, as shown in the data, in 82 per cent of the cases (*vis-à-vis* an 18 per cent rate for rebels to install their own establishments), the existing régime survived after the rebellious bombardment (see Appendix J). In those 82 per cent of crisis-outliving cases, the rebellions activated the self-regulating mechanisms of the state, which were otherwise severely stifled by corruption. Once the self-regulating mechanisms began to work again, there was often a tug-of-war between the state and the rebels in the race to restore the trinary equilibrium. Often the state had advantages in communication, administrative expertise and political experience, which tilted the scale in favour of the existing government. A good example was the Tongzhi Restoration and Reforms (1862–74) as a counter-measure to the Taiping Rebellion, the most powerful rebellion since 1368. Both sides offered tax cuts, land redistribution and better administration. In the end, the Qing state won. Together with the role of a deterrent to corruption, the role of catalyst indicates again that the seemingly low success rate of rebellions does not reflect the true weight of the rebellions in the whole process of equilibrium restoration. It also indicates that the maintenance of the trinary structure and equilibrium did not entirely rely on the overthrow and replacement of the existing dynasties.

Third, the rebellions worked as the terminator of the corrupt state apparatus. But the peasantry did not destroy the corrupt state apparatus just for the sake of relief of political pressure. It was the way to change government economic policies. The purposely established, rebellion-backed authorities would have to reform the tax and/or land ownership systems to achieve the goal of the rebels.

Fourth, rebellions worked as a redistributor of wealth. Regardless of whether the rebels succeeded in toppling the corrupt régime, redistribution of wealth normally took place in the rebel-controlled areas.

Last but not least, the rebellions worked as the first step towards restoration of the trinary equilibrium. It is not the case that the rebels were only a destructive force as they were also responsible for the establishment of new dynasties. The role of rebellion was essentially to steer the society back to its old course, as Mencius maintains in his *Master Meng's Book* (Mengzi Warning States Period.) Wars are meant to rescue people from crises and should be ended with the establishment of a small landholding- and landowning-based economy (*ibid.*: ch. 'Lianghuiwang I'). Thus, the differences between the Chinese rebellions and their counterparts in the rest of the premodern world were not just quantitative but qualitative as well.

The formula is illustrated in Figure 4.12. Portraying the two extremes, this diagram does not include the 'tug-of-war' situation between the government and the rebel forces. Here, the rebellions are seen both as the 'beginning of the end' in terms of the crises, and the 'end of the beginning' in terms of a new régime. Consequently, the Chinese state did not remain unchecked for long. If the state had been the sole instrument with which maintain the equilibrium, without the rebellion as the ultimate terminator for state corruption, Chinese civilisation as we know it might have met its demise long ago.

Following rebellions, restoration of the trinary equilibrium began. This included: (1) a return to the ideology of agricultural fundamentalism; (2) the redistribution of land among peasants and the re-ensuring of land and property rights in society; (3) the reintroduction of restraint of trade, exempting taxation and reducing corvée in rural areas, and so forth. To take taxation as an example, the tax rate of the Qin, about 50 per cent of the household output, was sharply reduced to 3.3 per cent in the early Han period in the wake of the major rebellion, the extent of the decrease being 93 per cent (Zhang S. and Zheng X. 1983: 20). No doubt rebels' demands were largely met under the new régime. In comparison, although rural protests in eighteenth-to-twentieth-century Ireland appear from the records to have broken out

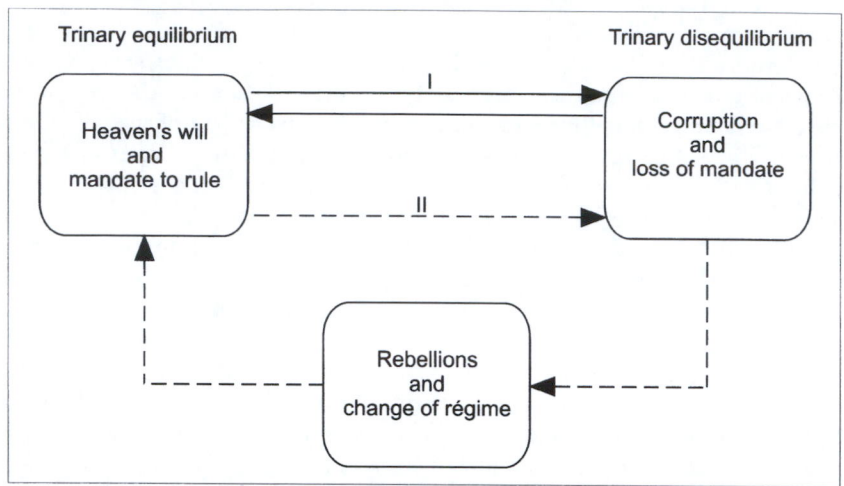

*Figure 4.12.* A full circle of the equilibrium

*Note*
Two loops: 1) the return though self-regulation of the state; 2) the return with peasant inter-ference after the failure of the self-regulating mechanisms.

often, no clear pattern is seen (Clark and Donnelly 1983: 25–6, 173). The same can be said about the Japanese rebellions: in the heyday of peasant upris-ings in premodern Japan (1590–1884), 3,001 events were reported, yet they lack a pattern (Bowen 1980; Bix 1986). In other words, those rebellions were not an organic part of the socio-economic mechanism to regulate social struc-ture and social life. They were external shocks to the system.

It is worth knowing that the components to restore the trinary equilibrium were present most of the time in society: (1) peasant rebellions, and (2) Confu-cianism and the record or memory of the trinary Golden Ages. Peasant rebel-lions served to bust the superstructure, the precondition for restoring the trinary system. Confucianism worked as a moral and theoretical back-up to the post-rebellion reconstruction (including re-establishment of the socio-eco-nomic structure and resumption of the policy repertoire). The dynastic cycle was the actual process. Therefore, the hostilities between the standing army loyal to the ruling elite and the rebels' forces formed not only the major action during the trinary crises, but also the major solution to the malfunction of the system. It is worth noting that to this day peasant rebellion still represents the sword of Damocles to the state of the People's Republic (Kelliher 1992: 167–8).

### 4.6.4 *Consequences*

The consequences of rebellions as *force majeure* were mainly twofold. First, the rebellions periodically reaffirmed the social status of the peasantry as the dominant stratum in society. Second, the periodic rebellions whereby China was brought back to the trinary equilibrium was the periodic resetting of the 'clock' for the economy in what can be called an 'agrarian deadlock'. However, the Chinese economy was by no means statically fossilised. It was actively confined within the trinary limits.

After rebellions, farming was always the first economic activity to recover wherever labour and arable land were available, and the landholding and land-owning peasantry was always rebuilt ahead of the other social groups/classes. Thus, the peasantry were always in an advantageous position to fight for their own interests. Not only that, immediately after civil wars the non-peasant classes often took up agriculture in order to survive. By analogy, insurrections worked as do periodical bushfires for eucalyptus in Australia. The fire kills off the rival species and helps only the eucalyptus to seed. In addition, like the eucalyptus trees, which always come alive in a more suitable natural environment from the ashes, the Chinese peasantry always recovered in a more favourable socio-economic condition from the civil wars. Therefore, no matter how disastrous rebellions may have been to the other strata, they were indeed a blessing to the Chinese peasantry.

Evidently, the rebellions brought about little structural change, which reveals the very nature of the Chinese armed peasant rebellions (see Figure 4.12). A way to oppose the corrupt monarchs and officials, the peasant rebellions never acted against the trinary pattern itself. During the crises and rebellions, the ruling class, the peasantry and the trinary relationships did not perish together; the relationship between them was readjusted. Therefore, the function of rebellions was to fulfil the task of ending the trinary crises (see Li Z. 1993; Sun Y. 1994).

Equally important were the side-effects of the rebellions. From the viewpoint of economics, the periodic loss of a proportion of the population had at least two consequences. First, at the macro level, per capita resources (especially land) increased as a trade-off with the inevitable drop in total output that was caused by war destruction. Second, at the micro level, the loss of labour enabled the grass-roots units of the economy to undo the deterioration in the marginal product of labour as well as the diminished returns from the total output. Third, with the combination of the macro and micro mechanisms, the post-war economy was almost guaranteed to experience a boom because of the improved resource conditions and improved labour productivity. This was undoubtedly a part of the Chinese peasant economic ecology. With favourable institutions, policies and technology, such a boom could even grow to a period of great socio-economic prosperity, of the kind recognised by the ancient Chinese as a Golden Age. After the civil war, all these things could be done within the trinary framework.

It is thus easy to understand that although the Chinese experienced some promising changes, both technical and structural, prominent events being 'economic revolution in the Han Dynasty' (206 BC – AD 220) (Bray 1984) and 'economic growth in the Song Dynasty' (AD 907–1271) (Elvin 1973), and although China's man-to-land ratio was from time to time improved greatly owing to the heavy losses of population during the numerous rebellions, invasions and conquests, neither a pattern of industrial production of the European style nor a phase of quasi-industrial capitalism took place in China (Hartwell 1963, 1967; Elvin 1973; Skinner 1977; Ronan 1978: 54; Bray 1984).

Not surprisingly, any fundamental changes in China became possible only when the country encountered another culture which was superior to China in technology and economy. It is not merely accidental that the traditional Chinese trinary equilibrium began to collapse only in the mid-nineteenth century after the Opium War. The Westerners were not just another foreign tribe: they came from the ocean rather than the traditional northern steppes and represented industrial capitalism and the world market instead of nomadism at a subsistence level. Encountering this superiority, the Chinese were no longer able to integrate the invaders but were forced to be integrated. Thus, the Opium War of 1840, in which a small number of British troops defeated the gigantic Manchu forces, heralded the end of the era of China's premodern power in technological, economic and military aspects.

Here an explanation of why China failed to develop industrial capitalism emerges: in premodern China, an equilibrium between the dominant pattern of production and interlocking institutions was maintained. Any major change in this pattern, namely the trinary equilibrium, was recognised by the rulers and/or the peasantry as a threat to the social order. This equilibrium was structural and institutional rather than technical and ideological. This structural equilibrium effectively precluded the separation of peasants from their land, which was a prerequisite for an industrial revolution in providing a labour supply which industry needed. It also substantially precluded a growth of the market economy to its full potential with the rise of the indigenous merchant class.

## 4.7 Further evaluation

### 4.7.1 Dynamics of the model

Previously, in Chapter 3, the impact of the trinary equilibrium was examined. At that stage, for the convenience of the analysis it is assumed that the equilibrium was self-regulated and self-adjusted and that China was a place of tranquillity. Now corruption and disequilibrium are introduced into the model and it is obvious that such an equilibrium was full of crises and chaos. Because of this, the trinary equilibrium should be redefined as the cataclysm–equilibrium cycle.

### 4.7.2 *New insights*

The Chinese rebellion had few parallels in world history, a phenomenon which has been widely recognised by both political and economic historians (see, for example, Fairbank 1957, 1965; Elvin 1973: 245–6). But very few have viewed the rebellions as a part of China's socio-economic system. At best, revolts are viewed as a consequence of or an exogenous shock to the system. For example, historiography in mainland China follows the Marxian class struggle hypothesis and views popular revolts as simply a counteraction to state coercion in the fashion of physics: force and reacting force. What is often ignored is that the Chinese merchant class, which was also subject to state coercion, was able to put up with the pressure. The 'force versus reacting force' paradigm explains little if anything. A chief contribution of this study is the establishment of the missing link between the rebellions and the socio-economic institutions of premodern China.

In J. A. Goldstone's book *Revolution and Rebellion in the Early Modern World*, probably the best work so far in terms of studying armed rebellions both from a comparative perspective and as a part of Eurasian economic history, armed rebellions are taken as a result of a long chain of malfunctions of a socio-economic system. However, population growth is taken as the ultimate drive for rebellions. Moreover, Goldstone sees no structural differences in his case-study societies across Eurasia: peoples rebelled for the same reasons and rebellions were even synchronised in time (Goldstone 1991: ch. 1). Furthermore, Goldstone fails to recognise the fact that Chinese armed rebellions in the Ming–Qing Period were part of a much longer tradition which can be traced back to 208 BC, in an incident known as the 'Chensheng Wuguang Uprising', which terminated the glorious Qin. Evidence shows that the Chinese popular revolts were almost completely independent of outside influence till 1840 (see Appendix J). Another contribution of this study is to show that the Chinese rebellions were unique because of their unique institutional entourage.

Second, the traditional view is that rebellions broke the Confucian norms of moderation, harmony and order. There are two schools of thought. Marxists–Leninists see insurrections as progressive forces while the non-communist view sees the rebels unfavourably as being creators of instability (Parsons 1970: 252–5). Both schools, however, view rebellions as interrupters. The new insight offered by this study is that rebellions restored the Confucian norm, instead of breaking it. Or, more correctly, the rebellion was a part of the Confucian norm considering the idea of 'people as the foundation', physiocracy and the right to rebel, and so forth. The guilty party that did break the Confucian norm was the corrupt state.

Third, in the Fairbankian view of China's dynastic cycle, it is not clear who played the central role in the process of the cycle as if the ruling clique and the peasantry worked in some kind of coincidental cooperation (Fairbank 1965: ch. 4; Fairbank and Reischaver 1979: 70–5). The present research shows that it was the peasantry who played the central role in the dynastic cycle. In the Fairbankian model, the Chinese Empire went from government control to chaotic rebellions and to government control again (Fairbank 1965: ch. 4; Parsons 1970: 256). Now this process can be viewed as China moving from an equilibrium to a disequilibrium and back to the equilibrium, reflecting the dynamic nature of the process. In this context, it is superficial to say that the Chinese were backward-looking. They were in effect trinary equilibrium-looking and equilibrium-aiming.

Barrington Moore is right about the difference between the Indian and Chinese peasantries (Moore 1966: 339). Unlike the Indian peasants, who did not really need a government under the village–caste system, the Chinese peasants needed a 'good' central government as one of the basic conditions for their livelihood. Thus, 'to get a good government' was what the phenomenon of periodic peasant rebellions in China was all about. The present study provides the new insight that popular peasantry-based rebellions formed a part of the macro-economic system in premodern China: rebellion had a violent and politicised façade but was in essence an economic act from the general public of the empire.

### 4.7.3 *The role of the key factors involved in the equilibrium cycle*

Here the key factors were the rebellion, the peasantry, Chinese philosophies and the Confucian elite. They formed more or less a joint force in what can be called the trinary equilibrium cycle.

#### 4.7.3.1 *Role of rebellions in the equilibrium cycle*

In the long term, the frequency of rebellions suggests that trinary crises occurred regularly. In turn, regular trinary crises suggest regular restoration of the trinary equilibrium without which the civilisation would have gone long ago. The peasant rebellions formed a transition link between the two poles: equilibrium and disequilibrium. In Europe, political decentralisation offset the malfunctioning of the state (Jones 1981: 237), while in China society had to depend to a great extent on rebellions to do the job if the governing institutions (monarch and bureaucracy) failed to stop a malfunction of the system. The rebellion was thus the endogenous factor of the self-regulating machines of the empire, and the peasant rebellions in China formed the axis of dynastic vicissitudes. This pattern was uniquely Chinese.

The incidents in China easily make China the champion country for rebellions. However, those rebellions seldom brought about any significant changes towards further socio-economic development. The mass armed rebellion in China was only the safeguard of the perpetuation of the trinary equilibrium. There is a common misunderstanding that the Chinese Empire crumbled from time to time (see Fairbank and Reischaver 1979: 70–1). If we allow short-term readjustments, only the dynasties crumbled, not the empire *per se*. While changing dynasties periodically with the rebellions, the empire preserved its entity over time.

Whereas the Chinese rebellions contributed greatly to the Chinese conservativeness, in Europe and Japan what the rebels demanded was often something new, such as political and economic equality and property rights for the lower strata, which were largely absent prior to the rebellions and which were meant to end the existing feudal system. A good example was the demand for equality in the 1381 peasant revolts in England (Dobson 1983: 164–5, 365–6, 371), which was indeed revolutionary although sounding 'romantic' (*ibid.*: 363). In contrast, the same concept of equality implied a timeless model of the Chinese 'Golden Ages' under the trinary equilibrium, neither revolutionary nor romantic.

### 4.7.3.2 Role of the peasantry in the equilibrium cycle

It has been recognised by scholars in the field of Chinese studies that chaos in China eventually led to equilibrium. But what they have not been clear about is that (1) the rebellions were the necessary process by which to bring about the trinary equilibrium, and (2) the peasantry was responsible for safeguarding and restoring the equilibrium. In that sense, the peasantry was the rescuer and saviour of the Chinese Empire, which experienced severe periodic crises. From an institutionalist viewpoint, these armed rebellions played a central role in protecting the Chinese socio-economic structure in which the peasantry were beneficiaries.

From the role of the peasant rebellions, it is easy to judge the quality of the Chinese peasants. They were fundamentally reactionary and conservative, not revolutionary by any standard (*cf.* Moore 1966: ch. 9). As described in Chesneaux's phrase (1973: 9–10), '[In premodern China] peasant revolts, far from threatening the principle of established order, are finally accepted as functional, as capable of restoring order in troubled times'. Here, Chesneaux's 'troubled times' were no doubt those period of trinary crises (see also Fairbank 1965: ch. 7). Marsh's conclusion was even more straightforward (1961: 43):

> The Chinese have been called the most rebellious but the least revolutionary of peoples: even the overthrow of a dynasty did not legitimate a basic, revolutionary change.... It signaled a return to a traditional, ideal *status quo ante*, which had been outraged in the downward swing of the dynasty cycle.

It is therefore sensible to argue that the universal conservativeness is to be attributed to the elite and peasants alike, a new insight which is radically different from the conventional theories, which mainly blame the upper classes (see, for example, Fairbank 1965; Qian 1985). After all, the peasantry reset the clock for the economy in accordance with the trinary equilibrium. So, categorically, the peasant rebels were not social outcast bandits and desperadoes. They had a historical mission to perform.

### 4.7.3.3 Role of Chinese philosophies in the equilibrium cycle

The Chinese Golden Ages and Confucianism played an important role during the second stage in ending the trinary crises, which was also the first step towards recovery: it provided a blueprint with a set of criteria with which to restore the trinary equilibrium, including information about how to establish a good government and what economic policies the society needed. The reason why Confucianism played such a role was not because it was a Hegelian 'absolute spirit' but because it legitimised the trinary equilibrium that Chinese society was long in favour of. The Confucian value of 'collective existence and the search for harmonious social and political frameworks' (Mitchell 1977: 46) makes sense only if the peasantry was content.

It is interesting to know that Taoism often played a significant role in government policy-making during and immediately after the rebellions. The Taoist belief in the 'natural way' or *laissez-faire* (*wuwei erzhi*, literally 'doing little leads to a good order') in administration meant less or no tax, less or no interference in peasant life. It allowed the pendulum to swing back towards the trinary equilibrium. The great believers in this principle were Emperor Gaozu (r. 206–195 BC) and Emperor Wendi (r. 179–157 BC) of the Han Dynasty, both known as wise rulers who delivered desirable policy results (Xiao L. 1987: 147–84). Such a shift to Taoism is often regarded as the result of concessions made by the Confucian ruling class to console and reassure the peasantry (Fan W. 1964–5; Bai 1982). However, during the Taoist policy period in post-Qin times, the Chinese social structure did not fall into anarchy; nor did it generate any structural changes. Rather, the practice of Taoism achieved the same goal in economic recovery as Confucianism. This shows just how compatible Confucianism and Taoism were in Chinese politics. What made Taoism different from Confucianism was tactics: the former used the visible hand to manipulate social forces while the latter used an 'invisible hand'.

### 4.7.3.4 Role of the elite in the equilibrium cycle

The Confucian elite played a key role during the recovery of the trinary equilibrium. After the insurrections the Chinese peasantry customarily handed over power to the elite, who then took on the responsibility of forming a new government to implement what the previous governing institutions had failed to do. The peasantry then quietly withdrew from the political arena.

Marxist scholars often blame the Chinese upper classes for 'hijacking' the peasant cause and 'stealing' the fruit of the lower classes after the bloody insurrections. This assertion has raised interesting questions: (1) Why did the Chinese peasants almost always end up losing their trophies as if they were guaranteed to be fooled by the upper classes? and (2) If the peasants were caught in such a 'no-win' situation, what was the point of their rising up later on? From the Marxist point of view, the submission of the victory by the Chinese peasantry was utterly irrational.

If we understand the result of the rebellions, such an illusion is uprooted. First, as the main task force, the peasant undertaking was to challenge and destroy the unqualified régimes. Once this had been done, the reconstruction work was passed on to the specialised elite who had the knowledge and expertise to set up the administrative framework. The elite members were also best qualified to staff the bureaucracy. These two critical areas, designing and running the state apparatus, were those which the ordinary peasants were least qualified to perform. So, the reason why the Chinese elite came under the spotlight on the political stage after the rebellions was because of the division of labour or specialisation in the Chinese society, not because of the upper classes' dirty tricks.

Although the peasant hand-over of power was the norm, the elite needed the mandate from the population, especially from the rebels, who were often the comrades-in-arms of many members of the elite class during the civil wars. The divergence of interests between the peasantry and the elite was negligible as long as what the new governing institutions did satisfied the rebels and general public. So, it was a case of cooperation, not hijacking or stealing.

With this division of labour, the worst thing that could happen was betrayal by the elite. But the rule was that if the peasantry were not happy with the new government, they came back and smashed the state apparatus again; this made the existence of the dynastic cycle possible. So, overall, the peasantry were always the winner, though only in terms of their short-run interest.

## 4.8 A comparison with post-1789 France

Chapters 3 and 4 reveal from different angles the landholding pattern, and political and economic influence of the Chinese peasantry over time. The question here is just how unique the Chinese system was in world history. Evidently, post-Qin China had a lot in common with post-1789 France.

It has been argued that the Declaration of the Rights of Man in 1789 marked the triumph of agrarian individualism with private property rights underwritten along with the principle of individual liberty (Moulin 1991: 29). An agrarian reform then followed (*ibid.*: 27–32). As a result, although it did not create small landholding *per se*, which had begun before, the

1789 Revolution certainly resulted in a large number of small owner–cultivators after a sweeping scheme of sale of national lands, a process called 'parcelisation of land' (Wright 1964: 5–6; Hohenberg 1972: 235; see also Dallas 1982: 120–3; Moulin 1991: 30–1, 36–7, 41). As Barrington Moore points out, the Revolution destroyed the landed aristocracy and at the same time created small-peasant property (1966: 107). This reform continued under Napoleon, as revealed by the phrase 'land chopping machine' (Wright 1964: 6). It has been estimated that by 1802, after the first wave of change, half of all the land had fallen into the hands of small cultivators (Moulin 1991: 36). Meanwhile, during the revolutionary decade attempts were made to privatise communal rights over village common land and all the land after harvest (Wright 1964: 5; Moulin 1991: 30). The changes were both dramatic and decisive. In Annie Moulin's phrase, 'The Revolution paved the way for a period of some 150 years in which the small family farm, based on subsistence production and the intensive use of family labour, dominated the economic and social régime of the countryside' (1991: 47) in spite of some hiccups like the local peasant resistance to the Revolution in the Vendée (1793–6) and the short-lived restoration of the aristocratic landholding (1815–30) under the Bourbon reign (Moore 1966: 92–4, 106).

Most significantly, these changes – the destruction of the feudal structure, the abolition of seigneurial rights and the establishment of private land ownership – were all institutionalised by the Civil Code of 1804 (Moulin 1991: 36, 40, 47). That the Napoleonic Code abolished primogeniture and established equal inheritance rights to force 'every peasant to split his holding among all his sons' certainly helped to strengthen the smallholders class in spite of the question of just how effective the law was at that time (Wright 1964: 6; Moulin 1991: 40). Hand in hand with these changes, physiocratic ideas prevailed in society and bore fruit in the Rural Code of 1801 (Moulin 1991: 29, 40). All these made a profound impact on French economic concepts. As Gregor Dallas points out, unlike in England, the concept of 'property' in France included not only the physical territory but also the complete cadastral record, which had two functions: (1) legal recognition of land ownership, and (2) liability for tax payment, a stark exchange between political protection from the state and financial payment from the peasantry (Dallas 1982: 198). He even goes so far as to say that in France the concept of 'home' implied land ownership whereas in England it meant merely a dwelling-place (*ibid.*).

Steadily, during the century after the Revolution, the number of farms reached a peak of 3.5 million *vis-à-vis* some 16 million peasants with an average of 4.8 persons per farm. Given that in the period between 1836 and 1886 an average household in the Orléanais and Nantais had 3.9 and 4.3 persons respectively (Dallas 1982: 146), it is almost certain that a high proportion of family farms existed in the economy (Wright 1964: 6, 9 and photos 1–3). This landholding pattern was very stable over time, as shown in two cadastres for the Loire Country, one for 1821–44 and the other for 1913 (Dallas 1982: 76–7, 210–11; see also 203, 208, 212–15, 218):

| Subregion | Property size (0.01–25 ha) | | Property size (25.01–100 ha) | |
|---|---|---|---|---|
| | Percentage in total | Index | Percentage in total | Index |
| *Orléanais* | | | | |
| 1822–37 | 96.5 | 100 | 2.2 | 100 |
| 1913 | 97.2 | 101 | 1.9 | 86 |
| *Nantais* | | | | |
| 1821–44 | 97.7 | 100 | 2.1 | 100 |
| 1913 | 98.6 | 101 | 1.2 | 57 |

This stability was also reflected by the proportion of the full-time farming population in the total working population in the region. In 1851, the proportion was 78–81 per cent. In 1901, it remained at the level of 70 per cent (Dallas 1982: 23, 115).

In terms of the weight of the agricultural sector in the French economy, similar stability existed across the country. Here, although the data are incomplete, a pattern can still be detected (based on Wright 1964: 13; Burns 1984: 12; Moulin 1991: 57, 114, 141; cf. Heywood 1981: 361, 362):

| Year | Small farms as a proportion of all farms | Landowners as a proportion among farmers | Farmers as a proportion of total workers | Rural population as a proportion of the total |
|---|---|---|---|---|
| 1826–58 | 84–86% | — | — | — |
| 1882 | — | 75% | — | — |
| 1891 | — | — | 45% | 63% |
| 1900 | — | — | 45% | — |
| 1931 | — | — | 49% | — |

With such stability, it is not surprising that during the early 1960s France still had large numbers of these small landholders: as many as 50 per cent of the farms had less than 10.1 hectares and another 30 per cent had less than 20.2 hectares (Wright 1964: 178, 231, 248). It was not until 1985 that the medium landholding (20–50 ha) became equal to the upper small landholding (5–20 ha) in the share of the total farming land. Even so, the aggregate share of the small and medium landholders was still some 10 per cent ahead of that of the large landholders in France's total (Moulin 1991: 203). This arguably laid the foundation for a situation in which 'two agricultures' coexisted – one modern and the other left behind (Wright 1964: 147–8).

To change the landholding peasantry proved to be a tall order and the land-holding concentration process was exceedingly slow. The reason was three-fold. First, the French peasants had the incentive to maintain the ownership type that benefited them. Second, 'peasantist doctrine' or agricultural funda-mentalism 'remained too strongly entrenched in French emotions' since a large mass of smallholders was still 'held up as a *sine qua non* of national stab-ility and strength' (Wright 1964: 1, 148). This included, of course, the milit-ary power, which depended to a great extent upon the service of young peasants (Moulin 1991: 46, 103, 117–18, 133). Third, French law leaned towards inefficient small farms (Wright 1964: 164–7, 169). In this context, the overwhelming political influence of the landholding peasantry reached its pinnacle after the 1848 Revolution: universal suffrage made the peasantry the 'arbiter of the nation's political life' (Moulin 1991: 84). Such influence remained strong as recently as the 1940s (*ibid.*: 151–4). In addition, the peasantry at times showed their muscle, as reflected in the rural revolts in 1789–91, 1791–3 (*ibid.*: 23, 26–7, 33–4) and 1961 (Wright 1964: 164–7, 169) to protect their vested interests.

During the nineteenth century, one consequence of the making of this landholding peasantry was an agricultural revolution in the first half of the nineteenth century (Newell 1973) which was similar to the Meiji *noho* pheno-menon in Japan after the land-tax reform (Francks 1992: 120–8). However, the positive impact of the French agricultural revolution on the country's eco-nomic performance was cancelled out to a degree by another consequence of the making of this landholding peasantry: a noticeable attitude of indifference towards industrial progress and urbanisation (as well as towards a proletarian social revolution in France as Karl Marx hoped for) (Wright 1964: 9–10). There was the resistance within the agricultural sector to transforming the French agricultural sector to the type found in Britain and the American Mid-dle West, a type which required landholding concentration, critical to achieve economies of scale and modernisation (*ibid.*: 178). Overall, as commonly accepted, the French peasantry or the French smallholders' agriculture played a major role in slowing down the pace of modernisation of the economy (Hohenberg 1972: 236–7; Cameron and Freedeman 1983: 17–19; see also Crafts 1984).

Here it is obvious that France had a structural equilibrium (or a near-equilibrium) among the type of land ownership, state philosophy and govern-ment policy. Such an equilibrium was characterised, paradoxically, by micro-level flexibility with macro-level stability and a degree of intra-sectoral dualism (Hohenberg 1972: 238–9; Heywood 1981). So, China was not alone.

## Notes

1 According to Fairbank's conversion, the salary for the first rank was the equivalent of US$300 per annum at the present value (Fairbank 1983: 115).

2 History indeed repeats itself: in contemporary mainland China, the age-old power-pulled and low income-pushed corruption functions well, and communist officials, the so-called 'professional revolutionaries' and 'people's liberators', of all levels, are notorious for their lust for extra-legal incomes and non-monetary comforts and possessions of all kinds. Chairman Mao himself, the 'beloved great leader', was no exception: his corrupt life began soon after the communist takeover of mainland China (Li 1994).

3 Not surprisingly, Mao blamed the alleged bad weather for the starvation of tens of millions of Chinese peasants between 1959 and 1961, a period which in the Communist Party's line has been called the 'three-year natural disasters' (*sannian ziran zaihai*). All the scientifically serious data show, however, that the weather was not at all unfavourable in most of the country during that period.

4 In 1966, when Mao launched his manipulative Cultural Revolution under the banner of 'rebellion is justified' (*zaofan youli*), the rebellion became a farce simply because under his Communist leadership the socio-economic basis for mass rebellions to function in China was gone. He was hoist by his own petard when his most loyal disciples, including his own wife, ended up in prison.

5 Strictly speaking, the alleged attempted military *coup d'état* in 1971 led by the most senior communist officer, Marshal Lin Biao (1907–71), involving the commanding officers of the Chinese army, navy and air force, was a tyrannicidal attempt *ex ante* to eliminate Mao Zedong. Five years later, in 1976, a month after the death of the tyrant, a military *coup d'état* led by Marshal Ye Jianying (1897–1986) finally succeeded in eliminating Mao's diehard allies called the 'Gang of Four', which was a tyrannicide *ex post*. Both coup attempt were just by the Confucian standard.

6 This is applicable to the peaceful civilian protests against the rampant corruption of the Chinese Communist state in 1989. Although the unarmed protesters were ruthlessly suppressed, the Communist leadership speeded up their economic reform in the hope that material benefits would eventually outweigh the damage caused by the corruption and suppression. So, the 'warning shot' from the 'powerless' public was well heeded.

# 5

# EXTERNAL PRESSURE AND SHOCK

## The reinforcement of the pattern

### 5.1 Agrarian China: the constant attraction to invaders

Throughout history, nomadic peoples in the north and west along the Chinese borders constituted a constant threat of invasion, plunder and conquest to Chinese settled agriculture (Hegel 1975: 192–3; McGovern 1939; Lattimore 1962; Fairbank 1965: 68–82). This is demonstrated in Table 5.1, which includes in all 1,109 main military conflicts between the Chinese and the nomads from 215 BC to AD 1684.

The reason China became so attractive to invaders was twofold. First, as a society of settled agriculture, China was evidently wealthier than its nomadic neighbours and the economic returns from plundering China were higher than those from hunting and animal husbandry. Second, as a society based on free landholding peasants who were individualistic by nature, China was vulnerable before the militant nomadic tribes. This was a problem of military supremacy of the northern nomads vis-à-vis the economic affluence of the Chinese.

*Table 5.1* Main military conflicts between the Chinese and the nomads

| Period | Number of conflicts | Period | Number of conflicts |
|---|---|---|---|
| 215–116 BC | 23 | 785–884 | 11 |
| 115–16 BC | 36 | 885–984 | 22 |
| 15 BC–AD 84 | 22 | 985–1084 | 39 |
| 85–184 | 96 | 1085–1184 | 66 |
| 185–284 | 26 | 1185–1284 | 109 |
| 285–384 | 56 | 1285–1384 | 107 |
| 385–484 | 74 | 1385–1484 | 60 |
| 485–584 | 21 | 1485–1584 | 89 |
| 585–684 | 54 | 1585–1684 | 145 |
| 685–784 | 53 | Total | 1,109 |

*Source*: Based on Fu Z. *et al.* 1985, 1986.

It should be noted that between the Chinese and the nomads there was a long history of arranged intermarriages among the upper classes and voluntary trade (of silk, tea and horses, for example), activities which were predominantly peaceful. It is not the task of the present study to examine such relationships since they were normally not a threat to China.

## 5.2 External pressure and its internalisation

### 5.2.1 The 'Walled Empire'

Nothing could be as evident as the construction and maintenance of the Great Wall, commonly regarded as the longest wall on this planet, in demonstrating the Chinese preventive response to the pressure of alien invasion and conquest. The last overhaul/reconstruction of the Great Walls took place in the Ming Period (1368–1644). Stretching over 14,000 *li* (7,300 km;, see Yu 1986: 81–2; Guo R. *et al.* 1988: 225–33), the Ming walls had two lines. The outer wall was called the 'Border Wall' (*bianqiang*), and the inner, the 'Second Wall' (*cibian*). They lay between 94°E and 120°E, from Dunhuang, where the 'Western Corridor' (*hexi zoulang*) – a narrow oasis (100 km × 1,000 km) between the Steppes and the Qilian Range – ended, to Shanhaiguan, where the Bohai Sea begins. The reason was simply that the North Plain of China (*huabei pingyuan*) was not a natural fortress for defence but an open road for invaders.

It is appropriate to use the term 'Great Walls' in the plural form since there were at least four main lines of walls along China's northern and northwestern borders prior to the seventeenth century. More importantly, the plural form shows the dynamics of the wall construction, reconstruction and maintenance over time. The walls were specifically for defence against the northern nomads; although non-Chinese groups, such as the Miaos and Viets (*baiyue*) also operated in the south, no long wall was built along China's southern border. Instead of building walls against each other, all the warring Chinese kingdoms (Yan, Zhao, Qi, Wei, Qin, Zheng, Han, Chu and Wu) formed a collective defence system with their walls facing the Tungus, Huns, Yuezhis and Qiangs (see Figure 5.1). Here it is only too evident that the common enemy came from the Steppes during the internally turbulent era of the Warring States Period.

Having the walls represented a long-term commitment by the Chinese on two accounts. First, the materialisation of the Great Walls, as they were known during the Warring States Period (Yu 1986: 97), began no later than *c*.400 BC. Second, throughout the post-Warring States Period till the end of the Ming, the Great Walls were rebuilt at least three times – during the Qin, Han and Ming periods, respectively (*ibid.*: 97–8). In between, the walls were maintained. As a result, the walls, the longest permanent defence line in world history in both time and space (McGovern 1939: 113–14; Lattimore 1962: 97–118), made China the only 'walled empire' in world history.

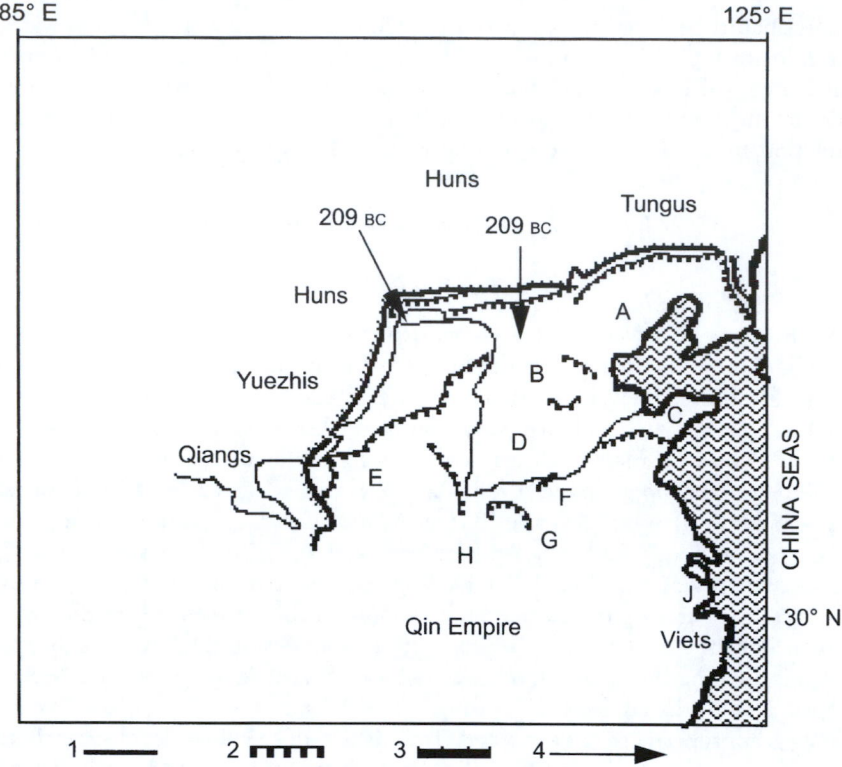

*Figure 5.1* The Great Walls during the Warring States and the Qin, 475–207 BC

*Source*: Based on information from Yu 1986: 97; ZDC 1990; Zhao X. *et al*. 1991: 69–84, 111–13; and Hou W. 1992: 784, 1332–3.

Notes

1, The Yellow River (with its modern course); 2, the Great Walls, *c.*400 BC 3, the unified Great Wall under the Qin, *c.*207 BC; kingdoms as at *c.* 400 BC; A, Yan; B, Zhao; C, Qi; D, Wei; E, Qin; F, Zheng; G, Han; H, Chu; J, Wu; 4, main nomadic invasions with dates.

But the walls were costly in terms of construction, maintenance and guarding. During the Ming Period, the Chinese government ran eighteen main construction projects to rebuild the walls. These projects lasted two hundred years commencing from the beginning of the dynasty in 1368, or 72 per cent of the life span of the Ming (Zhao X. *et al*. 1991: 247). Thus, the walls were built and maintained out of China's desperation rather than the strength of an army of peasants. In other words, the walls were the ultimate substitution for the poor quality of Chinese soldiers and thus were imperative for the survival of Chinese civilisation, rather than a luxury. To show the importance of the walls, the founder of the Ming Dynasty, Zhu Yuanzhang, sent two of his own sons, the Duke of Yan and the Duke of Jin, to the northern border to take charge of the Great Wall defence. The two made their life-long careers there (Zhao X. *et al.* 1987: 408).

Four main phases can be identified in the establishment of China's northern and western defence line in which the walls played a central part. During the first phase, from 400 to 207 BC the defence line was firmly established. The groundwork was completed by individual kingdoms during the Warring States Period. What the Qin Empire achieved was (1) linking the three existing north-facing walls together, and (2) enclosing the rest of the Great Bend of the Yellow River (*hetao*) in the walled region (see Figure 5.2). Given that the newly walled area in the Great Bend has inferior soil types for farming (ZKY 1978: appendix 3), this expansion was chiefly of military importance. The main progress, made during the second phase in around 100 BC under the Western Han Dynasty (206 BC–AD 24), was stretching China's defence line outwards following the historic triumph of the Chinese army over the Huns in four main military campaigns during 121–119 BC along China's northern and northwestern frontiers (Sima Q. 91 BC: ch. 'History of the Huns'; Ban G. AD 82: ch. 'History of the Huns'; see also Hou W. 1992: 313). To secure the victory, two parallel walls along the new borderline were in construction in 102 BC (Hou W. 1992: 579). Known in Chinese history as the 'Outer Walls', the Han defence line was moved radically northward and westward, embracing parts of the Steppes and the so-called 'Western Region' (*xiyu*), traditionally homes of the nomads (*ibid.*: 312–14, 1265–7). From then on, on the western flank, the Chinese no longer depended on the Yellow River for their national defence. Rather, they left it with a series of mountain ranges of heights 3,000–5,000 m above sea level where the construction of a wall was beyond the Chinese capacity and where the nomad population was thin and less threatening. Consequently, the Western Region Governorate (*xiyu zhangshifu*) was formally established in AD 83 to rule this non-Chinese region, making sure the region was pro-China. This governorate system was maintained until the fifth centruy when nomad tribes moved in and claimed much of Northwest China. The system was promptly resumed under the Tang (AD 618–907) and the Northern Song (AD 960–1127). The Western Region became a part of the Monogol Empire and remained in Mongol hands during the Ming. It once again became directly controlled by the Empire during the Qing (1644–1911) (see Hou W. 1992: 320, 478, 971, 1089, 1282–3). The new Chinese defence line proved to be effective in the following Eastern Han Period (AD 25–220): after a final contest of military strength in AD 91 the defeated Huns withdrew from the Steppes and migrated westward out of the East Asian scene, which paved the way for the later rise of the Xianbei in the Steppes (*ibid.*: 328–9).

However, during the third phase in the Tang Period (AD 618–907), from AD 659 onwards, in spite of four consecutive peace treaties between the Tang Empire and the Kingdom of Tibet, the nomads staged a comeback on a large scale from the west, outflanking the Chinese border guards via the

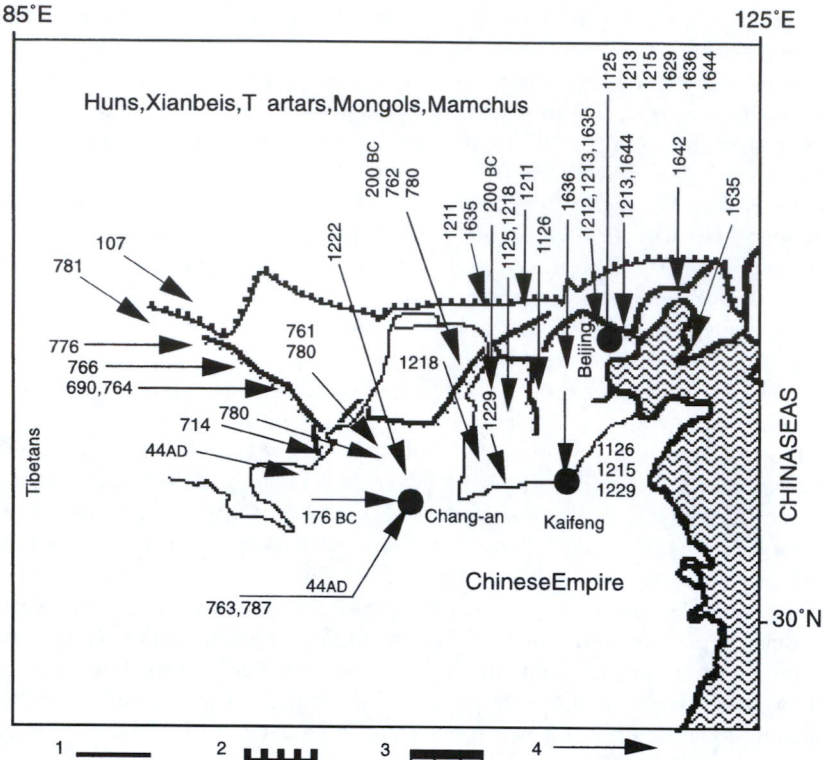

*Figure 5.2* The walls and invasions from the Han to the Ming, 206 BC–1644

*Source*: Based on information from Yu 1986: 98; ZDC 1990; Zhao D. *et al.* 1991: 111–18, 244–8; and Hou W. 1992: 312, 452–5, 580, 805–6, 1120–2, 1332–3.

*Notes*

1, The Yellow River (with its modern course); 2, the Han Great Wall line, *c.* 100 BC; 3, the Ming Great Walls, *c.* 1560; 4, main nomadic invasions from the north and west with dates. Three capital cities of various periods are shown: Chang-an (202 BC–AD 190, 304–420, 535–907), Kaifeng (960–1126, 1214–35) and Beijing (1414–1911). The main nomad groups in the north are listed according to chronological order from the Huns to the Manchus

Western Corridor and the mountain ranges, attacking Hexi (now Gansu), Longyou (now Qinghai) and Jiannan (now Sichuan). Thus, the seemingly impenetrable northern defence line of the Tang had the same problem as the modern French Maginot Line. It is groundless to claim that the Tang were too strong to need the walls (*cf.* Waldron 1990: ch. 1). Instead, the Tang were too confident in their northern defence. The Tang Empire paid a heavy price: the capital, Chang-an, alone was attacked twice, in 763 and 768 (see Figure 5.2). Unable to build a wall, the defending Chinese troops erected castles and walled barracks along the western borders. It took the half of the Chinese standing army to block the first wave of the invaders (Hou W. 1992: 1120–2). This incidence exposed the soft belly of the Chinese defence, a problem which haunted the empire for another one and a half centuries until the establishment of the Northern Song (AD 960–1127), including the capture of the capital, Chang-an, in 763 and occupation of China's western provinces in the upper reaches of the Yellow River in the second half of the eighth century (*ibid*.: 1121–3). By then, China's defence line on the western flank had been pushed back to its Qin origin although its northern front was intact. During the last phase in the Ming Period, China's northern front was pushed more or less back to its Qin origin although the Western Corridor was secured and the territorial loss in the north was compensated for by the repossession of China's territory on the western flank. This was arguably the outcome of the Mongol conquest of China during the thirteenth to fourteenth centuries, which affected the circumscription of the Chinese territory.

It seemed that after some two thousand years of struggling, there was a draw between the nomads and the Chinese, a phenomenon which is consistent with the perpetual presence of the nomadic threat.

The walls themselves were only a part of the Chinese anti-nomad defence line. They also required men to guard them. As in the Ming case, the Chinese had a five-layer system which consisted of (1) strategic points (*zhen*), (2) main branches (*lu*), (3) passes (*guan*), (4) castles (*cheng*), and (5) beacon towers (*tai*) (for the complexity of the Great Wall defence system, see Zhao X. *et al*. 1991: 111–36, 244–79). According to *History of the Ming Dynasty*, the distribution of the troops among the eleven strategic points along the walled defence line is as follows (based on Zhang T. 1735: ch. 'Military'):

| Location | Province | Troops |
|---|---|---|
| Beizhen | Liaoning | 99,875 |
| Qianxi | Hebei | 107,813 |
| Changping | Hebei | 19,039 |
| Baoding | Hebei | 34,697 |
| Xuanhua | Hebei | 151,452 |
| Datong | Shanxi | 135,778 |
| Taiyuan | Shanxi | 57,611 |
| Yulin | Shaanxi | 80,196 |
| Yinchuan | Ningxia | 71,693 |
| Guyuan | Ningxia | 126,919 |
| Zhangye | Gansu | 91,571 |
| Total | | 6976,644 |

On average, 134 soldiers were allocated to each kilometre of the Wall with a density of one soldier per 7.5 metres. In this respect, the Great Wall defence line was not only capital intensive but also labour intensive.

This was not all. There was the second Ming echelon with 400,000–500,000 combatants under 72 divisions (called *jingjun*, literally 'the Army for the Capital') stationed in the capital city, Beijing, less than 100 km away from a main point along the Walls, the Juyongguan Pass (Zhao X. *et al.* 1987: 411–14, 417). This meant that the Great Wall-related troops under the Ming numbered 1.4–1.5 million. Given that the total number of the Ming armed forces was between 1.8 and 2.8 million men (*ibid.*: 404), the standing army for the Great Walls thus occupied 50–83 per cent of China's total.

It is worth noting that the Ming was not an unusual period of heavy border defence. It has been estimated that under Emperors Oin Shihuang (r. 221–210 BC) and Wudi (r. 140–88 BC) the Chinese border troops (*bianbing*) numbered 800,000–900,000 (Huang and Chen 1997: 91). Given that (1) normally the northern border troops occupied 30 per cent of China's total armed forces (*ibid.*), (2) a quarter of the population was probably qualified to serve in the army, and (3) in AD 2, China had a peak of population growth at around 60 million (Liang F. 1980: 4), the participation rate in China's defence would be at least 15 per cent of the total population. In some periods, the Great Wall defence system alone involved 19 per cent of China's total population (Chao 1986: 50). Considering the size and the long borderline of the empire, the heavy concentration of military presence along the northern and northwestern frontiers shows the equally heavy pressure from the nomads.

### 5.2.2 Debate on the Great Walls and their significance

As one of the focal point of studies of premodern Chinese history, the Great Walls have caused both attention and debate. Among Western scholars, there have been some doubts about the walls and their significance in premodern Chinese history. Such doubts are reflected in a recent work by Arthur Waldron entitled *The Great Wall of China: From History to Myth* (1990). Methodologically, Waldron's work is a case study of the Ming supplemented by textual study of earlier times and modern observations. The key points raised by the author are, first, that it is doubtful whether the Chinese ever completed the walls in pre-Ming times (more precisely from 221 BC to 1368); second, that it is doubtful whether the Chinese could really afford the costs of building and maintaining the walls; third, that it is doubtful whether the Chinese depended on the walls to defend their territory even if their northern boundary could be clearly marked; and fourth, it is doubtful whether the walls were effective in discouraging and stopping the northern invaders. In essence, it is doubtful whether the walls ever functioned as more than a national or political symbol. It is crucial for the present study to clarify these doubts before a proper judgement can be made regarding the impact of the invaders and conquerors on the Chinese socio-economic structure.

First of all, the identification of most of the pre-Qin walls has been the result of modern archaeological excavations rather than the study of ancient Chinese records (Zhao X. *et al.* 1991: 69–84). Indeed, this lack of record concerning the Great Walls was consistent throughout the entire pre-Ming history. On the basis of those archaeological findings, one naturally asks which is more reliable, the tangible objects or the written record. This is not a new problem. To a great extent, the establishment of archaeology as a field of study is based on this problem. The high Chinese propensity for keeping records in the past does not remove the problem. It can be justifiably argued that physical relics are more trustworthy than written records. Judging from the Chinese literature alone is risky. It is thus beyond question that the Chinese began the Great Walls' construction long before the Qin Empire was established in 221 BC.

Second, in the beginning, these early walls were obviously smaller and shorter and thus more affordable in terms of labour, material and capital inputs. After all, in the entire pre-Qin period there was no record of a popular rebellion resulting from the unbearable burden incurred by the walls' construction. Here again, the timing of the first round of the construction of the walls was important: Chinese civilisation had just entered the Iron Age; a new horizon for growth was to take place, which marked a rapid increase in China's agricultural output and newly established private land ownership. With the new technology and new institutions, a surplus was produced in greater quantities and spread more widely across the economy. This almost certainly made China a more attractive target for the northern nomads to plunder. On the other hand, with iron tools readily available and with more surplus from farming, there was no technological or financial barrier preventing the Chinese from building those walls. In the eyes of the Warring States Chinese, building the walls must have been a cost-effective insurance policy in guarding their farming regions and their newly found wealth against the nomads. It was no accident that during the Warring States Period (475–221 BC) all the main kingdoms rushed into wall construction until the activity reached its first climax under the first emperor, Qin Shihuang (r. 221–210 BC). The affordability of the Walls is not in doubt.

Third, to see the function of the Great Walls one needs to go back all the way to the history of pre-Qin times to see (1) why the Chinese (or the proto-Chinese) had their walls facing certain directions but not others, and especially (2) why those different units did not build the walls between themselves as shown in Table 5.1. The only sensible explanation is that the Chinese civilisation as a whole felt the common threat from the northern nomads and that building the walls was a common strategy from the settled agrarian Chinese to protect themselves from the nomadic tribes. Here it is worth noting that the timing of the first round of the wall constructions was during the Warring States Period (475–221 BC), a period of the most chaotic and lasting civil wars in China's written history. So, the threat from the north must have

271

been real. Not only that, the threat must have been greater than that from the rival kingdoms of the same Chinese race. If so, the need and incentive for a permanent defence line must have been real.

Fourth, the effectiveness of the Great Walls was evident in that after 200 BC, without exception, all the nomad conquerors (the Xianbeis, the Five Barbarians, the Tartars, the Mongols and Manchus) had to cross the walls to claim their prey. As shown in Figure 5.2, there were 45 main nomadic invasions along the walls from the Han to the Ming periods. In other words, the walls formed a permanent physical barrier to prevent those alien nomadic groups from entering China's farming region. In comparison, it only took the Manchus a single-line willow fence some 1,300 kms long (erected between 1644 and 1700, called *liutiao bian*) to stop the agrarian Chinese from infiltrating Manchuria. The Manchu willow fence followed the same idea as the Chinese Great Walls. It differed from the walls only in the material used. This means that an artificially built *cordon sanitaire* was needed from either side to demarcate political borders between the Chinese and non-Chinese. The difference in materials was determined by the physical strength of the enemy. Obviously, it required a greater physical mass to stop those northern nomads, who were equipped with the power of horses. So, a brick wall instead of a willow fence was appropriate for the defending Chinese.

Fifth, to understand the phenomenon of the lack of record for the walls one must bear in mind that there were certain areas that the Chinese literati had distaste for and thus did not want to touch. The Great Walls happened to be one of these areas for at least two reasons. The first reason lay in the Confucian vision of the great harmony (*datong*) and sense of mission to 'civilise' the souls of both the Chinese and the non-Chinese (*jiaohua*). This vision and mission in principle rejected the need for keeping the 'barbarians' out. This was crystallised in the Zhou system of 'five-level circles' (*wufu*), as recorded in the chapter 'Tribute to King Yu' ('Yugong') of the Confucian classic *Book of History* (*Shangshu*) (see Wu G. 1993: 118–19). The Zhou system radiated from the Zhou capital in all directions with a radius of 500 *li* for each level with five levels, covering an area with an aggregate radius of 2,500 *li*. Given that one Zhou *li* is equivalent to 346.5 m (Liang F. 1980: 540–4), the entire area liable to pay tributes to the Zhou was thus 2,356,222 square kilometres, some 24.5 per cent of the territory of China today. The five levels were (1) 'king's land' (*dianfu*), (2) 'lords' land' (*houfu*), (3) 'vassals' land' (*binfu*), (4) 'semi-barbarians' land' (*yaofu*) and (5) 'barbarians' land' (*huangfu*). Different types and quantities of goods were demanded by the Zhou authorities as tributes from each level. It is interesting that beyond the 'king's land' circle, no grain was required as tribute, which suggests that the farming land diminished with distance. The Zhou system was an open system and was thus incompatible with walls designated to separate different groups. Confucius and his followers took this Zhou system as a perfect social order and the basis on which to apply their ideal of civilising souls far and near. What the early Confucians did not predict, though, was that at the end of the Spring and Autumn Period (770–476 BC), China entered the Iron Age and had a sudden increase in labour and land productivities. As a result, the income gap between the farming Chinese and the non-farming nomads was enlarged at an increasing speed. Thus, although China had not been so attractive a prey to the nomads, it certainly became one by the end of the Spring and Autumn Period. Regardless of this new development, Confucians still held on to the five-level circle order as a matter of principle and stuck to their classics. So, ideologically, the walls were viewed as unsound and consequently excluded from Confucians' writings. The second reason came from the wall project itself. In the following Qin Dynasty (221–207 BC), the construction was partly responsible for leading to the first mass, dynasty-smashing rebellion in Chinese history. From then on, wall construction and maintenance became closely associated with people's miseries: because of the Great Wall, an excessive corvée burden was imposed on the general public and the Legalist coercive approach became rampant in administration. The ever-popular and touching story in Chinese literature on the legendary Meng Jiangnü reflects such a mentality. A young woman, Meng had travelled thousands of *li* to reunite with her husband serving corvée to build the wall and discovered that her loved one had been worked to death and buried under the wall. Her wailing caused the collapse of the section of the wall under which her husband was buried. On the part of the ruling class, wall construction and maintenance were closely associated with tyranny, with a disastrous outcome for the governing institutions (see Ban G. AD 82 vol. 24: ch. 'Shihuo Zhi'), something that was to be avoided at all costs. The Qin Great Wall was thus China's Wailing Wall for both the ruled (in terms of human suffering) and the ruling (in terms of dethronement), and was condemned. Throughout post-Qin history, wall construction and maintenance became more or less a political taboo and was always kept low-key or unpublicised, even though such projects were imperative for the survival of the empire. This ambivalence in the Chinese attitude towards the walls explains why they were deliberately overlooked in Chinese literature and official records so completely and for so long.

Sixth, it is naive to believe that the walls were effective all the time in discouraging and stopping the nomad invasion. Soon after the Northern Song's defence collapsed before the mighty Jin Tartars (Jin: 1115–1234), the walls, swallowed up by the Jin territory, became irrelevant to both the Chinese and the Tartars. The same situation continued after the Mongol Yuan (1271–1368) took over the Jin's territory in a 'second-hand' conquest. After the Ming general Wu Sangui (1612–78) opened the gate of the wall fortress at the Shanhaiguan Pass for the Manchus, the same fate recurred, as the Qing Empire pushed its territory further north to Siberia and further northwest to Turkistan. Consequently, the Ming walls now stood in the middle of China's hinterland. So, for at least 520 years in China's pre-modern period (253 years during Jin–Yuan times, 267 years during Qing times), the walls were obsolete. If the modern period (1840 onwards) is taken into account the obsolete time is well over 600 years, since the Qing territory has been inherited by both the Nationalist and Communist states. What happened to the walls when they became useless for defence purposes? The Chinese simply recycled them – or, more precisely, the bricks, flagstones, timber and so forth – to build houses, temples, bridges and tombs. Such recycling was an open secret. After all, once the border-guards were gone, the walls belonged to free-riders. This was a case of the 'tragedy of the commons'. Once the brick surface was cut open, the earth body of the walls was subject to rapid weathering and erosion. It is not surprising that after some ten generations under the Jin and Yuan, the Song wall was gone and the Mings had to start it all over again. Similarly, after another ten generations under the Qing, apart from sections near urban centres and remote mountains, much of the Ming walls disappeared. Given that Qing law protected only the Ming royal tombs, not the Ming walls, the wall recycling was in effect legal. Therefore, since the turn of the twentieth century what modern observers have seen are only the remains of the Ming walls after being recycled over a long time. If they had visited all the villages and towns in a radius of 500 km along the Ming walls, they would know what the walls have been reincarnated as. This process was finally reversed in Deng Xiaoping's era (1978–97) under a politically motivated propaganda programme first to stop the wall recycling and then to restore the Ming walls.

Last but not least, the fact that China practised a policy of peaceful coexistence through regular border trade (*quechang*) and intermarriage (*heqin*) with its nomadic neighbours, a policy which had almost as long a history as the Great Walls themselves, should not be regarded as the abandonment of China's northern military defence. Data for the Ming and recent periods show that China's national security–territorial policy was based on violence (Wilkenfeld *et al.* 1988). It was merely a strategy to complement the Great Wall defence in accordance with the strategy of Sun Wu (Spring and Autumn Period), the ancient military theorist and a rational economic thinker, called 'to win all the battles is not always the most desirable strategy, to subdue your enemy without fighting is the best' (*baizhan baisheng fei shanzhishan zheye, buzhan erquren zhibin, shanzhishan zheye*) (Tian Z. *et al.* 1990: 82; see also Griffith 1963: vii). So, it is incorrect to think that China was less ready to fight than her nomadic neighbours. Under the guidance of Sun Wu, China was merely more calculating than the nomads and had an accommodationist strategy of peaceful, and sometimes even humiliating, intercourse with aliens (through diplomacy, intermarriages, trade, reparations and so forth). Empirically, China did not hesitate to switch from the dimension of peace to the dimension of violence when the cost of the accommodationist strategy exceeded that of war (Johnson 1995).

Interestingly, most national heroines in Chinese history had much to do with either fighting the war against the northern nomads or marrying

them. The best examples of the former were Mu Lan, a legendary ranking officer of around the Tang Period (AD 618–907), who disguised herself as a man
to replace her father for a 12-year-long military service along China's northern
borders (see Wang Z. *et al.* 1992 vol. 1: 414–16), and the legendary female
warriors of General Yang Ye's family (Tang Ye, AD ?–986) of the Northern
Song (Anon. *c.* 1606). The best examples of the latter were Wang Zhaojun,
an Imperial concubine of the Han Dynasty, who in 33 BC volunteered to
marry the Hun king Huhanxie in a bilateral peace deal between the Chinese
and the Huns, and the Tang princess Wencheng (?–630), who in AD 641
married the Tibetan king Songzan Ganbu (*c.* AD 617–50) to strengthen the
tie between the two countries. This dual utility of the Chinese women to
the Empire was undoubtedly determined by the 'carrot and stick' approach
of the Chinese northern defence policy.

Thus, it is ahistorical to overemphasise the importance of Chinese written
records regarding the existence and utility of the Great Walls. It is equally
ahistorical to judge the function of the Great Walls by examining the Ming
carcass after the walls had been obsolete for generations. It is misleading to
take the policy of peaceful coexistence as a fundamental change in China's
northern defence.

### 5.2.3 Impacts on military competitiveness and the economy

#### 5.2.3.1 Military competitiveness

The threat and pressure from the nomadic peoples along the northern borders
formed a type of competition between the Chinese and the non-Chinese
throughout the history of the East Asian mainland. This competition provided
the Chinese with incentives to invent more for the sake of their national
defence. In this context, there is little doubt that the competition with the
nomads sharpened the competitive edge of the Zhuo and Qin, both being the
'front-line' units of their times respectively against the Huns, Tungus, Yuezhis
and Qiangs. The Shaanxi Region, where both the Zhou and Qin were based,
faced the nomad pressure from two flanks instead of one, and was thus unique
among all the Chinese units; the Zhou and Qing thus bore a double pressure
compared to the rest of the front-line units. Under these circumstances, it
was no accident that the Zhou and Qin kingdoms were able to defeat their Chinese rivals: the competition with the nomads made the Zhou and Qin super-
strong within China. Consequently, during the pre-Tang Period, there was a
rigorous pecking order coordinating the geographic zones from the north to
the south in the East Asian mainland: (1) the non-Chinese nomads from the
Steppes; (2) the Chinese from the front-line regions; (3) the Chinese in interior
China; and (4) the non-Chinese in south China (see Weng D. 1990).

What is of significance is that both the Zhou and Qin maintained their
agrarian preference from where their military strength was drawn (see

Chapter 3). The pressure from the nomads was thus internalised and contributed positively to the formation and spread of the Chinese trinary structure from its beginning.

### 5.2.3.2 Impact on the economy

The impact on the Chinese economy was profound in terms of inputs of capital and labour in the walled defence line. Modern research shows that the total lengths of the Great Walls under the Qin and Han were over 5,000 km. The Ming walls were considerably longer: 7,300 km (Yu 1986: 81–2; Guo R. et al. 1988: 225–33). The total length of the Warring States' walls, as shown in Figure 5.1, was easily another 5,000 km. So, the aggregate length of the walls of the Warring States, Qin, Han and Ming periods was 22,300 km. This figure can be used for input estimation.

#### MATERIAL INPUTS

Behind this aggregate length of the walls were huge inputs of construction materials (earth, sand, bricks and stone blocks). It has been estimated that the materials used in building the Ming walls had a volume of over 200 million cubic metres, which would build a wall 1m thick and 5m high capable of encircling the earth at the equator (Yu 1986: 82), or simply of 'walling this planet'. Conservatively, to suppose that all the inputs to the walls from 400 BC to 1367 AD were twice that for the Ming walls, the aggregate inputs to the walls over time would have been 600 million cubic metres. Given that the relevant period for the construction of the walls was 1,960 years (400 BC– AD 1560), the annual inputs were about 306,100 cubic metres. It is known that between AD 57 and 1560, the long-term average of the Chinese population was 40.7 million people (Liang F. 1980: 4–10). To use this figure as the base, the annual per capita inputs must have been enough to build a piece of the wall of volume 7,530.7 cubic centimetres over the 1,960 years. In reality, the aggregate input was almost certainly much greater if (1) the total inputs to the walls exceeded 600 million cubic metres; (2) the capital inputs to the wall construction are taken into account; (3) the capital and material inputs for the transportation of building materials to the contraction sites along the border are included; and (4) the capital and material inputs in the routine maintenance are considered.

As China's elite troops, during the Song and Ming, the standing army along the walls was equipped with the best weapons, including crossbows and firearms (Wei Z. et al. 1993: ch. 3). So there must have been at least 1.4–1.5 million pieces of equipment. Here, the deduction of arms from the non- combatant was cancelled out by the minimum arms stock required to sustain combat capacity, which, according to History of the Song Dynasty, totalled 12.7 million pieces a year (Tuo T. 1345: 'Military, Entry 11'). In

1007, the stock of arms accumulated was reported to be enough for the next thirty years (Wei Z. *et al*. 1993: 164). The capital and material inputs in arms should also be included in the total northern defence line.

## LABOUR INPUTS

According to *Complete Records of Institutions and Regulations*, compiled in AD 801, it took 1 man-day to build a section of 2 cubic *chi* of wall for military defence purposes (or 0.0602 cubic metres; 1 Tang *chi* = 0.311 m) (Du Y. AD 801: ch. 'Military, Entry 5'). The above-mentioned 600 million cubic metres would need 9,966.8 million man-days with an average of 5.1 million man-days per annum for 1,960 years. To show the proportion of this labour input in the economy as a whole, it is reasonable to assume that a half of the total population could have worked 300 days a year, giving an aggregate of 6,105 million man-work days per annum (to use the long-term average population size of 40.7 million). The total labour input in the construction of the walls is thus likely to have been 163.3 per cent of China's annual total. Moreover, if the 9,966.8 million man-days had been paid at the subsistence level of 500g of grain per man per day, a total of 5 million tonnes of grain, sufficient to maintain 27.3 million people for a year, would be needed, which can be taken as the minimum labour cost of the wall construction.

If a labourer worked 300 days a year, this average annual workload required some 17,000 full-time workers. Here the travel time needed to move the labourers to the construction site is not included. This does not include the periodic maintenance of the walls, either, which was evidently not trivial. In AD 607, 1 million labourers were sent to maintain the Great Wall; a year later, a total of 200,000 people were employed for the task (Fan W. 1964–5 vol. 3: 30–47). These estimates are likely to be conservative, as evidence shows that the number of man-days per rural labourer per year was only 172 during the 1920s and 250 under the brutal commune system in the 1950s (Stover 1974: 273).

Considering that the walls were built in a limited period, which was dictated by military emergency, all the inputs (capital, labour and materials) were made in a spurt rather than in a trickle. Thus, the economy must have had sufficient surplus at its disposal to cope with such spurts. To take the Ming case as an example, the walls were built over a period of two hundred years; the annual input of materials was likely to have been 1 million cubic metres, which was 3.3 times as high as the long-term average of 306,100 cubic metres. This 1 million cubic metres of wall would require 16.6 million man-days each year, or 55,370 full-time workers. If the 1.4–1.5 million border-guards and workers in the arms industry are also taken into account, the total labour inputs in the walled defence line were much greater.

### SURPLUS REQUIRED FROM THE AGRICULTURAL SECTOR

Construction labourers and border-guards had to be fed by agricultural surplus. If it is supposed that all the wall constructors and border-guards were paid at the subsistence level of 500g of grain a day, then (1) the total annual wage bill in kind for the wall construction (5.09 million man-days) is 2,545 tonnes; (2) the annual cost in kind of the maintenance of the 1.4–1.5 million border-guards was 255,500–273,750 tonnes. These two are combined as 258,045–276,295 tonnes a year at the Ming level.

According to *History of the Ming Dynasty*, an army of 190,000 needed 40,000 farmers to feed it, with a soldier-to-farmer ratio of 4.75:1 (Zhang T. 1735: ch. 'Economy'). To use this ratio as a base, the 1.4–1.5 million Great Wall-based troops would need 294,700–315,800 farmers to support them. To include the 5.09 million man-days, or 17,000 full-time construction workers, another 3,580 farmers were required. Moreover, the food had to be transported to the border where the army was stationed. So, there was another army, an army of logistics personnel, to fulfil the task. The second army had to be fed, too. Furthermore, workers in the arms industry were dependent on the agricultural surplus as well. According to a modern survey, the 22,300-km-long wall aggregate is only a half of the total length of all the walls ever constructed in different periods (*ibid.*). Within the territory of Inner Mongolia in contemporary China, a theatre for battles between the Chinese and the northern nomads in the past, the aggregate length of walls is some 15,000 km (Yu 1986: 82). Therefore, all the above estimates are almost certainly much lower than was the case in reality.

Ultimately, all the labour inputs in terms of wall construction, weapon manufacturing and border patrol depended upon China's agricultural sector and its performance. More precisely, they depended on the surplus capacity of Chinese agriculture. Indeed, the Great Wall defence line itself was the materialisation of the Chinese economic surpluses over time. Obviously, the Chinese strategy was to turn China's economic superiority in terms of sustained surpluses to enhance China's military strength. It worked like an insurance premium, a necessary price against risks.

### 5.2.3.3 *Impact on public expenditure and government policy*

### DEFENCE EXPENDITURE ON THE NORTHERN BORDER TROOPS

It has been estimated that during the Western Han Period (206 BC–AD 24), the defence expenditure on the 800,000–900,000 northern border troops was likely to be around 21.3 million *shi* of grain, or 39 per cent of the land-tax revenue in grain, and 6,038.2 bronze coins, equivalent to 92.3 per cent of China's monetary tax revenue (Huang J. and Chen X. 1997). If the land tax was 10 per cent of the total agricultural output, and if the agricultural sector produced 70–80 per cent of the total gross national product (GNP), the food alone cost 2.7–3.1 per cent of China's GNP. If the same tax rate had been applied to the non-agricultural sectors which occupied the remaining 20–30 per cent of China's GNP, the cash payment to the troops was likely to have been another 1.8–2.8 per cent of China's GNP. The total share was probably 4.5–5.9 per cent of the total GNP. Bear in mind, this was only one-third of the Western Han's total defence expenditure.

IMPACT ON GOVERNMENT POLICY

Although China's northern defence line was a deadweight on the economy from 400 BC to the end of the Ming, the Chinese preventive response to the threat of alien invasion and conquest worked as an inducement to promote the agricultural sector to produce more and better. If the surplus capacity of the agricultural sector dropped below the minimum level, China's northern defence suffered and the outcome was often disastrous. Prosperous agriculture meant stronger national defence, a correlation that the Chinese evidently recognised long before the country's unification under the reign of Emperor Qin Shihuang (r. 221–209 BC) (Fan W. 1964–5 vol. 2: ch. 2). The well-known 'Tillage and Arms Policy' (*gengzhan zhengce*) of Shang Yang (*c.* 390–338 BC) can be taken as a good example. In history, the great success in economic reform and in the simultaneous defence of China against the Huns by Emperor Wudi (r. 140–88 BC) of the Han Dynasty provides a classic proof of the correlation. Conversely, China's defence failures often resulted directly or indirectly from a weakening of the agricultural economy. Evidence can be found in the demise of the Jin (AD 265–420), Song (AD 960–1279) and Ming (1368–1644) dynasties (Lee 1969: 33–133).

Through preventive response to the alien threat, the external pressure was internalised in the Chinese economy and the alien pressure functioned as a stimulus. From the institutional viewpoint, the barbarian threat provided the Chinese with an incentive to strengthen the Chinese trinary structure.

## 5.3 External shock and its internalisation

### 5.3.1 The shock

However, what China's northern defence line was able to achieve was not to eliminate but to minimise foreign invasions and conquests. In Chinese history as a whole, from the Qin to the Qing periods, there were in all 25 nomadic régimes that lasted more than five years (CBW 1989: 2357–405; see also Weng D. 1990). This was about a 2.3 per cent success rate out of the total of 1,109 main military conflicts between the Chinese and the nomads from 215 BC to 1684, compatible with a long-term 'draw' between the nomads and the Chinese along the Great Walls. Although the odds were clearly against the nomads, the empire was conquered several times, partly so by nomads such as the Xianbeis and Tartars, and entirely by Mongols and Manchus.

For China, alien invasions and conquests incurred both accounting costs (in terms of looting and destroying products, factors of production and lives) and opportunity costs (in terms of how the economy would have performed without invasion and conquest). These were socio-economically disastrous, as has been recognised by modern observers (Jones 1981, 1988). Invasions and conquests were thus external shocks to the Chinese system.

This shock was clearly revealed by the aftermath of the Mongol conquest. In terms of the loss of lives, by 1291 China's total population had dropped by 31 per cent from its level under the Tartar Jin and the Southern Song combined. In north China, where the population was hit the hardest, the decrease was as high as 85 per cent, which marks this as one of the bloodiest pages in pre-modern Chinese history (Liang F. 1980: 4–11, 164, 185). From the heavy losses of Chinese lives, it is easy to understand that a genocidal policy was at that time suggested to the Mongol chief to the effect that 'Since the Chinese are useless to our cause, they should be killed off so that their land can be converted to grazing land' (Song L. 1371 vol. 153: no. 146; see also Wright and Twitchett 1962: 19–20, 189–216). Among those Chinese who survived, millions were enslaved (*quding*). Horses belonging to the Chinese were confiscated. Vast agrarian areas were enclosed as Mongol grazing land. The taxation burden increased enormously in the south, where the Mongols milked 70 per cent of the Yuan annual revenue (Wang Q. 1586; Perkins 1969: 23–4, 197–9; ZNK 1984 vol. 2: 51–3; Zheng X. *et al.* 1984: 242–4, 254–5).

As with external pressure, the shock from invasions and conquests was also internalised by the Chinese system. First, to prevent invasions the Chinese were forced to pay even more attention than would have been neccessary otherwise to their agriculture, the physiocratic government and the free peasantry. As a result, the trinary equilibrium was better maintained in normal times. Second, when invasions and conquests did occur, the trinary structure managed to survive through a process of cultural integration whereby the conquerors accepted the Chinese socio-economic way of life. So, the nomadic invasions and conquests were mainly military victories; and the conquerors were unable to win their war in the field of culture and the economy. There was no exception till the end of the eighteenth century. Thus the damage caused by invasions and conquests was only temporary, and the Chinese civilisation survived from the ashes.

### 5.3.2 Cases of integration

The best examples of 'willing integratees' of the Chinese trinary structure are the Xianbeis during the Northern and Southern Dynasties (AD 420–581) and the Manchus during the Qing (Bai C. 1987).

### 5.3.2.1 The Xianbeis

The Northern and Southern Dynasties (AD 420–581) was a period of warfare and schism during which China was broken in pieces by the 'Five Nomadic Barbarians' (*wuhu*) from the north and west (Elvin 1973: 44). The Xianbeis, one of the nomadic groups who had replaced the Huns on the Steppes, conquered north China in AD 386 and their North Wei régime lasted some one and a half centuries.

During the initial period of invasion and conquest a large number of Chinese farmers were killed, cultivated land was abandoned, and agriculture in the north was brutally disrupted. But subtle changes began to take place immediately after the Xianbei military triumph. In AD 386, at the very beginning of the Xianbei reign, Emperor Daowu (r. AD 386–408) hired Chinese scholars as his courtiers. Politically, the emperor's principal policy was 'encouraging agriculture in order to calm the Chinese' (*wunong ximin*) (Fan W. 1964–5 vol. 2: 455). Meanwhile, economically, the Xianbei herdsmen realised that tillage was more productive than pasturage. Therefore, in AD 400, acting like a Chinese monarch, Emperor Daowu set an example for all the Xianbeis by ploughing his own farm (*ibid.*: 458). A policy quantum leap occurred in AD 485 under Emperor Xiaowen (r. AD 471–99). Adopting the suggestion from his Chinese adviser, the emperor launched an economic reform. The core of the reforms was the establishment of the Land Equalisation System (*juntianzhi*), which enabled citizens to obtain state land so that all able-bodied adults, Chinese and Xianbeis alike, had the basic resources with which to start their own household farming and hence the government began to gain tax revenue (Tang Z. 1956; Elvin 1973: 47–51). In this way, the Chinese family farms were rebuilt. More significantly, under this system the Xianbeis voluntarily departed from their pastoral past and successfully converted themselves to an agrarian people. This Land Equalisation System worked so well that it was adopted for three centuries by the following Chinese dynasties.

The establishment of the Land Equalisation System marked the systematic recovery of Northern Wei agriculture from the regression caused by the lengthy upheavals that followed the alien intrusion and conquest. With it, a renaissance of Chinese agricultural technology took place which was marked by the *Essential Techniques for the Peasantry*, the first comprehensive agronomic treatise in Chinese history. Jia Sixie, the author of the book, was a Chinese working for the Xianbeis as a local official. In his preface, Jia took the advantage to remind his reader of physiocracy:

In the past sage king Shen Nong [Master of Agriculture] invented the spade and the plough to benefit the people; King Yao asked four scholars to make the calendar; King Shun taught the young that agriculture was to be the first priority in government policy-making.

And,

> *Master Guan's Book* [*Guanzi*] reads that: an idle farmer makes some-
> one hungry and an idle weaver makes someone cold. People start to
> know courtesy only when their granaries are full. People start to
> understand honour or disgrace only when clothing and food supply
> are sufficient.
>
> (Jia S. *c.* AD 534 AD 1985: 1, 5)

To judge from the Xianbei policies, this physiocratic attitude was well
received among the ruling class.

A similar integration process took place in the other four of the Five Barbarians: the Dis (responsible for the establishment of the Early Qin, AD 350–
94, and the Late Liang, AD 386–403), Huns (responsible for the establishment
of the Early Zhao, AD 304–29), Jies (responsible for the establishment of the
Late Zhao, AD 311–34) and Qiangs (responsible for the establishment of
the Late Qin régime, AD 384–417). Unfortunately, these régimes did not
last long enough to complete the conversion. But, since their territories
were eventually annexed by the mighty Xianbeis, who did complete the conversion, it is safe to suggest that integration was the norm for those nomads
(Weng D. 1990: pt 2).

### 5.3.2.2 The Manchus

Long before the Manchu invasion of China, Chinese classics such as *The
Four Books* (*Sishu*), *The Five Classics* (*Wujing*) and *A General History for Administrative Purposes* (*Zizhi Tongjian*), Chinese law books such as *Record of
the Administrative Statutes of the Ming Dynasty* (*Ming Huidian*) and even Chinese novels such as *Romance of the Three Kingdoms* (*Sanguo Yanyi*) had been
translated into Manchu (Zuo B. 1986). So, the Manchus began to adopt
Chinese culture even before they had crossed the Great Wall (Fairbank
1965: 77), which gave them the confidence to claim the Qing to be the
orthodox successor to the overthrown Ming. As Fairbank points out
(*ibid.*), 'The essential point about the Manchu conquest of 1644 is that the
Manchus by the time they came to power in China had already mastered
the Confucian art of government and reconciled their own political institutions with it.'

The Manchu voluntary integration with the Chinese was not just lip-
service to win the support of the Chinese. The Ming political system was
religiously followed; the Chinese language was an official language; and the
Manchu emperors were all strictly educated from a very young age by
Chinese scholars (Zuo B. 1986). The Ming imperial palaces (*zijincheng*,
literally 'The City of the Monarch Star', commonly mistranslated as 'The Forbidden City') were carefully preserved (including the names of the buildings

and gardens). In the palace compound, there was little sign of nomadic van-
dalism by the Manchus, nor were many amendments made by the new
masters.

To some extent, the Manchus became more Confucian than the Chinese: 40
official positions were established called 'Executor of Confucius Temple
Affairs' in charge of regular ceremonies (*kongmiao zhishiguan*), the first of
their type in the entire Chinese premodern history (see Lü Z. 1994: 190,
911–13). These executors were ranked from the Third Grade Plus (two
posts) to the Ninth Grade Plus (ten posts) at seven levels. With it, a dual
ranking system was invented by the Xianbei Northern Wei and was later
passed on to the Tang. The system was characterised by two subranks, plus
and minus, at each grade. Given that the Governor-General of a province
(*xunfu*) was ranked the Second Grade Plus, the weight of the Confucian affairs
in the Manchu state was thus remarkable. This 'Confucianisation' can also be
seen from Emperor Kangxi's activities. In the winter of 1684, Emperor
Kangxi (r. 1662–1722) paid his personal respects in Nanjing to the mauso-
leum of Zhu Yuanzhang, the founder of the Manchu Qing's predecessor
Ming. It was reported that at the mausoleum the emperor took the side
path instead of the boulevard and ordered his entourage to dismount. He
then deigned to kneel three times and kowtowed nine times (*sangui jiukou*)
at the tomb, the highest etiquette and one that was observed by officials
and citizens exclusively towards the throne (Wei Z. *et al.* 1995: 193). So,
instead of behaving like an arrogant conqueror, the emperor was extremely
humble and obviously apologetic to the Mings and thus to the Chinese.
Not surprisingly, Emperor Kangxi treated the Ming royal tombs as his ancestors'. In 1716, he ordered two grave robbers to be executed immediately
by beheading and hanging, emphasising that it was a capital crime to
disturb the tombs (*ibid.*: 251). As the most civilised conquerors in Chinese
history, the Manchus gradually lost their own cultural identity – so much
so that the word 'Mandarin', literarily meaning the 'Manchu language',
came to refer to the Chinese language and the original Manchu Mandarin
was lost, becoming a dead language.

Not surprisingly, the importance of tillage was well addressed and agriculture was given the highest priority in the Qing policies. Each year, the Qing
emperor was expected to perform the Opening of Tillage Ceremony (*gengjili*)
and to hold a memorial ceremony in the Temple of the First Agriculturist
(*Xiannong Tan*), authentic Chinese ceremonies with a clear physiocratic gesture (E E. 1742/1956: 1073, 1077–8, 1083–4). Emperor Kangxi knew so
much about farming that he was responsible for the discovery of a new type
of early-ripening rice at his own Fengzeyuan Farm (Elvin 1982: 14).

It is evident that the Manchus integrated themselves, both culturally
and economically, with the Chinese. As a result, the Chinese Ming and the
Manchu Qing are customarily considered as a single, integrated historical
period.

### 5.3.3.3 The Mongols

The Mongols won two wars on China's soil. The first was aimed at the Tartars, who had taken over the northern half of the Chinese Empire in 1126 from the Northern Song Dynasty. The Mongols triumphed in 1234 and then began to annexe south China, now under the Southern Song, a task which took them four decades to achieve. The Mongols finally gained control over all of China proper in 1279 and ruled the country under a stratocracy till 1368.

In this process, as already mentioned, Chinese agricultural regions were first ruined by the Mongols' physical attacks and then stifled by their policies of enclosure and heavy taxation. In administration, Mongol racial discrimination against the indigenous Chinese further harmed the economy. However, a turning point occurred when the genocidal Mongol policy was rebutted by Yelü Chucai, a man from Persia working as a high-ranking courtier of the Yuan. He argued that the Chinese could be exploited as a source of productive labour so the killing should be stopped, a point that was well taken by the Mongols (Wright and Twitchett 1962: 19–20, 189–216). This sharp policy U-turn reflected the Mongol need for a production base to finance further invasions elsewhere. So, after they had captured north China, the Mongols began to see the importance of Chinese agriculture in their ambitious course and, consequently, made efforts to restore the damaged agrarian economy in north China.

In this context, new institutions were created by the Mongols to promote agriculture on China's soil. In 1261, the Mongols established the Agriculture Promotion Bureau (*quannongsi*). It was upgraded in 1270 to the Bureau for Agriculture (*sinongsi*), with four Agriculture Inspection Bureaux (*xunxing quannongsi*) under its command. In 1271, the bureau was once again upgraded to Grand Bureau for Agricultural Extension (*da sinongsi*), in charge of agricultural and sericultural planning and production, water control and famine relief (Li C. 1370: 'Biography of Emperor Shizu' vols. 4, 7; Lü Z. 1994: 34). The mission of these organisations was, as their names implied, to rebuild and protect Chinese agriculture, something completely foreign to the Mongol tradition and diametrically opposite to the genocidal Mongol policy of earlier years.

In terms of the sharp change in Mongol attitude, the most telling case was the publication of agricultural treatises in the Chinese language for the Mongol officials to improve production across the country. In 1273, the first Mongol government-sponsored project under an imperial edict resulted in the compilation of an official agricultural treatise, entitled *Fundamentals of Agriculture and Sericulture* (*Nongsang Jiyao*) (Shi S. 1980: 50–1). It referred mainly to the existing knowledge of Chinese agriculture up to the Song Period, which is consistent with the urgent need for agricultural restoration at that time. It also had a section dealing with cotton-growing and processing, which was the first systematic description of cotton production in Chinese literature (Appendix K; see also Ji Y. 1782 vol. 730: 220–1). Given that the Mongol Yuan had a great incentive to save as much silk as possible for the lucrative foreign trade, this new information was almost certainly disseminated widely among the farming regions. Known for its quality, this book is recognised as among the five most important agricultural books in premodern Chinese history (Hu D. 1985: 58–9). This shows just how serious the Mongols became about farming and the Chinese farmers.

The book was repeatedly published by the Mongol authorities. Copies were first issued in the Mongol-controlled regions in North and West China (including the Yellow River Valley and the Sichuan Basin) and publication was later extended to South China after the Mongol conquest was completed (Qu Z. 1960: 51–2; Shi S. 1980: 50, 55; Li C. 1982). Given that by around 1234 the Mongols had gained control of six of China's provinces, including 650 counties, and later, in 1279, ruled the entire country of eleven provinces and 1,110 counties (Liang F. 1980: 178–84), the copies almost certainly reached county level (see Table 5.2).

The scope of the distribution was large by premodern standards. *Fundamentals of Agriculture and Sericulture* was not the only technical manual that was published by the Mongol Establishment. In 1318, Emperor Renzong (r. 1311–19) ordered 1,000 copies of *Illustrations of Mulberry-Growing (Zaisang Tushuo)* to be printed and issued across the country (Li C. 1370: 'Biography of Emperor Renzong').

The Mongols' new attitude was best demonstrated in their promotion of another agronomic work entitled *Wangzhen's Agricultural Treatise (Wangzhen*

Table 5.2 *Fundamentals of Agriculture and Sericulture* and its publication history

| Edition | Year | Copies | Recipients |
|---|---|---|---|
| 1st[a] | 1273 | — | — |
| 1st[a] | 1286 | 1,000 | — |
| 2nd[a] | 1314 | 1,500 | Court and provinces |
| 2nd[a] | 1316 | 1,500 | — |
| 2nd[a] | 1322 | 1,500 | — |
| 2nd[a] | 1329 | 3,000 | — |
| 2nd[a] | 1332 | 1,500 | — |
| 2nd[a] | 1339 | — | — |
| —[b] | 1314–23 | — | — |
| —[b] | 1372 | — | — |
| Total | | 10,000[c] | |

*Sources*: Based on Hu D. 1985: 57–68; Han R. 1986: 372–3.

*Notes*
a Central government sponsored publications.
b Local government sponsored publications.
c The minimum number.

*Nongshu*), written in 1304 by an indigenous scholar, Wang Zhen. The Yuan Emperor Chengzong (r. 1295–1307) even issued an edict concerning Wang's work:

> Wang Zhen, Magistrate of Yongfeng County of Xinzhou Province, is a well-known Confucian of Shandong. He is senior in age and advanced in learning. He has served the country in different regions from the north to the south and obtained wide experience. Wang has completed his works entitled *General Rules of Agriculture and Sericulture* [*Nongsang Tongjue*], *Flora of All Crop Types* [*Baigupu*] and *Illustration of Agricultural Implements* [*Nongqi Tupu*]. His works are based on thorough study. The knowledge is clearly presented, including both knowledge from the classics, from ancient times onwards, and knowledge of northern and southern agriculture. Wang's book can be thus used to guide both the commoners in their everyday practice and the authorities in their encouragement of agriculture. Although certain old agricultural books are available on the market such as *Essential Techniques for the Peasantry* [*Qimin Yaoshu*] and *Fundamentals of Basic Practice* [*Wuben Jiyao*], they are not as comprehensive as Wang's book. If the book is not printed and issued, it may be lost. It is beneficial to have it printed and issued as an official book.
>
> (Wang Z. 1304/1981: 446)

This was one of the few occasions on which the ruling Mongols openly applauded Confucian scholars' achievements. It is worth noting that in his preface, Wang revisited the age-old physiocratic ideas as follows:

> Agriculture is essential to society: 'One idle man results in hunger and one idle woman results in cold.' The ancient sages served people and gave the first priority to agriculture. They exhaustively taught people how to plough, how to weave, how to raise plants and animals.
>
> (*ibid.*:1)

Wang and Emperor Chengzong must have reached consensus on this physiocratic viewpoint, another sign of the integration of the Mongols.

The integration is further shown by the fact that in 1313 the Chinese Imperial Examination system for bureaucratic recruitment was copied by the Yuan state, although the original Chinese rule was slightly modified for political reasons. Instead of producing one Imperial Examination Champion (*zhuangyuan*) each round, the Mongols decided to have two. From 1315 to 1366, 16 such examinations were held and a balance of champions was carefully kept between the Chinese and the Mongols. For 15 of the 16 examinations there was one Mongol champion and one Chinese champion, the exception being 1354, when the champions were both Chinese (Zhou Y. 1995: 406–29). At the lower levels, many more Chinese candidates passed the examinations: at least a quarter of the total (Deng C. 1967: 195–9, 337–8). This indicates that Yuan official positions were taken by Confucian Chinese. All these were alien to the Mongol nomadic culture and their original plan for China and the Chinese.

To show the nature of the change, among 17 of the best-known Chinese poets of the Yuan Period, 16 held Yuan official positions, or 94 per cent of the total (Wang Z. *et al.* 1992: 1584–669). This means that the Chinese who served the Mongol Yuan régime were not solely Mongol collaborators. The transformed Mongol régime identified itself to a great extent with indigenous Chinese socio-economic life and thus became a source of attraction to the indigenous scholars. This phenomenon is also revealed by evidence on the Mongol side. The three poets of the Mongol origin who are regarded as among the top 20 Yuan poets were so Sinicised that little trace of their ethnic and political backgrounds was left in their works (*ibid.*: 1614–24, 1634–38). One of the three, Sa Dula (*c.* 1284–1348), wrote a piece under the title of *On a Trip along the Yellow River* (*Zaofa Huanghe Jishi*). It reads in part:

> Sailing off on the river with a ship-load of dawn light,
> I see cooking smoke curling around thatched cottages
> And autumn rice piling up on ridges,
> Before having the chance to taste their new harvest
> Farmers are already urged to pay the government tax.
> Do the city dwellers in the capital
> Understand the hardships of the country folks?
> (Sa D. *c.* 1348)

It is easy to judge that Sa Dula was living an agriculture-based urban life.

In summary, although reluctant, the Mongol conquerors slowly became integrated with the Chinese. The Mongol promotion of Chinese agriculture may well have been a temporary expedient and technology-oriented at the beginning. But it grew, with the adoption of Chinese physiocracy, into the all-round conversion of Mongol socio-economic life to that of the Chinese. By the time the Chinese finally rose up to topple the Mongols, the gap between the behaviour and guiding policy of the Mongols and those of the Chinese had greatly narrowed.

### 5.3.4 *Quasi- and full trinary status*

What concerns the current study is not the integration *per se* but the restoration of the Chinese trinary structure and trinary equilibrium. Evidence suggests that nomadic conquests in China ended up with a quasi- or full trinary status which can be demonstrated in three areas: (1) restoration and enhancement of Chinese agriculture as seen by agricultural technology; (2) invention of new physiocratic institutions; and (3) restoration of the peasant household economy.

### 5.3.4.1 Restoration and enhancement of Chinese agriculture from the viewpoint of agricultural technology

The recovery of Chinese agriculture was positively reflected by the recovery of Chinese agricultural technology. It is thus not surprising that the North Wei, Yuan and Qing periods had one thing in common: great emphasis was placed and initiatives taken on the restoration and enhancement of Chinese agricultural technology. The afore-mentioned *Fundamentals of Agriculture and Sericulture* was in effect the first agricultural book resulting from a central government project in premodern Chinese history (Shi S. 1980: 50–1). In this respect, it is no coincidence that in premodern Chinese agronomy, some of the best treatises were produced under the reigns of the Xianbeis, Mongols and Manchus (see Deng 1993a).

The involvement of the Manchu monarch in promoting Chinese agricultural technology was unprecedented. Emperor Yongzheng (r. 1723–35) ordered the compilation of *Imperial Collection of Books, Past and Present* (*Gujin Tushu Jicheng*), which was completed in 1726; and Emperor Gaozong (r. 1736–95) had *Complete Collection of Books for the Four Imperial Libraries* (*Siku Quanshu*) published in 1782. Both collections contained agronomic treatises, including *Essential Techniques for the Peasantry* (*Qimin Yaoshu*), *Chen Fu's Treatise on Agriculture* (*Chenfu Nongshu*) and *Wang Zhen's Treatise on Agriculture* (*Wangzhen Nongshu*) (Lo 1986; Guy 1987; Deng 1993a: ch. 5). In addition, new treatises were completed under imperial edicts. Emperors Kangxi and Yongzheng sponsored two series of illustrations under the same title, *Pictures of Tillage and Weaving* (*Gengzhi Tu*). The two emperors themselves wrote prefaces and instructive poems for the artistically illustrated agricultural processes. Emperor Kangxi also had a botanic encyclopaedia compiled entitled *Complete Thesaurus of Botany Enlarged* (*Guang Qunfangpu*): the sections on cereals, textile fibre plants, vegetables, bamboo and trees account for 43 per cent of the total length of the book with information of 25 varieties of wheat and barley, 100 varieties of rice and 167 varieties of millet (Wang H. 1708: vols 7–10).

Individual efforts to diffuse agricultural technology were also made and encouraged. Apart from the Chinese agronomists such as Jia Sixie of the Northern Wei and Wang Zheng of the Yuan, there was Lu Mingshan, a Uighur who served the Mongols as an official of the 'coloured-eye' race (called *semuren*, a preferred group under Mongol racial discrimination[1]). In 1314, Lu compiled a monthly ordinance book entitled *Selected Essentials of Agriculture, Sericulture and Household Economy* (*Nongsang Yishi Cuoyao*) which referred mainly to the agricultural technology of South China to inform the farming

*Table 5.3* Estimates of grain yield levels

| Period | Wheat (per mu) | Change index | Rice (per mu) | Change index | Mean (per mu) | Change index |
|---|---|---|---|---|---|---|
| Pre-Qin | 0.732 *shi* | 100 | — | — | — | — |
| Han | 0.804 *shi* | 110 | 0.536 *shi* | 100 | 101 *jin* | 100 |
| Wei* and Jin | 0.791 *shi* | 108 | 0.791 *shi* | 148 | 172 *jin* | 170 |
| Southern Dynasty | — | — | 1.111 *shi* | 207 | — | — |
| North Dynasty | 0.686 *shi* | 94 | — | — | 258 *jin* | 255 |
| Sui and Tang | 0.757 *shi* | 103 | 1.136 *shi* | 212 | 334 *jin* | 331 |
| Song | 0.694 *shi* | 95 | 1.387 *shi* | 259 | 309 *jin* | 306 |
| Yuan* | 0.964 *shi* | 132 | 1.927 *shi* | 360 | 338 *jin* | 335 |
| Ming and Qing* | 1.302 *shi* | 178 | 2.604 *shi* | 486 | — | — |
| (Ming only) | | | | | (346 *jin* | 343) |
| (Qing* only) | | | | | (367 *jin* | 363) |

*Sources*: Based on Yu Y. 1980; Wu H. 1985: 194; ZNK 1984 vol. 1: 242.
*Note*
An asterisk indicates a period under alien conquests. *Shi* is a capacity measure, *jin* a weight measure.

population as to what was best practice. In view of Lu's own nomadic background and northwestern origin, the integration of the Yuan officials into the Chinese socio-economic way of life was undeniable. This was especially evident since his work was the first comprehensive book on Chinese agronomy written by a non-Chinese, which means that the previously exclusive Chinese knowledge was cracked by nomads for the first time. His treatise also reflects the fact that the Mongol administration was very conscious of the importance of agriculture in China, and that some of the officials of non-Chinese origin were thoroughly integrated with the local Chinese: they mastered the Chinese language and understood Chinese society and culture. Lu's achievement undoubtedly derived from the general political atmosphere in favour of Chinese farmers and Chinese agriculture.

The result of the enhancement of Chinese agricultural technology (owing either to invention and innovation or to the better spread of good practice, or both) can be demonstrated by the data in Table 5.3. There was no dramatic drop in the Chinese grain yield levels after the Xianbei, Mongol and Manchu conquests. Regardless of the difference in estimates, the upward trend of the yield levels of wheat and rice during these much-condemned conquests is unmistakable.

### 5.3.4.2 *Invention of new physiocratic institutions*

Among the most important new physiocratic institutions under the alien conquests were (1) the Xianbei Land Equalisation System (*juntianzhi*),

(2) the Mongol Grand Bureau for Agricultural Extension (*da sinongsi*), and (3) the Qing Farming Expert System.

## LAND EQUALISATION SYSTEM

The Xianbeis were responsible for the invention of the Land Equalisation System (*juntianzhi*), which was formally established in AD 477 by the Northern Wei government (Wei S. AD 554 vol. 7: 'Biography of Emperor Gaozu'). At the beginning, the new system was an emergency measure to re-establish the damaged rural economy through resource allocation for sustainable family farms. Aspects covered by government supervision ranged from the size of each farm to the crops that could be grown. For example, in AD 485 the system allowed each married couple to till 80 *mu* of land, of which 60 *mu* was to be used to grow grain and 20 *mu* to grow 50 mulberry trees, 5 jujube trees and 3 elm trees. The size of the family plot was doubled if the environment was less favourable (called *beitian*) (Wei S. AD 554: ch. 'Economy'; Gao M. 1987: 186–219; Zhao D. 1990: 225–6). The advantage of the Land Equalisation System was that it lowered the threshold for rebuilding household farms.

Such a package is often regarded as state land ownership of the 'Asiatic Mode of Production' type. Superficially, it seems to have been. However, one should not be confused by the face value of land ownership. The essence of the Land Equalisation System was twofold: (1) it was a lifetime tenure, and (2) it was convertible to private land ownership through privatisation. A lifetime lease was the next best thing after private land ownership, with secured landholding for farming without the impact of market mechanisms. As a good alternative, the system was inherited by the following Sui and Tang dynasties and was carried out on a larger scale (Li L. AD 738: vol. 3; Liang F. 1980: 476–85). Not only did the affected area expand to south China, where the Xianbeis had not reached, but also the land plot for each family increased: according to statistics collated by Liang Fangzhong (1980: 7), under the Tang the average land area per household was 160.45 *mu* (in AD 755), much larger than the Xianbei norm. More importantly, there was no difficulty for the state in privatising the land plots under the system when the surveillance costs grew to an unmanageable level, as happened during the Tang (Zheng X. *et al.* 1984: 171–93).

After the Tang, attempts were made twice more under the Tartar Jin and Ming to revive the universal Land Equalisation System, both short-lived because of the mounting surveillance costs, or simply the diminishing returns. The Tartars' system was called 'Land Allocation According to Clan Members' (*jiko shoudi*), mainly designed for the Tartars themselves. It played a central role in converting the nomad conquerors (now in north China) to settled farmers. The land was soon privatised (Zhao D. 1990: 444–5). The Ming state adopted a scheme called 'Land Allocation According to Population' (*jimin shoutian*) in 1370–2 as a temporary means to re-establish landholding family farms. The scheme was applied to unclaimed land after the war. Again the land was later privatised (*ibid.*: 497).

But the system continued in the form of 'Agricultural Colonies' (*tuntian*), which were established under all the dynasties after the Tang (Lee 1969: 73, 85–6, 104, 113, 117; Liang F. 1980: 322–8, 360–4, 420–2, 464; Zhao D. 1990: 444–5, 497). By 1887, for example, Qing agricultural colonies spread in 18 of the 23 provinces and occupied 3.4 million hectares (509,300 *qing*), about 6 per cent of the total cultivated land of the country (Liang F. 1980: 384–5). To the colonies, the same principle of the long leasehold of land was applied with the same propensity to privatise land.

## GRAND BUREAU FOR AGRICULTURAL EXTENSION

Before the Mongol Yuan, the Chinese bureaucracy had had a long history of official posts in charge of agricultural production. But these officials often did not run a government department devoted exclusively to agriculture. A turning point occurred around 1200 when the Agriculture Promotion Bureau (*quannongsi*) was patented by the Tartar Jin, a nomadic conquest régime in north China. The new organisation lasted, on and off, for a total of five years during about 1200–22 (Lü Z. 1994: 189, 313). It seems that the Tartars had problems in agricultural administration. Before they were able to solve them, the Mongols came, so the new system had no time to develop fully.

The idea did not, however, die with the demise of the Tartar Jin. It was taken over by the Mongols, who reinvented the administration with a well-structured network with Grand Commissioner of Agriculture (*dasinong*) at the top, Grand Minister of Agriculture (*dasinongqing*) and Junior Minister of Agriculture (*dasinong shaoqing*) in the middle and numerous officers at the bottom. The agricultural officials at the lower ranks were assigned specialised missions: the Commissioner of Agricultural Colonies (*tuntianshi*) dealt with the establishment and maintenance of agricultural colonies, often in remote regions; while the Commissioner of Rice Cultivation (*dushui yongtianshi*) took charge of paddy farming in the south (Lü Z. 1994: 664, 901–4; see also Langlois 1981: 41). At the grass-roots level, the Yuan rural population was systematically organised into farming groups of 50 households each (*she*), and a skilful elderly farmer was appointed head (*shezhang*) to take charge of tillage and vigilance (Zheng Z. 1938: 202). Considering the coercive discipline of the militant Mongols, the impetus they gave to the recovery and growth of Chinese agriculture was likely to be very great.

The Grand Bureau for Agricultural Extension system showed the Mongol government priorities in terms of policy. This is particularly evident when the highest ranks of the officials in charge of agriculture in different periods are compared to those under the Yuan (see Table 5.4). At the First Grade Minus (*congyipin*), the rank of the Mongol Grand Commissioner of Agriculture was next only to that of Prime Minister. It was the highest for an agricultural

*Table 5.4* Comparison of ranks of agricultural officials

| Period | Name | Grade[a] |
|--------|------|-------|
| Xia | *Nongshi* (Agriculturist) | — |
| Zhou | *Nongzheng* (Agriculturist) | — |
| | *Daoren* (Master of Rice Production) | — |
| Spring and Autumn | *Nong* (Agriculturist) | — |
| Qin | *Nongcheng* (Minister of Agriculture) | — |
| Han | *Dasinongcheng* (Grand Minister of Agriculture) | 5th |
| Three Kingdoms | *Diannong zhonglangjiang* | |
| | (Agricultural Supervisor, the Middle Rank) | 6th |
| Jin | *Danong* (Grand Agriculturist) | 6th |
| Song (Southern Dynasties) | *Danong* (Grand Agriculturist) | 6th |
| Northern Wei | *Dasinongqing* (Grand Minister of Agriculture) | 3rd⁺ |
| Northern Qi | *Sinongqing* (Minister of Agriculture) | 3rd |
| Sui, Tang, Song | *Sinongqing* (Minister of Agriculturae) | 3rd⁺ |
| Tartar Jin | *Quannongshi* (Agriculture Commissioner) | 3rd⁺ |
| Ming | *Sinongsiqing* (Minister of Agriculture) | 3rd⁺ |
| Qing | — | — |
| | | |
| Mongol Yuan | *Dasinong* (Grand Commissioner of Agriculture) | 1st⁻ |
| | *Dasinongqing* (Grand Minister of Agriculture) | 2nd⁺ |
| | *Dasinong shaoqing* (Junior Minister of Agriculture) | 2nd⁻ |
| | *Tuntianshi* (Commissioner of Agricultural Colonies) | 3rd⁺ |
| | *Dushui yongtianshi* (Commissioner of Rice Cultivation) | 3rd⁺ |
| | *Dasinongcheng* (Agricultural Officer) | 3rd⁻ |
| | *Yingtianshi* (Officer of Agricultural Colonies) | 5th⁺ |
| | *Dasinongsi jingli* (Office Secretary of Ministry of Agriculture) | 5th⁻ |

*Sources*: Based on Anon. *c.* 3rd century BC: ch. 'Duan'; ZW 1963: 1893; Lü Z. 1994: 313, 400–1, 497, 664, 850, 871, 874, 878, 881, 890, 898, 901–4.

*Note*

a The dual ranking system with plus and minus for each grade.

official throughout the entire history of China. Other Yuan ranks for agriculture-related posts were much higher than their counterparts during other periods (the smaller the number, the higher the ranking). The new policies and institutions in the Mongol campaign to promote farming yielded handsome economic returns for the Mongols. Between 1282 and 1329, collected from the south as tax and administered by Ministry of Revenue (*hubu*), a total of 6.2 million tonnes of grain (83 million *shi*) was shipped from south China to north China under the government food supply scheme (see Liang F. 1980: 329–30). The importance of the southern grain supply was shown by the fact that (1) the shipping was organised in a military fashion to ensure its delivery; and (2) soon after a peasant rebellion cut the grain transport routes, the Mongol régime collapsed (Li C. 1370: ch. 'Shihuo, Haiyun').

The Mongol government also acted like an authentic Chinese one in controlling domestic and international trade. For instance, tax payment in silk was imposed on the Chinese, and the government monopolised the silk sold to the Arabs for revenue. By the end of the Mongol conquest the tradition of agricultural dominance and physiocracy were both re-established by the Mongols, which can be defined as a status of quasi-trinary structure. When Zhu Yuanzhang and his rebel followers tore down the Mongol Yuan, the first thing he did was to make good his early promise of land and land ownership to the peasantry, a promise which had been manifested along with the restoration of Chinese rule. Before long, the full-blooded trinary structure was rebuilt under the Ming. Indeed, regarding the trinary structure, the difference during the fourteenth century between the Yuan and Ming was only marginal. Even without the interference of the Ming rebels, the pendulum would have swung back in full to the trinary optimum.

QING FARMING EXPERT SYSTEM

Under Qing law, successful farmers were regarded as farming experts and awarded the formal position of Eighth Grade Plus (*bapin*) to assist scholar-officials with agricultural planning and management (Cheng Q. 1865 vol. 9: 635; Lee 1969: 117). Evidence shows that some agricultural experts were promoted to posts at the Qing court. Li Yinggui, an experienced rice grower who specialised in double cropping, became a personal friend of Emperor Kangxi and was assigned to a nationwide project to promote a new high-yield rice variety which was discovered by the emperor himself (Kong X. 1983).[2]

### 5.3.4.3 Restoration of the peasant household economy

Under the Land Equalisation System, free peasants began to operate their household economy, which is explained in Jia Sixie's *Essential Techniques for the Peasantry* (*Qimin Yaoshu*). First, peasants had a wide range of choices after meeting the requirements of the government. In Jia's book, such choices include 16 cereal species, 18 vegetable species, 15 tree species and 10 domestic animal species. Second, details are given regarding the making of compost (four plant types with their sowing, growing and cutting times), essential for the maintenance of soil nutrients under the relatively intensive farming of the family farms. This shows the self-sufficient nature of these household farms (Miao Q. 1982: 24, 111, 128, 143). Third, great emphasis was placed on the management of the household economy, which occupies as much as 37 per cent of the book's length. The instruction for trade management exemplifies the author's precepts:

Go to market often and observe with care. Whenever you come across pregnant animals, buy them. Foals and calves become independent weanlings in 150 days. For lambs, it takes only 60 days.... The dams can be resold to get the investment money back. The sale of the foals and calves then becomes the profit. The money can be used to buy more pregnant animals. Within a year the capital is able to circulate twice on cattle, horses and donkeys, four times on sheep and goats.

(Jia S. *c.* AD 534/1982: 319)

With instructions for handling market activity, Jia frankly claims that 'To become rich, handicrafts are preferable to agriculture, and commerce to handicrafts' (*ibid.*: 350). There is little doubt that the individual household economy was restored and thrived under the Xianbei Land Equalisation System, which was highly compatible with the Chinese trinary structure.

The Qing was known as a period of hyper-growth of population: the population took off after about 1740. Not only did it pass China's long-term average mark of 40.7 million, but it grew exponentially until by 1833 it had reached nearly 400 million (see Appendix I). Given (1) that the Chinese had a high 'population elasticity to income' (see Chapter 3), (2) that any significant increase in China's population depended on the general income level among the vast number of small farmers, and (3) that China's food importation and emigration/immigration were negligible prior to 1850, a growing population was a proxy for the general income and thus a proxy for the performance of the household economy. The Chinese peasant household economy not only recovered from the early Qing turmoil but also grew at an unprecedented rate.

## 5.4 Reinforcement of the trinary structure

It is convenient to blame external shocks such as invasions and conquests for economic damage and interruptions in economic development. But in pre-nineteenth-century China invasions and conquests can at most be viewed as factors delaying the 'expected process' of economic development. A reliable test lies in whether any fundamental change took place in China in the wake of the alien shocks. If such changes did occur, invasions and conquests should then bear the blame. However, if China returned to its old track after the ordeals, the external shocks had little to do with the consequence or fate of the society in the longer term no matter how unpleasant and destructive the shocks were. Thus, it is not very convincing to use invasions and conquests to explain why capitalist industrialisation did not grow fully in premodern China (see Tian C. 1986).

All things considered, although there is little doubt that the alien invasion and conquest of China were initially destructive, the restoration of the

Chinese system and socio-economic life largely cancelled out the negative impact of the conquests. The secret lies in the ability of the Chinese system to internalise, or more precisely its capacity to internalise, external shocks. All nomadic conquerors, no matter how reluctant they were, ended up being absorbed culturally and economically by the Chinese in the process of integration, as clearly demonstrated by the restoration of the Chinese socio-economic structure (particularly in the areas of bureaucracy and landholding) and the continuation of Chinese civilisation (typically in terms of the use of the Chinese language, the adoption of the Chinese state philosophy and the compilation of the official histories of the overthrown native Chinese dynasties.

Ultimately, it was the overwhelming material returns from the process of 'Sinicisation' that gave the nomadic conquerors the incentive to integrate with the Chinese. These returns were the result of the way the trinary structure worked. For the Chinese, this integration was a process of counter-conquest. It was in nature a long-term economic victory of the Chinese over an immediate, short-term military triumph of the nomads. It was the former that counted in the end.

Like the peasant rebellions, the barbarian conquests – violent and brutal as they were – actually consolidated the trinary structure and equilibrium, a result which was almost certainly contrary to the initial intention of the invaders. This phenomenon can be defined as the 'Trojan horse effect': the Chinese cultural and economic achievements worked as the horse to the captors, a spoil of war that delivers unexpected consequences in favour of the original owner of the horse. Arguably, the efficiency of the reinforcement lay in the long-term unchallenged superiority of Chinese technology and economy over China's nomadic neighbours in premodern times.

The reinforcement was constant both in terms of external pressure due to the nomads' standing by for a kill and in the form of external shock as the invaders marched in. It can be argued that the Chinese–nomad competition resulted in a 'ratchet effect' to upgrade Chinese technology. In the long term, China's superiority was thus underpinned, rather than undermined, by the lasting pressure from the northern nomads who stood by for a kill across the Great Walls, as illustrated in Figures 5.1 and 5.2. For the Chinese trinary structure, it was a win–win situation regardless, as long as the pressure and shocks were from an economy that was less advanced than China's.

So, until European penetration in East Asia, the Chinese system remained virtually unbreakable. It was no accident that fundamental changes in Chinese society took place only after China's hard-earned supremacy suddenly disappeared when the Chinese navy, army and Boxer militias were defeated one after another by a small number of troops of the industrial powers following the Opium War (1840–2), when China's new-found inferiority was repeatedly exposed as seen in the disastrous outcomes of the Second Opium

War (1856–60, with Britain, France and the United States), the Sino-Franco War (1883–5) and Sino-Japanese War (1894–5).

## 5.5  Answer to the first paradox about China

China's resilience was deeply rooted in both micro- and macro-components of the Chinese system. The former was the landholding family farm and the latter the trinary framework. Evidently, the Chinese system managed to regulate internal corruption (peacefully or with violence by rebellions) and to internalise external shocks (so long as the shocks came from an inferior economy). As a result, through repeated 'reincarnations' back to the same species, China became the champion of the premodern world with the longest continuous history. This provides the key to understanding the first paradox about China: the long-term coexistence of shocks/disasters and perpetuation of the Chinese system.

## Notes

1  The designation *semuren* was at that time applied to Caucasians of Asia Minor and beyond with coloured eyes. The Mongols employed them in large numbers to undertake administrative duties at different levels in China. That was the reason why Marco Polo was appointed as a high-ranking official working for the Yuan Imperial Court.

2  The Qing farming expert system set up a precedent for Communist China. Under Mao's wing, Chen Yonggui (1914–86), an ordinary farmer in rural Shanxi, was promoted at breakneck speed in a space of less than ten years to Deputy Prime Minister and Member of the Politburo of the Chinese Communist Party.

# 6

# CONCLUSION

Deadlock in economic development

## 6.1 Supra-stability of the trinary structure

The essence of this study is to show how ideology (including Confucianism), the state (including the monarch and elite administrative class) and landholding system (freehold and leasehold) interacted with and matched each other, and what impacts they had on the economy.

The establishment of the trinary structure, which wove the economic, social and political lives of the Chinese neatly together, was the result of long trial and error. During the process, the sustained military strength played a critical role among the vying political units on the East Asian mainland. After that, the structure was jealously guarded by the winner, first the Zhou Kingdom, which laid the foundation for Chinese civilisation, and later the Qin, which built the Chinese Empire. From the Han Period onwards, the system gradually perfected itself with self-regulating devices to check corruption/alienation of the system, either from the top down, involving initiatives of the state, or from the bottom up, with the activities of rebelling masses. The self-regulation mechanism also included a 'side way', by which nomadic invasions and conquests could be internalised.

The way in which the trinary structure benefited Chinese society was fourfold: (1) to allocate resources, labour, land and capital, as seen from the stability of the economy of the empire; (2) through such allocation, to provide the population with employment and to ensure adequate basic living standards for ordinary people most of the time, as seen from China's population growth and the expansion of the economy; (3) to accommodate non-agricultural activities in society most of the time, as shown from the high degree of commercialisation, urbanisation and monetarisation of the economy as well as the maintenance of a standing army and bureaucracy, both of stable size; and (4) to improve ordinary people's living standards from time to time as shown by China's periodical prosperity and glory until the eighteenth century. These in turn formed the ultimate *raison d'être* for the structure to continue. This *raison d'être* was as much socio-political as socio-economic.

The main achievement under the structure was the periodic trinary equilibrium, although some demanding conditions were to be met, especially the balancing of the internal tensions within the structure. The main consequences of the structure were two: (1) spatially speaking, the expansion of China's territory to the geographic limits for an agrarian economy to operate; (2) and temporally speaking, the perpetuation of the empire. So, although it experienced crisis after crisis, the empire revived, which differentiated China from the other dinosaurs – the Egyptian, Babylonian, Byzantine, Roman and Mayan empires.

The core of the Chinese trinary structure was China's landholding system; and both the state and ideology (here, Confucianism) can be regarded as economic devices to maintain this structure (see North 1981: chs 3, 5 and 6). As explained in Chapter 2, the foundation of this landholding system was 'absolute land ownership by individuals' (for the term see Macfarlane 1978: ch. 4). Such ownership type went hand in hand with the formation, development and perpetuation of the Chinese peasantry as we know it. It is claimed that in England the development of such ownership marked the demise of the traditional peasantry (*ibid.*: especially p. 94). In terms of the making of the Chinese institutions, the Chinese peasantry did contribute to the early victory of the agrarian kingdoms of the Zhou and Qin. The nomadic conquests are owed the credit in 'fine-tuning' the institution as reflected by things like the Land Equalisation System.

As a macro-institution, the trinary structure was designed to equalise social and private costs and to balance social and private benefits, and thus to reward both individuals and society at the same time. The structure enabled the lowering and regulation of transaction costs (see North 1981). At the trinary equilibrium, where the transaction costs reached their lowest, China's economy flourished at a height that few other premodern societies were able to match. During the lower ebbs of socio-economic performance, deviations were, under normal circumstances, detected and corrected by the Chinese state to avoid crises simply in the state's interests. If this device failed, a peasant rebellion would reset the clock for the structure. Although unintentionally, the alien invasion and conquest of the nomads reinforced the structure. The present study shows that instead of gloating over the ruins of the Chinese trinary structure, the indigenous peasantry and alien nomads participated actively in its maintenance. All these made the trinary structure convergent, resilient and stable, as shown by China's two-millennium record until the end of the nineteenth century.

Moreover, the Chinese trinary structure was flexible enough to operate across seven time zones and three climatic zones with ten main soil types on the East Asian mainland (as at the end of the nineteenth century) where the Han Chinese maintained their position as the farming majority in society. It was also flexible enough to accommodate commercialisation as well as pressures and shocks, internal and external, from political corruption, armed rebellions, invasions and conquests. The structure was not a closed system. China sometimes welcomed foreign ideas, technology and peoples with open arms: for example, the wholesale adoption of Buddhism from the fifth century to around the tenth century; the persistent diffusion of wheat, rice, tea, cotton, maize, sweet potatoes and irrigation from prehistoric to early modern times; and the making of the Muslim ethnic group, the Hui (*huihui* or *huizu*, literally 'returnees [to Mecca]'), part-Middle-Eastern and part-Chinese, a result of intermarriage between Arab and Persian merchants and Chinese women since Tang times with the inflow of Muslim maritime activists. Forming the second largest ethnic group next to the Han Chinese in contemporary China, the Hui numbered 6.49 million people in 1980 (Grosvenor 1980).

It is thus not surprising that until the third quarter of the nineteenth century, China's political, military and economic power, which was generated under the trinary structure and its equilibrium, met little challenge from China's neighbouring civilisations. This unique structure differentiated China (relatively affluent and stable) from the ancient Egyptian Empire (stable but poor) and the ancient Roman Empire (well-off but unstable) (see North 1981: ch. 9). This was the third consequence in addition to the aforementioned spatial and temporal achievements.

China's stability meant, however, that the Chinese system was unable to generate sustained growth and revolutionary changes in the long term. Occasionally, though, the refraction of another path glimmered along China's 'designated path' as described in Chapters 2–4, which happened during the Han, Song and Qing periods. Most significant was the Song, during which China experienced multidimensional changes prior to any European influence: higher yields in farming were achieved, cash crops were produced, irrigation and transportation systems were improved, labour division and specialisation were furthered, internal migration and urbanisation increased, and trade grew. New inventions and innovations were achieved including credit and paper money (see Hartwell 1963, 1966; Shiba 1970; Elvin 1972: pt 2). Compared to its European counterpart, according to Eric L. Jones, Song China's superiority was of an all-round nature: in technology, commerce, transportation and public-goods investment (1988: 75). Most important of all, the Song economy appeared to have been well on its way to shaking off its timeless dependence on the agrarian sector (Jones 1988: 83). China came very close to the production level for the preparatory phase of industrialisation: the Song's total iron output (as in the eleventh century) reached 150,000 tons, which was approximately the same as that produced in Europe some seven hundred years later in 1700 on the eve of the Industrial Revolution (Jones 1981: 202). Given that the Chinese population in the first half of the eleventh century varied from 16.3 million to 22.3 million (Liang F. 1980: 7–8), China's per capita iron output is likely to have been 6.7–9.2 kg. Although such a comparison of face values of economic performance can sometimes be misleading (for the Indian case see Chandavarkar 1985: 628), the Song growth was real. It was quite another matter that it withered almost as quickly as it blossomed.

What strikes us most are two interrelated questions/problems. First, why did the Song growth wither so quickly? Or, although Ming–Qing growth was at times impressive, why did China not repeat its Song economic glory until the Opium War? Second, why did the long gap exist between 'economic revolutions', as they may be called, in premodern China? From the Han Period (which was marked by technological change in farming, with a new iron plough and a new cropping system) to the Song Period (during which change was not only technical but also structural to a degree), there was a gap of a millennium. From the Song revolution to the next breakthrough in the Westernisation Movement (*yangwu yundong*, 1870–95) and the 1898 'One-Hundred-Day Reform' (*bairi bianfa*), masterminded by high-ranking officials and involving Emperors Muzong (r. 1862–74) and Dezong (r. 1875–1908) – the Chinese version of the Japanese Meiji reform (1869–89) aiming at transplanting Western technology and institutions to boost the strength of the indigenous system – another millennium passed. The fruition of these revolutions was absorbed by the trinary structure. Therefore, although China has had sufficient time for indigenous sustained intensive growth, capitalism and industrialisation to take place, even today, the end of the twentieth century, mainland China still has difficulties in adopting and diffusing industrialisation and/or capitalism that have been imported from outside under various official schemes for modernisation. Obviously, from the Chinese experience 'sufficient time' was not the sufficient condition for those changes to take place. From the Meiji Japanese experience 'sufficient time' was not even a necessary condition for those changes. From this viewpoint, the approach of the 'sprouting of indigenous capitalism in China' (which suggests that China would have automatically entered capitalist or market industrialisation if sufficient time had been given) is utterly misleading, not to mention its naked counter-factual bias (for the approach see Han D. 1957; Sanlian Books 1957; Yin J. 1980; Fang X. 1981; Li W. 1981; Xu D. and Wu C. 1985).

Given the long life span of the Empire, the short-lived, one-off flirtation with revolutionary changes during the Han and Song periods indicates that premodern China had a higher threshold for socio-economic change in favour of sustained intensive growth and industrialisation than some societies across the Eurasian world. As the fourth consequence, a trade-off between the empire's spatial–temporal achievements and its further development, China was a hostile land for indigenous intensive growth and industrialisation to bear fruit.

The seemingly repeated failure to spearhead industrialisation with or without capitalism has been the core of China's enigma, especially as to why China did not maintain her momentum in progress after she came 'within a hair's breadth of industrialising' (Jones 1981: 160). Here, the use of the term of 'deadlock' can be justified in describing China's situation in comparison to other civilisations that managed to continue their growth (in terms of either 'industrialisation' or 'sustained intensive growth'). In essence, China's paradoxes, discussed in Chapter 1, and China's developmental deadlock are the two faces of the same coin: the paradoxes appear on one face and China's deadlock appears on the other. It reminds us of the dead-end path taken by some species extinct in the natural world in their evolutionary processes. If Darwin is right about natural selection, the number of species that fall into this category has been significant. One only has to mention the long list of species extinct prior to any human interference. This view should not be interpreted as static. The empire expanded and contracted all the time under the trinary structure and its economy fluctuated with identifiable cycles. Neither should the view be regarded as Eurocentric since this study does not judge China's performance according to a West European norm. Nor does it see anything 'wrong' with China's sterility in sustained intensive growth, industrialisation and/or capitalism. As in dealing with the natural world, where a comparison among different species is useful to see how they have coped with and adapted to their environments (as long as one does not impose the idea of converting the seemingly inferior species to another), a comparison between China and some other civilisations helps deepen our understanding of China's long saga. This necessitates a retrospect of the Song economic revolution.

## 6.2 The song and its extraordinariness

The Song challenges any view that China was completely sealed off from a higher degree of industrial and commercial development. The fundamental question is whether the Song was a normal dynasty. If the answer is 'yes', then why did such normality not repeat itself? If the answer is 'no', then what made the Song so different from the other mainstream dynasties?

### 6.2.1 *How did it begin and continue?*

The Song (both Northern and Southern) was a period of chronic crises: the government was extraordinarily weak, pressure from the Tartars and Mongols was mounting to an unprecedented degree, and the polarisation among landholders reached a record level. However, these factors alone did not make the Song unique since they had occurred before, although to different degrees. So, they themselves did not create a flaw in the Chinese system that allowed some unprecedented commercial growth to take place. Rather, the distinctiveness of this period lay in (1) a change in the governmental structure, (2) a change in landholding structure, and (3) a change in demographic distribution and redistribution between north and south. They were all related to Song institutions.

301

CONCLUSION

## 6.2.1.1  The Northern Song

### CHANGE IN THE GOVERNMENTAL STRUCTURE, ITS REASON AND IMPACT

The Song state was known for its impotence, which began to show from the very beginning of the dynasty. The failure successfully to defend China's frontiers, and then the whole of north China, was just one of the symptoms. The weak government was a result of a deliberate policy from the beginning of the dynasty under the first Song monarch, Zhao Kuangyin (Emperor Taizu, r. AD 960–76). Zhao was a shrewd conspirator who grabbed the throne by a military *coup d'état* (see Tuo T. 1345: ch. 'Biography of Emperor Taizu'). In constant fear of being toppled himself by a *coup d'état*, he copied Emperor Qin Shihuang (r. 221–210 BC) by systematically stripping army officers and civilian bureaucrats of their power, claiming military, financial, judicial decision-making as the exclusive responsibility of the Imperial Court (Zhao X. *et al.* 1987: 293–354; Tang J. and Zheng C. 1993: ch. 7). The Song administrative reform in essence aimed at removing the links between commanding officers and troops in the army and divorcing the nexus between official position and administrative responsibility in the bureaucracy. This policy was carried out over the entire life of the Northern Song.

On the other hand, with the legitimacy of the Song always questionable, Zhao Kuangyin needed to gain recognition and support from the citizens, especially the administrative class of Confucians. To win the support of Zhao's usurpatory régime among the literati and to compensate the bureaucrats for their loss of power, a package was delivered: not only were the Song bureaucrats paid higher salaries than any of their counterparts among all dynasties, but also, extra official positions were created to accommodate members of the literati. In terms of salaries, according to Song official records (Tuo T. 1345: pt 'Official Appointments'; Xu S. 1809: pt 'Official Appointments'; CBW 1978: 151), a scale in cash and in rent can be demonstrated as follows, excluding numerous regular allowances in kind such as fuel and materials for clothes (as during 1063–77):

| Position | Monthly salary (in coin) | Salary land (mu) |
| --- | --- | --- |
| Prime Minister | 300,000–400,000 | – |
| Deputy Prime Minister | 200,000 | – |
| Minister | 150,000 | 2,000 (116.0 ha) |
| Deputy Minister | 50,000 | – |
| Army General, First Rank | 60,000–200,000 | – |
| Army General, Second Rank | 25,000–80,000 | – |
| Army General, Third Rank | 20,000–30,000 | – |
| County magistrate | 12,000–22,000 | 100–200 (5.8–11.6 ha) |

As a comparison, it is known that during the Qing Period the salary of the highest rank, First Rank (*yipin*), was only 15 *liang* of silver, or 559.5 g (Sun X. 1988: 192–3), which was in nominal terms 15,000–30,000 bronze coins. Taking inflation into account, the Qing salary was probably even lower. In terms of multiplication of official posts, the increase was fivefold at the prefecture (*zhou*) and country (*xian*) levels. Officials were also allowed to hold as many as ten concurrent paid posts to fill the created vacancies for which they were paid but did not take charge (Yang Z. 1992: 283; Tian Z. 1994: 228–9). Moreover, positions were allowed to be inherited by officials' descendants, which to a great extent made the Imperial Examination-based bureaucrat recruitment system and meritocratic promotion mechanisms obsolete, these having been crucial in underpinning social mobility and maintaining the physiocratic touch to society (Pu J. 1990: 378–9; Yang Z. 1992: 277–9).

This change in government structure was a huge step away from the evolutionary trend of the Chinese bureaucratic development of the previous millennium which started at the beginning of the Han Dynasty. It clashed with the post-Han tradition in many areas. First, by the time the Song was established, Chinese society had developed to such a stage that a functional, sophisticated bureaucracy to run the empire was imperative. The Song's reshaping of the bureaucracy inevitably upset or even destroyed the existing social fabric and social order, as clearly shown by the large shifts of Chinese population between regions. Seond, by the tenth century AD, the Chinese Empire and its economy had developed to such a degree of complexity that it was impossible for a single centre to make all the decisions for the whole country. Attempts of this type led only to the paralysis of the system and, possibly, anarchy in society, which the Song state experienced and survived, having teetered on the brink of total collapse in its defence and administration. Third, through the one-thousand-year-long competition since the Qin Period between the Chinese and their neighbouring northern nomads, a 'ratchet effect' on technology and tactics developed to such a degree that any weakening on either side along the Great Walls became fatal. This was particularly true for the defending, agrarian Chinese. As shown in Table 5.1, between 985 and 1284 there were in all 214 major military conflicts between the nomads and the Chinese, by far the greatest frequency for any of the main dynasties. In most of these cases, China was the victim of an alien invasion (Fu Z. *et al.* 1986: 3–185). Obviously, China's weakness along the Great Wall defences created opportunities for the nomads to attack the empire. In the last resort, the Song's payment of annual ransom to the Tartars from AD 1005 onwards did not stop the Tartars' further invasion and conquest (Tian Z. 1994: 228). The fact that the Northern Song lost half its territory shows how heavy a price the Song paid. The competition between the northern nomads and the Chinese constantly sharpened the military edge of those nomadic tribes. It was thus no sheer accident that after they conquered the Chinese Empire, technically the most advanced society in Eurasia at that time, the Mongols swept triumphantly across much of the Eurasian continent.

The Song practices were in nature a systematic bribery on the largest scale that Chinese history had ever experienced. They effectively bought loyalty and defused attempts at a *coup d'état* but with severe side-effects in four main areas: (1) the collapse of bureaucratic surveillance which was designed to keep official corruption at a manageable level; (2) as a result, uncurbed corruption, official incompetence and government impotence, which the empire had tried to minimise or avoid; (3) a crack in the trinary structure due to the lack of physiocratic control over the economy which, after trial and error, had appeared to be an efficient device for China; and (4) weakening of Chinese national defence on which the survival and development of the Chinese civilisation heavily depended. In summary, the distrust of bureaucrats backfired and resulted in government inefficiency. This created opportunities for nomadic tribes to win the war against China, which in turn aggravated China's internal crises.

### CHANGE IN LANDHOLDING STRUCTURE, ITS REASON AND IMPACT

With the collapse of the government physiocratic surveillance, a change in landholding structure emerged. It is reported in the government census that record high tenancy rates – 41.7 per cent (in AD 980–9), 43.1 per cent (in 1029), 41.1 and 41.6 per cent (in 1034 and 1037, respectively) – were reached (Liang F. 1980: 126–9). From 980 through to 1099, the long-term average tenancy rate was 34.5 per cent among all farmers (*ibid.*), one of the longest-lasting periods with such a high tenancy rate ever reported in the empire's history.

The rise in the tenancy rate was at least partly due to the relaxation, or more correctly the impotence, of government landholding control. Although the empire was under pressure from the Tartars, the Northern Song territory was stable in the beginning with a size similar to that in the previous Han, Sui and Tang periods. Further, the Northern Song population peak (46.7 million as at AD 1110) was lower than the peaks of the previous Han (59.6 million at AD 2 and 56.5 million at AD 157) and Tang (52.9 million at AD 755), about the same as the Sui (46 million at AD 609) (Liang F. 1980: 4–8).[1] Thus, there is no reason to assume that the Song Period had experienced a population explosion since an absolute shortage of land in terms of absolute deterioration in the man-to-land ratio did not occur. Rather, the high tenancy rate, probably 5–10 percentage points higher than the 'physiocratic norm', was caused by landholding concentration with fewer landowners having the same land in aggregate, which was a situation of relative land shortage.

This change in landholding structure resulted in a landless mass, which from time to time became an explosive issue. To respond to deteriorating landholding and land ownership, from AD 990 to the end of the Northern Song (1127), several mass rebellions broke out under the leadership of Wang Xiaobo and Li Shun (AD 993), Zhao Yanshun (AD 1000), Wang Lun and Zhang Hai (1043), Wang Ze (1047), Fang La (1120–1) and Song Jiang (1120–7) (see Zhang S. and Zheng X. 1983: 450–1; Fu Z et al. 1986: 24–5, 41, 71).

The government response to the tenancy problem and its resulting rebellions was to enlarge the standing army. The Song armed forces increased from 120,000 in AD 960 to 378,000 in 976, and continued to rise to 666,000 by 997 (out of a total population of some 16 million), to 912,000 (out of a total population of 19.9 million) by 1021, then to 1,259,000 by 1048 and finally to a record level of 1,400,000 in 1049 (out of a total population of some 22.3 million) (Liang F. 1980: 7–8; Zhao X. et al. 1987: 300–1; Tian Z. 1994: 228). In absolute terms, the increase was over elevenfold with an annual increase rate of 2.8 per cent. In relative terms, the increase was 150 per cent regarding the proportion of soldiers in the total population. The idea was to kill two birds with one stone: (1) to reduce unemployment so as to reduce civil unrest, and (2) to strengthen national defence to minimise external shocks.

The Song soldiers were exceptionally well paid. It is recorded that during the reign of Zhiping (1064–7) each soldier of the elite troops (jinjun) was paid 50,000 bronze coins per year and each soldier in the ordinary troops (xiangjun) 30,000. It was compulsory by Song law for a soldier to remain in service till the age of 61 (Zhao X. et al. 1987: 334). The troops thus formed a permanent deduction from the taxpaying labour force. It is reasonable to assume that (1) on average each solder had an immediate family of five persons, and (2) the families of those soldiers were able to live on the army allowance. Therefore, the Song defence budget was likely to have maintained as much as 21–32 per cent of the total population. To maintain this large and well-fed army cost the Song 48,000–50,000 million bronze coins a year, about 80 per cent of total government expenses (see Zhao X. et al. 1987: 334–5; Wang S. 1995: 771–3; cf. P. J. Smith 1991: 8).

No doubt, this practice greatly offset the impact of the high tenancy rate and brought the unemployment rate down to a manageable level. But at the same time it resulted in an enormous financial burden on the economy. The strategy to buy peace from the Tartars with silver (100,000–200,000 liang, or 3.7–7.4 tonnes a year) and silk cloth (200,000–300,000 rolls a year) added more to the defence expenditure (Tian Z. 1994: 228). But with the number of landowners declining and the powerful large landowners enjoying tax exemption, the tax base shrank sharply. It has been estimated that before the 1069 land-tax reform under Wang Anshi (AD 1021–86) only 30 per cent of the land under cultivation actually bore tax (Zhou B. 1981: 249). Although the information is scattered, government overspending, which occurred from the beginning of the Northern Song, reflected such a situation (based on Wang S. 1995: 678–86):

| Year | Revenue ($10^6$ coins) | Expenditure ($10^6$ coins) | Balance |
|---|---|---|---|
| Northern Song | | | |
| 997 | 70,893 | 86,950 | −16,057 |
| 1007(?) | 47,211 | 49,749 | −2,538 |
| 1021 | 140,298 | 168,044 | −27,746 |
| 1048 | 122,592 | 111,785 | 10,807 |
| 1049 | 126,252 | ±126,252 | ±0 |
| 1064 | 101,906 | 100,399 | 1,507 |
| 1065 | 116,138 | 120,343 | −4,205 |
| 1086 | 82,491 | 91,910 | −9,419 |
| Southern Song | | | |
| 1190 | 68,001 | ±68,001 | ±0 |
| 1253(?) | 120,000 | 250,000 | −130,000 |

The Treasury then introduced a discount on the tax payments (*zhebian*) at a rate as high as 50 per cent to increase the actual tax revenue (Zheng X. *et al.* 1984: 255). Also, a poll tax on males aged between 20 and 60 years (*shending qian*) was introduced. In 1011, the poll tax revenue reached 45 million coins, about three times that from the tax on agriculture (*xiashui*) (Hou W. 1992: 913). Desperate measures, they helped little. It is reported in 1065 that the Song Treasury had a total budget deficit of 157,200 million bronze coins (Tuo T. 1345: entry 'Accounting' of ch. 'Economy'). From the data for the Song defence budget (48,000–50,000 million bronze coins a year) and its share in the government expenses (80 per cent), this amount of deficit was equivalent to 2.5–2.6 years of total government expenses. There is little doubt that by the time Wang Anshi launched his land-tax reform, the Song state had practically gone broke.

To reverse the crisis, the Song state was forced to seek alternative sources of revenue beyond the traditional agricultural sector. Commerce was chosen as the income generator. Since China's traditional overland trading routes linking China and Asia Minor were lost to the Tartars and Mongols, new routes had to be found in the south, mainly across the waters to connect China with South and Southeast Asia and East Africa. Maritime trade was thus viewed particularly favourably by the authorities as a source of easy money, and comprehensive methods were employed to promote foreign trade. First, an initiative was taken by the Northern Song government to reach out to lure foreign traders. In AD 987, Emperor Taizong (r. AD 977–97) sent eight court officials along four sea routes to advertise Sino-foreign trade opportunities (see Xu S. 1809: ch. 'Zhiguan 44'). Second, customs law was established in 1080 to reassure the merchants of non-interference from individual officials and of the fixed duty rates (Li C. 1370: ch. 'Shihuo Zhi, Shibo'). The Northern Song tax rate on traded goods varied between 2 and 5 per cent (Tuo T. 1345 vol. 186 ch. 'Economy'; see also Li Z. 1991), which was favourable to traders. Third, both stick and carrot were used to keep merchants astir. Official titles were granted to those who were able to attract imports (Xu S. 1809: ch. 'Zhiguan 44'). The beneficiaries included foreigners: for example, the title of 'General of Submission to Virtue' ( *guide jiangjun*) was conferred by the Imperial Court on Xinya Tuoluo, a merchant of Arab origin (see Deng D. 1986: 85). Meanwhile, customs officials closely watched merchants' performance. On some occasions, officials picked up names from a government registration list and sent reluctant merchants overseas by force (Xu S. 1809: chs 'Zhiguan' and 'Xingfa'). Fourth, under a quasi-privatisation scheme, a less profitable market was left for professional merchants to operate so that the government was able to concentrate on the most profitable ones. The former included the traditionally monopolised 'key markets' of salt, tea and wine (Zhou B. 1981: 269–75), and the latter included imported medicine. Under the 'Law of Market Trade' (*shiyi fa*), the Pharmacy of the Imperial Medical Bureau (*taiyiju maiyaosuo*) monopolised imported medicine for guaranteed revenue through resale (Wang H. 1982: 64). In 1077, at Port Canton (Guangzhou) alone, some 19 tonnes (32,000 *jin*) of frankincense was dealt with by this system (Liang T. *c.* 1861: vol. 3); and between 1076 and 1078 an amount of frankincense worth 1,536.6 million bronze coins was resold by the Song state to the domestic market, averaging 512.2 million a year (see Deng D. 1986: 100). Fifth, government direct investment in profiteering was made. The scale of this activity was such that in 1125, the government budgeted and allocated 100 million bronze coins for each of the three Bureaux for Maritime Trade in Ningbo, Hangzhou and Guangzhou (Xu S. 1809: ch. 'Zhiguan 44'). If it is supposed that (1) a total yearly investment through these three bureaux was 300 million bronze coins, as in 1125 (*ibid.*), and (2) all the investment was used for the trade of frankincense, the profit rate would be as high as over 70 per cent. Finally, port cities were deliberately nurtured to lay 'golden eggs'. Quanzhou in Fujian Province was one of them. In AD 976 alone, the city paid the government a levy in kind of (1) imported goods of 105 tonnes (176,000 *jin*), including 6 tonnes of ivory (10,000 *jin*), and (2) 61,000 rolls (*pi*) of silk cloth. In addition, there were monetary payments of 1 tonne of silver (27,000 *liang*) and 2,010 million bronze coins (see Zhuang W. *et al.* 1989: 16–19). Given that in AD 980, the population in Quanzhou consisted of 96,581 households (see Liang F. 1980: 135), each household would have to bear a burden of 1.8 *jin* of imported goods, 0.6 roll of silk cloth, 0.3 *liang* of silver and 20,800 bronze coins. Not surprisingly, it was during the Northern Song Period that China's maritime trade first flourished: according to Zhao Rukuo's work written in 1125, entitled *Records of Foreign Peoples* (*Zhufan Zhi*), there were 17 foreign destinations for China's porcelain exports.

Meanwhile, the Song government invented an inflationary policy with a steady increase in the money supply. From AD 1024 onwards, the Northern

Song government regularly issued paper currency (*jiaozi* and *qianyin*) to meet the payment requirements and thus kept the economy going. The face value of the first batch aggregated 3,884.6 million bronze coins. The face value of the issue increased to 13,316.3 million coins in 1103 and 1105, respectively (Liu S. 1993a; 1993b: 24–6)

It is obvious that the Song trade policy was in nature a contingent measure to ease the financial crisis of the government rather than a well-thought-out development plan for the economy. Ultimately, the crisis was caused by the changes in government structure and landholding structure. From the practice of 'sending merchants to do business by force' and the monopoly on imported medicine, there is good reason to believe that the traders' activities were not all free and voluntary. The heavy levy imposed on port cities reveals further the rent-seeking nature of the Song trade policy (see P. J. Smith 1991: 305–18). Nevertheless, the Song proto-mercantilism did create some room for large-scale trade to grow.

LARGE-SCALE POPULATION SHIFTING TO THE SOUTH: ITS REASON AND IMPACT

After the tenth century, during the Tang Period, the empire's southward expansion came to a halt. The new territory was reclaimed and southern agriculture developed with its characteristic of paddy farming. Northerners began to migrate to the new land to make a living. During the Northern Song, the south became doubly appealing because in the north, where the government control was tighter, the heavy taxes killed farmers' incentive to till. In contrast, the south, where land was less controlled by powerful landowners and population was less controlled by the Song state, offered hope. That the emigrants from the north were labelled 'tax dodgers' (*taohu*) explains well the nature of this phenomenon (Li J. 1957: 184–5). It was thus to a great extent an institution-pushed migration.

This southbound migration took place on a large scale. It is reported that in AD 996, within a month 10,285 households 'escaped' from 14 counties in Shaanxi Province in the north to evade taxation (Li J. 1957: 185). With the northern and northwestern frontiers now blocked by the Tartars, these tax dodgers almost certainly went south. Meanwhile, in China's southernmost province, Guangdong, the northern immigrants made up some 40 per cent of the total population during the Song (Tian F. and Chen Y. 1986: 49–50; see also Eberhard 1962; Elvin 1973: 204–15), and their language, which was basically a northern dialect called *kejia* (or *hakka*, meaning 'the dialect of the immigrants'), has been the most spoken dialect in Guangdong next to the indigenous Cantonese. Other provinces on the way to Guangdong (such as Hubei, Hunan, Jiangxi, Fujian and Guizhou) were almost certainly hit equally hard by this wave of immigrants.

This migration quickly changed the geographic distribution of China's population. At the beginning of the Northern Song Period, the ratio between the northern residents and their southern counterparts was close to unity (0.91:1). In 1102, as the official census shows, the ratio became 0.5:1 (Liang F. 1980: 152–60). By then, the population in the south had surpassed that of the north by 115 per cent as some 70 per cent of the population were now living in the area south of the Yangzi River (see Table 6.1). Soon, the south became overcrowded and a problem of land scarcity developed. Desperate farmers in the south built plots on wooden rafts in order to use water-surface space, as recorded and recommended in *Chen Fu's Treatise on Agriculture*, written in 1149 and dealing exclusively with southern agricultural practice (Ji Y. 1782 vol. 730: 174).

Abandoning physiocratic control, the Northern Song state did little, from an institutional point of view, to ease the land shortage crisis. However, the Song state did make efforts to improve the grain-yield level to ease the demographic pressure on land resources in the south. It is reported that Emperor Renzong (r. 1023–63) sent his envoy from Fujian to Champa (now in Vietnam) with treasure to exchange for an early-ripening rice variety,

*Table 6.1*  Changes in geographic distribution of China's population

| Year (AD) | South | North | North:South ratio |
|---|---|---|---|
| A | *Tang (in $10^6$)* | *Tang (in $10^6$)* | |
| 713 | 3.2* | 4.3* | 1.3 |
| B | *Northern Song (in $10^6$)* | *Northern Song (in $10^6$)* | |
| 980 | 3.2* | 2.9* | 0.9 |
| 1085 | 9.7* | 5.7* | 0.6 |
| 1102 | 31.1 | 14.4 | 0.5 |
| C | *Southern Song (in $10^6$)* | *Tartar Jin (in $10^6$)* | |
| 1159 | 16.8 | — | — |
| 1187 | 24.3 | 44.7 | 1.8 |
| 1190 | 28.5 | 45.4 | 1.6 |
| 1195 | 27.8 | 48.5 | 1.7 |
| 1207 | 27.8 | 53.3 | 1.9 |
| 1234 | 28.3 | — | — |
| 1264 | 13.0 | — | — |
| D | *Mongol Yuan (in $10^6$)* | *Mongol Yuan (in $10^6$)* | |
| 1290 | 50.4 | 9.1 | 0.2 |
| E | *Ming (in $10^6$)* | *Ming (in $10^6$)* | |
| 1393 | 45.1 | 15.5 | 0.3 |

*Source*: Based on Liang F. 1980: 96–113, 130–7, 141–8, 152–60, 168, 207.

*Note*
An asterisk indicates number of households.

which was then distributed in the Yangzi River Valley region. As targeted, land utilisation in the south was dramatically intensified by the adoption of the introduced species (see Ho 1956; Eberhard 1977: 254–6). Although the impact of the spread of the early-ripening rice was revolutionary in China,[2] it did not completely offset the impact of population pressure in the south. As we will see, the population shifted back to the north on the same scale during the Southern Song, partly for landholding purposes.

Eventually, many immigrants to the south had to give up farming completely and to take up careers outside the agricultural sector, such as silk processing and commerce. Reflecting such a trend, the Southern Song government downplayed the importance of the tax on farming and concentrated on the poll tax (Hou W. 1992: 913). Fortunately, the agricultural productivity in the south was high enough to have little difficulty in supporting a large non-agricultural population. This is compatible with Perkins's estimation that during the Song Period around 20 to 30 per cent of China's farm produce was exchanged within local areas (1969: 117), almost certainly between the tillers and the local non-farming individuals.

In this context, not only did the attitude of the bureaucracy towards merchants shift, but the overpaid, financially well-off officials had the greatest ever propensity to participate in commercial ventures. It is reported that profit-seeking became the priority of Song officialdom, with officials involved in commercial activities, violating laws and insatiably pursuing profits (see Tuo T. 1345: ch. 'Lizong San'). Their operations covered a wide range of interests such as hotels, wineries, and the wholesale and retailing of tea and salt in both the domestic and overseas markets (Tang K. 1993). Not only were public funds embezzled by officials for their commercial ventures, but also sweatshops were established in the government sector, even including the imperial army (*ibid.*: 120–1). Although some efforts were made by the Imperial Court to curb what may be called the 'commercialisation of the Song bureaucracy' with symbolic dismissals and executions of some notorious offenders,[3] there is little evidence to show any fundamental behavioural change among Song officials. One thesis explaining the failure of China's northern border defence during the Northern Song is that the strength of the imperial army was significantly weakened by the rampant commercial activities of officers (*ibid.*: 122). Here, what would surprise Weberians is that on the whole in Song times there was very little check from orthodox Confucianism on such a trend of business–bureaucracy collaboration: for the Northern Song authorities, the main concern about commercialisation in bureaucracy was not that trade should be banned but whether officials should be allowed to scramble too much for profit in the market *vis-à-vis* ordinary citizens (see Tang K. 1993). This departing from orthodox Confucianism was part of the Song institutional change.

One consequence was that the power of the market was unleashed in the short run to reach its potential at the time with the unprecedented development of commercialisation. The Song economic revolution was born.

### 6.2.1.2 The Southern Song

The loss of the north to the Tartars cut back the Song revenue source almost overnight. Considering that what was lost was the well-established northern breadbaskets, the Loess Plateau and North Plain, the impact on the Song economy was devastating. However, the trends of the Northern Song continued during the Southern Song, namely changes in government and land-holding and the rise of commercialisation, and so did the problems such as weak government, broken national defence, heavy taxation and a budget deficit. The only change was a shift in the direction of people's migration.

It is clear from Table 6.1 that from the early eighth century to the fourteenth century, the overall direction of internal migration in the long term was to the south. What seems puzzling is that the tide changed in the opposite direction during the Southern Song Period when the Tartar Jin and Southern Song régimes coexisted. First, considering the coexistence of these two régimes, one would think that it would have been natural for the Han Chinese population to have packed into the south to avoid the alien conquerors in the north. Second, considering that the south was not a war zone, one would expect that the south not to have lost a large proportion of its population. Third, considering the violent process of alien conquest, one would imagine that north China would lose a sizeable proportion of its population and that its recovery would have needed time. Yet by 1187 the northern population under the Tartars had increased over threefold from its pre-conquest level in 1102 with a minimum annual increase rate of 1.3 per cent, as if the war had never taken place. If the population loss during the war of conquest is taken into account, the rate of increase in the north is certainly much greater. Comparatively, in the south, where peace was to a great extent retained, the population dropped by 46 per cent in 1102–59, with an annual negative growth rate of 1.4 per cent. Percentagewise, the gain and loss matched nicely, maybe too nicely. But if the natural population growth rates in the north and south were similar, and thus constant, this would happen. The dramatic population shift thus indicates two things: first, the loss of the Southern Song population was to a great extent a gain of the Tartar Jin; second, the reverse migration of the Chinese population to the north was voluntary and ethnicity was not a consideration.

REASONS FOR THE REVERSE MIGRATION

At least four key factors, two from the Song side and two from the Tartar side, contributed to the reverse population shift. First, owing to the structural changes during the Northern Song Period, China was weakened and consequently lost its northern half. The Song's humiliating failure to defend China along the Great Walls dramatically changed the image of the indigenous government in the eyes of the Chinese population, which seriously undermined the government's credibility, legitimacy and authority. What made it worse was that in 1129, to escape from the Tartars, Emperor Gaozong (r. 1127–62) exiled himself with a fleet from Mingzhou (now Ningbo, Jiangsu Province) and remained at sea for four long months (Zhang X. 1986: 54). History repeated itself later. To escape from the Mongols, the last Song emperors, the brothers Zhao Shi (r. 1276–8) and Zhao Bing (r. 1278–9), followed in Emperor Gaozong's footsteps and once again found refuge at sea, this time for four years (Zhang X. 1986: 54–5). The Song monarch in effect abandoned the empire in order to save his own neck. This was the ultimate betrayal of his Chinese subjects and a total violation of the Confucian rule of 'People as the Foundation' (*minben*). This was particularly serious given the overcentralisation of the Song state, with which the emperor's responsibility increased exponentially. It was a miracle that the Southern Song did not collapse within these crucial months.

Second, when the exiled Song government withdrew to the south, a large number of bureaucrats and troops went with it. The old problems of overspending and budget deficit recurred under the Southern Song. Evidence shows that by 1196 the Southern Song government payroll had some 42,000 officials and over 400,000 military personnel. The total wage bills for theses two groups reached 5,000 million and 80,000 million bronze coins, respectively, considerably higher than under the Northern Song (Wang S. 1995: 144–5). In addition, to resist further Tartar aggression, the Southern Song urgently built a new defence line along the Yangzi River. In 1274, in Ezhou alone (in what is now Wuhan, Hubei Province) the build-up of Song warships reached 10,000; another 1,000 were stationed in Yingcheng (now Jiangling, Hubei Province), and an armada of 2,500 warships took charge of patrolling the river (Li C. 1370 vol. 8: ch. 'Shizu Jiwu'). The Song Yangzi fleet thus totalled 13,500 ships. The cost of building and maintaining this armada was very high. In Song times, a small ship of 15.4 m × 3.7 m (5 *zhang* × 1.2 *zhang*) cost 400,000 bronze coins; a warship of medium size cost 1 million coins; and a large ship cost 10–20 million (Xu S. 1809: ch. 'Shihuo Zhi'; Lin S. 1990: 33). If it is supposed that all the ships were of medium size at 1 million coins each, the initial cost of the Song fleet would be 13,500 million bronze coins. That was not all. Evidence shows that ships were pulled out of service for maintenance as frequently as once a year at a cost of about half the initial purchase price (Chen X. 1991: 56). So, the total cost of the yearly maintenance would be 6,750 million bronze coins. These two items alone, namely the aggregate government wage bill and the cost of the naval fleet, totalled some 91,000 million bronze coins.

Conceivably, all these expenses were translated into a tax burden on the residents in the south. The tax burden can be simulated by using the limited figures for the total wage bill (5,000 plus 80,000 million coins) and the cost of ship maintenance at 6,750 million coins. Given that the Southern Song population averaged 23.8 million (see Table 6.1), the per capita tax would be at least 3,800 bronze coins per year. According to Li Xinchuan (1167–1244), a scholar and high-ranking official of the Southern Song, the revenue under the Southern Song rocketed from its rather humble start of less than 10,000 million bronze coins in 1127 to 65,300 million bronze coins in 1189 (Li X. *c.* 1202 vol. 14: entry 'Revenue'), an increase of over 650 per cent with an annual increase rate of 3.1 per cent over 62 years. In comparison with the Northern Song revenue peak of 60,000 million bronze coins in the period 1068–85, this must have resulted from redoubling of tax-collecting efforts. Considering that this was done within half of the territory, with a declining population, the real increase in the per capita tax burden was phenomenal. It was openly admitted by a high-ranking official, Li Xun, that during the first three years of the Southern Song (1127–30), the rate of land tax was seven times as high as under the previous Tang Dynasty (Tuo T. 1345: ch. 'Economy'). From Appendix G, it is known that the Tang land tax rate was 3.3 per cent in nominal terms; the Southern Song land tax was therefore 23.1 per cent, which was a long way from the physio-cratic norm. This has caused modern scholars to regard the Southern Song state as parasitic (P. J. Smith 1991: 313).

With the southward move of the state apparatus, Song control over the south intensified, which brought the southern tax-evasion haven to an end. Meanwhile, the south was infected by the landholding concentration disease. During the Northern Song, someone possessing 580 heactares (10,000 *mu*) was rated a large landowner; in the Southern Song, Zhang Jun, a high-ranking army officer, had a private estate of 37,120 heactares (640,000 *mu*), an amount which was almost unheard of under the Northern Song (Li J. 1957: 192–3). This was not all: the Southern Song government joined in and scrambled for land. By law, the state had the power to purchase up to one-third of the estates that fell into certain categories. Under this scheme, the state brought a total of 203,000 heactares (3.5 million *mu*) from six prefectures to yield rents (Tuo T. 1345 vol. 173: ch. 'Economy', entry 'Agricultural Land'). The payments were made by the Song government with paper currency. Given the way the Song paper currency was issued, this was close to land robbery. Not surprisingly, legal disputes over land ownership, land tax and duties of military services accelerated at the grassroots level (McKnight 1971: 47).

Third, in Olson's view (Olson 1982: chs 3–4), the war of the Tartars against the Song in North China eliminated the entrenched Song administration and influential officials and large landowners, vested interest groups who proved to be less tolerable to the Chinese than the alien conquerors. The adoption of the trinary structure in the Tartar-controlled north, marked by the 'Land Allocation According to Clan Members' (*jiko shoudi*), made remigration back to the north more attractive.

Last, the Tartar Jin made the Chinese peasantry feel relatively comfortable: the régime actively encouraged farming through (1) the *meng-an moke* system, characterised by Tartar land ownership and Chinese tenancy; (2) a reasonably fair tax system copied from the Tang output-based 'Two Seasonal Taxes' (*liangshui fa*); and (3) systematic confinement of merchant activities, also copied from the Tang (Tuo T. 1344: vol. 7: 'Biography of Emperor Shizong', vol. 9: 'Biography of Emperor Zhangzong', vol. 47: 'Economy', vol. 49: 'Economy'; see also Wang Z. 1993).

Consequently, the direction of internal migration began to reverse, given the unprecedented distrust of the Song government, and for the same purposes of tax evasion and landholding. So, the unthinkable happened: large numbers of Chinese defected from the Southern Song régime and joined the Tartars. The fact that many of the immigrants were tenants and traders made their reverse migration easier since the opportunity costs for the landless or near-landless to move were normally lower than those for landowners. That so many people managed to emigrate back to the north indicates that the Song government was further weakened. This was reflected by the quality of the Southern Song census, which was considerably poorer than that of the Tartar Jin (see Liang F. 1980: 130–1, 167–74). Arguably, the reverse migration during the Southern Song was institution-pushed, too.

IMPACT OF THE REVERSE MIGRATION

The impact of the reverse migration was to further the Song's proto-mercantilism to compensate for the loss of population and the consequent reduction in tax revenue. Now the government depended more than ever on trade to finance its existence.

In this context, some changes took place to cement the association between the government and commerce. In the Northern Song Dynasty, there were in all eight Bureaux for Maritime Trade, located in Hangzhou, Mingzhou (now Ningbo), Guangzhou, Quanzhou, Mizhou (now Zhucheng, Shandong Province), Huating (Fujian Province), Zhenjiang (Jiangsu Province) and Pingjiang (now Suzhou) (Xu S. 1809: ch. 'Zhiguan 44'). In the Southern Song Dynasty, although the territory had been halved, the number of bureaux was kept at seven, the highest in per capita terms in Chinese history. Moreover, between 1163 and 1276, Quanzhou Prefecture, the most active sea trade region of that time, supplied the Chinese bureaucracy with 14 top-ranking officials (Prime Ministers and *de facto* Prime Ministers), averaging one every eight years for over a century (see Fu Z. 1991: 128). Given that in 1123 the population of Fujian Province made up some 13.5 per cent of the total population of South China (see Liang F. 1980: 161–3) and that Quanzhou was only a small part of Fujian and home to no more than 20 per cent of the population in the province (as in 1102; see Liang F. 1980: 157), or less than 3 per cent of the southern total, such a disproportionately high concentration of top-ranking officials from Quanzhou implies strong trade orientation in the Southern Song administration. In one celebrated case, Pu Shougeng, an Arab immigrant to Southern Song China, was appointed Director (*tiju*) in Quanzhou. He remained in the post for thirty years (Wu Z. 1334).

Support for commercial undertakings also came from the highest level. Emperor Gaozong (r. 1127–62) of the Southern Song is recorded as saying that

> The profit from overseas trade is the greatest. If the trade is handled in the right way, the profit can easily reach millions of bronze coins. Isn't the revenue from trade better than that from taxing ordinary people? Thus, I should pay more attention to overseas trade to relieve the tax burden of the people.
>
> (Xu S. 1809: ch. 'Zhiguan 44')

Here, considering that huge numbers of the 'ordinary people' left South China, profiteering from maritime trade was indeed an easy choice. So, in 1137 when Pu Yali, an Arab sea merchant who made his fortune in trade with China, decided to retire, the emperor issued an edict to persuade him to continue his career (see Deng D. 1986 vol. 1: 91).

To strengthen the incentive for trading activities, the Southern Song government employed various innovative methods. Understanding the correlation between tax revenue from maritime trade and the turnover rate of the trading ships, in 1164 the Southern Song authorities established the 'Discriminatory Duties' (*raoshui*) to encourage a fast turnover in overseas trade: if a ship returned to China within five months, a low tax rate was imposed; if a ship returned within a year, the normal rate was applied; if a ship returned after longer than a year, the owner was subject to official investigation (Xu S. 1809: ch. 'Zhiguan 44'). Tax on commerce was cut too (Li Z. 1991).

No doubt, during the Southern Song, more commercial growth was generated, at least in the short run. From the point of view of its geographic scope, archaeological discovery shows that the extent of the Southern Song commercial activities reached much of the northern Indian Ocean. From a medium-sized Southern Song shipwreck discovered in Quanzhou Bay of Fujian Province in the mid-1970s, a full shipload of materials – spices, perfume and medicine – imported from overseas was excavated (Lin G. 1982). A chromatographic analysis of samples showed that some of the goods came from the east coast of Africa (Zhang W. 1982). In terms of the total value of the goods and services traded, although data concerning the value of goods traded during the Southern Song are rare, it is known that in 1242, a total of 100 million Song bronze coins (100,000 *min*) were shipped to Japan through trade, an equivalent to one year's monetary supply of the Song Treasury in the twelfth century (Luo Y. 1992: 80; Liu S. 1992: 117). To show the volume of the metal, according to the Southern Song mintage standard, to cast 1,000 bronze coins needed 2.5 *jin* of copper, 1.94 *jin* of lead, 0.19 *jin* of tin and 5 *jin* of charcoal (Wang S. 1995 vol. 1: 371–2). Given that the Song measure of *jin* is 596.82 g, these 100 million coins took 276.3 tonnes of metals (149.2 tonnes of copper, 115.8 tonnes of lead and 11.3 tonnes of tin) and 298.4 tonnes of charcoal to make. The total value of the Southern Song's foreign trade must have been greater since Japan was only one of the many trading partners of Southern Song China.

The initial result of the Southern Song trade policy can also be seen from the composition of the government revenue: the component from commercial activities increased exponentially. This is reflected by the tax revenues from taxes on maritime trade (based on Wang S. 1995: 723–4):

| Period | Annual tax revenue ($10^6$ coins) | Rate of increase |
|--------|-----------------------------------|------------------|
| 1087–99 | 416 | 100 |
| 1102–6 | 1,110 | 267 |
| ?–1159 | 2,000 | 481 |

By 1131 overseas trade alone had grown to 20 per cent of the government's total cash revenue while the taxes on trade made up half of the government's total revenue (Merson 1989: 61). Later, according to Wang Yinglin, a Southern Song scholar, by the end of the twelfth century the revenue from indirect taxes on commodities such as tea, salt and wine amounted to 44,900 million bronze coins, some 70 per cent of the total revenue (65,300 million bronze coins) (Wang Y. *c*. 1296 vol. 186: entries 'Economy', 'Financial Management' and 'The Song Revenue').

Along with the commercial boom, there was a boom in shipbuilding, partly owing to the Yangzi defence line and partly owing to the growth in China's maritime trade. Apart from the aforementioned 13,500 ships, the Mongol army captured 7,000 Song sea-vessels along the Fujian coast in 1276 (Li C. 1370 vol. 162: ch. 'Gaoxing Zhuan'), which indicates that the Southern Song fleet had at least 20,500 ships. It is known that under Ming–Qing regulations, all government transport vessels had a ten-year service life and were to be replaced in the tenth year (Zhang T. 1735: ch. 'Shihuo Zhi'; see also Barbosa 1518/967 vol. 2: 172–4; Wang G. 1991: 43). Thus, a fleet had to replace 10 per cent of its ships each year regardless of the maintenance requirement. It is easy to work out the size of the Southern Song shipbuilding industry: it must have had the capacity to produce at least 2,050 ships a year just to keep the fleet size unchanged.

If routine maintenance is taken into account, the capacity of the industry would have to be much greater, which seems to be the case, as evidence indicates that the Song technology of shipbuilding and ship maintenance technology was inferior, in that the ships were pulled out of service for maintenance once a year, five times as frequently as the Ming–Qing rate (Zhang T. 1735: ch. 'Shihuo Zhi'; Chen X. 1991: 56). Given that during the Song, maintenance cost about half the initial purchase price of a ship (Chen X. 1991: 56), half the labour and materials were required for the maintenance each time. If all the maintenance workload had been converted to that of shipbuilding, the Southern Song shipbuilding sector would have had the capacity to build in all over 10,000 ships every year. The estimation of the maintenance workload is as follows:

$$W = s \cdot mn \tag{6.1}$$

where $W$ is the converted workload to shipbuilding; $S$, the existing fleet; $m$, the maintenance rate; and $n$, the convertor. In our case, the value of $S$ is the Southern Song naval fleet of 20,500 ships. The value of $m$ is 90 per cent (100 per cent of the fleet minus 10 per cent of ship replacement). The value of $n$ is 50 per cent because of the ship maintenance:construction cost ratio (50:100). The resulting $W$ is thus 9,225. To combine this figure with the 2,050 new ships totals 11,275.

Commerce and shipbuilding were only two of the many areas where changes took place. To facilitate trade, goods for trade such as silk, ceramics, stationery and metal wares including monetary coins had to be produced, which would trigger a further chain reaction in the economy.

Commercialisation also spilled over to and penetrated other areas of Chinese life. To increase revenue, the Song authorities sold Official Certificates for Monks (*dudie*) and official titles to the public on a large scale. The following data show the number of Official Certificates for Monks sold and the revenues collected (Wang S. 1995: 741–3):

| Period | Certificates sold | Total revenue ($\times 10^6$ coins) |
|---|---|---|
| 1057–67 | 78,000 | — |
| 1068–75 | 89,000 | 11,570 |
| 1078–83 | 50,918 | 6,619 |
| 1001–2 | 36,000 | 7,920 |
| 1109 | 30,000 | 6,000 |
| 1129 | 20,000 | 2,400 |
| 1134 | 10,000 | 1,200 |
| 1139 | — | 2,000 |
| 1163–9 | 120,000 | 48,000 |

Since both the certificates and titles bore the privilege of tax and corvée exemption, it was a type of tax advance. There was even a black market for these products (Wang S. 1995: 745). It has been argued that in the France of Henri IV (r. 1589–1610) and Louis XIV (r. 1643–1715) the sale of official positions for the revenue purposes caused commercialisation of the bureaucracy which created cracks in the French system for the bourgeoisie to gain access to economic and political power (Moore 1966: 57–9). The Song practice seems to have led to a similar result.

The change in revenue sources and the growth in industries imply that some structural change in the economy did happen. The Song revolution continued. However, one should not overestimate the commercial achievement of the Southern Song. The Southern Song government was more inflation-addicted than that of the Northern Song. After 1161, when the face value of the paper currency supply (23,736 million bronze coins) first passed the Northern Song peak, there was no turning back in inflationary crisis. In all, from 1127 to 1255, there were 49 issues with a total face value of 608,917.3 million bronze coins, 5.5 times higher than the Northern Song's total (93,449.7 million bronze coins) (Liu S. 1993b: 24–6, 56–9). When this is taken together with the tax increase, one might think that inflation would have eased the tax burden. That would indeed be the case at the macro or national level. But it would not to some strata. From the weight of the indirect tax revenue extracted from low-value goods for everyday consumption (tea, salt and wine) in the total government income, the ordinary people were hit hard. Because of inflation, the Southern Song commercial growth to a great extent was cancelled out. This included the growth in the printing industry on which the mass production of paper currency depended.

### 6.2.2 How did it end?

From the aspect of commercial development, Southern Song indeed seemed to be heading for an extensive transformation of the economy. However, like its predecessor in the Han Dynasty a millennium before, the Song economic revolution came to a premature end. That the very nature of the Song economic revolution was derived from some changes in government, landholding and demographic distribution sowed the seed for its brief flowering. Three factors can be identified regarding the non-sustainability of the Song growth.

First, the Song stick-and-carrot way of dealing with the merchant class implies a lack of property rights in the commercial sector. This was particularly true when the well-defined and well-protected land property rights are used as a yardstick for comparison. To judge from the fact that large numbers of people emigrated from the commercially advanced Southern Song territory to the less commercialised north, the transaction cost in the south was high and so was the economic risk/uncertainty.

Seond, from the initial migration and the following reverse migration within the life span of the Song Period (including both Northern and Southern), it is very obvious that government economic policy, rather than relative scarcity of land, dictated the direction of internal migration in China. It also shows that the Chinese population was highly conditioned after having lived under the trinary structure for so long. This means that the Chinese needed a de-programming hand in hand with a structural change in the economy. The de-programming process required not only time but also compatible institutions. The passiveness of the Song policies indicates that, if not completely uninventive, the Song state was at least very weak in implementing new institutions. Most evident of all, the Song failed to transfer its commercial growth to its military strength, which the empire desperately needed to keep the Tartars and Mongols away.

Third, from the heavy loss of the Song population to the Tartar Jin, it was obvious that there were two types of economies competing against each other, regardless of cultural, ethnical and political differences. The fact that the Southern Song régime turned out to be very unpopular means that the Song régime unplugged itself when throwing away the old trinary structure, and it did not meet the public expectations of a rise in income and improvement in living standards. At this point, it is worth noting that during the period 1130–5, soon after the Southern Song became a reality, 200,000 peasants rebelled in the south under the leadership of Zhong Xiang and Yang Yao. Elite Song troops were used to crack down on the rebels. But mass rebellion recurred in 1143, 1165 and 1176 (Zhang S. and Zheng X. 1983: 452–3). In contrast with the socio-economic mutation under the Song, there was, in accordance with the 'genetic code' of the Tang, a marked return to the trinary structure in the Tartar territory.

In essence, the reverse migration was a peaceful mass rebellion which was almost certainly 'cheaper' than a violent, bloody one. The Song régime was successful in bribing the bureaucrats and the soldiers, who at most occupied 40 per cent of the total population. However, it was not able to win over the majority. If we use maximal figures for soldiers and officials, the assumptions are (1) 1,400,000 troops (as at AD 1049); (2) 20,000 officials (as at 1196); (3) a total population of some 22.3 million (as at 1049); (4) on average each soldier/official had an immediate family of five persons (Li A. 1183: vol. 301; Liang F. 1980: 7–8; Zhao X. et al. 1987: 300–1; Tian Z. 1994: 228). In that case, the proportion of the bribed was 32 per cent of the Song's total. In other words, the Song institution was unable to equalise 'social cost' and 'private cost' and 'social benefit' and 'private benefit' (North and Thomas 1973: 1–3). So, when the Tartars showed their interest in rebuilding the trinary structure, the Chinese took the opposing side. The Song–Jin competition was indeed a competition between the old trinary structure and the new Song structure. The Song not only lost the war against the alien invaders, but also lost the war against the Chinese trinary structure established by the Song's predecessors.

To have identified this reverse migration and the loss of the Song population to the Tartar Jin is one of the main findings of the present study. So far, this part of the Chinese population has been excluded from the history of the

Song. This is understandable because of the prejudice from the prevailing 'Sino-centricism': those who left the Chinese-controlled territory and joined the barbarians were regarded as 'de-Sinicized' expatriates (*tianchao qimin*, literally 'the abandoned by the Heavenly Empire'), and downgraded from the viewpoint of Chinese culturalism. It was a cultural taboo. But, as demonstrated in Chapter 5, there was no such a thing as 'pure Chinese' or 'pure Chinese culture'. The Chinese race and culture as we know them have considerable 'barbarian inputs'. More seriously, the exclusion of the part of the Song population that joined the Tartar Jin has led to miscalculation and mis-measuring of the Chinese economic performance from the early twelfth to the late thirteenth centuries. At the very least, there are four implications. First, the participation rate among the Chinese population in the Song economic revolution was much lower than has been thought. In other words, the scale and impact of the revolution are prone to exaggeration. Second, through losing a large number of its people, the Song enjoyed a much better man-to-resource ratio than otherwise would have been the case, which almost certainly helped the revolution. In other words, the Song did not play solo. It had a co-star, in the shape of the Tartar Jin, that carried the population burden on its shoulders for the Song. So, when talking about the Song economic revolution, one needs to take the Tartar Jin's role into full account. Third, to many Song Chinese, there were economic and political choices as presented by the Song on the one hand and the Tartars on the other. Considering the consequence of 'de-Sinicisation', the choice to join the Tartars must have been well balanced and thus highly rational. In other words, among those who left the Song territory, 'Sinicist membership' was worth much less than membership of the 'trinary club'. Fourth, the population gain in North China helped to maintain and reinforce the adopted trinary structure under the Tartars. In other words, the reverse migration indicated that the pendulum swung back to the old trinary structure (which was now represented by the Tartar Jin) much earlier than was previously thought. So, ultimately, the Song economic revolution was undermined by the outflow of its own people, who should have benefited from the revolution.

As the other face of the same coin, the double-edged role (as a supporter and competitor at the same time) played by the Tartar Jin régime was extremely important in determining the fate of the Song economic revolution. However, owing to deeply rooted Confucian cultural and political prejudice and Chinese chauvinism, few have given positive credit to the Tartars. Typically, the Tartars have been portrayed as backward, excessively rent-seeking and racially discriminatory, although the Jins were in effect much closer to the authentic Chinese trinary structure than the Songs.

Superficially, the Song economic revolution was interrupted by the Mongol invasion and conquest. This view sees the ending of the Song achievement as completely accidental. After all, in thirteenth-century Eurasia few civilisations escaped the same fate when encountering the galloping Mongol cavalry.

So, a causal link between the Mongol invasion and the ending of the Song economic revolution is highly plausible.

But, in the light of the present analysis, it is obvious that the Song's failure was not caused by external shocks only. Internal factors played an equally important role. In particular, the Song economic revolution did not provide the economy with some basic conditions: (1) minimum financial stability in balancing the government budget and in controlling inflation; (2) relative equity among citizens to share the fruits of commercial growth; (3) reasonable socio-economic and political stability for the growth to be sustained; (4) national defence to secure the fruits of the Song growth from the alien invasion and conquest; and (5) minimal expenditure on public goods. In terms of public expenditure, Song records show (1) that the total wage bill for the bureaucrats occupied some 20 per cent of the total government expenditure, and (2) that the other 80 per cent was the defence budget (Wang S. 1995: 771–3), suggesting that little was left for the repertoire projects such as water control and famine relief. If so, the standards of living among ordinary citizens were almost certainly worsened due to the lack of provision of these public goods.

So, the Song growth was in essence by, of and for the privileged. As a result, far from saving the Song from its socio-economic crises, the commercial growth was very unpopular among many Chinese. This unpopularity eventually cost the very survival of the Song régime: the dynasty died in the cross-fire between alien invasions and people's rebellions, armed or peaceful (in the form of tax-evading migrants).

## 6.3 Final remarks

### 6.3.1 *The nature of the Song growth*

The nature of the Song growth phenomenon is reflected in a range of changes that the Song underwent. These changes crystallised in a jump in urbanisation as shown in Table 3.4: the Song proportion of non-agricultural population in China's total reached the highest among all the main dynasties from 2 BC onwards. With a minimum of over 10 per cent of its population living in urban centres, Song China matched the degree of urbanisation in Europe in 1800 (for Europe see, for example, De Vries 1984: tables 2.2, 3.1, 3.2, 3.5, 3.6 and appendix 1). Together with a rise in industrial outputs and trade activities, such an increased urban population suggests a structural change in the economy. No doubt Song public expenditure and the consequent inflationary policies played an important part in the making of the Song economic revolution. The unleashed market and mutant institutions played another.

A close scrutiny of the Song growth phenomenon rejects the view that there was no drama during the Song but merely a gradual build-up of growth momentum from the previous periods. For example, according to Morgan Kelly, (1) before the Song, China had had extensive waterways, numerous

321

markets and a range of technologies, none of which had realised its full commercial and production potential; and (2) the Song reached a break-point for qualitative changes (Kelly 1997: 952–62). However, his study does not consider institutional factors and their changes, as if the Song growth were purely technical and thus could have occurred at some other time and was not Song-specific. Kelly's view that the Song growth ended because it ran out of steam, as any Smithian growth does, is consistent with his technological approach. The present study shows the opposite. The unprecedented reverse migration of a large number of Chinese who decided to distance themselves from the spectacular Song growth and to re-enter the world of the trinary structure under the Tartars is a clear indication that the institutional changes were equally dramatic, too much so for many ordinary Chinese to cope with. In essence, the Song was not only a period of drama with a new production function with technological and production frontiers being suddenly outstretched but also an epoch of institutional changes. Factually, the Song growth was cut short not by Smithian exhaustion but by the cross-fire of invasions and rebellions, which suggests a sharp U-turn for the institutions. So, the growth was highly institution-conditional and Song-specific. In the following Yuan, Ming and Qing the pendulum swung back to the 'norm', as indicated by the long-term average proportion of urban population in China's total (see Table 3.4). This swing marked the Song economic revolution as a one-off event. Such a one-off growth had occurred at least once before: Western Han China (206 BC–AD 24) reached the level of urbanisation that Europe reached in around AD 1500 (for Europe see De Vries 1984: tables 2.2, 3.1, 3.2, 3.5, 3.6 and appendix 1). However, from the Eastern Han onward, the degree of urbanisation declined until the Tang (AD 618–907), which coincided with China's commitment first to the 'King's Land Scheme' (*wangtianzhi*) during the late Western Han Period under Wang Mang (r. AD 9–23) and then to the 'Land Equalisation Scheme' (*juntianzhi*) from the Jin (AD 265–420) to the Tang (AD 618–907). So, if one takes a very long-term view, the Song economic growth was an episode of extraordinariness, an epiphenomenon outside China's mainstream.

This one-off phenomenon suggests at least three things. First, prior to the British Industrial Revolution, sustained economic growth of the intensive type or the proto-industrial type occurred only randomly or accidentally with a cluster of conditions met. Because it was random, there was a high 'casualty rate'. After the Industrial Revolution, with a model readily available for the later-comers to copy, the process has become artificially controlled and programmed, as revealed by scholars like Alexander Gerschenkron. Since it is no longer random, the 'casualty rate' has dropped sharply, as the history of industrialisation shows. So, the Chinese early failure is understandable. Second, however, even if one takes into full account the random nature of the Han and Song events, that China had a 100 per cent failure rate in its two promising attempts means that premodern China was not a land suitable for sustained intensive growth. Such growth was unable to repeat itself until the end of the eighteenth century. Instead, the Song revolution gave way to the time-tested trinary structure. Third, the fate of the Song growth thus shows the convergence of the trinary structure. The occasional flowering of commerce and industry at a higher degree was like many life forms in the desert that become visible only when the stifling and suppressing drought and heat are temporarily overpowered by occasional, unusual rainfalls. Thus, the Song, as well as the Han, was merely an unusual rainfall, not an oasis. In short, China's problem was internal or endogenous deficiencies, mainly structural and institutional.

In the context of China's long-term growth pattern, it is misleading to view the Song episode as a 'natural' developmental step in premodern China. Otherwise, it is hard to explain the enormous resistance in China to other developmental alternatives as seen not only from China's return to its old track after the Song, but also from the facts that (1) after the Chinese elite recognised the necessity for change, around the second half of the nineteenth century, it has taken China an awfully long time to limp towards modernisation, and (2) China's reforms have been characterised by a low success rate, although the country has tried just about all the main models available. From the 1870s to the 1980s, China was virtually a huge testing ground for a wide range of socio-economic models of modernisation. The main events included, in the first round, the Westernisation Movement (1870–95), which was masterminded by high-ranking officials, and the 1898 'One-Hundred-Day Reform' which involved Emperor Guangxu (r. 1875–1908), both being a Chinese version of the Japanese Meiji reform (1869–89) and both aimed at transplanting Western technology and institutions to rebuild the strength of the Chinese Empire. In the second round, there was the Nationalist Movement, organised first from overseas bases under Dr Sun Yat-sen (or Sun Zhongshan, 1866–1925), a genuine republican who copied the French model of the 1789–94 Revolution to end the Qing monarchy. The third round, immediately after the 1949 Communist takeover of the mainland, was marked by the establishment of an administrative command economy of the Soviet style in the wake of a wholesale package of nationalisation of private and corporate industrial assets and collectivisation of peasant private properties. The fourth round began in 1978 in two dimensions: to re-establish the market economy and non-state ownership on the one hand and to adopt the 'technocracy'-operated 'export-led growth' strategy on the other. The former, called 'socialist market economy', was patented by Tito (r. 1953–80) in former Yugoslavia, and the latter was copied from the post-war Asian newly industrialised countries (NICs). Still, success in China's conversion is not guaranteed since (1) the per capita income gap between the advanced and the developing economies has widened fivefold during the past 250 years (O'Brien 1997: 85–6); and (2) since 1850 'catching up' and 'keeping up' by an economy in the 'periphery' of the world-system has proved to be difficult if not impossible (Wallerstein 1974–86). After all, the Soviet model was a complete failure and the 'Asian tigers' – fast-growing in the 1980s and quickly sickening in the later 1990s – have yet to prove themselves more than paper tigers.

### 6.3.2 Answer to the second paradox about China

Unlike the paradox of the coexistence of disasters and perpetuation of the Chinese system, the paradox of China's degeneration from development to underdevelopment is not a straightforward one. One needs to go beyond Chinese economic history *per se* to see the problem because within the trinary structure it seems like 'business as usual'. It becomes a paradox only when the observer uses a particular reference or a benchmark with which to measure China. When compared with premodern Eurasia, China was developed: until five hundred years ago, China's technology took the lead in Eurasia and only two hundred years ago its standards of living were still ahead of those of most civilisations. After the Industrial Revolution, the West surpassed and then marginalised China. Many developing economies also outgrew China (Bairoch 1977: 36, 38, 75, 84, 193, 246–9; Tan 1996: 27, 115). The comparative benchmark is capitalist industrialisation. Consequently, China was no longer looked up to nor was it regarded as a model for Europe (after the eighteenth century, see Waverick 1946) or for Japan (after the 1840–2 Opium War, see Francks 1992: ch. 2). China became underdeveloped owing to external peripeteia. So, the paradox is a relative term, and China appeared in a deadlock only comparatively.

Here, the fundamental problem was not so much one of why China did not have growth. Under the trinary structure, growth did take place in the forms of more total output (GDP), more goods and services traded (both within and without China), more urban centres and a greater population. China also had occasional increases in factor productivities with better technology and practice (such as the windfall of new crops from the New World). Rather, the problem is what growth path China took. Here, the term 'path dependency' is deliberately avoided, although it captures some features of the Chinese past. A better phrase is 'dynamic returns to the equilibrium', which means more than merely a sequence in development.

Evidently, the very growth path that allowed the Chinese economy to develop ahead of the rest of the premodern world effectively prevented China from going further to match that of the modern West. To judge from the Song and post-Song experiences, the path was overshadowed by the trinary equilibrium. The Song saga thus shows that science, technology, output surplus, urbanisation and commercialisation were not sufficient conditions for capitalist industrialisation to take place even if they were all present. Institutional factors – including socio-economic structure, property rights, ideology, values and government policies – determined the developmental path for a society, which in turn determined whether that society was able to develop capitalist industrialisation. China's trinary structure and equilibrium resulted in an overall environment unsuited for growth of the Western type along a different path. So, it was the 'dynamic returns to the equilibrium' that set the limits for economic growth and development in premodern China. At best, until the end of the eighteenth century China had pseudo-capitalism which sometimes looked like the kind of development in Western Europe. But it was unable to give birth to an industrial revolution. After the eighteenth century, the entire socio-economic ecology in the Asian world was disturbed by the industrialising West and then turned upside down by the industrialised West. So, strictly speaking, there was no longer any indigenous capitalist development in China. China remained a land of capitalist sterility. This is not fatalism but an evolutionary process over a very long period of time.

In most cases, to end an equilibrium requires an external push from a force of another type. Likewise, China's trinary equilibrium continued until a push from a superior force, a *force majeure*, caused the collapse of the system. The humiliating defeats by the West embodied the working of such an external push. Japanese history provides positive proof. With thousands of warships, the Mongol naval invasion during 1274–93 was far more spectacular and violent than that led by Captain Perry in the mid-nineteenth century (Li C. 1370; Chen B. 1606: vol. 5; Ke S. 1920: chs 'Riben Zhuan' and 'Zhaowa Zhuan'; Elvin 1973: 220). But it was the latter that forced the Japanese to kneel: the Japanese door was prized open, trade treaties imposed and the economy transformed. Obviously, although reaching Japan's shore, the Mongols did not enjoy the same degree of military and economic supremacy over Japan as the USA did, and consequently did not inspire any significant change in Japan. Later on the Japanese chose militarism, which led their economy to total ruin. It was the US occupation that steered devastated Japan out of its self-made crisis and paved the way for Japan's healthy development in the post-war period. With its external *force majeure* the USA was undeniably responsible for the so-called 'creative destruction' in modern Japanese history of the past hundred and fifty years, which has been the source of Japan's ambivalent relationship with the USA.

Until the mid-nineteenth century, the main difference between Tokugawa Japan and Qing China lay in that the latter was far wealthier, far more powerful, far more successful in premodern growth, and thus far less flexible in coping with a changing world. At this point, one only has to mention two facts. First, in 1900, to capture Beijing took the joint elite force of as many as eight industrial powers (*baguo lianjun*); overkill maybe, but certainly unprecedented in modern history of the world. Second, not until the eve of the Pacific War did Japan manage to impose roughly the same influence – military, political and economic – on the Asian world as the Chinese Empire enjoyed at its pinnacles during the Ming and Qing (see Deng 1997: Frank 1978: 137–8; Reid 1997: *passim* and especially chs 1 and 4).

So, although China and Japan were each presented with similar options/choices, China's opportunity costs for reform were far higher than Japan's. Given that opportunity costs are what a rational choice largely depends on, from China's point of view the slowness in adapting changes has been indeed natural: 'Don't fix it if it isn't broken.' Meiji Japan, with very little to lose, certainly had the advantage of being more backward than Qing China. Even if Qing China had been just as willing to change as Meiji Japan, it would have experienced a considerable time lag between plans and modernisation because of the task of de-programming the trinary structure, which was absent in Japan. To move China off its old orbit thus required a much greater force and took a much longer time than to change Japan, owing to the enormous inertia generated by China's medieval success, *fons et origo* of China's problem in modern times. There was a similar situation in Western Europe when one compares the different speeds in industrialisation in nineteenth-century France and Germany.

This is portrayed in Figure 6.1, where diagram A shows that opportunity costs are direct ratios of medieval economic performance. The shape of the curve indicates diminishing returns. In diagram B, speed of reform is a reciprocal function of the opportunity costs. Qing China was at the upper end of both curves, and early Meiji Japan at the lower end.

Indeed, the utility of the 'Song drama' lies in that it not only unveils what China's growth path really was but also testifies just how difficult it was for the country to shake off the entrenched deadlock of trinary equilibrium from within. Post-Song economic history, on the other hand, indicates why an external push was the only way to end China's equilibrium. As a whole, Song and post-Song economic history attest that if a civilisation cannot

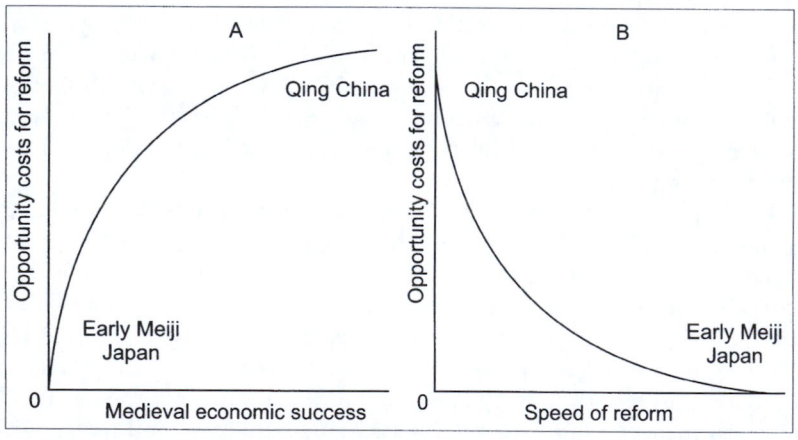

*Figure 6.1.* Medieval success, opportunity costs and speed of reform, China versus Japan

nourish the required conditions, capitalist industrialisation, or simply 'capitalismisation', will have to be transplanted from outside with the local conditions and institutions altered and new conditions created, which has been suggested by numerous recent and contemporary studies (see, for example, Gerschenkron 1962; Cameron 1974; Fairbank and Reischaver 1979; Shue 1980; Rozman 1981; Kraus 1982; Kueh 1984, 1985; Hao 1986; Nee et al. 1989; Rawski 1989; Chu 1990; Crane 1990; Hinton 1990; Kamath 1990; Myers 1991; Hay 1993; Selden 1993; Solinger 1993; Wong 1997).

In China, such a process of 'social reverse engineering' has been neither 'natural', painless nor smooth. This is too evident in the 1870s through to the 1970s from the basic facts including mainland China's regrettably missing, so many times, 'windows of opportunity' to modernise; its blindly landing in fanatic, meaningless, tasteless and costly campaigns under Maoism that claimed the heaviest losses of human lives in a non-war situation in modern world history; and its religiously following the wrong growth path of the Soviet type until the economy virtually went broke at the death of Mao. This is also seen in the 1980s and 1990s, behind the façade of spectacular growth figures and official promises, from the rampant corruption, soaring inflation and unemployment, increasing socio-economic inequality, and, above all, the constant tension between the disillusioned ordinary citizens and the vested interest group of rent-seekers from the Communist Party and the party-cum-bureaucracy and -military.

It is up to the reader to speculate on China's future development.

## Notes

1 Some guesstimates have pushed the Tang population to 80 million and the Song to 100 million, mainly on the basis of the technological capacity of Chinese agriculture (see, for example, Ge J. 1993: 43). Although flattering, these sensational figures imply that over 50 per cent of China's population was not counted in the government censuses under the Tang and Song periods. In practice, with such a huge error margin in the census, the empire would have collapsed either because of the severe malfunctioning of the bureaucracy or owing to the persistent centrifugal force among the population to pull the system apart. These guesstimates therefore make little socio-economic and socio-political sense.

2 First, it made possible a multi-cropping system in both south and north, and with it a dramatic increase in the yield capacity of land. Second, it made possible the use of marginal land such as seasonal flood areas which otherwise would lie idle. Third, it greatly reduced the risk from disasters such as typhoons because the shorter the growing period, the less chance for the crop to be exposed. Fourth, it greatly increased the chance to fight disasters: the failure of one crop could be compensated for by the success of another within the limit of the growth season. Fifth, with the already existing middle-ripening and late-ripening varieties, the new early-ripening variety gave a complete range of rice types for the Chinese farmers to choose from, which would almost certainly improve their management and

output. Lastly, almost overnight, the new variety stretched the rice-growing belt towards the Yellow River Valley and further north, the limited frost-free period in these areas no longer being a barrier for the high-yield crop rice (see Deng 1993: ch. 4, section B). As a result, to this day, rice is grown in China over a geographic span between 18° N (Hainan Island) and 50° N (Heilongjiang in Manchuria).

3 Those include the Governor of Lizhou (named Bai Jinshao), Taxation Commissioner of Qinzhou (named Cao Feigong) and Deputy Governor of Hailing–Yancheng Colony (named Zhang Ai) (Tang K. 1993: 122).

# APPENDIX A

## Government profiteering

Government profiteering in premodern China took two directions: (1) through trade monopoly with or without an agent, and (2) via participation in trade as a partner or agent.

### Profiteering through trade monopoly

Officially beginning from the Western Han Period, systematic profiteering through trade monopoly by the Chinese government was marked by Sang Hongyang's policy of 81 BC towards the 'key' domestic markets (wine, iron and salt). Government profiteering thus had a history as long as the empire itself.

During the Tang Dynasty, government profiteering first expanded to the foreign trade field via imposing an indirect tax on imports through the compulsory purchase of imported goods at government unilateral prices called 'proportional procurement' (*choumai*). The proportion of imports subject to this tax régime varied from 30 to 60 per cent of the total shipment (see Xia Z. 1989: 770). Through such a scheme, the Chinese government became the sole dealer in imports. This practice continued till the beginning of the sixteenth century. To show the revenue-yielding capacity of this tax on trade, in the Southern Song Dynasty the revenue, including customs duty and government monopolistic profit, collected in Port Quanzhou and Port Guangzhou alone amounted to 2 billion bronze coins a year (Li X. *c.* 1202: vol. 183; Sun G. 1989: 473). In 1128 and 1158 the sea trade-related income constituted 20 per cent and 15 per cent, respectively, of the Song annual revenue (see Deng D. 1986 vol. 1: 88; Ye T. 1991: 104; Zhang S. 1992).

The high profit yield from this practice is indicated by the Ming tax reform. At the beginning of the Ming, the government abandoned customs duty (at 30 per cent) and imposed a monopoly on importing (see Xia Z. 1989: 770). It is reasonable to guess that the profit rate of the Ming monopoly must have offset the customs duty rate at 30 per cent (see Zhu Y. 1119: vol. 2; Ma D. 1307 vol. 20: ch. 'Shidi Yi'). To facilitate the attempted monopoly in sea trade, the Ming administration established the 'Chartered Trading Houses' (*shibosi yahang*) in port cities. In Guangzhou alone, the trading houses numbered 13 at first and increased to 36 (see Deng D. 1986: 160–2). This was one step forward in that the government decided to use agents for profiteering instead of dirtying its own hands. This trend continued till the Qing with four trading ports to the outside world. Among four officially permitted foreign trade seaports in four provinces, Jiangsu, Zhejiang, Fujian and Guangdong, the customs revenue from Guangzhou in Guangdong occupied some 40 per cent of the total, twice as much as the average amount for the other three (see Peng Z. 1990: 53; also Deng D. 1986: 200–3). This led to 'one-port-ism', which became officially effective in 1760. Guangzhou was later chosen as the sole port for Sino-foreign sea trade. The underlying consideration of the Manchu authorities for such a geographic arrangement was arguably monopolistic profiteering by erecting a barrier to entry to the market. This caused a great row among China's trading partners and then extensive smuggling. The fact that it took the West several wars (the best known being the two Opium Wars of 1840–1 and 1856–60) to stop such a practice indicated just how efficient the Chinese monopoly was and just how profitable it was for the Qing government.

## Profiteering via participation in trade

Government profiteering via participation in trade as a partner often took the form of government–merchant joint ventures or government quasi-companies.

Government–merchant joint ventures were actively promoted by the Mongol Yuan state, combining government ships with merchant expertise to undertake maritime trade (Li C. 1370: ch. 'Shundi Ji'; also Yu C. 1991). Profit was shared at a 7:3 ratio between the two parties (Li C. 1370 vol. 49: ch. 'Shihu Zhi, Shibo'). It is recorded that in 1285 the Yuan government allocated 100,000 ingots (*ding*) of silver (18.7–37.3 tonnes, 1 *ding* = 5 or 10 *liang*) to building ships for joint ventures (see Yu C. 1991: 96). The government further institutionalised the operation by establishing a Joint Venture Bureau (*motuo zongguanfu*) and providing sea merchants with cash funds of several tens of thousands of ingots of silver at an interest rate of over 30 per cent a year (see Yao S. 1371: vol. 13; Yu C. 1991: 93). Such a rate reveals the profit-making capacity of the maritime sector as well as the rent-seeking mentality of the Mongols.

Government quasi-companies for trade appeared from time to time in Chinese history as an alternative since they required expertise that the Confucian officials did not have. In 1363, Zhu Yuanzhang, the founder of the Ming Dynasty (r. 1368–98), sent his official, Wang Shi, by sea with 3,000 *liang* of silver (112 kg) to trade for horses (Cao Y. 1984: 57). In 1375–6, he sent Li Hao, Deputy Minister of Punishment, to Ryukyu with 220 rolls of silk cloth, 1,000 iron cookers and 70,500 pieces of ceramics to exchange for horses and sulphur (Dong L. *c.* 1399: vols 95, 105). Aware of Ryukyu's lack of sailors and vessels, Zhu went to the length of sending ships with 36 sailor families from Fujian to the king of Ryukyu as a gift to facilitate bilateral trade (Cao Y. 1988: 305–8; Yang G. 1991). Admiral Zheng He of the Ming Imperial Navy often traded extensively with countries his fleet visited, exchanging porcelain, silver, gold, tin and silk cloth for sulphur (Qiu X. 1993: 128). Zheng even stocked Chinese goods in a transfer station in Malacca to facilitate trade, the only recorded overseas trading station in the entire history of China (Huang X. 1520/1982: 43).

# APPENDIX B

## The Ming–Qing price revolution and population growth

By definition, a price revolution is a substantial reduction in the relative price of a currency in relation to all the other 'ordinary goods'. It occurs as a result of a rightwards shift of the supply curve of the 'monetary good' after a supply shock. A price revolution takes the form of a general price increase among ordinary goods even though the relative price ratios among those goods remain more or less constant. It can thus be viewed as a type of inflation. In other words, the price change during a price revolution differs in nature from a price change resulting from a change in the scarcity of ordinary goods and services.

### Silver imports over time

During the Ming–Qing, over a period of about two and half centuries (from 1570 to 1840) China imported large quantities of monetary silver. During the first stage, from 1571 to 1644, the total amount of silver received by China has been estimated as 53–100 million pesos (38.1–71.9 million *liang*, averaging 55 million *liang*; or 1,422–2,683 tonnes, averaging 2,050 tonnes) (Liang F. 1989: 178–9; Chen X.W. 1991: 50). During the third stage, between 1700 and 1840, the West was responsible for exporting 6,340 tonnes (170 million *liang*) of silver to China (Zhuang G. 1995: 71). During the second stage (1645–99) in between, it is known that (1) the Manila galleon trade ended in 1640 when the Spaniards ran out of silver to pay for silk from China (see Wallerstein 1974–86 vol. 1: 338) and (2) in the second half of the sixteenth and the first half of the seventeenth centuries, Japan became an important silver supplier to China, exporting 122–223 tonnes a year (Quan H. 1993: 8; Iwao 1967: 11; Ni L. and Xia W. 1990: 51; see also Reid 1993: 27). If it is assumed that from 1645 to 1699 Japan was the sole silver supplier to China with an average of 178 tonnes a year (Wallerstein 1974–86 vol. 1: 338), there would be another 9,600 tonnes or so. The estimated total silver sum is thus 18,000 tonnes. Such an intake of large quantities of monetary silver for such a long period of time caused the money supply curve to shift to the right by a great margin. The impact was a price revolution.

### Change in money supply over time

However, an absolute increase in the quantity of monetary silver alone does not necessarily lead to a price revolution simply because the equilibrium of the monetary market is unknown. In an expanding market, more money is demanded. So, an increase in monetary supply at the same rate as demand increases will not cause a price revolution. If the increase in monetary supply lags behind demand, it will result in deflation instead. One way to detect a landslide supply shock which outdid the increase in demand is to use the total population as a proxy for the market scale and to examine the ratio between monetary supply and population (MP ratio).

## Pre-Qing

During the Tang Period, the MP ratio showed a tendency to decline: in AD 713–41 the annual bronze coin supply was 1 million *min* (1,000 *wen*) (Sima G. 1084 vol. 242: 'Tangmuzong Changqin Yuannian'). During this period, China had a population of 41.4–48.1 million (see Liang F. 1980: 69). The MP ratio was thus 20.8–24.2 *wen*. In AD 742–56, the annual coin supply was 327,000 *min* for a population of 48.9–52.9 million (see Ouyang X. 1060: ch. 'Shihuozhi 4'; Liang F. 1980: 69–70). The MP ratio dropped to 6.2–6.7 *wen*. In AD 785–805, the annual coin supply was as low as 135,000 *min*, while the Tang population dropped to 12–19 million people (2.4–3.8 million households, five persons per household) (see Ouyang X. 1060: ch. 'Shihuozhi 4'; Liang F. 1980: 70). The MP ratio rose to 7.1–11.3 *wen*. In the 820s AD the annual monetary supply reached 150,000 *min*, but dropped to 100,000 *min* in AD 834 (see Sima G. 1084 vol. 242: 'Tangmuzong Changqin Yuannian'; Ouyang X. 1060: ch. 'Shihuozhi 4'). The MP ratios in these two cases were as low as 9.5 *wen* (against a population of 15.8 million in AD 820) and 4.5 *wen* (22 million people, converted from 4.4 million households in AD 834) (Liang F. 1980: 70–1). As expected, the monetary supply curve shifted leftwards and caused deflation: the grain price dropped 75 per cent from AD 641 to 820 and that of silk halved during the period AD 785–820 (Xue P. 1995: 65–6).

During the following Northern Song, in the eleventh century AD, the annual supply of bronze coins was 6 million *min* plus iron coins of 200,000–500,000 *min*, or a total of 6.2–6.5 million *min* a year. With the population peak of 29 million as in 1066, there was a new record MP ratio of 214–224 *wen*, some nine times higher than the previous record under the Tang (Liang F. 1980: 7–8; Liu S. 1992: 117, 1993). In the Southern Song Dynasty, money supply declined to around 100,000 *min* a year (as in the twelfth century) against a population of 29.5 million (a peak in 1179) (Liang F. 1980: 130; Liu S. 1992: 117). The MP ratio was as low as 3.4 *wen*. Paper currency was circulated to ease the monetary shortage.

Here, the long-term mean value of MP ratio is 43.5–46.5 *wen*, excluding the Ming–Qing Period, during which a thorough monetary reform took place to replace base metal with imported silver.

## Change during the early Qing

The Qing monetary situation was transitional. On the one hand, the age-old bronze standard tailed off, and on the other imported silver played an increasingly dominant role. Before 1662 under the Qing, the annual supply of bronze coins was 30 to 33 *mao* (1 *mao* = 12,880,000 coins). The coin issuing increased by 33 per cent in 1662 (see Wang Q. 1858/1985: 207). China's population was 16.1 million in 1651–61 and

17.2–26.4 million between 1662 and 1735 (Liang F. 1980: 251–2). So, the MP ratios were 24–26.4 *wen* and 19.5–29.9 *wen*, respectively. In 1773, the Qing money supply in bronze coins reached its peak of 75 *mao*; the MP ratio decreased to 4.4 *wen* with a population of 218.7 million (*ibid.*: 252). Finally, the coin supply dropped back to 30 *mao* a year at the end of the eighteenth century (see Wang Q. 1858/1985: 207). At this time, China's population had reached 293.3 million (as in 1799; Liang F. 1980: 251–2) and the MP ratio was only 1.3 *wen*, the poorest since the Tang. The steady drop in the MP ratio during the Qing reflects such a change.

As mentioned earlier, about 2,050 tonnes of silver had been imported by China by 1644 (Liang F. 1980: 178–9; Chen X.W. 1991: 50). The MP ratio for a population of 16.1 million (as in 1651–61) is thus 127.3 g, or 3.41 *liang*. According to the lowest government rate of exchange of silver and bronze currencies in Ming–Qing times, this amount of silver equalled 3,410 bronze coins (*wen*) (Xie G. 1981: 166). The combined MP ratio for the early Qing period is 3,436 *wen* (26 *wen* + 3,410 *wen*). The converted Qing MP ratio in copper terms was 73 to 78 times the long-term MP mean value (43.5–46.5 *wen*) and 15 to 16 times the Song MP record (214–224 *wen*). Since the silver was obtained and circulated by trade, measured by weight (1 *liang* = 37.3 g), not by government issue (Sun Z. 1989; Sun Z. *et al.* 1991; Su Y. and Li J. 1992), there was a good chance it was underrated because of the tendency to under-report.

As Skinner indicates, during the Qing there were in all some 45,000 market towns in China (1971: 272–3); this 2,050 tonnes of silver could thus add to the existing currency in circulation in each town a sum of 1,221 *liang* (45.6 kg), an equivalent of a minimum 1.2 million bronze coins at the government exchange rate. In this context, China was qualified to have a genuine price revolution. The minimum threefold increase in the general price level in late Ming and early Qing times showed just that (Xie G. 1981: 162; Sun X. 1988: 153; Guo C. 1996; Wang Y. 1996; see also Geiss 1979: 159–64; Cartier 1981: 464).

However, the increase in monetary supply is only one side of the market. The Ming–Qing Period is also marked as a period of rapid expansion of market activities which in turn increased the demand for more money to facilitate this. The difference between the increase rate in MP ratio and that in general price level is consistent with the increase in monetary demand owing to the market expansion, which can be estimated by the following equation:

$$X_m = \frac{MP_D}{P_D} \tag{B.1}$$

where $X_m$ is the market expansion rate in value of goods and services traded. $MP_D$ is the degree of MP ratio change, measured by the MP ratios of comparable periods $MP_i$ over $MP_{i-1}$ and $P_D$ is the degree of the price revolution, measured by $P_i$ over $P_{i-1}$ (standing for the price levels at period $i-1$ and period $i$). Hence:

$$X_m = \frac{MP_i : MP_{i-1}}{P_i : P_{i-1}} \tag{B.2}$$

Given that the value of $MP_D$ is 15–16, $MP_{i-1}$ being 214 to 224 *wen* (as the peak by 1400) and $MP_i$ 3,436 *wen* (by 1644), and that of $P_D$ is 3, shown by the net increase of the general price level by period $P_i$, the value of $X_m$ is 5–5.3. Clearly, the market expansion cancelled out to a considerable degree the inflationary effect generated by the price revolution.

One may argue that the practice of silver bullion hoarding in China should be taken into account and that the result will be very different. Hoarding by its nature is a deduction of the currency in circulation from the supply side and it thus eases the pressure for a price revolution. If, say, 50 per cent of the imported silver was hoarded, the potential $P_D$ value without hoarding was double the actual $P_D$ value, which may help the market by acting as a safety valve. Also, the fact that all the hoarded silver represents tangible wealth in the form of a trade surplus sedimenting via market exchange demonstrates that the capacity of the economy is greater rather than lesser, which is compatible with the market expansion process. Therefore, on the whole, hoarding as such should not be viewed as a sign of economic weakness but rather of economic strength because of the undeniable wealth behind it. On the other hand, hoarding and market demand expansion work in the same direction in cancelling the effect/degrees of the supply shock. Therefore, $X_m$ needs to be further defined as 'expansion rate of market activities and hoarding'. The reciprocal of $X_m$ can be used to measure the degree of such cancellation $(1 - Y_c)$:

$$Y_c = \frac{1}{X_m} = \frac{1}{\dfrac{MP_i : MP_{i-1}}{P_i : P_{i-1}}} = \frac{P_i : P_{i-1}}{MP_i : MP_{i-1}} \tag{B.3}$$

Obviously, when $Y_c$ is unity, hence $(1 - Y_c)$ is zero, there is no cancellation. The more closely $Y_c$ approaches zero, hence the closer $(1 - Y_c)$ is to unity, the greater the cancellation. In the Ming–Qing case, the value of $Y_c$ is 0.19–0.20 and $(1 - Y_c)$ 0.80–0.81, very high indeed.

## Change during the late Qing

By the end of the eighteenth century, the Qing copper MP ratio had become a negligible 1.3 *wen* (Wang Q. 1858/1985: 207; Liang F. 1980: 251–2). At this point, China had a silver standard for the first time in history. Evidence shows that the MP ratio more or less maintained with China's population growth. As stated earlier, by AD 1840, a total of 18,000 metric tons of silver had been absorbed by the Chinese economy. Given that in 1833 China's population reached a new height of 398.9 million (Liang F. 1980: 10), the MP ratio can be calculated as 41.1 g, or 1.1 *liang* of silver, an equivalent of between 2,200 *wen* at the lowest government exchange rate in 1845 and 4,400 *wen* at the provincial market rate, averaging 3,300 *wen* (Sun X. 1988: 204). Although during the eighteenth century the price of rice in the Yangzi Delta fluctuated between 0.94 and 2.18 *liang* per *shi* without further upsurge (see Wang 1992: 40–7), the aftermath of the price revolution was still felt from 1750 to 1864, during which the general price level increased by probably another 150 per cent and then became relatively stable from 1864 to 1910 (Wang 1973: 61). This indicates that a new equilibrium was finally reached and the price revolution was over. This is revealed by the close synchronisation of China's silver currency exchange rate with six other Asian currencies from 1860 to 1915 (Eng 1993: 3).

## Price revolution without a Malthusian crisis

During the Ming–Qing Period, China experienced a seemingly classical situation of Malthusian crisis as its population quadrupled, a convenient fact that can be and has been used in explaining China's misfortune in economic growth.

However, a closer examination of the population movement and other economic indicators such as price change makes one realise that they did not go hand in hand. In particular, prices accelerated before the upsurge of population: arguably, large quantities of monetary silver importation began in China in the sixteenth century when China's population was stable. It continued to remain stable till the beginning of the eighteenth century; rapid population growth began around AD 1700. The starting point of this growth is inferred from the average growth rate of 1.45 a year based on the data for 1741–1851 and 1863–87. With this rate, it would take about 45 years for the population to double (Liang F. 1980: 4–11; 251–4, 256–7). There was thus a noticeable gap of some two centuries (1571–1699). During this period, as mentioned earlier, a total of 10,050 tonnes of silver, or 56 per cent of the entire silver intake by China (18,000 tonnes), was absorbed by the economy. This pile of monetary silver left China an MP ratio of 495 g or 13.3 *liang* (10,050 tonnes versus 20.3 million people if the Qing official data are taken as the base; Liang F. 1980: 251). Even if the population estimate for 1700 is increased four- or fivefold with an outrageous exaggeration (thus 81.2 million and 101.5 million), the MP ratio is still high at 2.7–3.3 *liang*, twice as high as that for 1833–40.

It is not at all surprising to see that the index of food price moved ahead of that of the population in the entire period 1500–1700. Between 1500 and 1600, when the population increased by only 50 per cent, the food price doubled. Later, during 1600–50, when the population dropped some 5 per cent, the food price kept increasing, by about another 90 per cent (Goldstone 1991: 358). In this context, the Malthusian synchronisation of change in food price and growth in population may well have been the case in Japan and Western Europe between 1500 and 1800 (*ibid.*: 83–8, 179, 298; Feeney and Hamano 1990), but it is certainly not applicable in their Chinese counterpart. Therefore, it is reasonable to state that China's price revolution commenced much earlier than the Qing population explosion and thus had little to do with the latter.

# APPENDIX C

## Dissemination of agricultural technology in China

Farming technology was actively obtained by the proto-Chinese in the early stages of Chinese civilisation. So far, three cases have been investigated: crop species, the plough and irrigation.

### Crop species: the diffusion of rice and wheat

Archaeological findings show that a distinctive pattern of divergence in Neolithic agriculture existed in China. Between 7000 and 5000 BC, the Yellow River Region was predominantly a millet cultivation area with two varieties: glutinous millet (*shu*, *Panicum miliaceum*) and non-glutinous millet (*su*, *Setaria italica*) (see Huang Q. 1982–3); whereas the Yangzi River Valley and the area further south formed a rice-growing region with two rice species: japonica rice (*jingdao*, *Oryza stativa subsp. Keng*) and indica rice (*xiandao*, *Oryza stativa subsp. Hsien*) (see Guo W. 1988: 27–9; and also Yan W. 1982; Lin C. 1987; Liu Y. 1987). If such an observation is credible, it can safely be suggested that the invention of rice cultivation was achieved by the indigenous 'Southern Barbarians' (*man*) and had very little to do with the northern proto-Chinese group which was based in the Yellow River Valley. It was much later that the proto-Chinese group moved to the Yangzi and Pearl River regions.

Such regional divergence is often blurred as a result of either ignorance or deliberation. A common practice is to take some historical record of crops as evidence without analytical identification of their origin and diffusion. It is true that in the Inscriptions on Bones and Tortoise Shells (*jiaguwen*), an early form of the Chinese written language dating back 4,500–5,000 years (Su M. 1987), at least six species of domestic crops were recorded (Yu X. 1957: 88; Hu D. 1985: 138–44): two varieties of glutinous millet (*Panicum miliaceum*), *shu* and *ji*; and two varieties of non-glutinous broomcorn millet (*Setaria italica*), *he* and *liang*; *dan*, soya bean (*Glycine max*) or adzuki bean (*Phaseolus calcalatus*); *mai*, or wheat (*Triticum aestivum*); and *ni*, or rice (*Oryza sativa*). However, there is an identification problem here. The record of crop species was one thing and the actual cultivation of them was another. Thus, the location where the record was discovered was not necessarily the region where the crop originated and was grown. The record of rice in the Inscriptions on Bones and Tortoise Shells may well have reflected the curiosity of the proto-Chinese in the Yellow River Valley: they recorded some things in the alien south.

As for wheat and wheat cultivation, from ancient times to this day, north China, especially the Yellow River Region, has been known as a wheat-growing zone. Thus, it has been taken for granted that wheat should be related to the Chinese. However, if we trace back the origin of wheat (*Triticum aestivum*), the discovery and invention of wheat cultivation also had little to do with the proto-Chinese group. Wheat was first called *lai* in the Chinese language, which is often interpreted as '[species] coming [from a foreign land]' (see Bray 1984). It has been commonly guessed that wheat came from Central Asia to the Yellow River Valley. According to recent research, wheat originated in the Laimu Region (in what is now Laiwu City) of Shandong Province, which was traditionally the centre of the 'Eastern Barbarians' (*yi*). Also, the name *lai* for wheat came from the name of Laimu (Hu X. 1958: 244; Tang Q. 1986: ch. 2). That wheat cultivation in China dates back 6,000–7,000 years does not change the fact that the species was introduced (Guo W. 1988: 30). Even if we accept the theory that wheat was introduced from Central Asia to the Yellow River Valley, it will not change the nature of the statement: Central Asia was the region occupied by the 'Western Barbarians' (*di* and *rong*). Moreover, there is the possibility that wheat was introduced from two independent sources, one in the east and another in the west.

The advantages of wheat-growing were so great that it gradually replaced the indigenous millet in the Yellow River Region (Tang Q. 1986: 57–60), the very home base of the earliest farming people in East Asia. Later, rice-growing claimed an even larger share of China's land under cultivation. In the Ming Dynasty, approximately 70 per cent of the total grain output in China was rice (Song Y. 1637: 1). These two crops thus changed China's landscape and the Chinese diet. Their entrenchment helped shape the agricultural dominance on the East Asian mainland.

# The plough

Related to the divergence between dry farming in the Yellow River Region and wet farming in the Yangzi and Pearl River regions was the difference in farming equipment. Neolithic hoes and sickles made of stone and bones have been unearthed mainly in the north, while stone adzes and ploughs have been discovered only in the south (see Guo W. 1988: 32–5). Based on archaeological evidence, recent studies convincingly argued that in China the plough originated in the south, not in the north (Mu Y. and Song Z. 1981; also Wen S. 1987).

The plough was invented because of the heavy texture of the soil types in South China. Thus, given the physical environment in the Yangzi and Pearl River regions during the Neolithic Period the invention of the plough was indeed a solution for the expansion of agriculture in the south. In contrast, as Ping-ti Ho convincingly argued (1969), North China had a large area of extremely fine and soft loess which made cultivation easy: it could be done with wooden sticks if not fingernails.

It is worth knowing that the materials used for farming tools were more or less the same in both the north and south, the differences being mainly in their design. In the Yellow River Region the fine loess soil made the spade a sufficient tool to dig holes in fields whereas the forest land of the south required much heavier tools, and the plough was ideal to open up and turn over the soil. In addition, in dry farming, the visibility during the process of soil preparation is far better than that in the paddies, where soil is sometimes submerged by water. The advantage of the use of a plough is twofold: (1) the tilling depth of soil is predetermined by the angle of the plough head so that invisibility of the soil is no longer a problem; and (2) the water in the paddies works as a lubricating agent to save energy. It is thus plausible to suggest that in the Neolithic Period, the plough was first invented in the south as a tool to reclaim arable land.

The plough was absent in the north, not only during the Neolithic Period but also throughout the entire Bronze Age of the Xia–Shang (c. 2000–1030 BC), although spades and sickles made of bronze were common (see Zheng X. et al. 1984: 14–19; Wang J. 1985; Guo W. 1988: 49–52; ZNK 1984 vol. 1: 26–34). By the time of *The Book of Odes* (*Shijing*), which was written in the Western Zhou Dynasty (c. 1030–771 BC), there was still no sign that the plough was used in the north; in contrast, the ancient spade (*lei*) was extensively referred to (Anon. Zhou Dynasty). The earliest evidence for the use of the plough in the north was during the Spring–Autumn and Warring States periods (770–221 BC), the Iron Age of Chinese civilisation (Guo W. 1988: 73–6). This makes sense because the iron plough can be made very thin to reduce resistance from the soil during ploughing with or without water as a lubricant. Although the iron material used to make the plough was indeed superior to the wood, stone and bone used in the south, this does change the fact that the use of the plough in the north began several millennia later than in the south.

Evidence also shows that the imperial government of China had to step in to popularise the use of the plough in the north. During the Western Han Dynasty (206 BC– AD 24), Emperor Wudi (r. 140–88 BC) launched a massive campaign in the north to promote Zhao Guo's 'Alternate Ride Cultivation' (*daitianfa*), a new method of intensive dry farming which was characterised by the use of the cattle-drawn plough to prepare soil and to divide a field into rides and furrows (Ban G. AD 82: ch. 'Shihuo Zhi'; Fan W. 1964–5 vol. 2: 53–4; ZNK 1984 vol. 1: 151–6). The idea was to replace the timeless practice of fallow by alternating the rides and furrows each year and thus to save land.

The illusion that the proto-Chinese group first invented the plough has mainly come from some scattered written records. In the Inscriptions on Bones and Tortoise Shells, *lei* (ancient spade) and *li* (plough) were first recorded (Sun C. 1964: 1–2; Li B. 1981: 20–32; Fan W. 1964–5 vol. 2: 113). Such a record is far from sufficient for modern researchers to know just how wide the distribution of these tools was. Thus, it is risky to assume that these two types of tools were used together in the north. Given that the word *li* was not exclusively used for the farming tool, and was used as people's names as well (see Zhang Z.M. 1987: 47), such doubt is further fuelled.

The illusion has been reinforced by some later historical records. For instance, in the Han Dynasty, Sima Qian recorded that the southerners practised slash-and-burn cultivation (Sima Q. 91 BC: vol. 129). Liu Xu of the Tang Dynasty reported the same phenomenon (Liu X. AD 945 vol. 158: entry 'Biography of Yan Zhen'). Here, two questions have to be asked: (1) To what extent did the southerners practise slash-and-burn cultivation when it was recorded? and (2) Just how often was this technique applied? Before these questions are satisfactorily answered, it is risky to assume that the use of the plough did not exist in the south.

Since the written record in the Inscriptions on Bones and Tortoise Shells shows that the northerners knew of the existence of the southern agricultural technology in rice cultivation and of the use of the plough before the northerners themselves grew rice and used the plough, it rules out the possibility of reinvention of these two things by the northerners, although it does not rule out the possibility of north-erners having modified the southern inventions. But there is a fundamental difference between invention and innovation, creation and adoption.

## Irrigation

Irrigation is an indispensable process in rice cultivation. Given the long history of rice cultivation in the south by the *man* peoples ('Southern Barbarians'), it is only logical to assume that irrigation developed first in the south and was diffused to the proto-Chinese group with the waves of migration of the proto-Chinese group to the south. Evidence shows (Zuoqiu *c.* 454b BC: ch. 'Xuangong Shiyinian') that the earliest large-scale irrigation project was constructed not by the proto-Chinese but by the *chu* tribe in the south: in 598 BC under the instruction of Sun Shu-ao, a technical official of King Zhuang of the Chu Kingdom (613–591 BC), the Qisibei Irrigation Network was built in the Hubei Region. Chu was a kingdom of the *man* in the area where the Han River and Yangzi River meet (see Han L. 1986: 139; Zhang Z.M. 1987).

Large irrigation projects built under Chinese, as apposed to *man*, rule began only in the Qin Kingdom: King Zhao (306–251 BC) appointed Li Bing the Governor of Shu (in what is now Sichuan Province) and ordered him to build the Dujiangyan Irrigation System. The Shu Region was a peripheral region at that time, newly captured from the non-Chinese. The first irrigation system built in the heartland of the Chinese domain in present day Shanxi Province dates back to no earlier than 246 BC; it is known as the Zhengguo Canal (Sima Q 91 BC: ch. 'Hequ Shu') and was constructed by order of King Zheng of Qin (246–221 BC). The Zhengguo Canal was a medium-sized work of its kind. The era of large-scale irrigation networks in the Chinese heartland began only in the Western Han Period (206 BC–AD 24): seven canals were built connecting three rivers (the Wei, Jing and Luo) in the Guanzhong Region (in what is now Shanxi Province) (Fan W. 1964–5 vol. 2: 52–62; ZNK 1984: 139–40; Guo W. 1988: 146–7). It is worth noting that the beginning of the era of irrigation in the Yellow River Region coincided with the timing of the southwards expansion of the Chinese.

Thus, it is safe to suggest that the *man* peoples were about three centuries ahead of the proto-Chinese group in large-scale irrigation (598–306 BC) and several millennia ahead of the proto-Chinese in small-scale irrigation (7000–598 BC).

But a general impression has been given that the proto-Chinese group invented irrigation. The first evidence given to support such a theory is that there is no written record to show that the non-Chinese peoples practised irrigation. Fortunately, such a myth has now been resolved by archaeological findings of early rice cultivation in the south. The second evidence is from the water control effort made by King Yu of the Xia Period (Xia: *c.* 2000–1520 BC), a ruler who was later regarded and worshipped as the model agricultural administrator in Chinese history (Fan W. 1964–5 vol. 1: 92–5; Lee 1969: 35–43, 46). However, if we look closely, it is clear that Yu's contribution was explicitly drainage or flood control (*zhishui*), not irrigation (see Ma Z. 1982; Wang K. 1983). By definition, flood control seeks to get rid of excess water in order to control damage while irrigation is intended to maintain water supply in order to support production. The third evidence is from the chessboard-field system (*jingtianzhi*) of the Western Zhou Dynasty (see Li J. 1962: ch. 9; Ma Z. 1985), a system which has been widely taken as that of irrigation by the proto-Chinese group in the eleventh century BC (see, for example, Zheng X. *et al*. 1984: 23–4; Han L.Q. 1986: 18–20, 29). In effect, as a system of the distribution of land, the chessboard-field system had nothing to do with the well, or with irrigation (Fan W. 1964–5 vol. 1: 142–5; Han L. 1986: 57–68). The common misunderstanding about the chessboard-field system comes from (1) misinterpretation of the word *jing*, and (2) misinterpretation of the function of ditches in the fields. The word *jing* in the Chinese language can mean two things: the well and the chessboard shape. The ditches in the chessboard-field system were likely to be landmarks for both the calculation of workloads for the farmers and the boundaries between individual land and community land. The reasons are simple. First, digging ditches was a cheap way to mark land. Second, there is no evidence to show that in Western Zhou times (*c*. 1030–771 BC) rice was grown extensively in the Yellow River Region, where the chessboard-field system was used; instead, evidence shows that millet and wheat were the main, crops and these relied on the monsoons and needed no artificial water supply from irrigation. Third, With the drought-resistant crops millet and wheat, the main concern by the proto-Chinese farmers was flooding, and efforts were made to keep excess water out of the farming areas as much as possible by means of the ditches rather than allowing the flood water to run into the fields (Sima Q. 91 BC: ch. 'Wudi Benji'). Fourth, during the Spring and Autumn Period (770–476 BC) when the chessboard-field system finally collapsed and was replaced by individual private land ownership, the ditches were abandoned. There was no sign that the change had any negative impact on agricultural production. It can thus safely be assumed that no irrigation existed under the chessboard-field system.

# APPENDIX D

## Peasant behavioural patterns

### Peasant behavioural paradox

One of the enigmas about the Chinese peasantry is why peasants did not leave the agricultural sector in large numbers and open up a second front in the economy, given the high productivity in Chinese agriculture and the long history of non-agricultural sectors, namely industries, trade and services.

It is hypothesised that the reason the Chinese did not break away from agricultural dominance was population pressure and limited land. According to Kang Chao, the man-to-land ratio deteriorated continuously and the impoverished peasantry was unable to leave the land for social mobility (Chao 1986: ch. 10). But, by definition, when the peasantry became poorer and poorer, this often meant that the number of unemployed soared. It also meant that the marginal product of labour dropped and probably approached zero. In turn, it meant that the opportunity cost for peasants of leaving agriculture was lowered. These were exactly the conditions needed for peasants to establish a livelihood somewhere else. They were not fools. They would have reversed their fate, had quitting farming helped. Such a process can be demonstrated by the marginal analysis and by Lewis's model of the dual economy.

### Theoretical models

#### A neo-classical approach: when to leave agriculture

According to the marginal analysis, under intensive farming, if labour input keeps increasing while the inputs of land, capital and technology are held constant, the total output (TP) will increase but the marginal product of labour (MPL) will decrease, and so will the average product of labour (APL). This is determined by the law of diminishing returns. Three equations can be presented. First,

$$TP = aL^2 + bL + c \tag{D.1}$$

where TP is the total output level of a farm, L is the labour input and a, b and c are constants. Second,

$$APL = \frac{TP}{L} \tag{D.2}$$

where APL is the average product of labour, which is an indicator of labour productivity. In the formula, the value of APL is inversely related to $L$. Third,

$$\text{MPL} = \frac{\text{d}TP}{\text{d}L} \tag{D.3}$$

where MPL is the marginal physical product of labour. In the formula, the value of MPL is also inversely related to $L$.

The correlations among the total output level, the average product of labour and the marginal physical product of labour are illustrated in Figure D.1. In the figure, a, b and c are the optimal value points of MPL, APL and TP, respectively. Owing to the law of diminishing returns, beyond these points MPL, APL and TP become downwards-sloping, reflecting the decreases in marginal output, average output and total output, which shows the limit for a factor input (here labour). When MPL

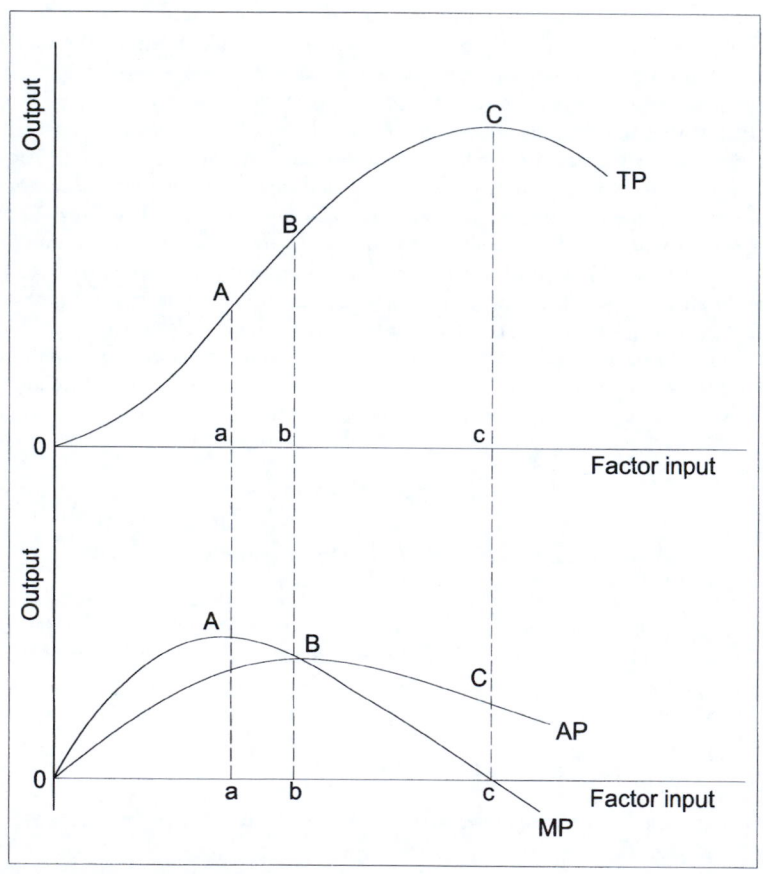

*Figure D.1* Operational basis of capitalism

drops to zero, intersecting the $x$ axis, any further labour input will make no neo-classical economic sense, and should thus be stopped. MPL equal to zero is thus the floor for labour input, indicating where peasants should leave the agricultural sector. Otherwise they will become impoverished. Thus, impoverishment, or the fear of it, is a stimulus, not a preventer, for peasants to leave agriculture.

Certainly, the condition here is that no technological change takes place. However, even if we take technological progress into account, for each level of technology applied there will still be a labour input floor which is dictated by MPL $= 0$.

Naturally, the next question is where should the surplus rural population go. The model established by Arthur Lewis (1954) shows us not only when but also how to dispose of these extra people from the agricultural sector.

### Chayanovian behavioural pattern: not to leave agriculture

In reality, traditional agriculture may well coexist with modern and semi-modern industries. A pioneering work in this field by A. V. Chayanov points out that tradi-tional peasants seek not a high wage rate but 'total employment' (not Keynesian full employment under the market economy) (see also Dalton 1972: 409). Thus, their aim and behaviour are not to maximise returns, which are often measured by the mar-ginal product of labour (MPL) and profit, but to maximise the total output (TP). This means by definition that in their economy the marginal product of labour equals zero (Chayanov 1925). His theory also implies that once this maximum output is reached the peasant tends to maintain it by staying at the point where the marginal product of labour is zero, given that negative marginal product of labour means destruction of product, which is irrational for a peasant household economy. This is particularly true since traditional agriculture produces little waste: undesirable pro-duct can be turned to fodder, fertiliser and many other side-products. Therefore a higher wage offers peasants no inducement to move from agricultural to industry. This is a society which is largely immune from the Lewisian transition, as in China Chayanovian behaviour was evident.

If we stick to the marginal analysis, the Chayanovian theory can be interpreted as follows: through 'self-exploitation' the peasant economy has so perfectly inelastic a labour supply curve that the curve is virtually vertical, as shown by S in Figure D.2. Such a supply curve means that the peasantry can work at any wage rate from 0 and above. It also means that the labour force is totally employed because the peas-antry has very few choices. There is thus is not at all a normal or perfect market. The nature of such an economy determines that the zero MPL is not only tolerable but also the key factor in reaching 'total employment' status with a corresponding low wage rate. This is illustrated by $Qt$ (an intersection between the labour supply curve S and the $x$ axis), and $W$ (a derived intersection between point a, an equilibrium between demand and supply, and the $y$ axis for wage level).

In short, four prominent features mark the fundamental difference between a mar-ket economy and the Chayanovian economy: (1) unlike $OS'$ the supply curve OS is not a normally behaved one; (2) society pursues total employment at $Qt$, but not Keynesian full employment at $Qf$; (3) the wage rate is at $W$, much lower than $W'$; and (4) the total income of labour under the non-market economy (the area which is marked by O, $W$, a and $Qt$) is much lower than under the market economy (the area which is marked by O, $W'$, $a'$ and $Qf$). Here, the concept of marginal product becomes irrelevant.

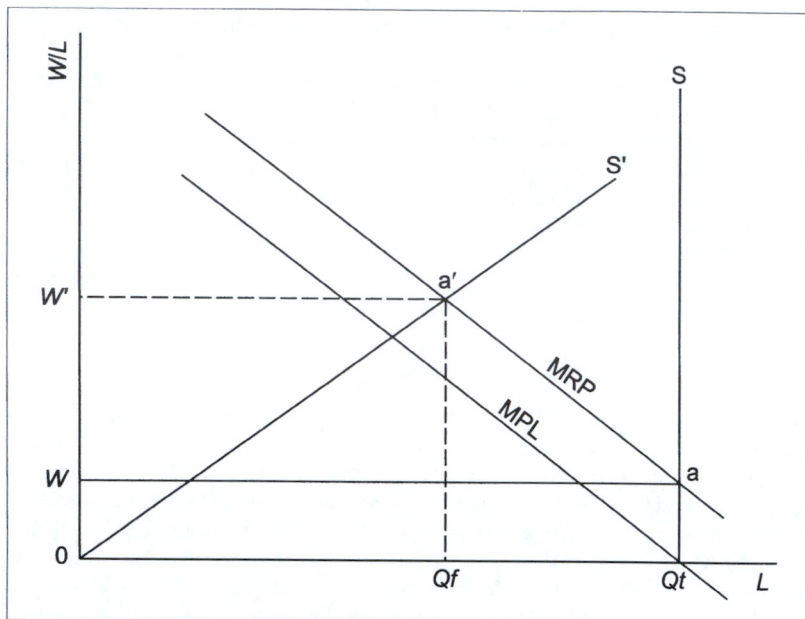

*Figure D.2* Peasant economy: labour demand and supply

*Notes*

L, Labour; W/L, wage rate; W, subsistence wage rate; W', market wage rate; S and S', supply curves; MRL, marginal product of labour; MRP, physical product of labour; Qt, total employment level; Qf, neo-classical full employment level.

a The supply curve is perfectly inelastic and intersects with the MPL at zero.

b Accordingly, the wage rate is very low, which can be seen by using a hypothetical supply curve as a reference system.

 c The economy reaches 'total employment' (Qt), as distinct from the hypothetical neo-classical 'full employment' (Qf).

So, the non-market sector is not compatible with the market one, which simply means that the threshold of 'surplus labour' was so high in the agricultural sector that the labour will not move out for a higher wage offer. This can be illustrated by point C along TP in Figure D.3. The marginal product of labour must reach zero (point c along the *x* axis).

The problem is this: once the economy reaches point C the marginal product of labour reaches zero, whether or not peasants stop further labour input in agriculture. If we consider the maximal total output as the only optimal object for the Chayanovian peasants, input of labour should stop at point C, and any further increase of input is irrational because the diminishing returns will drag down the total output. However, the Chayanovian peasants have two other objectives: (1) to reach 'total employment' and (2) to maintain a minimal/subsistence wage rate. To achieve total employment, labour input must be continued regardless of the marginal output of labour. To maintain a minimal/subsistence wage rate, peasants only need only to calculate the average output of labour (APL).

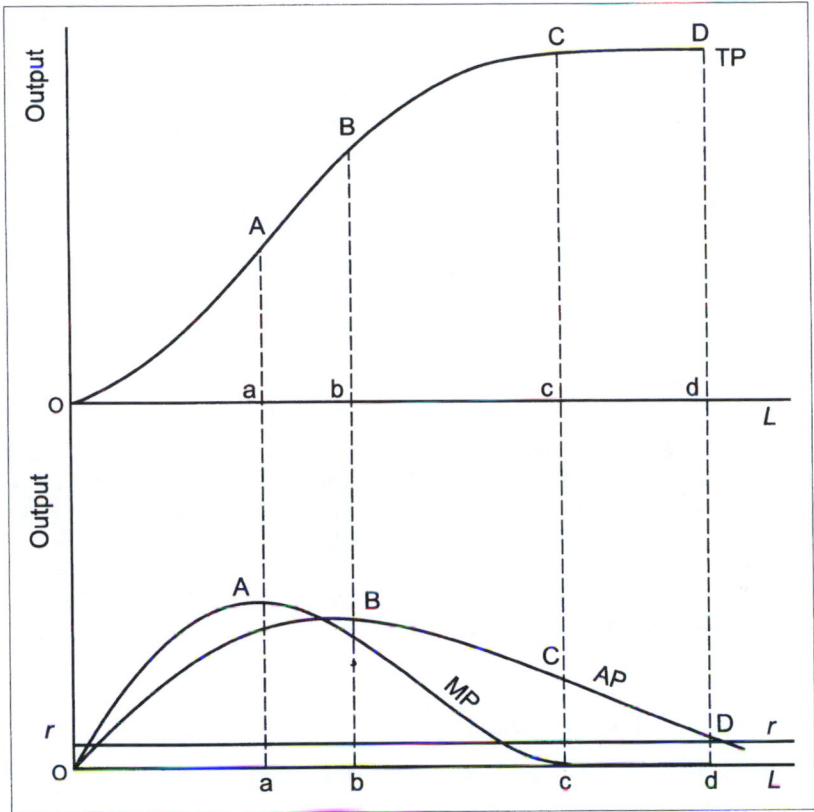

*Figure D.3* A Chayanovian economy

From Figure D.3, we do not know the subsistence wage level because wages are determined by consumption and thus to a great extent are independent of production. Supposing that the subsistence wage rate is r, when production reaches point C, the actual wage, which is determined by AP, is still higher than the subsistence wage. This means that a further increase in labour input, $d - c$, is still feasible to maintain total employment. The limit for labour input is at point D, where the actual wage level (represented by APL) intersects the subsistence wage level $r$, a threshold which is also called the 'Chayanovian labour–consumption balance' (Dallas 1982: 27–9). Once this is achieved, the agricultural surplus is exhausted and the peasants have to decide whether they should reclaim new land or change farming technology. If new land is not readily available, technological progress is the only way to avoid poverty and starvation. This is consistent with an Chayanovian notion of 'self-exploitation'.

In essence, in the Chayanovian economy, with an increase of labour input the marginal product of labour will not only reach zero but also stay at zero. In other words, the impact of the extra labour input after point C on total output is neutral, not negative. Because of this neutral impact, after point C the curve of marginal product of labour becomes flat along the $x$ axis. Accordingly, the total product curve becomes flat, too. As long as an output is produced, a certain level of individual income (average output) will be produced, and the peasant wage will never become zero. Society tolerates a large population with a low wage rate.

This is described in the following formula, where $w$ is the income level of the total output divided by labour input. It shows: (1) the income level is the dependent variable on both the total output and labour input; (2) the optimal point is where MPL reaches zero and TP is maximal, (3) by definition income is always positive if TP is positive, which is the basis of 'total employment'.

$$w = APL = \frac{TP}{L} \quad (\lim TP \rightarrow maximum)$$
$$MPL \rightarrow 0$$

(D.4)

Disagreeing with Chayanov, who views the peasant non-market behaviour as an endogenous factor, T. W. Schultz sees such behaviour as a result of impacts by exogenous factors, mainly market imperfection. Thus, a peasant can by nature be as entrepreneurial as any capitalist but will not leave farming when his labour becomes of the 'surplus' type within the agricultural sector (Schultz 1964). According to Schultz's analysis, the end result is the same as Chayanov's: the peasantry is not responsive, or not responsive enough, to the market and stays on in agriculture regardless of the progress of the commercialisation of the economy as a whole.

## Evidence of the Chayanovian Pattern

Chayanov's model is largely based on the Russian experience with little influence from the market and competing non-agricultural sectors, commerce and industry. In his model there is no room for social mobility, either. Thus it is a static model. Technically, Chayanov did not go further from his self-exploitation notion to explore correlations among total output, average output, marginal output and income levels. In addition, Chayanov's work has not solved the problems of (1) what was the pattern and mechanism of technological development in such a self-perpetuating peasant economy, a critical factor for the peasantry to counterbalance population pressure; (2) why in some places the peasantry behaved so differently from others, and why this model obviously cannot explain the pattern of most of Europe from the eighteenth century onwards; and (3) what was the basis of such a behavioural pattern. Nevertheless, the Chayanovian model offers a useful insight in explaining a non-capitalist path of development.

This production–distribution pattern has been positively proved by some field studies of rural economies in Asia. For example, one study of Java indicates that (1) rice farmers reached the point where marginal product of labour equalled zero and maintained it in the process of 'agricultural involution', and (2) the total output was equally divided among labourers in the fashion of 'shared property' (Geertz 1963: 80, 97). Another observation reveals the same situation on a broader scope in Asia (Bray 1984).

Similarly, James Scott argues that in Southeast Asia the behaviour of the peasantry is not to maximise profit, but to avoid risk and to maintain subsistence living. In other words, they are a very different economic species in comparison to capitalists (Scott 1972, 1976).

Such a non-profit-seeking pattern, or a 'non-optimal solution' by the neo-classical standard, explains why in traditional China (1) peasants did not leave agriculture even if the marginal product of labour dropped to zero and remained zero; (2) peasants had a high 'population elasticity to agricultural output' and were not able to achieve a higher living standard as Chinese agricultural technology promised; and (3) to increase total output level per unit of land became a millennia-long national concern of not only the peasantry itself but also the intelligentsia (Deng 1993a).

The main contribution of the Chayanovian model lies in that, as a 'non-communist and non-capitalist' manifesto, it shows that a peasant economy could perpetuate itself under the pressure of population growth and could coexist with an industrial/commercial sector. The main problem for the model seems to be how a peasant society manages to avoid diminishing returns when the total output level approached the maximum, point C. Fortunately, the model allows technological changes: by definition, total output can be produced by a range of technical combinations. Therefore, the model is theoretically feasible.

## The Chinese case versus the models

China seems to have had all the conditions for Lewis's model to work: (1) in premodern China, commerce and industry were both actively competing against agriculture, and non-agricultural sectors offered higher wages; (2) people were able to change their jobs with social mobility. The evidence is undeniable. First, in premodern China the investment returns and wages among all the economic sectors were ranked as follows: the highest from commerce, the second from craft industries and the lowest from agriculture (Fu Z. and Wang Y. 1982: 358; Han L.Q. 1986). Second, as legally free citizens, the ordinary Chinese were allowed to change their occupations, and there was no legal barrier to stop a Chinese farmer from becoming a merchant, for example.

In Lewis's logic, the Chinese economy should have easily moved towards and achieved industrialisation. Certainly, China seems to have started a few times, but, disappointingly, never went far enough to fulfil such a transition. If the Han, Song and late Qing periods are taken as three such periods, the intervals were a millennium each in spite of the fact that China kept a growing supply of labour and capital within the agricultural sector at the expense of improvements in labour and capital productivities. What puzzles us more is that China for a long time had a noticeable market system and remarkable urbanisation. China had every reason to become the most suitable candidate for industrialisation.

The paradox is apparent, given the economic dualism in premodern China (Elvin 1973: 304–5, 314). If the Chinese peasants were rational and thus were able to escape impoverishment by leaving agriculture, why did they not do just that like their counterparts in Europe and Japan?

It seems that there must have been some other mechanisms regulating or restraining peasant behaviour. Obviously, the problem was not purely technical since the

Chinese had an impressive record of inventions and innovations. Neither was it structural in a conventional sense (namely economic structure) because China had economic dualism.

It is suggested that there were intra-structural and intra-institutional barriers in China: the trinary equilibrium in China blocked a cross-sectoral labour supply to industry and commerce, and thus blocked diversity in economic development.

## Summary

It is clear that neither land scarcity (as in the man-to-land ratio approach), labour intensiveness-oriented tillage (as in 'rice paddy farming black hole hypothesis'), class struggle (as in so-called 'feudal landlordism'), nor cultural values (as in Confucian determinism) can satisfactorily spell out the causality in Chinese economic development.

Despite all the problems, Chayanov's ingenious system appears to explain premodern China better. If premodern China proves the validity of the Chayanovian model, a new insight into world economic history emerges simply because premodern China had the world's largest peasant population, and the largest single agrarian economy with one of the longest histories.

# APPENDIX E

## China's pseudo-feudalism

Many Chinese scholars, obsessed by the Marxist development phase model, have been using the term 'feudalism' to describe the nature of post-Qin China as a precapitalist society. Their dogmatic logic is that since precapitalist Europe, as described by Marx, was feudal, then precapitalist China must have been feudal, too.

In their hands, the concept of feudalism has been badly corrupted and become extremely misleading. According to these scholars, the word 'feudalism' in post-Qin China really means (1) the existence of large landowners who exploited landless tenants; (2) peasants confined in villages and agrarian life; and (3) a coercive and parasitical central government. Obviously, none of these characteristics has much to do with feudalism, because (1) a large number of post-Qin peasants had full or partial ownership of the land they tilled; (2) post-Qin peasants were legally free, not belonging to other people as a form of property, although the degree of freedom was not high by modern standards; and (3) a centralised government is by definition non-feudal.

Three other commonly used models for post-Qin China are also misleading: (1) the so-called 'Asiatic Mode of Production' put forward by Marx (Krader 1975; Brook 1989); (2) the so-called feudal 'landlordism' of the Maoists (Mao 1965 vol. 2: 306–14; Fan W. 1964–5; Bai 1982: ch. 4; Sun J. 1990); and (3) the so-called 'centralised bureaucratic feudalism' of Joseph Needham (1969: 31–2, 150–2, 175–88).

First, the Asiatic Mode of Production labels China as a slave-based society, controlled by a bureaucracy mainly through the managing of hydraulic infrastructure imperative for agriculture (see Brook 1989), the key evidence being that China had some state-owned land and the Chinese built huge irrigation networks which required a strong commanding centre to organise labour, capital and materials used for construction and maintenance of the networks. The logic is that if land was owned by the state there must have been no private land ownership, and that if public works on a large scale were built it must have been the result of a hydraulic bureaucracy. Thus, China must have belonged to the category of the Asiatic Mode of Production. Such rationale is indeed arbitrary simply because (1) what has been taken for state land ownership was in effect a dual system of communal/tribal land ownership and state ownership, by definition neither of which is slavery or feudalism; (2) there is little evidence to show the link between the hydraulic needs of the peasantry and the establishment of a centralised bureaucracy in China: Qin Shihuang, the first 'crowned' emperor and the unifier of China, made little effort to build and maintain any hydraulic works on a large scale. Instead, he built and maintained the Great Walls and thus began the legacy of centralised national bureaucracy.

Second, although landlordism did exist in post-Qin Chinese history, it always went together with a small, family landholding system. The very practice of equal inheritance among all the sons and the existence of the market for land estates caused landholding of any size to be unstable. So, in China landholding by large landlords was never static, which differed fundamentally from the feudal system. Most obvious of all, large land estates in post-Qin China did not incur compulsory military and administrative service, which was the very core of feudalism.

Finally, the terms 'feudal landlordism' and 'bureaucratic feudalism' are confusing, simply because the very existence of the landlord class and that of the centralised bureaucracy were themselves signs of a non-feudal system or structure. To combine these contradicting concepts shows a strong unscientific bias, if not ignorance. An equivalent of such bias is to call someone a 'pagan Christian'.

In summary, the Chinese landholding pattern, administrative system and their ramifications differed noticeably from those under a feudal system characterised by stratified military duties, exclusive aristocratic landholding, tenant peasantry and political decentralisation. At best, the Chinese system can be described as pseudo-feudal.

# APPENDIX F

## Choices of a dualistic peasant household economy

### Micro-level choices

Theoretically, there are five possible situations in which a dualistic peasant household makes its choice between 'subsistence farming and related activities' and 'commercial farming and related activities', as displayed one by one in Figure F.1 with a choice range between two poles and three return curves, sectoral and total.

In the first situation (Figure F.1a), returns (with all risks and uncertainties counted) from subsistence farming and commercial farming are the same. Therefore, there is no difference in choosing a corner solution (100 per cent subsistence farming or 100 per cent commercial farming) or any combination of activities in both sectors. In the second situation (Figure F.1b), returns from one sector are higher than those from any combination of the two sectors, which indicates some sort of penalty incurred when the economic agent shows a lack of total commitment to one sector. The peasant household will choose a corner solution as the rational response. In the third situation (Figure F.1c), returns from a combination of subsistence farming and commercial

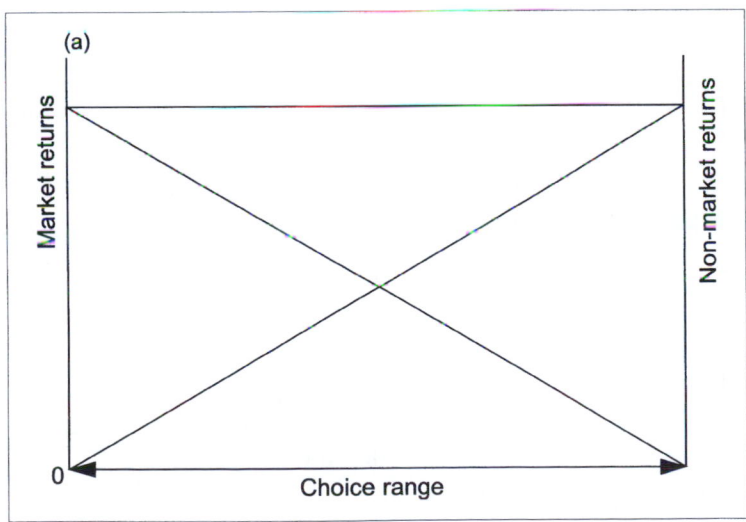

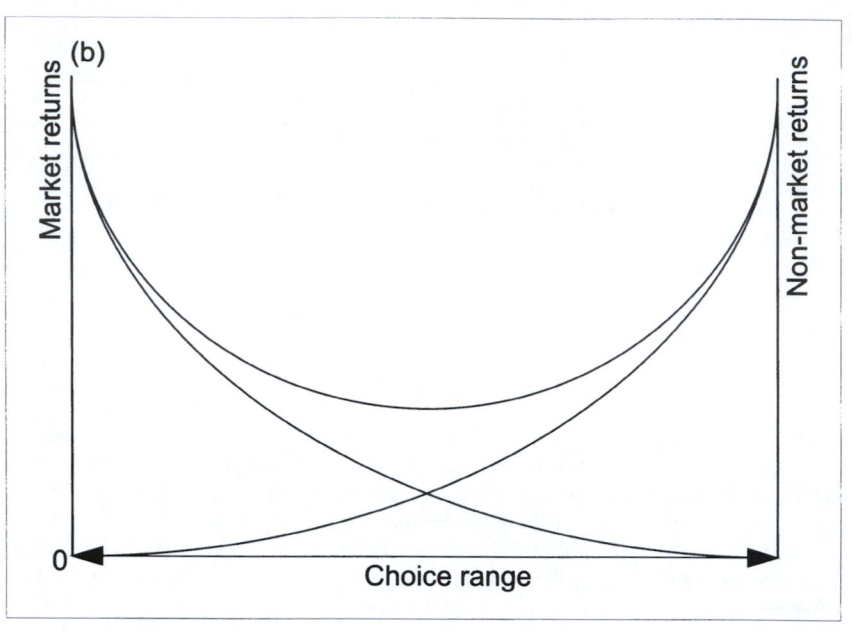

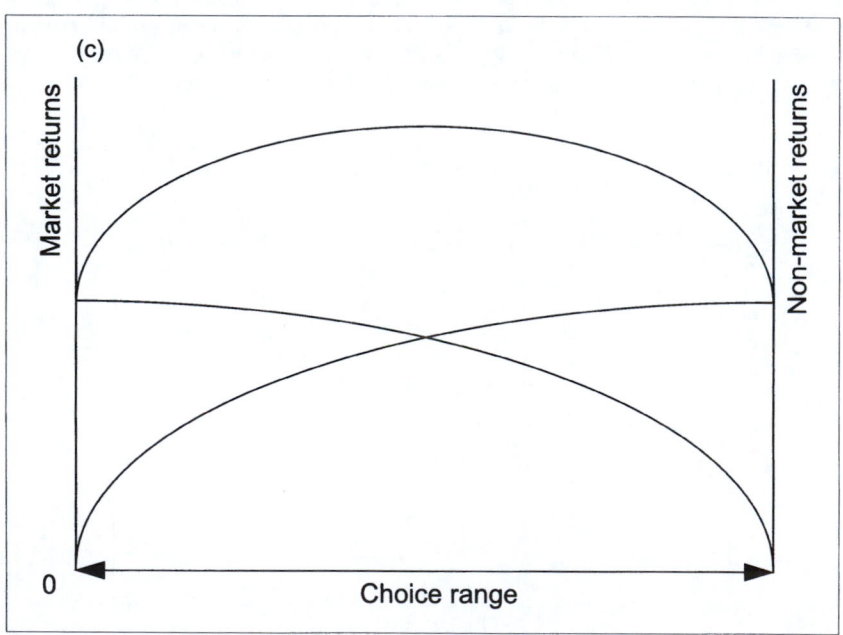

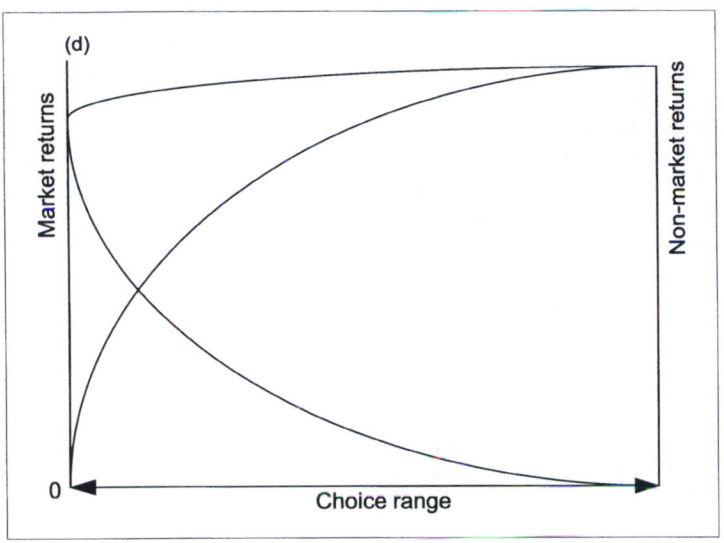

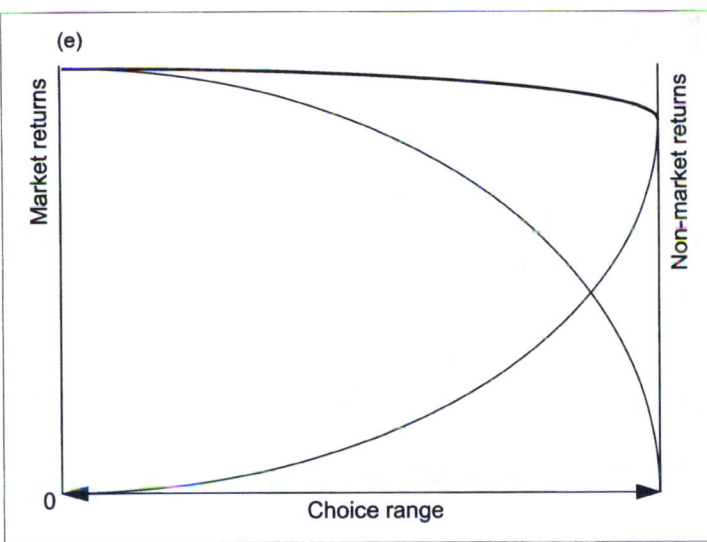

*Figure F.1* Choice patterns for a dualistic peasant household

*Notes*

(a) A corner solution equal to the summation of the two sectors; (b) a corner solution greater than the summation of the two sectors; (c) A corner solution less than the summation of the two sectors; (d) The non-market corner solution greater than either the market corner solution or the summation of the two sectors; (e) The market corner solution greater than either the non-market corner solution or the summation of the two sectors.

farming are higher than those from a corner solution. The household will thus avoid total commitment to one sector but undertake activities in both. In the fourth situation (Figure F.1d), returns from subsistence farming are greater than the returns either from the commercial-farming corner solution or from a combination of the two sectors, indicating unfavourable conditions for commercial farming. The household will lean towards subsistence farming. The fifth situation (Figure F.1e), is the diametric opposite: returns from commercial farming are greater than those either from the subsistence-farming corner solution or from any combination of the two sectors, indicating unfavourable conditions for subsistence farming. The household will move away from subsistence farming.

In reality, the shapes of the return curves are almost certainly less smooth with numerous variants and one situation will certainly change to another over time. But a peasant household will face choices between the two poles no matter how favourable or unfavourable the conditions may be.

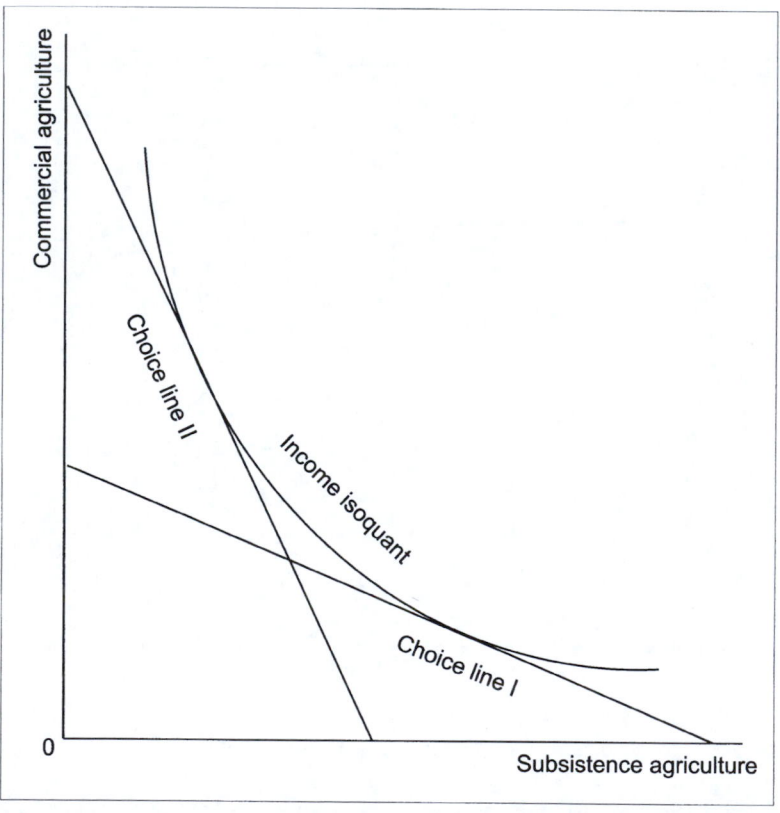

*Figure F.2* Macro pattern: equal bearing of commercial and subsistence agricultures

## Macro-level choices

At the macro level, to sustain the same income level (shown by the income isoquant curve) a peasant society may lean towards commercial farming (the budget line of choice II) or subsistence farming (the budget line of choice I). In other words, commercial farming is not always superior, especially considering the market-related risks, bankruptcy and loss of income (see Figure F.2).

In theory, the locus of the points of tangency of the income isoquants with the budget lines can form developmental paths. There are at least three (Figure F.3): (1) a path of commercialisation, which is characterised by a decline in subsistence agriculture and rise in commercial farming (OC); (2) a path of de-commercialisation with a decline in commercial farming and a rise in subsistence farming (OD), a situation common after wars; and (3) a path of semi-commercial and semi-subsistence (OS), a situation of well-kept balance between the two poles. The OS dividing line also serves as the critical point locus. Once OC or OD passes this line, a structural change in the agricultural economy becomes decisive.

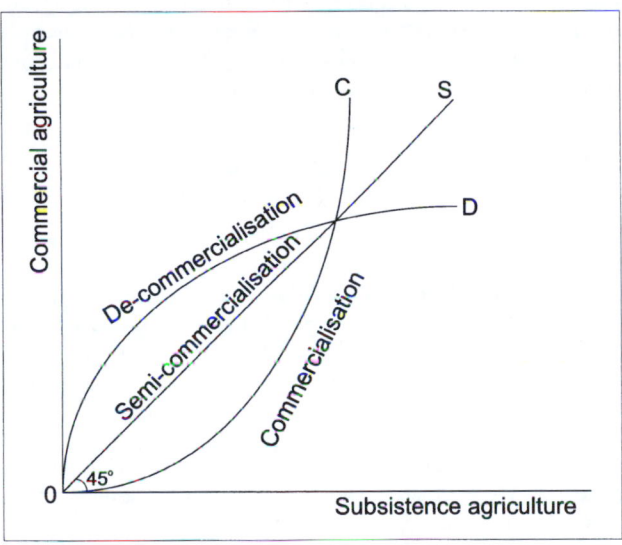

*Figure F.3* Macro pattern: structural dynamics

## Summary

Obviously, peasant choice is a complex process. Commercialisation does not always lead to an increase in real income. Commercial farming may well coexist with subsistence agriculture without taking over and converting the latter.

# APPENDIX G
## Estimation of tax rates

During the post-Qin period, the major forms of government taxation in China, from which the government gained most of its revenue, were land tax and household/poll tax. It is commonly taken that the tax rate was 10 per cent of the total output of an economic unit (the household according to the standard practice). However, from time to time, historical records show very different rates, which necessitates investigation. Here, the periods from the Han (206 BC–AD 220) to the Tang (618–907) are chosen to show the long-term trend and a 'trinary norm'.

### Land tax rates

During the Jian-an Period (AD 196–219) of the Eastern Han Dynasty, the land tax was 4 litres (*sheng*) of grain per *mu* (Zhou B. 1981: 153). From the Eastern Jin (AD 317–420) to the Northern Dynasties (AD 420–589), the land tax and poll tax were combined at 5 piculs or hectolitres (*shi*) per male adult a year (*ibid*.: 158, 160). From the information that, under the long-lasting Land Equalisation System, each household possessed an average of 160.45 *mu* of land, the tax burden can be estimated as not greater than 3 *sheng* per *mu* (Liang F. 1980: 7). In the Sui Dynasty, the tax rate was higher, ranging between 3 and 7.5 *sheng* per *mu* (Zhou B. 1981: 195–6). During the following Tang Dynasty, according to a law issued in AD 624, the rate was 3.3 *sheng* per *mu* (*ibid*.: 198–9). Based on these data, the estimation of land tax rates is shown in Table 3.2. The estimated land tax rate is within a range of 0.7 to 5.2 per cent of the total grain output of a household, an average of 1.6–2.5 per cent. Such rates are not high.

One may argue that the estimated grain output was likely to be at the top of the scale and thus the land tax burden would appear higher than it would have been otherwise. Such a problem can easily be solved by including some weights in the calculation. For instance, the estimated yield levels can be reduced to half. This makes the tax burden rise to 1.4–10.4 per cent, averaging 5.9 per cent. Even so, it was still very light.

### Corvée

Household/poll tax (see section 3.4.2.2 of Chapter 3) was sometimes imposed as corvée (*yaoyi* or *laoyi*) to construct public projects, such as the Great Walls and the

Grand Canal, or to serve in the army. In the Qin Dynasty, there were a million people constantly on corvée (Zhou B. 1981: 76). During the Northern and Southern Dynasties (AD 420–581), the corvée was between 20 and 45 days per annum for each able-bodied male adult (*ibid*.: 180–1), the proportion of each year (365 days) being 5.5–12 per cent, with an average of 8.8 per cent. Later, in the Sui Dynasty (AD 581–618), the land tax was imposed in conjunction with military service under the *fubing* (Regional Recruitment) system (*ibid*.: 184). Sometimes land tax and household/poll tax were combined: examples include, as mentioned before, the 'Two Seasonal Taxes' (*liangshui fa*) in the Tang Dynasty, the 'Single Whip Tax' (*yitiaobian fa*) in the Ming Dynasty and the 'Poll Tax from Land' (*tanding rudi*) in the Qing. According to Tang law, in AD 769, under the 'Two Seasonal Taxes', the tax collected was 7–11 *sheng* of grain per *mu* (*ibid*.: 206), which can be converted to modern measures of 5.14–8.07 *sheng* per *mu*. Considering that the estimated grain yields were between 75.7 *sheng* per *mu* of wheat and 113.6 *sheng* per *mu* of rice (Deng 1993a: 160), the tax rate was between 6.8 and 7.1 per cent.

Although it fluctuated from time to time, the tax rate was normally around 10 per cent of the household's total output. Such a rate was institutionalised by all Confucian governments from Han to Tang times.

# APPENDIX H

## Land reforms and anti-concentration of landholding

In the more recent past, Japan and India came across the same problem as premodern China in terms of landholding concentration after the establishment of a small landholding pattern. In both countries, the government had to intervene (in the form of regulating the farm size and controlling the grain price) in the post-reform period to keep the smallholders' heads above water and thus to avoid the inevitable landholding concentration which is bound to take place after a significant number of smallholders go into bankruptcy.

The 1873–6 Land-Tax Reform under the Meiji régime (1) created an owner farmers' class through the abolition of the Tokugawa feudal land ownership, and (2) provided the government with a greater taxation basis through the abolition of the Tokugawa feudal power of rent- and taxation-collecting (Francks 1992: 102–3). However, the tendency towards land concentration began soon after the redistribution of land, because (1) with its inelastic supply, land is a perfect commodity for speculation; and (2) when individual farming households have financial difficulties (crop failure, market failure and so forth), they first run into debt and later lose their land. So, even if all the farmers had an equal footing in the beginning when the Meiji reform took place, by the interwar period peasant land ownership had eroded. As a result, a large number of land-hungry Japanese emigrated during the interwar period to Manchuria to re-establish the owner-farmers' sector. By the end of the Second World War, there was a marked increase in tenancy rate with a marked 300 per cent rise in landlord–tenant disputes between 1921 and 1936 (Waswo 1988: 548–9). The second, and timely, reform was imposed by the US occupation forces during 1946–7. Land owned by absentee landlords was virtually confiscated and then sold to tenants at low prices. This was an attempt to redistribute land and get rid of rent and the rent-seeking class. Three years later, in 1950, the percentage of land farmed by tenants had dropped from 46 per cent of the land total to 10 per cent, a good indication of the impact of the land redistribution (Ito 1992: 54–5). However, this was only half the battle. Unless every farmer were able to make a decent living from land, the land ownership concentration cycle would start all over again. The Japanese approach was to subsidise farmers to ensure that this would not happen: a floor price was applied to agricultural products as a safety net for the small and inferior farmers (Hara 1990). This was one reason why Japan has been so reluctant to open its domestic market for cheap foreign food imports.

Similarly, in post-independence India, a land reform was launched and the idea was to eliminate rent for the landlord class and to create a large base for government taxation. This in turn allowed an increase in government revenue to facilitate indigenous industrialisation. Before the reform, India had a rather polarised peasantry. Under the *zamindari* system, which was protected by the British, large landholders were absentee landlords, obviously rent-seeking. This type of landholding was common in West Bengal and North Madras. Before the land reform, over half of the land was owned by a minority of less than 10 per cent of the owner-farmers, while at the other end of the spectrum, as many as 57 per cent of farmers owned only 17 per cent of the total land. Among all the farming households, 15 per cent were landless. In per capita terms, a rich peasant produced 2.5 times more marketed surplus than a middle-ranking peasant, and 13 times more marketed surplus than a poor peasant (Byres 1974: 235, 237–8). These ratios can be taken as the proxies of their income gaps. What the Indian land reform did was to impose a ceiling on landholding size through land legislation after independence. The *zamindari* landholding was successfully abolished. Land was redistributed. In addition, to complement the reform the Indian government instituted an agricultural price policy to support the peasantry: in the 1960s and 1970s, the government was responsible for the purchase of 21 to 25 per cent of the food demand from the agricultural sector. The share was great enough to influence the market price. This arguably improved the terms of trade for the agricultural sector: from 1960 to 1975, the terms of trade for food grain increased steadily at an average rate of 2.6 per cent per annum; for all agricultural products, 1.7 per cent per annum (Balasubramanyam 1984: 98).

In both Japan and India, the land reform was the end of the beginning: to sustain the small landholding peasantry, an institutional package was needed almost immediately after the land reform.

# APPENDIX I

## Population growth and arable land

Table I.1 contains data concerning the long-term Chinese population growth *vis-à-vis* arable land. The main economic indicators are in columns C (index of change), E (land scarcity index) and F (land productivity index).

*Table I.1* Trends of population and registered land under cultivation[a]

| $A^b$ | B | $C^c$ | D | $C^c$ | E | F |
|---|---|---|---|---|---|---|
| **Han** | | | | | | |
| 2 | 59.60 | 100 | 57.15 | 100 | 9.6 | 0.104 |
| | (12.23) | (100) | | | | |
| 105 | 53.26 | 89 | 53.51 | 94 | 10.0 | 0.100 |
| | (9.24) | (76) | | | | |
| 146 | 47.57 | 79 | 50.66 | 8 9 | 10.6 | 0.094 |
| | (9.35) | (76) | | | | |
| **Three Kingdoms** | | | | | | |
| 263–80 | (1.47) | (12) | — | — | — | — |
| **Sui** | | | | | | |
| 589 | — | — | 220.24 | 385 | — | — |
| 609 | 46.02 | 77 | — | — | — | — |
| | (8.91) | (73) | | | | |
| **Tang** | | | | | | |
| 650 | (3.80) | (31) | — | — | — | — |
| 705 | 37.14 | 62 | — | — | — | — |
| | (6.16) | (50) | | | | |
| 726 | 41.42 | 69 | 116.67 | 204 | 28.2 | 0.035 |
| | (7.07) | (58) | | | | |
| 755 | 52.92 | 89 | 115.86 | 203 | 21.9 | 0.046 |
| | (8.91) | (73) | | | | |
| 820 | 15.76 | 26 | — | — | — | — |
| | (2.38) | (19) | | | | |
| 847–59 | — | — | 94.68 | 166 | — | — |

*Table I.1 (contd)*

| $A^b$ | B | $C^c$ | D | $C^c$ | E | F |
|---|---|---|---|---|---|---|
| **Five Dynasties** | | | | | | |
| 959 | (2.31) | (19) | 9.39 | 16 | — | — |
| **Northern Song** | | | | | | |
| 996 | (4.57) | (37) | 27.03 | 47 | — | — |
| 1053 | 22.29 | 37 | 19.72 | 36 | 8.8 | 0.114 |
| | (10.79) | (88) | | | | |
| 1085 | — | — | 21.5 | 38 | — | — |
| 1100 | 44.91 | 75 | — | — | — | — |
| | (19.96) | (163) | | | | |
| 1159 | 16.84 | 28 | — | — | — | — |
| | (11.09) | (91) | | | | |
| 1193 | 27.85 | 47 | — | — | — | — |
| | (12.30) | (100.6) | | | | |
| 1264 | 13.03 | 22 | — | — | — | — |
| | (5.70) | (47) | | | | |
| **Southern Song and Jin** | | | | | | |
| 1290 | 73.95 | 124 | — | — | — | — |
| | (19.29) | (158) | | | | |
| **Yuan** | | | | | | |
| 1291 | 59.85 | 100.4 | — | — | — | — |
| | (13.43) | (110) | | | | |
| 1330 | (13.40) | (110) | — | — | — | — |
| **Ming** | | | | | | |
| 1381 | 59.87 | 100.5 | 38.14 | 67 | 6.4 | 0.156 |
| | (10.65) | (87) | | | | |
| 1426 | 51.96 | 87 | 42.90 | 75 | 8.3 | 0.120 |
| | (9.92) | (81) | | | | |
| 1484 | 62.89 | 106 | 50.56 | 88 | 8.0 | 0.125 |
| | (9.21) | (75) | | | | |
| 1532 | 61.71 | 103.5 | 44.60 | 78 | 7.2 | 0.139 |
| | (9.44) | (77) | | | | |
| 1578 | 60.70 | 101.8 | 72.95 | 128 | 12.0 | 0.083 |
| | (10.62) | (87) | | | | |
| 1626 | 51.66 | 87 | 77.37 | 135 | 15.0 | 0.067 |
| | (9.84) | (80) | | | | |
| **Qing** | | | | | | |
| 1680 | 17.10 | 29 | 54.37 | 95 | 31.8 | 0.031 |
| 1734 | 27.36 | 46 | 92.57 | 162 | 33.8 | 0.030 |
| 1766 | 208.10 | 349 | 77.11 | 135 | 3.7 | 0.270 |
| 1812 | 361.70 | 607 | 82.32 | 144 | 2.3 | 0.435 |
| 1833 | 398.94 | 669 | — | — | — | — |

*Table I.1 (contd)*

| $A^b$ | B | $C^c$ | D | $C^c$ | E | F |
|------|------|------|------|------|------|------|
| 1887 | 377.64 | 634 | 94.86 | 167 | 2.5 | 0.400 |
| 1911 | 341.42 | 573 | — | — | — | — |
|      | (92.70) | (760) | | | | |

*Source*: Based on Liang F. 1980: 4–13, 122–5.

*Notes*

A, period (AD); B, population ($\times 10^6$); C, index of change; D, land under cultivation ($\times 10^7$ *mu*); E, land scarcity index (man:land); F, land productivity index or intensification of land utilisation index (land:man). Household numbers, which in many cases are the only data available, are presented in brackets as the second best source to complement the bare population data. Adjusted measure of land is used (based on Liang F. 1980 and Chao 1986: 66).

a Government-registered land under cultivation was not necessarily consistent with the expansion of the farming zone and thus should be taken as the minimum.

b The interval is roughly 50 years, if the data are available.

c The data for AD 2 are taken as 100.

# APPENDIX J

## Data concerning mass rebellions

Periodic mass rebellions were carefully recorded in Chinese history. As a result, a set of data can be extracted as shown in Table J.1, including who were the rebels and when, where and for how long the rebellions took place.

*Table J.1* Data concerning main rebellions, 210 BC–1900

| Period | Incident | Leader | Rebels' number | Original region | Affected area (in province) | Duration |
|---|---|---|---|---|---|---|
| Qin | 208 BC | Chen Sheng, Wu Guang | X · 100,000 | Suxian (AH) | AN, HeN, HeB, SD, SX, JS, S'X | 0.5 y |
| Han | 208 | Xiang Liang, Xiang Yu, Liu Bang | 6–70,000 | Tengxian (SD) | 7 provinces with the Han | 2 y |
| | 99 | Xu Bo | X · 1,000 | Tai-an (SD) | SD | — |
| | 99 | Mei Mian, Bai Zheng | X · 1,000 | Nanyang (HeN) | HeN | — |
| | 99 | Duan Zhong, Du Shao | X · 1,000 | HuB | HuB | — |
| | 99 | Jian Lu, Fan Zhu | X · 1,000 | HeB | HeB | — |
| | 69–6 | peasants | | Heb, SD | HeB, SD | — |
| | 30 | Beng Zong | X · 100 | Chang-an (S'X) | S'X | 1 y+ |
| | 26 | Hou Wupi | — | Chiping (SD) | SD | — |
| | 22 | Shen Tusheng (iron worker) | — | Yuxian (HeN) | HeN (9 prefectures) | — |
| | 20 | Ma Zheng | — | — | — | — |
| | 18 | Zheng Gong | 10,000+ | Guangha (SC) | SC (4 prefectures) | 1 y |
| | 14 | Su Ling (iron worker) | — | Jinxiang (SD) | 40 prefectures | 1 y+ |
| | 14 | Fan Bing | 13 | Weishi (HeN) | HeN | 1 y+ |
| | 13 | Liang Zixiao | X · 1,000 | Huxian (S'X) | S'X | — |
| | 3 | — | X · 1,000 | — | 26 prefectures | — |
| AD | 3 | Ren Heng | | Gaoling (S'X) | S'X | — |
| | 7 | Zhao Ming, Huo Hong | 100,000+ | Chang-an (S'X) | 23 counties | 1 y+ |
| | 11 | peasants and soldiers | — | SX, NM | SX, NM | — |
| | 15 | — | X · 1,000 | NM, SX | MN, SX | 1 y+ |
| | 17 | Gua Tianyi | — | Fengyang (AH) | JS, AH | — |
| | 17 | Lu Mu (female) | 10,000+ | Rizhao (SD) | SD | — |
| | 17 | Wang Kuang, Wang Feng ('Lulin Army') | 100,000+ | Jingmen (HuB) | HuB | — |
| | 17 | Tongma (15 branches) | X · 1,000,000 | HeB, SD | HeB, SD | — |

364

| Period | Year | Leader ('Army') | Strength | Place | Provinces | Duration |
|---|---|---|---|---|---|---|
| 18 | | Fan Chong ('Chimei Army') | 100,000+ | Juxian (SD) | SD, JS (AD 25 Chang-an captured) | 7 y |
| | 18 | Lusuo Hui | 300,000 | Dongping (SD) | AH, SD, HeN | — |
| | 22 | Liu Xiu, Liu Yan ('Lulin Army') | X · 100,000+ | Zhaoyang (HuB) | 10 provinces with the Eastern Han | — |
| | 23 | Du Yu | — | Chang-an | S'X (Wang Mang, the Usurper, killed) | — |
| | 106–88 | 67 uprisings | | — | — | |
| | 184 | Zhang Jiao ('Huangjin Army') | X · 100,000 | HeB, HeN, AH | HeB, HeN, AH | 1 y |
| | 184 | Zhang Xiu (Wudoumi) | — | Chongqing (SC) | SC | 30 y |
| | 184 | Beigong Bozhi, Li Wenhou | — | Lanzhou (GS) | GS | 6 y |
| | 184 | Guo Jia | — | Jiayuguan (GS) | GS | — |
| | 184 | Zhutian Jiangjun | — | Hepu (GX) | GX | — |
| | 185 | Zhang Niujiao ('Heishan Army') | X · 1,000,000 | Ningji (HeB) | HeB | 20 y |
| | 187 | — | | Yingyan (HeN) | HeN | — |
| | | Guan Hu | | Chenxian (HuN) | HuN | — |
| | 188 | Guo Tai ('Huangjin Army') | | Lishi (SX) | SX | 7 y |
| | 188 | 'Huangjin Army' | | HeN | HeN | 8 y |
| | 188 | Ma Xiang, Zhao Di ('Huangjin Army') | 100,000+ | Deyang (SC) | SC | — |
| | 188 | 'Huangjin Army' | X · 1,000,000 | SD, HeN | SD, HeN | 4 y |
| | 189 | Zhang Rao | 200,000 | Changle (SD) | SD | — |
| | 191 | Zhang Lu, Zhang Xiu (Wudoumi or 'Five Decilitre Rice') | — | S'X | S'X | 24 y |
| 3 Ks | 221 | Liu Bei | X · 100,000 | Peixian (JS) | JS, HeN, HuB, SC (Shu established) | 42 y |
| Jin | 294 | Hao San (Hun ethnic minority) | — | Shangzhi (SX) | SX | 3 y |
| | 296 | Qi Wannian | 70,000 | — | — | — |

Table J.1 (contd)

| Period | Incident | Leader | Rebels' number | Original region | Affected area (in province) | Duration |
|---|---|---|---|---|---|---|
| | 301 | Li Te, Li Xiong | 100,000+ | Mianzhu (SC) | SC (Chenghan established) | 46 y |
| | 303 | Zhang Chang | 30,000 | Anlu (HuB) | HuB | 1 y |
| | 306 | Tian Yin | 50,000 | — | — | — |
| | 307 | Wei Zhi | 50,000 | — | — | — |
| | 309 | migrants | X · 10,000 households | — | — | — |
| | 310 | Wang Ru | 4–50, 000 | HeN | HeN, HuB | 2 y |
| | 311 | Du Tao (migrant) | X · 10,000 households | HuN, HuB | HuN, HuB | 4 y |
| | 389 | Sun Tai (*Wudoumi*) | — | Zhucheng (SD) | SD | — |
| | 399 | Sun En, Lu Xun, Xu Daofu (*Wudoumi*) | X · 100,000 | Shangyu (ZJ) | ZJ, JS, FJ, GD, JX, HuB, HuN | 19 y |
| Northern | 432 | Zhao Guang | 100,000+ | SC | SC | 5 y |
| and | 445 | Gai Wu | — | Huangling (S'X) | S'X, GS | 1 y |
| Southern | 445 | Xue Yongzong (joint with Gai Wu) | | | | |
| | 446 | Bian Jiong, Liang Hui | 3,000 | Yongji (SX) | SX | — |
| | 446 | Wang Yuanda | X · 1,000 | Tianshui (GS) | GS | — |
| | 460 | migrants | 3,000 | Qin-an (GS) | GS | — |
| | 469 | Tian Liu | 1,000+ | AH | AH | — |
| | 471 | Zhang Feng | — | Linhai (ZJ) | ZJ | — |
| | 473 | Li Chengming | — | JX | JX | — |
| | 479 | Zhang Qun | — | SC | SC | — |
| | | | — | Xinyang (HeN) | HeN | — |

| Year | Leader | Location | Region | Number | Duration |
|---|---|---|---|---|---|
| 485 | Tang Yuzhi | Fuyang (ZJ) | ZJ (Xingping regime established) | 30,000 | 1 y |
| 499 | Zhao Xubo | Santai (SC) | SC | — | — |
| 500 | Bo Yang | Suining (SC) | SC (Jianyi regime established) | 10,000+ | — |
| 500 | Yong Daoyi | SC | SC | — | — |
| 500 | Cheng Yansi | SC | SC | — | — |
| 500 | Zhao Xubo (second revolt) | Shehong (SC) | SC | 20,000 | — |
| 505 | Jiao Senghu | SC | SC | X · 10,000 | — |
| 510 | Wu Chengbo | Xuancheng (AH) | AH | — | — |
| 511 | Yao Jing | Baxi (SC,) | SC | — | — |
| 523 | Poliu Hanbaling (Hun Ethnic Minority) | | GS, SC, S'X (Zhen established) | — | 1 y+ |
| 524 | Xue Zhen, Liu Qing | GS | GS | — | — |
| 524 | Mozhe Dati (Qiang) | Qingzhou (GS) | GS, NX, S'X (Tianjian established) | X · 100,000 | 7 y |
| 525 | Du louzhou (soldier) | Yanqiang (HeB) | HeB (Zhen regime established) | X · 100,000 | 3 y |
| 526 | Xianyu Xiuli | Tangxian (HeB) | HeB, HeN (Luxing regime established) | X · 100,000 | 3 y |
| 528 | Qi Gou-er | Liyang (SC) | SC | 100,000 | — |
| 529 | Shanxi peasants, dozen times | Taiyuan (SX) | SX | 200,000 | — |
| 542 | Liu Jinggong | Nanchang (SC) | SC (Yonghan regime established) | X · 10,000 | — |
| 544 | Wang Qinzong | Chongren (JX) | JX | — | — |
| 611 | Meng Rang, Wang Bo | Zhangqiu (SD) | SD, HeB | 100,000+ | — |
| 612 | Zhen Baoche | SD | SD | 10,000 | — |
| 613 | Meng Haigong | Caoxian (SD) | SD | X · 10,000 | — |
| 613 | Guo Fangyu | Yidu (SD) | SD | 30,000 | — |
| 613 | Zhang Jicheng, Sun Xianya | | | | |
| 613 | Hao Xiaode | Xinyang (SD) | SD | 100,000 | — |
| 613 | Hao Xiaode | HeB | HeB | — | — |
| 613 | Ge Qian | Hejian (HeB) | HeB | — | — |
| 613 | Han Jinluo | Liaocheng (SD) | SD | X · 10,000 | — |

Sui

Table J.1 (contd)

| Period | Incident Leader | Rebels' number | Original region (HeN) | Affected area (in province) | Duration |
|---|---|---|---|---|---|
| 613 | Yang Xuangan, Han Xiangguo | 100,000+ | Xunxian (HeN) | Yellow, Yangzi and Pearl rivers (10 provinces) | — |
| 613 | Bai Yusha (herdsman) | X · 10,000 | Lingwu (NX) | GS, S'X | — |
| 613 | herdsmen | — | Guyuan (NX) | NX | — |
| 613 | Liu Yuanjin | X · 10,000 | ZJ | ZJ | — |
| 613 | Guan Chong | 100,000 | JS | JS | — |
| 613 | Cheng Zhen | 30,000 | GD | GD | — |
| 613 | Wu Hailiu, Peng Xiaocai | X · 10,000 | JS | JS | — |
| 613 | Liang Huishang | 40,000 | GD | GD | — |
| 613 | Li San-er, Xiang Danzi | X · 10,000 | ZJ | ZJ | — |
| 613 | Xiang Haiming | X · 10,000 | S'X | S'X | — |
| 613–15 | Other rebellions: widely spread with thousands of incidents (History of the Sui Dynasty: ch. 'Report of the Imperial Historians') | | | | |
| 613–15 | Du Fuwei, Meng Rang, Li Zitong | min. 100,000 | Mt Changbai (SD) | SD, AH, HeN (Mingzheng established) | 5 y |
| 614 | Liu Jialun | 100,000 | S'X | S'X (Dashi regime established) | — |
| 614 | Zheng Wenya, Lin Baohu | 30,000 | S'X | S'X | — |
| 614 | Yang Gongqing | 8,000 | HeB | HeB | — |
| 614 | Liu Maowang | X · 10,000 | SX | SX | — |
| 614 | Wang Deren | X · 10,000 | HeN | HeN | — |
| 614 | Zuo Xiaoyou | 10,000 | SD | SD | — |
| 615 | Lu Mingxing | 100,000 | Mt. Changbai (SD) | SD, HeN | — |
| 615 | Wang Xuba, Wei Dao-er | 100,000 | HeB | HeB | — |
| 615 | Wei Qilin | 10,000 | SD | SD | — |

| | Year | Name | Number | Location | Area/Notes | Duration |
|---|---|---|---|---|---|---|
| | 615 | Li Zitong | 10,000 | AH | AH | — |
| | 615 | Zhu Can | 100,000 | AH | AH (Changda regime established) | — |
| | 616 | Zuo Caixiang | X · 10,000 | Mt. Changbai (SD) | SD, HeN | — |
| | 616 | Zhai Rang | 10,000 | HeN | HeN | — |
| | 616 | Li Mi ('Wagang Army') | 300,000 | HeN, HeB | HeN, HeB (Wei regime established) | 1 y |
| | 616 | Dou Jiangde | 100,000+ | HeB | HeB (in 617, Xia regime established) | 3 y |
| | 616 | Du Fuwei | X · 10,000 | AH | AH, JS | 6 y |
| | 616 | Zhai Songbai | X · 10,000 | SX | SX | — |
| | 616 | Lu Gongxian | X · 10,000 | SD | SD | — |
| | 616 | Zhao Wanhai | X · 100,000 | — | — | — |
| | 616 | Cao Shiqi | 100,000 | JS, ZJ, HuN, GD | JS, ZJ, HuN, GD | — |
| | 617 | Li Yuan | — | Taiyuan (SX) | Tang established (15 provinces first) | 7 y |
| | 617 | Xue Ju | — | GS | Entire GS (Qinxing regime established) | — |
| | 617 | Xiao Xian | 400,000 | HuN, GD | HuN, GD (Liang regime established) | 2 |
| | 618 | Yuwen Huaji | 100,000 | JS | JS (Emperor Suiyang, the Terrible, killed) | — |
| Tang | 621 | Liu Heita | X · 10,000 | HeB | Heb | 2 y |
| | 621 | Dong Dingming (joint with Liu Heita) | — | Guantao (HeB) | HeB | 2 y |
| | 623 | Fu Gongshi | — | Nanjing | JS (Song regime established) | 1 y |
| | 648 | Minority | — | SC | SC | — |
| | 653 | Chen Shuozhen | — | Jiande (ZJ) | ZJ | — |
| | 700 (?) | peasants | 30,000 | SC | SC | — |
| | 762 | Yuan Chao | 200,000 | Zhoushan Island (ZJ) | ZJ, JX | 1 y |

Table J.1 (contd)

| Period | Incident | Leader | Rebels' number | Original region | Affected area (in province) | Duration |
|---|---|---|---|---|---|---|
| | 762 | Fang Qing | X · 10,000 | Yixian (AH) | AH | 4 y |
| | 763–4 | Gao Zhi | — | HeN, S'X | HeN, S'X | — |
| | 860 | Qiu Pu | 30,000+ | Shengxian (ZJ) | ZJ (Luoping regime established) | 0.5 y |
| | 863 | Pang Xun | 200,000 | Guilin (GX) | AH | 6 y |
| | 875 | Wang Xianzhi, Huang Chao | 600,000 | Changhe (HeN) and Hezhe (SD) | SD, HeN, AH, HuB, HuN, ZJ, FJ, GD, JS, S'X, JX, GX (capital captured, Qi regime established) | 9 y |
| 5 Ds | 920 | Mu Yi, Dong Yi | — | Huayang (HeN) | AH, HeN | — |
| | 942 | Zhang Yuxian | 100,000 | Huiyang (GD) | JX | 1 y |
| N. Song | 993 | Wang Xiaobo, Li Shun | X · 100,000 | Chongqing (SC) | SC (in 994, Yingyun established) | 3 y |
| | 997 | — | — | Luoyang (HeN) | HeN | |
| | 1043 | Wang Lun | | Linyi (SD) | JS | 7 m |
| | 1043 | Zhang Hai, Guo Maoshan | 1,000+ | Shangxian (SX) | HeN, S'X, HuB boarder | — |
| | 1043 | Yao ethnic minority | 5,000 | Lanshan (HuN) | HuN | 4 y |
| | 1047 | Wang Ze | — | Qinghe (HeB) | HeB (Dasheng regime established) | 2 m |
| | 1119 | Fang La | 1,000,000 | Chun-an (ZJ) | ZJ, AH, HeN (capital captured, Yongle regime established) | 2 y |
| | 1120 | Song Jiang | — | Yuncheng (SD) | SD, HeB, HeN, JS | 3 y |
| | 1124 | Zhang Xian | 50,000 | SD | SD | — |
| | 1124 | Zhang Di | 50,000 | SD | SD | — |
| | 1124 | Jia Jin | 100,000 | SD | SD | — |
| | 1124 | Xu Jin | 50,000 | SD | SD | — |
| | 1124 | Hu Wu | 10,000 | SD | SD | — |

370

| Year | Name | Number | Location | Region | Duration |
|---|---|---|---|---|---|
| 1124 | Liu Daliang | 10,000 | | SD | — |
| 1124 | Xu Daliang | 10,000 | | SD | — |
| 1124 | Gao Tuoshan | 300,000 | | HeB | — |
| 1130 | Zhong Xiang, Yang Yao | 3–400,000 | Changde (HuN) | HuN, HuB (Tianzai and Dasheng established) | 5 y |
| 1130 | Fan Ruwei | 100,000+ | Jian-ou (FJ) | FJ, ZJ | 2 y |
| 1160 | Zhang Wang, Xu Yuan | — | Donghai (JS) | JS | — |
| 1161 | Wang Youzhi | — | Daming (HeB) | HeB | — |
| 1161 | Geng Jing | — | SD | SD | — |
| 1163 | Fa Tong (Buddhist monk) | — | Liaoyang (LN) | LN | — |
| 1164 | Jiang Zhi | — | Xuzhou (JS) | JS | — |
| 1165 | Li Jin | — | Yizhang (HuN) | HuN, GD, GX | 4 m |
| 1166 | He Zhu | — | Fuyu (JL) | JL | — |
| 1169 | Zhang He | — | Jixian (HeB) | HeB | — |
| 1171 | Zang An-er | — | Guide (SD) | SD | — |
| 1172 | Cao Gui | — | Beijing | HeB | — |
| 1172 | Wang Qiong | — | Jixian (HeB) | HeB | — |
| 1173 | — | X · 1,000 | Luoyang (HeN) | HeN | — |
| 1175 | Lai Wenzheng | | HuB | HuB, HuN, JX, GD | 5 m |
| 1178 | Yin Xiao-er | — | Xianxian (HeB) | HeB | — |
| 1179 | Xu Tong | — | Mixian (HeN) | HeN | — |
| 1179 | Liu Xizhong | — | Jinan (SD) | SD | — |
| 1179 | Li Ji | — | GX | GX, GD | 0.5 m |
| 1181 | Zhu Zhou | — | Liaozhou (LN) | LN | — |
| 1197 | Chen Dong | — | Chenzhou (HuN) | HuN | — |
| 1209 | Li Yuanli | — | Chenzhou (HuN) | JX, GD | 1 y |
| 1212 | Yang An-er | X · 100,000 | Yidu (SD) | SD (in 1214, Tianshun established) | 5 y |
| 1212 | Li Jin | — | Weifang (SD) | SD, JS | 5 y |

Jin and S. Song

Table J.1 (contd')

| Period | Incident | Leader | Rebels' number | Original region | Affected area (in province) | Duration |
|---|---|---|---|---|---|---|
| | 1212 | Liu Erzu | — | Tai-an (SD) | SD | — |
| | 1229 | Yan Biao | — | Changting (FJ) | FJ | 2 y |
| | 1233–4 | Zhang Mowang, Chen Sanqiang | — | Ganzhou (JX) | JX, FJ, GD | — |
| | 1234 | — | X · 1,000 | Jianyang (FJ) | FJ | — |
| | 1278 | Li Er | — | Linfen (SX) | SX | — |
| Yuan | 1280 | Chen Jilong, Chen Diaoyan | X · 10,000 | Zhangzhou (FJ) | FJ | 2 y |
| | 1283 | Lin Guifang, Zhao Lianqin | 10,000+ | Xinhui (GD) | GD | — |
| | 1283 | Huang Hua | 100,000 | Jianning (FJ) | FJ | — |
| | 1284 | Li Yizhu | — | Renqiu (HeB) | HeB | — |
| | 1285 | Zhao Heshang (Buddhist monk) | — | SC | SC | — |
| | 1288 | Dong Xianju | 10,000+ | GD | GD | — |
| | 1288 | Zan Yizi | 10,000+ | HuN | HuN | — |
| | 1288 | Yang Zhenlong, Liu Shiying | 10,000+ | ZJ | ZJ | — |
| | 1288 | Zhong Mingliang | 10,000+ | Huizhou (GD) | JX | — |
| | 1289 | — | — | Jiangnan | – | X y |
| | 1292 | Huang Shengxu | 20,000 | Shangsi (GX) | GX | — |
| | 1296 | Liu Liushi | 10,000+ | Ganzhou (JX) | JX | — |
| | 1301 | Song Longji | 4,000 | GZ | GZ | 3 y |
| | 1312 | A Shi Dai-er, Ta Hai | — | Cangzhou (HeB) | HeB, SD | — |
| | 1325 | Zhao Chousi, Guo Pusa | — | HeN | HeN | — |
| | 1337 | Bang Hu | 100+ | Huaiyang (HeN) | HeN | — |
| | 1337 | Bi Si | 36 (defeat 10,000) | Nanjing | JS | — |
| | 1338 | Peng Yingyu (Buddhist monk) | 5,000 | Yichun (JX) | JX | — |
| | 1348 | Fang Guozhen | — | Huangyan (ZJ) | ZJ | — |

| Year | Leader | Number | Place | Region | Duration |
|---|---|---|---|---|---|
| 1351 | Liu Futong, Xu Shouhui ('Hongjin Army') | 1,000,000 | HeB, AH, JS / HuB, JS | SD, SX, HeB, S'X, GS, SC, LN, FJ, ZJ, JX, HuB, HuN, GD, GX (Tianwan established) | 12 y |
| 1352 | Guo Zixing, Zhu Yuanzhang | X · 100,000 | AH | 20 provinces with the Ming | 16 y |
| 1353 | Zhang Shicheng | 100,000 | Taixian (JS) | Lower Yangzi (6 provinces) (Zhou regime established) | 14 y |
| **Ming** | | | | | |
| 1375 | Chang Delin (soldier) | — | S'X | S'X | — |
| 1376 | Chen Huasi (soldier) | X · 1,000 | Hexian (GX) | GX | — |
| 1378 | Shan Dan (soldier) | — | Lingwu (NX) | NX | — |
| 1379 | Peng Pugui | — | Meixian (SC) | SC | — |
| 1381 | Chanping Wang (Ever-Equal King) | X · 10,000 | GD | GD | — |
| 1385 | Wu Po | 200,000 | SC | SC | 10 y |
| 1397 | Tian Jiucheng, Gao Fuxing | — | S'X | S'X, GS (Longfeng established) | — |
| 1398 | A Sun | — | Liancheng (FJ) | FJ | — |
| 1409 | Li Faliang | — | Xiangtan (HuN) | JX | — |
| 1420 | Tang Sai-er | X · 10,000 | Putai (SD) | SD | 6 y |
| 1445–7 | Ye Zongliu (miner) | X · 10,000 | Shangrao (JX) | ZJ, JX, FJ | 1 y |
| 1448 | Deng Maoqi | X · 10,000 | Shaxian (FJ) | FJ, JX, ZJ, GD | 2 y |
| 1448 | Huang Xiaoyang | 100,000+ | Guangzhou | GD (Dongyang regime established) | — |
| 1450 | Wang Biao | 400,000 | SD | SD, HeN, S'X, HuB, SC | 22 y |
| 1456 | Hou Dagou (Ethnic Yao) | — | Guiping (GX) | GX, GD | — |
| 1457 | Hou Zheng-ang (Ethnic Yao) | — | Luzhai (GX) | GX | — |
| 1464 | Zhao Feng | — | Deyang (SC) | SC | — |
| 1465 | Liu Tong, Shi Long | 1,000,000 | Jingzhou (HuB) | HuB, SC, HeN, S'X | 1 y |
| 1470 | Li Yuan | X · 100,000 | Nanzhang (HuN) | HuB, HuN | 1 y |
| 1508 | Liu Lie | 100,000+ | Baohe (SC) | SX, HuB, HuN, GD, GX | — |

Table J.1 (contd)

| Period | Incident Leader | Rebels' number | Original region | Affected area (in province) | Duration |
|---|---|---|---|---|---|
| 1510 | Liu Liu, Liu Qi | 130,000 | Baxian (HeB) | HeB, HeN, SD, HuB, JS, AN, SX, JX | 3 y |
| 1510 | — | — | Guiping (GX) | GX | — |
| 1511 | Cao Pu, Fang Si | 200,000 | Jiangjin (SC) | SC, GZ | — |
| 1511 | Wang Yuwu (with six groups) | — | JX | JX | — |
| 1512 | Liao Gongguang | — | GD | GD | — |
| 1517 | Xie Jieshan, Lan Tianfeng | — | JX | JX | — |
| 1517 | Chen Yueneng, Chi Zhongrong | — | GD | GD | — |
| 1517 | Gao Kuaima | — | GD | GD | — |
| 1517 | Gong Fuquan | — | HuN | HuN | — |
| 1517 | Zan Shifu | — | FJ | FJ | — |
| 1524 | Li Wenji | X · 1,000 | GD | GD | — |
| 1536 | Hou Shenghai, Hou Gongding | — | Guiping (GX) | GX | 3 y |
| 1550 (?) | Lai Qinggui | — | Longnan (JX) | JX | 10 y |
| 1572 | Lin Daoqian | X · 1,000 | Chaozhou (GD) | GD | — |
| 1588 | Mei Tang, Liu Ruguo | — | Huanggang (HuB) | HuB | 1 y |
| 1599 | merchants | X · 1,000 | Jingzhou (HuB) | HuB | — |
| 1599 | merchants | 10,000 | Wuchang (HuB) | HuB | — |
| 1599 | residents | 10,000+ | Tianjin | HeB | — |
| 1601 | Ge Xian (worker) | 2,000 | Suzhou | JS | — |
| 1606 | residents | 10,000 | YN | YN | — |
| 1622 | Xu Hongru | X · 10,000 | Yuncheng (SD) | SD (Dacheng Xingsheng established) | 0.5 y |

| Year | Leader(s) | Number | Location | Provinces affected / Notes | Duration |
|---|---|---|---|---|---|
| 1627 | Zhang Xianzhong, Li Zicheng | 100,000+ | S'X | S'X, HeB, HeN, SX, SD, HuB, JS, JX, SC, GD (Dashun and Daxi established) | 9 y |

**Qing**

| Year | Leader(s) | Number | Location | Provinces affected / Notes | Duration |
|---|---|---|---|---|---|
| 1630 | Wang Gang | 200,000 | SX | SX | 41 y |
| 1641 | Li Zicheng | 1,000,000 | HeN | in 1644, Beijing captured | 5 y |
| 1644 | 'Yuyuan Army' | 1,000,000 | SD | SD | 11 y |
| 1646 | 13 allays | min. 300,000 | — | HuN, SC, HuB | 19 y |
| 1721 | Zhu Yigui | 350,000 | TW | TW (Yongye regime established) | — |
| 1774 | Wang Lun | — | SD | SD | — |
| 1781 | Su Sishisan, Han Er | — | Linxia (GS) | GS | — |
| 1783 | Tian Wu | — | Gangu (GS) | GS | 1 y |
| 1786 | Lin Shuangwen | 100,000+ | Zhanghua (TW) | TW (Shuntian regime established) | 1 y |
| 1795 | Shi Liudeng, Wu Longdeng | X · 1,000 | GZ, HuN | GZ, HuN | 12 y |
| 1796 | Nie Jieren, Zhang Zhengying | X · 100,000 | Yidu, Zhijiang (HuB) | SC, HuB, HeN, S'X, GS | 9 y |
| 1813 | Li Wencheng, Lin Qing | X · 10,000 | Huaxian (HeN) | Imperial Palace in Beijing attacked | — |
| 1851 | Hong Xiuquan | — | Jintian (GX) | JS, JX, HuB, HuN, GD, GX, SC, FJ (Taiping Tianguo established) | 15 y |
| 1853 | Liu Lichuan (Xiaodaohui, or 'Stab Society') | — | Shanghai | JS | 1.5 y |
| 1861 | Song Jingshi ('Heiqi Army') | 10,000+ | SD | SD | 1 y |
| 1863 | Boke Maizi Muzate | X · 100,000 | Yili (XJ) | XJ (Sultan established) | 10 y |
| 1864 | Yi Sa | 5–6,000 | Tulufan (XJ) | XJ | 9 y |
| 1864 | — | — | Kuche (XJ) | XJ | 9 y |
| 1866 | — | — | Hami (XJ) | XJ | 7 y |
| 1884 | Jin Xiangyin, A Gubai | — | Kashi (XJ) | XJ (Sultan established) | 13 y |
| 1898 | Guangxi Rebels | 100,000 | GX | GX, GD | 10 y |

Table J.1 (contd)

| Period | Incident | Leader | Rebels' number | Original region | Affected area (in province) | Duration |
|---|---|---|---|---|---|---|
| Total | 2106 | 269 (minimum) | 23,266,400 (minimum) | (minimum) | 424 (minimum) | (minimum)589.9 y |
| Cases counted | | | 103 | | 166 | 81 |
| Mean of the counted cases | | | 225,887 | | 2.6 provinces | 7.3 y |

*Sources:* Li G. *et al.* 1958; Fan W. 1964–5; Liu Z. *et al.* 1979; CBW 1979: 4766–4816; Zhang S. and Zheng X. 1983.

*Notes*

For the convenience of the reader provinces of modern China are used.

Numbers are aggregated for each period recorded.

For each rebellion, the rebels' numbers and occupied/affected areas are measured at the peak period of each incident.

The symbol 'X' represents 'several' (su), which means 'more than two'. Thus in counting rebel numbers, 'X' is replaced by 2 to obtain a minimal value.

Abbreviations of regions (in the form of provinces of modern China): AH, Anhui; FJ, Fujian; GD, Guangdong; GS, Gansu; GX, Guangxi; GZ, Guizhou; HeB, Hebei; HeN, Henan; HuB, Hubei; HuN, Hunan; JL, Jilin; JS, Jiangsu; JX, Jiangxi; LN, Liaoning; NM, Neimeng; NX, Ningxia; QH, Qinghai; SC, Sichuan; SD, Shandong; SX, Shanxi; S'X, Shaanxi; TW, Taiwan; XJ, Xinjiang; YN, Yunnan; ZJ, Zhejiang.

# APPENDIX K

## Cotton and its diffusion in China

Cotton (*mian* or *mumian*, *Gossypium* spp.) was known to the Chinese before the Han Dynasty, as it was recorded by Fan Ye in *The History of the Eastern Han Dynasty* (*Huo-han Shu*) that the Lao-ai tribe in the southwest produced good-quality cotton cloth (Fan Y. AD 445 vol. 26: ch. 'Xinanyi Zhuan'). Later on, cotton cloth was supplied to China from outside. According to Tang regulations, the authorities of Port Quanzhou were responsible for obtaining 20 *jin* of cotton (11.9 kg) a year for the Imperial Court (see Zhuang W. *et al.* 1989: 9).

Recent research shows that three cotton species were introduced to China through three routes: (1) the African–Arabian species (*Gossypium herbaceum*) through a northern route overland from Central Asia to China's Gansu and Shanxi; (2) the South Asian species (*Gossypium arboreum* and *Gossypium barbadense*) through a southern route overseas from India to Burma, Vietnam and to China's Hainan Island, Yunnan, Guangxi and Guangdong; (3) the American species (*Gossypium hirsutum*) through an eastern route overseas either directly to the east coast of China or to Manchuria via Korea (Tang Q. 1986: ch. 12; see also Zhao G. and Chen Z. 1983: chs 1–2).

Among these three, it was the South Asian species that formed the main stream because of its scale and duration. It was introduced first to the non-Chinese peoples in the southern border region of China around the third century AD (Fan Y. AD 445 vol. 26: ch. 'Xinanyi Zhuan'; see also Tang Q. 1986: 476–7; Weng D. 1990: 582–3), and then arrived in China in about the tenth century AD (see Han E. *c.* AD 907). Ancient literature indicates that by the late Southern Song Dynasty cotton had gained a firm footing in Fujian Province and spread along the coast to Zhejiang and Jiangsu (Qi X. 1992). It took at least another two hundred years for cotton to spread within North China (Xu G. *c.* 1628: ch. 8; Shi S. 1979: 973). By the end of the Ming Dynasty, cotton dominated China's fibre production. Such a long time-lag may have resulted from the strength of the traditional fibre sources in China: silk and hemp (*ma*, *Cannabis sativa*).

The impact of the cotton diffusion in China's economy was revolutionary. First, it provided the population with a cheap fibre of good quality which silk and hemp could not match. Second, cotton's side-products such as cotton seed-oil and oil-cake were good sources of food and fertiliser which silk and hemp could not match either. Third, the establishment of cotton cultivation and processing paved the way for China's silk exports from the sixteenth century to this day.

# BIBLIOGRAPHY

## Chinese-language references

An Zhimin (1988) 'Zhongguode Shiqian Nongye' ('Prehistoric Agriculture in China'), *Kaogu Xuebao* (*Archaeological Bulletin*), 4: 369–81.

Anon. (*c.* Eleventh Century BC) *Yijing* (*Book of Changes*), publisher unknown.

Anon. (*c.* Third Century BC) *Zhouli* (*Rite of the Zhou Dynasty*), in Sun Yirang (ed.) (1934) *Zhouli* (*Rite of the Zhou Dynasty*), Shanghai: Commercial Press.

Anon. (Zhou Dynasty) *Shangshu* (*The Book of History*), publisher unknown.

Anon. (Spring and Autumn) *Shijing* (*Book of Odes*), publisher unknown.

Anon. (*c.* 1606 AD) *Yangjiafu Yanyi* (*The Romance of General Yangye's Family*), reprinted in 1980, Shanghai: Shanghai Classics Publisher.

Anon. (1980a) *Yinxu Fuhaomu* (*Excavation of Fuhao's Tomb at the Yin City Ruins*), Beijing: Cultural Relics Press.

Anon. (1985) 'Quangou Yangshao Wenhua Xuehui Taolunhui Zai Shengchi Zhaokai' ('Report of the National Yangshao Culture Symposium at Shengchi'), *Guangming Ribao* (*Guangming Daily*), 8 November, p. 1.

Anon. (1986) 'Zhonghua Wenming Faxiangdi You Si Da Quyu' ('The Four Major Regions of the Origins of Chinese Civilisation'), *RR*, 23 September, p. 1.

Anxi Culture Bureau (1987) 'Gansu Anxixian Faxian Yichu Xinshiqi Shidai Yizhi' ('New Excavation of the Neolithic Site in Anxi County, Gansu Province'), *KG*, 1: 91.

Bai Cuiqin (1987) 'Lun Weijing Nanbeichao Shiqi Minzhude Qianxi He Ronghe' ('On the Migration and Integration of Peoples in the Jin, Northern and Southern Dynasties'), *Zhongyang Minzu Xueyuan Xuebao* (*Bulletin of the Central National College*), 1: 8–13.

Bai Yunxiang (1985) 'Yindai Xizhou Shifou Daliang Shiyong Qingtong Nongjude Kaoguxue Guancha' ('An Archaeological Observation of Whether Bronze Farming Tools Were Used Extensively in the Shang and Western Zhou Periods'), *NK*, 1: 70–81.

Balinyouqi Museum (1987) 'Nemenggu Balinyouqi Nasitai Yizhi Diaocha' ('Investigation into the Neolithic Site at Nasitai, Baliyou Banner, Inner Mongolia'), *KG*, 6: 507–18.

Ban Gu (AD. 82) *Han Shu* (*History of the Han Dynasty*), reprinted in 1982, Beijing: Zhonghua Books.

Cao Guanyi (1989) *Zhongguo Nongye Jingjishi* (*An Agricultural-Economic History of China*), Beijing: China's Social Sciences Press.

Cao Shuji (1995) 'Hongwu Shiqi Hebei Diqude Renko Qianyi' ('Immigration in Hebei during the Hongwu Reign [1368–98]'), *ZNS*, 3: 12–27.

Cao Wanru (1987) 'Zailun Yujitude Zuozhe' ('The Author of *King Yu's Hydrography*'), *WW*, 3: 76–8.

Cao Xueqin (c. 1763) *Hongloumeng* (*Dream of the Red Chamber*), reprinted in 1970, Beijing: People's Press.

Cao Yonghe (1984) 'Shilun Mingtaizude Haiyang Jiaotong Zhengce' ('On Emperor Taizu's Maritime Policy in the Ming Dynasty'), in Editing Committee for *Maritime History of China* (ed.) *Zhongguo Haiyang Fazhanshi Lunwenji* (*Selected Essays on the Maritime History of China*), vol. 1, Taipei: Academia Sinica, pp. 41–70.

——(1988) 'Ming Hongwuchaode Zhongliu Guanxi' ('Relationship between China and Ryukyu under the Hongwu Reign [1368–98] of the Ming Dynasty'), in Zhang Yanxian (ed.), *Zhongguo Haiyang Fazhanshi Lunwenji* (*Selected Essays on the Maritime History of China*), vol. 3, Taipei: Academia Sinica, pp. 284–312.

CBW (1978) Cihai: Jingji (*Encyclopaedia: Economics*), ser. 3, Shanghai: Encyclopaedia Publisher.

——(1979) *Cihai* (*Encyclopaedia*), Shanghai: Encyclopaedia Publisher.

——(1980) *Cihai: Zhexue* (*Encyclopaedia: Philosophy*), ser. 2, Shanghai: Encyclopaedia Publisher.

——(1989) *Cihai* (*Encyclopaedia*), Shanghai: Encyclopaedia Publisher.

Chao Fulin (1996) 'Zhanguo Shiqide Tudi Siyouhua Jiqi Shehui Yingxiang' ('Private Land Ownership and Its Socio-economic Impact during the Warring States Period'), *Jianghai Xuekan* (*The Jianghai Journal*), 4: 108–14.

Chen Bangzhan (1606) *Yuanshi Jishi Benmo* (*Complete Record of the Yuan Dynasty*), reprinted in 1979, Beijing: Zhonghua Books.

Chen Changyuan (1995) 'Cong Qi Deming Kan Gudai Qidi Fangzhiye' ('The Textile Industry and the Naming of Qi Kingdom'), *Guanzi Xuekan* (*Journal of the Guanzi Tradition*), 2: 57–60.

Chen Dunyi and Hu Jishan (1983) *Zhongguo Jingji Dili* (*Economic Geography of China*), Beijing: China's Perspective Press.

Chen Fu (1149) *Chenfu Nongshu* (*Chen Fu's Treatise on Agriculture*), reprinted in 1981, Beijing: Agriculture Press.

Chen Gaoyong (1939) *Zhongguo Lidai Tianzai Renhou Biao* (*Chronological Tables of Chinese Natural and Man-made Disasters*), Shanghai: Shanghai Books.

Chen Guo-en and Yuan Hui (eds) (1995) *Zhongguo Gudai Dexing Xindian* (*A New Collection of Cases of Moral Integrity in Premodern China*), Beijing: China's Workers' Press.

Chen Mengjia (1956) *Yinxu Buci Zongshu* (*Survey of the Oracle Inscriptions from the Yin City Ruins of the Shang Dynasty*), Beijing: Sciences Press.

Chen Shou (*c.* AD 280) *Sanguo Zhi* (*History of the Three Kingdoms*), reprinted in 1982, Beijing: Zhonghua Books.

Chen Tiemin (ed.) (1994) *Qiyi Lingxiu Zhuan* (*Biographies of Rebel Leaders in the Chinese Dynastic Histories*), Haiko: Hainan Press.

Chen Xiyu (1991) 'Songdai Daxing Shangchuan Jiqi Liaode Jisuan Faze' ('Large Commercial Vessels in Song Times and the Formulae for the Estimation of their Sizes'), *HJY*, 1: 53–9.

Chen Xuewen (1991) 'Wanli Shiqide Zhongfei Maoyi' ('Sino-Philippine Trade during the Wanli Reign [1573–1619]'), *ZSY*, 1: 44–52.

Chen Zugui (ed.) (1958) *Dao* (*Rice*), Beijing: Zhonghua Books.

Cheng Qi (1865) *Qinding Hubu Zeli* (*Regulations of Ministry of Revenue, Made by Imperial Order*), reprinted in 1968, Taipei: Chengwen Press.

Cheng Xiaojun, Tang Zhaomei and Tan Songlin (eds) (1994) *Diwang Jiaxun* (*Private Instructions of Chinese Monarchs*), Wuhan: Hubei People's Press.

Cui Xuan (1987) 'Neimenggu Xinshiqi Shidai Kaogude Zhongyao Tupo' ('An Important Breakthrough in Neolithic Archaeology in Inner Mongolia'), *Neimenggu Sehuikexue* (*Social Sciences of Inner Mongolia*), 1: 66–9.

Cultural Bureau of Shandong Province and Jinan Museum (1974) *Dawenkou* (*The Neolithic Site at Dawenkou*), Beijing: Cultural Relics Press.

Dai Sheng (Western Han Period) *Liji* (*The Book of Rites*), in Wang Yunwu (ed.) (1969) *Liji Jinzhu Jinyi* (*Annotated Edition of the Book of Rites*), Taipei: Taiwan Commercial Press.

Deng Ciyu (1967) *Zhongguo Kaoshi Zhidu Shi* (*History of the Chinese Imperial Examination System*), Taipei: Xuesheng Books.

Deng Duanben (ed.) (1986) *Guangzhou Gangshi* (*A History of Port Guangzhou*), Beijing: Maritime Press.

Dong Lun (*c.* 1399) *Ming Taizu Shilu* (*Veritable Records of Emperor Taizu of the Ming Dynasty*), publisher unknown, reprinted in 1961, Taipei: Academia Sinica.

Dong Shucheng (1995) *Lidai Quanchen Fajide Aomiao* (*Secrets of the Rise of the Powerful Officials in Premodern China*), Beijing: China's International Broadcasting Press.

Dong Zhongshu (*c.* 104 BC) *Chunqiu Fanlu* (*Many Dewdrops of Spring and Autumn*), reprinted in 1975, Beijing: Zhonghua Books.

Du Shaoshun (1996) 'Tangdai Juntianzhi Pingmin Yingshoutian Biaozhun Xintan' ('A New Insight into the Land Distribution under the Tang Land Equalization System'), *ZJY*, 3: 132–8.

Du You (AD 801) *Tongdian* (*Complete Record of Institutions and Regulations*), publisher unknown.

E Ertai (AD 1742) *Shoushi Tongkao* (*Compendium of Works and Days*), reprinted in 1956, Beijing: Zhonghua Books.

Fan Wenlan (1964–5) *Zhongguo Tongshi Jian Bian* (*A Brief Panorama of Chinese History*), Beijing: People's Press.

Fan Ye (AD 445) *Houhan Shu* (*The History of the Eastern Han Dynasty*), reprinted in 1984, Beijing: Zhonghua Books.

Fan Yuzhou (1995) 'Jiangnan Diqude Shiqian Nongye' ('Prehistoric Agriculture in the Yangzi Delta Region'), *ZNS*, 2: 1–8.

Fang Jiedeng (1995) 'Yueguode Shangye' ('Commerce in Yue Kingdom'), *Zhejiang Shehui Kexue* (*Social Sciences of Zhejiang*), 1: 53–9.

Fang Xing (1981) 'Zhongguo Fengjian Shehui De Jingzi Jie Gou Yu Ziben Zhuyi Meng Ya' ('Economic Structure of China's Medieval Society and the Sprouting of Capitalism'), *LY*, 4: 126–36.

——(1984) 'Qingdai Qianqi Xiaonong Jingjide Zai Shangchan' ('Reproduction of the Petty Peasant Economy in Early Qing Times'), *LY*, 5: 129–41.

——(1986) 'Lun Qingdai Qianqi Nongmin Shangpin Shengchande Fazhan' ('On the Development of Peasant Commercial Production in Early Qing Times'), *ZJY*, 1: 53–66.

Fang Xuanling (AD 646) *Jin Shu* (*History of the Jin Dynasty*), reprinted in 1989, Beijing: Zhonghua Books.

Fang Zhongpu (1983) 'Yinren Hangdu Meizhou Zaitan' ('Further Investigation of the Shang Tribe's Sailing to America'), *Shijie Lishi* (*World History*), 3: 47–57.

FDL (Fudan Daxue Lishixi [History Department of Fudan University]), Lishi Yanjiu Bianjibu (Editorial Board of Research in History) and Fudan Xuebao Bianjibu (Editorial Board of Bulletin of Fudan University) (eds) (1983) *Jindai Zhongguo Zichan Jieji Yanjiu* (*Study of the Bourgeoisie in Modern China*), Shanghai: Fudan University Press.

Fu Yiling (1966) *Ming Qing Nongcun Shehui Jingji* (*Rural Economy in Ming and Qing Times*), Beijing: Sanlian Books.

Fu Zhongxia, Zhang Xing, Tian Zhaolin and Yang Boshi (1985) *Zhongguo Junshishi Fujuan Shang* (*A Military History of China, Supplement I*), Beijing: PLA Press.

Fu Zhongxia, Zhang Xing, Tian Zhaolin and Yang Boshi (1986) *Zhongguo Junshishi Fujuan Xia* (*A Military History of China, Supplement II*), Beijing: PLA Press.

Fu Zhufu (1980) *Zhongguo Jingjishi Luncong* (*Essays on Chinese Economic History*), Shanghai: Sanlian Books.

——(1981) *Zhongguo Fengjian Shehui Jingjishi* (*An Economic History of Feudal China*), Beijing: People's Press.

Fu Zhufu and Wang Yuhu (1982) *Zhongguo Jingjishi Ziliao Qin Han Sanguo Bian* (*Materials on Chinese Economic History during the Qin, Han and Three Kingdoms Periods*), Beijing: China's Social Sciences Press.

Fu Zongwen (1991) 'Citong Gangshi Chutan' ('A History of Port Citong [Quanzhou], Continued'), *HJY*, 2: 105–51.

Gao Min (1987) *Weijin Nanbeichao Sehui Jingjishi Tantao* (*On the Economic History of the Northern and Southern Dynasties*), Beijing: People's Press.

Gao Wende (1996) 'Zhongguo Lishishang Youmu Jingjide Gongxing He Texing' ('Generality and Peculiarity of the Nomadic Economy in Chinese History'), *ZJY*, 4: 109–21.

Ge Jianxiong (1993) 'Songdai Renko Xinzheng' ('New Evidence of Population during the Song Period'), *LY*, 6: 34–45.

Gong Weiying (1987) 'Shilun Zhongguo Shanggu Yi Xia Zhenyude Xiaoshi' ('On the Disappearance of the Differences between the Yi and Xia Peoples in Ancient China'), *Renwen Zazhi* (*Humanities Journal*), 1: 81–6.

Gongyang Gao (Warring States Period) *Gongyang Zhuan* (*A Political History of the Spring and Autumn Period by Master Gongyang*), reprinted in 1980, Beijing: Zhonghua Books.

Guan Zhong (Warring States Period) *Guanzi* (*Master Guan's Book*), reprinted in 1988, Beijing: Zhonghua Books.

Guo Baojun (1978) *Zhongguo Qingtongqi Shidai* (*China's Bronze Age*), Beijing: Sanlian Books.

Guo Chengkang (1996) 'Shiba Shiji Zhongguo Wujia Wenti He Zhengfu Duice' ('Inflation in Eighteenth-Century China and Government Responses'), *Qingshi Yanjiu* (*Studies in Qing History*), 1: 8–19.

Guo Moruo (1977) *Zhongguo Gudai Shehui Yanjiu* (*Study of the Ancient Society of China*), Beijing: People's Press.

Guo Qian (1979) 'Nanshui Beidia Guanxi Zhongguo Beifang Nongye Dazhengchande Gongcheng' ('Manoeuvring River Water from the South to the North: A Project for a Substantial Increase in North China's Agricultural Production'), *Mingbao Yuekan* (*Ming Monthly*), 6: 33–8.

Guo Rugui, Deng Zezong, Tan Qijin, Yao Zhihong and Liang Mingquan (1988) *Zhongguo Junshishi* (*A Military History of China*), vol. 4, Beijing: PLA Press.

Guo Wentao (1988) *Zhongguo Nongyie Keji Fazhan Shilue* (*A Brief History of the Development of Agricultural Science and Technology in China*), Beijing: China's Science and Technology Press.

Han Dacheng (1957) 'Mingdai Shang Pin Jingji De Fazhan Yu Ziben Zhuyi De Meng Ya' ('The Development of a Commercial Economy in Ming Times and Sproutings of Capitalism'), Shanghai: Department of History of Chinese People's University.

——(1986) *Mingdai Shehui Jingji Chutan* (*A Study of Society and the Economy of the Ming Period*), Beijing: People's Press.

Han E (*c.* AD 907) *Sishi Zuanyao* (*Important Rules for the Four Seasons*), in Miao Qiyu (ed.) (1979) *Sishi Zhuan Yao Jiaoshi* (*Annotated Edition of 'Important Rules for the Four Seasons'*), Beijing: Agriculture Press.

Han Lianqi (1986) *Xianqin Lianghanshi Luncong* (*On the History of Pre-Qin to Han Times*), Jinan: Qilu Books.

Han Longfu (1986) 'Lun Suiyangdide Lishi Zuoyong' ('The Role of Emperor Suiyang in Chinese History'), *Anhui Shixue* (*Anhui History*), 3: 13–34.

Han Rulin (ed.) (1986) *Yuanchao Shi* (*A History of the Yuan Dynasty*), Beijing: People's Press.

Han Yu (*c.* AD 824) *Yuandao* (*Original Way*), publisher unknown.

Hao Tiechuan (1987) 'Zhouchao Guojia Jiegou Kaoshu' ('On the Political Structure of the Zhou Dynasty'), *Huadong Shifan Xueyuan Xuebao* (*Bulletin of East China Normal University*), 2: 75–8.

He Bochuan (1992) *China on the Edge*, San Francisco: China Books.

Hong Zou, Er Ertai, Fu Min and Xu Yuanmeng (1735) *Baqi Manzhou Shizu Tongpu* (*The Complete Genealogies of the Manchu Eight Banners*), reprinted in 1989, Shenyang: Liaoshen Books.

Hou Wailu (ed.) (1992) *Zhongguo Dabaike Quanshu Zhongguo Lishi* (*Encyclopaedia of Chinese History*), Beijing and Shanghai: China's Encyclopaedia Publisher.

Hu Daojing (1985) *Nongshu Nongshi Lunji* (*Selected Works on Agricultural Books and Agronomic History*), Beijing: Agriculture Press.

Hu Ji (1983) 'Cong Gengsan Yuyi Shuoqi' ('On Three-year Farming for Four-year Food'), *ZNS*, 4: 14–22.

Hu Xiwen (ed.) (1958) *Mai* (*Wheat*), Beijing: Zhonghua Books.

Huan Kuan (Han Dynasty) *Yantie Lun* (*Discourses on Salt and Iron Policies*), publisher unknown.

Huang Jinyan and Chen Xiaoming (1997) 'Hanchao Bianfangjunde Guimo Jiqi Yangbing Feiyongzhi Tantao' ('Estimation of the Size of the Border Forces and their Costs during the Han Period'), *ZJY*, 1: 86–102.

Huang Qixu (1982–3) 'Huanghe Liuyu Xinshiqi Shidai Nonggeng Wenhua Zhongde Zuowu' ('Domestic Crops of the Neolithic Period in the Yellow River Valley'), *NK*, 2 (1982): 55–61; *NK*, 1 (1983): 39–50.

Huang Xingzeng (1520) *Xiyang Chaogong Dianlu* (*Records of Tributes from South Asia*), reprinted in 1982, Beijing: Zhonghua Books.

Institute of Archaeology (1965) *Jingshan Qujialing* (*Ch'uchialing, Chinshan*), Beijing: Sciences Press.

——(1987) 'Neimenggu Aohanqi Xiaoshan Yizhi' ('Excavation of the Neolithic Site at Xiaoshan, Aohan Banner, Inner Mongolia'), *WW*, 6: 481–3.

Ji Xianlin (1955) 'Zhongguo Canshi Shuru Yindu Wentide Chubu Yanjiu' ('A Historical Survey of the Export of Silk from China to India'), *LY*, 4: 51–94.

Ji Yun (1782) *Qinding Siku Quanshu* (*Complete Collection of Books for the Four Imperial Libraries under the Qing Imperial Edict*), reprinted, n.d., Taipei: Taiwan Commercial Press.

Jia Sixie (*c.* AD 534) *Qimin Yaoshu* (*Essential Techniques for the Peasantry*), reprinted in 1985, Beijing: Agriculture Press; also in Miao Qiyu (ed.) (1982) *Qimin Yaoshu Jiaoshi* (*Annotated Edition of 'Essential Techniques for the Peasantry'*), Beijing: Agriculture Press.

Jia Yi (*c.* 200–168 BC) *Guo Qin Lun* (*On the Experience of the Qin*), in Shanghai Classics Publisher (ed.) *Jiayi Xinshu* (*New Edition of Jia Yi's Works*), Shanghai: Shanghai Classics Publisher.

Jian Bozan (1983) *Qin Han Shi* (*A History of the Qin and Han Dynasties*), Beijing: Peking University Press.

Jian Bozan and Zheng Tianting (eds) (1962) *Zhongguo Tongshi Cankao Ziliao* (*Selected Materials on a Panorama of Chinese History*), Beijing: Zhonghua Books.

Jiang Chao (1987) 'Xiaozhan He Xiaozhandao' ('Xiaozhan and Xiaozhan Rice'), *KR*, 5 May, p. 4.

Jiang Xiaoyuan (1995) *Xingzhangli Xiade Zhongguoren* (*Chinese under Sexual Tension*), Shanghai: Shanghai People's Press.

Jin Guantao and Liu Qingfeng (1984) *Xingsheng Yu Weiji (Prosperity and Crises)*, Changsha: Hunan People's Press.

Jing Junjian (1981) 'Lun Qingdai Shehuide Dengji Jiegou' ('On the Social Strata of the Qing Dynasty'), in The Institute of Economics (ed.) *Zhongguo Shehui Kexueyuan Jingji Yanjiusuo Jikan (Bulletin of the Institute of Economics of the Chinese Academy of Social Sciences)*, vol. 3, Beijing: China's Social Sciences Press, pp. 1–64.

JKY (Junshi Kexueyuan, Institute of Military Sciences) (ed.) (1987) *Zhongguo Junshi Dili Gaikuang (Survey of Military Geography on China)*, Beijing: Military Sciences Press.

Ke Shaomin (1920) *Xin Yuan Shi (A New History of the Yuan Dynasty)*, Tianjin: Xushi Tuigengtan Press.

Kong Qiu (Confucius) (*c.* 479 BC) *Lunyu (The Analects)*, reprinted in 1985, Hong Kong: Kongxue Press.

Kong Xiangxian (1983) 'Jiangnan Geshengde Shuangjidao Shizai Kangxi Houqi Kaishi Tuiguangde' ('Promotion of Double-Cropping Rice in the Late Years of the Kangxi Reign'), *NK*, 1: 33–8.

Lai Qi and Chen Shen (eds) (1995) *Songtaizu Zhiguo Shengxun (Emperor Songtaizu's Instructions on State Management)*, Beijing: Expatriates' Press.

Lan Yong (1996a) 'Cong Tiandisheng Zonghe Yanjiu Jiaodu Kan Zhonghua Wenming Dongyi Nanqiande Yuanyin' ('The Climatic and Ecological Causes for the Chinese Civilisation to Shift Eastwards and Southwards'), *XW*, 3: 69–72.

——(1996b) 'Mingqing Sanxia Diqu Nongye Kenzhi Yu Nongtian Shuili Jianshe Yanjiu' ('Land Reclamation and Construction of Irrigation Networks in the Three-Gorges Region during the Ming–Qing Period'), *ZNS*, 2: 59–69.

Le Shouming (1986) 'Woguo Tangsong Yihou Fuojiaode Tedian' ('Characteristics of Buddhism in China after Tang and Song Times'), *Jianghuai Luntan (Jianghuai Regional Tribune)*, 3: 90–6.

Li Ao (1183) *Xu Zizhi Tongjian Changbian (Enlarged Comprehensive References for State Management)*, reprinted in 1956, Beijing: Zhonghua Books.

Li Bincheng (ed.) (1985) *Zhongguo Nongmin Zhanzhengshi, Suitang Wudai Shiguo (A History of Peasant Wars in China: Sui, Tang and Five Dynasties)*, Beijing: People's Press.

Li Bo (1981) *Zhongguo Gunongju Fazhanshi Jianbian (A Brief History of Ancient Chinese Agricultural Implements)*, Beijing: Agriculture Press.

Li Bozhong (1984) 'Mingqing Shiqi Jiangnan Shuidao Shengchan Jiyue Chengdude Tigao' ('Intensification of Rice Production in the Yangzi Delta during the Ming–Qing Period'), *ZNS*, 1: 24–37.

——(1985) 'Mingqing Jiangnan Nongye Ziyuande Heli Liyong' ('Rational Application of Agricultural Resources in the Yangzi Delta during the Ming–Qing Period'), *Nongye Kexue (Agricultural Sciences)*, 2: 150–63.

——(1996a) 'Rengen Shimu Yu Mingqing Jiangnan Nongminde Jingying Guimo' ('The Practice of "Ten *Mu* per Farmer" and the Scale of the Traditional Peasant Economy'), *ZNS*, 1: 1–14.

——(1996b) 'Cong Fufu Bingzuo Dao Nangeng Nuzhi' ('From "Husband and Wife Tilling Together" to "Husband Tilling and Wife Weaving"'), *LY*, 3: 99–107.

——(1996c) 'Qingdai Qianzhongqi Jiangnan Renkode Disu Zengzhang Jiqi Yuanyin' ('The Low Population Growth in the Yangzi Delta and its Reason during Early and Mid-Qing Times'), *Qingshi Yanjiu (Study of Qing History)*, 2: 10–19.

Li Changnian (ed.) (1982) *Nongsangjing Jiaozhu (Annotated Classic of Agriculture and Sericulture)*, Beijing: Agriculture Press.

Li Changshan (ed.) (1370) *Yuan Shi (History of the Yuan Dynasty)*, publisher unknown.

Li Fang (AD 983) *Taiping Yulan (The Imperial Classified Collection of Books of the Taiping Régime)*, publisher unknown.

Li Guangbi, Qian Junye and Lai Xinxia (1958) *Zhongguo Nongmin Qiyi Lunji (On Chinese Peasant Rebellions)*, Beijing: Sanlian Books.

Li Guihai (1987) *Zongguo Lidai Mingchen (Outstanding Bureaucrats in Premodern China)*, Zhengzhou: Henan People's Press.

Li Hongzhang (*c.* 1901) *Li Hongzhang Jiashu (Li Hongzhang's Letters to his Family)*, reprinted in 1994, Beijing: China's Expatriates' Press.

Li Ji (1990) *Anyang (The Shang Ruins at Anyang)*, Beijing: China's Social Sciences Press.

Li Jiannong (1957) *Song Yuan Ming Jingjishi Gao (An Economic History of the Song, Yuan and Ming Periods)*, Beijing: Sanlian Books.

—— (1962) *Xianqin Lianghan Jingjishi Gao (An Economic History of the Period from Pre-Qin to the Western and Eastern Han Dynasties)*, Beijing: Zhonghua Books.

Li Jinming (1990) *Mingdai Haiwai Maoyishi (A History of Overseas Trade in the Ming Period)*, Beijing: China's Social Sciences Press.

Li Longji (Emperor Xuanzong) (AD. 738) *Tang Liudian (Law of the Tang Dynasty)*, reprinted in 1991, Beijing: Zhonghua Books.

Li Min (1986) 'Luelun Zhongguo Gudai Shizu Zhidude Jieti' ('On the Disintegration of the Ancient Clan System in China'), *Zhongzhou Xiekan (Study of Central China)*, 6: 121–6.

Li Min, Yang Zeling, Sun Shunlin and Shi Daoxiang (1990) *Guben Zhushu Jinian Yizhu (Annotated Edition of Bamboo Strip Chronicles)*, Zhengzhou: Zhongzhou Classics Press.

Li Ruilan (1986) 'Li Kui Bianfazhongde Jin Dili Zhijiao' ('The Policy of "Maximising Agricultural Production" in Li Kui's Socio-economic Reform'), *Lishi Jiaoxue (History in Education)*, 6: 33–5.

Li Sanmou (1995) 'Lun Mingqing Nanfang Zhudianzhide Teshuxing' ('On the Characteristics of the Ming–Qing Tenancy System in South China'), *ZNS*, 2: 39–48.

Li Shaobai (1984) *Kexue Jishu Shi (History of Science and Technology)*, Wuhan: Central China's Institute of Engineering Press.

Li Shaolian (1987) 'Zhongguo Wenmingde Kaogu Xiansuo Jiqi Qishi' ('Archaeological Clues to the Origin of Chinese Civilisation and their Implications'), *XW*, 4: 90–4.

Li Shimin (*c.* AD 649a) *Difan (The Norm for Monarchs)*, in Cheng Xiaojun, Tang Zhaomei and Tan Songlin (eds) (1994) *Diwang Jiaxun (Private Instructions of Chinese Monarchs)*, ch. 10, Wuhan: Hubei People's Press.

—— (AD 649b) *Zijian Lu (Self-Warming)*, in Cheng Xiaojun, Tang Zhaomei and Tan Songlin (eds) (1994) *Diwang Jiaxun (Private Instructions of Chinese Monarchs)*, Wuhan: Hubei People's Press, ch. 11.

Li Shiyu (ed.) (1994) *Qingguan Tanguan Zhuan (Biographies of Upright and Venal Officials in the Chinese Dynastic Histories)*, Haiko: Hainan Press.

Li Wenzhi (1981) 'Lun Zhongguo Dizhu Jingji Yu Nongye Ziben Zhuyi Mengya' ('On China's Landlord Economy and the Sprouting of Capitalism in Agriculture'), *Zhongguo Shehui Kexue (Social Sciences of China)*, 1: 143–60.

—— (1994) 'Xizhou Fengjian Lun–Cong Zhufa Kaocha Xizhoude Shehui Xingzhi' ('On the Feudal Nature of the Western Zhou Dynasty: To Reveal the Nature of the Western Zhou Society from the Tax in Labour'), *ZJY*, 4: 85–93.

Li Xiaodong (1986) *Zhongguo Fengjian Jiali (Chinese Family Etiquette and Obligations)*, Xi-an: Shaanxi People's Press.

Li Xinchuan (*c.* 1202) *Jianyan Yilai Xinian Yaolu* (*Annuals of Important Events since 1128*), reprinted in 1956, Beijing: Zhonghua Books.

Li Yan (1996) 'Sanlun Zhongguo Fengjian Tudi Guoyouzhi' ('The Third Essay on the State Land Ownership in Premodern China'), *Sixiang Zhanxian* (*Ideological Front*), 1: 57–63.

Li Yanshou (AD 659) *Nan Shi* (*History of the Southern Dynasties*), reprinted in 1975, Beijing: Zhonghua Books.

Li Zhaochao (1991) 'Luexi Songdai Guanshi Zhizheng' ('Brief Analysis of Commodity Tax in the Song Period'), *Jingji Kexue* (*Economic Sciences*), 5: 70–6.

Li Zude (1990) *Zhongguo Lidai Kaiguo Diwangzhuan* (*Biographies of Founders of the Chinese Dynasties*), Hefei: Huangshan Books.

——(1993) *Zhongguo Lidai Wangguo Diwangzhuan* (*Biographies of the Overthrown Dynasts*), Hefei: Huangshan Books.

Liang Fangzhong (1980) *Zhongguo Li Dai Huko Tiandi Tianfu Tongji* (*Dynastic Data on China's Households, Cultivated Land and Land Taxation*), Shanghai: Shanghai People's Press.

Liang Jichong and Wang Yulin (eds) (1995) *Mingtaizu Zhiguo Shengxun* (*Emperor Mingtaizu's Instructions on State Management*), Beijing: Expatriates' Press.

Liang Tingran (*c.* 1861) *Yue Haiguan Zhi* (*History of the Customs of Guangdong*), publisher unknown.

Lin Chengkun (1987) 'Changjiang Qiantanjiang Zhongxiayou Diqu Xinshiqi Shidai Dili Yu Daozuode Qiyuan He Fenbu' ('The Origin and Geographic Distribution of Rice Cultivation during the Neolithic Period in the Middle and Lower Reaches of the Yangzi and Qiantang Rivers'), *NK*, 1: 283–91.

Lin Gengsheng (1982) 'Gudai Cong Hailu Yinjin Fujiande Zhiwu' ('Introduced Plants in Premodern Fujian through Sea Routes'), *HJY*, 4: 87–91.

Lin Manhong (1991) 'Zhongguode Baiyin Wailiu Yu Shijie Jinyin Jianchan [1814–1850]' ('China's Silver Outflow and Decline in Gold and Silver Outputs in the World [1814–1850]'), in Wu Jianxiong (ed.) *Zhongguo Haiyang Fazhanshi Lunwenji* (*Selected Essays on the Maritime History of China*), vol. 4, Taipei: Academia Sinica, pp. 1–44.

Lin Shimin (1990) *Haishang Sichouzhi Lude Zhuming Haigang Mingzhou* (*Ningbo – A Port known for Trade along the 'Maritime Silk Road'*), Beijing: Maritime Press.

Lin Weiwen (1986) 'Gudai Yuerende Hanghai Nengli Ji Dongdu Meizhou' ('Sailing Capacity of the Ancient Viets and Voyages Crossing the Pacific to America'), *HJY*, 1: 38–46.

Lin Xianggeng (1987) 'Yiqi Zhouqi Shidai Shehui Xingzhi Zairenshi' ('The Reappraisal of the Zhou Dynasty when the Deeds of Yin were First Abandoned'), *LY*, 2: 47–63.

Liu An (179–122 BC) *Huainanzi* (*Duke of Huinan*), reprinted in 1989, Shanghai: Shanghai Classics Publisher.

Liu Bima (1987) 'Xiandai Zhongguoren Tizhi Tezheng Yanjiude Xishouhuo' ('New Achievements in the Study of Modern Chinese Physical Characteristics'), *KR*, 6 October, p. 4.

Liu Chang (1982) 'Weishenme Ziben Zhuyi Buceng Zai Zhongguo Fazhan Qilai' ('Why Capitalism Never Developed in China'), *LY*, 5: 188–98.

Liu Dajun (1992) *Yijing Quanyi* (*The Annotated Book of Changes*), Chengdu: Bashu Books.

Liu Dajun and Lin Zhongjun (1993) *Zhouyizhuanwen Baihua Jie* (*Annotated Commentaries on 'The Book of Changes'*), Chengdu: Bashu Books.

Liu Lu (1996) 'Qingdai Yu Shijie Kejide Jiaoliu' ('Intake of Western Science and Technology by the Qing Court'), *RR* (Overseas Edition), 23 November, p. 3.

Liu Sen (1992) 'Songdai Qianjian Yanjiu' ('Study of the Mints of the Song Dynasty'), *ZSY*, 3: 117–23.

Liu Sen (1993a) 'Songdaide Tieqian Yu Tie Chanliang' ('Monetary Iron and Iron Outputs in the Song Dynasty'), *ZJY*, 2: 86–90.

—— (1993b) *Songjin Zhibishi* (*A History of Paper Currencies during the Song and Jin Periods*), Beijing: China's Finance Press.

Liu Xiao (1988) 'Qin Shihuang Yu Dahai' ('Emperor Qin Shihuang and the Sea'), *RR*, 11 May, p. 8.

Liu Xinglin (1995) 'Lu Shangdai Nongyede Fazhan' ('On Agricultural Development in Shang Times'), *ZNS*, 4: 14– 24.

Liu Xu (945) *Tang Shu* (*History of the Tang Dynasty*), reprinted in 1975, Beijing: Zhonghua Books.

Liu Yongming. 1987. 'Xiaoyi Hemudu Nongye' ('Brief Survey of the Agriculture of Hemudu Neolithic Culture'), *NK*, 2: 100–2.

Liu Zehua (1987) 'Zhanguo Shiqide Shi' ('The Literati Stratum in the Warring States Period'), *LY*, 4: 42–55.

Liu Zehua and Zhang Fentian (1991) 'Lun Zhenguan Shiqi Junchende Minben Sixiang' ('On "People as the Foundation" in State Politics during the Zhiguan Reign'), *XW*, 7: 70–5.

Liu Zehua, Yang Zhijiu, Wang Yuzhe, Yang Yixiang, Feng Erkang, Nan Bingwen, Tang Gang, Zheng Kesheng and Sun Liqun (1979) *Zhongguo Gudaishi* (*History of Pre-modern China*), Beijing: People's Press.

Lü Buwei (Warring States Period), *Lushi Chunqiu* (*Master Lu's Spring and Autumn Annals*), reprinted in 1989, Shanghai: Shanghai Classics Publisher.

Lu Xuhui (1991) 'Zhongguo Xianguan Zhidu Yange Shulue' ('Survey of the Change of the County Magistrate System'), *XW*, 6: 74–7.

Lü Zhenyu (1983) *Yinzhou Shidaide Zhongguo Shehui* (*Chinese Society of the Shang–Zhou Period*), Beijing: Sanlian Books.

Lü Zongli (ed.) (1994) *Zhongguo Lidai Guanzhi Dacidian* (*Encyclopaedia of Dynastic Official Positions*), Beijing: Beijing Press.

Luan Baoqun and Qin Jincai (eds) (1994) *Zhichen Jianchen Zhuan* (*Biographies of Upright and Treacherous Court Officials in the Chinese Dynastic Histories*), Haiko: Hainan Press.

Luo Cunkang (1996) 'Shilun Shangdaide Cansiye' ('On the Silk-Making Industry of the Shang Period'), *Sichuan Shifan Xueyuan Xuebao* (*Bulletin of Sichuan Teachers' College*), 1: 113–17.

Luo Yaping (1992) 'Nansong Qianhuang Chengyin Tantao' ('On the Causes of Monetary Shortage under the Southern Song Dynasty'), *Huangzhou Daxue Xuebao* (*Bulletin of the University of Hangzhou*), 3: 77–82.

Luo Zhiye (1995) *Yijing Xinyi* (*A New Translation of 'The Book of Changes'*), Qingdao: Qingdao Press.

Ma Duanlin (1307) *Wenxian Tongkao* (*Comprehensive Study of Historical Records*), publisher unknown.

Ma Xueqin (1996) 'Mingdai Henan Wangzhuang Nongye Jingji Yanjiu' ('A Study of the Agricultural Economy of the Royal Estates in Henan Province during the Ming Period'), *ZJY*, 4: 61–70.

Ma Zhenduo (1993) *Ren Rendao–Kongzide Zhexue Sixiang* (*Humanity and Confucius's Philosophy*), Beijing: China's Social Sciences Press.

Ma Zongshen (1982) 'Guanyu Woguo Gudai Hongshui He Dayu Zhishuide Tantao' ('Discussion on Floods in Ancient China and Yu's Harnessing of Rivers'), *NK*, 2: 3–11.

—— (1985) 'Xizhou Nongye Shuifa Kao' ('Agricultural Taxation in Western Zhou Times'), *NK*, 2: 50–60.

Mao Hanwen (1987) 'Zhonghua Minzude Liang Da Fayandi' ('Two Major Geographic Origins of the Chinese'), *XW*, 1: 199–200.

Mengzi (Mencius) (Warring States Period) *Mengzi (Book of Mencius)*, reprinted in 1957, Beijing: People's Literature Press.

Miao Qiyu (ed.) (1982) *Qimin Yaoshu Jiaoshi (Annotated Edition of 'Essential Techniques for the Peasantry')*, Beijing: Agriculture Press.

Mu Yongkang and Song Zhaolin (1981) 'Jianzhede Shili He Puotuqi, Shilun Woguo Ligengde Qiyuan' ('The Stone Ploughshares and Soil-Breaking Implements of the Yangtze Delta, a Hypothesis on the Origins of Chinese Ploughing'), *NK*, 2: 75–84.

Ni Lai-en and Xia Weizhong (1990) 'Waiguo Baiyin Yu Mingdiguode Bengkui' ('Foreign Silver and the Demise of the Ming Dynasty'), *ZJY*, 3: 46–56.

Niu Chuangping and Qin Guojing (1992) *Zhongguo Lidai Wuzheng Sanbaili (Three Hundred Error Cases in the History of Chinese Government)*, Beijing: Beijing Normal University Press.

Ouyang Xiu (1060) *Xin Tangshu (The New History of the Tang Dynasty)*, reprinted in 1975, Beijing: Zhonghua Books.

Peng Bo and Gong Fei (1989) *Zhongguo Jiancha Zhidushi (A History of Surveillance Systems in China)*, Beijing: China's University of Political Sciences and Law.

Peng Zeyi (1990) 'Qingdai Caizheng Guanli Tizhi Yu Shouzhi Jiegou' ('Financial Administration and Structure of the Qing Dynasty'), *Zhongguo Shehui Kexueyuan Yanjiushengyuan Xuebao (Bulletin of the Graduate School of the Chinese Academy of Social Sciences)*, 2: 48–59.

Pu Jian (1990) *Zhongguo Gudai Xingzheng Lifa (Administrative Legislation of Premodern China)*, Beijing: Peking University Press.

Qi Xia (1992) 'Songdai Zhimian Xukao' ('Further Study of Cotton Cultivation in the Song Dynasty'), *Shixue Yuekan (History Studies Monthly)*, 5: 18–21.

Qiu Xuanyu (1993) 'Mingchu Yu Nanhai Zhu Fanguozhi Chaogong Maoyi 1368–1449' ('Regular Tributes of Exotic Goods and Bestowal of Chinese Goods between China and Countries in South Asia, 1368–1449'), in Zhang Bincun and Liu Shiji (eds) *Zhongguo Haiyang Fazhanshi Lunwenji (Selected Essays on the Maritime History of China)*, vol. 5, Taipei: Academia Sinica, pp. 111–51.

Qu Zhisheng (1960) *Zhongguo Gunongshu Jianjie (A Survey of Traditional Chinese Agricultural Treatises)*, Taipei: Economics Research Society.

Quan Hansheng (1993) 'Lielun Xinhanglu Faxianhoude Zhongguo Haiwai Maoyi' ('On China's Overseas Trade after the Discovery of a New Asia–Europe Sea Route'), in Zhang Bincun and Liu Shiji (eds) *Zhongguo Haiyang Fazhanshi Lunwenji (Selected Essays on the Maritime History of China)*, vol. 5: 1–16, Taipei: Academia Sinica.

Sa Dula (*c.* 1348) *Zaofa Huanghe Jishi (On a Trip along the Yellow River)*, in Wang Zhengyuan, Yang Ming, Li Mengsheng, Zhao Changping, Huan Baohua and Jiang Jianyuan (eds) (1992) *Gushihai (Collection of Ancient Chinese Poems)*, Shanghai: Shanghai Classics Publisher, p. 1616.

Sanlian Books (1957) *Zhongguo Ziben Zhuyi Meng Ya Wen Ti Tao Lun Ji (Collected Papers on the Issue of Sproutings of Capitalism in China)*, Beijing: Sanlian Books.

SGC (Shanghai Guji Chubanshe, Shanghai Classics Press) (1991) *Shida Jianchen (Biographies of Ten Treacherous Officials)*, Shanghai: Shanghai Classics Press.

Shang Xiaoyuan (1989) *Zhongguo Guominde Ziwo Yizhixing Renge (Self-restrained Personality of the Chinese)*, Kunming: Yunnan People's Press.

Shang Yang (338 BC) *Shangjun Shu (Master Shang's Book)*, reprinted in 1986, Beijing: Zhonghua Books.

Shao Qin (1985) 'Xi Minben, Dui Xianqin Zhi Xihan Minben Sixiangde Kaocha' ('The Idea of the People as the Foundation in the Pre-Qin to Western Han Periods'), *LY*, 6: 3–16.

Shen Yucheng (ed.) (1994) *Shengshi Huangdi Zhuan* (*Biographies of Emperors during the Piping Times of Great Peace and Prosperity in the Chinese Dynastic Histories*), Haiko: Hainan Press.

Shen Zhong (ed.) (1995) *Tangdai Mingren Keju Kaojuan Yiping* (*Annotated Essays by Prominent Scholars for the Imperial Examination during the Tang Period*), Nanchang: Jiangxi Tertiary Education Press.

Shi Fengyi (1987) *Zhongguo Gudai Hunyin Yu Jiating* (*Marriage and Family in Premodern China*), Changsha: Hubei People's Press.

Shi Naiyan (Early Ming Period) *Shuihu Zhuan* (*Water Marsh*), reprinted in 1980, Beijing: Zhonghua Books.

Shi Shenghan (1979) *Nongzheng Quanshu Jiaozhu* (*Annotated Edition of the 'Complete Treatise on Agricultural Administration'*), Shanghai: Shanghai Classics Publisher.

——(1980) *Zhongguo Gudai Nongshu Pingjie* (*A Critical Introduction to the Ancient Chinese Agricultural Books*), Beijing: Agriculture Press.

Shi Weiqing (1986) 'Guanyu Qinhan Yaoyide Ruogan Wenti' ('Issues Related to Corvée Services during the Qin-Han Period'), *ZSY*, 2: 17–30.

Shi Yanting (1992) *Zhongguo Lidai Jianchenzhuan* (*Biographies of Treacherous Officials in Premodern China*), Beijing: International Culture Press.

Si Weizhi (1957) 'Guanyu Yinzhou Tudi Suoyouzhi Wenti' ('On the Land-Ownership Type of the Shang and Zhou Periods'), in Editorial Board of *Research in History* (ed.) *Zhongguo Gudaishi Fenqi Wenti Taolunji* (*Essays on Division of Eras in Premodern Chinese History*), Beijing: Sanlian Books, pp. 151–78.

Sima Guang (1084) *Zizhi Tongjian* (*Comprehensive References for State Management*), reprinted in 1956, Beijing: Zhonghua Books.

Sima Qian (91 BC) *Shi Ji* (*The Book of History*), reprinted in 1982, Beijing: Zhonghua Books.

Song Lian (1371) 'Yeluchucai Zhuan' ('Biography of Yeluchucai'), *Yuan Shi* (*History of the Yuan Dynasty*), vol. 153, entry no. 146.

Song Xinchao (1991) *Yinshang Wenhua Quyu Yanjiu* (*A Study of Regional Cultures of the Shang Dynasty*), Xi-an: Shaanxi People's Press.

Song Xishang (1954) *Lidai Zhishui Wenxian* (*Essays and Documents on Water Control in Premodern Periods*), Taipei: China's Cultural Publication Committee.

Song Yingxing (1637) *Tiangong Kaiwu* (*Exploitation of the Works of Nature*), reprinted in 1978, Hong Kong: Zhonghua Books, Hong Kong Branch.

Song Yuanqiang (1992) *Qingchaode Zhuangyuan* (*Imperial Examination Champions in the Qing Period*), Changchun: Jilin Culture and History Press.

Su Jin (1985) *Qinlü Tonglun* (*A Comprehensive Analysis of the Qin Law*), Jinan: Shandong People's Press.

Su Minsheng (1987) 'Woguo Wenzide Lishi Jiujing You Duojiu' ('Beginning of the Chinese Written Language'), *Liaowang'* (*Observation*) 9: 44–45.

Su Ye and Li Ju (1992) *Gubi Zongheng* (*Survey of Ancient Currencies*), Beijing: China's Finance Press.

Sun Changjiang (1986) 'Jingxue Yu Zhongguo Wenhua' ('Orthodox Confucianism and Chinese Culture'), in Department of History of Fudan University (ed.) *Zhongguo Chuantong Wenhuade Zai Guji* (*Re-Evaluation of Chinese Traditional Culture*), Shanghai: Shanghai People's Press, pp. 613–32.

Sun Changxu (1964) *Leishide Qiyuan Jiqi Fazhan* (*Origin and Development of Chinese Tillage Implements*), Shanghai: Shanghai People's Press.

Sun Guangqi (1989) *Zhongguo Gudai Hanghaishi* (*A Nautical History of Premodern China*), Beijing: Maritime Press.

Sun Jingtan (1990) 'Zhongguo Gushi Fenqi Xintan' ('Reinterpretation of the Phases of Premodern Chinese History') *XW*, 4: 64–9.

Sun Xugang (ed.) (1988) *Jianming Zhongguo Caizhengshi* (*A Compact History of Finance of Premodern China*), Beijing: China's Finance and Economy Press.

Sun Yancheng (ed.) (1994) *Modai Huangdi Zhuan* (*Biographies of the Last Dynasts in the Chinese Dynastic Histories*), Haiko: Hainan Press.

Sun Zhonghui (1989) *Guqianbi Tujie* (*Illustrations of Ancient Currencies*), Shanghai: Shanghai Books.

Sun Zhonghui, Shi Xinbiao, Zhou Xiang, Hu Wei and Huang Ximing (eds) (1991) *Jianming Qianbi Cidian* (*Compact Dictionary of Ancient Chinese Currencies*), Shanghai: Shanghai Classics Publisher.

Sun Zuoyun (1966) *Shijing Yu Zhoudai Shehui Yanjiu* (*'Book of Odes' and Study of Society of the Zhou Period*), Beijing: Zhonghua Books.

Tang Gaocai (ed.) (1988) *Tangsong Ci Jianshang Cidian* (*Encyclopaedia of Poems of the Tang–Song Period*), Shanghai: Shanghai Encyclopaedia Publisher.

Tang Jing and Zheng Chuanshui (1993) *Zhongguo Guojia Jigoushi* (*A History of Administrative Structures in China*), Shenyang: Liaoning People's Press.

Tang Keliang (1993) 'Shilun Beisong Shiqide Guanli Jingshang' ('On Officials' Involvement in Commercial Activities in the Northern Song Dynasty'), *Qiusuo* (*Pursuits*), 6: 120–4.

Tang Qiyu (1986) *Zhongguo Zuowu Zaipei Shigao* (*A History of Cultivation of Crops in China*), Beijing: Agriculture Press.

Tang Zhangru (1956) 'Juntian Zhidude Chansheng Yu Puohuai' ('Formation and Decline of the Land Equalisation System'), *LY*, 2: 1–30.

Tian Changwu (1986) 'Zhongguo Fengjian Shehui Changqi Tingzhilun Zhiyi' ('On Long-Term Socio-economic Stagnation in Premodern China'), *Zhengzhou Daxue Xuebao* (*Bulletin of Zhengzhou University*), 4: 72–81.

Tian Fang and Chen Yijun (1986) *Zhongguo Yimin Shilue* (*Brief History of Migration in China*), Beijing: Knowledge Press.

Tian Zaoyang (1994) *Zhongguo Gudai Xingzheng Shilue* (*A History of Administration in Premodern China*), Beijing: New World Press.

Tian Zhaolin, Tao Wenhuan, Chen Xijin, Zhao Xiukun, Shi Shengbi, Chen Yangping, Deng Zezong, Yao Zhihong and Yang Qi (1990) *Zhongguo Junshishi* (*A Military History of China*), vol. 5, Beijing: PLA Press.

Tomlinson, B.R. (1985) 'Writing History Sideways: Lessons for Indian Economic Historians from Meiji Japan', *Modern Asian Studies*, 3: 669–98.

Tong Zhuchen (1986) 'Zhongguo Xinshiqi Shidai Wenhuade Duozhong Xi Fazhan Lu He Fazhan Bu Pingheng Lun' ('On the Multi-centre Nature and Heterogeneity of the Chinese Neolithic Age'), *WW*, 2: 16–39.

Tuo Tuo (ed.) (1344) *Jin Shi* (*History of the Jin Dynasty*), reprinted in 1985, Beijing: Zhonghua Books.

—— (ed.) (1345) *Song Shi* (*History of the Song Dynasty*), reprinted in 1985, Beijing: Zhonghua Books.

Wang Bicheng (1979) *Zhoudai Chengbang* (*City State of the Zhou Period*), Taipei: Lianjing Books.

Wang Cun (1987) 'Jin Wuqian Yu Nian Lai Wuoguo Zhongyuan Diqiu Qihou Zai Nian Jiangshuiliang Fangmiande Bianqian' ('Fluctuations in Annual Precipitation over 5,000 Years in North China'), *Zhongguo Kexue* (*Scientia Sinica*), 1: 104–12.

Wang Dezhao (1982) *Qingdai Keju Zhidu Yanjiu* (*A Study of the Civil Examinations of the Qing Dynasty*), Hong Kong: The Chinese University Press.

Wang Guanzhuo (1991) *Zhongguo Guchuan* (*Ancient Ships of China*), Beijing: Maritime Press.

Wang Hao (1708) *Guang Qunfangpu* (*Complete Thesaurus of Botany, Enlarged*), reprinted, 1936, Shanghai: Commercial Press.

Wang Huifang (1982) 'Quanzhouwan Chutu Songdai Haichuande Jinko Yaowu Zai Zhongguo Yiyaoshishangde Jiazhi' ('Importance in Chinese Medical History of the Imported Raw Medicine Discovered from the Song Wreck in Quanzhou Bay'), *HJY*, 4: 60–5.

Wang Jingyu (1984) 'Lue Lun Zhongguo Ziben Zhuyi Chan Sheng De Lishi Tiao Jian' ('On the Historical Conditions of the Emergence of Capitalism in China'), *LY*, 2: 95–110.

Wang Kelin (1983) 'Luelun Woguo Gouxude Qiyuan He Yongtu' ('The Origin and Function of Canals and Ditches in China'), *NK*, 2: 65–69.

Wang Qi (1586) *Xu Wenxian Tongkao* (*Imperially Commissioned Continuation of the Comprehensive Study of Literature*), vol. 1, publisher unknown.

Wang Qingyun (1858) *Shiqu Yuji* (*A Personal Record of the Qing Dynasty*), reprinted 1985, Beijing: Beijing Classics Press.

Wang Shengduo (1995) *Liangsong Caizhengshi* (*A History of Government Finance of the Northern and Southern Song Periods*), Beijing: Zhonghua Books.

Wang Xianming (1987) 'Jindai Zhongguo Shenshi Jiecengde Fenhua' ('The Change in the Chinese Literati in Modern Times'), *Shehui Kexue Zhanxian* (*Social Science Front*), 3: 165–74.

Wang Xiantang (1985) *Yanhuang Shizu Wenhua Kao* (*On Cultures of the Proto-Chinese Tribes, Yan and Huang*), Jinan: Qilu Books.

Wang Xiaotian (1991) 'Zhongguo Gudai Jiancai Zhidu Shulun' ('Surveillant Systems in Premodern China'), *XW*, 7: 75–8.

Wang Xingya (1996) 'Qingdai Henan Jishide Fazhang' ('Development of the Rural Markets in Henan during the Qing Period'), *Nandu Xuetan* (*Nandu Academia*), 1: 70–4.

Wang Yinglin (*c.* 1296) *Yuhai* (*Jade Sea Encyclopaedia*), reprinted in 1883, Hangzhou: Zhejiang Books.

Wang Yuhu (1964) *Zhongguo Nongxue Shulu* (*Bibliography of Chinese Classical Agronomy*), Beijing: Agriculture Press.

Wang Yunsen (1980) *Zhongguo Gudai Turang Kexue* (*Knowledge of Soil in Ancient China*), Beijing: Science Press.

Wang Yuru (1996) 'Zhongguo Jindai Wujia Zongshuiping Biandong Qiushi Yanjiu' ('A Study in the Trend of the General Price Change in Modern China'), *ZJY*, 2: 50–63.

Wang Zengyu (1993) 'Jinchao Huko Fenlei Zhidu He Jieji Jiegou' ('The Household Classification System and Class Structure under the Jin Dynasty'), *LY*, 6: 46–62.

Wang Zhaolin and Bian Jiang (1996) 'Qijin Zuida Xizhou Xunzang Chemakeng Zai Shan Faxian' ('Discovery of the Largest Western Zhou Funerary Pit of Horses with Carts in Shaanxi'), *Xinhua Wenzhai* (*New China Compilation*), 11: 84.

Wang Zhaotang and Xu Yongkang (eds) (1986) *Zhongguo Fazhi Shigang* (*A Brief History of the Legal System in China*), Hangzhou: Zhejiang People's Press.

Wang Zhen (1304) *Wangzhen Nongshu* (*Wang Zhen's Treatise on Agriculture*), in Wang Yuhu (ed.) (1981) *Wangzhen Nongshu* (*Annotated Edition of Wang Zhen's Treatise on Agriculture*), Beijing: Agriculture Press.

Wang Zhengyuan, Yang Ming, Li Mengsheng, Zhao Changping, Huan Baohua and Jiang Jianyuan (eds) (1992) *Gushihai* (*Collection of Ancient Chinese Poems*), Shanghai: Shanghai Classics Publisher.

Wang Zhigong (1986) 'Zhongguo Nongyiede Qiyang Jiqi Jingji Diwei' ('The Origin of Agriculture in China and its Significance'), *Shantou Daxue Xuebao* (*Bulletin of Shantuo University*), 4: 87–90.

Wang Zhigong and Wei Liying (1995) 'Ronghe Yu Fazhang' ('Integration and Development'), *Gansu Shehui Kexue* (*Social Sciences of Gansu*), 6: 69–72.

Wei Qingyuan (1989) *Zhongguo Zhengzhi Zhidushi* (*A History of the Political Systems in China*), Beijing: Chinese People's University Press.

Wei Shou (AD 554) *Wei Shu* (*History of the Wei Kingdom*), reprinted in 1974, Beijing: Zhonghua Books.

Wei Zaitian, Xu Xuechu and Li Yawei (eds) (1995) *Kangxi Zhiguo Shengxun* (*Emperor Kangxi's Instructions on State Management*), Beijing: Expatriates' Press.

Wei Zheng (AD 656) *Sui Shu* (*History of the Sui Dynasty*), reprinted in 1989, Beijing: Zhonghua Books.

Wei Zuhui and Yan Jihe (1992) *Zhongguo Lidai Qingguanzhuan* (*Biographies of Upright Officials in Premodern China*), Beijing: International Culture Press.

Wen Shanfeng and Yuan Tingdong (1983) *Yinxu Buci Yanjiu* (*A Study of the Oracle Inscriptions from the Yin City Ruins of the Shang Dynasty*), Chongqing: Sichuan Social Sciences Press.

Wen Shidan (1987) 'Changjiang Zhongyoude Xianqin Nongju' ('Farming Tools of Pre-Qin Times Unearthed in the Middle Reach of the Yangzi Valley'), *NK*, 1: 157–72.

Wen Zhenfu, Tian Shaolin, Yi Xiuliang and Huang Yibing (1993) *Zhongguo Junshishi* (*A Military History of China*), vol. 1, Beijing: PLA Press.

Weng Dujian (ed.) (1990) *Zhongguo Minzu Guanxishi Gangyao* (*A Compact History of Relationships among Ethnic Groups in China*), Beijing: China's Social Sciences Press.

Wu Chengming (1985) *Zhongguo Zibenznuyi Yu Guonei Shichang* (*Capitalism and Domestic Market of China*), Beijing: China's Social Sciences Press.

Wu Genyou (ed.) (1993) *Sishu Wujing* (*The Annotated Four Books and Five Classics of Confucianism*), Beijing: China's Friendship Press.

Wu Hui (1984) *Zhongguo Gudai Liuda Jingji Gaigejia* (*Six Outstanding Economic Reformers in Chinese History*), Shanghai: Shanghai People's Press.

—— (1985) *Zhongguo Lidai Liangshi Muchan Yanji* (*Research in the Dynastic Grain Output per Mu in China*), Beijing: Agriculture Press.

Wu Jianguo (1996) 'Lun Wudai Shiguode Fengjian Tudi Guoyouzhi' ('On State Land Ownership in the Ten Kingdoms during the Five Dynasties Period'), *ZJY*, 1: 128–39.

Wu Yumin (1988) *Wuxingde Wangluo* (*The Invisible Network: Chinese Traditional Culture from the Angle of Communication*), Beijing: International Culture Press.

Wu Zimu (1334) *Mengliang Lu* (*Recorded Dreams*), reprinted in 1980, Beijing: China's Commercial Press.

Xia Zhengnong (ed.) (1989) *Cihai* (*Encyclopaedia*), Shanghai: Encyclopaedia Publisher.

Xiao Li (1987) *Zhongguo Lidai Mingjun* (*Outstanding Dynasts of Premodern China*), Zhengzhou: Henan People's Press.

Xiao Zixian (AD 514–26) *Nanqi Shu* (*History of the Southern Qi Dynasty*), reprinted in 1972, Beijing: Zhonghua Books.

Xie Guozhen (1956) *Qingchu Nongmin Qiyi Ciliao Jilu* (*Records of the Peasant Uprisings in Early Qing Times*), Shanghai: Xinzhishi Books.

—— (1980) *Mingdai Shehui Jingji Shiliao Xuanbian* (*Selected Materials of the Socio-economic History of the Ming Dynasty*), vol. 1, Fuzhou: Fujian People's Press.

—— (1981) *Mingdai Shehui Jingji Shiliao Xuanbian* (*Selected Materials of the Socio-economic History of the Ming Dynasty*), vol. 2, Fuzhou: Fujian People's Press.

Xie Tianyou and Jian Xiuwei (1980) *Zhongguo Nongmin Zhanzheng Jianshi* (*A Short History of Peasant Wars in China*), Shanghai: Shanghai People's Press.

Xie Weiyang (1990) *Zhoudai Jiating Xingtai* (*Family Types during the Zhou Period*), Beijing: China's Social Sciences Press.

Xin Li (1987) 'Kongzide Deliguan' ('The Confucian View on Morality and Etiquette'), *Beijing Shifan Daxue Xuebao* (*Bulletin of Beijing Normal University*), 4: 87–93.

Xing Tie (1995) 'Woguo Gudaide Zhuzi Pingjun Xichan Wenti' ('On Equal Inheritance among Sons in Premodern China'), *ZSY*, 4: 3–15.

Xu Changli and Li Yaowu (eds) (1995) *Qianlong Zhiguo Shengxun* (*Emperor Qianlong's Instructions on State Management*), Beijing: Expatriates' Press.

Xu Dixin and Wu Chengming (eds) (1985) *Zhongguo Ziben Zhuyide Mengya* (*Sprouting of Capitalism in China*), Beijing: People's Press.

Xu Guangqi (*c.* 1628) *Nongzheng Quanshu* (*Complete Treatise on Agricultural Administration*), reprinted in 1979, Shanghai: Shanghai Classics Publisher.

Xu Min and Jing Cheng (1992) *Zhongguo Lidai Gaigejia Zhuan* (*Reformers in Chinese History*), Beijing: International Culture Press.

Xu Song (1809) *Song Huiyao Jigao* (*Edited Administrative Statutes of the Song Dynasty*), reprinted in 1957, Beijing: Zhonghua Books.

—— (1838) *Denkeji Kao* (*Review of the Successes of the Tang Imperial Examinations*), reprinted in 1984, Beijing: Zhonghua Books.

Xu Tan (1995) 'Mingqing Shiqi Shandong Jingjide Fazhan' ('Economic Growth of Shandong during the Ming–Qing Period'), *ZJY*, 3: 40–63.

Xu Tianchun and Li Yawei (eds) (1995) *Tangtaizong Zhiguo Shengxun* (*Emperor Tangtaizong's Instructions on State Management*), Beijing: Expatiates' Press.

Xu Tianlin (Southern Song Period) *Donghan Huiyao* (*Record of the Eastern Han Dynasty*), publisher unknown.

Xuan Ye (*c.* 1772) *Tingxun Geyan* (*Maxims from Family Instructions*), in Cheng Xiaojun, Tang Zhaomei and Tan Songlin (eds) (1994) *Diwang Jiaxun* (*Private Instructions of Chinese Monarchs*), Wuhan: Hubei People's Press, ch. 20.

Xuanzong, Emperor (AD 738) *Tang Liudian* (*Law of the Tang Dynasty*), reprinted in 1991, Beijing: Zhonghua Books.

Xue Pingshuan (1995) 'Zhongwantang Qianzhong Wuqing Shitan' ('Analysis of Deflation during Mid- and Late Tang Times'), *Shaanxi Shida Xuebao* (*Bulletin of Shaanxi Normal University*), 3: 61–7.

Xun Kuang (*c.* 238 BC) *Xunzi* (*Master Xun's Book*), reprinted in 1979, Beijing: Zhonghua Books.

Yan Buke (1986) 'Qinzheng Hanzheng Yu Wenli Rusheng' ('Scholars, Officials and Policies of the Qin and Han Dynasties'), *LY*, 3: 143–59.

Yan Huicong (1994) 'Songdai Taociye Xingshengde Yuanyin' ('On the Rise of the Ceramics Industry during the Song Period'), *Nanchang Daxue Xuebao* (*Bulletin of the University of Nanchang*), 2: 105–10.

Yan Shoucheng (1988) 'Zhongnong Yishang Shixi' ('On Physiocracy and the Policy of Restraining Commercial Activity in Chinese History'), *LY*, 4: 136–46.

Yan Wenming (1982) 'Zhongguo Daozuo Nongyede Qiyuan' ('The Origin of Rice Cultivation in China'), *NK*, 1: 19–31.

—— (1987) 'Zhongguo Shiqianwenhuade Tongyixing Yu Duoyangxing' ('The Unity and Variety of Chinese Prehistorical Culture'), *WW*, 3: 38–50.

Yang Baolin (1982) 'Woguo Yinjin Fanshude Zuizao Zhiren He Yinjin Fanshude Zuizao Zhidi' ('Evidence of the Earliest Adoption of Sweet Potatoes in China'), *NK*, 2: 79–83.

Yang Chunqiu and Shen Guoqing (1993) *Zhongguo Lidai Kaiguo Huangdi* (*Founders of Chinese Dynasties*), Beijing: China's Personnel Press.

Yang Guozhen (1988) *Mingqing Tudi Qiyue Wenshu Yanjiu* (*A Study of Documents of Land Deeds of the Ming–Qing Period*), Beijing: People's Press.

—— (1991) 'Mingdai Minnan Tong Liuqiu Hanglu Shishi Gouchen' ('A Study of Sea Routes between South Fujian and Ryukyu in the Ming Period'), *HJY*, 2: 16–20.

Yang Shanqun (1984) 'Guanyu Xizhou Fenfengzhide Jige Wenti' ('Issues Related to Feudalism of the Western Zhou Dynasty'), *Qiushi Xuekan* (*Facts*), 3: 78–83.

Yang Shengnan (1992) *Shangdai Jingjishi* (*An Economic History of the Shang Period*), Guiyang: Guizhou People's Press.

Yang Zhengtai (1994) *Mingdai Yizhan Kaofu* (*Attachment to the Study of the Ming Post and Post Roads*), Shanghai: Shanghai Classics Publisher.

Yang Zhijiu (1992) *Zhongguo Gudai Guanzhi Jiangzuo* (*Bureaucracy of Premodern China*), Beijing: Zhonghua Books.

Yao Sui (1371) *Mu-an Wenji* (*A Collection of Tablets*), publisher unknown.

Ye Tan (1991) 'Songdai Gongshangye Fazhande Lishi Tezheng' ('Features of the Development of Industries and Commerce in the Song Period'), *Shanghai Shehui Kexueyuan Jikan* (*Quarterly Bulletin of Shanghai Academy of Social Sciences*), 2: 103–11.

Ye Wenxian (1991) 'Zhongguo Guojia Xingcheng Zhilu' ('Pattern of the Establishment of the State in China'), *XW*, 3: 63–6.

Yin Jin (1980) 'Guanyu Zhongguo Nongyie Zhong Ziben Zhuyi Meng Ya Wen Ti' ('A Historical Research on the Sproutings of Capitalism in Chinese Agriculture'), *LY*, 2: 107–20.

Yu Changsen (1991) 'Yuandai Guanbenchuan Haiwai Maoyi Zhidu' ('Joint Ventures between Government and Commercial Sailors and the Foreign Trade System in the Yuan Dynasty'), *HJY*, 2: 92–8.

Yu Huaqing (1993) *Zhongguo Huangguan Zhidushi* (*A History of the Institution of Eunuchs in China*), Shanghai: Shanghai People's Press.

Yu Xingwu (1957) 'Shangdaide Gulei Zuowu' ('Domestic Cereals in the Shang Dynasty'), *Dongbei Renmin Daxue Renwen Kexue Xuebao* (*Humanities Bulletin of the Northeast People's University*), 1: 87–107.

Yu Yenbo (1987) 'Tudi, Renkou, Shengtai Huanjing' ('Land, Population and Environment'), *KR*, 20 July, p. 3.

Yu Yiefei (1980) 'Zhongguo Lidai Liangshi Pingjun Muchanliang Kaolue' ('An Investigation of the Dynastic Average Grain Output per *Mu* in China'), *Chongqing Shiyuan Xuebao* (*Bulletin of Chongqing Teachers' College*), 3: 8–21.

Yu Yingshi (1987) *Shi Yu Zhongguo Wenhua* (*The Literati and Chinese Culture*), Shanghai: Shanghai People's Press.

ZDB (1985) *Zhongguo Dabaike Jiaoyu* (*Encyclopaedia Sinica: Education*), Beijing and Shanghai: Encyclopaedia Sinica Publisher.

ZDC (ed.) (1990) *Zhonghua Renmin Gongheguo Fensheng Dituji* (*Collected Provincial Maps of the People's Republic of China*), Beijing: China's Atlas Press.

Zeng Shen (*c.* 436 BC) *Daxue* (*The Great Learning*), in Wu Genyou (ed.) (1993) *Sishu Wujing* (*The Annotated Four Books and Five Classics of Confucianism*), ch. 1, Beijing: China's Friendship Press.

Zeng Xueyou (1996) 'Qingdai Ganjiang Zhongyou Diqu Nongcun Shichang Chutan' ('A Study of the Rural Market Economy in the Middle Reaches of the Gan River in the Qing Period'), *ZJY*, 1: 38–50.

Zhang Baoming and Mu Zhengguo (1987) 'Bixu Gaodu Zhongshi Liangshi Shengchan' ('Great Importance Must Be Attached to Grain Production'), *KR*, January 22 (1987), p. 3.

Zhang Dainian (1987) 'Zhongguo Chuantong Zhexue Pipan Jicheng' ('Criticism and Inheritance of the Chinese Traditional Philosophy'), *Lilun Yuekan* (*Theory Monthly*), 1: 21.

Zhang Dechang (1970) *Qingji Yige Jingguande Shenghuo* (*Life of a Qing Official in Beijing*), Hong Kong: The Chinese University Press.

Zhang Haipeng and Zhang Haiying (1993) *Zhongguo Shida Shangbang* (*Ten Merchant Groups in Traditional China*), Hefei: Mount Yellow Books.

Zhang Jiaju (1957) *Liansong Jingji Zhongxinde Nanyi* (*Southern Shift of the Economic Centre in Song Times*), Wuhan: Hubei People's Press.

Zhang Jiayan (1995) 'Mingqing Jianghan Pingyuande Nongye Kaifa Dui Shangren Huodong He Shizhen Fazhande Yingxiang' ('Impact of Agricultural Development in the Yangzi–Han Plain on Commercial Activities and Urbanisation during the Ming–Qing Period'), *ZNS*, 4: 40–8.

Zhang Jiguang, Sun Jianhua and Li Kehe (1993) *Zhongguo Lidai Quanjian* (*Treacherous Officials in Premodern China*), Beijing: China's Personnel Press.

Zhang Kai and Li Genpan (1983) 'Yumi Zai Woguo Liangshi Zuowuzhong Diweide Bianhua' ('The Changing Place of Maize in China's Domestic Crops'), *NK*, 2: 94–9.

Zhang Shaoliang and Zheng Xianjin (1983) *Zhongguo Nongmin Geming Douzhengshi* (*A History of Revolutionary Struggle of the Chinese Peasantry*), Beijing: Qiushi Press.

Zhang Shen (1992) 'Xifeng Bianfa Shiqide Haiwai Maoyi' ('Sino-Foreign Trade during the Song Reform in 1068–85'), *Hebei Xuekan* (*Hebei Journal*), 5: 79–84.

Zhang Shudong and Li Xiuling (1990) *Zhongguo Hunyin Jiatingde Shanbian* (*Changes in Marriages and Families in Chinese History*), Hangzhou: Zhejiang People's Press.

Zhang Tingyu (ed.) (1735) *Ming Shi* (*History of the Ming Dynasty*), reprinted in 1974, Beijing: Zhonghua Books.

Zhang Wengong (1982) 'Quanzhouwang Songdai Chenchuanzhong Ruxiangde Boceng Sepu Jianding' ('Chromatographic Analysis of the Frankincense from the Song Shipwreck in Quanzhou Bay'), *HJY*, 4: 56–9.

Zhang Xun (1986) *Woguo Gudaide Haishang Jiaotong* (*Sea Traffic in Premodern China*), Beijing: Commercial Press.

Zhang Yaonan, Li Baiguang and Ziao Weizhong (1995) *Guanchang Wenhua* (*Culture of Chinese Officialdom*), Beijing: China's Economy Press.

Zhang Zhengming (1987) *Chuwenhua Shi* (*History of the Chu Culture*), Shanghai: Shanghai People's Press.

Zhang Zhengming (1995) *Jinshang Xingshuaishi* (*Rise and Decline of the Shanxi Merchants in History*), Taiyuan: Shanxi Classics Publisher.

Zhang Zhongmin (1996) 'Xiaoshengchan Daliutong–Qian Jindai Zhongguo Shehui Zaishengchande Jiben Moshi' (Petty Production at the Household Level and Great Circulation of Commodities in the Economy: A Basic Production Model in Traditional China), *ZJY*, 2: 42–9.

Zhang Zhongpei (1987) 'Qiantan Zhongguo Kaoguxuede Xianzai Yu Weilai' ('The Current State and Future of Chinese Archaeology'), *Liaowang* (*Observation*), 36: 42–3.

Zhang Zhongxun (1986) 'Qing Jiaqing Nianjian Minzhe Haidao Zuzhi Yanjiu' ('On Pirates' Organisations in the Fujian and Zhejiang Regions during the Jiaqing Reign [1796–1820] of the Qing Dynasty'), in Editing Committee for *Maritime History of China* (ed.) *Zhongguo Haiyang Fazhanshi Lunwenji* (*Selected Essays on the Maritime History of China*), vol. 2, Taipei: Academia Sinica, pp. 161–98.

Zhang Zigao (1977) *Zhongguo Gudai Huaxue Shi* (*A History of Chemistry in China*), Hong Kong: Commercial Press.

Zhao Dexin (ed.) (1990) *Zhongguo Jingjishi Cidian* (*Dictionary of Chinese Economic History*), Wuhan: Hubei Dictionary Press.

Zhao Gang and Chen Zhongyi (1983) *Zhongguo Mianye Shi* (*A History of the Cotton Industry in China*), Beijing: Lianjing Publishing Co.

Zhao Keyao (1984) 'Lun Tangtaizongde Nongben Sixiang Yu Zhongnong Zhengce' ('On the Idea of Agricultural Fundamentalism and the Physiocratic Policies of the Tang Emperor Taizong'), *XW*, 11: 67–71.

Zhao Kuangyin (*c.* AD 976) *Songtaizu Zhiguo Shengxun* (*Emperor Songtaizu's Instructions on State Management*), in Lai Qi and Chen Shen (eds) (1995) *Songtaizu Zhiguo Shengxun* (*Emperor Songtaizu's Instructions on State Management*), Beijing: Expatriates' Press.

Zhao Tongmao (1986) 'Zhonghua Minzu Qiyuandide Xin Tansuo' ('A New Inquiry into the Original Regions of the Chinese'), *Dazong Yixue* (*Popular Medical Science*), 3: 5–6.

Zhao Xiukun, Tian Zhaolin, He Shaohuan and Cai Zhipu (1987) *Zhongguo Junshishi* (*A Military History of China*), vol. 3, Beijing: PLA Press.

Zhao Xiukun, Tian Zhaolin, Kang Ning, Tao Wenhuan, Shi Shibi, Chen Yangping, Zhu Ansheng, Xu Fei, Zhang Chunyi and Zhang Shufang (1991) *Zhongguo Junshishi* (*A Military History of China*), vol. 6, Beijing: PLA Press.

Zheng Liangshu (1989) *Shangyang Jiqi Xuepai* (*Shang Yang and his School of Thought*), Shanghai: Shanghai Classics Publisher.

Zheng Ruokui (1987) 'Shilun Shangdaide Chemazang' ('On Funerary Horses with Carts of the Shang Period'), *KG*, 5: 462–9.

Zheng Xuemeng, Jiang Zhaocheng and Zhang Wenqi (1984) *Jianming Zhongguo Jingji Tongshi* (*A Brief Panorama of Chinese Economic History*), Harbin: Heilongjiang People's Press.

Zheng Ziming (1938) *Zhongguo Lidaide Xianzheng* (*County Administration in Premodern China*), Shanghai: Cangjie Publishing Co.

Zhou Bodi (1981) *Zhongguo Caizhengshi* (*Financial History of China*), Shanghai: Shanghai People's Press.

Zhou Luanshu (1997) *Qiangu Yicun Liukeng Lishi Wenhuade Kaocha* (*A Thousand-Year Old Village: A Study of Liukeng's Culture in History*), Nanchang: Jiangxi People's Press.

Zhou Yafei (1995) *Zhongguo Lidai Zhuangyuanklu* (*Records of 'Number One Scholars' in the Dynastic Palace Examinations*), Shanghai: Shanghai Culture Press.

Zhou Yuanlian and Xie Zhaohua (1986) *Qingdai Zudianzhi Yanjiu* (*Study of Tenancy in the Qing Period*), Shenyang: Liaoning People's Press.

Zhu Dawei (ed.) (1985) *Zhongguo Nongmin Zhanzhengshi, Weijin Nanbeichao Juan* (*A History of Peasant Wars in China: Wei, Jin and Northern and Southern Dynasties*), Beijing: People's Press.

——(ed.) (1994) *Kaiguo Huangdi Zhuan* (*Biographies of the Dynastic Founders in the Chinese Dynastic Histories*), Haiko: Hainan Press.

Zhu Delan (1986) 'Qingchu Qianjieling Shi Zhongguo Chuan Haishang Maoyizhi Yanjiu' ('On Trade Activities of Chinese Ships under the Qing Law of Anti-maritime Immigration from the Coastal Region'), in Editing Committee for *Maritime History of China* (ed.) *Zhongguo Haiyang Fazhanshi Lunwenji* (*Selected Essays on the Maritime History of China*), vol. 2, Taipei: Academia Sinica, pp. 105–59.

Zhu Kezhen (Chu, Kho-chen) (1979) 'Zhongguo Jin Wuqiannian Lai Qixiang Bianqiande Chubu Yanjiu' ('A Preliminary Study of Climatic Change during the Past Five Thousand Years in China'), in his *Zhukezhen Wenji* (*Collected Works of Zhu Kezhen*), Beijing: Science Press.

Zhu Shaohou (1985) *Zhongguo Gudaishi* (*A History of Ancient China*), Fuzhou: Fujian People's Press.

Zhu Xi (*c.* 1200) *Yu Lei* (*Philosophical Analects*), publisher unknown.

Zhu Yanjun and Lin Yeshang (1992) *Zhongguo Gudai Renshi Zhidu* (*Personnel Management Systems in Premodern China*), Lanzhou: Gansu People's Press.

Zhu Yu (1119) *Pingzhou Ketan* (*Pingzhou Table Talk*), publisher unknown.

Zhuang Guotu (1995) 'Chaye Baiyin He Yapian: 1750–1849 Nian Zhongxi Maoyi Jiegou' ('Tea, Silver and Opium: The Sino-Western Trade Pattern, 1750–1840'), *Zhongguo Jingjishi Yanjiu* (*Study of Chinese Economic History*), 3: 64–76.

Zhuang Weiji, Zhuang Jinghui and Wang Lianmao (1989) *Haishang Sichou Zhilude Zhuming Gangko Quanzhou* (*Quanzhou: A Port Known for Trade along the 'Maritime Silk Road'*), Beijing: Maritime Press.

Zi Si (n.d.) *Zhongyong* (*The Doctrine of the Mean*), publisher unknown.

ZKY (1978) *Zhongguo Turang* (*Soil in China*), Beijing: Sciences Press.

ZNK (1984) *Zhongguo Nongxue Shi* (*History of Chinese Agronomy*), Beijing: Sciences Press.

ZNZ (ed.) (1982) *Zhongguo Nongmin Zhanzhengshi Luncong* (*Essays on Peasant Wars in China*), Zhengzhou: Henan People's Press.

——(1985) *Zhongguo Nongmin Zhanzhengshi Yanjiu* (*On the History of Peasant Wars in China*), Shanghai: Shanghai People's Press.

Zuo Buqing (1986) 'Chuantong Wenhua Yu Qingwangchaode Xingshuai' ('Chinese Traditional Culture vis-à-vis the Rise and Fall of the Qing Dynasty'), *RR*, 28 November, p. 5.

Zuo Shu-er (1986) 'Mingdai Ningxia Tuntianlun' ('On the Ming Agricultural Colonies in Ningxia Province'), *Ningxia Shehui Kexue* (*Ningxia Social Sciences*), 3: 85–90.

Zuo Zongtang (*c.* 1885 AD) *Zuo Zongtang Jiashu* (*Zuo Zongtang's Letters to His Family*), reprinted in 1994, Beijing: China's Expatriates' Press.

Zuoqiu Ming (*c.* 454a BC) *Guo Yu* (*Histories of the Eight Kingdoms*), reprinted in 1981, Beijing: Zhonghua Books.

——(*c.* 454b BC) *Zuo Zhuan* (*Master Zuo's Chronicle*), reprinted in 1981, Beijing: Zhonghua Books.

ZW (ed.) (1962–8) *Zhongwen Dacidian* (*An Encyclopaedic Dictionary of the Chinese Language*), Taipei: Institute of Chinese Culture.

## 2 Non-Chinese references

An Jinhuai (1984) 'Henan: Birthplace of Chinese Civilization', *CR*, 10: 65–7.

Anon. (1980b) 'The Peoples of China', *NGM*, July, n.p.

Anon. (1991) 'Maps of Chinese History', *NGM*, July, n.p.

Anon. (1995) *Times Atlas of the World, Reference Edition*, London: Times Books.

Aston, T. H. and Philpin, C. H. E. (1985) *The Brenner Debate: Agrarian Structure and Economic Development in Pre-industrial Europe*, Cambridge: Cambridge University Press.

Bagchi, A. K. (1992) 'Land Tax, Property Rights and Peasant Insecurity in Colonial India', *JPS*, 1: 1–49.

Bai Shouyi (ed.) (1982) *An Outline History of China*, Beijing: Foreign Language Press.

Bainbridge, A. A. (1988) 'Pitcher Irrigation', *Drylander* (University of California), 2 (2): 3.

Bairoch, P. (1977) *The Economic Development of the Third World since 1900*, translated by C. Postan, Berkeley and Los Angeles: University of California Press.

—— (1986) 'Historical Roots of Underdevelopment: Myths and Realities', in W. J. Mommsen and J. Osterhammel (eds) *Imperialism and After: Continuities and Discontinuity*, London: Allen and Unwin, pp. 192–4.

—— (1993) *Economics and World History: Myths and Paradoxes*, Hemel Hempstead: Harvester Wheatsheaf.

Balasubramanyam, V. N. (1984) *The Economy of India*, London: Weidenfeld and Nicolson.

Balazs, E. (1972) *Chinese Civilization and Bureaucracy*, New Haven: Yale University Press.

Barbosa, D. (1518 AD.) *The Book of Duarte Barbosa: An Account of the Countries Bordering on the Indian Ocean and their Inhabitants*, translated by M. L. Dames in 1812, reprinted in 1967, Nendeln: Kraus Reprint.

Barker, R., Herdt, R. W. and Rose, B. (1985) *The Rice Economy of Asia*, Washington, DC: Resources for the Future, Inc.

Barrow, J. (1804) *Travels in China*, London: A. Strahan.

Bercé, Y.-M. (1990) *History of Peasant Revolts: The Social Origins of Rebellion in Early Modern France*, Cambridge: Polity Press.

Bix, H. P. (1986) *Peasant Protest in Japan, 1590–1884*, New Haven: Yale University Press.

Blunden, C. and Elvin, M. (1983) *Cultural Atlas of China*, Oxford: Phaidon Press.

Boserup, E. (1965) *The Conditions of Agricultural Growth*, London: Allen and Unwin.

—— (1970) *Woman's Role in Economic Development*, London: Earthscan Publications.

—— (1981) *Population and Technical Change: A Study of Long-Term Trends*, Chicago: University of Chicago Press.

Bowen, R. W. (1980) *Rebellion and Democracy in Meiji Japan*, Berkeley: University of California Press.

Bray, F. (1983) 'Patterns of Evolution in Rice-Growing Societies', *JPS*, 1: 3–33.

—— (1984) 'Section 41: Agriculture', in J. Needham (ed.) *Science and Civilisation in China*, vol. 6, Cambridge: Cambridge University Press.

—— (1986) *The Rice Economies: Technology and Development in Asian Societies*, Oxford: Basil Blackwell.

Brenner, R. (1982) 'The Agrarian Roots of European Capitalism', *PP*, 97: 16–113.

Broadbent, K. (1978) *A Chinese/English Dictionary of Chinese Rural Economy*, Farnham Royal: Commonwealth Agricultural Bureaux.

Brook, T. (ed.) (1989) *The Asiatic Mode of Production in China*, New York: M. E. Sharpe.

Buck, J. L. (1937) *Chinese Farm Economy*, Nanking: The University of Nanking and the China Council of the Institute of Pacific Relations.

—— (ed.) (1968) *Land Utilization in China*, New York: Paragon.

Burns, M. (1984) *Rural Society and French Politics*, Princeton: Princeton University Press.

Byres, T. J. (1974) 'Land Reform, Industrialisation and Marketed Surplus', in D. Lehmann (ed.) *Agrarian Reform and Agrarian Reformism*, London: Faber and Faber.

Cameron, M. E. (1974) *The Reform Movement in China, 1898– 1912*, Stanford: Stanford University Press.

Cameron, R. and Freedeman, C. E. (1983) 'French Economic Growth: A Radical Revision', *Social Sciences History*, 1: 3–30.

Cartier, M. (1981) 'Les importations de métaux monétaires en Chine: essai sur la conjoncture chinoise', *Annales*, 36: 454–66.

Cavalli-Sforza, L. L. (1974) 'The Genetics of Human Population', *SA*, 231(3): 81–9.

Chambers, J. D. (1972) *Population, Economy, and Society in Pre-industrial England*, Oxford: Oxford University Press.

Chandavarkar, R. (1985) 'Industrialization in India before 1947: Conventional Approaches and Alternative Perspectives', *MAS*, 3: 623–68.

Chang, Chung-li (1955) *The Chinese Gentry: Studies on their Role in Nineteenth-century Chinese Society*, Seattle: University of Washington Press.

Chao, Kang (1981) 'New Data on Land Ownership Patterns in Ming–Ch'ing China', *JAS*, 4: 719–34.

——(1986) *Man and Land in Chinese History: An Economic Analysis*, Stanford: Stanford University.

Chayanov, A. V. (1925) *The Theory of Peasant Economy*, reprinted in 1986, Madison: University of Wisconsin Press.

Chen, Huan-chang (1911) *The Economic Principles of Confucius and his School*, New York: Columbia University.

Ch'en, K. K. S. (1973) *The Chinese Transformation of Buddhism*, Princeton, NJ: Princeton University Press.

Chen Shen (1994) 'Early Urbanization in the Eastern Zhou in China (770–221 BC): An Archaeological View', *Antiquity*, 68: 724–44.

Chen Wenxiang (1984) 'Rare Sacrificial Horse Pit', *CR*, 9: 59.

Chesneaux, J. (1973) *Peasant Revolts in China, 1840– 1949*, London: Thames and Hudson.

Chinn, D. L. (1979) 'Team Cohesion and Collective-Labour Supply in Chinese Agriculture', *JCE*, 3: 375–94.

Chu, L. (1990) 'The Chimera of the Chinese Market', *The Atlantic Monthly*, October, pp. 56–68.

Chu, R. W. and Saywell, W. G. (1984) *Career Patterns in the Ch'ing Dynasty: The Office of the Governor General*, Ann Arbor: Center for Chinese Studies of the University of Michigan.

Cipolla, C. (1970) *The Economic Decline of Empires*, London: Methuen.

——(1978) *The Economic History of World Population*, Brighton: Harvester Press.

Clark, S. and Donnelly, J. S. Jr (eds) (1983) *Irish Peasants Violence and Political Unrest, 1780– 1914*, Manchester: Manchester University Press.

Coleman, D. and Schofield, R. (eds) (1986) *The State of Population Theory: Forward from Malthus*, Oxford: Basil Blackwell.

Cotterell, A. (1986) *A Dictionary of World Mythology*, Oxford: Oxford University Press.

Crafts, N. F. R. (1984) 'Economic Growth in France and Britain, 1830–1910: A Review of the Evidence', *JEH*, 1: 49– 67.

Crane, G. T. (1990) *The Political Economy of China's Special Economic Zones*, New York: M. E. Sharpe.

Cressey, G. B. (1934) *China's Geographic Foundations: A Survey of the Land and Its People*, New York: McGraw-Hill.

Critchley, J. S. (1978) *Feudalism*, London: George Allen and Unwin.

# BIBLIOGRAPHY

Dallas, G. (1982) *The Imperfect Peasant Economy: The Loire Country, 1800–1914*, Cambridge: Cambridge University Press.

Dalton, G. (1969) 'Theoretical Issues in Economic Anthropology', *CA*, 1: 63–102.

—— (1972) 'Peasantries in Anthropology and History', *CA*, June–October, pp. 383–415.

Davies, R. W. (ed.) (1990) *From Tsarism to the New Economic Policy*, London: Macmillan.

De Vries, J. (1984) *European Urbanization, 1500–1800*, London: Methuen.

—— (1993a) *Development versus Stagnation: Technological Continuity and Agricultural Progress in Premodern China*, New York: Greenwood.

—— (1993b) 'Property Rights and China's Reform', *Policy* (Australia), 3: 57–9.

—— (1997) *Chinese Maritime Activities and Socio-economic Consequences, c. 2100* BC.*–1900* AD., New York: Greenwood.

Diamond, J. M. (1998) 'Peeling the Chinese Onion', *Nature*, 29 January, pp. 433–4.

Dobson, R. B. (1983) *The Peasants' Revolts of 1381*, London: Macmillan.

Eberhard, W. (1962) *Social Mobility in Traditional China*, Leiden: E. J. Brill.

—— (1977) *A History of China*, Berkeley: University of California Press.

Ellis, F. (1988) *Peasant Economics, Farm Households and Agrarian Development*, Cambridge: Cambridge University Press.

Ellis, H. (1818) *Journal of the Proceedings of the Late Embassy to China*, London: John Murray.

Elvin, M. (1973) *The Pattern of the Chinese Past*, Stanford: Stanford University Press.

—— (1975) 'Skills and Resources in Late Traditional China', in D. H. Perkins (ed.) *China's Modern Economy in Historical Perspective*, Stanford: Stanford University Press, pp. 85–113.

—— (1988) 'China as a Counterfactual', in J. Baechler, J. A. Hall and M. Mann (eds) *Europe and the Rise of Capitalism*, Oxford: Basil Blackwell.

Eng, P. van der (1993) 'The Silver Standard and Asia's Integration into the World Economy, 1850–1914', Working Paper, no. 175, Research School of Pacific Studies, The Australian National University.

Engels, F. (1942) *The Origin of the Family, Private Property and the State in the Light of the Researches of Lewis H. Morgan*, Sydney: Current Book Distributors.

Ennew, J., Hirst, P. and Tribe, K. (1977) ' "Peasantry" as an Economic Category', *JPS*, 4: 295–322.

Fairbank, J. K. (ed.) (1957) *Chinese Thought and Institutions*, Chicago: University of Chicago Press.

—— (1965) *The United States and China*, Cambridge, MA: Harvard University Press.

—— (1980) *The Cambridge History of China*, New York: Cambridge University Press.

—— (1983) *The United States and China*, 4th edition, Cambridge, MA: Harvard University Press.

Fairbank, J. K. and Reischaver, E. O. (1979) *China: Tradition and Transformation*, London: Allen and Unwin.

Feeney, G. and Hamano, K. (1990) 'Rice Price Fluctuations and Fertility in Late Tokugawa Japan', *Journal of Japanese Studies*, 1: 1–30.

Feeny, D. (1983) 'The Moral or the Rational Peasant: Competing Hypothesis of Collective Action', *JAS*, 42: 769–89.

Fei Hsiao-t'ung (1939) *Peasant Life in China; A Field Study of Country Life in the Yangtze Valley*, London: Paul, Trench, Trubner.

Fei, J. C. H. and Liu, T. J. (1977) 'Population Dynamics of Agrarianism in Traditional China', in Hou Chi-ming and Yu Tzong-shian (eds) *Modern Chinese Economic History*, Taipei: The Institute of Economics, Academia Sinica, pp. 23–54.

Feuerwerker, A. (1975) *Rebellion in Nineteenth-Century China*, Ann Arbor: Center for Chinese Studies of the University of Michigan.

——(1976) *State and Society in Eighteenth-Century China: The Ch'ing Empire in its Glory*, Ann Arbor: Center for Chinese Studies of the University of Michigan.

——(1984) 'The State and the Economy in Late Imperial China', *Theory and Society*, 13: 297–326.

Fitzgerald, C. P. (1972) *The Southern Expansion of the Chinese People*, London: Barrie and Jenkins.

Fogel, R. W. (1964) *Railroads and American Economic Growth: Essays in Economic History*, Baltimore: Johns Hopkins University Press.

Francks, P. (1992) *Japanese Economic Development: Theory and Practice*, London: Routledge.

Frank, A. G. (1978) *World Accumulation, 1492–1789*, New York and London: Monthly Review Press.

Fukuyama, F. (1992) *The End of History and the Last Man*, London: Hamish Hamilton.

Fullard, H. (ed.) (1968) *China in Maps*, London: George Philip.

Galeski, B. (1972) *Basic Concepts of Rural Sociology*, Manchester: Manchester University Press.

Gardiner, Juliet and Wenborn, Neil (1995) *The History Today Companion to British History*, London: Collins & Brown.

Gates, H. (1996), *China's Motor: A Thousand Years of Petty Capitalism*, Ithaca, NY: Cornell University Press.

Gatrell, P. (1986) *The Tsarist Economy, 1850–1917*, London: B. T. Batsford.

Geelan, P. J. M. and Twitchett, D. C. (eds) (1974) *The Times Atlas of China*, London: Times Books.

Geertz, C. (1963) *Agricultural Involution: The Process of Ecological Change in Indonesia*, Berkeley: University of California Press.

Geiss, J. P. (1979) 'Peking under the Ming, 1368–1644', Ph.D. thesis, Princeton, NJ: Princeton University.

Gerschenkron, A. (1962) *Economic Backwardness in Historical Perspective*, Cambridge: Harvard University Press.

Goldstone, J. A. (1991) *Revolution and Rebellion in the Early Modern World*, Berkeley: University of California Press.

Goudsblom, J., Jones, E. L. and Mennell, S. (1996) *The Course of Human History*, Armonk, NY: M. E. Sharpe.

Gregory, P. R. and Stuart, R. C. (1994) *Soviet and Post-Soviet Economic Structure and Performance*, 5th edition, New York: Harper Collins.

Griffith, S. (1963) *Sun Tzu: The Art of War*, Oxford: Oxford University Press.

Grigg, D. (1980) *Population Growth and Agrarian Change: An Historical Perspective*, Cambridge: Cambridge University Press.

Grosvenor, G. M. (1980) 'Map of the Peoples of China', *National Geographic Magazine*, 7: n.p.

Guisso, R. W. L., Pagani, C. and Miller, D. (1989) *The First Emperor of China*, London: Sidgwick and Jackson.

Guo Xu (1986) 'The Search for China's Earliest City', *CR*, 5: 29–31.

Guy, R. K. (1987) *The Emperor's Four Treasuries*, Cambridge, MA: Harvard University Press.

Hall, D. L. and Ames, R. T. (1987) *Thinking through Confucius*, New York: State University of New York Press.

Hall, J. W. (1991) *The Cambridge History of Japan*, Cambridge: Cambridge University Press.

Hao, Yen-p'ing (1986) *The Commercial Revolution in Nineteenth-Century China: The Rise of Sino-Western Mercantile Capitalism*, Berkeley: University of California Press.

Hara, Y. (1990) 'Agricultural Development and Policy in Modern Japan', in C. H. Lee and I. Yamazawa (eds) *The Economic Development of Japan and Korea: A Parallel with Lessons*, New York: Praeger, pp. 123–35.

Harley, C. K. (1991) 'Substitution for prerequisites: endogenous institutions and comparative economic history', in R. Sylla and G. Toniolo (eds) *Patterns of European Industrialisation: The Nineteenth Century*, London: Routledge, pp. 29–44.

Harrison, M. (1977) 'The Peasant Mode of Production in the Work of A. V. Chayanov', *JPS*, 4: 323–36.

Hartwell, R. M. (1963) *Iron and Early Industrialism in Eleventh-Century China*, Chicago: University of Chicago Library.

—— (1966) 'Markets, Technology, and the Structure of Enterprise in the Development of the Eleventh-Century Chinese Iron and Steel Industry', *JEH*, 1: 29–58.

—— (1967) 'A Cycle of Economic Change in Imperial China: Coal and Iron in Northwest China, 750–1350', *Journal of the Economic and Social History of the Orient*, 10 (1): 102–59.

Hasan, P. and Rao, D. C. (eds) (1979) *Korea, Policy Issues for Long-Term Development: The Report of a Mission Sent to the Republic of Korea by the World Bank*, Baltimore: Johns Hopkins University Press.

Hay, D. A. (1993) *Economic Reform and State-Owned Enterprises in China, 1979–1987*, Oxford: Clarendon Press.

Hayami, Y. and Ruttan, V. W. (1971) *Agricultural Development: An International Perspective*, London: Johns Hopkins University Press.

Hazell, P., Ramasamy, C. and Aiyasamy, P. K. (1991) *The Green Revolution Reconsidered: The Impact of High-Yielding Rice Varieties in South India*, Baltimore: Johns Hopkins University Press.

He Zhaowu, Bu Jinzhi, Tang Yuyuan and Sum Kaitai (1991) *An Intellectual History of China*, Beijing: Foreign Language Press.

Hegel, G. W. F. (1975) *Lectures on the Philosophy of World History*, translated by H. B. Nisbet, Cambridge: Cambridge University Press.

Heywood, C. (1981) 'The Role of the Peasantry in French Industrialisation, 1815–80', *EHR*, 3: 359–76.

Hicks, J. (1969) *A Theory of Economic History*, London: Clarendon Press.

Hinton, W. (1990) *The Great Reversal: The Privatization of China*, New York: Monthly Review Press.

Ho, Ping-ti (1956) 'Early-Ripening Rice in Chinese History', *EHR*, ser. 2 (1956–8): 200–18.

—— (1962) *The Ladder of Success in Imperial China: Aspects of Social Mobility, 1368–1911*, New York: Columbia University Press.

—— (1969) 'The Loess and the Origin of Chinese Agriculture', *American Historical Review*, 75: 1–36.

—— (1970) 'An Estimate of the Total Population of Sung-Ching China', *Studies Song*, 1: 33–5.

Hohenberg, P. (1972) 'Change in Rural France in the Period of Industrialisation, 1830–1914', *JEH*, 1: 219–40.

Hsiao, Kung-ch'uan (1979) *A History of Chinese Political Thought*, translated by F. W. Mote, Princeton, NJ: Princeton University Press.

Hsieh, Chiao-min (1973) *Atlas of China*, New York: McGraw-Hill.

Hsu, Cho-yun (1965) *Ancient China in Transition: An Analysis of Social Mobility, 722–222 BC*, Stanford: Stanford University Press.

—— (1980) *Han Agriculture*, Seattle: University of Washington Press.

Huang, P. C. C. (1990) *The Peasant Family and Rural Development in the Yangzi Delta, 1350–1988*, Stanford: Stanford University Press.

Huang, R. (1981) *1597, A Year of No Significance: The Ming Dynasty in Decline*, Westford, MA: The Murray Printing Co.

Hucker, C. (1985) *A Dictionary of Official Titles in Imperial China*, Stanford: Stanford University Press.

Hummel, A. W. (ed.) (1967) *Eminent Chinese of the Ch'ing Period (1644–1912)*, Taipei: Ch'eng-Wen Publishing Co.

Huntington, S. P. (1996) *The Clash of Civilisations and the Remaking of World Order*, New York: Simon and Schuster.

Institute of Archaeology (1984) *Recent Archaeological Discoveries in the People's Republic of China*, Paris: UNESCO.

Ito, T. (1992) *The Japanese Economy*, Cambridge, MA: MIT Press.

Iwao, S. (1967) 'Japanese Foreign Trade in the 16th and 17th Centuries', *Acta Asiatica*, 30: 1–18.

Jennings, J. D. (ed.) (1978) *Ancient South Americans*, San Francisco: W. H. Freeman.

Johnson, A. I. (1995) *Cultural Realism: Strategic Culture and Grand Strategy in Chinese History*, Princeton, NJ: Princeton University Press.

Jones, E. L. (1968) 'Agricultural Origins of Industry', *PP*, 40: 58–71.

——(1969) *Agrarian Change and Economic Development: The Historical Problems*, London: Methuen.

——(1974) *Agriculture and Industrial Revolution*, Oxford: Basil Blackwell.

——(1981) *The European Miracle*, Cambridge: Cambridge University Press.

——(1988) *Growth Recurring: Economic Change in World History*, Oxford: Clarendon Press.

——(1990) 'The Real Question about China: Why Was the Song Economic Achievement not Repeated?' *AEHR*, 2: 5–22.

——(1991) 'A Framework for the History of Economic Growth in Southeast Asia', *AEHR*, 1: 5–19.

Kamath, S. J. (1990) 'FDI in a Centrally Planned Developing Country: The Chinese Case', *Economic Development and Cultural Change*, 39 (1): 107–30.

Kelliher, D. (1992) *Peasant Power in China: The Era of Rural Reform 1979–1989*, New Haven: Yale University Press.

Kelly, M. (1997) 'The Dynamics of Smithian Growth', *Quarterly Journal of Economics*, 3: 939–64.

Kennedy, P. (1987) *The Rise and Fall of the Great Powers*, New York: Ramdom House.

Krader, L. (1975) *The Asiatic Mode of Production: Sources, Development and Critique in the Writings of Karl Marx*, Assen: Van Gorcum.

Kraus, W. (1982) *Economic Development and Social Changes in the People's Republic of China*, translated by E. M. Holz, New York: Springer-Verlag.

Kroeber, A. L. (1948) *Anthropology*, New York: Harcourt Brace Jovanovich.

Kueh, Y. Y. (1984) 'China's New Agricultural Policy Program: Major Economic Consequences, 1979–1983', *JCE*, 4: 353–75.

——(1985) 'The Economics of the "Second Land Reform" in China', *China Quarterly*, 101: 122–31.

Kuhn, P. A. (1970) *Rebellion and Its Enemies in Later Imperial China*, Cambridge, MA: Harvard University Press.

Kuznets, S. (1966) *Modern Economic Growth: Its Rate, Structure and Spread*, New Haven: Yale University Press.

Landes, D. S. (1994) 'What Room for Accident in History?: Explaining Big Changes by Small Events', *EHR*, 4: 637–56.

Landsberger, H. A. (ed.) (1974) *Rural Protest: Peasant Movements and Social Change*, London: Macmillan.

Langlois, J. D. (ed.) (1981) *China under Mongol Rule*, Princeton, NJ: Princeton University Press.

Lardy, N. R. (1983) *Agriculture in China's Modern Economic Development*, Cambridge: Cambridge University Press.

—— (1986) 'Agricultural Reforms in China', *Journal of International Affairs*, 2: 91–104.

Latourette, K. S. (1964) *The Chinese, their History and Culture*, New York: Macmillan.

Lattimore, O. (1962) *Studies in Frontier History*, London: Oxford University Press.

Lau, D. C. (tran.) (1984) *Mencius*, Hong Kong: The Chinese University Press.

Lee, M. P. (1969) *The Economic History of China, with Special Reference to Agriculture*, New York: AMS Press.

Lee, R. D. (1986) 'Malthus and Boserup: A Dynamic Synthesis', in D. Coleman and R. Schofield (eds) *The State of Population Theory: Forward from Malthus*, London: Basil Blackwell, pp. 96–130.

Lenin, V. I. (1960) 'Imperialism the Highest Development Stage of Capitalism', in *Collected Works of Lenin*, Moscow: Foreign Language Publishing House.

Leveson, J. and Schurmann, F. (1969) *China: An Interpretive History*, Berkeley: University of California.

Lewin, R. (1997) 'Ancestral Echoes', *New Scientist*, 155 (2089): 32–7.

Lewis, A. (1954) 'Economic Development with Unlimited Supplies of Labour', *The Manchester School*, 22: 139–91.

Li, Zhisui (1994) *The Private Life of Chairman Mao*, London: Arrow Books.

Lin, J. (1987) 'The Household Responsibility System Reform in China: A Peasant Institutional Choice', *American Journal of Agricultural Economics*, 2: 410–15.

Lippit, V. D. (1987) *The Economic Development of China*, Armonk, NY: M. E. Sharpe.

Lipton, M. (1968) 'The Theory of the Optimising Peasant', *Journal of Development Studies*, 4: 327–51.

Llewellyn-Jones, D. (1975) *People Populating*, London: Faber and Faber.

Lo, Jiu-jung (1986) 'The Literary Way to Retribution', *Free China Review*, 8/9: 28–33.

McAlpin, M. B. (1975) 'The Effects of Expansion of Markets on Rural Income Distribution in Nineteenth Century India', *EEH*, 12: 283–302.

McEvedy, C. and Jones, R. (1978) *Atlas of World Population History*, London: Penguin Books.

Macfarlane, A. (1978) *The Origin of English Individualism, the Family, Property and Social Transition*, Oxford: Balckwell.

McGovern, W. M. (1939) *The Early Empires of Central Asia*, Chapel Hill: University of North Carolina Press.

McKnight, B. (1971) *Village and Bureaucracy in Southern Sung China*, Chicago: University of Chicago Press.

McMillan, J., Whalley, J. and Zhu, L. (1989) 'The Impact of China's Economic Reforms on Agricultural Productivity Growth', *Journal of Political Economy*, 4: 781–807.

McNeill, W. H. (1963) *The Rise of the West*, Chicago: University of Chicago Press.

—— (1979) *A World History*, New York: Oxford University Press.

Malthus, T. R. (1914) *An Essay on Population*, London: Dent.

Mao, Tse-Tung (1965) *Selected Works of Mao Tse-Tung*, vol. II, Peking: Foreign Languages Press.

—— (1967) *Selected Works of Mao Tse-Tung*, vol. I, Peking: Foreign Languages Press.

Marks, R. B. (1991) 'Rice Prices, Food Supply, and Market Structure in Eighteenth-Century South China', *Late Imperial China*, 2: 64–116.

Marsh, R. M. (1961) *The Mandarin: Circulation of Elite in China, 1600–1900*, New York: Free Press of Glencoe.

Marx, K. (with F. Engels) (1976a) 'Manifesto of the Communist Party', in *Karl Marx and Frederick Engels, Collected Works*, vol. 6: 477–519, London: Lawrence and Wishart.

Marx, K. (1976b) 'Economic Works', in *Karl Marx and Frederick Engels, Collected Works*, London: Lawrence and Wishart, vols 28–33.

Mathias, P. and Postan, M. M. (eds) (1978) *The Cambridge Economic History of Europe*, vol. 7, pt 2, Cambridge: Cambridge University Press.

Maverick, L. A. (1946) *China A Model for Europe*, San Antonio, TX: Paul Anderson.

Merson, J. (1989) *Roads to Xanadu, East and West in the Making of the Modern World*, Frenchs Forest, NSW: Child and Associates and ABC.

Minami, R. (1986) *The Economic Development of Japan*, London: Macmillan.

Mishra, S. C. (1985) 'Agricultural Trends in Bombay Presidency 1900–1920: The Illusion of Growth', *MAS*, 4: 733–59.

Mitchell, P. M. (1977) *China: Tradition and Revolution*, Toronto: Macmillan.

Mokyr, J. (1990) *The Lever of Riches*, New York and Oxford: Oxford University Press.

Moore, B. (1966) *Social Origins of Dictatorship and Democracy: Lord and Peasant in the Making of the Modern World*, Boston: Beacon Press.

Morse, J. L. (ed.) (1969) *Funk and Wagnalls Standard Reference Encyclopedia*, vol. 10, New York: Standard Reference Library.

Moulder, F. V. (1977) *Japan, China and the Modern World Economy: Towards a Reinterpretation of East Asia Development ca. 1600–ca. 1918*, New York: Cambridge University Press.

Moulin, A. (1991) *Peasantry and Society in France since 1789*, translated by M. C. Cleary and M. F. Cleary, Cambridge: Cambridge University Press.

Mousnier, R. (1971) *Peasant Uprisings in Seventeenth Century France, Russia and China*, London: George Allen and Unwin.

Munro, D. J. (1985) *Individualism and Holism: Studies in Confucian and Taoist Values*, Ann Arbor: Center for Chinese Studies of the University of Michigan.

Murphey, R. (1954) 'The City as a Centre of Change: Western Europe and China', *Annual of the Association of American Geographers*, 44: 349–62.

Myers, R. H. (1970) *The Chinese Peasant Economy: Agricultural Development in Hopei and Shang-tung, 1890–1949*, Cambridge, MA: Harvard University Press.

——(1991) *Two Societies in Opposition, the Republic of China and the People's Republic of China*, Stanford: Hoover Institution Press.

Nee, V. and Sijin Su (1990) 'Institutional Change and Economic Growth in China: The View from the Villages', *JAS*, 1: 3–25.

Nee, V., Stark, D. and Seldon, M. (1989) *Remaking the Economic Institutions of Socialism: China and Eastern Europe*, Stanford: Stanford University Press.

Needham, J. (ed.) (1954–94) *Science and Civilisation in China*, Cambridge: Cambridge University Press.

——(1959) 'Mathematics and the Sciences of the Heavens and the Earth', in J. Needham (ed.) *Science and Civilisation in China*, vol. 3, Cambridge: Cambridge University Press.

——(1962) 'History of Scientific Thought', in J. Needham (ed.) *Science and Civilisation in China*, vol. 2, Cambridge: Cambridge University Press.

——(1969) *The Grand Titration*, London: Allen and Unwin.

Newell, W. H. (1973) 'The Agricultural Revolution in Nineteenth- Century France', *JEH*, 4: 697–731.

North, D. C. (1981) *Structure and Change in Economic History*, New York and London: W. W. Norton.

North, D. C. and Thomas, R. P. (1973) *The Rise of the Western World: A New Economic History*, Cambridge: Cambridge University Press.

Nove, A. (1992) *An Economic History of the USSR, 1917–1991*, 3rd edition, London: Penguin Books.

O'Brien, P. K. (1997) 'Intercontinental Trade and the Development of the Third World since the Industrial Revolution', *Journal of World History*, 1: 75–133.

Olson, M. (1982) *The Rise and Decline of Nations: Economic Growth, Stagflation, and Social Rigidities*, New Haven: Yale University Press.

Osborn, F. (1960) 'Outline of Present Conditions', in M. Book (ed.) *On Population, Three Essays*, New York: The New American Library.

Pannell, C. W. and Ma, L. J. C. (1983) *China: The Geography of Development and Modernization*, London: Edward Arnold.

Parsons, J. B. (1970) *The Peasant Rebellions of the Late Ming Dynasty*, Tucson: University of Arizona Press.

Patnaik, U. (1979) 'Neo-Populism and Marxism: The Chayanovian View of the Agrarian Question and its Fundamental Fallacy', *JPS*, 4: 375–420.

Perkins, D. (1967) 'Government as an Obstacle to Industrialization: The Case of Nineteenth Century China', *JEH*, 27: 478–92.

—— (1969) *Agricultural Development in China, 1368– 1968*, Edinburgh: Edinburgh University Press.

Pomeranz, K. (1997) 'Rethinking Eighteenth-Century China: A High Standard of Living and Its Implications', Paper for All – U.C. Group in Economic History Conference, Davis, California, November 1997.

Popkin, S. L. (1979) *The Rational Peasant: The Political Economy of Rural Society in Vietnam*, Berkeley: University of California Press.

Pryor, F. L. (1980) 'The Asian Mode of Production as an Economic System', *JCE*, 4: 437–42.

Putterman, L. (1988) 'Group Farming and Work Incentives in Collective-Era China', *Modern China*, 4: 419–50.

Qian Wen-yuan (1985) *The Great Inertia: Scientific Stagnation in Traditional China*, Sydney: Croom Helm.

Rawski, E. S. (1972) *Agricultural Change and the Peasant Economy of South China*, Cambridge, MA: Harvard University Press.

—— (1979) *Education and Popular Literacy in Ch'ing China*, Ann Arbor: University of Michigan Press.

Rawski, T. G. (1989) *Economic Growth in Prewar China*, Berkeley: University of California Press.

Redfield, R. (1965) *Peasant Society and Culture*, Chicago: University of Chicago Press.

Reid, A. (1993) *Southeast Asia in the Age of Commerce, 1450–1680*, New Haven and London: Yale University Press.

—— (ed.) (1997) *The Last Stand of Asian Autonomies*, Basingstoke: Macmillan.

Rickett, W. A. (trans.) (1985) *Guanzi: Political, Economic, and Philosophical Essays from Early China*, Princeton, NJ: Princeton University Press.

Riskin, C. (1975) 'Surplus and Stagnation in Modern China', in D. H. Perkins (ed.) *China's Modern Economy in Historical Perspective*, Stanford: Stanford University Press.

Ronan, C. (1978) *Shorter Science and Civilisation in China*, Cambridge: Cambridge University Press.

Rosenberg, N. (1994) *Exploring the Black Box: Technology, Economics, and History*, Cambridge: Cambridge University Press.

Rostow, W. W. (1960) *The Stages of Economic Growth: A Non-communist Manifesto*, Cambridge: Cambridge University Press.

——(1975) *How It All Began: Origins of the Modern Economy*, London: Methuen.

Rothermund, D. (1993) *An Economic History of India, from Pre-colonial Times to 1991*, London: Routledge.

Rozman, G. (1973) *Urban Networks in Ch'ing China and Tokugawa Japan*, Princeton: Princeton University Press.

——(ed.) (1981) *The Modernization of China*, New York: Free Press.

Sadao, N. (1978) 'The Economics and Social History of Former Han', in D. Twitchett and M. Loewe (eds) *The Cambridge History of China*, vol. 1, New York: Cambridge University Press, pp. 545–607.

Scherer, F. M. and Perlman, M. (eds) (1992) *Entrepreneurship, Technological Innovation and Economic Growth*, Ann Arbor: University of Michigan Press.

Schultz, T. W. (1964) *Transforming Traditional Agriculture*, New Haven: Yale University Press.

Schumpeter, J. A. (1954) *History of Economic Analysis*, New York: Oxford University Press.

Scott, J. (1972) 'The Erosion of Patron–Client Bonds and Social Change in Rural Southeast Asia', *JAS*, 1: 5–38.

——(1976) *The Moral Economy of the Peasant Rebellion and Subsistence in Southeast Asia*, New Haven: Yale University Press.

Selden, M. (1993) *The Political Economy of Chinese Development*, New York: M. E. Sharpe.

Sen, A. K. (1981) *Poverty and Famines: An Essay on Entitlement and Deprivation*, Oxford: Clarendon.

Shanin, T. (1973–4) 'The Nature and Logic of the Peasant Economy', *JPS*, no. 1 (1973): 63–80 and no. 2 (1974): 186–206.

Shiba, Y. (1970) *Commerce and Society in Sung China*, translated by M. Elvin, Ann Arbor: Center for Chinese Studies of the University of Michigan.

Shih, V. Y. C. (1967) *The Taiping Ideology: Its Sources, Interpretations, and Influences*, Seattle: University of Washington Press.

Shue, V. (1980) *Peasant China in Transition: The Development towards Socialism, 1949–1956*, Berkeley: University of California Press.

Siskind, J. (1978) 'Kinship and Mode of Production', *American Anthropologist*, 80: 860–72.

Skinner, G. W. (1964–5) 'Marketing and Social Structure in Rural China', *JAS*, 24: 3–44, 195–228, 363–400.

——(1971) 'Chinese Peasants and Closed Community: An Open and Shut Case', *Comparative Studies in Society and History*, 13: 270–81.

——(1977) *The City in Late Imperial China*, Stanford: Stanford University Press.

Smith, C. J. (1991) *China, People and Places in the Land of One Billion*, Boulder, CO: Westview Press.

Smith, P. J. (1991) *Taxing Heaven's Storehouse*, Cambridge, MA: Council on East Asian Studies, Harvard University.

Solinger, D. J. (1993) *China's Transition from Socialism: Statist Legacies and Market Reforms, 1980–1990*, New York: M. E. Sharpe.

Spencer, J. and Thomas, W. (1971) *Asia East by South*, New York: Wiley.

406

Stover, L. E. (1974) *The Cultural Ecology of Chinese Civilisation: Peasants and Elites in the Last of the Agrarian States*, New York: Pica Press.

Sullivan, R. J. (1984) 'Measurement of English Farming Technological Change: 1523–1900', *EEH*, 21: 270–89.

Swaminathan, M. S. (1984) 'Rice', *SA*, 250: 62–71.

Sylla, R. and Toniolo, G. (eds) (1991) *Patterns of European Industrialisation: The Nineteenth Century*, London: Routledge.

Tan, G. (1996) *Asean: Economic Development and Co-operation*, Singapore: Times Academic Press.

Tawney, R. H. (1926) *Religion and the Rise of Capitalism*, London: John Murray.

—— (1964) *Life and Labour in China*, New York: Octagon Books.

Thaxton, R. (1983) *China Turned Rightside Up: Revolutionary Legitimacy in the Peasant World*, New Haven: Yale University Press.

Tomlinson, B. R (1985) 'Writing History Sideways: Lessons for Indian Economic Historians from Meiji Japan', *Modern Asian studies*, 3: 669–98.

Torbert, P. W. (1977) *The Ching Imperial Household Department*, Cambridge, MA: Harvard University Press.

Tregear, T. R. (1970) *An Economic Geography of China*, London: Butterworths.

Tu Wei-ming (1974) 'Reconstituting of the Confucian Tradition', *JAS*, May, pp. 441–54.

Twitchett, D. (1968) 'Merchant, Trade and Government in Late T'ang', *Asia Major*, 14 (1): 63–95.

Waldron, A. (1990) *The Great Wall of China: From History to Myth*, Cambridge: Cambridge University Press.

—— (1995) *From War to Nationalism: China's Turning Point, 1924–1925*, Cambridge: Cambridge University Press.

Wallerstein, I. (1974–86) *The Modern World-System I–III*, New York: Academic Press.

Wang, Gungwu (1958) 'The Nanhai Trade', *Journal of the Malayan Branch, Royal Asiatic Society*, 2: 1–135.

Wang, Yie-chien (1973) *Land Taxation in Imperial China, 1750–1911*, Cambridge, MA: Harvard University Press.

—— (1992) 'Secular Trends of Rice Prices in the Yangzi Delta, 1638–1935', in T. G. Rawski and L. M. Li (eds) *Chinese History in Economic Perspective*, Berkeley: University of California Press, pp. 35–68.

Wang, Yu-ch'uan (1936) 'The Rise of Land Tax and the Fall of Dynasties in Chinese History', *Pacific Affairs*, 2: 201– 20.

Waswo, A. (1988) 'The Transformation of Rural Society, 1900– 1950', in P. Duus (ed.) *Cambridge History of Japan*, vol. 6, Cambridge: Cambridge University Press, pp. 541–605.

Watanabe, T. (1992) *Asia: Its Growth and Agony*, Honolulu: East–West Centre.

Waverick, L. A. (1946) *China: A Model for Europe*, San Antonio, TX: Paul Anderson.

Weber, M. (1930) *The Protestant Ethic and the Spirit of Capitalism*, translated by T. Parsons, London: Allen and Unwin.

Werner, E. T. C. (1961) *A Dictionary of Chinese Mythology*, New York: Julian Press.

Wilkenfeld, J., Brecher, M. and Morser, S. (1988) *Crises in the Twentieth Century*, vol. 2, Oxford: Pergamon Press.

Will, P.-E. (1990) *Bureaucracy and Famine in Eighteenth-Century China*, translated by E. Forster, Stanford: Stanford University Press.

Will, P.-E. and R. B. Wong (1991) *Nourish the People: the State Civilian Granary System in China, 1650–1850*, Ann Arbor: University of Michigan Center for Chinese Studies.

407

Wittfogel, K. A. (1957) *Oriental Despotism: A Comparative Study of Total Power*, New Haven: Yale University Press.

Wolf, E. (1966) *Peasants*, Englewood Cliffs, NJ: Prentice-Hall.

Wong, R. B. (1997) *China Transformed*, Ithaca and London: Cornell University Press.

Wood, F. (1995) *Did Marco Polo Go to China?*, London: Secker and Warburg.

Wright, A. F. and Twitchett, D. (eds) (1962) *Confucian Personalities*, Stanford: Stanford University Press.

Wright, G. (1964) *Rural Revolution in France*, Stanford: Stanford University Press; London: Oxford University Press.

Wright, M. C. (1957) *The Last Stand of Chinese Conservatism*, Stanford: Stanford University Press.

Wright, T. (ed.) (1854) *The Travels of Marco Polo*, reprinted in 1968, New York: AMS Press.

Yamamura, K. (1979) 'Pre-industrial Landlording Patterns in Japan and England', in A. M. Craig (ed.) *Japan: A Comparative View*, Princeton, NJ: Princeton University Press.

Yang, C. K. (1961) *Religion in Chinese Society*, Berkeley: University of California Press.

Yu Jin (ed.) (1986) *The Great Wall*, 4th edition, Beijing: Cultural Relics Press.

Zeng Qi (1988) 'The Characteristics and Sequence of Development of Neolithic Cultures in China', *Chinese Sociology and Anthropology* (New York), 4: 73–92.

# INDEX